Information Architecture
for the World Wide Web

Other resources from O'Reilly

Related titles
Ambient Findability

Information Dashboard
   Design

Designing Interfaces

Web Design in a Nutshell

Ajax Design Patterns

Head First HTML
   with CSS & XHTML

oreilly.com
oreilly.com is more than a complete catalog of O'Reilly books. You'll also find links to news, events, articles, weblogs, sample chapters, and code examples.

oreillynet.com is the essential portal for developers interested in open and emerging technologies, including new platforms, programming languages, and operating systems.

Conferences
O'Reilly brings diverse innovators together to nurture the ideas that spark revolutionary industries. We specialize in documenting the latest tools and systems, translating the innovator's knowledge into useful skills for those in the trenches. Visit *conferences.oreilly.com* for our upcoming events.

Safari Bookshelf (*safari.oreilly.com*) is the premier online reference library for programmers and IT professionals. Conduct searches across more than 1,000 books. Subscribers can zero in on answers to time-critical questions in a matter of seconds. Read the books on your Bookshelf from cover to cover or simply flip to the page you need. Try it today for free.

THIRD EDITION

Information Architecture for the World Wide Web

Peter Morville and Louis Rosenfeld

O'REILLY®

Beijing · Cambridge · Farnham · Köln · Paris · Sebastopol · Taipei · Tokyo

Information Architecture for the World Wide Web, Third Edition
by Peter Morville and Louis Rosenfeld

Copyright © 2007, 2002, 1998 O'Reilly Media, Inc. All rights reserved.
Printed in the United States of America.

Published by O'Reilly Media, Inc., 1005 Gravenstein Highway North, Sebastopol, CA 95472.

O'Reilly books may be purchased for educational, business, or sales promotional use. Online editions are also available for most titles (*safari.oreilly.com*). For more information, contact our corporate/institutional sales department: (800) 998-9938 or *corporate@oreilly.com*.

Editor: Simon St.Laurent	**Cover Designer:** Karen Montgomery
Production Editor: Rachel Monaghan	**Interior Designer:** David Futato
Proofreader: Rachel Monaghan	**Illustrators:** Robert Romano and Jessamyn Read
Indexer: Reg Aubry	

Printing History:

February 1998:	First Edition.
August 2002:	Second Edition.
December 2006:	Third Edition.

Nutshell Handbook, the Nutshell Handbook logo, and the O'Reilly logo are registered trademarks of O'Reilly Media, Inc. *Information Architecture for the World Wide Web*, the image of a polar bear, and related trade dress are trademarks of O'Reilly Media, Inc.

Many of the designations used by manufacturers and sellers to distinguish their products are claimed as trademarks. Where those designations appear in this book, and O'Reilly Media, Inc. was aware of a trademark claim, the designations have been printed in caps or initial caps.

While every precaution has been taken in the preparation of this book, the publisher and authors assume no responsibility for errors or omissions, or for damages resulting from the use of the information contained herein.

 This book uses RepKover™, a durable and flexible lay-flat binding.

ISBN-13: 978-0-596-52734-1
[M] [5/08]

Table of Contents

Part I.   Introducing Information Architecture

Part II. Basic Principles of Information Architecture

Part III. Process and Methodology

Part IV. Information Architecture in Practice

Part V. Information Architecture in the Organization

Foreword

On the Web, if a site is difficult to use, most people will leave. On an intranet, if employees perform their tasks more slowly due to difficult design, the company bears the cost of the reduced productivity. In fact, I estimate that low intranet usability costs the world economy $100 billion per year in lost employee productivity. This may not be the most important problem facing the planet, but it's not a trifling issue either.

Usability is an important, though not the only, determinant for the success of a web site or an intranet. Information architecture is an important, though not the only, determinant for the usability of a design. There are other issues, but you ignore information architecture at your peril.

In our recent book, *Prioritizing Web Usability*, Hoa Loranger and I reported on a study we conducted of how people used a broad spectrum of 25 web sites. We recorded hundreds of usability problems on those sites, but only some of these issues were so severe that they caused users to fail their task or abandon the site. Search and findability problems accounted for a whopping 42 percent of these usability catastrophes. Other issues, such as page design, content usability, task support, and even annoying multimedia were definitely important as well, accounting for the remaining 58 percent of task failures. But the very first step is to get to the correct page, and if that fails, the entire site might as well not exist. This is why information architecture is so important.

Critics may say that users don't care about information architecture. They don't want to learn how a web site is structured; they just want to get in, get their task done, and get out. Users focus on tasks, not on structure. But it's because users don't care about the structure of a web site that it is so important to get the information architecture right in the design. If users did bother to study our web sites, they could surely learn how an obscure or illogical structure works and utilize that knowledge to improve their task performance. Humans are flexible creatures and can adapt to hostile environments if they choose to do so.

But since we know that users won't spend time learning our information architecture, we have to spend resources to design the best information architecture we can. Allow users to focus on their tasks, and let information architects be the ones to spend time worrying about the structure of the web site or intranet. This is a good division of labor, and the pay-off from good information architecture is immense. The more often that answers are located in the places you look for them, the easier the design will feel to users, and the more successful the project. There will be more sales (for e-commerce sites), better reputation for good service (for marketing sites), and less loss of productivity (for intranets).

I am a great believer in having professional information architects design the structure of professional information projects such as corporate web sites and intranets. But I also think there will be an increasing role for personal information architecture in the future. It will soon be time to teach a simplified version of the discipline to high school students, and possibly even to bring it into elementary schools as well.

The modern world is one of information overload; we are constantly bombarded by an inflow of messages, and we ought to read much more information than we have time for. Keeping yourself from drowning in this morass of information will require personal information architecture skills for problems like structuring email folders and computer files, as well as the ability to manage advanced search features.

In the long run, personal information architecture may turn out to be even more important than corporate information architecture. For now, though, read this third edition of *Information Architecture for the World Wide Web* and get your web site and intranet in shape to support your customers and employees. Good information architecture makes users less alienated and suppressed by technology. It simultaneously increases human satisfaction and your company's profits. Very few jobs allow you to do both at the same time, so enjoy.

—Jakob Nielsen
www.useit.com

Dr. Jakob Nielsen is principal of Nielsen Norman Group and author of *Designing Web Usability: The Practice of Simplicity*, *Homepage Usability: 50 Websites Deconstructed*, and *Prioritizing Web Usability*.

Preface

The mind is slow to unlearn what it learnt early.
—Seneca

Since 1994, when we first began organizing web sites, we have enjoyed a rare opportunity to participate in the birth of a new discipline. In the early days, we were pioneers and evangelists, exhorting web designers to learn about library science, even as we struggled to apply traditional principles in a new medium. To improve our craft, we embraced relevant fields such as human–computer interaction, integrating user research and usability engineering into the process. And to spread the word, we spoke at conferences, wrote the *Web Architect* column, and in 1998, published the first "polar bear" book on information architecture.

In the intervening years, it's been exciting to see information architecture mature into an established profession and an international community of practice. We have all learned so much from our work and from one another. And therein lies one of our biggest challenges. As our body of knowledge grows deeper, our discipline becomes more resistant to change. Individually and collectively, we find it harder to unlearn.

And yet, unlearn we must, for technology relentlessly transforms the playing field, changing not just the answers but the questions as well. In a post-Ajaxian Web 2.0 world of wikis, folksonomies, and mashups, how do we structure for co-creation? How do we document the rich interfaces of web applications? How do we design for multiple platforms and mobile devices? What has changed, and what remains the same?

In writing the third edition, it was these questions that kept us awake at night. There are no easy answers. We have done our best to balance old and new. We have addressed emerging technologies while maintaining a focus on fundamentals. And, we have tried to emphasize goals and approaches over specific tactics or technologies. In this way, we hope to provide not only knowledge about information architecture, but a framework that will enable you to learn and unlearn over an extended period of time.

What's New in the Third Edition

We've maintained the overall organization of the book while bringing the concepts, examples, and illustrations in each chapter up to date. We received substantial help from the information architecture community in the form of responses to a series of surveys we conducted in 2006.* The chapters on organization and navigation systems have been expanded to address tagging, folksonomies, social classification, and guided navigation. The chapter on design and documentation includes new sections on the role of diagrams in the design phase and the when, why, and how behind blueprints and wireframes. The Education and the Tools and Software chapters have been revised based on survey feedback. The chapter on enterprise information architecture enjoyed a major rewrite to accommodate lessons learned over the past few years. Finally, we've updated the Appendix to include the most useful information architecture resources available today.

Organization of This Book

This book is divided into six sections and twenty-one chapters, progressing from fundamentals to advanced topics. It breaks down as follows.

Part I, *Introducing Information Architecture*, provides an overview of information architecture for those new to the field and experienced practitioners alike, and comprises the following chapters:

Chapter 1, *Defining Information Architecture*
> This chapter offers definitions and analogies, shows how information architecture relates to other fields, and explains why it matters at all.

Chapter 2, *Practicing Information Architecture*
> This chapter discusses the qualities and skills essential to the professional information architect, and explains where and when the work should happen.

Chapter 3, *User Needs and Behaviors*
> This chapter sets the stage for information architecture design by helping us better understand how people interact with information.

Part II, *Basic Principles of Information Architecture*, includes chapters on the fundamental components of an architecture, illustrating the interconnected nature of these systems. It comprises the following chapters:

Chapter 4, *The Anatomy of an Information Architecture*
> This chapter helps you visualize the nuts and bolts of an architecture and introduces the systems covered in subsequent chapters.

---

* For complete survey results, see *http://iainstitute.org/pg/polar_bear_book_third_edition.php*.

Chapter 5, *Organization Systems*

This chapter describes ways to structure and organize sites to meet business goals and user needs.

Chapter 6, *Labeling Systems*

This chapter presents approaches for creating consistent, effective, and descriptive labels for a site.

Chapter 7, *Navigation Systems*

This chapter explores the design of browsing systems that help users understand where they are and where they can go within a site.

Chapter 8, *Search Systems*

This chapter covers the nuts and bolts of searching systems, and describes approaches to indexing and the design of search result interfaces that can improve overall performance.

Chapter 9, *Thesauri, Controlled Vocabularies, and Metadata*

This chapter shows how vocabulary control can connect these systems and improve the user experience.

Part III, *Process and Methodology*, covers the tools, techniques, and methods to take you from research to strategy and design to implementation of an information architecture. It comprises the following chapters:

Chapter 10, *Research*

This chapter explains the discovery process necessary to create a foundation of understanding.

Chapter 11, *Strategy*

This chapter presents a framework and methodology for defining the direction and scope of your information architecture.

Chapter 12, *Design and Documentation*

This chapter introduces the deliverables and processes required to bring your information architecture to life.

Part IV, *Information Architecture in Practice*, is a series of short essays that provide practical tips and philosophical advice for those doing the work of information architecture, and comprises the following chapters:

Chapter 13, *Education*

This chapter explains how to enter the field and how to keep learning, drawing from traditional and novel educational forums.

Chapter 14, *Ethics*

This chapter exposes the moral dilemmas in information architecture practice.

Chapter 15, *Building an Information Architecture Team*

This chapter introduces the specialist roles emerging within the field and addresses the transition from performing short-term projects to building sustainable programs.

Chapter 16, *Tools and Software*

This chapter covers a diverse set of software applications and technologies that can assist information architects and power information architectures.

Part V, *Information Architecture in the Organization*, addresses the business context of practicing and promoting information architecture, and comprises the following chapters:

Chapter 17, *Making the Case for Information Architecture*

This chapter provides guidance for those who must sell the value of information architecture to clients and colleagues.

Chapter 18, *Business Strategy*

This chapter notes similarities and dependencies between the fields of information architecture and business strategy, explaining how we can work toward competitive advantage.

Chapter 19, *Information Architecture for the Enterprise*

This chapter lays out a broad entrepreneurial framework for supporting the creation of information architecture services to serve the organization over a long period of time.

Part VI, *Case Studies*, describes the evolution of two large and very different information architectures, illustrating best practices along the way. It comprises the following two chapters:

Chapter 20, *MSWeb: An Enterprise Intranet*

This chapter presents the story of how a small team at one of the world's most powerful corporations has been able to create a successful and sustainable intranet information architecture.

Chapter 21, *evolt.org: An Online Community*

This chapter shows how a well-designed participation economy can produce an emergent information architecture that can be used and maintained by a distributed community of volunteers.

The Appendix, *Essential Resources*, is a selective list of pointers to the most useful information architecture resources available today.

Audience for This Book

Who do we hope to reach with this new edition? In short, anyone who's interested in information architecture, and maybe a few who aren't. We're information architecture evangelists at heart.

This third edition is necessary because *you*, the readers and practitioners of information architecture, have changed dramatically over the past few years. Many of you are completely new to the field, while some of you now have years of experience under your belts. For better or for worse, we've tried to meet the needs of both groups. While we intend this edition to serve as a useful introduction, we hope many battle-scarred practitioners will find the new material helpful as they make their way through today's information technology and business environments.

Finally, this is *our* take on information architecture. Many of our colleagues are also now writing about the subject, and we are grateful that so many smart people are sharing their experiences and insights. We look forward to continuing to learn from them. You should, too. Buy their books, read their articles, and find ways to share what you know. The more perspectives, the better. Only by sharing as individuals can we learn as a community.

Conventions for This Book

Italic
> Used for URLs, email addresses, and for emphasis.

`Constant width`
> Used for code examples.

 Indicates a tip, suggestion, or general note.

 Indicates a warning or caution.

Contacting the Authors

Please direct all suggestions, kudos, flames, and other assorted comments to us *both* via email:

> Peter Morville, Semantic Studios (*morville@semanticstudios.com*)
> Lou Rosenfeld, Louis Rosenfeld LLC (*lou@louisrosenfeld.com*)

Contacting O'Reilly

You can also address comments and questions concerning this book to the publisher:

> O'Reilly Media, Inc.
> 1005 Gravenstein Highway North
> Sebastopol, CA 95472
> 800-998-9938 (in the United States or Canada)
> 707-829-0515 (international/local)
> 707-829-0104 (fax)

There is a web page for this book, which lists errata and additional information. You can access this page at:

http://www.oreilly.com/catalog/9780596527341

To comment or ask technical questions about this book, send email to:

bookquestions@oreilly.com

For more information about books, conferences, Resource Centers, and the O'Reilly Network, see the O'Reilly web site at:

http://www.oreilly.com

Safari® Enabled

 When you see a Safari® Enabled icon on the cover of your favorite technology book, that means the book is available online through the O'Reilly Network Safari Bookshelf.

Safari offers a solution that's better than e-books. It's a virtual library that lets you easily search thousands of top tech books, cut and paste code samples, download chapters, and find quick answers when you need the most accurate, current information. Try it for free at http://safari.oreilly.com.

Acknowledgments

It's not easy to write about such a complex, dynamic area. Fortunately, we've had a lot of help from many smart, generous people. While we can't begin to thank all of the teachers, colleagues, friends, and family members who helped, permit us to acknowledge those most influential in shaping this third edition.

We're grateful to our technical reviewers, whose words of criticism and encouragement made this a much better book. They include: Austin Govella, Chris Farnum, Dan Brown, Donna Maurer, Fred Leise, Gene Smith, Greg Notess, James Melzer, Javier Velasco, Jeff Lash, Keith Instone, Margaret Hanley, Michael Crandall, Richard Dalton, Samantha Starmer, Sarah Rice, Stacy Surla, Tanya Rabourn, and Todd Warfel.

We truly appreciate the help we received from Beth Koloski, our editorial assistant. From surveys to screenshots, Beth was invaluable in keeping us on track. We also wish to thank the Information Architecture Institute for publishing our survey results.

It's always a privilege to work with the great team at O'Reilly Media. For the third edition, our editor Simon St.Laurent did a wonderful job of prodding and praising us through the process. Endless thanks to Simon, his colleagues, and the entire production crew at O'Reilly.

Finally, we can never fully express our appreciation and admiration for our wives, Mary Jean Babic and Susan Joanne Morville, who patiently supported our labors, and reminded us that there would indeed be light at the end of the tunnel, again.

—Louis Rosenfeld and Peter Morville
Ann Arbor, MI, USA

PART I

Introducing Information Architecture

CHAPTER 1

Defining Information Architecture

We shape our buildings: thereafter they shape us.
—Winston Churchill

What we'll cover:
- What is (and isn't) information architecture
- Why information architecture is important
- The value of explaining and illustrating IA concepts

What is it about buildings that stirs us? Whether we're architectural connoisseurs or just plain folks, we are all emotionally engaged by the physical structures we experience throughout our lives.

Each building serves a different purpose. A bustling café with hardwood floors and large windows facing Main Street provides the ideal place for a quick breakfast meeting. A steel-and-glass high-rise with its mix of cubes and offices envelops inhabitants in a collaborative, high-energy work environment. A dark, smoky bar with tin ceilings and exposed brick walls becomes a sanctuary from the whirl of modern life. And a medieval Gothic cathedral adorned with granite sculptures, stained-glass windows, and towers that reach for the heavens provides an experience both humbling and inspirational.

Each building serves its purpose uniquely. Architecture, design, construction, furnishings, inhabitants, and location all play major roles in shaping the overall experience. All elements must work together. In successful buildings, the whole is greater than the sum of its parts.

Why begin a book about web sites by writing about buildings? Because the architectural analogy is a powerful tool for introducing the complex, multidimensional nature of information spaces. Like buildings, web sites have architectures that cause us to react.

Some web sites provide logical structures that help us find answers and complete tasks. Others lack any intelligible organization and frustrate our attempts to navigate through them. We can't find the product we need; we can't locate the report we found last week; we're lost inside an online shopping cart. These web sites may remind us of buildings that fail: houses with flat roofs that leak, kitchens with no counter space, office towers with windows you can't open, and mazelike airports with misleading signs.

Bad buildings and bad web sites share similar architectural roots. First, many architects don't inhabit the structures they design. They don't fully understand the needs of their customers, and they're not around to suffer the long-term consequences of poor decisions. Second, creating structures to stand the test of time is really difficult. Needs change. Surprises are the rule. The desire for stability must be balanced against the value of flexibility and scalability. Architects are often faced with complex requirements, competing goals, and high levels of ambiguity. Transforming this chaos into order is extremely hard work that requires rare vision and perspective.

However, as designers of web sites, we should not become trapped by the metaphor of building architecture. Throughout this book, we'll also talk about information ecologies, knowledge economies, digital libraries, and virtual communities. We learn what we can from each analogy, and we leave the baggage behind.

A Definition

If you're new to the field, you may still be wondering: what exactly is information architecture? This section is for you.

> in·for·ma·tion ar·chi·tec·ture n.
>
> 1. The structural design of shared information environments.
>
> 2. The combination of organization, labeling, search, and navigation systems within web sites and intranets.
>
> 3. The art and science of shaping information products and experiences to support usability and findability.
>
> 4. An emerging discipline and community of practice focused on bringing principles of design and architecture to the digital landscape.

Were you expecting a single definition? Something short and sweet? A few words that succinctly capture the essence and expanse of the field of information architecture? Keep dreaming!

The reason we can't serve up a single, all-powerful, all-purpose definition is a clue to understanding why it's so hard to design good web sites. We're talking about the challenges inherent in language and representation. No document fully and accurately represents the intended meaning of its author. No label or definition totally captures the meaning of a document. And no two readers experience or understand a particular document or definition or label in quite the same way. The relationship between words and meaning is tricky at best.*

---

* For a humorous perspective on the trickiness of the English language, see Bill Bryson's *The Mother Tongue: English & How It Got That Way* (William Morrow).

We'll now descend from our philosophical soapbox and get down to basics. Let's expand on our definitions to explore some basic concepts of information architecture.

Information

> We use the term *information* to distinguish information architecture from data and knowledge management. Data is facts and figures. Relational databases are highly structured and produce specific answers to specific questions. Knowledge is the stuff in people's heads. Knowledge managers develop tools, processes, and incentives to encourage people to share that stuff. Information exists in the messy middle. With information systems, there's often no single "right" answer to a given question. We're concerned with information of all shapes and sizes: web sites, documents, software applications, images, and more. We're also concerned with *metadata*: terms used to describe and represent content objects such as documents, people, processes, and organizations.

Structuring, organizing, and labeling

> It's what information architects do best. Structuring involves determining the appropriate levels of granularity* for the information "atoms" in your site, and deciding how to relate them to one another. Organizing involves grouping those components into meaningful and distinctive categories. Labeling means figuring out what to call those categories and the series of navigation links that lead to them.

Finding and managing

> Findability is a critical success factor for overall usability. If users can't find what they need through some combination of browsing, searching, and asking, then the site fails. But user-centered design isn't enough. The organizations and people who manage information are important, too. An information architecture must balance the needs of users with the goals of the business. Efficient content management and clear policies and procedures are essential.

Art and science

> Disciplines such as usability engineering and ethnography are helping to bring the rigor of the scientific method to the analysis of users' needs and information-seeking behaviors. We're increasingly able to study patterns of usage and subsequently make improvements to our web sites. But the practice of information architecture will never be reduced to numbers; there's too much ambiguity and complexity. Information architects must rely on experience, intuition, and creativity. We must be willing to take risks and trust our intuition. This is the "art" of information architecture.

---

* *Granularity* refers to the relative size or coarseness of information chunks. Varying levels of granularity might include: journal issue, article, paragraph, and sentence.

Tablets, Scrolls, Books, and Libraries

Humans have been structuring, organizing, and labeling information for centuries. Back in 660 B.C., an Assyrian king had his clay tablets organized by subject. In 330 B.C., the Alexandria Library housed a 120-scroll bibliography. In 1873, Melvil Dewey conceived the Dewey Decimal System as a tool to organize and provide access to the growing number of books.

In modern times, most of us become familiar with the basics of information organization through our experiences with books and libraries. Table 1-1 shows how the concepts of information architecture (IA) apply to the world of print and the World Wide Web.

Table 1-1. Differences between books and web sites

IA concept	Books	Web sites
Components	Cover, title, author, chapters, sections, pages, page numbers, table of contents, index	Main page, navigation bar, links, content pages, sitemap, site index, search
Dimensions	Two-dimensional pages presented in a linear, sequential order	Multidimensional information space with hyper-textual navigation
Boundaries	Tangible and finite with a clear beginning and ending	Fairly intangible with fuzzy borders that "bleed" information into other sites

As we go beyond books to collections of books, the comparisons become even more interesting. Imagine a bookstore with no organization scheme. Thousands of books are simply tossed into huge piles on table tops. Such a bookstore does, in fact, exist: Gould's Book Arcade in Newtown, Australia. It's shown in Figure 1-1.

Figure 1-1. Gould's Book Arcade (image courtesy of Seth Gordon)

From a philosophical perspective, you might feel that this casual jumble of books represents a refreshing break from the rigid structures of everyday life. And this bookstore really can provide a wonderful browsing experience filled with adventure and serendipity. But if you arrive seeking a specific book or if you have a particular author or topic in mind, you're almost guaranteed to have a long and painful needle-in-the-haystack experience.

Compare the chaos of this bookstore to the order of a library (see Figure 1-2). Even on the surface, the contrast is like night and day. But look deeper and you'll see that a library is more than a warehouse for books, magazines, and music. There are complex systems and well-trained professionals operating behind the scenes to select, evaluate, label, describe, structure, and organize the collection so that users of the library can find what they need. And though the library's information environment is highly structured, the subject-oriented approaches of the Dewey Decimal and Library of Congress classification schemes also support exploratory browsing and serendipity.

Figure 1-2. Browsing in a library (image courtesy of http://intergate.sdmesa.sdccd.cc.ca.us/lrc/ stacks.jpg)

In short, a major way that libraries and librarians add value to printed materials is by placing them within the framework of an information architecture that facilitates access to those materials. Information architects perform a similar role, but we typically do it within the context of web sites and digital content. Of course, there are major differences between libraries and web sites. Table 1-2 shows just a few.

Table 1-2. Differences between libraries and web sites

IA Concepts	Libraries	Web sites
Purpose	Provide access to a well-defined collection of formally published content.	Provide access to content, sell products, enable transactions, facilitate collaboration, and on and on…
Heterogeneity	Diverse collections with books, magazines, music, software, databases, and files.	Huge diversity of media types, document types, and file formats.
Centralization	Highly centralized operations, often within one or a few physical library buildings.	Often very decentralized operations, with subsites maintained independently.

Developing an information architecture for a library presents many challenges, but a library is a relatively well-defined environment, and there is much collective experience and wisdom to draw upon. Web sites, on the other hand, present an array of new challenges. Virtual spaces are more flexible than physical spaces and can therefore be more complex. And at this point, we have precious few guidelines for creating information architectures for digital spaces.

Obviously, we've made some gross generalizations in these comparisons, and have oversimplified to illustrate key points. As you try to communicate information architecture concepts to others, you'll probably have to do the same.

Explaining IA to Others

One of the most frustrating things about being an information architect is the fact that most of your family members and neighbors will never have a clue what you do. The more you try to explain it, the more confused or bored they become. Their eyes glaze over. They nod politely. Then comes the desperate attempt to change the subject. "Hey, speaking of information architecture, did you hear tomorrow's weather report?"

Friends and relatives aren't the only tough audience. Sometimes you have to sell the concept to colleagues, clients, or managers. Each audience presents its own set of challenges. There's no magic bullet, but it's helpful to be prepared with an "elevator pitch" and an analogy suited to your particular audience.

The elevator pitch explains what you do in a sentence or two of plain language. If you can combine an analogy that resonates with your audience, even better!

Here are a few approaches to try out:

- "I'm an information architect. I organize huge amounts of information on big web sites and intranets so that people can actually find what they're looking for. Think of me as an Internet librarian."

- "I'm an information architect. I help my company by making it easy for customers to find our products on our web site. I'm a kind of online merchandiser. I apply one-to-one marketing concepts on the Internet."

- "I'm an information architect. I'm the one who takes on that information overload problem that everyone's been complaining about lately."

Sometimes we're too close to what we do. That's when it's a good idea to call for help. Ask someone who's familiar with you and your job to describe what you do in one or two sentences. Often you'll be amazed by how well they nail it, and grateful for their clarity and brevity.

What Isn't Information Architecture?

One of the most effective ways to define something is to identify its boundaries. We do this all the time. This is my property. That's your property. This is England. That's Scotland. She's a brain surgeon. He's an ophthalmologist.

Sometimes it's very easy to explain the differences. Mammals breathe with their lungs and give birth to live young. Dogs, cats, dolphins, and humans are all clearly mammals. Fish live in water, breathe with their gills, and lay eggs. Salmon, bass, and guppies are all clearly fish.

But as with many classifications, you quickly run into problems. What about fish with lungs? What about fish that don't look like fish? Are sharks, skates, eels, and sea horses really fish? (Yes, they are.) And where do we put that darned platypus?[*] Biological taxonomists have argued about these classification issues for centuries.

Mapping the boundaries of information architecture is even more slippery. Some things are clearly not information architecture:

- Graphic design is NOT information architecture.
- Software development is NOT information architecture.
- Usability engineering is NOT information architecture.

Makes sense, right? But as soon as you start working within the messy reality of web site design and construction, you find yourself in the gray areas between disciplines. For example, consider the ubiquitous global navigation bars in Figure 1-3.

Figure 1-3. Top and bottom navigation bars on the United Nations web site

The navigation bars feature labels and links that lead to other sections and pages within the web site. These labels are dependent upon the underlying structure and categorization of the site. The creation of categories and choice of labels fall clearly inside the domain of information architecture.

---

[*] To find out, read *The Platypus and the Mermaid: And Other Figments of the Classifying Imagination*, by Harriet Ritvo (Harvard University Press).

But wait a second. What about the look and feel of the navigation bar? What about the choice of colors, images, font styles, and sizes? Now we enter the realms of graphic design, interaction design, and information design. And what if a designer challenges the labels proposed by an information architect? Perhaps those labels are too long to fit on the navigation bar. What happens then?

What if the information architect wants a search link on the navigation bar, but the software developer says that adding a search capability to the web site is too expensive and time-consuming? And what if the usability engineer says that user tests indicated there are too many options on the navigation bar? What happens then?

These are the questions and challenges that live in the gray areas between disciplines. These gray areas drive some people crazy. Lots of heated arguments have resulted from attempts to draw clear lines. We believe the gray areas are necessary and valuable. They force interdisciplinary collaboration, which ultimately results in a better product.

Gray areas and caveats aside, here is our attempt to draw some boundaries between information architecture and a number of closely related disciplines.

Graphic design

> Traditionally, a graphic designer was responsible for all aspects of visual communication, from the design of corporate logos and identities to the layout of individual pages. On the Web, we're seeing increasing specialization due to the complexity of the environment. Even so, many graphic designers do a great deal of information architecture as part of their work.

Interaction design

> Interaction designers are concerned with the behavior of tasks and processes that users encounter in software and information systems at the interface level. They often have a background in human–computer interaction, and are focused on helping users successfully achieve goals and complete tasks.

Usability engineering

> Usability engineers understand how to apply the rigors of the scientific method to user research, testing, and analysis. Their background in human–computer interaction and their experience observing users provide them with useful insights into design. They are often concerned with testing all aspects of the user experience, inclusive of information architecture and graphic design.

Experience design

> Experience design is an umbrella term that encompasses information architecture, usability engineering, graphic design, and interaction design as components of the holistic user experience. You'll find relatively few "experience designers," as there aren't many people with skills in all these areas. The term is useful insofar as it encourages cross-disciplinary awareness and collaboration.

Software development

> People rarely confuse software development and information architecture, but the two fields are highly interdependent. Information architects rely on developers to

bring our ideas to fruition. Developers help us understand what is and isn't possible. And as the Web continues to blur the distinction between software applications and information systems, these collaborations will become even more important.

Enterprise architecture

In the 80s and 90s, a movement calling itself *enterprise architecture* arose in the information systems discipline. While the early stages of this movement were focused on data and system integration, later definitions have encompassed business, process, information, and technology architecture.

Content management

Content management and information architecture are really two sides of the same coin. IA portrays a "snapshot" or spatial view of an information system, while CM describes a temporal view by showing how information should flow into, around, and out of that same system over time. Content managers deal with issues of content ownership and the integration of policies, processes, and technologies to support a dynamic publishing environment.

Knowledge management

Knowledge managers develop tools, policies, and incentives to encourage people to share what they know. Creating a collaborative knowledge environment means tackling tough issues surrounding corporate culture such as "information hoarding" and "not-invented-here syndrome." Information architects focus more on making accessible what has already been captured.

Why Information Architecture Matters

You now understand what information architecture is and what it isn't. So, why is it important? Why should you care? Why should your company or your clients invest time and money in the design of their information architectures? What is the return on investment (ROI)?

We'll tackle these tough questions in detail later in the book, but for now, let's hit the highlights without getting bogged down in subtleties. When you calculate the importance of information architecture to your organization, you should consider the following costs and value propositions:

The cost of finding information

What does it cost if every employee in your company spends an extra five minutes per day struggling to find answers on your intranet?* What is the cost of frustrating your customers with a poorly organized web site?

---

* Jakob Nielsen deserves credit for publicizing the fact that the costs of poor navigation-system design in a large enterprise can add up to millions of dollars of lost employee productivity.

The cost of not finding information

How many bad decisions are made every day in your organization because employees didn't find the information they needed? How much duplication of effort results from this disconnect? How many customers do you lose because they can't find the product they want on your web site? How much do you spend every day providing telephone support to existing customers because they hate navigating your online technical-support database?

The value of education

What is the value of educating your customers about new products and services related to the ones they're actively seeking on your web site?

The cost of construction

What does it cost to design and build a web site? How much does it cost to redo it six months later because it doesn't support findability or doesn't scale?

The cost of maintenance

Similarly, what does it cost to ensure that good designs don't crumble over time? Will the people who maintain your site know where to put new content and when to remove outdated content?

The cost of training

For internal, mission-critical information systems that support call centers, for example, what does it cost to train employees to use that system? How much could you save if it wasn't so complicated to use?

The value of brand

No matter how beautiful your web site is, if customers can't find what they need, your brand loses value in their eyes. How much did you spend on those brand-building TV commercials?

And the list goes on. In your particular situation, there are sure to be a whole slew of opportunities to make money, save money, improve employee or customer satisfaction, or just plain make the world a better place. Figure out what they are and communicate them as clearly and directly as possible.

We're not saying this is easy. In fact, it's very difficult to calculate an exact return on an information architecture investment—there are simply too many variables. This is really no different from most other areas of activity within the business world. It's just that people in more traditional areas like sales, marketing, engineering, human resources, and administration have had more time to get their stories straight.

Bringing Our Work to Life

Information architecture lives beneath the surface. Users rarely look at a web site and exclaim, "Wow, check out this brilliant classification scheme!" In fact, much of our work is intangible; many people who are directly involved in web design have only a superficial understanding of information architecture. They may recognize the need for clear labels in a navigation bar, but have no clue how a controlled vocabulary could improve the search experience. If you can't see it, touch it, taste it, or smell it, it doesn't exist.

This invisibility is fine with respect to users. We don't want to force users to see our hard work; we want them to complete tasks and find information in blissful ignorance of our labors. But invisibility is a major problem when it comes to justifying our existence to colleagues and making the case for investments to decision makers. We must constantly work to help people see the complexity of the challenges we face and the long-term value of our solutions.

We must find ways to articulate the key concepts of our craft, helping people to understand the sophisticated nature of user needs and behavior. We must show the interconnections between people and content that underpin knowledge networks, and explain how these concepts can be applied to transform static web sites into complex adaptive systems (Figure 1-4*).

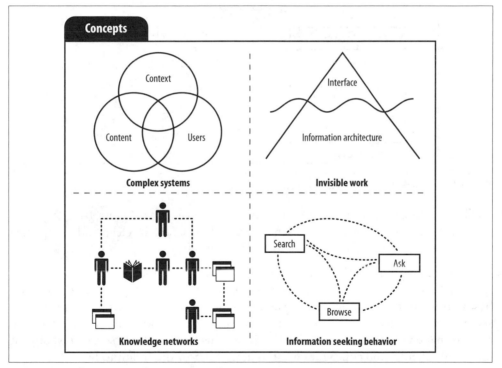

Figure 1-4. Information architecture concepts

---

* This series of images was designed by Myra Messing Klarman of Studio Mobius (*http://studiomobius.com*).

We must be prepared to dive into detail, identifying and defining the component systems that support our sites (Figure 1-5). We must show how semantic networks can provide a foundation for fluid navigation. And we must convince our clients and colleagues that an effective searching experience requires not just a good engine or a nice interface, but a carefully integrated system of interdependent parts.

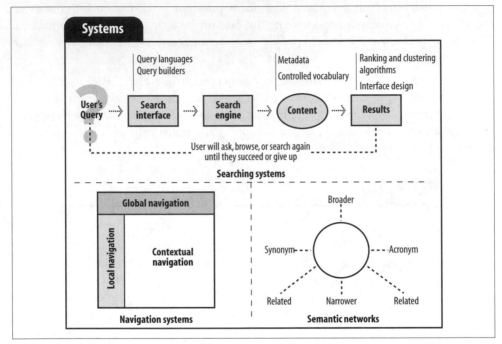

Figure 1-5. Information architecture systems

Finally, we must be ready to produce concrete deliverables (Figure 1-6). We must learn to render our constructs of semantics and structure in clear and compelling ways. In short, we must help people to see the invisible.

In this book, we explain the concepts, systems, and deliverables of information architecture. By drawing upon words, stories, metaphors, and images, we've done our best to bring our work to life. However, no single collection of words and images can serve all purposes. A key to the craft of information architecture is understanding how to shape your message for your audience. This requires some sense of what your managers, clients, and colleagues want to hear and how they want to hear it.

Did we mention that information architecture involves a little magic? How else would you read minds and make the invisible visible? So put on a black hat, bring along your sense of humor, and prepare to enter the secret society of information architects.

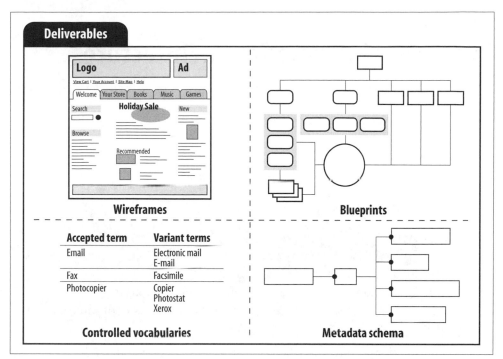

Figure 1-6. Information architecture deliverables

CHAPTER 2
Practicing Information Architecture

What we'll cover:
- Information architecture is everywhere
- Whether the world needs information architects
- Qualifications and source disciplines for information architects
- Information ecologies and their impact on the practice of information architecture

What is information architecture? Is it an art, a science, or a craft? Who should do this work? What qualifications are required? These are the questions we grapple with as a community of information architects. We write articles and publish books. We debate on discussion lists and argue passionately at conferences. We pull out our hair. We lose sleep. This is serious stuff.

And yet, independent of our intellectual theories and existential agonies, something very powerful is taking place. We are being surrounded, quite literally, by information architecture.

Have you ever walked through Times Square in New York City at night? It's quite a spectacle. You're on the corner of 42nd and Broadway. The glassy facades of buildings are pulsing with real-time information, courtesy of the latest in flat-panel display and projection technologies. Business news, financial data, corporate logos, and URLs are lit up in neon. Taxicabs sport billboards on their roofs as they honk their way through traffic. Pedestrians (or shall we say "users") hustle past one another, chattering into their cell phones or stopping on the corner to check email or get directions on their wireless PDAs. This is William Gibson's cyberspace turned inside out, physical architecture meets information architecture, a world of content, labels, and metadata all competing for your attention.[*]

---

[*] See the Flickr photo pool "Everyday Information Architecture": *http://www.flickr.com/groups/everyday-information-architecture/pool*.

And that's nothing compared to the real cyberspace, a new reality where we spend increasing amounts of time. How many hours do you spend staring at a computer monitor each day? How often do you check email or pop open your web browser? When your Internet connection is broken, how do you feel?

The World Wide Web has lived up to its name. It has connected and transformed the world. Want to know what's going on? Check out nytimes.com, bbc.co.uk, or your favorite blogs. Planning a trip? orbitz.com and kayak.com will meet your every need. Having trouble with your green iguana? No need to leave the house. You'll find the answer at iguana.com.

Billions of web pages have sprung up since the Web began. And guess what? Information architects played no role in designing most of them. This has been an emergent, bottom-up, grass-roots phenomenon. But every single web site that exists does have an information architecture. They're riddled with labels and taxonomies, vocabularies and metadata, sitemaps and indexes. There are portals linking to portals linking to search engines. Pure navigation. Some is good. Much of it isn't. We can critique it and we can make fun of it, but we can't stop it. Information architecture happens!

Do We Need Information Architects?

Since information architecture happens anyway, does the world really need information architects? If you've attended any of the IA Summits* in recent years, you know this has been a hot topic. A few speakers in particular have stirred the pot. Andrew Dillon is fond of saying, "I know we need information architecture. I'm not so sure we need information architects." And Peter Merholz suggests that "we need to teach everyone to do information architecture, rather than isolating the practice to a handful of professionals."

We have to give credit to the information architecture community for having the guts to ask these questions in public. But we'd like to respond with a firm assertion that *we absolutely do need information architects*. We're not too particular about the specific job title; if you prefer to call them user-experience designers, knowledge managers, or findability engineers, that's fine with us. What we're focused on is the need for professionals with specialized skills and experience, who know how to create useful, usable information systems within massively complex environments.

Programmers and graphic designers are great at what they do. They're not great at what we do. And information architecture design is not a skill you can pick up by taking a half-day seminar. There's real depth to the discipline. Information architecture resembles the games of *Othello* and *Go*. A minute to learn, a lifetime to master.

---

* Sponsored by the American Society for Information Science & Technology, the Information Architecture Summit is held in February or March each year. Learn more on the IA Summit web site: *http://iasummit.org*.

Does this mean that all web developers will need a licensed information architect on board before they write their first line of code? Of course not. Information architecture happens, with or without information architects, and that's just fine with us. That's why Peter Merholz is right to emphasize the vital role information architects must play in education. We can have a major positive impact on the world by sharing what we know with all those people who do information architecture in the course of doing something else.

But the most important and complex information environments already rely on professional information architects. Large organizations like IBM, Microsoft, and Vanguard already have teams of information architects dedicated to the long-term strategy and design of their web sites and intranets. Smaller organizations tend to involve information architects in a consulting capacity during a site redesign. This allows the information architect to make a major contribution without breaking the bank.

This selective use of expertise is not isolated to the field of information architecture; in fact, it is quite common. Consider, for example, the practice of law. A huge percentage of legal decisions are made every day by business managers rather than by their lawyers.

> Manager #1: "Should we approve this nondisclosure agreement?"
>
> Manager #2: "Yes, that's fine. It's no big deal. Let's move on."

Most companies don't have lawyers on staff. They get lawyers involved when the situation is particularly messy, complex, or important. The same happens and will continue to happen with information architects.

In fact, as web sites and intranets become more sophisticated and mission-critical, the demand for information architects will only rise. This demand will be partly offset as other professionals learn the basics of information architecture. Our responsibility as information architects will be to continue to push the envelope, to learn how to do what we do faster and better, and then to share our knowledge and experience with those around us. We all have so much to learn and so much to do. We fully expect information architects to be very busy for at least the next few hundred years.

Who's Qualified to Practice Information Architecture?

Unlike medicine and law, the field of information architecture has no official certification process. There are no university consortia, boards, or exams that can prevent you from practicing information architecture. As we explain in Chapter 13, a number of academic programs are emerging to serve the needs of prospective information architects, but for now very few people have a degree in information architecture.

Disciplinary Backgrounds

As you look over this list, you might not find your home discipline listed. Don't be daunted: any field focused on information and its use is a good source of information architects. And the field is still young enough that just about anyone will have to rely on experience from the School of Hard Knocks to practice IA effectively and confidently.

If you're looking for IA talent, keep in mind that, because the field is relatively new and because demand for information architects continues to explode, you can't just post a job description and expect a flock of competent and experienced candidates to show up on your doorstep. Instead, you'll need to actively recruit, outsource, or perhaps *become* the information architect for your organization.

Of course, if you are looking for someone else to fill this role, you might consider the following disciplines as sources for information architects. If you're on your own, it might not be a bad thing to learn a little bit about each of these disciplines yourself. In either case, remember that no single discipline is the obvious source for information architects. Each presents its own strengths and weaknesses.

OK, on to the list:

Graphic design and information design
> Many of the people who have written about and practice information architecture are graphic designers by training. This is not surprising, as both graphic design and information design involve much more than creating pretty pictures. These professions are geared more toward creating relationships between visual elements and determining how those elements can be integrated as a whole to communicate more effectively.

Information and library science
> Our backgrounds in information science and librarianship have proven very useful in dealing with the relationships between pages and other elements that make up a whole site. Librarians have a long history of organizing and providing access to information and are trained to work with searching, browsing, and indexing technologies. Forward-looking librarians understand that their expertise applies in new arenas far beyond the library walls.

Journalism
> Journalists, like librarians, are trained at organizing information, but in a setting that places special emphasis on timeliness. If your web site is geared toward delivering dynamic information, such as a news service or online magazine, someone with a background in journalism might have a great sense of how this information could be best organized and delivered. Because of their writing experience, journalists are also good candidates for architecting sites that will have high levels of edited content.

Usability engineering

Usability engineers are experts at testing and evaluating how people work with systems. These human–computer interaction professionals measure such criteria as how long it takes users to learn how to use a system, how long it takes them to complete tasks and find answers, and how many errors they make along the way. Of all the disciplines we list, usability engineering is probably the most scientific in its view of users and the quality of their experiences.

Marketing

Marketing specialists are expert at understanding audiences and communicating messages effectively. They are particularly valuable in the design of customer-facing web sites, where product sales and brand are critical to success. Marketing expertise can ensure that the message is presented in the language of the target audience. We've run into a number of "online merchandisers" who have become expert information architects.

Computer science

Programmers and software developers bring important skills and sensitivities to information architecture, especially to "bottom-up" processes. For example, developers are often excellent at modeling content and metadata for inclusion in a database or content management system. They're also great at figuring out how all of the component systems and technologies of an information architecture fit together.

Technical writing

Professionals who have spent time writing technical documentation or developing online help systems are often well-sensitized to both the needs of users and the potential for structuring, labeling, and describing textual content.

Architecture

While the transition from bricks and mortar to bits and bytes is obviously a big move, we actually know quite a few building architects turned information architects. These folks tend to have a great deal of experience studying people's needs and seeking behaviors, and an excellent foundation in the concepts and challenges surrounding strategy and design.

Product management

Many information architects play the role of "orchestra conductor." They understand how to tap the motivations and talents of a diverse group of professionals, creating a whole that's greater than the sum of its parts. People with a background in product, program, or project management can become very effective information architects, particularly in the areas of strategy formation and interdisciplinary team management.

…And many more

This list is far from comprehensive. There are dozens of established fields from which we can learn (see Figure 2-1). No list or picture will ever capture the true diversity of practicing information architects.

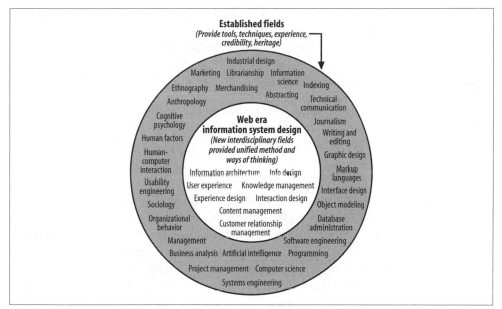

Figure 2-1. Information system design in the Web era (designed with help from Jess McMullin)

Innies and Outies

When staffing an information architecture project, it's also worth considering trade-offs between insider and outsider perspectives. On one hand, there's value in having an information architect who can think as an "outsider," take a fresh look at the site, and be sensitive to the needs of users without being weighed down by internal political baggage. On the other hand, an "insider" can really understand the organization's goals, content, and audiences, and will also be around for the long haul, helping to design, implement, and manage the solution.

Because it's difficult to choose between these two perspectives, many intelligent organizations put together a balanced team of consultants and employees. The consultants often help with major strategy and design initiatives, and provide highly specialized varieties of IA consulting, while the employees provide continuity as projects transition into programs. Even if you're the lone in-house information architect, you should seek to work with outies—whether by convincing management to hire consultants or specialists for you to collaborate with, or simply by hanging out with and learning from other IAs at local meetups and conferences.

Really, the fact that both innies and outies are flourishing is a sign of the field's maturation: in IA's early years (coinciding with this book's first edition), most practitioners were outies, working at agencies and consultancies. After the bubble burst (see the second edition), many of us ran for cover in the security of working in-house, often assisting with the implementation and customization of large applications like CMS and search engines. And now, as our third edition comes out, the field is in balance—there is room for both innies and outies, and a symbiotic relationship exists between them. It's truly indicative of a healthy profession, and good insurance against the vagaries of the next sudden economic downturn. We're not going away.

Gap Fillers and Trench Warriors

IA's early practitioners got their jobs by taking on work that no one else wanted or realized existed. Structuring information? Indexing it? Making it findable? Even if these tasks sounded appealing, few had the vocabulary, much less the skills, to address them. So stone-age information architects were, by definition, natural gap fillers who often tackled these tasks out of opportunism or simply because *someone* had to.

Over the past five or seven years, the field has matured and the practice of IA has solidified. What an information architect does is now much better understood and documented; you'll even detect a whiff of standardization among job descriptions. In effect, IA has moved from the exotic to the everyday, and more and more the people filling those roles are heads-down crack experts in the nuts-and-bolts of IA practices. These are the information architects that you'll want and need down in the trenches, grinding out an information architecture amid the guts and gore of your organization's users, content, and context. These trench warriors aren't pioneers, but providers of an important commodity service.

Of course, as trench warriors began to take over, gap fillers didn't disappear. They saw other opportunities that needed filling—only this time, the gaps popped up in the field of IA itself, rather than within specific teams or organizations. Information architects are now making livings as independent consultants, often working in such specialized areas such as taxonomy development, or as user experience team leaders, or as teachers and trainers for in-house IAs. Increasingly, many of us have become independent entrepreneurs who are developing own IA-infused products and services; there are always new gaps to be filled.

As the field continues its healthy evolution, gap fillers and trench warriors will continue to fill changing roles. Whether you're looking to staff your team, hire a consultant, or determine if IA is in your future, it's important to know that the field is now large and healthy enough to accommodate many personality types.

Putting It All Together

Whether you're looking to become an information architect or hire one, keep this in mind: everyone (including the authors) is biased by their disciplinary perspective. If at all possible, try to ensure that various disciplines are represented on your web site development team to guarantee a balanced architecture.

Additionally, no matter what your perspective, the information architect ideally should be responsible solely for the site's architecture, *not* for its other aspects. It can be overly distracting to have to deal with other, more tangible aspects of the site, such as its graphic identity or programming. In that case, the site's architecture can easily, if unintentionally, get relegated to second-class status because you'll be concentrating, naturally, on the more visible and tangible stuff.

However, in the case of smaller organizations, limited resources mean that all or most aspects of the site's development—design, editorial, technical, architecture, and production—are likely to be the responsibility of one person. Our best advice for someone in this position is obvious but still worth considering. First, find a group of friends and colleagues who are willing to be a sounding board for your ideas. Second, practice a sort of controlled schizophrenia in which you make a point to look at your site from different perspectives: first from the architect's, then from the designer's, and so on. And look for company among others who are suffering similar psychoses; consider joining the Information Architecture Institute* and attending the annual ASIS&T Information Architecture Summit.

Information Architecture Specialists

These general discussions about the role, value, and qualifications of information architects are worthwhile but incomplete. The community of information architects is experiencing what evolutionary biologists call a period of "punctuated equilibrium," marked by rapid change and specialization.

Particularly in large organizations, people who began as all-purpose information architects are gravitating towards specialized niches that match their strengths to their organization's needs. Here are just a few of the titles that already exist:

- Thesaurus Designer
- Search Schema Content Editor
- Metadata Specialist
- Content Manager
- Information Architecture Strategist
- Manager, Information Architecture
- Director, User Experience

There are so many possible variations and so many different facets. For example, information architects can specialize by:

- Industry lines (e.g., financial services, automotive)
- Functional department (e.g., human resources, engineering, marketing)
- Type of system (e.g., intranets, web sites, extranets, online magazines, digital libraries, software, online communities)
- Audience (e.g., small business owners, elementary school teachers, rocket scientists, teenagers, grandparents)

---

* Information Architecture Institute: *http://www.iainstitute.org*.

Finally, much IA work is centered on making large-scale applications work as advertised. So many information architects find their specializations centered on a variety of tools, most commonly:

- Content management systems
- Search engines
- Portals

As our use of networked information environments grows, the possibilities for specialization are unlimited and unpredictable. We're watching evolution in fast-forward. This is part of what makes it so much fun to be part of the information architecture community.

Practicing Information Architecture in the Real World

Users. Content. Context. You'll hear these three words again and again throughout this book. They form the basis of our model for practicing effective information architecture design. Underlying this model is a recognition that you can't design useful information architectures in a vacuum. An architect can't huddle in a dark room with a bunch of content, organize it, and emerge with a grand solution. It simply won't hold up against the light of day.

Web sites and intranets are not lifeless, static constructs. Rather, there is a dynamic, organic nature to both the information systems and the broader environments in which they exist. This is not the old world of yellowing cards in a library card catalog. We're talking complex, adaptive systems with emergent qualities. We're talking rich streams of information flowing within and beyond the borders of departments, business units, institutions, and countries. We're talking messiness and mistakes, trial and error, survival of the fittest.

We use the concept of an "information ecology"* composed of users, content, and context to address the complex dependencies that exist. And we draw upon our trusty Venn diagram (see Figure 2-2) to help people visualize and understand these relationships. The three circles illustrate the interdependent nature of users, content, and context within a complex, adaptive information ecology.

In short, we need to understand the business goals behind the web site and the resources available for design and implementation. We need to be aware of the nature and volume of content that exists today and how that might change a year from now. And we must learn about the needs and information-seeking behaviors of our major audiences. Good information architecture design is informed by all three areas.

---

* For more about information ecologies, read *Information Ecology* by Thomas Davenport and Lawrence Prusak (Oxford University Press, USA) and *Information Ecologies* by Bonnie Nardi and Vicki O'Day (MIT Press). Nardi and O'Day define an information ecology as "a system of people, practices, values, and technologies in a particular local environment."

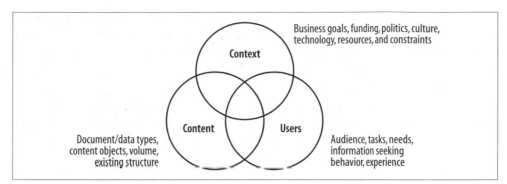

Figure 2-2. The infamous three circles of information architecture

Is this an oversimplified view of reality? Yes. Is it still useful? Absolutely. We've been using this model for over 10 years. It's held up well in all sorts of environments, from global web sites of Fortune 100 corporations to standalone intranet applications within small nonprofits. More importantly, we find these three circles incredibly helpful whenever we're confronted by a difficult question. After mouthing the trusty phrase "It depends"—as all smart information architects do—we develop our answer by deconstructing the question into three parts that coincide with our three circles. For example, when asked what are the most important qualities that an information architect should have, the answer becomes quite simple: some knowledge of users and their needs (which might come from exposure to human–computer interaction and a variety of other fields), content (think technical communication and journalism), and context (read a book on organizational psychology).

The three circles help with other tough questions, too, such as:

- What research and evaluation methods should information architects be familiar with?
- What's the ideal education for an information architect?
- What kinds of people should be part of an information architecture team?
- What kinds of books and blogs should I read to keep up with the field and its practice?
- What should go into the IA strategy that I propose to my new prospect?

The answer to each starts with a balance among the three areas: users, content, and context.

Should technology have its own circle? Maybe. But we find that technology usually gets too much attention—and it would look silly to add a fourth circle.

Incidentally, we think it's important for information architects to have a good sense of humor. Perhaps you've already figured this out. The work we do involves high levels of abstraction, ambiguity, and occasionally absurdity, and to some degree we're all still making it up as we go along. A good information architect knows how to get the work done while having some fun along the way.

If there's one thing that many years of information architecture consulting has taught us, it's that every situation is unique. We don't just mean that web sites are different from intranets or that extranets should vary by industry. We mean that, like finger-prints and snowflakes, every information ecology is unique.

The DaimlerChrysler intranet is vastly different from that of Ford or GM. Fidelity, Vanguard, Schwab, and Etrade have each created unique online financial-service experiences. Despite all the copycatting, benchmarking, and definitions of industry best practices that have surged throughout the business world in recent years, each of these information systems has emerged as quite distinctive.

That's where our model comes in handy. It's an excellent tool for learning about the specific needs and opportunities presented by a particular web site or intranet. Let's take a look at how each of our three circles contributes to the emergence of a totally unique information ecology.

Context

All web sites and intranets exist within a particular business or organizational con-text. Whether explicit or implicit, each organization has a mission, goals, strategy, staff, processes and procedures, physical and technology infrastructure, budget, and culture. This collective mix of capabilities, aspirations, and resources is unique to each organization.

Does it then follow that the information architecture of each organization must be unique? After all, companies buy generic office furniture. They invest in standard technology platforms. They even outsource important activities to vendors that ser-vice their competitors.

Still, the answer is a resounding yes. Information architectures must be uniquely matched to their contexts. The vocabulary and structure of your web site and your intranet is a major component of the evolving conversation between your business and your customers and employees. It influences how they think about your prod-ucts and services. It tells them what to expect from you in the future. It invites or limits interaction between customers and employees. Your information architecture provides perhaps the most tangible snapshot of your organization's mission, vision, values, strategy, and culture. Do you really want that snapshot to look like that of your competitor?

As we'll explain later in more detail, the key to success is understanding and align-ment. First, you need to understand the business context. What makes it unique? Where is the business today and where does it want to be tomorrow? In many cases, you're dealing with tacit knowledge. It's not written down anywhere; it's in people's heads and has never been put into words. We'll discuss a variety of methods for extracting and organizing this understanding of context. Then, you need to find ways to align the information architecture with the goals, strategy, and culture of the busi-ness. We'll discuss the approaches and tools that enable this custom configuration.

Content

We define "content" very broadly to include the documents, applications, services, schema, and metadata that people need to use or find on your site. To employ a technical term, it's the *stuff* that makes up your site. Our library backgrounds will be evident here in our bias toward textual information, and that's not such a bad thing, given the heavily textual nature of many web sites and intranets. Among other things, the Web is a wonderful communication tool, and communication is built upon words and sentences trying to convey meaning. Of course, we also recognize the Web as a tool for tasks and transactions, a flexible technology platform that supports buying and selling, calculating and configuring, sorting and simulating. But even the most task-oriented e-commerce web site has "content" that customers must be able to find.

As you survey content across a variety of sites, the following facets bubble to the surface as distinguishing factors of each information ecology.

Ownership

Who creates and owns the content? Is ownership centralized within a content authoring group or distributed among functional departments? How much content is licensed from external information vendors? The answers to these questions play a huge role in influencing the level of control you have over all the other dimensions.

Format

Web sites and intranets are becoming the unifying means of access to all digital formats within the organization. Oracle databases, product catalogs, Lotus Notes discussion archives, technical reports in MS Word, annual reports in PDF, office-supply purchasing applications, and video clips of the CEO are just a few of the types of documents, databases, and applications you'll find on a given site.

Structure

All documents are not created equal. An important memo may be fewer than 100 words. A technical manual may be more than 1,000 pages. Some information systems are built around the document paradigm, with the fully integrated document as the smallest discrete unit. Other systems take a content component or digital asset approach, leveraging some form of structural markup (XML or SGML, for example) to allow management and access at a finer level of granularity.

Metadata

To what extent has metadata that describes the content and objects within your site already been created? Have documents been tagged manually or automatically? What's the level of quality and consistency? Is there a controlled vocabulary in place? Or have users been allowed to supply their own "folksonomic" tags to the content? These factors determine how much you're starting from scratch with respect to both information retrieval and content management.

Volume
> How much content are we talking about? A hundred applications? A thousand pages? A million documents? How big is your web site?

Dynamism
> What is the rate of growth or turnover? How much new content will be added next year? And how quickly will it go stale?

All of these dimensions make for a unique mix of content and applications, which in turn suggests the need for a customized information architecture.

Users

When we worked on the first corporate web site for Borders Books & Music, back in the mid-90s before Amazon became a household name, we learned a lot about how customer research and analysis was applied towards the design and architecture of physical bookstores.

Borders had a clear understanding of how the demographics, aesthetic preferences, and purchasing behaviors of their customers differed from those of Barnes & Noble. It is no mistake that the physical layout and the selection of books differ significantly between these two stores, even within the same town. They are different by design. And that difference is built upon an understanding of their unique customer or market segments.

Differences in customer preferences and behaviors within the physical world translate into different information needs and information-seeking behaviors in the context of web sites and intranets. For example, senior executives may need to find a few good documents on a particular topic very quickly. Research analysts may need to find all the relevant documents and may be willing to spend several hours on the hunt. Managers may have a high level of industry knowledge but low navigation and searching proficiency. Teenagers may be new to the subject area but really know how to handle a search engine.

Do you know who's using your web site? Do you know how they're using it? And perhaps most importantly, do you know what information they want from your site? These are not questions you can answer in brainstorming meetings or focus groups. As our friend and fellow information architect Chris Farnum likes to say, you need to get out there in the real world and study your "users in the mist."

What Lies Ahead

So, information architecture happens. Information architectures are being created every day by generalists and specialists, by innies and outies, risk takers and people who get things done, and by people who've never heard the term "information architecture." They're being created inside all manner of information ecologies with unique combinations of users, content, and context.

Herein lies the dual challenge to the information architecture discipline. As professionals, we must advance our own understanding and our ability to perform this very difficult work inside massively complex environments. We still have so much to learn! And as a community, we must strive to advance the practice of information architecture by educating those around us who create or influence information architectures while they're focused on doing something else. We still have so much to teach!

In any case, we hope we've done a good job of setting the stage. Now it's time to delve into the guts of information architecture, so roll up your sleeves and dig in.

CHAPTER 3

User Needs and Behaviors

What we'll cover:

- The dangers of an oversimplified view of how we find information
- How our information needs vary
- How our information-seeking behaviors vary
- How and why to learn more about determining users' information needs and information-seeking behaviors

In the last two chapters, we've defined information architecture and placed it within the broader context of where, when, and by whom it's practiced. But before we jump into the actual "stuff" of information architecture—the components that make up an architecture, the methodologies that drive its design, and so on—let's first take a look at users. Information architecture is not restricted to taxonomies, search engines, and the other things that help users find information on a site. Information architecture starts with users and the reason they come to a site in the first place: they have an information need.

This is a truism, but there's more to it than meets the eye. Information needs can vary widely, and each type of information need causes users to exhibit specific information-seeking behaviors. Information architects need to understand those needs and behaviors, and their designs should correspond accordingly. There is no goal more important to designing information architecture than to satisfy users' needs.

For example, if your site is a staff directory, looking up a staff member's phone number is probably a very common information need among your site's users; in fact, this type of need may describe most of your users' finding sessions. When confronted by such a need, users will likely perform a search, and you'd be wise to make sure your information architecture supports searching by name. On the other hand, if your site helps non-savvy investors learn about and select mutual funds for investment, your users may satisfy this need through some other means. They might really benefit from a site wizard that leads them through a tutorial, or they may wish to wander by browsing through categories.

Seeking something you know is there, like your colleague's phone number, is quite a different information need than learning about a topic, like small-cap mutual funds, and your site's information architecture should be designed with those differences in mind. These needs are examples of information-seeking behaviors and, not surprisingly, searching for something you know is a very different behavior than browsing for the unknown. Distinguishing between these needs and behaviors and determining which are your users' highest priorities is an extremely valuable pursuit—it helps you determine where to invest your efforts, resources, time, and money as you design your architecture.

The "Too-Simple" Information Model

There are different models of what happens when users look for information. Modeling users' needs and behaviors forces us to ask useful questions about what kind of information the user wants, how much information is enough, and how the user actually interacts with the architecture.

Unfortunately, "too-simple" is the most common information model, and it's also the most problematic. It looks something like Figure 3-1.

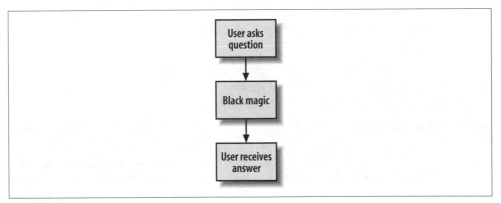

Figure 3-1. The "too-simple" model of information needs

Or, expressed as a simple algorithm:

1. User asks a question.
2. Something happens (i.e., searching or browsing).
3. User receives the answer.
4. Fin.

Input, output, end of story. This is a very mechanistic and ultimately dehumanizing model for how users find and use information on web sites. In fact, in this model, the user, like the site itself, is just another system—predictable in behavior, rational in motivation.

Why do we have a problem with this "too-simple" model? Because it rarely happens this way. There are exceptions—for example, when users know what they're looking for, as in the staff directory scenario. Here, users have a question for which there is a right answer, they know where to find the answer, they know how to state the question, and they know how to use the site to do so.

But users don't always know exactly what they want. Have you ever visited a site just to poke around? By exploring the site, you're trying to find information of a sort; you just don't exactly know what you're looking for. Even when you do, you may not have the language to express it: is it "PDA," "Palm Pilot," or "handheld computer"?

Users often complete their efforts at finding information in a state of partial satisfaction or outright frustration. Example: "I was able to find information on synchronizing my Palm Pilot, but nothing specific on syncing to a Macintosh." Or, during the process of finding, they may learn new information that changes what they're looking for altogether. Example: "I realized that a Keough retirement plan is ideal for me, even though when I started I was trying to learn about IRAs."

We also dislike the "too-simple" model because it narrowly focuses on what happens while the user is interacting with the information architecture. The information need's context—all the related stuff that happens before and after the user ever touches the keyboard—gets left out. It also assumes an ignorant user who brings little, if any, prior knowledge to the table. So the model essentially ignores any context for this scenario.

Finally, by oversimplifying, this model cedes so many great opportunities to understand what goes on in users' heads and observe the richness of what happens during their interactions with an information architecture.

This model is dangerous because it's built upon a misconception: that finding information is a straightforward problem that can be addressed by a simple, algorithmic approach. After all, we've solved the challenge of retrieving data—which, of course, is facts and figures—with database technologies such as SQL. So, the thinking goes, let's treat the abstract ideas and concepts embedded in our semi-structured textual documents the same way.

This attitude has led to the wasting of many millions of dollars on search engine software and other technological panaceas that would indeed work if this assumption were true. Many user-centered design techniques carry this misconception forward, assuming that the process of finding is simple enough to be easily measured in a quantifiable way. So we think we can measure the experience of finding by how long it takes, or how many mouse clicks it takes, or how many viewed pages it takes to find the "right" answer, when often there is no right answer.

OK, enough complaining about this model. Let's take a closer look at information needs and seeking behaviors so that we can build better models.

Information Needs

When a user comes to a web site to find something, what does she really want? In the "too-simple" model, she wants the "right answer" to her question. Indeed, right answers do come from searching databases, which store facts and figures and answer questions that really do have right answers, such as "What is the population of San Marino?" To many of us, database searching is the most familiar model of searching.

But web sites store much more than highly structured data. Not surprisingly, text is the most common type of data stored, and text itself is made up of ambiguous, messy ideas and concepts. When we go to a web site for advice on retirement investing, to learn about restaurants in Mendocino County, or to find out what's happening with the Manchester United football team, we are essentially looking for ideas and concepts that inform us and help us make decisions. The answer, if there is one, is an ambiguous moving target.

So back to the question: What do users want? Let's use the metaphor of fishing to get at the answer.

The perfect catch

Sometimes users really are looking for the right answer. Let's think of that as fishing with a pole, hoping to hook that ideal fish. What is the population of San Marino? You go to the CIA Fact Book or some other useful site that's jam-packed with data, and you hook in that number (it's 29,251, by the way). And you're done, just as the too-simple model would have it.

Lobster trapping

What about the times you're looking for more than just a single answer? Let's say you're hoping to find out about good bed-and-breakfast inns in Stratford, Ontario. Or you want to learn something about Lewis and Clark's journey of exploration. Or you need to get a sense of what sort of financial plans can help you save for retirement. You don't really know much about what you're looking for, and aren't ready to commit to retrieving anything more than just a few useful items, or suggestions of where to learn more. You're not hoping to hook the perfect fish, because you wouldn't know it if you caught it. Instead, you're setting out the equivalent of a lobster trap—you hope that whatever ambles in will be useful, and if it is, that's good enough. Perhaps it's a few candidate restaurants that you'll investigate further by calling and checking their availability and features. Or maybe it's a motley assemblage of Lewis and Clark stuff, ranging from book reviews to a digital version of Clark's diary to information about Lewis & Clark College in Oregon. You might be happy with a few of these items, and toss out the rest.

Indiscriminate driftnetting

Then there are times when you want to leave no stone unturned in your search for information on a topic. You may be doing research for a doctoral thesis, or performing competitive intelligence analysis, or learning about the medical condition affecting a close friend, or, heck, ego surfing. In these cases, you want to catch every fish in the sea, so you cast your driftnets and drag up everything you can.

I've seen you before, Moby Dick…

There's some information that you'd prefer to never lose track of, so you'll tag it so you can find it again. Thanks to social bookmarking services like del.icio.us—which were primarily intended to support refindability—it's now possible to toss a fish back in the sea with the expectation of finding it again.

This fishing metaphor is helpful because it illustrates four common information needs. When you're hoping to make the perfect catch, you usually know what you're looking for, what to call it, and where you'll find it—this is called *known-item seeking*. An example is when you search the staff directory to find a colleague's phone number.

When you're hoping to find a few useful items in your traps, you're doing something called *exploratory seeking*. In this case, the user is not exactly sure what he's looking for. In fact, whether he realizes it or not, he is looking to learn something from the process of searching and browsing. For example, the user may go to his employer's human resources site to learn something about retirement plans that the company offers. In the process, he may encounter some basic information on IRA plans, and then change his search to learning more about such plans. As he learns more about the IRA, he shifts his search again to learning whether the simple or Roth IRA plan is best for him. Exploratory seeking is typically open-ended; there is no clear expectation of a "right" answer, nor does the user necessarily know how to articulate what exactly he is looking for. He is happy to retrieve a few good results, and use them as a springboard for the next iteration of the search. It's not always possible to definitively determine when exploratory searching is finished.

When you want everything, you're performing *exhaustive research*. The user is looking for everything on a particular topic, hoping to leave no stone unturned. In this case, the user often has many ways to express what she's looking for, and may have the patience to construct her search using all those varied terms. For example, someone who is trying to learn more about a friend's medical condition might execute multiple searches for "AIDS," "HIV," "acquired immuno-deficiency syndrome," and so forth. Again, there isn't necessarily a "right" answer. And in this case, the user must be patient enough to wade through more results than is typical with other information needs.

Finally, our failing memories and busy schedules continually force us to engage in refinding a piece of useful information that we've happened upon before. For example, while you're at work, you might surf for a few minutes and stumble on a great but long explanation of Django Reinhardt's guitar technique. Naturally, you won't read it now and risk losing your job. You'll refind it later instead. It's no surprise that del.icio.us users often assign such tags as "readme," "toread," or "readlater" to their bookmarks.

Figure 3-2 illustrates these four different types of information needs.

These four information needs are by no means the only ones, but many of your users' needs will fall into these categories.

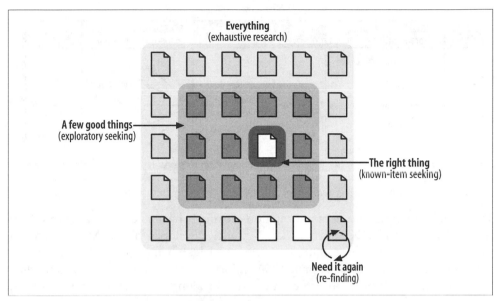

Figure 3-2. Four common information needs

Information-Seeking Behaviors

How do web site users find information? They enter queries in search systems, browse from link to link, and ask humans for help (through email, chat interfaces, and so forth). *Searching*, *browsing*, and *asking* are all methods for finding, and are the basic building blocks of information-seeking behavior.

There are two other major aspects to seeking behaviors: integration and iteration. We often integrate searching, browsing, and asking in the same finding session. Figure 3-3 shows how you might search your corporate intranet for guidelines on traveling abroad. You might first browse your way through the intranet portal to the HR site, browse the policies area, and then search for the policy that includes the string "international travel." If you still didn't get your question answered, you might send an email to Biff, the person responsible for that policy, to ask exactly what your per diem will be while spending the week in Timbuktu. Let's hope your intranet's information architecture was designed to support such integration!

Figure 3-3 also illustrates the iteration you may go through during one finding session. After all, we don't always get things right the first time. And our information needs may change along the way, causing us to try new approaches with each new iteration. So, while you may have begun with a broad quest for "guidelines on traveling abroad," you might be satisfied to find something as specific as "recommended per diem in Timbuktu" by the time you're done. Each iteration of searching, browsing, asking, and interacting with content can greatly impact what it is we're seeking.

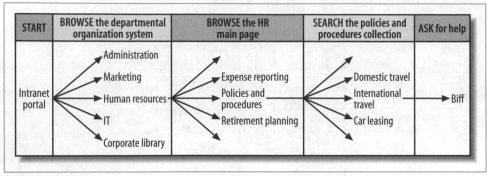

Figure 3-3. Integrated browsing, searching, and asking over many iterations

These different components of information-seeking behaviors come together in complex models, such as the "berry-picking" model* developed by Dr. Marcia Bates of the University of Southern California. In this model (shown in Figure 3-4), users start with an information need, formulate an information request (a *query*), and then move iteratively through an information system along potentially complex paths, picking bits of information ("berries") along the way. In the process, they modify their information requests as they learn more about what they need and what information is available from the system.

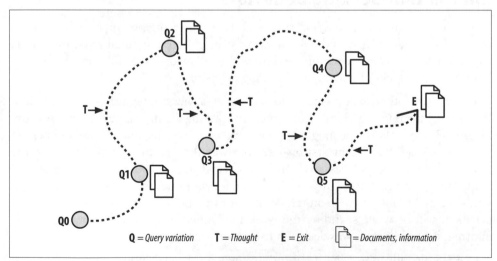

Figure 3-4. The "berry-picking" model of how users move through an information system

The berry-picking diagram looks messy, much more so than the "too-simple" model. It should; that's the way our minds often work. After all, we're not automatons.

---

* Bates's seminal paper, "The design of browsing and berrypicking techniques for the online search interface" (in *Online Review*, vol.13, no.5, 1989), is required reading for every information architect. See *http://www.gseis.ucla.edu/faculty/bates/berrypicking.html*.

If the berry-picking model is common to your site's users, you'll want to look for ways to support moving easily from search to browse and back again. Yahoo! provides one such integrated approach to consider: you can search within the subcategories you find through browsing, as shown in Figure 3-5. And you can browse through categories that you find by searching, as shown in Figure 3-6.

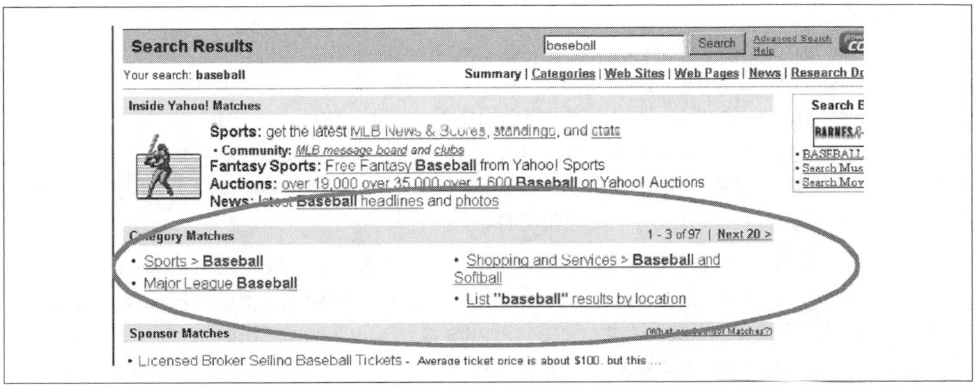

Figure 3-5. First search, then browse: searching Yahoo! for "baseball" retrieves categories that can be browsed

Figure 3-6. First browse, then search: Yahoo!'s categories are themselves searchable

Another useful model is the "pearl-growing" approach. Users start with one or a few good documents that are exactly what they need. They want to get "more like this one." To meet this need, Google and many other search engines allow users to do just that: Google provides a command called "Similar pages" next to each search result. A similar approach is to allow users to link from a "good" document to documents indexed with the same keywords. In sites that contain scientific papers and other documents that are heavy with citations, you can find other papers that share many of the same citations as yours or that have been co-cited with the one you like. Del.icio.us and Flickr are recent examples of sites that allow users to navigate to items that share something in common; in this case, the same user-supplied tag. All of these architectural approaches help us find "more like this one."

Corporate portals and intranets often utilize a "two-step" model. Confronted with a site consisting of links to perhaps hundreds of departmental subsites, users first need to know where to look for the information they need. They might search or browse through a directory until they find a good candidate or two, and then perform the second step: looking for information within those subsites. Their seeking behaviors may be radically different for each of these two steps; certainly, the information architectures typical of portals are usually nothing like those of departmental subsites.

Learning About Information Needs and Information-Seeking Behaviors

How does one learn about their users' information needs and seeking behaviors? There are a variety of user research methods to consider—too many to cover in detail here—so we'll recommend a pair of our favorites: search analytics and contextual inquiry. Search analytics* involves reviewing the most common search queries on your site (usually stored in your search engine's logfiles) as a way to diagnose problems with search performance, metadata, navigation, and content. Search analytics provides a sense of what users commonly seek, and can help inform your understanding of their information needs and seeking behaviors (and is handy in other ways, too, such as developing task-analysis exercises).

While search analytics is based on a high volume of real user data, it doesn't provide an opportunity to interact with users and learn more about their needs directly. Contextual inquiry,† a user research method with roots in ethnography, is a great complement to search analytics because it allows you to observe how users interact with information in their "natural" settings and, in that context, ask them why they're doing what they're doing.

Other user research methods you might look to are task analysis, surveys, and, with great care, focus groups. Ultimately, you should consider any method that might expose you to users' direct statements of their own needs, and when you can, use a combination of methods to cover as many bases as possible.

Finally, remember that, as an information architect, your goal is to do your best to learn about your users' major information needs and likely information-seeking behaviors. A better understanding of what users actually want from your site will, naturally, help you determine and prioritize which architectural components to build, which makes your job much simpler, especially considering how many ways a particular information architecture could be designed. You'll also have great user data to help counterbalance the other drivers that too often influence design, such as budget, time, politics, entrenched technologies, and designers' personal preferences.

---

* For more on search analytics, read the forthcoming book by Rosenfeld and Wiggins, *Search Analytics for Your Site: Conversations with Your Customers*, which will be published in 2007 (Rosenfeld Media).

† For more on contextual inquiry, read Beyer and Holtzblatt's *Contextual Design: Defining Customer-Centered Systems* (Morgan Kaufmann).

PART II

Basic Principles of Information Architecture

CHAPTER 4

The Anatomy of an Information Architecture

What we'll cover:
- Why it's important (and difficult) to make an information architecture as tangible as possible
- Examples that help you visualize an information architecture from both the top down and the bottom up
- Ways of categorizing the components of an information architecture so you can better understand and explain IA

In the preceding chapters, we discussed information architecture from a conceptual perspective. This chapter presents a more concrete view of what information architecture actually is to help you recognize it when you see it. We also introduce the components of an architecture; these are important to understand because they make up the information architect's palette. We'll cover them in greater detail in Chapters 5–9.

Visualizing Information Architecture

Why is it important to be able to visualize information architecture? There are several answers. One is that the field is new, and many people don't believe that things exist until they can see them. Another is that the field is abstract, and many who might conceptually understand the basic premise of information architecture won't really "get it" until they see it and experience it. Finally, a well-designed information architecture is invisible to users (which, paradoxically, is quite an unfair reward for IA success).

IA's lack of tangible qualities forces all information architects to be salespeople to some degree. Because it's highly probable that you'll need to explain information architecture to several important people, including colleagues, managers, prospects, clients, and perhaps your significant other, it's in your interest to be able to help them visualize what an information architecture actually is.

Let's start by looking at a site's main page. Figure 4-1 shows the main page for Gustavus Adolphus College in Saint Peter, Minnesota, USA.

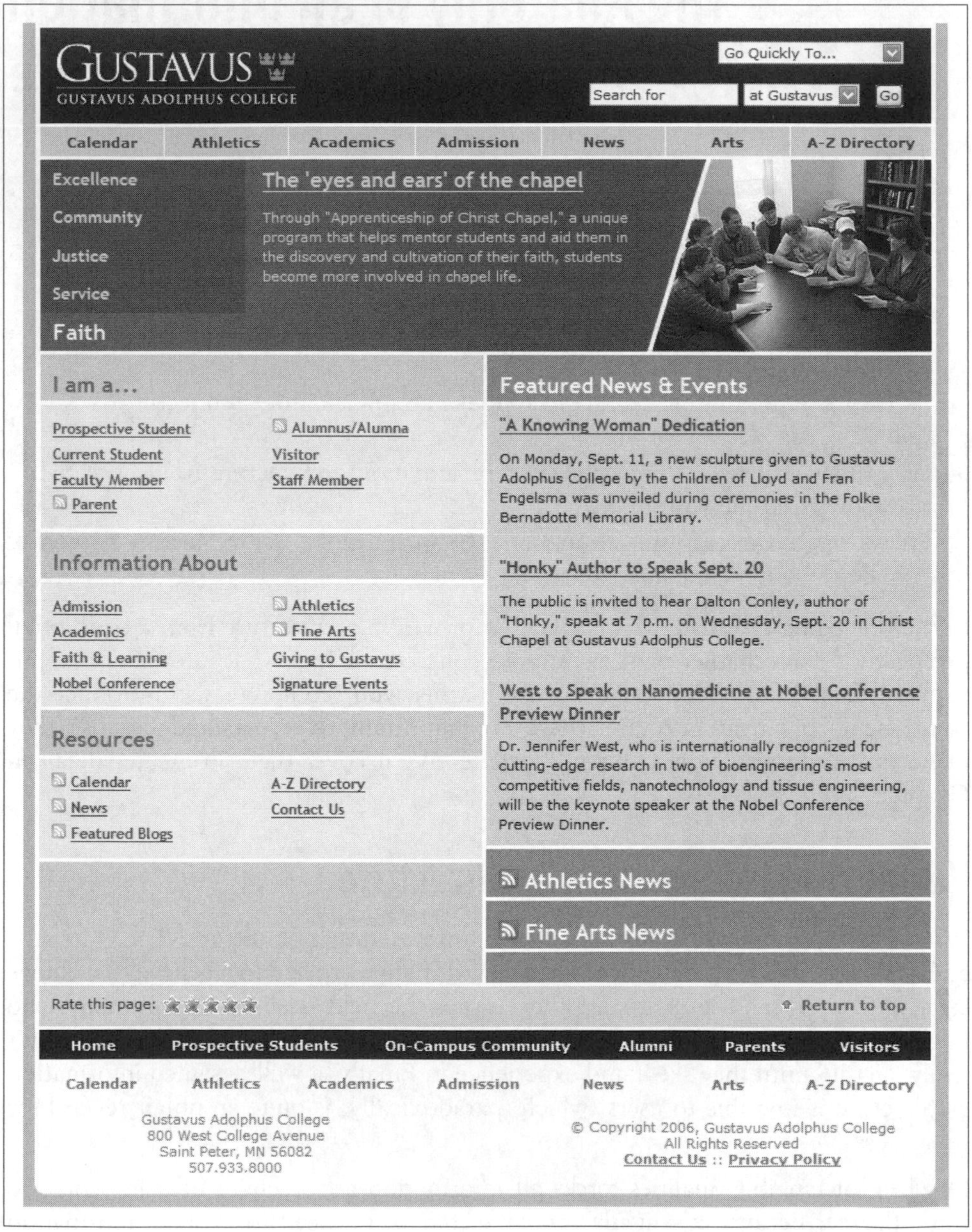

Figure 4-1. Gustavus Adolphus College's main page

What's obvious here? Most immediately, you see that the site's visual design stands out. You can't help but notice the site's colors (you'll have to take our word for it), typeface choices, and images. You also notice aspects of the site's information design; for example, the number of columns—and their widths—changes throughout the page.

What else? With a careful eye, you can detect aspects of the site's interaction design, such as the use of mouseovers (over main menu choices) and pull-down menus for "Go Quickly To" and search options. Although the college's logo and logotype are prominent, the site relies on textual content (e.g., "Excellence," "Community," and so forth) to convey its message and brand. And although this particular site functions well, you'd learn something about its supporting technology (and related expertise) just from the main page—for example, if it didn't load properly in a common browser, you might guess that the designers weren't aware of or concerned with standards-compliant design.

Thus far, we've noticed all sorts of things that aren't information architecture. So what *is* recognizable as information architecture? You might be surprised by how much information architecture you can see if you know how to look. For example, the information has been structured in some basic ways, which we'll explain in later chapters:

Organization systems
Present the site's information to us in a variety of ways, such as content categories that pertain to the entire campus (e.g., the top bar and its "Calendar" and "Academics" choices), or to specific audiences (the "I am a…" area, with such choices as "Prospective Students" and "Staff Member").

Navigation systems
Help users move through the content, such as the "A–Z Directory" and the "Go Quickly To…" menu of popular destinations.

Search systems
Allow users to search the content. Here, the default is set to search the Gustavus site, but one could also search the Gustavus calendar, its directory, or the whole web from the site's search interface.

Labeling systems
Describe categories, options, and links in language that (hopefully) is meaningful to users; you'll see examples throughout the page, some (e.g., "Admission") more understandable than others ("Nobel Conference").

Figure 4-2 provides a visualization of these architectural components.

As we can see from this figure and from Figure 4-3, these areas are just the tip of the iceberg. Categories group pages and applications throughout the site; labels systematically represent the site's content; navigation systems and a search system can be used to move through the site. That's quite a lot of information architecture to cram into one screenshot!

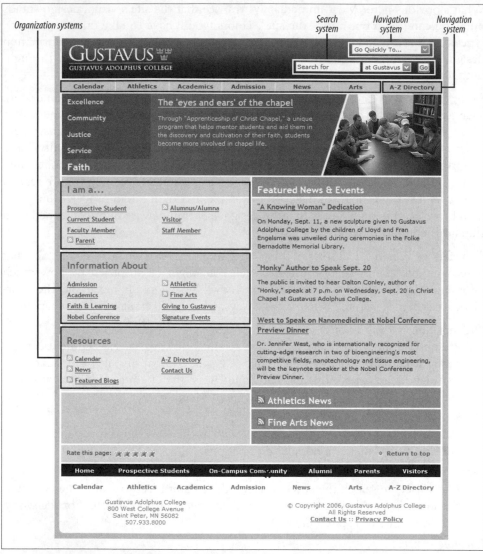

Figure 4-2. This page is crammed with architectural components

In effect, the Gustavus main page tries to anticipate users' major information needs, such as "How do I find out about admissions?" or "What's going on this week on campus?" The site's information architects have worked hard to determine the most common questions, and have designed the site to meet those needs. We refer to this as *top-down information architecture*, and the Gustavus main page addresses many common "top-down" questions that users have when they land on a site, including:

1. Where am I?
2. I know what I'm looking for; how do I search for it?

3. How do I get around this site?

4. What's important and unique about this organization?

5. What's available on this site?

6. What's happening there?

7. Do they want my opinion about their site?

8. How can I contact a human?

9. What's their address?

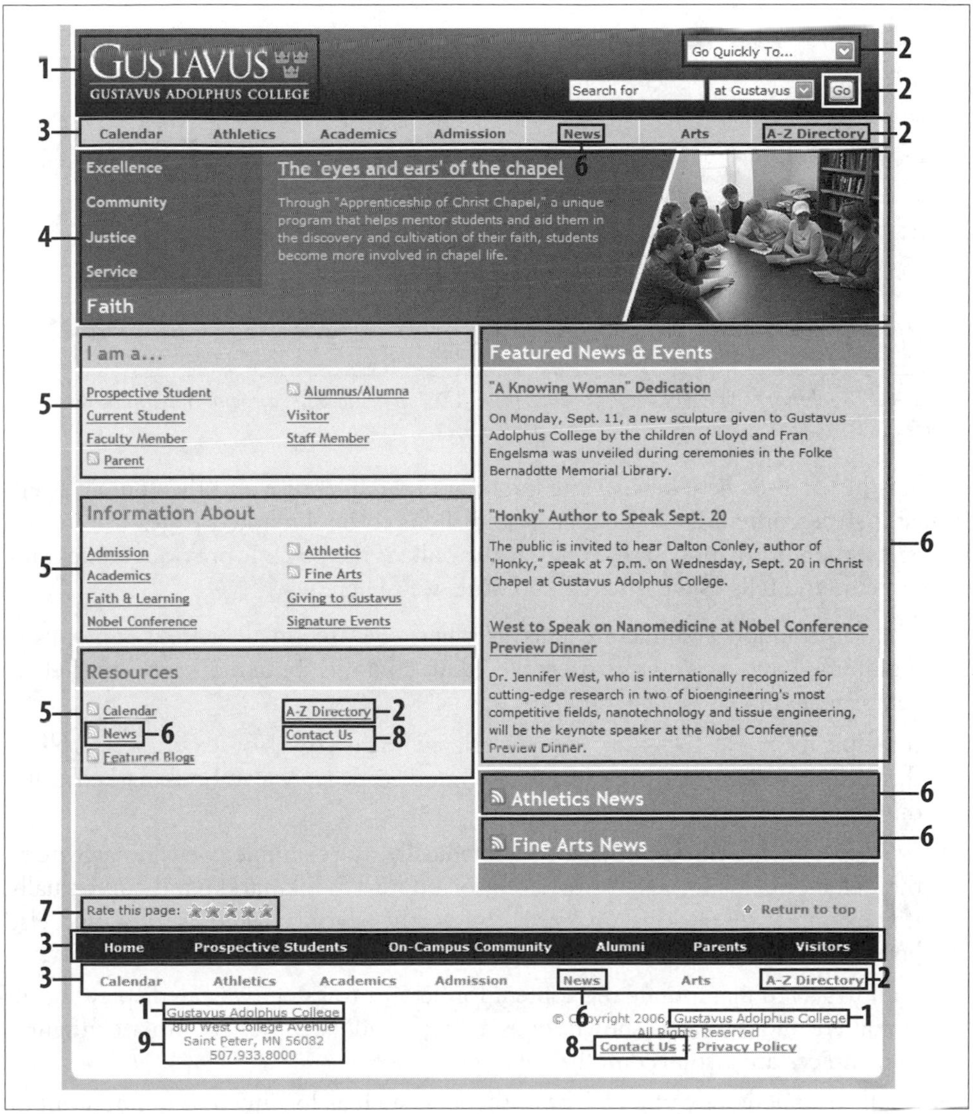

Figure 4-3. A site's main page is crammed with answers to users' questions

Figure 4-4 shows a slightly different example—pages tagged by one of the authors as relevant to enterprise user experience in del.icio.us, a social bookmarking service.

Figure 4-4. Bookmarks tagged as about "enterprise_UX" in del.icio.us, a social bookmarking service.

There is little to see here besides the information architecture and the content itself. In fact, as the content is just a collection of links to bookmarked pages from other web sites, the information architecture is the bulk of the page. It provides context for the content, and tells us what we can do while we're here.

- The information architecture tells us where we are (in del.icio.us, on a page maintained by user "louisrosenfeld" that contains bookmarks he tagged as "enterprise_ux").

- It helps us move to other, closely related pages (by, for example, scrolling through results ("<< earlier | later >>") and to pages we've bookmarked using different tags (under "tags" and "related tags").

- It helps us move through the site hierarchically (for example, we can navigate to the del.icio.us main page, or to recent or popular bookmarks) and contextually (for example, by clicking on "saved by 4 other people" or by seeing who else bookmarked pages using the same tag).

- It allows us to manipulate the content for better browsing (we can display tags in alphabetical order, as is shown, or as a "tag cloud"; a variety of other configuration choices are displayed in the "options").

- It tells us where we can go for basic services, such as logging into our account or getting help ("contact us" and "help").

In many respects, this page from del.icio.us is nothing but information architecture.

Content itself can have information architecture embedded within it. The recipe in Figure 4-5 shows a nutritious drink from the Epicurious site.

Figure 4-5. A recipe for the thirsty from Epicurious.com

Beyond the navigational options at the top of the page, there's not much information architecture here. Or is there?

The recipe itself has a clear, strong structure: a title at the top, a list of ingredients, then preparation directions and serving information. This information is "chunked" so you know what's what, even without subtitles for "ingredients" or "directions." The recipe's native chunking could also support searching and browsing; for example, users might be able to search on the chunks known as "recipe titles" for "salty dog" and retrieve this one. And these chunks are sequenced in a logical manner; after all, you'll want to know the ingredients ("Do I have four ounces of grapefruit juice?") before you start mixing the drink. The definition and sequential placement of chunks help you to recognize that this content is a recipe before you even read it. And once you know what it is, you have a better idea what this content is about and how to use it, move around it, and go somewhere else from it.

So, if you look closely enough, you can see information architecture even when it's embedded in the guts of your content. In fact, by supporting searching and browsing, the structure inherent in content enables the answers to users' questions to "rise" to the surface. This is *bottom-up information architecture*; content structure, sequencing, and tagging help you answer such questions as:

- Where am I?
- What's here?
- Where can I go from here?

Bottom-up information architecture is important because users are increasingly likely to bypass your site's top-down information architecture. Instead, they're using web-wide search tools like Google, clicking through ads, and clicking links while reading your content via their aggregators to find themselves deep in your site. Once there, they'll want to jump to other relevant content in your site without learning how to use its top-down structure. A good information architecture is designed to anticipate this type of use; Keith Instone's simple and practical Navigation Stress Test is a great way to evaluate a site's bottom-up information architecture (*http://user-experience.org/uefiles/navstress/*).

You now know that information architecture is something that can be seen, if you know what to look for. But it's important to understand that information architecture is often invisible. For example, Figure 4-6 shows some search results from the BBC's web site.

Figure 4-6. BBC's search results include three "Best Links"

What's going on here? We've searched for "chechnya," and the site has presented us with a couple of different things, most interestingly three results labeled as a "BBC Best Link." As you'd imagine, all search results were retrieved by a piece of software—a search engine—that the user never sees. The search engine has been configured to index and search certain parts of the site, to display certain kinds of information in each search result (i.e., page title, extract, and date), and to handle search queries in certain ways, such as removing "stop words" (e.g., "a," "the," and "of"). All of these decisions regarding search system configuration are unknown to users, and are integral aspects of information architecture design.

What's different is that the "Best Link" results are manually created: some people at the BBC decided that "chechnya" is an important term and that some of the BBC's best content is not news stories, which normally come up at the top of most retrieval sets. So they applied some editorial expertise to identify three highly relevant pages and associated them with the term "chechnya," thereby ensuring that these three items are displayed when someone searches for "chechnya." Users might assume these search results are automatically generated, but humans are manually modifying the information architecture in the background; this is another example of invisible information architecture.

Information architecture is much more than just blueprints that portray navigational routes and wireframes that inform visual design. Our field involves more than meets the eye, and both its visible and invisible aspects help define what we do and illustrate how challenging it really is.

Information Architecture Components

It can be difficult to know exactly what components make up an information architecture. Users interact directly with some, while (as we saw above) others are so behind the scenes that users are unaware of their existence.

In the next four chapters, we'll present and discuss information architecture components by breaking them up into the following four categories:

Organization systems
How we categorize information, e.g., by subject or chronology. See Chapter 5.

Labeling systems
How we represent information, e.g., scientific terminology ("Acer") or lay terminology ("maple"). See Chapter 6.

Navigation systems
How we browse or move through information, e.g., clicking through a hierarchy. See Chapter 7.

Searching systems
How we search information, e.g., executing a search query against an index. See Chapter 8.

Like any categorization scheme, this one has its problems. For example, it can be difficult to distinguish organization systems from labeling systems (hint: you organize content into groups, and then label those groups; each group can be labeled in different ways). In such situations, it can be useful to group objects in new ways. So before we delve into these systems, we'll present an alternative method of categorizing information architecture components. This method is comprised of browsing aids, search aids, content and tasks, and "invisible" components.

Browsing Aids

These components present users with a predetermined set of paths to help them navigate the site. Users don't articulate their queries, but instead find their way through menus and links. Types of browsing aids include:

Organization systems
> The main ways of categorizing or grouping a site's content (e.g., by topic, by task, by audiences, or by chronology). Also known as taxonomies and hierarchies. Tag clouds (based on user-generated tags) are also a form of organization system.

Site-wide navigation systems
> Primary navigation systems that help users understand where they are and where they can go within a site (e.g., breadcrumbs).

Local navigation systems
> Primary navigation systems that help users understand where they are and where they can go within a portion of a site (i.e., a subsite).

Sitemaps/Tables of contents
> Navigation systems that supplement primary navigation systems; provide a condensed overview of and links to major content areas and subsites within the site, usually in outline form.

Site indices
> Supplementary navigation systems that provide an alphabetized list of links to the contents of the site.

Site guides
> Supplementary navigation systems that provide specialized information on a specific topic, as well as links to a related subset of the site's content.

Site wizards
> Supplementary navigation systems that lead users through a sequential set of steps; may also link to a related subset of the site's content.

Contextual navigation systems
> Consistently presented links to related content. Often embedded in text, and generally used to connect highly specialized content within a site.

Search Aids

These components allow the entry of a user-defined query (e.g., a search) and automatically present users with a customized set of results that match their queries. Think of these as dynamic and mostly automated counterparts to browsing aids. Types of search components include:

Search interface
> The means of entering and revising a search query, typically with information on how to improve your query, as well as other ways to configure your search (e.g., selecting from specific search zones).

Query language
> The grammar of a search query; query languages might include Boolean operators (e.g., AND, OR, NOT), proximity operators (e.g., ADJACENT, NEAR), or ways of specifying which field to search (e.g., AUTHOR="Shakespeare").

Query builders
> Ways of enhancing a query's performance; common examples include spell checkers, stemming, concept searching, and drawing in synonyms from a thesaurus.

Retrieval algorithms
> The part of a search engine that determines which content matches a user's query; Google's PageRank is perhaps the best-known example.

Search zones
> Subsets of site content that have been separately indexed to support narrower searching (e.g., searching the tech support area within a software vendor's site).

Search results
> Presentation of content that matches the user's search query; involves decisions of what types of content should make up each individual result, how many results to display, and how sets of results should be ranked, sorted, and clustered.

Content and Tasks

These are the users' ultimate destinations, as opposed to separate components that get users to their destinations. However, it's difficult to separate content and tasks from an information architecture, as there are components embedded in content and tasks that help us find our way. Examples of information architecture components embedded in content and tasks include:

Headings
> Labels for the content that follows them.

Embedded links
> Links within text; these label (i.e., represent) the content they link to.

Embedded metadata

Information that can be used as metadata but must first be extracted (e.g., in a recipe, if an ingredient is mentioned, this information can be indexed to support searching by ingredient).

Chunks

Logical units of content; these can vary in granularity (e.g., sections and chapters are both chunks) and can be nested (e.g., a section is part of a book).

Lists

Groups of chunks or links to chunks; these are important because they've been grouped together (e.g., they share some trait in common) and have been presented in a particular order (e.g., chronologically).

Sequential aids

Clues that suggest where the user is in a process or task, and how far he has to go before completing it (e.g., "step 3 of 8").

Identifiers

Clues that suggest where the user is in an information system (e.g., a logo specifying what site she is using, or a breadcrumb explaining where in the site she is).

"Invisible" Components

Certain key architectural components are manifest completely in the background; users rarely (if ever) interact with them. These components often "feed" other components, such as a thesaurus that's used to enhance a search query. Some examples of invisible information architecture components include:

Controlled vocabularies and thesauri

Predetermined vocabularies of preferred terms that describe a specific domain (e.g., auto racing or orthopedic surgery); typically include variant terms (e.g., "brewskie" is a variant term for "beer"). Thesauri are controlled vocabularies that generally include links to broader and narrower terms, related terms, and descriptions of preferred terms (aka "scope notes"). Search systems can enhance queries by extracting a query's synonyms from a controlled vocabulary.

Retrieval algorithms

Used to rank search results by relevance; retrieval algorithms reflect their programmers' judgments on how to determine relevance.

Best bets

Preferred search results that are manually coupled with a search query; editors and subject matter experts determine which queries should retrieve best bets, and which documents merit best bet status.

Whichever method you use for categorizing architectural components, it's useful to drill down beyond the abstract concept of information architecture and become familiar with its more tangible and, when possible, visual aspects. In the following chapters, we'll take an even deeper look at the nuts and bolts of an information architecture.

CHAPTER 5

Organization Systems

The beginning of all understanding is classification.
—Hayden White

What we'll cover:
- Subjectivity, politics, and other reasons why organizing information is so difficult
- Exact and ambiguous organization schemes
- Hierarchy, hypertext, and relational database structures
- Folksonomies, tagging, and social classification

Our understanding of the world is largely determined by our ability to organize information. Where do you live? What do you do? Who are you? Our answers reveal the systems of classification that form the very foundations of our understanding. We live in towns within states within countries. We work in departments in companies in industries. We are parents, children, and siblings, each an integral part of a family tree.

We organize to understand, to explain, and to control. Our classification systems inherently reflect social and political perspectives and objectives. We live in the first world. They live in the third world. She is a freedom fighter. He is a terrorist. The way we organize, label, and relate information influences the way people comprehend that information.

As information architects, we organize information so that people can find the right answers to their questions. We strive to support casual browsing and directed searching. Our aim is to design organization and labeling systems that make sense to users.

The Web provides information architects with a wonderfully flexible environment in which to organize. We can apply multiple organization systems to the same content and escape the physical limitations of the print world. So why are many large web sites so difficult to navigate? Why can't the people who design these sites make it easy to find information? These common questions focus attention on the very real challenge of organizing information.

Challenges of Organizing Information

In recent years, increasing attention has been focused on the challenge of organizing information. Yet this challenge is not new. People have struggled with the difficulties of information organization for centuries. The field of librarianship has been largely devoted to the task of organizing and providing access to information. So why all the fuss now?

Believe it or not, we're all becoming librarians. This quiet yet powerful revolution is driven by the decentralizing force of the global Internet. Not long ago, the responsibility for labeling, organizing, and providing access to information fell squarely in the laps of librarians. These librarians spoke in strange languages about Dewey Decimal Classification and the Anglo-American Cataloging Rules. They classified, cataloged, and helped you find the information you needed.

As it grows, the Internet is forcing the responsibility for organizing information on more of us each day. How many corporate web sites exist today? How many blogs? What about tomorrow? As the Internet provides users with the freedom to publish information, it quietly burdens them with the responsibility to organize that information. New information technologies open the floodgates for exponential content growth, which creates a need for innovation in content organization (see Figure 5-1).

And if you're not convinced that we're facing severe information-overload challenges, take a look at an excellent study* conducted at Berkeley. This study finds that the world produces between one and two exabytes of unique information per year. Given that an exabyte is a billion gigabytes (we're talking 18 zeros), this growing mountain of information should keep us all busy for a while.

As we struggle to meet these challenges, we unknowingly adopt the language of librarians. How should we *label* that content? Is there an existing *classification scheme* we can borrow? Who's going to *catalog* all of that information?

We're moving toward a world in which tremendous numbers of people publish and organize their own information. As we do so, the challenges inherent in organizing that information become more recognized and more important. Let's explore some of the reasons why organizing information in useful ways is so difficult.

Ambiguity

Classification systems are built upon the foundation of language, and language is ambiguous: words are capable of being understood more than one way. Think about

---

* "How Much Information?" is a study produced by the faculty and students at the School of Information Management and Systems at the University of California at Berkeley. See *http://www2.sims.berkeley.edu/ research/projects/how-much-info-2003*.

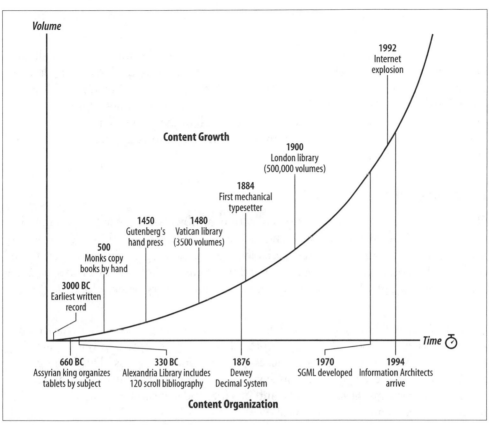

Figure 5-1. Content growth drives innovation

the word *pitch*. When I say pitch, what do you hear? There are more than 15 definitions, including:

- A throw, fling, or toss
- A black, sticky substance used for waterproofing
- The rising and falling of the bow and stern of a ship in a rough sea
- A salesman's persuasive line of talk
- An element of sound determined by the frequency of vibration

This ambiguity results in a shaky foundation for our classification systems. When we use words as labels for our categories, we run the risk that users will miss our meaning. This is a serious problem. (See Chapter 6 to learn more about labeling.)

It gets worse. Not only do we need to agree on the labels and their definitions, we also need to agree on which documents to place in which categories. Consider the common tomato. According to Webster's dictionary, a tomato is "a red or yellowish fruit with a juicy pulp, used as a vegetable: botanically it is a berry." Now I'm confused. Is it a fruit, a vegetable, or a berry?*

If we have such problems classifying the common tomato, consider the challenges involved in classifying web site content. Classification is particularly difficult when you're organizing abstract concepts such as subjects, topics, or functions. For example, what is meant by "alternative healing," and should it be cataloged under "philosophy" or "religion" or "health and medicine" or all of the above? The organization of words and phrases, taking into account their inherent ambiguity, presents a very real and substantial challenge.

Heterogeneity

Heterogeneity refers to an object or collection of objects composed of unrelated or unlike parts. You might refer to grandma's homemade broth with its assortment of vegetables, meats, and other mysterious leftovers as heterogeneous. At the other end of the scale, homogeneous refers to something composed of similar or identical elements. For example, Ritz crackers are homogeneous. Every cracker looks and tastes the same.

An old-fashioned library card catalog is relatively homogeneous. It organizes and provides access to books. It does not provide access to chapters in books or collections of books. It may not provide access to magazines or videos. This homogeneity allows for a structured classification system. Each book has a record in the catalog. Each record contains the same fields: author, title, and subject. It is a high-level, single-medium system, and works fairly well.

Most web sites, on the other hand, are highly heterogeneous in many respects. For example, web sites often provide access to documents and their components at varying levels of *granularity*. A web site might present articles and journals and journal databases side by side. Links might lead to pages, sections of pages, or other web sites. And, web sites typically provide access to documents in multiple formats. You might find financial news, product descriptions, employee home pages, image archives, and software files. Dynamic news content shares space with static human-resources information. Textual information shares space with video, audio, and interactive applications. The web site is a great multimedia melting pot, where you are challenged to reconcile the cataloging of the broad and the detailed across many mediums.

The heterogeneous nature of web sites makes it difficult to impose any single structured organization system on the content. It usually doesn't make sense to classify

---

* The tomato is technically a berry and thus a fruit, despite an 1893 U.S. Supreme Court decision that declared it a vegetable. (John Nix, an importer of West Indies tomatoes, had brought suit to lift a 10 percent tariff, mandated by Congress, on imported vegetables. Nix argued that the tomato is a fruit. The Court held that since a tomato was consumed as a vegetable rather than as a dessert like fruit, it was a vegetable.) "Best Bite of Summer," by Denise Grady, July 1997.

documents at varying levels of granularity side by side. An article and a magazine should be treated differently. Similarly, it may not make sense to handle varying formats the same way. Each format will have uniquely important characteristics. For example, we need to know certain things about images, such as file format (GIF, TIFF, etc.) and resolution (640×480, 1024×768, etc.). It is difficult and often misguided to attempt a one-size-fits-all approach to the organization of heterogeneous web site content. This is a fundamental flaw of many enterprise taxonomy initiatives.

Differences in Perspectives

Have you ever tried to find a file on a coworker's desktop computer? Perhaps you had permission. Perhaps you were engaged in low-grade corporate espionage. In either case, you needed that file. In some instances, you may have found the file immediately. In others, you may have searched for hours. The ways people organize and name files and directories on their computers can be maddeningly illogical. When questioned, they will often claim that their organization system makes perfect sense. "But it's obvious! I put current proposals in the folder labeled */office/clients/ green* and old proposals in */office/clients/red*. I don't understand why you couldn't find them!"*

The fact is that labeling and organization systems are intensely affected by their creators' perspectives.† We see this at the corporate level with web sites organized according to internal divisions or org charts, with groupings such as *marketing*, *sales*, *customer support*, *human resources*, and *information systems*. How does a customer visiting this web site know where to go for technical information about a product she just purchased? To design usable organization systems, we need to escape from our own mental models of content labeling and organization.

We employ a mix of user research and analysis methods to gain real insight. How do users group the information? What types of labels do they use? How do they navigate? This challenge is complicated by the fact that web sites are designed for multiple users, and all users will have different ways of understanding the information. Their levels of familiarity with your company and your content will vary. For these reasons, even with a massive barrage of user tests, it is impossible to create a perfect organization system. One site does not fit all! However, by recognizing the importance of perspective, by striving to understand the intended audiences through user research and testing, and by providing multiple navigation pathways, you can do a better job of organizing information for public consumption than your coworker does on his desktop computer.

---

* It actually gets even more complicated because an individual's needs, perspectives, and behaviors change over time. A significant body of research within the field of library and information science explores the complex nature of information models. For an example, see "Anomalous States of Knowledge as a Basis for Information Retrieval" by N.J. Belkin, *Canadian Journal of Information Science,* 5 (1980).

† For a fascinating study on the idiosyncratic methods people use to organize their physical desktops and office spaces, see "How Do People Organize Their Desks? Implications for the Design of Office Information Systems" by T.W. Malone, *ACM Transactions on Office Information Systems 1* (1983).

Internal Politics

Politics exist in every organization. Individuals and departments constantly position for influence or respect. Because of the inherent power of information organization in forming understanding and opinion, the process of designing information architectures for web sites and intranets can involve a strong undercurrent of politics. The choice of organization and labeling systems can have a big impact on how users of the site perceive the company, its departments, and its products. For example, should we include a link to the library site on the main page of the corporate intranet? Should we call it *The Library* or *Information Services* or *Knowledge Management*? Should information resources provided by other departments be included in this area? If the library gets a link on the main page, why not corporate communications? What about daily news?

As an information architect, you must be sensitive to your organization's political environment. In certain cases, you must remind your colleagues to focus on creating an architecture that works for the user. In others, you may need to make compromises to avoid serious political conflict. Politics raise the complexity and difficulty of creating usable information architectures. However, if you are sensitive to the political issues at hand, you can manage their impact upon the architecture.

Organizing Web Sites and Intranets

The organization of information in web sites and intranets is a major factor in determining success, and yet many web development teams lack the understanding necessary to do the job well. Our goal in this chapter is to provide a foundation for tackling even the most challenging information organization projects.

Organization systems are composed of *organization schemes* and *organization structures*. An organization scheme defines the shared characteristics of content items and influences the logical grouping of those items. An organization structure defines the types of relationships between content items and groups.

Before diving in, it's important to understand information organization in the context of web site development. Organization is closely related to navigation, labeling, and indexing. The hierarchical organization structures of web sites often play the part of primary navigation system. The labels of categories play a significant role in defining the contents of those categories. Manual indexing or *metadata tagging* is ultimately a tool for organizing content items into groups at a very detailed level. Despite these closely knit relationships, it is both possible and useful to isolate the design of organization systems, which will form the foundation for navigation and labeling systems. By focusing solely on the logical grouping of information, you avoid the distractions of implementation details and can design a better web site.

Organization Schemes

We navigate through organization schemes every day. Telephone books, supermarkets, and television programming guides all use organization schemes to facilitate access. Some schemes are easy to use. We rarely have difficulty finding a friend's phone number in the alphabetical organization scheme of the white pages. Some schemes are intensely frustrating. Trying to find marshmallows or popcorn in a large and unfamiliar supermarket can drive us crazy. Are marshmallows in the snack aisle, the baking ingredients section, both, or neither?

In fact, the organization schemes of the phone book and the supermarket are fundamentally different. The alphabetical organization scheme of the phone book's white pages is exact. The hybrid topical/task-oriented organization scheme of the supermarket is ambiguous.

Exact Organization Schemes

Let's start with the easy ones. Exact or "objective" organization schemes divide information into well-defined and mutually exclusive sections. The alphabetical organization of the phone book's white pages is a perfect example. If you know the last name of the person you are looking for, navigating the scheme is easy. "Porter" is in the Ps, which are after the Os but before the Qs. This is called *known-item* searching. You know what you're looking for, and it's obvious where to find it. No ambiguity is involved. The problem with exact organization schemes is that they require users to know the specific name of the resource they are looking for. The white pages don't work very well if you're looking for a plumber.

Exact organization schemes are relatively easy to design and maintain because there is little intellectual work involved in assigning items to categories. They are also easy to use. The following sections explore three frequently used exact organization schemes.

Alphabetical

An alphabetical organization scheme is the primary organization scheme for encyclopedias and dictionaries. Almost all nonfiction books, including this one, provide an alphabetical index. Phone books, department-store directories, bookstores, and libraries all make use of our 26-letter alphabet for organizing their contents. Alphabetical organization often serves as an umbrella for other organization schemes. We see information organized alphabetically by last name, by product or service, by department, and by format. Figure 5-2 provides an example of a departmental directory organized alphabetically by last name.

Figure 5-2. A directory of people at Microsoft Research

Chronological

Certain types of information lend themselves to chronological organization. For example, an archive of press releases might be organized by the date of release. Press release archives are obvious candidates for chronological organization schemes (see Figure 5-3). The date of announcement provides important context for the release. However, keep in mind that users may also want to browse the releases by title, product category, or geography, or to search by keyword. A complementary combination of organization schemes is often necessary. History books, magazine archives, diaries, and television guides tend to be organized chronologically. As long as there is agreement on when a particular event occurred, chronological schemes are easy to design and use.

Geographical

Place is often an important characteristic of information. We travel from one place to another. We care about the news and weather that affects us in our location. Political, social, and economic issues are frequently location-dependent. And, in a world where mobile devices such as Blackberries and Treos are becoming location-aware, while companies like Google and Yahoo! are investing heavily in local search and directory services, the map as interface is enjoying a resurgence of interest.

With the exception of border disputes, geographical organization schemes are fairly straightforward to design and use. Figure 5-4 shows an example of a geographical organization scheme. Users can select a location from the map using their mouse.

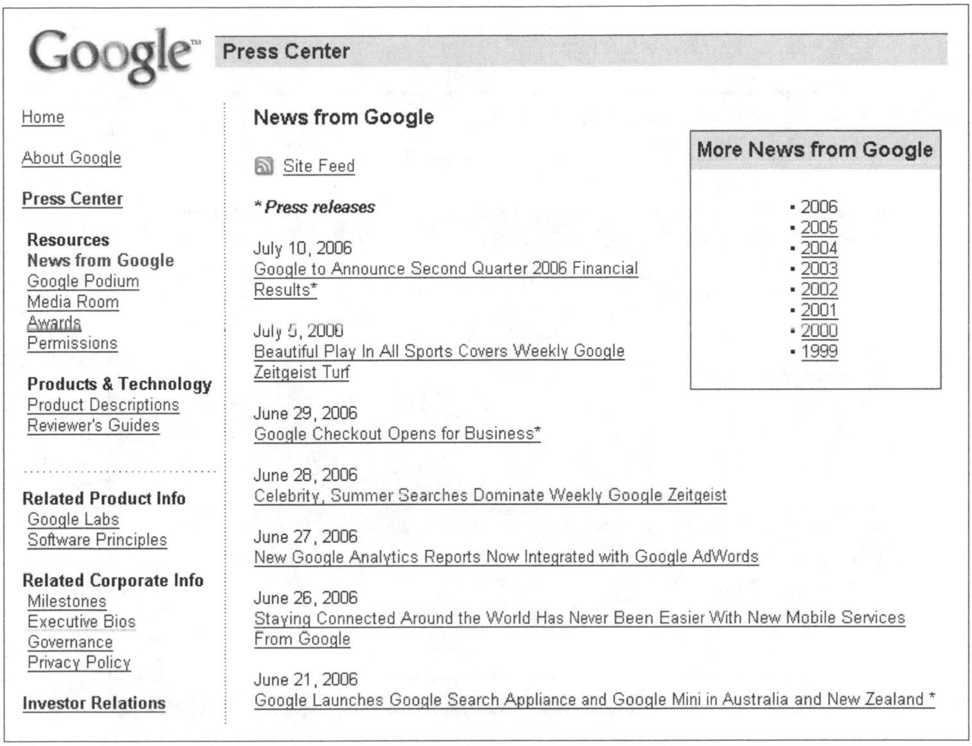

Figure 5-3. Press releases in reverse chronological order

Ambiguous Organization Schemes

Now for the tough ones. Ambiguous or "subjective" organization schemes divide information into categories that defy exact definition. They are mired in the ambiguity of language and organization, not to mention human subjectivity. They are difficult to design and maintain. They can be difficult to use. Remember the tomato? Do we classify it under fruit, berry, or vegetable?

However, they are often more important and useful than exact organization schemes. Consider the typical library catalog. There are three primary organization schemes: you can search for books by author, by title, or by subject. The author and title organization schemes are exact and thereby easier to create, maintain, and use. However, extensive research shows that library patrons use ambiguous subject-based schemes such as the Dewey Decimal and Library of Congress classification systems much more frequently.

There's a simple reason why people find ambiguous organization schemes so useful: we don't always know what we're looking for. In some cases, you simply don't know the correct label. In others, you may have only a vague information need that you can't quite articulate. For these reasons, information seeking is often iterative and interactive. What you find at the beginning of your search may influence what you

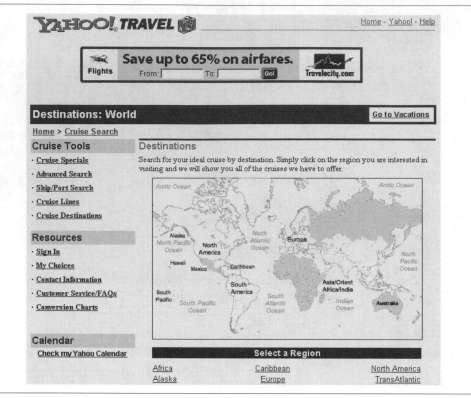

Figure 5-4. A geographical organization scheme

look for and find later in your search. This information-seeking process can involve a wonderful element of associative learning. Seek and ye shall find, but if the system is well designed, you also might learn along the way. This is web surfing at its best.

Ambiguous organization supports this serendipitous mode of information seeking by grouping items in intellectually meaningful ways. In an alphabetical scheme, closely grouped items may have nothing in common beyond the fact that their names begin with the same letter. In an ambiguous organization scheme, someone other than the user has made an intellectual decision to group items together. This grouping of related items supports an associative learning process that may enable the user to make new connections and reach better conclusions. While ambiguous organization schemes require more work and introduce a messy element of subjectivity, they often prove more valuable to the user than exact schemes.

The success of ambiguous organization schemes depends upon the quality of the scheme and the careful placement of individual items within that scheme. Rigorous user testing is essential. In most situations, there is an ongoing need for classifying new items and for modifying the organization scheme to reflect changes in the industry. Maintaining these schemes may require dedicated staff with subject matter expertise. Let's review a few of the most common and valuable ambiguous organization schemes.

Topic

Organizing information by subject or topic is one of the most useful and challenging approaches. Phone book yellow pages are organized topically, so that's the place to look when you need a plumber. Academic courses and departments, newspapers, and the chapters of most nonfiction books are all organized along topical lines.

While few web sites are organized solely by topic, most should provide some sort of topical access to content. In designing a topical organization scheme, it is important to define the breadth of coverage. Some schemes, such as those found in an encyclopedia, cover the entire breadth of human knowledge. Research-oriented web sites such as Consumer Reports (shown in Figure 5-5) rely heavily on their topical organization scheme. Others, such as corporate web sites, are limited in breadth, covering only those topics directly related to that company's products and services. In designing a topical organization scheme, keep in mind that you are defining the universe of content (both present and future) that users will expect to find within that area of the web site.

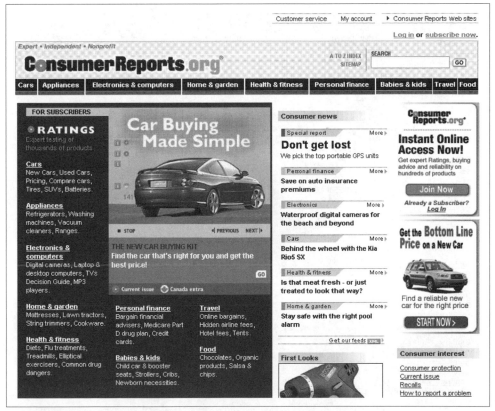

Figure 5-5. This topical taxonomy shows categories and subcategories

Task

Task-oriented schemes organize content and applications into a collection of processes, functions, or tasks. These schemes are appropriate when it's possible to anticipate a limited number of high-priority tasks that users will want to perform. Desktop software applications such as word processors and spreadsheets provide familiar examples. Collections of individual actions are organized under task-oriented menus such as *Edit*, *Insert*, and *Format*.

On the Web, task-oriented organization schemes are most common in the context of e-commerce web sites where customer interaction takes center stage. Intranets and extranets also lend themselves well to a task orientation, since they tend to integrate powerful applications or "e-services" as well as content. You will rarely find a web site organized solely by task. Instead, task-oriented schemes are usually embedded within specific subsites or integrated into hybrid task/topic navigation systems, as we see in Figure 5-6.

Figure 5-6. Task and topic coexist on the eBay home page

Audience

In cases where there are two or more clearly definable audiences for a web site or intranet, an audience-specific organization scheme may make sense. This type of scheme works best when the site is frequented by repeat visitors who can bookmark their particular section of the site. It also works well if there is value in customizing the content for each audience. Audience-oriented schemes break a site into smaller, audience-specific mini-sites, thereby allowing for clutter-free pages that present only the options of interest to that particular audience. The main page of dell.com, shown in Figure 5-7, presents an audience-oriented organization scheme (on the right) that invites customers to self-identify.

Figure 5-7. Dell invites users to self-identify

Organizing by audience brings all the promise and peril associated with any form of personalization. For example, Dell understands a great deal about its audience segments and brings this knowledge to bear on its web site. If I visit the site and identify myself as a member of the "Home & Home Office" audience, Dell will present me with a set of options and sample system configurations designed to meet my needs. In this instance, Dell might make the educated guess that I probably need a modem to connect to the Internet from my home. However, this guess would be wrong, since I now have affordable broadband access in my community. I need an Ethernet card instead. All ambiguous schemes require the information architect to make these educated guesses and revisit them over time.

Audience-specific schemes can be open or closed. An open scheme will allow members of one audience to access the content intended for other audiences. A closed scheme will prevent members from moving between audience-specific sections. This may be appropriate if subscription fees or security issues are involved.

Metaphor

Metaphors are commonly used to help users understand the new by relating it to the familiar. You need not look further than your *desktop* computer with its *folders*, *files*, and *trash can* or *recycle bin* for an example. Applied to an interface in this way, metaphors can help users understand content and function intuitively. In addition, the process of exploring possible metaphor-driven organization schemes can generate new and exciting ideas about the design, organization, and function of the web site.

While metaphor exploration can be useful while brainstorming, you should use caution when considering a metaphor-driven global organization scheme. First, metaphors, if they are to succeed, must be familiar to users. Organizing the web site of a computer-hardware vendor according to the internal architecture of a computer will not help users who don't understand the layout of a motherboard.

Second, metaphors can introduce unwanted baggage or be limiting. For example, users might expect a digital library to be staffed by a librarian that will answer reference questions. Most digital libraries do not provide this service. Additionally, you may wish to provide services in your digital library that have no clear corollary in the real world. Creating your own customized version of the library is one such example. This will force you to break out of the metaphor, introducing inconsistency into your organization scheme.

In the Teletubbies example in Figure 5-8, the games area is organized according to the metaphor of a physical place, populated by creatures and objects. This colorful approach invites exploration, and children quickly learn that they must go "inside Home Hill" to play with the machine called "Nu Nu." Since most of the target audience can't read, an overarching visual metaphor is a great solution. But unless your web site is aimed at young children, metaphor should probably play only a niche role.

Hybrids

The power of a pure organization scheme derives from its ability to suggest a simple mental model that users can quickly understand. Users easily recognize an audience-specific or topical organization. And fairly small, pure organization schemes can be applied to large amounts of content without sacrificing their integrity or diminishing their usability.

Figure 5-8. The Teletubbies' metaphor-driven games area

However, when you start blending elements of multiple schemes, confusion often follows, and solutions are rarely scalable. Consider the example in Figure 5-9. This hybrid scheme includes elements of audience-specific, topical, metaphor-based, task-oriented, and alphabetical organization schemes. Because they are all mixed together, we can't form a mental model. Instead, we need to skim through each menu item to find the option we're looking for.

The Mixed-Up Library

Adult	*audience-oriented*
Arts and Humanities	*topical*
Community Center	*metaphor-based*
Get a Library Card	*functional*
Learn About Our Library	*functional*
Science	*topical*
Social Science	*topical*
Teen	*audience-oriented*
Youth	*audience-oriented*

Figure 5-9. A hybrid organization scheme

The exception to these cautions against hybrid schemes exists within the surface layer of navigation. As illustrated by eBay (see Figure 5-6), many web sites successfully combine topics and tasks on their main page and within their global navigation. This reflects the reality that both the organization and its users typically identify finding content and completing key tasks at the top of their priority lists. Because this includes only the highest-priority tasks, the solution does not need to be scalable. It's only when such schemes are used to organize a large volume of content and tasks that the problems arise. In other words, shallow hybrid schemes are fine, but deep hybrid schemes are not.

Unfortunately, deep hybrid schemes are still fairly common. This is because it is often difficult to agree upon any one scheme, so people throw the elements of multiple schemes together in a confusing mix. There is a better alternative. In cases where multiple schemes must be presented on one page, you should communicate to designers the importance of preserving the integrity of each scheme. As long as the schemes are presented separately on the page, they will retain the powerful ability to suggest a mental model for users. For example, a look at the Stanford University home page in Figure 5-10 reveals a topical scheme, an audience-oriented scheme, an alphabetical index, and a search function. By presenting them separately, Stanford provides flexibility without causing confusion.

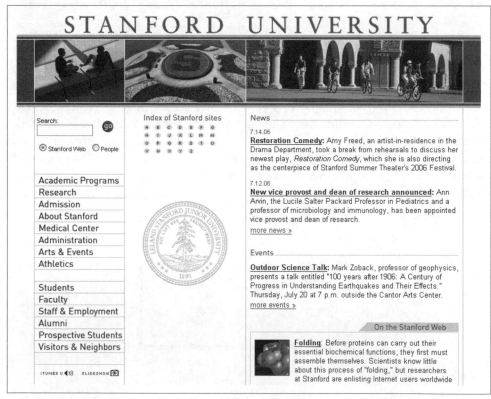

Figure 5-10. Stanford provides multiple organization schemes

Organization Structures

Organization structure plays an intangible yet very important role in the design of web sites. Although we interact with organization structures every day, we rarely think about them. Movies are linear in their physical structure. We experience them frame by frame from beginning to end. However, the plots themselves may be non-linear, employing flashbacks and parallel subplots. Maps have a spatial structure. Items are placed according to physical proximity, although the most useful maps cheat, sacrificing accuracy for clarity.

The structure of information defines the primary ways in which users can navigate. Major organization structures that apply to web site and intranet architectures include the hierarchy, the database-oriented model, and hypertext. Each organization structure possesses unique strengths and weaknesses. In some cases, it makes sense to use one or the other. In many cases, it makes sense to use all three in a complementary manner.

The Hierarchy: A Top-Down Approach

The foundation of almost all good information architectures is a well-designed hierarchy or *taxonomy*.[*] In this hypertextual world of nets and webs, such a statement may seem blasphemous, but it's true. The mutually exclusive subdivisions and parent–child relationships of hierarchies are simple and familiar. We have organized information into hierarchies since the beginning of time. Family trees are hierarchical. Our division of life on earth into kingdoms, classes, and species is hierarchical. Organization charts are usually hierarchical. We divide books into chapters into sections into paragraphs into sentences into words into letters. Hierarchy is ubiquitous in our lives and informs our understanding of the world in a profound and meaningful way. Because of this pervasiveness of hierarchy, users can easily and quickly understand web sites that use hierarchical organization models. They are able to develop a mental model of the site's structure and their location within that structure. This provides context that helps users feel comfortable. Figure 5-11 shows an example of a simple hierarchical model.

Because hierarchies provide a simple and familiar way to organize information, they are usually a good place to start the information architecture process. The top-down approach allows you to quickly get a handle on the scope of the web site without going through an extensive content-inventory process. You can begin identifying the major content areas and exploring possible organization schemes that will provide access to that content.

[*] In recent years, the business world has fallen in love with the term "taxonomies." Many biologists and librarians are frustrated with the exploding abuse of this term. We use it specifically to refer to a hierarchical arrangement of categories within the user interface of a web site or intranet. If you can't beat them, join them.

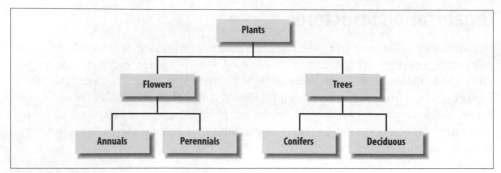

Figure 5-11. A simple hierarchical model

Designing taxonomies

When designing taxonomies on the Web, you should remember a few rules of thumb. First, you should be aware of, but not bound by, the idea that hierarchical categories should be mutually exclusive. Within a single organization scheme, you will need to balance the tension between exclusivity and inclusivity. Taxonomies that allow cross-listing are known as *polyhierarchical*. Ambiguous organization schemes in particular make it challenging to divide content into mutually exclusive categories. Do tomatoes belong in the fruit, vegetable, or berry category? In many cases, you might place the more ambiguous items into two or more categories so that users are sure to find them. However, if too many items are cross-listed, the hierarchy loses its value. This tension between exclusivity and inclusivity does not exist across different organization schemes. You would expect a listing of products organized by format to include the same items as a companion listing of products organized by topic. Topic and format are simply two different ways of looking at the same information. Or to use a technical term, they're two independent *facets*. See Chapter 9 for more about metadata, facets, and polyhierarchy.

Second, it is important to consider the balance between breadth and depth in your taxonomy. Breadth refers to the number of options at each level of the hierarchy. Depth refers to the number of levels in the hierarchy. If a hierarchy is too narrow and deep, users have to click through an inordinate number of levels to find what they are looking for. The top of Figure 5-12 illustrates a narrow-and-deep hierarchy in which users are faced with six clicks to reach the deepest content. In the (relatively) broad-and-shallow hierarchy, users must choose from 10 categories to reach 10 content items. If a hierarchy is too broad and shallow, as shown in the bottom part of Figure 5-12, users are faced with too many options on the main menu and are unpleasantly surprised by the lack of content once they select an option.

When considering breadth, you should be sensitive to people's visual scanning abilities and to the cognitive limits of the human mind. Now, we're not going to tell you

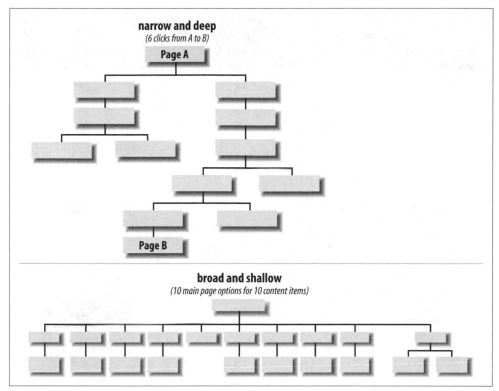

Figure 5-12. Balancing depth and breadth

to follow the infamous seven plus-or-minus two rule.[*] There is general consensus that the number of links you can safely include is constrained by users' abilities to visually scan the page rather than by their short-term memories.

Instead, we suggest that you:

- Recognize the danger of overloading users with too many options.
- Group and structure information at the page level.
- Subject your designs to rigorous user testing.

Consider the National Cancer Institute's award-winning main page, shown in Figure 5-13. It's one of the government's most visited (and tested) pages on the Web, and the portal into a large information system. Presenting information hierarchically at the page level, as NCI has done, can make a major positive impact on usability.

[*] G. Miller, "The Magical Number Seven, Plus or Minus Two: Some Limits on Our Capacity for Processing Information," *Psychological Review* 63, no. 2 (1956).

Figure 5-13. The National Cancer Institute groups items within the page

There are roughly 75 links on NCI's main page, and they're organized into several key groupings:

Group	Notes
Global Navigation	Global navigation (e.g., Cancer Topics, Clinical Trials, Cancer Statistics) has 7 links plus Search.
Types of Cancer	Includes 13 Common Cancer Types and 4 alternate ways to explore All Cancer Types.
Clinical Trials	Includes 4 links.
Cancer Topics	Includes 6 links.
Quick Links	Includes 8 links.
NCI Highlights	There are 7 headlines plus a link to the archive.
Features	On the right, there are 5 feature tiles.
Footer Navigation	Includes 11 links.

These 75 links are subdivided into eight discrete categories, with a limited number of links per category.

In contrast to breadth, when considering depth, you should be even more conservative. If users are forced to click through more than two or three levels, they may simply give up and leave your web site. At the very least, they'll become frustrated.

An excellent study conducted by Microsoft Research suggests that a medium balance of breadth and depth may provide the best results.[*]

For new web sites and intranets that are expected to grow, you should lean toward a broad-and-shallow rather than a narrow and deep hierarchy. This allows for the addition of content without major restructuring. It is less problematic to add items to secondary levels of the hierarchy than to the main page for a couple of reasons. First, the main page serves as the most prominent and important navigation interface for users. Changes to this page can really hurt the mental model users have formed of the web site over time. Second, because of the main page's prominence and importance, companies tend to spend lots of care (and money) on its graphic design and layout. Changes to the main page can be more time consuming and expensive than changes to secondary pages.

Finally, when designing organization structures, you should not become trapped by the hierarchical model. Certain content areas will invite a database or hypertext-based approach. The hierarchy is a good place to begin, but it is only one component in a cohesive organization system.

The Database Model: A Bottom-Up Approach

A database is defined as "a collection of data arranged for ease and speed of search and retrieval." A Rolodex provides a simple example of a flat-file database (see Figure 5-14). Each card represents an individual contact and constitutes a *record*. Each record contains several *fields*, such as name, address, and telephone number. Each field may contain data specific to that contact. The collection of records is a database.

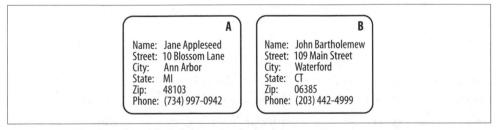

Figure 5-14. The printed card Rolodex is a simple database

---

[*] "Web Page Design: Implications of Memory, Structure and Scent for Information Retrieval," by Kevin Larson and Mary Czerwinski, Microsoft Research. See *http://research.microsoft.com/users/marycz/p25-larson.pdf.*

In an old-fashioned Rolodex, users are limited to searching for a particular individual by last name. In a more contemporary, computer-based contact-management system, we can also search and sort using other fields. For example, we can ask for a list of all contacts who live in Connecticut, sorted alphabetically by city.

Most of the heavy-duty databases we use are built upon the relational database model. In relational database structures, data is stored within a set of relations or tables. Rows in the tables represent records, and columns represent fields. Data in different tables may be linked through a series of keys. For example, in Figure 5-15, the au_id and title_id fields within the Author_Title table act as keys linking the data stored separately in the Author and Title tables.

So why are database structures important to information architects? After all, we made a fuss earlier in the book about our focus on information access rather than data retrieval. Where is this discussion heading?

In a word, metadata. Metadata is the primary key that links information architecture to the design of database schema. It allows us to apply the structure and power of relational databases to the heterogeneous, unstructured environments of web sites and intranets. By tagging documents and other information objects with controlled vocabulary metadata, we enable powerful searching, browsing, filtering, and dynamic linking. (We'll discuss metadata and controlled vocabularies in more detail in Chapter 9.)

The relationships between metadata elements can become quite complex. Defining and mapping these formal relationships requires significant skill and technical understanding. For example, the entity relationship diagram (ERD) in Figure 5-16 illustrates a structured approach to defining a metadata schema. Each entity (e.g., Resource) has attributes (e.g., Name, URL). These entities and attributes become records and fields. The ERD is used to visualize and refine the data model before design and population of the database.

We're not suggesting that all information architects must become experts in SQL, XML schema definition, the creation of entity relationship diagrams, and the design of relational databases—though these are all extremely valuable skills. In many cases, you'll be better off working with a professional programmer or database designer who really knows how to do this stuff. And for large web sites, you will hopefully be able to rely on Content Management System (CMS) software to manage your metadata and controlled vocabularies.

Instead, information architects need to understand how metadata, controlled vocabularies, and database structures can be used to enable:

- Automatic generation of alphabetical indexes (e.g., product index)
- Dynamic presentation of associative "see also" links
- Fielded searching
- Advanced filtering and sorting of search results

A Relational Data Base

AUTHOR

au_id	au_lname	au_fname	address	city	state
172-32-1176	White	Johnson	10932 Bigge Rd.	Menlo Park	CA
213-46-8915	Green	Marjorie	309 63rd St. #411	Oakland	CA
238-95-7766	Carson	Cheryl	589 Darwin Ln.	Berkeley	CA
267-41-2394	O'Leary	Michael	22 Cleveland Av. #14	San Jose	CA
274-80-9391	Straight	Dean	5420 College Av.	Oakland	CA
341-22-1782	Smith	Meander	10 Mississippi Dr.	Lawrence	KS
409-56-7008	Bennet	Abraham	6223 Bateman St.	Berkeley	CA
427-17-2319	Dull	Ann	3410 Blonde St.	Palo Alto	CA
472-27-2349	Gringlesby	Burt	PO Box 792	Covelo	CA
486-29-1786	Locksley	Charlene	18 Broadway Av.	San Francisco	CA

TITLE

title_id	title	type	price	pub_id
BU1032	The Busy Executive's Database Guide	business	19.99	1389
BU1111	Cooking with Computers	business	11.95	1389
BU2075	You Can Combat Computer Stress!	business	2.99	736
BU7832	Straight Talk About Computers	business	19.99	1389
MC2222	Silicon Valley Gastronomic Treats	mod_cook	19.99	877
MC3021	The Gourmet Microwave	mod_cook	2.99	877
MC3026	The Psychology of Computer Cooking	UNDECIDED		877
PC1035	But Is It User Friendly?	popular_comp	22.95	1389
PC8888	Secrets of Silicon Valley	popular_comp	20	1389
PC9999	Net Etiquette	popular_comp		1389
PS2091	Is Anger the Enemy?	psychology	10.95	736

PUBLISHER

pub_id	pub_name	city
736	New Moon Books	Boston
877	Binnet & Hardley	Washington
1389	Algodata Infosystems	Berkeley
1622	Five Lakes Publishing	Chicago
1756	Ramona Publishers	Dallas
9901	GGG&G	München
9952	Scootney Books	New York
9999	Lucerne Publishing	Paris

AUTHOR_TITLE

au_id	title_id
172-32-1176	PS3333
213-46-8915	BU1032
213-46-8915	BU2075
238-95-7766	PC1035
267-41-2394	BU1111
267-41-2394	TC7777
274-80-9391	BU7832
409-56-7008	BU1032
427-17-2319	PC8888
472-27-2349	TC7777

Figure 5-15. A relational database schema (this example is drawn from an overview of the relational database model at the University of Texas at Austin)

The database model is particularly useful when applied within relatively homogeneous subsites such as product catalogs and staff directories. However, enterprise controlled vocabularies can often provide a thin horizontal layer of structure across the full breadth of a site. Deeper vertical vocabularies can then be created for particular departments, subjects, or audiences.

Hypertext

Hypertext is a relatively recent and highly nonlinear way of structuring information. A hypertext system involves two primary types of components: the items or chunks of information that will be linked, and the links between those chunks.

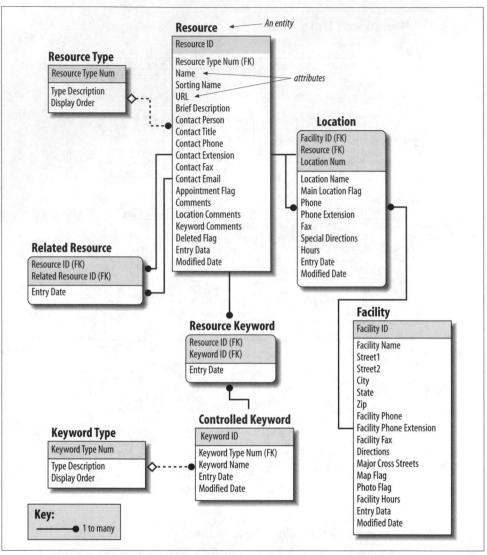

Figure 5-16. An entity relationship diagram showing a structured approach to defining a metadata schema (courtesy of InterConnect of Ann Arbor)

These components can form hypermedia systems that connect text, data, image, video, and audio chunks. Hypertext chunks can be connected hierarchically, non-hierarchically, or both, as shown in Figure 5-17. In hypertext systems, content chunks are connected via links in a loose web of relationships.

Although this organization structure provides you with great flexibility, it presents substantial potential for complexity and user confusion. Why? Because hypertext links reflect highly personal associations. As users navigate through highly hypertextual web

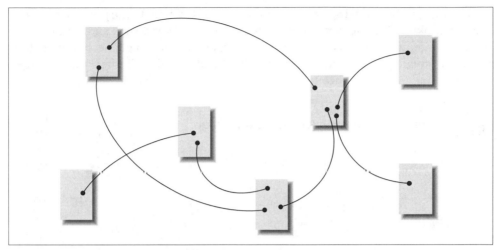

Figure 5-17. A network of hypertextual connections

sites, it is easy for them to get lost. It's as if they are thrown into a forest and are bouncing from tree to tree, trying to understand the lay of the land. They simply can't create a mental model of the site organization. Without context, users can quickly become overwhelmed and frustrated. In addition, hypertextual links are often personal in nature. The relationships that one person sees between content items may not be apparent to others.

For these reasons, hypertext is rarely a good candidate for the primary organization structure. Rather, it can be used to complement structures based upon the hierarchical or database models.

Hypertext allows for useful and creative relationships between items and areas in the hierarchy. It usually makes sense to first design the information hierarchy and then identify ways in which hypertext can complement the hierarchy.

Social Classification

In recent years, user participatory systems have captured the attention and imagination of many in the web design community. High profile successes such as Flickr and del.icio.us have demonstrated the potential to enlist users in content creation and classification, and they've sparked tremendous enthusiasm for tagging as a form of description and organization.

Free tagging, also known as collaborative categorization, mob indexing, and ethno-classification, is a simple yet powerful tool. Users tag objects with one or more keywords. The tags are public and serve as pivots for social navigation. Users can move fluidly between objects, authors, tags, and indexers. And when large numbers of people get involved, interesting opportunities arise to transform user behavior and tagging patterns into new organization and navigation systems.

For instance, in Figure 5-18, we see that the "IxDG Resource Library" is the most frequently bookmarked site that's been tagged with *interactiondesign*, and we can easily explore related tags such as *design*, *patterns*, *ia*, and *ui*. No single person or centralized team created a taxonomy to define these relationships. Rather, they emerged (and continue to emerge) through the tagging efforts of many individuals.

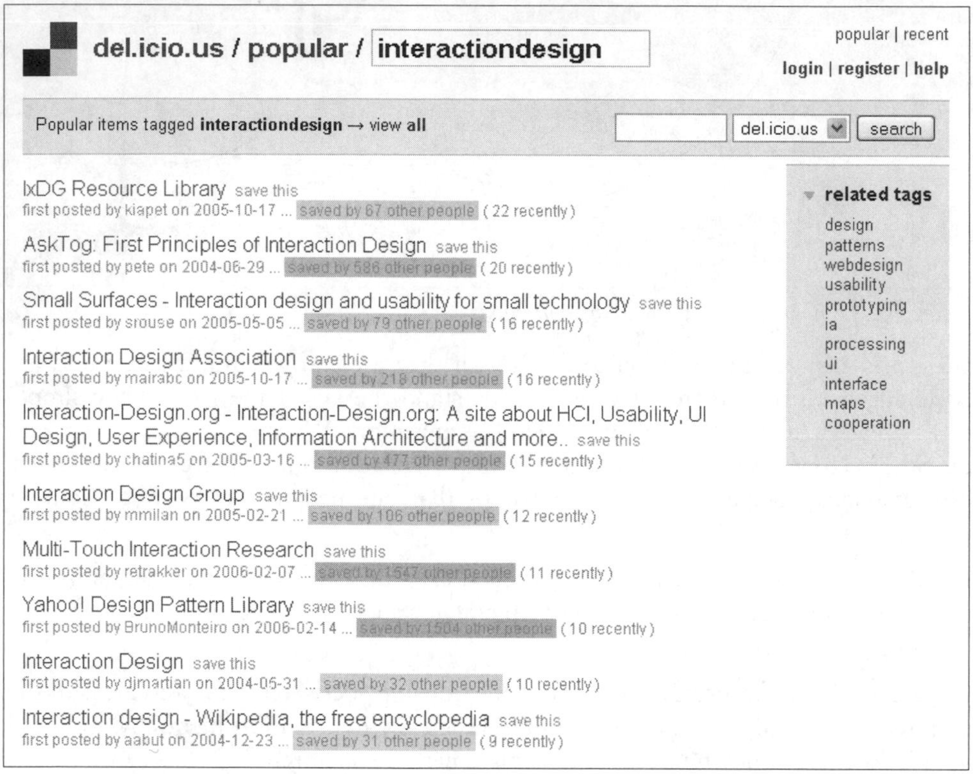

Figure 5-18. Popular items on del.icio.us

Similarly, Flickr has developed clustering algorithms (Figure 5-19) that group photos with overlapping tag sets, thereby creating emergent, self-describing taxonomies.

From an information architect's perspective, these experiments in the co-creation of structure and organization are fascinating. And, as you might expect, we can't resist labeling the new phenomenon. For instance, on an information architecture mailing list, Gene Smith described the growing use of user-defined tags to organize information, and asked, "Is there a name for this kind of informal social classification?" After a brief discussion, Thomas Vander Wal replied:

> So the user-created bottom-up categorical structure development with an emergent thesaurus would become a Folksonomy?[*]

---

[*] Posted on the members mailing list of the Information Architecture Institute on July 24, 2004.

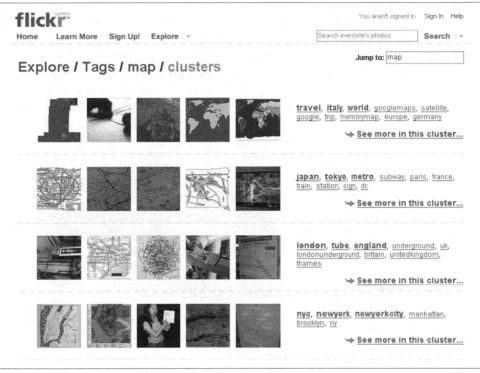

flickr GAMMA

You aren't signed in   Sign In   Help

Home   Learn More   Sign Up!   Explore ▾

Search everyone's photos   Search ▾

Jump to: map

Explore / Tags / map / clusters

travel, **italy**, **world**, googlemaps, satellite, google, trip, memorymap, europe, germany

↪ **See more in this cluster...**

japan, **tokyo**, **metro**, subway, paris, france, train, station, sign, dc

↪ **See more in this cluster...**

london, **tube**, **england**, underground, uk, londonunderground, britain, unitedkingdom, thames

↪ **See more in this cluster...**

nyc, **newyork**, **newyorkcity**, manhattan, brooklyn, ny

↪ **See more in this cluster...**

Figure 5-19. Clustering on Flickr

Of course, the tagging revolution hasn't come without a cost. In their enthusiasm for the new, many overzealous pundits have forecast the demise of traditional forms of organization. For example, David Sifry, founder and CEO of Technorati, stated:

> Tags are a simple, yet powerful, social software innovation. Today millions of people are freely and openly assigning metadata to content and conversations. Unlike rigid taxonomy schemes that people dislike, the ease of tagging for personal organization with social incentives leads to a rich and discoverable folksonomy. Intelligence is provided by real people from the bottom-up to aid social discovery. And with the right tag search and navigation, folksonomy outperforms more structured approaches to classification.*

And, in a debate with Lou Rosenfeld, Clay Shirky argued:

> The advantage of folksonomies isn't that they're better than controlled vocabularies, it's that they're better than nothing, because controlled vocabularies are not extensible to the majority of cases where tagging is needed...This is something the 'well-designed metadata' crowd has never understood...the cost of tagging large systems rigorously is crippling, so fantasies of using controlled metadata in environments like Flickr are really fantasies of users suddenly deciding to become disciples of information architecture.†

---

* This excerpt is from "Technorati Launches Tags," a January 17, 2005 post on the blog of David Sifry, founder and CEO of Technorati, the self-described "authority on what's going on in the world of weblogs."

† From the blog posting "folksonomies + controlled vocabularies" (*http://www.corante.com/many/archives/2005/01/07/folksonomies_controlled_vocabularies.php*).

These colorful statements play well in the blogosphere, but they are neither fair nor accurate. First, there's simply no evidence to suggest that folksonomy outperforms traditional approaches to organization, and anyone who searches Flickr can see first-hand the findability problems that come with the complete absence of vocabulary control. Second, these arguments ignore the critical importance of context. To date, tagging has flourished in a very limited set of environments. This is why the same examples, Flickr and del.icio.us, are used over and over again. It remains to be seen whether social classification can be successfully integrated into a wider range of web sites, intranets, and interactive products.

Hopefully, information architects will embrace this challenge, and play a leadership role in the synthesis of traditional and novel ways of organizing. In many contexts, we will continue to structure and organize information on behalf of our users. In others, we will design environments and tools that enlist our users in folksonomic acts of co-creation. And on some projects, we'll have the opportunity to bridge the gap, using both tags and taxonomies to connect users with the content they seek.

Creating Cohesive Organization Systems

Experience designer Nathan Shedroff suggests that the first step in transforming data into information is exploring its organization.* As you've seen in this chapter, organization systems are fairly complex. You need to consider a variety of exact and ambiguous organization schemes. Should you organize by topic, by task, or by audience? How about a chronological or geographical scheme? What about using multiple organization schemes?

You also need to think about the organization structures that influence how users can navigate through these schemes. Should you use a hierarchy, or would a more structured database model work best? Perhaps a loose hypertextual web would allow the most flexibility? Taken together in the context of a large web site development project, these questions can be overwhelming. That's why it's important to break down the site into its components, so you can tackle one question at a time. Also, keep in mind that all information-retrieval systems work best when applied to narrow domains of homogeneous content. By decomposing the content collection into these narrow domains, you can identify opportunities for highly effective organization systems.

However, it's also important not to lose sight of the big picture. As with cooking, you need to mix the right ingredients in the right way to get the desired results. Just because you like mushrooms and pancakes doesn't mean they will go well together. The recipe for cohesive organization systems varies from site to site. However, there are a few guidelines to keep in mind.

---

* For an interesting perspective on organizing things, see Nathan Shedroff's Unified Theory of Design at *http://www.nathan.com/thoughts/unified/6.html*.

When considering which organization schemes to use, remember the distinction between exact and ambiguous schemes. Exact schemes are best for known-item searching, when users know precisely what they are looking for. Ambiguous schemes are best for browsing and associative learning, when users have a vaguely defined information need. Whenever possible, use both types of schemes. Also, be aware of the challenges of organizing information on the Web. Language is ambiguous, content is heterogeneous, people have different perspectives, and politics can rear its ugly head. Providing multiple ways to access the same information can help to deal with all of these challenges.

When thinking about which organization structures to use, keep in mind that large web sites and intranets typically require several types of structure. The top-level, umbrella architecture for the site will almost certainly be hierarchical. As you are designing this hierarchy, keep a lookout for collections of structured, homogeneous information. These potential subsites are excellent candidates for the database model. Finally, remember that less structured, more creative relationships between content items can be handled through author-supplied hypertext or user-contributed tagging. In this way, myriad organization structures together can create a cohesive organization system.

CHAPTER 6
Labeling Systems

What we'll cover:
- What labeling is and why it's important
- Common types of labels
- Guidelines for developing labels
- Developing labels: borrowing from existing sources or starting from scratch

Labeling is a form of representation. Just as we use spoken words to represent concepts and thoughts, we use labels to represent larger chunks of information in our web sites. For example, "Contact Us" is a label that represents a chunk of content, often including a contact name, an address, and telephone, fax, and email information. You cannot present all this information quickly and effectively on an already crowded web page without overwhelming impatient users who might not actually need that information. Instead, a label like "Contact Us" works as a shortcut that triggers the right association in the user's mind without presenting all that stuff prominently. The user can then decide whether to click through or read on to get more contact information. So the goal of a label is to communicate information efficiently; that is, to convey meaning without taking up too much of a page's vertical space or a user's cognitive space.

Unlike the weather, hardly anyone ever talks about labeling (aside from a few deranged librarians, linguists, journalists, and, increasingly, information architects), but everyone can do something about it. In fact, we *are* doing something about it, albeit unconsciously: anyone developing content or an architecture for a web site is creating labels without even realizing it. And our label creation goes far beyond our web sites; ever since Adam named the animals, labeling has been one of the things that make us human. Spoken language is essentially a labeling system for concepts and things. Perhaps because we constantly label, we take the act of labeling for granted. That's why the labeling on web sites is often poor, and users suffer the consequences. This chapter provides some advice on how to think through a site's labeling before diving into implementation.

How does labeling fit with the other systems we've discussed? Well, labels are often the most obvious way to clearly show the user your organization and navigation systems. For example, a single web page might contain different groups of labels, with each group representing a different organization or navigation system. Examples include labels that match the site's organization system (e.g., Home/Home Office, Small Business, Medium & Large Business, Government, Health Care), a site-wide navigation system (e.g., Main, Search, Feedback), and a subsite navigation system (e.g., Add to Cart, Enter Billing Information, Confirm Purchase).

Why You Should Care About Labeling

Prerecorded or canned communications, including print, the Web, scripted radio, and TV, are very different from interactive real-time communications. When we talk with another person, we rely on constant user feedback to help us hone the way we get our message across. We subconsciously notice our conversation partner zoning out, getting ready to make her own point, or beginning to clench her fingers into an angry fist, and we react by shifting our own style of communication, perhaps by raising our speaking volume, increasing our use of body language, changing a rhetorical tack, or fleeing.

Unfortunately, when we "converse" with users through the web sites we design, the feedback isn't quite so immediate, if it exists at all. There are certainly exceptions—blogs, for example—but in most cases a site serves as an intermediary that slowly translates messages from the site's owners and authors to users, and back again. This "telephone game" muddies the message. So in such a disintermediated medium with few visual cues, communicating is harder, and labeling is therefore more important.

To minimize this disconnect, information architects must try their best to design labels that speak the same language as a site's users while reflecting its content. And, just as in a dialogue, when there is a question or confusion over a label, there should be clarification and explanation. Labels should educate users about new concepts and help them quickly identify familiar ones.

The conversation between user and site owner generally begins on a site's main page. To get a sense of how successful this conversation might be, look at a site's main page, do your best to ignore the other aspects of its design, and ask yourself a few questions: Do the prominent labels on this page stand out to you? If they do, why? (Often, successful labels are invisible; they don't get in your way.) If a label is new, unanticipated, or confusing, is there an explanation? Or are you required to click through to learn more? Although unscientific, this label testing exercise will help you get a sense of how the conversation might go with actual users.

Let's try it with an average, run-of-the-mill main page from the U-Haul site,* which is shown in Figure 6-1.

---

* In fairness to the good folks at U-Haul, their site is much improved since we grabbed this screen shot. But as the old design remains a wonderfully useful example of labeling problems, we've decided to keep it.

Figure 6-1. How do you respond to these labels?

The U-Haul main page's labels don't seem terribly out of the ordinary. However, mediocrity isn't an indicator of value or success; in fact, many trouble spots arise from an informal cruise through the page's labels. We've identified them as follows:

Main

"Main" refers to what? In web parlance, "Main" typically has something to do with a main page. Here, it describes a set of useful link labels such as "Get Rates & Reservations" and "Find a U-Haul Location." Why label these important links as "Main"? There are other possible labels, or visual design techniques could have been used to make the links stand out without mixing things up by using a conventional term like "Main." What exactly will be found under "College Connection"? It sounds like a branded program. Although it may represent useful content and functionality, that label sounds like part of U-Haul's corporate-speak, not the language of users.

Products & Services

If I wanted a hand truck, I'd look under "Hand trucks," not "Dollies." This disconnect may be due to regional differences: U-Haul is based in Phoenix, and I'm from New York. But which is the more common usage? Or if both labels are comparably common, should U-Haul list both terms?

SuperGraphics

Have you ever heard this term before? SuperGraphics are not graphics; they're apparently something better ("super"). English is wonderfully flexible, and new words are invented every day. But it's not realistic to expect impatient users to catch up with your linguistic creativity. Are "SuperGraphics" as important as "Products & Services"? What will we find behind the link "Pictorial Tribute to North America"—photos, a travelogue? And just what does such a tribute have to do with leasing trucks anyway?

Corporate

Do users understand what "Corporate" means? The term sounds, well, rather corporate, as if it might be intended for employees, suppliers, and others involved with the corporation. Perhaps the more conventional label "About Us" might be more appropriate. "Company Move" is a service for corporate relocations, not anything about U-Haul moving to new headquarters. Other links don't appear to belong here: like "Corporate Move," "Truck Sales" seems like it should go under "Products & Services." "Real Estate" and "Missing or Abandoned Equipment" are oddities that don't seem to belong anywhere. Is "Corporate" really another way of saying "Miscellaneous"?

Buy Online

Like "SuperGraphics," this label describes a single link, which is wasteful. And that link, "The U-Haul Store," seems to be a place to purchase or lease products and services. Why is "The U-Haul Store" set aside here? Does U-Haul want to accentuate it for some reason? If that reason has little to do with users, perhaps it's got everything to do with internal politics—perhaps one U-Haul VP owns "Products & Services," another owns "The U-Haul Store," and until they battle out their turf issues and one is extinguished, never the twain shall meet.

The results of this quick exercise can be summarized by these categories:

The labels aren't representative and don't differentiate

Too many of U-Haul's labels don't represent the content they link to or precede. Other than clicking through, users have no way to learn what "Corporate Move" means, or what the difference is between "Products & Services" and "The U-Haul Store." Groupings of dissimilar items (e.g., "Truck Sales," "Public Relations," and "Missing or Abandoned Equipment") don't provide any context for what those items' labels really represent. There is too much potential for confusion to consider these labels effective.

The labels are jargony, not user-centric

Labels like "College Connection" and "SuperGraphics" can expose an organization that, despite its best intentions, does not consider the importance of its customers' needs as important as its own goals, politics, and culture. This is often the case when web sites use organizational jargon for their labels. You've probably seen such sites; their labels are crystal clear, obvious, and enlightening, as long as you're one of the .01 percent of users who actually work for the sponsoring organization. A sure way to lose a sale is to label your site's product-ordering system as an "Order Processing and Fulfillment Facility."

The labels waste money

There are too many chances for a user to step into one of the many confusing cognitive traps presented by U-Haul's labels. And any time an architecture intrudes on a user's experience and forces him to pause and say "huh?", there is a reasonable chance that he will give up on a site and go somewhere else, especially given the competitive nature of this medium. In other words, confusing labels can negate the investment made to design and build a useful site and to market that site to intended audiences.

The labels don't make a good impression

The way you say or represent information in your site says a lot about you, your organization, and its brand. If you've ever read an airline magazine, you're familiar with those ads for some educational cassette series that develops your vocabulary. "The words you use can make or break your business deals" or something like that. The same is true with a web site's labeling—poor, unprofessional labeling can destroy a user's confidence in that organization. While it may have spent heavily on traditional branding, U-Haul doesn't seem to have given much thought to the labels on the most important piece of its virtual real estate—its main page. Customers might wonder if U-Haul will be similarly haphazard and thoughtless in the way it services its fleet of vehicles or handles the customer hotline.

Like writing or any other form of professional communication, labels do matter. It's fair to say that they're as integral to an effective web presence as any other aspect of your web site, be it brand, visual design, functionality, content, or navigability.

Varieties of Labels

On the Web, we regularly encounter labels in two formats: textual and iconic. In this chapter, we'll spend most of our time addressing textual labels (as they remain the most common despite the Web's highly visual nature), including:

Contextual links

Hyperlinks to chunks of information on other pages or to another location on the same page

Headings

Labels that simply describe the content that follows them, just as print headings do

Navigation system choices

Labels representing the options in navigation systems

Index terms

Keywords, tags, and subject headings that represent content for searching or browsing.

These categories are by no means perfect or mutually exclusive. A single label can do double duty; for example, the contextual link "Naked Bungee Jumping" could lead to a page that uses the heading label "Naked Bungee Jumping" and has been indexed as being about (you guessed it) "Naked Bungee Jumping." And some of these labels could be iconic rather than textual, although we'd rather not imagine a visual representation of naked bungee jumping.

In the following section, we'll explore the varieties of labeling in greater detail and provide you with some examples.

Labels As Contextual Links

Labels describe the hypertext links within the body of a document or chunk of information, and naturally occur within the descriptive context of their surrounding text. Contextual links are easy to create and are the basis for the exciting interconnectedness that drives much of the Web's success.

However, just because contextual links are relatively easy to create doesn't mean they necessarily work well. In fact, ease of creation introduces problems. Contextual links are generally not developed systematically; instead, they are developed in an ad hoc manner when the author makes a connection between his text and something else, and encodes that association in his document. These hypertext connections are therefore more heterogeneous and personal than, say, the connections between items in a hierarchy, where links are understood to be connecting parent items and child items. The result is that contextual link labels mean different things to different people. You see the link "Shakespeare" and, upon clicking it, expect to be taken to the Bard's biography. I, on the other hand, expect to be taken to his Wikipedia entry. In fact, the link actually takes us to a page for the village of Shakespeare, New Mexico, USA. Go figure....

To be more representational of the content they connect to, contextual links rely instead upon, naturally, context. If the content's author succeeds at establishing that context in his writing, then the label draws meaning from its surrounding text. If he doesn't, the label loses its representational value, and users are more likely to experience occasionally rude surprises.

Because Fidelity (Figure 6-2) is a site dedicated to providing information to investors, contextual links need to be straightforward and meaningful. Fidelity's contextual link labels, such as "stocks," "mutual funds," and "Learn how to invest," are representational, and draw on surrounding text and headings to make it clear what type of help you'll receive if you click through. These highly representational labels are made even clearer by their context: explanatory text, clear headings, and a site that itself has a few straightforward uses.

On the other hand, contextual links on a personal web log ("blog") aren't necessarily so clear. The author is among friends and can assume that his regular readers possess a certain level of background, or really, contextual knowledge. Or he knows that keeping his

Figure 6-2. The contextual links on this page from Fidelity are straightforward and meaningful

link labels less representational creates some mystery around what they'll lead to. So the author may choose to design contextual link labels that aren't so representational.

In Figure 6-3, the author expects us to know who "Eric Sinclair" is—perhaps he's been mentioned in this blog before. Or the author knows that we'll recognize the label "Eric Sinclair" as a person, and provides some minimal context—the fact that Eric wrote some comments—to entice the user to click through. "They Rule" is equally mysterious; we have no idea what this label represents, but the blog author contextualizes it as "fascinating" and "scary." Nonrepresentational labels have their place; as it's likely that we already trust the author's opinion, we'll probably want to click through and learn more. But without that degree of trust already in place, non-representational links can be damaging.

As we'll see, other varieties of labels derive context, and therefore meaning, from being part of larger sets of labels or labeling systems. But systematic consistency isn't

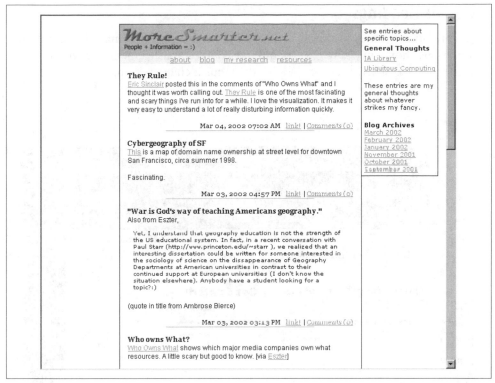

Figure 6-3. These contextual links aren't very representational, but that's acceptable when there is a high degree of trust for the author

quite so possible with link labels. These labels are instead glued together by the copy and context rather than membership in a peer group. However, consistency among these labels and the chunks of information to which they link remains an issue to keep in mind.

An information architect can ensure that contextual link labels are representational by asking herself, "What kind of information will the user expect to be taken to?" before creating and labeling a contextual link. Contextual links are created in such an ad hoc manner that simply asking this question will improve the quality of representation. (An easy way to study users' interpretations of labels is to provide a printout of a page with the labels clearly identified, and have subjects jot down what they'd expect each to link to.)

On the other hand, it's important to acknowledge that contextual links are often not within the information architect's control. Usually, content authors are responsible for contextual links. They are the ones who know the meaning of their content and how to best link it to other content. So while you may want to enforce rules for contextual link labels (such as what an employee's name should always link to), you may be better off suggesting guidelines to content authors (such as suggesting that employees' names link to a corresponding directory listing when possible).

Labels As Headings

Labels are often used as headings that describe the chunk of information that follows. Headings, as shown in Figure 6-4, are often used to establish a hierarchy within a text. Just as in a book, where headings help us distinguish chapters from sections, they also help us determine a site's subsites, or differentiate categories from subcategories.

Figure 6-4. Numbering, bullets, bolding, and vertical whitespace help the reader distinguish heading labels

The hierarchical relationships between headings—whether parent, child, or sibling—are usually established visually through consistent use of numbering, font sizes, colors and styles, whitespace and indentation, or combinations thereof. A visually clear hierarchy, often the work of information or graphic designers, can take some pressure off information architects by reducing the need to create labels that convey that hierarchy. So a set of labels that don't mean much can suddenly take on meaning when presented in a hierarchy. For example, this set of inconsistent headings may be quite confusing:

> Our Furniture Selection
> Office Chairs
> Our buyer's picks

```
Chairs from Steelcase
Hon products
Herman Miller
Aerons
Lateral Files
```

However, they are much more meaningful when presented in a hierarchy:

```
Our Furniture Selection
Office Chairs
        Our buyer's picks
                Chairs from Steelcase
                Hon products
                Herman Miller
                        Aerons
Lateral Files
```

It's also important not to be too rigidly bound to showcasing hierarchical relationships. In Figure 6-5, heading labels such as "Background" and "Scouting report" represent the text that follows them. Yet the statistics closer to the top of the page don't merit the same treatment because most readers could visually distinguish these without actually reading them. In other words, inserting the heading "Statistics" before the numbers and applying to it the same typographic style as "Background" and "Scouting report" wouldn't greatly benefit users, who, as baseball fans, would likely recognize them already.

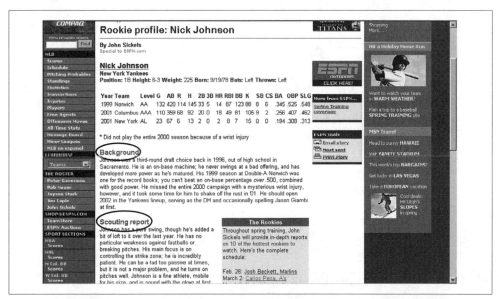

Figure 6-5. This hierarchy of heading labels is inconsistent, but that's OK

It is interesting to note, however, that it's difficult to distinguish one column of statistics from another, so each utilizes its own heading label.

We can be a bit more flexible when designing hierarchical headings, but it's especially important to maintain consistency when labeling steps in a process. To successfully navigate a process, it's typically necessary for users to complete each step along the way, so heading labels have to be obvious and must also convey sequence. Using numbers is an obvious way to communicate progression, and consistently framing the labels as actions—utilizing verbs—also helps tie together the sequence of steps. In effect, the labels should tell users where to start, where to go next, and what action will be involved in each step along the way. Figure 6-6 shows a page from Northwest Airlines in which the heading labels are clearly numbered, are consistently laid out, and utilize a consistent syntax that describes the question addressed in each step of the process.

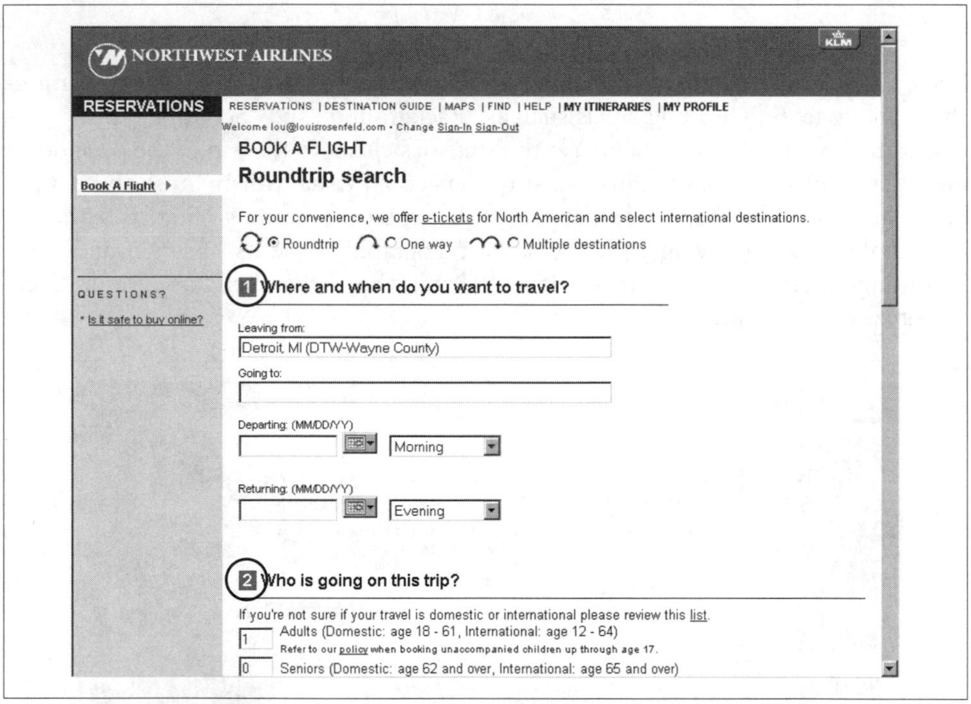

Figure 6-6. Sequential numbering and consistent syntax keep these labels clear

Heading labels, whether hierarchical or sequenced, come in multiples, and should be more systematically designed than contextual link labels.

Labels Within Navigation Systems

Because navigation systems typically have a small number of options, their labels demand consistent application more than any other type of label. A single inconsistent option can introduce an "apples and oranges" effect more quickly to a navigation system, which usually has fewer than ten choices, than to a set of index terms, which might have thousands. Additionally, a navigation system typically occurs again and again throughout a site, so navigation labeling problems are magnified through repeated exposure.

Users rely on a navigation system to behave "rationally" through consistent page location and look; labels should be no different. Effectively applied labels are integral to building a sense of familiarity, so they'd better not change from page to page. That's why using the label "Main" on one page, "Main Page" on another, and "Home" elsewhere could destroy the familiarity that the user needs when navigating a site. In Figure 6-7, the horizontal navigation system's four labels—"Getting Started," "Our Funds," "Planning," and "My Account"—are applied consistently throughout the site, and would be even more effective if colors and locations were also consistent.

Figure 6-7. Janus' navigation system labels remain consistent throughout the site

There are no standards, but some common variants exist for many navigation system labels. You should consider selecting one from each of these categories and applying it consistently, as these labels are already familiar to most web users. Here is a nonexhaustive list:

- Main, Main Page, Home
- Search, Find, Browse, Search/Browse
- Site Map, Contents, Table of Contents, Index
- Contact, Contact Us
- Help, FAQ, Frequently Asked Questions
- News, News & Events, News & Announcements, Announcements
- About, About Us, About <company name>, Who We Are

Of course, the same label can often represent different kinds of information. For example, in one site, "News" may link to an area that includes announcements of new additions to the site. In another site, "News" may link to an area of news stories describing national and world events. Obviously, if you use the same labels in different ways within your own site, your users will be very confused.

To address both problems, navigational labels can be augmented by brief descriptions (also known as *scope notes*) when initially introduced on the main page. In Figure 6-8, the navigation system labels appear in brief on the lefthand side, and are described with scope notes in the body of the main page.

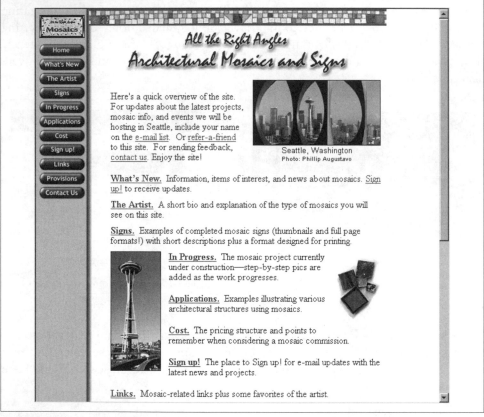

Figure 6-8. Scope notes are provided for each of the navigation system labels

In this case, if more representational navigation system labels had been used in the first place, they may have diminished the need to devote so much valuable main page real estate to scope notes. There are alternatives to scope notes that don't monopolize real estate, such as using JavaScript rollovers and other scripted mouseover effects to display the scope note, but these aren't an established convention. If you feel that your site will be regularly used by a loyal set of users who are willing to learn your site's conventions, then it's worth considering these alternatives; otherwise, we suggest keeping things simple by making your navigation labels representational.

Labels As Index Terms

Often referred to as keywords, tags, descriptive metadata, taxonomies, controlled vocabularies, and thesauri, sets of index term labels can be used to describe any type of content: sites, subsites, pages, content chunks, and so on. By representing the meaning of a piece of content, index terms support more precise searching than simply searching the full text of content—someone has assessed the content's meaning and described it using index terms, and searching those terms ought to be more effective than having a search engine match a query against the content's full text.

Index terms are also used to make browsing easier: the metadata from a collection of documents can serve as the source of browsable lists or menus. This can be highly beneficial to users, as index terms provide an alternative to a site's primary organization system, such as an information architecture organized by business unit. Index terms in the form of site indexes and other lists provide a valuable alternative view by "cutting across the grain" of organizational silos.

In Figure 6-9, this index of the BBC's site is generated from index term labels, which, in turn, are used to identify content from many different Sun business units. Much of the content already accessible through the BBC site's primary organization system is also accessible by browsing these index terms (e.g., keywords).

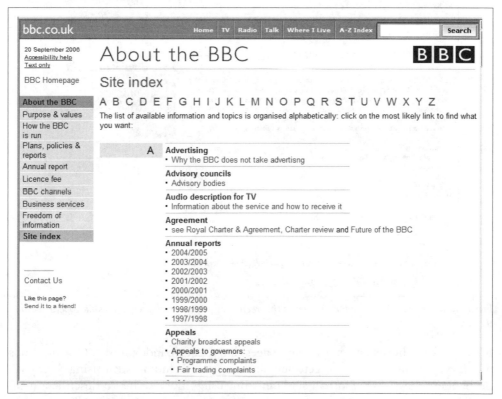

Figure 6-9. The BBC's site index

Frequently, index terms are completely invisible to users. The records we use to represent documents in content management systems and other databases typically include fields for index terms, which are often heard but not seen: they come into play only when you search. Similarly, index terms may be hidden as embedded metadata in an HTML document's <META...> or <TITLE> tags. For example, a furniture manufacturer's site might list the following index terms in the <META...> tags of records for its upholstered items:

```
<META NAME="keywords" CONTENT="upholstery, upholstered, sofa, couch,
loveseat, love seat, sectional, armchair, arm chair, easy chair,
chaise lounge">
```

So a search on "sofa" would retrieve the page with these index terms even if the term "sofa" doesn't appear anywhere in the page's text. Figure 6-10 shows a similar, more delectable example from Epicurious.com. A search for "snack" retrieves this recipe, though there is no mention of the term in the recipe itself. "Snack" is likely stored separately as an index term in a database record for this recipe.

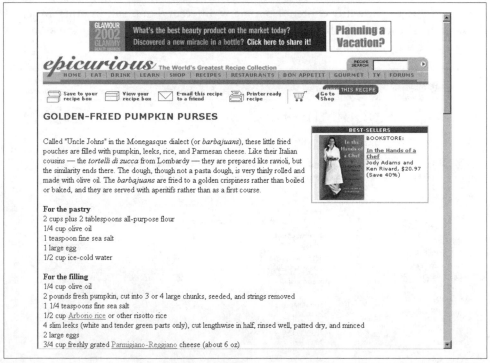

Figure 6-10. A search for "snack" retrieves this recipe, even though the term doesn't appear within the text

It's interesting how many sites' main pages don't feature index terms. Organizations do crazy, expensive things to get their sites noticed, including advertising their URL on banners flown over football stadiums. But using index terms to describe a main page is a much cheaper way for getting that page, and the site as a whole, indexed and "known" so that users who search the Web are more likely to find it.[*]

Getting your pages to stand out from one another is a different and much more daunting challenge. That's where a more systematic approach to labeling—using index terms from controlled vocabularies or thesauri—has more value. These sets of labels are designed to describe a delineated domain—such as products and services, or oncology—and to do so in a consistent, predictable manner. We'll describe these vocabularies in great detail in Chapter 9.

Iconic Labels

It's true that a picture is worth a thousand words. But which thousand?

Icons can represent information in much the same way as text can. We see them most frequently used as navigation system labels. Additionally, icons occasionally serve as heading labels and have even been known to show up as link labels, although this is rare.

The problem with iconic labels is that they constitute a much more limited language than text. That's why they're more typically used for navigation system or small organization system labels, where the list of options is small, than for larger sets of labels such as index terms, where iconic "vocabularies" are quickly outstripped. (They also can work well for less text-oriented audiences, like children.)

Even so, iconic labels are still a risky proposition in terms of whether or not they can represent meaning. Figure 6-11 is a navigation aid from jetBlue's web site. But what do the icons mean to you?

Figure 6-11. Icons from jetBlue's navigation system

Even given the fairly specific context of an airline's site, most users probably won't understand this language immediately, although they might correctly guess the meaning of one or two of these labels.

Since the iconic labels are presented with textual labels, our test wasn't really fair. But it is interesting to note that even the site's designers acknowledge that the iconic labels don't stand well on their own and hence need textual explanations.

---

[*] Search Engine Watch (*http://www.searchenginewatch.com*) is the most useful resource for learning how web-wide search engines and directories work, and how you can index your site's main and other major pages to "rise to the top" of retrieval results.

Iconic labels like these add aesthetic quality to a site, and as long as they don't compromise the site's usability, there's no reason not to use them. In fact, if your site's users visit regularly, the iconic "language" might get established in their minds through repeated exposure. In such situations, icons are an especially useful shorthand, both representational and easy to visually recognize—a double bonus. But it's interesting to note that jetBlue's subsidiary pages don't use iconic labels alone; they've chosen to maintain the icon/text pairing throughout their site. Unless your site has a patient, loyal audience of users who are willing to learn your visual language, we suggest using iconic labels only for systems with a limited set of options, being careful not to place form ahead of function.

Designing Labels

Designing effective labels is perhaps the most difficult aspect of information architecture. Language is simply too ambiguous for you to ever feel confident that you've perfected a label. There are always synonyms and homonyms to worry about, and different contexts influence our understanding of what a particular term means. But even labeling conventions are questionable: you absolutely cannot assume that the label "main page" will be correctly interpreted by 100 percent of your site's users. Your labels will never be perfect, and you can only hope that your efforts make a difference, as measuring label effectiveness is an extremely difficult undertaking.

If it sounds to you like labeling is an art rather than a science, you're absolutely correct. And, as in all such cases, you can forget about finding incontrovertible rules, and hope for guidelines instead. Following are some guidelines and related issues that will help you as you delve into the mysterious art of label design.

General Guidelines

Remember that *content*, *users*, and *context* affect all aspects of an information architecture, and this is particularly true with labels. Any of the variables attached to users, content, and context can drag a label into the land of ambiguity.

Let's go back to the term "pitch." From baseball (what's thrown) to football (the field where it's played in the United Kingdom), from sales (what's sometimes made on the golf course) to sailing (the angle of the boat in the water), there are at least 15 different definitions, and it's hard to make sure that your site's users, content, and context will converge upon the same definition. This ambiguity makes it difficult to assign labels to describe content, and difficult for users to rely on their assumptions about what specific labels actually mean.

So what can we do to make sure our labels are less ambiguous and more representational? The following two guidelines may help.

Narrow scope whenever possible

If we focus our sites on a more defined audience, we reduce the number of possible perspectives on what a label means. Sticking to fewer subject domains achieves more obvious and effective representation. A narrower business context means clearer goals for the site, its architecture, and therefore its labels.

To put it another way, labeling is easier if your site's content, users, and context are kept simple and focused. Too many sites have tried to take on too much, achieving broad mediocrity rather than nailing a few choice tasks. Accordingly, labeling systems often cover too much ground to truly be effective. If you are planning any aspect of your site's scope—who will use it, what content it will contain, and how, when, and why it should be used—erring toward simplicity will make your labels more effective.

If your site must be a jack of all trades, avoid using labels that address the entire site's content. (The obvious exception are the labels for site-wide navigation systems, which do cover the entire site.) But in the other areas of labeling, modularizing and simplifying content into subsites that meet the needs of specific audiences will enable you to design more modular, simpler collections of labels to address those specific areas.

This modular approach may result in separate labeling systems for different areas of your site. For example, records in your staff directory might benefit from a specialized labeling system that wouldn't make sense for other parts of the site, while your site-wide navigation system's labels wouldn't really apply to entries in the staff directory.

Develop consistent labeling systems, not labels

It's also important to remember that labels, like organization and navigation systems, are systems in their own right. Some are planned systems, some aren't. A successful system is designed with one or more characteristics that unify its members. In successful labeling systems, one characteristic is typically *consistency*.

Why is consistency important? Because consistency means predictability, and systems that are predictable are simply easier to learn. You see one or two labels, and then you know what to expect from the rest—if the system is consistent. This is especially important for first-time visitors to a site, but consistency benefits all users by making labeling easy to learn, easy to use, and therefore invisible.

Consistency is affected by many issues:

Style
> Haphazard usage of punctuation and case is a common problem within labeling systems, and can be addressed, if not eliminated, by using style guides. Consider hiring a proofreader and purchasing a copy of Strunk & White.

Presentation
> Similarly, consistent application of fonts, font sizes, colors, whitespace, and grouping can help visually reinforce the systematic nature of a group of labels.

Syntax

It's not uncommon to find verb-based labels (e.g., "Grooming Your Dog"), noun-based labels (e.g., "Diets for Dogs"), and question-based labels (e.g., "How Do You Paper-Train Your Dog?") all mixed together. Within a specific labeling system, consider choosing a single syntactical approach and sticking with it.

Granularity

Within a labeling system, it can be helpful to present labels that are roughly equal in their specificity. Exceptions (such as site indexes) aside, it's confusing to encounter a set of labels that cover differing levels of granularity. For example: "Chinese restaurants," "Restaurants," "Taquerias," "Fast Food Franchises," "Burger Kings."

Comprehensiveness

Users can be tripped up by noticeable gaps in a labeling system. For example, if a clothing retailer's site lists "pants," "ties," and "shoes," while somehow omitting "shirts," we may feel like something's wrong. Do they really not carry shirts? Or did they make a mistake? Aside from improving consistency, a comprehensive scope also helps users do a better job of quickly scanning and inferring the content a site will provide.

Audience

Mixing terms like "lymphoma" and "tummy ache" in a single labeling system can also throw off users, even if only temporarily. Consider the languages of your site's major audiences. If each audience uses a very different terminology, you may have to develop a separate labeling system for each audience, even if these systems are describing exactly the same content.

There are other potential roadblocks to consistency. None is particularly difficult to address, but you can certainly save a lot of labor and heartache if you consider these issues before you dive into creating labeling systems.

Sources of Labeling Systems

Now that you're ready to design labeling systems, where do you start? Believe it or not, this is the easy part. Unless you're dealing with ideas, concepts, and topics that until now were unknown to humanity, you'll probably have something to start with. And already having a few labels generally beats starting from scratch, which can be prohibitively expensive, especially with large vocabularies.

Existing labeling systems might include the labels currently on your site, or comparable or competitors' sites. Ask yourself who might have taken this on before. Study, learn, and "borrow" from what you find on other sites. And keep in mind that a major benefit of examining existing labeling systems is that they're systems—they're more than odd, miscellaneous labels that don't necessarily fit together.

As you look for existing labeling systems, consider what works and what doesn't. Which systems can you learn from, and, perhaps more importantly, which of those labels can you keep? There are a variety of sources for labels that you should examine.

Your site

Your web site probably already has labeling systems by default. At least some reasonable decisions had to have been made during the course of the site's creation, so you probably won't want to throw all those labels out completely. Instead, use them as a starting point for developing a complete labeling system, taking into consideration the decisions made while creating the original system.

A useful approach is to capture the existing labels in a single document. To do so, walk through the entire site, either manually or automatically, and gather the labels. You might consider assembling them in a simple table containing a list or outline of each label and the documents it represents. Creating a labeling table is often a natural extension of the content inventory process. It's a valuable exercise, though we don't recommend it for indexing term vocabularies, which are simply too large to table-ize unless you focus on small, focused segments of those vocabularies.

Following is a table for the navigation system labels on jetBlue's main page.

Label	Destination's heading label	Destination's <TITLE>label
Top-of-page navigation system labels		
Buy tickets	-	Online booking
Hotels/cars	Book hotels and rent cars online	Hotels - jetBlue
Travel info	-	Travel info - JetBlue
Work here	-	Work here - JetBlue
Learn more	Welcome from our CEO	Learn more - JetBlue
Speak up	-	Speak up - JetBlue
ShopBlue	Now you're ready to shopBlue	Welcome to shopBlue!
Body navigation system labels		
Track your flight	Real-Time Flight Tracking	Travel info - JetBlue
Our cities	Route map	Travel info - JetBlue
What to expect at the airport	Important security information	JetBlue Airways
Have fun	-	Have fun - jetBlue
Register with us	-	Member Profile
Bottom-of-page navigation system labels		
Home	jetBlue	JetBlue
Sitemap	Sitemap	siteMap - JetBlue
Faqs	FAQs	Get help - jetBlue
Your privacy	Privacy	Privacy policy - JetBlue
Contact us	Contacts	Learn more - JetBlue
Jobs	-	Learn more - JetBlue
Travel agents	Travel agency login	Agency and Corporate Bookings
Espanol	jetBlue en espanol	jetBlue en espanol

Arranging labels in a table provides a more condensed, complete, and accurate view of a site's navigation labels as a *system*. Inconsistencies are easier to catch; in jetBlue's case, we encounter three variants of the company's name alone: "jetBlue," "JetBlue," and "JetBlue Airways." We find inconsistencies for a single page's labels: the contact page is labeled "Contact us," "Contacts," and "Learn more - JetBlue." Many pages don't have main headings. We encounter various other style inconsistencies that may confuse users. We may decide that, personally, we just don't like certain labels. We may also decide that some of the problems aren't worth changing. In any case, we now have a sense of the site's current labeling system and how it could be improved.

Comparable and competitive sites

If you don't have a site in place or are looking for new ideas, look elsewhere for labeling systems. The open nature of the Web allows us to learn from one another and encourages an atmosphere of benevolent plagiarism. So, just as you might view the source of a wonderfully designed page, you can "borrow" from another site's great labeling system.

Determine beforehand what your audiences' needs are most likely to be, and then surf your competitors' sites, borrowing what works and noting what doesn't (you might consider creating a label table for this specific purpose). If you don't have competitors, visit comparable sites or sites that seem to be best in class.

If you surf multiple competitive or comparative sites, you may find that labeling patterns emerge. These patterns may not yet be industry standards, but they at least can inform your choice of labels. For example, in a recent competitive analysis of eight financial services sites, "personal finance" was found to be more or less a de facto label compared to its synonyms. Such data may discourage you from using a different label.

Figure 6-12 shows labeling systems from Compaq, Gateway, Dell, and IBM, all competing in the PC business. Do you notice a trend here?

Controlled vocabularies and thesauri

Another great source is existing controlled vocabularies and thesauri (a topic we'll cover in depth in Chapter 9). These especially useful resources are created by professionals with library or subject-specific backgrounds, who have already done much of the work of ensuring accurate representation and consistency. These vocabularies are often publicly available and have been designed for broad usage. You'll find these to be most useful for populating labeling systems used for indexing content.

But here's a piece of advice: seek out narrowly focused vocabularies that help specific audiences to access specific types of content. For example, if your site's users are computer scientists, a computer science thesaurus "thinks" and represents concepts in a way your users are likely to understand, more so than a general scheme like the Library of Congress subject headings would.

A good example of a specific controlled vocabulary is the Educational Resources Information Center (ERIC) Thesaurus. This thesaurus was designed, as you'd guess, to

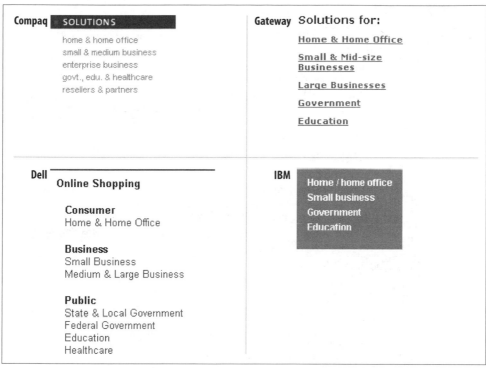

Figure 6-12. Labeling systems from Compaq, Gateway, Dell, and IBM

describe the domain of education. An entry in the ERIC Thesaurus for "scholarships" is shown in Figure 6-13.

If your site has to do with education or if your audience is comprised of educators, you might start with ERIC as the source for your site's labels. You can use a thesaurus like ERIC to help you with specific labeling challenges, like determining a better variant for a particularly knotty label. You might go as far as to license the entire vocabulary and use it as your site's labeling system.

Unfortunately, there aren't controlled vocabularies and thesauri for every domain. Sometimes you may find a matching vocabulary that emphasizes the needs of a different audience. Still, it's always worth seeing if a potentially useful controlled vocabulary or thesaurus exists before creating labeling systems from scratch. Try these four excellent lists as you hunt for sources of labels:

- Taxonomy Warehouse: *http://taxonomywarehouse.com/*

- ThesauriOnline (American Society of Indexers): *http://www.asindexing.org/site/thesonet.shtml*

- Controlled vocabularies (Michael Middleton): *http://sky.fit.qut.edu.au/~middletm/cont_voc.html*

- Web Thesaurus Compendium (Barbara Lutes): *http://www.ipsi.fraunhofer.de/~lutes/thesoecd.html*

Term:	Scholarships
Record Type:	Main
Scope Note:	Awards, usually of money or reduced tuition, given to students primarily in recognition of achievement or potential but also for other specific characteristics such as financial need, residence, or academic interest
Category:	620
Broader Terms:	Student Financial Aid;
Narrower Terms:	Merit Scholarships; Tuition Grants;
Related Terms:	Awards; Educational Finance; Educational Vouchers; Eligibility; Fellowships; Grants; Instructional Student Costs; Noninstructional Student Costs; Scholarship Funds; Student Costs;
Used For:	Endowed Scholarships
Use Term:	
Use And:	
Add Date:	07/01/1966

Figure 6-13. Controlled vocabularies and thesauri are rich sources of labels

Creating New Labeling Systems

When there are no existing labeling systems or when you need to do more customizing than you'd expected, you face the tougher challenge of creating labeling systems from scratch. Your most important sources are your content and your site's users.

Content analysis

Labels can come directly from your site's content. You might read a representative sample of your site's content and jot down a few descriptive keywords for each document along the way. It's a slow and painful process, and it obviously won't work with a huge set of documents. If you go this route, look for ways to speed up the process by focusing on any existing content representations like titles, summaries, and abstracts. Analyzing content for candidate labels is certainly another area where art dominates science.

There are software tools now available that can perform *auto-extraction* of meaningful terms from content. These tools can save you quite a bit of time if you face a huge body of content; like many software-based solutions, auto-extraction tools may get you 80 percent of the way to the finish line. You'll be able to take the terms that are output by the software and use them as candidates for a controlled vocabulary, but you'll still need to do a bit of manual labor to make sure the output actually makes sense. (And it's worth noting that auto-extraction tools—and the training and tuning to make them work well—can be quite expensive.) We provide pointers to some auto-extraction tools in Chapter 16.

Content authors

Another manual approach is to ask content authors to suggest labels for their own content. This might be useful if you have access to authors; for example, you could talk to your company's researchers who create technical reports and white papers, or to the PR people who write press releases.

However, even when authors select terms from a controlled vocabulary to label their content, they don't necessarily do it with the realization that their document is only one of many in a broader collection. So they might not use a sufficiently specific label. And few authors happen to be professional indexers.

So take their labels with a grain of salt, and don't rely upon them for accuracy. As with other sources, labels from authors should be considered useful candidates for labels, not final versions.

User advocates and subject matter experts

Another approach is to find advanced users or user advocates who can speak on the users' behalf. Such people may include librarians, switchboard operators, or subject matter experts (SMEs) who are familiar with the users' information needs in a larger context. Some of these people—reference librarians, for example—keep logs of what users want; all will have a good innate sense of users' needs by dint of constant interaction.

We found that talking to user advocates was quite helpful when working with a major healthcare system. Working with their library's staff and SMEs, we set out to create two labeling systems, one with medical terms to help medical professionals browse the services offered by the healthcare system, the other for the lay audience to access the same content. It wasn't difficult to come up with the medical terms because there are many thesauri and controlled vocabularies geared toward labeling medical content. It was much more difficult to come up with a scheme for the layperson's list of terms. There didn't seem to be an ideal controlled vocabulary, and we couldn't draw labels from the site's content because it hadn't been created yet. So we were truly starting from scratch.

We solved this dilemma by using a top-down approach: we worked with the librarians to determine what they thought users wanted out of the site. We considered their general needs, and came up with a few major ones:

1. They need information about a problem, illness, or condition.
2. The problem is with a particular organ or part of the body.
3. They want to know about the diagnostics or tests that the healthcare professionals will perform to learn more about the problem.

4. They need information on the treatment, drug, or solution that will be provided by the healthcare system.

5. They want to know how they can pay for the service.

6. They want to know how they can maintain their health.

We then came up with basic terms to cover the majority of these six categories, taking care to use terms appropriate to this audience of laypersons. Here are some examples:

Category	Sample labels
Problem/illness/condition	HIV, fracture, arthritis, depression
Organ/body part	Heart, joints, mental health
Diagnostics/tests	Blood pressure, X-ray
Treatment/drug/solution	Hospice, bifocals, joint replacement
Payment	Administrative services, health maintenance organization, medical records
Health maintenance	Exercise, vaccination

By starting with a few groupings, we were able to generate labels to support indexing the site. We knew a bit about the audience (laypersons), and so were able to generate the right kinds of terms to support their needs (e.g., *leg* instead of *femur*). The secret was working with people (in this case, staff librarians) who were knowledgeable about the kind of information the users want.

Directly from users

The users of a site may be telling you, directly or indirectly, what the labels should be. This isn't the easiest information to get your hands on, but if you can, it's the best source of labeling there is.

Card sorting. *Card sort* exercises are one of the best ways to learn how your users would use information. (Card sorting methodologies* are covered more extensively in Chapter 10.) There are two basic varieties of card sorts: open and closed. *Open card sorts* allow subjects to cluster labels for existing content into their own categories and then label those categories (and clearly, card sorting is useful when designing organization systems as well as labeling systems). *Closed card sorts* provide subjects with existing categories and ask them to sort content into those categories. At the start of a closed card sort, you can ask users to explain what they think each category label represents and compare these definitions to your own. Both approaches are useful ways to determine labels, although they're more appropriate for smaller sets of labels such as those used for navigation systems.

---

* We also anticipate that Donna Maurer's book, *Card Sorting: The Book* will be quite helpful here; it will be published by Rosenfeld Media in early 2007 (*http://www.rosenfeldmedia.com/books/cardsorting*).

In the example below, we asked subjects to categorize cards from the owner's section of a site for a large automotive company (let's call it "Tucker"). After we combined the data from this open card sort, we found that subjects labeled the combined categories in different ways. "Maintenance," "maintain," and "owner's" were often used in labels for the first cluster, indicating that these were good candidates for labels (see Table 6-1).

Table 6-1. Cluster 1

Subject	Categories
Subject 1	Ideas & maintenance
Subject 2	Owner's guide
Subject 3	Items to maintain car
Subject 4	Owner's manual
Subject 5	Personal information from dealer
Subject 6	-
Subject 7	Maintenance upkeep & ideas
Subject 8	Owner's tip AND owner's guide and maintenance

But in other cases, no strong patterns emerged (see Table 6-2).

Table 6-2. Cluster 2

Subject	Categories
Subject 1	Tucker features
Subject 2	-
Subject 3	Shortcut for info on car
Subject 4	Auto info
Subject 5	Associate with dealer
Subject 6	Tucker web site info
Subject 7	Manuals specific to each car
Subject 8	-

In a corresponding closed card sort, we asked subjects to describe each category label before they grouped content under each category. In effect, we were asking subjects to define each of these labels, and we compared their answers to see if they were similar or not. The more similar the answers, the stronger the label.

Some labels, such as "Service & Maintenance," were commonly understood, and were in line with the content that you'd actually find listed under this category (see Table 6-3).

Table 6-3. Service & Maintenance

Subject	Content
Subject 1	When to change the fluids, rotate tires; a place to keep track when I had my vehicle in for service (sic)
Subject 2	How to maintain vehicle: proper maintenance, features of car, where to find fuse box, etc., owner's manual
Subject 3	Find service that might be open on Sunday sometimes
Subject 4	When I will need service and where to go to get it
Subject 5	Reminders on when services is recommended (sic)
Subject 6	Timeline for service and maintenance
Subject 7	Maintenance schedule and tips to get best performance out of car and longevity of car
Subject 8	Maintenance tips, best place to go to fix car problem, estimated price

Other category labels were more problematic. Some subjects understood "Tucker Features & Events" in the way that was intended, representing announcements about automobile shows, discounts, and so on. Others interpreted this label to mean a vehicle's actual features, such as whether or not it had a CD player (see Table 6-4).

Table 6-4. Tucker Features & Events

Subject	Content
Subject 1	New items for my vehicle; upcoming new styles—new makes & models; financial news—like 0% financing
Subject 2	Local & national sponsorship; how to obtain Tucker sponsorship; community involvement
Subject 3	Mileage, CD or cassette, leg room, passengers, heat/AC control dull or not, removable seats, automatic door openers
Subject 4	All information regarding the Tucker automobile I'm looking for and any sale events going on regarding this auto
Subject 5	Looking for special pricing events
Subject 6	Site for outlining vehicles and options available. What automobile shows are available and where
Subject 7	About Tucker, sales, discounts, special events
Subject 8	No interested (sic)

Card sort exercises are very informative, but it's important to recognize that they don't present labels in the context of an actual site. Without this natural context, the labels' ability to represent meaning is diminished. So, as with all other techniques, card sorts have value but shouldn't be seen as the only method of investigating label quality.

Free-listing. While card sorting isn't necessarily an expensive and time-consuming method, free-listing is an even lower-cost way to get users to suggest labels.[*] Free-listing is quite simple: select an item and have subjects brainstorm terms to

---

[*] The best summary of this method is Rashmi Sinha's short but highly useful article in the Februrary 2003 *Boxes & Arrows*, "Beyond cardsorting: Free-listing methods to explore user categorizations" (*http://www.boxesandarrows.com/view/beyond_cardsorting_free_listing_methods_to_explore_user_categorizations*).

describe it. You can do this in person (capturing data with pencil and paper will be fine) or remotely, using a free or low-cost online-survey tool like SurveyMonkey or Zoomerang. That's really all there is to it.

Well, not quite: you'll want to consider your subjects: who (ideally representative of your overall audience) and how many (three to five may not yield scientifically significant results, but it is certainly better than nothing and may yield some interesting results). You might also consider asking subjects to rank the terms they've suggested as a way to determine which are the most appropriate.

You'll also need to choose which items to brainstorm terms for. Obviously you can only do this with a subset of your content. You could choose some representative content, such as a handful of your company's products. But even then, it'll be tricky—do you choose the most popular products or the more esoteric ones? It's important to get the labeling right for your big sellers, but conventions for their labels are already fairly established. The esoteric items? Well, they're more challenging, but fewer people care about them. So you may end up with a balance among the few items you select for a free-listing exercise. This is one of those cases where the art of information architecture is at least as important as the science.

What do you do with the results? Look for patterns and frequency of usage; for example, most of your subjects use the term "cell phone" while surprisingly few prefer "mobile phone." Patterns like these provide you with a sense of how to label an individual item, but may also demonstrate the tone of users' language overall. You might note that they use jargon quite a bit, or the reverse; perhaps you find a surprising amount of acronyms in their labels, or some other pattern emerges from free-listing. The result won't be a full-fledged labeling system, but it will give you a better sense of what tone and style you should take when developing a labeling system.

Indirectly from users

Most organizations—especially those whose sites include search engines—are sitting on top of reams of user data that describe their needs. Analyzing those search queries can be a hugely valuable way to tune labeling systems, not to mention diagnose a variety of other problems with your site. Additionally, the recent advent of folksonomic tagging has also created a valuable, if indirect, source of data on users' needs that can help information architects develop labeling systems.

Search-log analysis. Search-log analysis (also known as search analytics) is one of the least intrusive sources of data on the labels your site's audiences actually use. Analyzing search queries[*] is a great way to understand the types of labels your site's visitors

---

[*] Naturally, we have one more book to recommend that's not yet quite available at press time, but that should be useful nonetheless: *Search Analytics for Your Site: Conversations with Your Customers*, by Louis Rosenfeld and Rich Wiggins. It will be published by Rosenfeld Media and should be available in early 2007 (*http://www.rosenfeldmedia.com/books/searchanalytics*).

typically use (see Table 6-5). After all, these are the labels that users use to describe their own information needs in their own language. You may notice the use (or lack thereof) of acronyms, product names, and other jargon, which could impact your own willingness to use jargony labels. You might notice that users' queries use single or multiple terms, which could affect your own choice of short or long labels. And you might find that users simply aren't using the terms you thought they would for certain concepts. You may decide to change your labels accordingly, or use a thesaurus-style lookup to connect a user-supplied term (e.g., "pooch") to the preferred term (e.g., "dog").

Table 6-5. The top 40 most common queries from Michigan State University's site, February 8–14, 2006; each query tells us something about what the majority of users seek most often and how they label their information needs

Rank	Count	Cumulative	Percent of total	Query
1	1184	1184	1.5330	capa
2	1030	2214	2.8665	lon+capa
3	840	3054	3.9541	study+abroad
4	823	3877	5.0197	angel
5	664	4541	5.8794	lon-capa
6	656	5197	6.7287	library
7	584	5781	7.4849	olin
8	543	6324	8.1879	campus+map
9	530	6854	8.8741	spartantrak
10	506	7360	9.5292	cata
11	477	7837	10.1468	housing
12	467	8304	10.7515	map
13	462	8766	11.3496	im+west
14	409	9175	11.8792	computer+store
15	399	9574	12.3958	state+news
16	395	9969	12.9072	wharton+center
17	382	10351	13.4018	chemistry
18	346	10697	13.8498	payroll
19	340	11037	14.2900	breslin+center
20	339	11376	14.7289	honors+college
21	339	11715	15.1678	calendar
22	334	12049	15.6002	human+resources
23	328	12377	16.0249	registrar
24	327	12704	16.4483	dpps
25	310	13014	16.8497	breslin

Table 6-5. The top 40 most common queries from Michigan State University's site, February 8–14, 2006; each query tells us something about what the majority of users seek most often and how they label their information needs (continued)

Rank	Count	Cumulative	Percent of total	Query
26	307	13321	17.2471	tuition
27	291	13612	17.6239	spartan+trak
28	289	13901	17.9981	menus
29	273	14174	18.3515	uab
30	267	14441	18.6972	academic+calendar
31	265	14706	19.0403	im+east
32	262	14968	19.3796	rha
33	262	15230	19.7188	basketball
34	255	15485	20.0489	spartan+cash
35	246	15731	20.3674	loncapa
36	239	15970	20.6769	sparty+cash
37	239	16209	20.9863	transcripts
38	224	16433	21.2763	psychology
39	214	16647	21.5534	olin+health+center
40	206	16853	21.8201	cse+101

Tag analysis. The recent explosion in sites that employ folksonomic tagging (i.e., tags supplied by end users) means another useful indirect source of labels for you to learn from. In many of these sites, users' tags are publicly viewable. When you display them in aggregate, you'll find a collection of candidate labels that approximates the results of a free-listing exercise. Additionally, the data that comes from tag analysis can be used in much the same way as search-log analysis. Look for common terms, but also look for jargon, acronyms, and tone; even misspellings are useful if you're building a controlled vocabulary.

In the examples shown in Figures 6-14 and 6-15, you might be wondering how to develop labels for a new web-based iPod accessories store. To start, you might look at a popular folksonomic system like del.icio.us and see whether users have tagged a few common iPod accessories, and what terms they used. Let's try a pair of iPod accessories, a radio remote and a leather case. After searching both terms in del.icio.us, we found a variety of results, and chose those that had been bookmarked the most times.

Some of the tags are too broad to be particularly useful (e.g., "iPod" or "shopping"). But some will help you determine labels for categories; in the first example, "hardware" is more common than "media." Knowing that will clarify your category labeling. In the second example, you might choose "case" over the less popular "cases" as a product label.

```
common tags     cloud | list

141  ipod
 90  mac
 82  hardware
 66  apple
 63  shopping
 49  accessories
 37  audio
 29  technology
 27  music
 26  gadgets
 17  safari_export
 12  tech
 11  mp3
  9  cool
  9  electronics
  9  media
  7  computer
  7  design
  7  shop
  6  geek
  6  griffin
  6  macintosh
  6  osx
  6  software
  6  usb
```

Figure 6-14. Griffin Technology's IPod Radio Remote (as tagged by 298 del.icio.us users)

Tuning and Tweaking

Your list of labels might be raw, coming straight from the content in your site, another site, your site's users, or your own ideas of what should work best. Or, it may come straight from a polished controlled vocabulary. In any case, it'll need some work to become an effective labeling system.

First, sort the list of terms alphabetically. If it's a long list (e.g., from a search log), you'll likely encounter some duplicates; remove these.

Then review the list for consistency of usage, punctuation, letter case, and so forth, considering some of the consistency issues discussed earlier in this chapter. For example, you'll remember that the label table drawn from the jetBlue web site had inconsistencies that were immediately obvious: sometimes there were periods after labels, sometimes there weren't; the usage of link labels versus the heading labels on the corresponding pages was inconsistent; and so on. This is a good time to resolve these inconsistencies and to establish conventions for punctuation and style.

Decisions about which terms to include in a labeling system need to be made in the context of how broad and how large a system is required. First, determine if the labeling system has obvious gaps. Does it encompass all the possibilities that your site may eventually need to include?

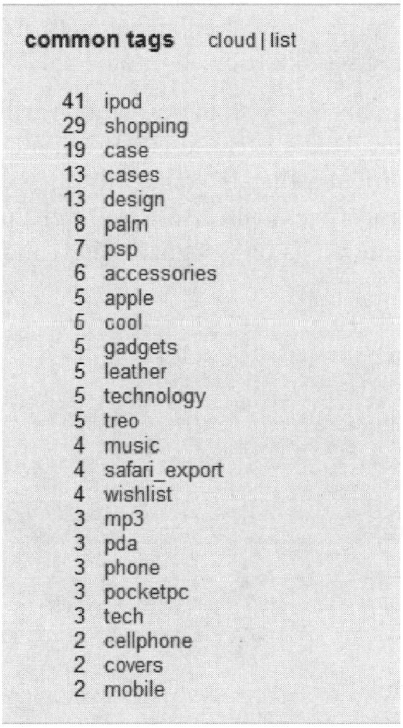

common tags cloud | list

```
41  ipod
29  shopping
19  case
13  cases
13  design
 8  palm
 7  psp
 6  accessories
 5  apple
 6  cool
 5  gadgets
 5  leather
 5  technology
 5  treo
 4  music
 4  safari_export
 4  wishlist
 3  mp3
 3  pda
 3  phone
 3  pocketpc
 3  tech
 2  cellphone
 2  covers
 2  mobile
```

Figure 6-15. Vaja's leather products for PDAs (as tagged by 92 del.icio.us users)

If, for example, your e-commerce site currently allows users to search only a portion of your product database, ask yourself if eventually it might provide access to all products. If you're not certain, assume it will, and devise appropriate labels for the additional products.

If the site's labeling system is topical, try to anticipate the topics not yet covered by the site. You might be surprised to see that the addition of these "phantom" labels has a large impact on your labeling system, perhaps even requiring you to change its conventions. If you fail to perform this predictive exercise, you might learn the hard way that future content doesn't fit into your site because you're not sure how to label it, or it ends up in cop-out categories such as "Miscellaneous," "Other Info," and the classic "Stuff." Plan ahead so that labels you might add in the future don't throw off the current labeling system.

Of course, this planning should be balanced with an understanding of what your labeling system is there to accomplish *today*. If you try to create a labeling system that encompasses the whole of human knowledge (instead of the current and antici-pated content of your web site), don't plan on doing anything else for the rest of your life. Keep your scope narrow and focused enough so that it can clearly address the requirements of your site's unique content, the special needs of its audiences, and the business objective at hand, but be comprehensive within that well-defined scope. This is a difficult pursuit, to be sure; all balancing acts are. Consider it justification #64 for information architects—like yourself—to be paid well.

Finally, remember that the labeling system you launch will need to be tweaked and improved shortly thereafter. That's because labels represent a relationship between two things—users and content—that is constantly morphing. Stuck between two moving targets, your labeling system will also have to change. So be prepared to perform user tests, analyze search logs on a regular basis, and adjust your labeling system as necessary.

CHAPTER 7

Navigation Systems

*Just wait, Gretel, until the moon rises, and then we
shall see the crumbs of bread which I have strewn
about; they will show us our way home again.*
—Hansel and Gretel

What we'll cover:
- Balancing context and flexibility in web navigation
- Integrating global, local, and contextual navigation
- Supplemental navigation tools such as sitemaps, indexes, guides, wizards, and configurators
- Personalization, visualization, tag clouds, collaborative filtering, and social navigation

As our fairy tales suggest, getting lost is a bad thing. It is associated with confusion, frustration, anger, and fear. In response to this danger, humans have developed navigation tools to prevent us from getting lost and to help us find our way home. From bread crumbs to compass and astrolabe, to maps, street signs, and global positioning systems, people have demonstrated great ingenuity in the design and use of navigation tools and wayfinding strategies.

We use these tools to chart our course, to determine our position, and to find our way back. They provide a sense of context and comfort as we explore new places. Anyone who has driven through an unfamiliar city as darkness falls understands the importance these tools and strategies play in our lives.

On the Web, navigation is rarely a life or death issue. However, getting lost in a large web site can be confusing and frustrating. While a well-designed taxonomy may reduce the chances that users will become lost, complementary navigation tools are often needed to provide context and to allow for greater flexibility. Structure and organization are about building rooms. Navigation design is about adding doors and windows.

In this book, we have split navigation and searching into individual chapters. This chapter focuses on navigation systems that support browsing; the next chapter digs deep into searching systems that are clearly components of navigation. In fact, structure, organization, labeling, browsing, and searching systems all contribute toward effective navigation.

Types of Navigation Systems

Navigation systems are composed of several basic elements, or subsystems. First, we have the global, local, and contextual navigation systems that are integrated within the web pages themselves. These *embedded navigation systems* are typically wrapped around and infused within the content of the site. They provide both context and flexibility, helping users understand where they are and where they can go. These three major systems, shown in Figure 7-1, are generally necessary but not sufficient in themselves.

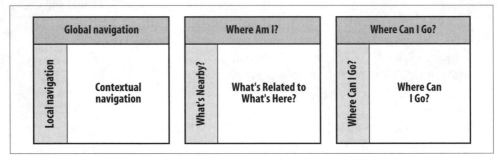

Figure 7-1. Global, local, and contextual embedded navigation systems

Second, we have *supplemental navigation systems* such as sitemaps, indexes, and guides that exist outside the content-bearing pages. These are shown in Figure 7-2.

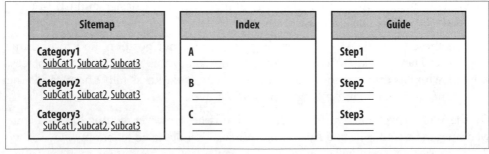

Figure 7-2. Supplemental navigation systems

Similar to search, these supplemental navigation systems provide different ways of accessing the same information. Sitemaps provide a bird's-eye view of the site. A to Z indexes allow direct access to content. And guides often feature linear navigation customized to a specific audience, task, or topic.

As we'll explain, each type of supplemental navigation system serves a unique purpose and is designed to fit within the broader framework of integrated searching and browsing systems.

Gray Matters

The design of navigation systems takes us deep into the gray area between information architecture, interaction design, information design, visual design, and usability engineering, all of which we might classify under the umbrella of user experience design.

As soon as we start talking about global, local, and contextual navigation, we find ourselves on the slippery slope that connects strategy, structure, design, and implementation. Does the local navigation bar work best at the top of the page, or is it better running down the left side? Should we use pull-downs, pop-ups, or cascading menus to reduce the required number of clicks? Will users ever notice gray links? Isn't it better to use the blue/red link color convention?

For better or for worse, information architects are often drawn into these debates, and we are sometimes responsible for making these decisions. We could try to draw a clear line in the sand, and argue that effective navigation is simply the manifestation of a well-organized system. Or we could abdicate responsibility and leave the interface to designers.

But we won't. In the real world, the boundaries are fuzzy and the lines get crossed every day. Information architects do design and designers do information architecture. And the best solutions often result from the biggest debates. While not always possible, interdisciplinary collaboration is the ideal, and collaboration works best when each of the experts understands something about the other areas of expertise.

So in this chapter, we roll up our sleeves, cross lines, step on toes, and get a little messy in the process. We tackle navigation design from the information architect's perspective. But before we drag you deep into this swampy gray matter, let us throw you a lifeline. In the Appendix, we have included references to a few truly excellent books that cover these topics from a variety of perspectives. We encourage you to read them all!

Browser Navigation Features

When designing a navigation system, it is important to consider the environment in which the system will exist. On the Web, people use web browsers such as Mozilla Firefox and Microsoft Internet Explorer to move around and view web sites. These browsers sport many built-in navigation features.

Open URL allows direct access to any page on a web site. Back and Forward provide a bidirectional backtracking capability. The History menu allows random access to pages visited during the current session, and Bookmark or Favorites enables users to save the location of specific pages for future reference. Web browsers also go beyond the Back button to support a "bread crumbs" feature by color-coding hypertext links. By default, unvisited hypertext links are one color and visited hypertext links are another. This feature helps users see where they have and haven't been and can help them to retrace their steps through a web site.

Finally, web browsers allow for a prospective view that can influence how users navigate. As the user passes the cursor over a hypertext link, the destination URL appears at the bottom of the browser window, hinting at the nature of that content. A good example is shown in Figure 7-3, where the cursor is positioned over "Pricing." The prospective view window at the bottom shows the URL of that page. If files and directories have been carefully labeled, prospective view gives the user context within the content hierarchy. If the hypertext link leads to a web site on another server, prospective view provides the user with basic information about this offsite destination.

Much research, analysis, and testing has been invested in the design of these browser-based navigation features. However, it is remarkable how frequently site designers unwittingly override or corrupt these navigation features. The most common design crimes are:

- Cluelessly modifying the visited/unvisited link colors
- Killing the Back button
- Crippling the Bookmark feature

Should you plan to commit any of these grave transgressions, make sure you've got a really good reason or an even better lawyer.

Building Context

With all navigation systems, before we can plot our course, we must locate our position. Whether we're visiting Yellowstone National Park or the Mall of America, the *You Are Here* mark on fixed-location maps is a familiar and valuable tool. Without that landmark, we must struggle to triangulate our current position using less dependable features such as street signs or nearby stores. The *You Are Here* indicator can be the difference between knowing where you stand and feeling completely lost.

When designing complex web sites, it is particularly important to provide context within the greater whole. Many contextual clues in the physical world do not exist on the Web. There are no natural landmarks, no north and south. Unlike physical travel, hypertextual navigation allows users to be transported right into the middle of an unfamiliar web site. Links from remote web pages and search engine results allow users to completely bypass the front door or main page of the web site. To further complicate matters, people often print web pages to read later or to pass along to a

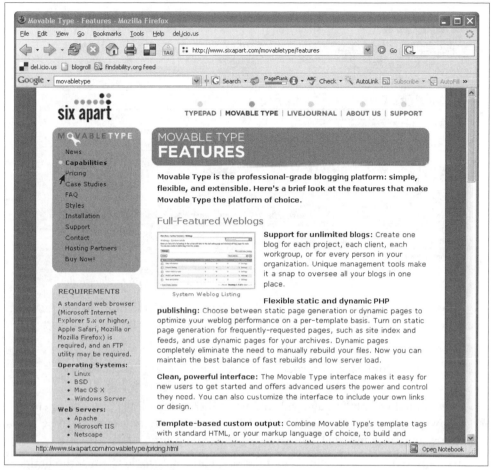

Figure 7-3. Prospective view is built into the browser

colleague, resulting in even more loss of context. For all these reasons, in the design of navigation systems, context is king!

You should always follow a few rules of thumb to ensure that your sites provide contextual clues. For example, users should always know which site they're in, even if they bypass the front door and enter through a search engine or a link to a subsidiary page. Extending the organization's name, logo, and graphic identity through all pages of the site is a fairly obvious way to accomplish this goal.

The navigation system should also present the structure of the information hierarchy in a clear and consistent manner, and indicate the user's current location, as shown in Figure 7-4. Wal-Mart's navigation system shows the user's location within the hierarchy with a variation of the You Are Here sign near the top of the page. This helps the user to build a mental model of the organization scheme, which facilitates navigation and helps her feel comfortable.

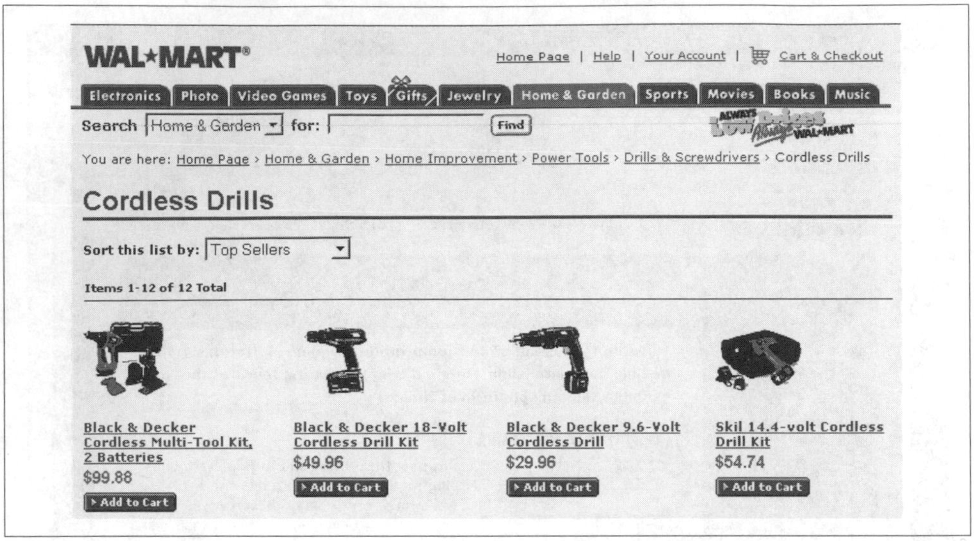

Figure 7-4. Wal-Mart's navigation system shows the user's location within the hierarchy

If you have an existing site, we suggest running a few users through a Navigation Stress Test.* Here are the basic steps as outlined by Keith Instone:

1. Ignore the home page and jump directly into the middle of the site.

2. For each random page, can you figure out where you are in relation to the rest of the site? What major section are you in? What is the parent page?

3. Can you tell where the page will lead you next? Are the links descriptive enough to give you a clue what each is about? Are the links different enough to help you choose one over another, depending on what you want to do?

By parachuting deep into the middle of the site, you will be able to push the limits of the navigation system and identify any opportunities for improvement.

Improving Flexibility

As we explained in Chapter 5, hierarchy is a familiar and powerful way of organizing information. In many cases, it makes sense for a hierarchy to form the foundation for organizing content in a web site. However, hierarchies can be limiting from a navigation perspective. If you have ever used the ancient information-browsing technology and precursor to the World Wide Web known as Gopher, you will understand the limitations of hierarchical navigation.† In Gopherspace, you were forced to move up

---

* Keith Instone popularized the notion of a Navigation Stress Test in his 1997 article, "Stress Test Your Site." See *http://user-experience.org/uefiles/navstress*.

† If you're too young to remember Gopher, consider the category/subcategory navigation on an iPod instead.

and down the tree structures of content hierarchies (see Figure 7-5). It was impractical to encourage or even allow jumps across branches (lateral navigation) or between multiple levels (vertical navigation) of a hierarchy.

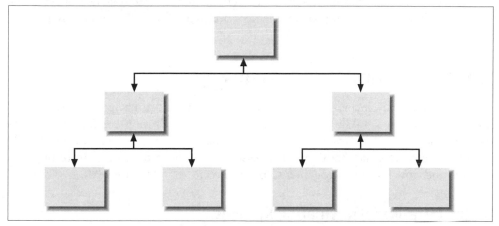

Figure 7-5. The pure hierarchy of Gopherspace

The Web's hypertextual capabilities removed these limitations, allowing tremendous freedom of navigation. Hypertext supports both lateral and vertical navigation. From any branch of the hierarchy, it is possible and often desirable to allow users to move laterally into other branches, to move vertically from one level to a higher level in that same branch, or to move all the way back to the main page of the web site. If the system is so enabled, users can get to anywhere from anywhere. However, as you can see in Figure 7-6, things can get confusing pretty quickly. It begins to look like an architecture designed by M.C. Escher.

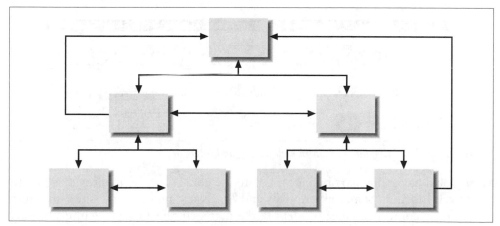

Figure 7-6. A hypertextual web can completely bypass the hierarchy

The trick to designing navigation systems is to balance the advantages of flexibility with the dangers of clutter. In a large, complex web site, a complete lack of lateral and vertical navigation aids can be very limiting. On the other hand, too many navigation aids can bury the hierarchy and overwhelm the user. Navigation systems should be designed with care to complement and reinforce the hierarchy by providing added context and flexibility.

Embedded Navigation Systems

Most large web sites include all three of the major embedded navigation systems we saw back in Figure 7-1. Global, local, and contextual navigation are extremely common on the Web. Each system solves specific problems and presents unique challenges. To design a successful site, it is essential to understand the nature of these systems and how they work together to provide context and flexibility.

Global (Site-Wide) Navigation Systems

By definition, a global navigation system is intended to be present on every page throughout a site. It is often implemented in the form of a navigation bar at the top of each page. These site-wide navigation systems allow direct access to key areas and functions, no matter where the user travels in the site's hierarchy.

Because global navigation bars are often the single consistent navigation element in the site, they have a huge impact on usability. Consequently, they should be subjected to intensive, iterative user-centered design and testing.

Global navigation bars come in all shapes and sizes. Consider the examples shown in Figure 7-7.

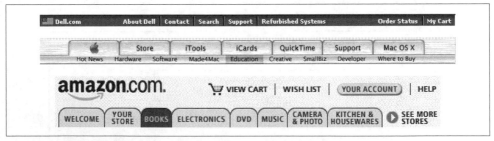

Figure 7-7. Global navigation bars from Dell, Apple, and Amazon

Most global navigation bars provide a link to the home page. Many provide a link to the search function. Some, like Apple's and Amazon's, reinforce the site's structure and provide contextual clues to identify the user's current location within the site. Others, like Dell's, have a simpler implementation and don't do either. This pushes the burden of providing context down to the local level and opens the door for inconsistency and disorientation. Global navigation system design forces difficult decisions that must be informed by user needs and by the organization's goals, content, technology, and culture. One size does not fit all.

It's often not possible to identify the global navigation system from the main page of a web site. The main page is sometimes the sole exception to the omnipresence of the global navigation bar. In some cases, designers choose to show an expanded view of the global navigation system on the main page. In other cases, the main page presents a variety of navigation options, and it's impossible to tell which ones have been carried throughout the site without exploring further.

This is the case with Microsoft's main page, as shown in Figure 7-8. There are three distinct navigation bars, and it's unclear whether any or all of them constitute a global navigation system. However, check out a few subsidiary pages, and it becomes obvious that only one is truly global. The other two are simply the designer's way of exposing important dimensions of the site's structure on the main page.

Figure 7-8. Microsoft's main page navigation

As Figure 7-9 shows, Microsoft's global navigation bar is very compact, and for good reason. This global navigation bar represents a massive investment in screen real estate, occupying a prominent position on several hundred thousand pages. These pages exist within dozens of subsites that are "owned" by powerful business units and functions within Microsoft.

Figure 7-9. Microsoft's global navigation bar

Despite convincing user-centered design arguments, it is still not easy to drive consistency throughout the subsites of modern, decentralized organizations. Most large enterprises are lucky if they can get the company logo and a simple global navigation bar implemented on 80 percent of their pages.

Local Navigation Systems

In many web sites, the global navigation system is complemented by one or more local navigation systems that enable users to explore the immediate area. Some tightly controlled sites integrate global and local navigation into a consistent, unified system. For example, the *New York Times* web site presents a global navigation bar that expands to provide local navigation options for each category of news. A reader who selects "Business" sees different local navigation options than a reader who selects "Sports," but both sets of options are presented within the same navigational framework (see Figure 7-10).

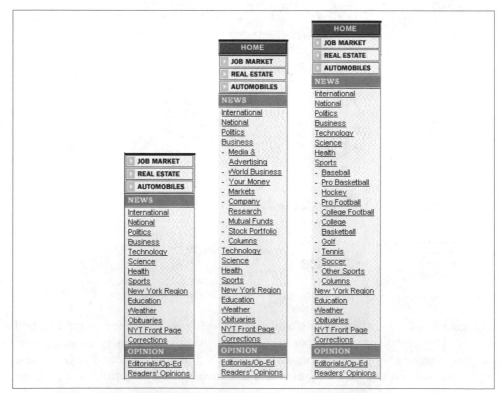

Figure 7-10. Local navigation at nytimes.com

In contrast, large sites like Microsoft.com (Figure 7-11) often provide multiple local navigation systems that may have little in common with one another or with the global navigation system.

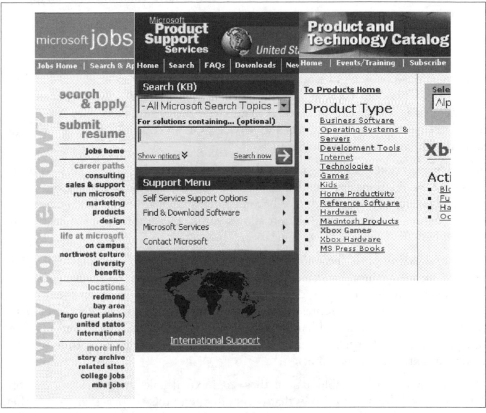

Figure 7-11. Local navigation at Microsoft.com

These local navigation systems and the content to which they provide access are often so different that these local areas are referred to as *subsites*,* or sites within sites. Subsites exist for two primary reasons. First, certain areas of content and functionality really do merit a unique navigation approach. Second, due to the decentralized nature of large organizations, different groups of people are often responsible for different content areas, and each group may decide to handle navigation differently.

In Microsoft's case, it makes sense to provide different ways to navigate the Jobs Area, the Support Database, and the Product Catalog. These local navigation systems are aligned with user needs and the local content. Unfortunately, there are

* The term *subsite* was coined by Jakob Nielsen in his 1996 article "The Rise of the Subsite" to describe a collection of web pages within a larger site that invite a common style and shared navigation mechanism unique to those pages. See *www.useit.com/alertbox/9609.html*.

many bad examples on the Web where the variation between local navigation systems is simply a result of multiple design groups choosing to run in different directions. Many organizations are still struggling with the question of how much central control to exercise over the look and feel of their local navigation systems. Grappling with these local navigation issues can make global navigation systems look easy.

Contextual Navigation

Some relationships don't fit neatly into the structured categories of global and local navigation. This demands the creation of *contextual* navigation links specific to a particular page, document, or object. On an e-commerce site, these "See Also" links can point users to related products and services. On an educational site, they might point to similar articles or related topics.

In this way, contextual navigation supports associative learning. Users learn by exploring the relationships you define between items. They might learn about useful products they didn't know about, or become interested in a subject they'd never considered before. Contextual navigation allows you to create a web of connective tissue that benefits users and the organization.

The actual definition of these links is often more editorial than architectural. Typically an author, editor, or subject matter expert will determine appropriate links once the content is placed into the architectural framework of the web site. In practice, this usually involves representing words or phrases within sentences or paragraphs (i.e., prose) as embedded or "inline" hypertext links. A page from Stanford University's site, shown in Figure 7-12, provides an example of carefully chosen inline contextual navigation links.

This approach can be problematic if these contextual links are critical to the content, since usability testing shows that users often tend to scan pages so quickly they miss or ignore these less conspicuous links. For this reason, you may want to design a system that provides a specific area of the page or a visual convention for contextual links. As you can see in Figure 7-13, REI designs contextual navigation links to related products into the layout of each page. Moderation is the primary rule of thumb for guiding the creation of these links. Used sparingly (as in this example), contextual links can complement the existing navigation systems by adding one more degree of flexibility. Used in excess, they can add clutter and confusion. Content authors have the option to replace or complement the embedded links with external links that are easier for the user to see.

The approach used on each page should be determined by the nature and importance of the contextual links. For noncritical links provided as a point of interest, inline links can be a useful but unobtrusive solution.

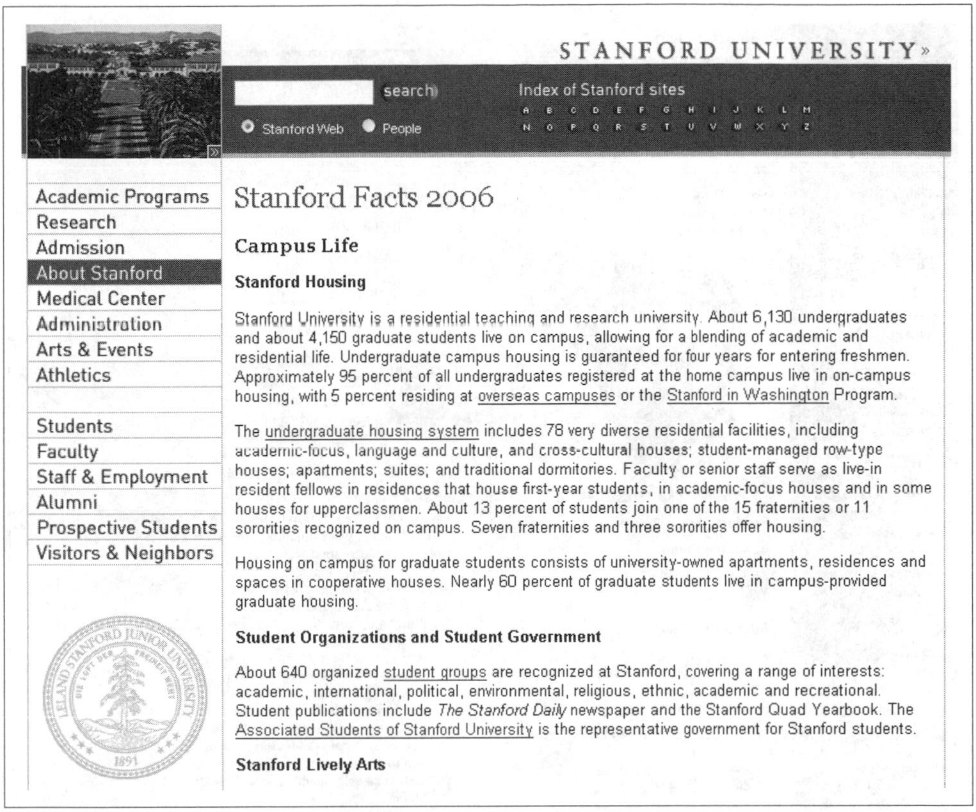

Figure 7-12. Inline contextual navigation links

When designing a contextual navigation system, imagine that every page on the site is a main page or portal in its own right. Once a user has identified a particular product or document, the rest of the site fades into the background. This page is now his interface. Where might he want to go from here? Consider the REI example. What additional information will the customer want before making a buying decision? What other products might he want to buy? Contextual navigation provides a real opportunity to cross-sell, up-sell, build brand, and provide customer value. Because these associative relationships are so important, we'll revisit this topic in Chapter 9.

Implementing Embedded Navigation

The constant challenge in navigation system design is to balance the flexibility of movement with the danger of overwhelming the user with too many options. One key to success is simply recognizing that global, local, and contextual navigation elements exist together on most pages (consider the representation of a web page shown in Figure 7-14). When integrated effectively, they can complement one another.

Figure 7-13. External contextual navigation links

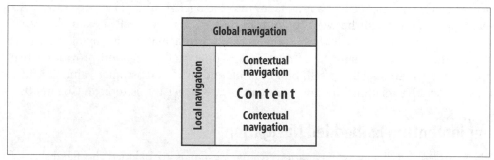

Figure 7-14. Navigation can drown out the content

But when designed independently, the three systems can combine to monopolize a great deal of screen real estate. Alone, they may each be manageable, but together on one page, the variety of options may overwhelm the user and drown out the content. In some cases, you may need to revisit the number of options within each navigation bar. In others, the problem may be minimized through careful design and layout.

In its simplest form, a navigation bar is a distinct collection of hypertext links that connect a series of pages, enabling movement among them. They can support global, local, and contextual navigation. You can implement navigation in all sorts of ways, using text or graphics, pull-downs, pop-ups, rollovers, cascading menus, and so on. Many of these implementation decisions fall primarily within the realms of interaction design and technical performance rather than information architecture, but let's trespass briefly and hit a few highlights.

For example, is it better to create textual or graphical navigation bars? Well, graphic navigation bars tend to look nicer, but can slow down the page-loading speed and are more expensive to design and maintain. If you use graphic navigation bars, you need to be sensitive to the needs of users with low bandwidth connections and text-only browsers. People who are blind and people using wireless mobile devices are two important audiences to consider. Appropriate use of the <ALT> attribute to define replacement text for the image will ensure that your site supports navigation for these users.

And where do the navigation bars belong on the page? It has become convention to place the global navigation bar along the top of the page and the local navigation bar along the lefthand side. However, all sorts of permutations can be successful. Just make sure you do lots of user testing, particularly if you deviate from convention.

What about textual labels versus icons? Textual labels are the easiest to create and most clearly indicate the contents of each option. Icons, on the other hand, are relatively difficult to create and are often ambiguous. It's difficult to represent abstract concepts through images. A picture may say a thousand words, but often they're the wrong words—particularly when you're communicating to a global audience.

Icons can successfully be used to complement the textual labels, however. Since repeat users may become so familiar with the icons that they no longer need to read the textual labels, icons can be useful in facilitating rapid menu selection. In Figure 7-15, Scott McCloud combines text and images to create a global navigation system that balances form and function. But can you guess what lies behind icons *b* through *e*? On this comic creator's web site, the mystery icons provoke curiosity and create a playful experience. On a business web site, they would simply be frustrating.

How about the increasingly common use of DHTML and JavaScript rollovers to show the navigation options behind a category or menu option (as shown in Figure 7-16)? Well, it depends. On one hand, this prospective view on steroids can make valuable

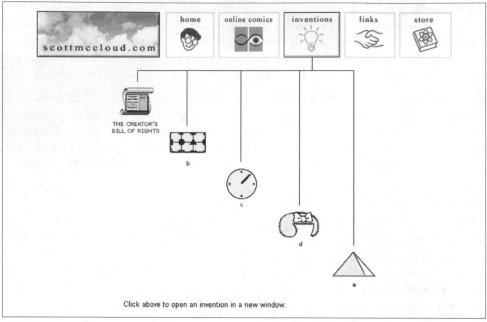

Figure 7-15. Navigation with integrated text and images

use of limited screen real estate, enhancing the scent of information and often reducing the number of pages and clicks, while simultaneously adding a dynamic, interactive feel to the web site. On the other hand, rollover navigation can be difficult to do well. Usability and accessibility often suffer due to poor design and implementation. Also, the use of rollover navigation is no substitute for the careful selection of the omnipresent major categories and labels, which lend themselves to rapid visual scanning. You can't expect the user to "mine sweep" her mouse cursor over every option.

And finally, what about frames? In the 1990s, designers went a little crazy with frames, implementing navigation bars and banner advertisements alike inside non-scrollable panes. We don't see too many frames these days, and that's a very good thing. Even beyond the technical design and performance problems, frames tend to cripple usability. After all, the Web is built upon a model of pages, each of which has a unique address or URL. Users are familiar with the concept of pages. Frames confuse this issue by slicing up pages into independent panes of content. By disrupting the page model, the use of frames frequently disables important browser navigation features such as bookmarking, visited and unvisited link discrimination, and history lists. Frames can also confuse users who are trying to perform simple tasks such as using the Back button, reloading a page, and printing a page. While web browsers have improved in their ability to handle frames, they can't remove the confusion caused by violating the page paradigm.

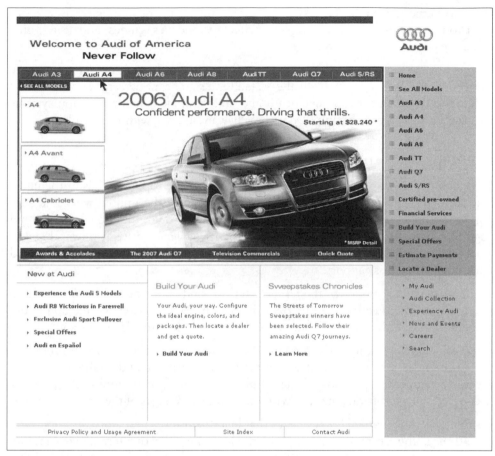

Figure 7-16. Audi's rollover navigation

Supplemental Navigation Systems

Supplemental navigation systems (shown back in Figure 7-2) include sitemaps, indexes, and guides. These are external to the basic hierarchy of a web site and provide complementary ways of finding content and completing tasks. Search also belongs to the supplemental navigation family but is so important that we've dedicated all of Chapter 8 to it.

Supplemental navigation systems can be critical factors for ensuring usability and findability within large web sites. However, they're often not given the care and feeding they deserve. Many site owners still labor under the misconception that if they could only get the taxonomy right, all users and all user needs would be addressed.

Usability pundits feed this fantasy by preaching the gospel of simplicity: users don't want to make choices, and they resort to sitemaps, indexes, guides, and search only when the taxonomy fails them.

Both statements are theoretically true but miss the point that the taxonomy and the embedded navigation systems will always fail for a significant percentage of users and tasks. You can count on this like death and taxes. Supplemental navigation systems give users an emergency backup. Do you really want to drive without a seatbelt?

Sitemaps

In a book or magazine, the table of contents presents the top few levels of the information hierarchy. It shows the organization structure for the printed work and supports random as well as linear access to the content through the use of chapter and page numbers. In contrast, a print map helps us navigate through physical space, whether we're driving through a network of streets and highways or trying to find our terminal in a busy airport.

In the early days of the Web, the terms "sitemap" and "table of contents" were used interchangeably. Of course, we librarians thought the TOC was a better metaphor, but *sitemap* sounds sexier and less hierarchical, so it has become the de facto standard.

A typical sitemap (Figure 7-17) presents the top few levels of the information hierarchy. It provides a broad view of the content in the web site and facilitates random access to segmented portions of that content. A sitemap can employ graphical or text-based links to provide the user with direct access to pages of the site.

A sitemap is most natural for web sites that lend themselves to hierarchical organization. If the architecture is not strongly hierarchical, an index or alternate visual representation may be better. You should also consider the web site's size when deciding whether to employ a sitemap. For a small site with only two or three hierarchical levels, a sitemap may be unnecessary.

The design of a sitemap significantly affects its usability. When working with a graphic designer, make sure he understands the following rules of thumb:

1. Reinforce the information hierarchy so the user becomes increasingly familiar with how the content is organized.
2. Facilitate fast, direct access to the contents of the site for those users who know what they want.
3. Avoid overwhelming the user with too much information. The goal is to help, not scare, the user.

Finally, it's worth noting that sitemaps are also useful from a search engine optimization perspective, since they point search engine spiders directly to important pages throughout the web site.

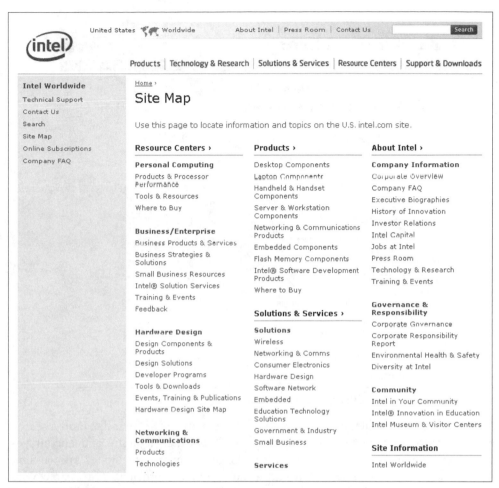

Figure 7-17. Intel's sitemap

Site Indexes

Similar to the back-of-book index found in many print materials, a web-based index presents keywords or phrases alphabetically, without representing the hierarchy. Unlike a table of contents, indexes are relatively flat, presenting only one or two levels of depth. Therefore, indexes work well for users who already know the name of the item they are looking for. A quick scan of the alphabetical listing will get them where they want to go; there's no need for them to understand where you've placed that item within your hierarchy. In Figure 7-18, AOL presents a simple but useful alphabetical site index. Handcrafted links within the index lead directly to destination pages.

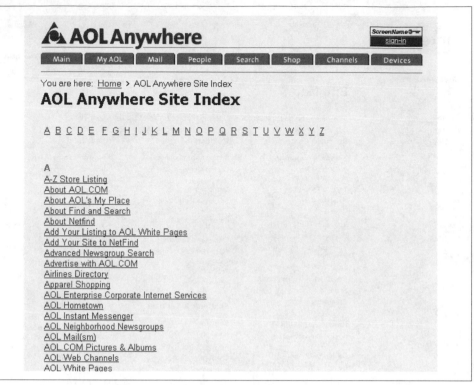

Figure 7-18. AOL's simple but useful alphabetical site index

Large, complex web sites often require both a sitemap and a site index (and a search capability, for that matter). The sitemap reinforces the hierarchy and encourages exploration, while the site index bypasses the hierarchy and facilitates known-item finding. For small web sites, a site index alone may be sufficient. On Usable Web (see Figure 7-19), Keith Instone has made his site index even more useful by indicating the number of items behind each link.

A major challenge in indexing a web site involves the level of granularity. Do you index web pages? Do you index individual paragraphs or concepts that are presented on web pages? Or do you index collections of web pages? In many cases, the answer may be all of the above. Perhaps a more valuable question is: what terms are users going to look for? The answers should guide the index design. To find those answers, you need to know your audience and understand their needs. You can learn more about the terms people will look for by analyzing search logs and conducting user research.

There are two very different ways to create a site index. For small web sites, you can simply create the index manually, using your knowledge of the full collection of content to inform decisions about which links to include. This centralized, manual

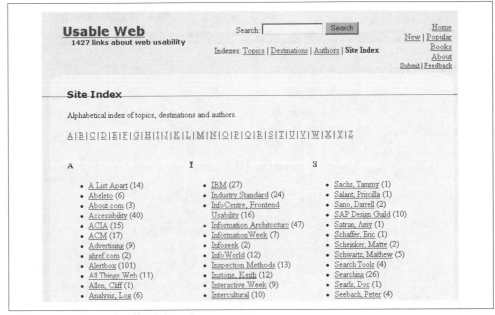

Figure 7-19. Usable Web's highly usable site index

approach results in a one-step index such as the one in Figure 7-18. Another example is shown in Figure 7-20, where Vanguard's dynamically generated two-step site index features term rotation and see/see-also references.

In contrast, on a large site with distributed content management, it may make sense to use controlled vocabulary indexing at the document level to drive automatic generation of the site index. Since many controlled vocabulary terms will be applied to more than one document, this type of index must allow for a two-step process. First the user selects the term from the index, and then selects from a list of documents indexed with that term.

A useful trick in designing an index involves *term rotation*, also known as *permutation*. A permuted index rotates the words in a phrase so that users can find the phrase in two places in the alphabetical sequence. For example, in the Vanguard index, users will find listings for both "refund, IRS" and "IRS refund." This supports the varied ways in which people look for information. Term rotation should be applied selectively. You need to balance the probability of users seeking a particular term with the annoyance of cluttering the index with too many permutations. For example, it would probably not make sense in an event calendar to present Sunday (Schedule) as well as Schedule (Sunday). If you have the time and budget to conduct focus groups or user testing, that's great. If not, you'll have to fall back on common sense.

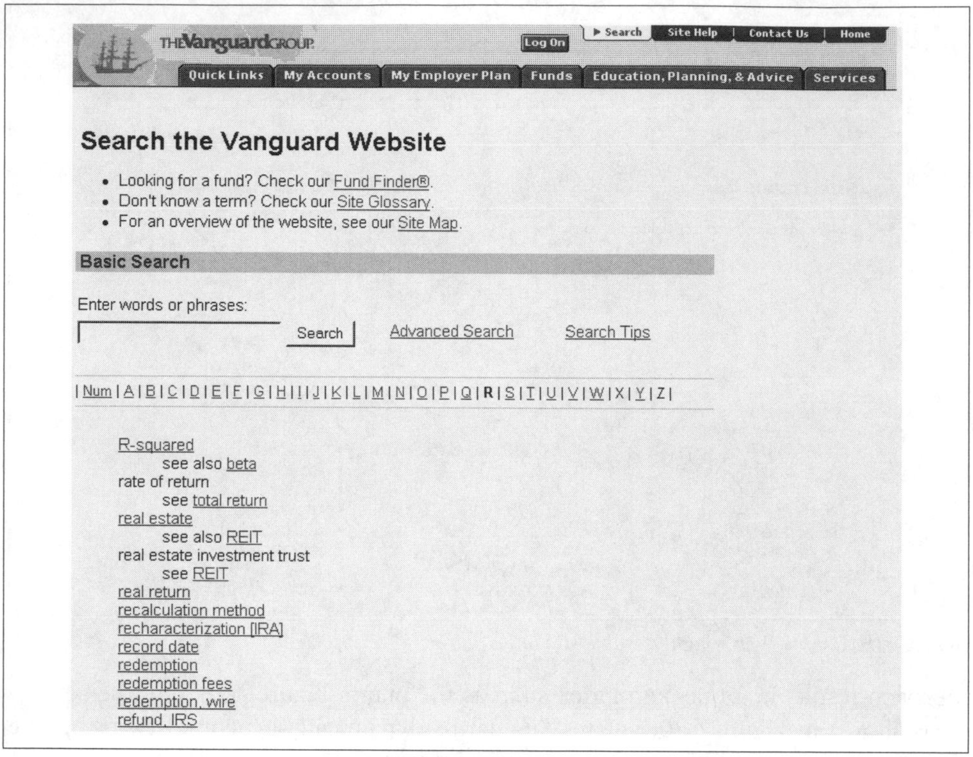

Figure 7-20. Vanguard's dynamically generated site index

Guides

Guides can take several forms, including guided tours, tutorials, and micro-portals focused around a specific audience, topic, or task. In each case, guides supplement the existing means of navigating and understanding site content.

Guides often serve as useful tools for introducing new users to the content and functionality of a web site. They can also be valuable marketing tools for restricted-access web sites (such as online publications that charge subscription fees), enabling you to show potential customers what they will get for their money. And, they can be valuable internally, providing an opportunity to showcase key features of a redesigned site to colleagues, managers, and venture capitalists.

Guides typically feature linear navigation (new users want to be guided, not thrown in), but hypertextual navigation should also be available to provide additional flexibility. Screenshots of major pages should be combined with narrative text that explains what can be found in each area of the web site.

The *Wall Street Journal*, shown in Figure 7-21, uses a guided tour to showcase navigation and editorial features of the web site that, for the most part, are accessible only to subscribers.

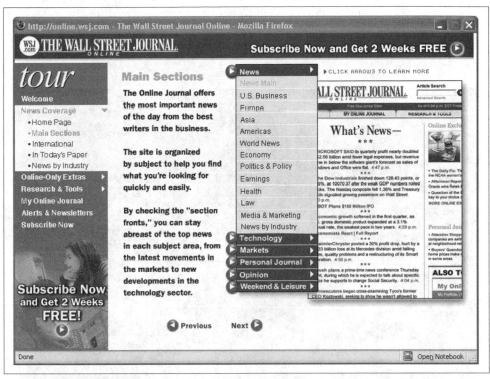

Figure 7-21. The Wall Street Journal's guided tour

Rules of thumb for designing guides include:

1. The guide should be short.

2. At any point, the user should be able to exit the guide.

3. Navigation (Previous, Home, Next) should be located in the same spot on every page so that users can easily step back and forth through the guide.

4. The guide should be designed to answer questions.

5. Screenshots should be crisp, clear, and optimized, with enlarged details of key features.

6. If the guide includes more than a few pages, it may need its own table of contents.

Remember that a guide is intended as an introduction for new users and as a marketing opportunity for the web site. Many people may never use it, and few people will use it more than once. You should balance the inevitable big ideas about how to create an exciting, dynamic, interactive guide with the fact that it will not play a central role in the day-to-day use of the web site.

Wizards and Configurators

Though they could be considered a special class of guide, wizards that help users to configure products or navigate complex decision trees deserve separate highlighting. Sophisticated configurators, like the Mini Cooper example shown in Figure 7-22, blur the lines between software application and web site.

Figure 7-22. The Mini Cooper configurator

Mini successfully combines a rich suite of navigation options without causing confusion. The user can move through a linear process or jump back and forth between steps, and the site's global navigation is always present, providing context and possible next steps.

Search

As we noted earlier, the searching system is a central part of supplemental navigation. Search is a favorite tool of users because it puts them in the driver's seat, allowing them to use their own keyword terms to look for information. Search also enables a tremendous level of specificity. Users can search the content for a particular phrase (e.g., "socially translucent systems failure") that is unlikely to be represented in a sitemap or site index.

However, the ambiguity of language causes huge problems with most search experiences. Users, authors, and information architects all use different words for the same things. Because the design of effective search systems is so important and so complex, we've devoted all of the following chapter to the topic.

Advanced Navigation Approaches

So far, we've focused attention on the bread-and-butter components of navigation systems, the elements that form the foundation of useful, usable web sites. Good navigation design is really important and really hard. Only after you've mastered the integration of these fundamental building blocks should you dare wander into the minefield of advanced navigation.

Personalization and Customization

Personalization involves serving up tailored pages to the user based upon a model of the behavior, needs, or preferences of that individual. In contrast, *customization* involves giving the user direct control over some combination of presentation, navigation, and content options. In short, with personalization, we guess what the user wants, and with customization, the user tells us what he wants.

Both personalization and customization can be used to refine or supplement existing navigation systems. Unfortunately, however, both have been hyped by consultants and software vendors as the solution to all navigation problems. The reality is that personalization and customization:

- Typically play important but limited roles
- Require a solid foundation of structure and organization
- Are really difficult to do well

Personalization has preoccupied marketing folks in recent years, partly due to the influential book by Don Peppers and Martha Rogers, *The One to One Future* (Doubleday). On a web site, you might use demographic data (e.g., age, sex, income level, zip code) and previous purchasing behavior to make educated guesses about which products to feature in the contextual navigation system during a customer's next visit. On an intranet, you might use role and job function as a basis for filtering views of news and e-service applications; for example, personalization is essential for controlling access to human-resource applications involving compensation and benefits.

Amazon is the most cited example of successful personalization, and some of the things it's done are truly valuable. It's nice that Amazon remembers our names, and it's great that it remembers our address and credit card information. It's when Amazon starts trying to recommend books based on past purchases that the system breaks down (see Figure 7-23). In this example, Peter already owns two of the top three recommended books, but the system doesn't know this because he didn't purchase them from Amazon. And this ignorance is not the exception but the rule. Because we don't have time to teach our systems, or because we prefer to maintain our privacy, we often don't share enough information to drive effective personalization. In addition, in many cases, it's really hard to guess what people will want to do or learn or buy tomorrow. As they say in the financial world, past performance is no guarantee of future results. In short, personalization works really well in limited contexts, but fails when you try to expand it to drive the entire user experience.

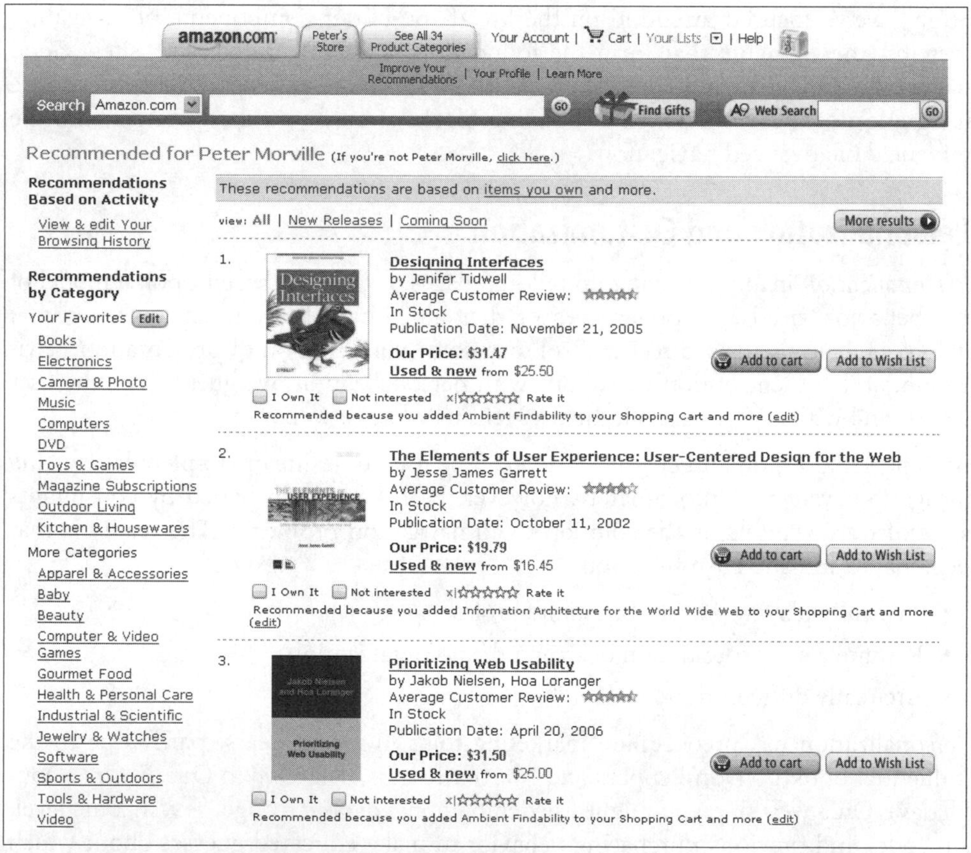

Figure 7-23. Amazon's personalized recommendations

Customization introduces a similar set of promises and perils. The idea of giving users control and thereby alleviating some of the pressures on design is obviously very compelling. And customization can sometimes deliver great value. My Yahoo! (Figure 7-24) and more recently, MySpace, are flagship examples and provide all sorts of customization capabilities, which many users take full advantage of—for better or for worse.

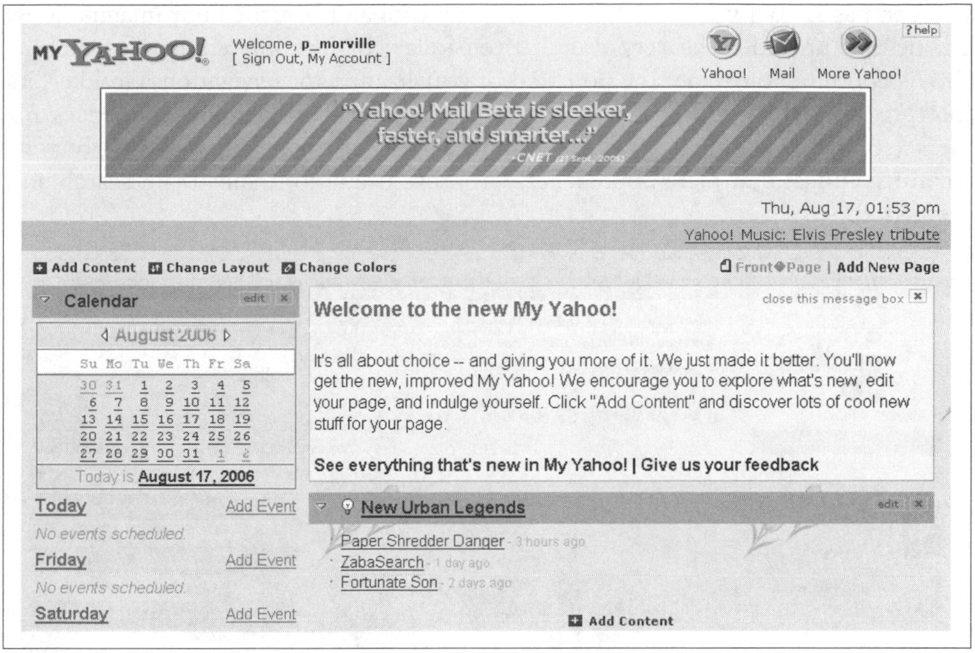

Figure 7-24. Customization at My Yahoo!

The problem with customization is that most people don't want to spend much (if any) time customizing, and will do this work only on a small handful of sites that are most important to them. Since corporate intranets have a captive audience of repeat visitors, customization has a much better chance of being used there than it does on most public web sites.

However, there's another problem. Even users themselves don't always know what they will want to know or do tomorrow. Customization works great for tracking the sports scores of your favorite baseball team or monitoring the value of stocks you own, but not so well when it comes to broader news and research needs. One day you want to know the results of the French elections; the next day you want to know when dogs were first domesticated. Do you really know what you might need next month?

Visualization

Since the advent of the Web, people have struggled to create useful tools that enable users to navigate in a more visual way. First came the metaphor-driven attempts to display online museums, libraries, shopping malls, and other web sites as physical places. Then came the dynamic, fly-through "sitemaps" that tried to show relationships between pages on a web site. Both looked very cool and stretched our imaginations. But neither proved to be very useful. Even today, high-profile companies such as Groxis continue to explore the potential of visualization for navigation. Grokker, its enterprise search product, allows you to create visual navigation experiences for users (see Figure 7-25). It's worth keeping an eye on these experiments, but we remain skeptical that these approaches will prove useful for mainstream search and navigation.

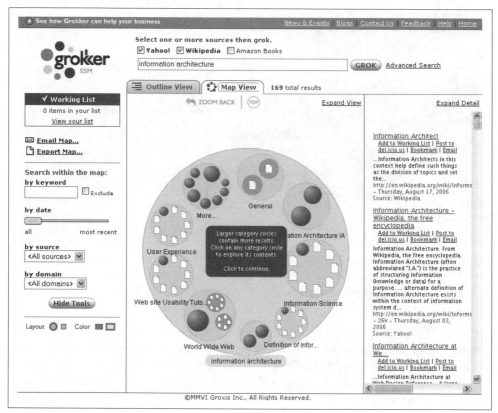

Figure 7-25. Grokker's visual search results

Social Navigation

On a more positive note, *social navigation*, built on the premise that value for the individual user can be derived from observing the actions of other users, continues to hold great promise and is already on the fast track to mainstream adoption. Simple examples include lists of most popular resources, such as the *New York Times*' Most Popular (see Figure 7-26).

The New York Times
Thursday, August 17, 2006

Most Popular

Search

E*TRADE FINANCIAL

WORLD | U.S. | N.Y. / REGION | BUSINESS | TECHNOLOGY | SCIENCE | HEALTH | SPORTS | OPINION | ARTS | STYLE | TRAVEL | **JOBS** | **REAL ESTATE** | **AUTOS**

25 years of The New York Times Archive — **TimesSelect** Only on NYTimes.com — Be There

MOST E-MAILED »

Articles most frequently e-mailed by NYTimes.com readers.

1. Coffee as a Health Drink? Studies Find Some Benefits
2. Overcoming Adoption's Racial Barriers
3. Skin Deep: Throw Your Tweezers Away
4. Elusive Proof, Elusive Prover: A New Mathematical Mystery
5. The Frugal Traveler: In San Francisco and Almost Home
6. A Food Web Site, Spiced With Attitude
7. Eye on Election, Democrats Run as Wal-Mart Foe
8. Singapore Acts as Haven for Stem Cell Research
9. Thomas L. Friedman: Big Talk, Little Will
10. Op-Ed Contributor: Muslim Myopia

Go to Complete List »

MOST BLOGGED »

Articles most frequently linked to by bloggers on the Web.

1. Conservative Pastor Steers Clear of Politics, and Pays
2. A Senate Race in Connecticut
3. Audit Finds U.S. Hid Actual Cost of Iraq Projects
4. Men Not Working, and Not Wanting Just Any Job
5. After Sluggish Start, Lieberman Hooded Warnings of Trouble
6. So Big and Healthy Nowadays That Grandpa Wouldn't Even Know You
7. Israeli Strike Is Deadliest in Fighting So Far
8. Newspapers to Use Links to Rivals on Web Sites
9. Fooling the Voters
10. A New Enemy Gains On the U.S.

Go to Complete List »

MOST SEARCHED »

Keywords most frequently searched by NYTimes.com readers.

1. immigration
2. china
3. india
4. college
5. gay
6. dell
7. iraq
8. iran
9. university
10. israel

Go to Complete List »

MOST POPULAR MOVIES »

Most popular movies among NYTimes.com readers.

1. Rocky Road to Dublin
2. World Trade Center
3. Kabhi Alvida Naa Kehna
4. Little Miss Sunshine
5. Half Nelson
6. House of Sand
7. Step Up
8. Talladega Nights: The Ballad of Ricky Bobby
9. Pulse
10. Conversations With Other Women

Go to Complete List »

Denotes a New York Times Critic's Pick

Figure 7-26. Most Popular at the New York Times

More sophisticated examples include Amazon's collaborative filtering (see Figure 7-27), Epinions' recommendation engine (see *http://www.epinions.com*), and Flickr's beloved tag clouds, shown in Figure 7-28, which use font size to show tag popularity. Perhaps there is a future for visualization after all.

Figure 7-27. Amazon's collaborative filtering

While most companies aren't yet employing social navigation approaches on their web sites and intranets, we expect the practice to become increasingly common in the coming years. At a minimum, companies will find ways to unlock the value currently trapped in their search logs, usage statistics, and customer databases to drive more effective contextual navigation. We also hope to see more ambitious solutions that tap this feedback loop between design and behavior, creating adaptive navigation systems that significantly advance the usability of our web sites and intranets.

Figure 7-28. Flickr's tag clouds

In the past several years, the design of navigation systems has improved in a rapid and highly visible manner. If you need convincing, just check out a few sites from the mid-90s using the Internet Archive's Wayback Machine (*http://www.archive.org/*). Let's hope we can keep up the pace, because there's still a long way to go.

CHAPTER 8

Search Systems

What we'll cover:
- Determining whether your site needs a search system
- The basic anatomy of a search system
- What to make searchable
- A basic understanding of retrieval algorithms
- How to present retrieval results
- Search interface design
- Where to learn more

Chapter 7 helped you create the best navigation system possible for your web site. This chapter describes another form of finding information: searching. Searching (and more broadly, information retrieval) is an expansive, challenging, and well-established field, and we can only scratch the surface here. We'll limit our discussion to what makes up a search system, when to implement search systems, and some practical advice on how to design a search interface and display search results.

This chapter often uses examples of search systems from sites that allow you to search the entire Web in addition to site-specific search engines. Although these web-wide tools tend to index a very broad collection of content, it's nonetheless extremely useful to study them. Of all search systems, none has undergone the testing, usage, and investment that web-wide search tools have, so why not benefit from their research? Many of these tools are available for use on local sites as well.

Does Your Site Need Search?

Before we delve into search systems, we need to make a point: think twice before you make your site searchable.

Your site should, of course, support the finding of its information. But as the preceding chapters demonstrate, there are other ways to support finding. And be careful not to assume, as many do, that a search engine alone will satisfy all users' information needs. While many users want to search a site, some are natural browsers, preferring to forego filling in that little search box and hitting the "search" button. We suggest you consider the following questions before committing to a search system for your site.

Does your site have enough content?

How much content is enough to merit the use of a search engine? It's hard to say. It could be 5, 50, or 500 pages; no specific number serves as a standard threshold. What's more important is the type of information need that's typical of your site's users. Users of a technical support site often have a specific kind of information in mind, and are more likely to require search than users of an online banking site. If your site is more like a library than a software application, then search probably makes sense. If that's the case, then consider the volume of content, balancing the time required to set up and maintain a search system with the payoff it will bring to your site's users.

Will investing in search systems divert resources from more useful navigation systems?

Because many site developers see search engines as the solution to the problems users have when trying to find information in their sites, search engines become Band-Aids for sites with poorly designed navigation systems and other architectural weaknesses. If you see yourself falling into this trap, you should probably suspend implementing your search system until you fix your navigation system's problems. You'll find that search systems often perform better if they can take advantage of aspects of strong navigation systems, such as the controlled vocabulary terms used to tag content. And users will often benefit even more from using both types of finding if they work together well. Of course, your site's navigation might be a disaster for political reasons, such as an inability among your organization's decision-makers to agree on a site-wide navigation system. In such cases, reality trumps what ought to be, and search might indeed be your best alternative.

Do you have the time and know-how to optimize your site's search system?

Search engines are fairly easy to get up and running, but like many things on the Web, they are difficult to implement effectively. As a user of the Web, you've certainly seen incomprehensible search interfaces, and we're sure that your queries have retrieved some pretty inscrutable results. This is often due to a lack of planning by the site developer, who probably installed the search engine with its default settings, pointed it at the site, and forgot about it. If you don't plan on putting some significant time into configuring your search engine properly, reconsider your decision to implement it.

Are there better alternatives?

Search may be a good way to serve your site's users, but other ways may work better. For example, if you don't have the technical expertise or confidence to configure a search engine or the money to shell out for one, consider providing a site index instead. Both site indexes and search engines help users who know what they're looking for. While a site index can be a heck of a lot of work, it is typically created and maintained manually, and can therefore be maintained by anyone who knows HTML.

Will your site's users bother with search?

It may already be clear that your users would rather browse than search. For example, users of a greeting card site may prefer browsing thumbnails of cards instead of searching. Or perhaps users do want to search, but searching is a lower priority for them, and it should be for you as you consider how to spend your information architecture development budget.

Now that we've got our warnings and threats out of the way, let's discuss when you should implement search systems. Most web sites, as we know, aren't planned out in much detail before they're built. Instead, they grow organically. This may be all right for smaller web sites that aren't likely to expand much, but for ones that become popular, more and more content and functional features get piled on haphazardly, leading to a navigation nightmare. The following issues will help you decide when your site has reached the point of needing a search system.

Search helps when you have too much information to browse

There's a good analogy of physical architecture. Powell's Books (*http://www. powells.com*), which claims to be the largest bookstore in the world, covers an entire city block (68,000 square feet) in Portland, Oregon. We guess that it started as a single small storefront on that block, but as the business grew, the owners knocked a doorway through the wall into the next storefront, and so on, until it occupied the whole block. The result is a hodgepodge of chambers, halls with odd turns, and unexpected stairways. This chaotic labyrinth is a charming place to wander and browse, but if you're searching for a particular title, good luck. It will be difficult to find what you're looking for, although if you're really lucky you might serendipitously stumble onto something better.

Yahoo! once was a web version of Powell's. At first, everything was there and fairly easy to find. Why? Because Yahoo!, like the Web, was relatively small. At its inception, Yahoo! pointed to a few hundred Internet resources, made accessible through an easily browsable subject hierarchy. No search option was available, something unimaginable to Yahoo! users today. But things soon changed. Yahoo! had an excellent technical architecture that allowed site owners to easily self-register their sites, but Yahoo!'s information architecture was not well planned and couldn't keep up with the increasing volume of resources that were added daily. Eventually, the subject hierarchy became too cumbersome to navigate, and Yahoo! installed a search system as an alternative way of finding information in the site. Nowadays, far more people use Yahoo!'s search engine instead of browsing through its taxonomy, which indeed disappeared from Yahoo!'s main page eons ago.

Your site probably isn't as large as Yahoo!, but it's probably experienced a similar evolution. Has your content outstripped your browsing systems? Do your site's users go insane trying to spot the right link on your site's hugely long category pages? Then perhaps the time has come for search.

Search helps fragmented sites

Powell's room after room after room of books is also a good analogy for the silos of content that make up so many intranets and large public sites. As is so often the case, each business unit has gone ahead and done its own thing, developing content haphazardly with few (if any) standards, and probably no metadata to support any sort of reasonable browsing.

If this describes your situation, you have a long road ahead of you, and search won't solve all of your problems—let alone your users' problems. But your highest priority should be to set up a search system to perform full-text indexing of as much cross-departmental content as possible. Even if it's only a stopgap, search will address your users' dire need for finding information regardless of which business unit actually owns it. Search will also help you, as the information architect, to get a better handle on what content is actually out there.

Search is a learning tool

Through search-log analysis, which we touched on in Chapter 6, you can gather useful data on what users actually want from your site, and how they articulate their needs (in the form of search queries). Over time you can analyze this valuable data to diagnose and tune your site's search system, other aspects of its information architecture, the performance of its content, and many other areas as well.

Search should be there because users expect it to be there

Your site probably doesn't contain as much content as Yahoo!, but if it's a substantial site, it probably merits a search engine. There are good reasons for this. Users won't always be willing to browse through your site's structure; their time is limited, and their cognitive-overload threshold is lower than you think. Interestingly, sometimes users won't browse for the wrong reasons—that is, they search when they don't necessarily know what to search for and would be better served by browsing. But perhaps most of all, users expect that little search box wherever they go. It's a default convention, and it's hard to stand against the wave of expectations.

Search can tame dynamism

You should also consider creating a search system for your site if it contains highly dynamic content. For example, if your site is a web-based newspaper, you might be adding dozens of story files daily via a commercial newsfeed or some other form of content syndication. For this reason, you probably wouldn't have the time each day to manually catalog your content or maintain elaborate tables of contents and site indexes. A search engine could help you by automatically indexing the contents of the site once or many times daily. Automating this process ensures that users have quality access to your site's content, and you can spend time doing things other than manually indexing and linking the story files as they come in.

Search System Anatomy

On its surface, search seems quite straightforward. Look for the box with the search button, enter and submit your query, and mutter a little prayer while the results load. If your prayers are answered, you'll find some useful results above the fold and can go on with your life.

Of course, there's a lot going on under the hood. A search engine application has indexed content on the site. All of it? Some of it? As a user, you'll probably never know. And what parts of the content? Usually the search engine can find the full text of each document. But a search engine can also index information associated with each document—like titles, controlled vocabulary terms, and so forth—depending on how it's been configured. And then there's the search interface, your window on the search engine's index. What you type there is looked up in the index; if things go well, results that match your query are returned.

A lot is going on here. There are the guts of the search engine itself; aside from tools for indexing and spidering, there are algorithms for processing your query into something the software can understand, and for ranking those results. There are interfaces, too: ones for entering queries (think simple and advanced search) and others for displaying results (including decisions on what to show for each result, and how to display the entire set of results). Further complicating the picture, there may be variations in query languages (for example, whether or not Boolean operators like AND, OR, and NOT can be used) and query builders (like spell checkers) that can improve upon a query.

Obviously, there's a lot to search that doesn't meet the eye. Additionally, there's your query, which itself usually isn't very straightforward. Where does your query come from? Your mind senses a gap that needs to be filled—with information—but isn't always sure how to express it. Searching is often iterative—not just because we don't always like the results we retrieve, but often because it takes us a few tries to get the words right for our query. You then interact with a search interface, heading for the simple, Google-like box or, if you're "advanced," grappling with the advanced search interface. And finally, you interact with results, which hopefully help you quickly determine which results are worth clicking through, which to ignore, and whether or not you should go back and try modifying your search. Figure 8-1 shows some of these pathways.

That's the 50,000-foot view of what's happening in a search system. Most of the technical details can be left to your IT staff; as an information architect, you are more concerned with factors that affect retrieval performance than with the technical guts of a search engine. But as we discuss in the following section, you don't want to leave *too* much in the hands of IT.

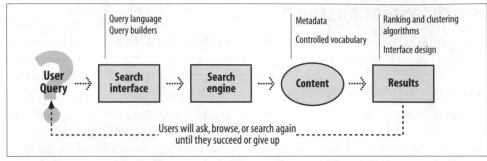

Figure 8-1. The basic anatomy of a search system (image from "In Defense of Search," Semantic Studios, http://www.semanticstudios.com/publications/semantics/search.html)

Search Is Not an IT Thing

Search engines are the foundation of search systems, and search engines are software applications. And software applications aren't your business; they're something for the IT people to worry about, and select, and install, and control. Right? Well, not exactly.

Setting up a web server is an IT thing, too, but we don't assign IT staff the tasks of writing a site's content, designing its visual aspects, or developing its information architecture; ideally, those are the responsibilities of people with other kinds of expertise. Why should setting up a search system be any different? Yet, it's all too common for information architects to be told that search is off-limits.

The reason is clear: a search engine is a complex piece of technology. It often requires someone who understands the technical issues—for example, load balancing for servers, platform limitations, and so on—to be involved in search engine selection and configuration.

But ultimately, search is there for users, and it's the responsibility of the information architect to advocate for users. An information architect will typically understand more than an IT specialist about how a search engine might benefit users by leveraging metadata, how its interface could be improved, or how it should be integrated with browsing. Additionally, consider all the aspects of a search system that we covered above; the search engine is just one piece of the puzzle. There are a lot of other decisions that must be made for the whole thing to behave, well, as a system that works well for users.

Ideally, the information architect, IT specialist, and people with other types of expertise will determine their respective needs, discuss how these might impact one another, and ultimately present a unified set of requirements when evaluating search-engine applications. Unfortunately, this is not always possible for political and other reasons. That's why the information architect must be prepared to argue strongly for owning at least an equal responsibility for selecting and implementing the search engine that will best serve users, rather than the one that runs on someone's favorite platform or is written in someone's favorite programming language.

Choosing What to Search

Let's assume that you've already chosen a search engine. What content should you index for searching? It's certainly reasonable to point your search engine at your site, tell it to index the full text of every document it finds, and walk away. That's a large part of the value of search systems—they can be comprehensive and can cover a huge amount of content quickly.

But indexing everything doesn't always serve users well. In a large, complex web environment chock-full of heterogeneous subsites and databases, you may want to allow users to search the silo of technical reports or the staff directory without muddying their search results with the latest HR newsletter articles on the addition of fish sticks to the cafeteria menu. The creation of *search zones*—pockets of more homogeneous content—reduces the apples-and-oranges effect and allows users to focus their searches.

Choosing what to make searchable isn't limited to selecting the right search zones. Each document or record in a collection has some sort of structure, whether rendered in HTML, XML, or database fields. In turn, that structure stores *content components*: pieces or "atoms" of content that are typically smaller than a document. Some of that structure—say, an author's name—may be leveraged by a search engine, while other parts—such as the legal disclaimer at the bottom of each page— might be left out.

Finally, if you've conducted an inventory and analysis of your site's content, you already have some sense of what content is "good." You might have identified your valuable content by manually tagging it or through some other mechanism. You might consider making this "good" stuff searchable on its own, in addition to being part of the site-wide search. You might even program your search engine to search this "good" stuff first, and expand to search the rest of the site's content if that first pass doesn't retrieve useful results. For example, if most of an e-commerce site's users are looking for products, those could be searched by default, and the search could then be expanded to cover the whole site as part of a revised search option.

In this section, we'll discuss issues of selecting what should be searchable at both a coarse level of granularity (search zones) and at the more atomic level of searching within documents (content components).

Determining Search Zones

Search zones are subsets of a web site that have been indexed separately from the rest of the site's content. When a user searches a search zone, he has, through interaction with the site, already identified himself as interested in that particular information. Ideally, the search zones in a site correspond to his specific needs, and the result is improved retrieval performance. By eliminating content that is irrelevant to his need, the user should retrieve fewer, more relevant, results.

On Dell's site (Figure 8-2), users can select search zones by audience type: home/home office, small business, and so on. (Note that "all" is the default setting.) These divisions quite possibly mirror how the company is organized, and perhaps each is stored in a separate filesystem or on its own server. If that's the case, the search zones are already in place, leveraging the way the files are logically and perhaps physically stored.

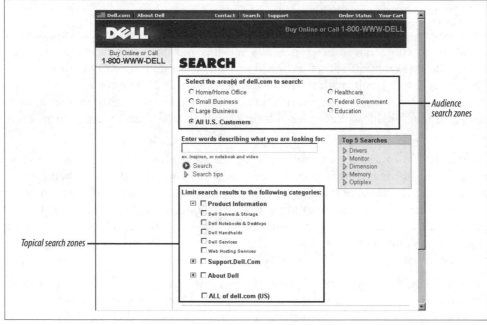

Figure 8-2. Two types of search zones: audience zones (top) and topical zones (bottom)

Additionally, users can select one or more of the site's categories or subcategories. It's probable that these pages come from the audience subsites, and that Dell allows its documents to be recombined into new search zones by indexing them by the keywords these zones represent. It's expensive to index specific content, especially manually, but one of the benefits of doing so is flexible search-zone creation: each category can be its own search zone or can be combined into a larger search zone.

You can create search zones in as many ways as you can physically segregate documents or logically tag them. Your decisions in selecting your site's organization schemes often help you determine search zones as well. So our old friends from Chapter 6 can also be the basis of search zones:

- Content type
- Audience
- Role
- Subject/topic
- Geography

- Chronology
- Author
- Department/business unit

And so on. Like browsing systems, search zones allow a large body of content to be sliced and diced in useful new ways, providing users with multiple "views" of the site and its content. But, naturally, search zones are a double-edged sword. Narrowing one's search through search zones can improve results, but interacting with them adds a layer of complexity. So be careful: many users will ignore search zones when they begin their search, opting to enter a simple search against the index of the entire site. So users might not bother with your meticulously created search zones until they're taking their second pass at a search, via an Advanced Search interface.

Following are a few ways to slice and dice.

Navigation versus destination

Most web sites contain, at minimum, two major types of pages: *navigation pages* and *destination pages*. Destination pages contain the actual information you want from a web site: sports scores, book reviews, software documentation, and so on. Navigation pages may include main pages, search pages, and pages that help you browse a site. The primary purpose of a site's navigation pages is to get you to the destination pages.

When a user searches a site, it's fair to assume that she is looking for destination pages. If navigation pages are included in the retrieval process, they will just clutter up the retrieval results.

Let's take a simple example: your company sells computer products via its web site. The destination pages consist of descriptions, pricing, and ordering information, one page for each product. Also, a number of navigation pages help users find products, such as listings of products for different platforms (e.g., Macintosh versus Windows), listings of products for different applications (e.g., word processing, book-keeping), listings of business versus home products, and listings of hardware versus software products. If the user is searching for Intuit's Quicken, what's likely to happen? Instead of simply retrieving Quicken's product page, she might have to wade through all of these pages:

- Financial Products index page
- Home Products index page
- Macintosh Products index page
- Quicken Product page
- Software Products index page
- Windows Products index page

The user retrieves the right destination page (i.e., the Quicken Product page) but also five more that are purely navigation pages. In other words, 83 percent of the retrieval obstructs the user's ability to find the most useful result.

Of course, indexing similar content isn't always easy, because "similar" is a highly relative term. It's not always clear where to draw the line between navigation and destination pages—in some cases, a page can be considered both. That's why it's important to test out navigation/destination distinctions before actually applying them. The weakness of the navigation/destination approach is that it is essentially an exact organization scheme (discussed in Chapter 6) that requires the pages to be either destination or navigation. In the following three approaches, the organization schemes are ambiguous, and therefore more forgiving of pages that fit into multiple categories.

Indexing for specific audiences

If you've already decided to create an architecture that uses an audience-oriented organization scheme, it may make sense to create search zones by audience breakdown as well. We found this a useful approach for the original Library of Michigan web site.

The Library of Michigan has three primary audiences: members of the Michigan state legislature and their staffs, Michigan libraries and their librarians, and the citizens of Michigan. The information needed from this site is different for each of these audiences; for example, each has a very different circulation policy.

So we created four indexes: one for each of the three audiences, and one unified index of the entire site in case the audience-specific indexes didn't do the trick for a particular search. Here are the results from running a query on the word "circulation" against each of the four indexes:

Index	Documents retrieved	Retrieval reduced by
Unified	40	-
Legislature Area	18	55%
Libraries Area	24	40%
Citizens Area	9	78%

As with any search zone, less overlap between indexes improves performance. If the retrieval results were reduced by a very small figure, say 10 or 20 percent, it may not be worth the overhead of creating separate audience-oriented indexes. But in this case, much of the site's content is specific to individual audiences.

Indexing by topic

Ameriprise Financial employs loosely topical search zones with its site. For example, if you're looking for information on investments that will help you achieve a financially secure retirement, you might preselect the "Individual" search zone, as shown in Figure 8-3.

The 85 results retrieved may sound like a lot, but if you'd searched the entire site, the total would have been 580 results, many dealing with topic areas that aren't germaine to personal retirement investing.

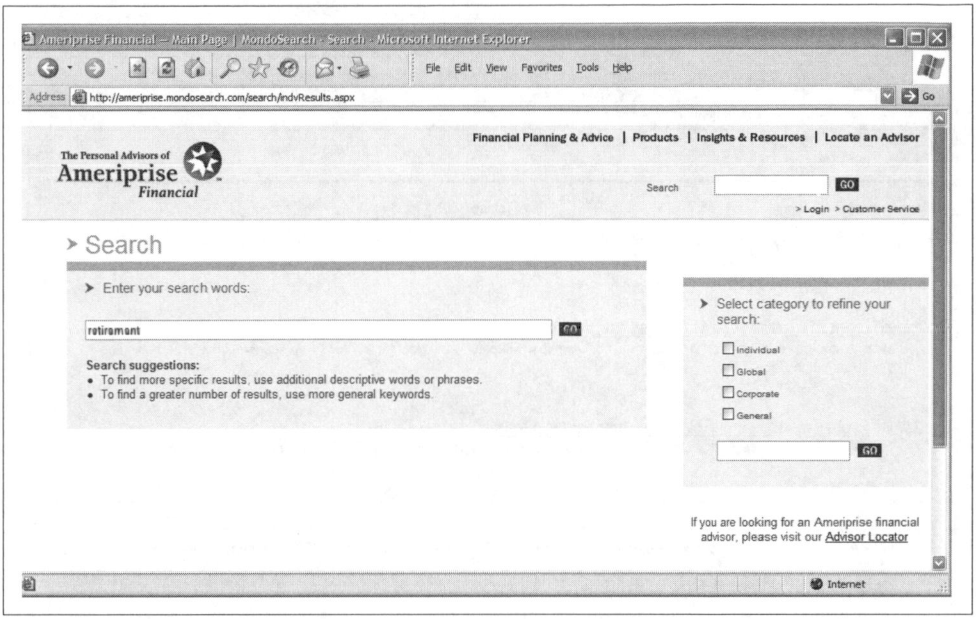

Figure 8-3. Executing a search against the "Individual" search zone

Indexing recent content

Chronologically organized content allows for perhaps the easiest implementation of search zones. (Not surprisingly, it's probably the most common example of search zones.) Because dated materials aren't generally ambiguous and date information is typically easy to come by, creating search zones by date—even ad hoc zones—is straightforward.

The advanced search interface of the *New York Times* provides a useful illustration of filtering by date range (Figure 8-4).

Regular users can return to the site and check up on the news using one of a number of chronological search zones (e.g., today's news, past week, past 30 days, past 90 days, past year, and since 1996). Additionally, users who are looking for news within a particular date range or on a specific date can essentially generate an ad hoc search zone.

Selecting Content Components to Index

Just as it's often useful to provide access to subsets of your site's content, it's valuable to allow users to search specific components of your documents. By doing so, you'll enable users to retrieve more specific, precise results. And if your documents have administrative or other content components that aren't especially meaningful to users, these can be excluded from the search.

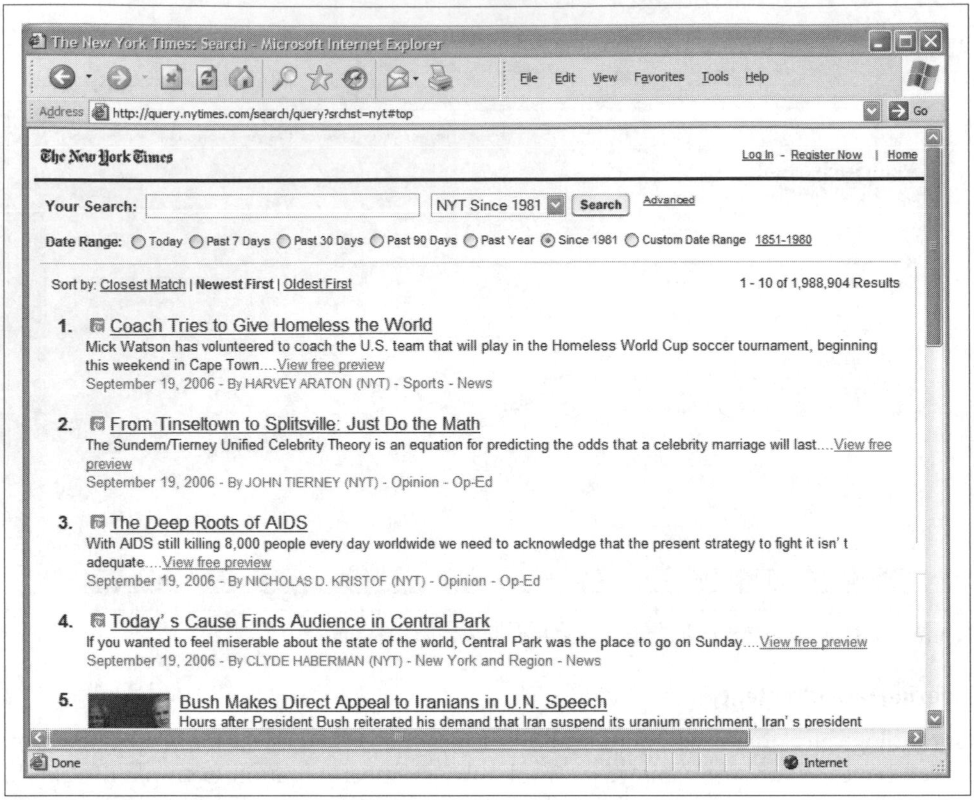

Figure 8-4. There are many ways to narrow your New York Times search by date

In the article from Salon shown in Figure 8-5, there are more content components than meet the eye. There is a title, an author name, a description, images, links, and some attributes (such as keywords) that are invisible to users. There are also content components that we don't want to search, such as the full list of categories in the upper left. These could confuse a user's search results; for example, if the full text of the document was indexed for searching, searches for "comics" would retrieve this article about finding a translator in Egypt. (A great by-product of the advent of content management systems and logical markup languages like XML is that it's now much easier to leave out content that shouldn't be indexed, like navigation options, advertisements, disclaimers, and other stuff that might show up in document headers and footers.)

Salon's search system allows users to take advantage of the site's structure, supporting searches by the following content components:

- Body
- Title
- URL

Figure 8-5. This article is jam-packed with various content components, some visible and some not

- Site name
- Link
- Image link
- Image alt text
- Description
- Keywords
- Remote anchor text

Would users bother to search by any of these components? In Salon's case, we could determine this by reviewing search-query logs. But what about in the case of a search system that hadn't yet been implemented? Prior to designing a search system, could we know that users would take advantage of this specialized functionality?

This question leads to a difficult paradox: even if users would benefit from such souped-up search functionality, they likely won't ever ask for it during initial user research. Typically users don't have much understanding of the intricacies and capabilities of search systems. Developing use cases and scenarios might unearth some reasons to support this level of detailed search functionality, but it might be better to instead examine other search interfaces that your site's users find valuable, and determine whether to provide a similar type of functionality.

There is another reason to exploit a document's structure. Content components aren't useful only for enabling more precise searches; they can also make the format of search results much more meaningful. In Figure 8-6, Salon's search results include category and document titles ("Salon Travel | In other words"), description ("The scoop on finding a translator in Egypt…"), and URL. Indexing numerous content components for retrieval provides added flexibility in how you design search results. (See the later section "Presenting Results.")

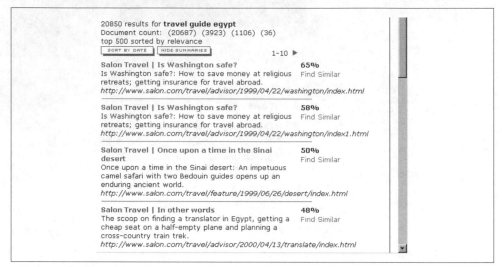

Figure 8-6. Title, description, and URL are content components displayed for each result

Search Algorithms

Search engines find information in many ways. In fact, there are about 40 different retrieval algorithms alone, most of which have been around for decades. We're not going to cover them all here; if you'd like to learn more, read any of the standard texts on information retrieval.*

We bring up the topic because it's important to realize that a retrieval algorithm is essentially a tool, and just like other tools, specific algorithms help solve specific problems. And as retrieval algorithms are at the heart of search engines, it's important to note that there is absolutely no single search engine that will meet all of your users' information needs. Remember that fact the next time you hear a search engine vendor claim that his product's brand-new proprietary algorithm is the solution to all information problems.

---

* A good starting point is *Modern Information Retrieval* by Ricardo Baeza-Yates and Berthier Ribeiro-Neto (Addison-Wesley).

Pattern-Matching Algorithms

Most retrieval algorithms employ pattern matching; that is, they compare the user's query with an index of, typically, the full texts of your site's documents, looking for the same string of text. When a matching string is found, the source document is added to the retrieval set. So a user types the textual query "electric guitar," and documents that include the text string "electric guitar" are retrieved. It all sounds quite simple. But this matching process can work in many different ways to produce different results.

Recall and precision

Some algorithms return numerous results of varying relevance, while some return just a few high quality results. The terms for these opposite ends of the spectrum are *recall* and *precision*. There are even formulas for calculating them (note the difference in the denominators):

> Recall = # relevant documents retrieved / # relevant documents in collection
> Precision = # relevant documents retrieved / # total documents in collection

Are your site's users doing legal research, learning about the current state of scientific research in a field, or performing due diligence about an acquisition? In these cases, they'll want high recall. Each of the hundreds or thousands (or more?) results retrieved will have some relevance to the user's search, although perhaps not very much. As an example, if a user is "ego-surfing," she wants to see every mention of her name—she is hoping for high recall. The problem, of course, is that along with good results come plenty of irrelevant ones.

On the other hand, if she's looking for two or three really good articles on how to get stains out of a wool carpet, then she's hoping for high-precision results. It doesn't matter how many relevant articles there are if you get a good enough answer right away.

Wouldn't it be nice to have both recall and precision at the same time? Lots and lots of very high quality results? Sadly, you can't have your cake and eat it, too: recall and precision are inversely related. You'll need to decide what balance of the two will be most beneficial to your users. You can then select a search engine with an algorithm biased toward either recall or precision or, in some cases, you can configure an engine to accommodate one or the other.

For example, a search tool might provide *automatic stemming*, which expands a term to include other terms that share the same root (or stem). If the stemming mechanism is very strong, it might treat the search term "computer" as sharing the same root ("comput") as "computers," "computation," "computational," and "computing." Strong stemming in effect expands the user's query by searching for documents that include any of those terms. This enhanced query will retrieve more related documents, meaning higher recall.

Conversely, no stemming means the query "computer" retrieves only documents with the term "computer" and ignores other variants. Weak stemming might expand the query only to include plurals, retrieving documents that include "computer" or "computers." With weak stemming or no stemming, precision is higher and recall is lower. Which way should you go with your search system—high recall or high precision? The answer depends on what kinds of information needs your users have.

Another consideration is how structured the content is. Are there fields, rendered in HTML or XML or perhaps in a document record, that the search engine can "see" and therefore search? If so, searching for "William Faulkner" in the author field will result in higher precision, assuming we're looking for books authored by Faulkner. Otherwise, we're left with searching the full text of each document and finding results where "William Faulkner" may be mentioned, whether or not he was the author.

Other Approaches

When you already have a "good" document on hand, some algorithms will convert that document into the equivalent of a query (this approach is typically known as *document similarity*). "Stop words," like "the," "is," and "he" are stripped out of the good document, leaving a useful set of semantically rich terms that, ideally, represent the document well. These terms are then converted into a query that should retrieve similar results. An alternative approach is to present results that have been indexed with similar metadata. In Figure 8-7, the first of WebMD's results for a search on "West Nile" is complemented by a link to "See More Content like this."

Approaches such as collaborative filtering and citation searching go even further to help expand results from a single relevant document. In the following example from CiteSeer (see Figure 8-8), we've identified an article that we like: "Application Fault Level Tolerance in Heterogeneous Networks of Workstations." Research Index automatically finds documents in a number of ways.

Cited by
> What other papers cite this one? The relationship between cited and citing papers implies some degree of mutual relevance. Perhaps the authors even know each other.

Active bibliography (related documents)
> Conversely, this paper cites others in its own bibliography, implying a similar type of shared relevance.

Similar documents based on text
> Documents are converted into queries automatically and are used to find similar documents.

Related documents from co-citation
> Another twist on citation, co-citation assumes that if documents appear together in the bibliographies of other papers, they probably have something in common.

Figure 8-7. Many WebMD search results are accompanied by a link to "See More Content like this"

There are other retrieval algorithms, more than we can cover here. What's most important is to remember that the main purpose of these algorithms is to identify the best pool of documents to be presented as search results. But "best" is subjective, and you'll need to have a good grasp of what users hope to find when they're searching your site. Once you have a sense of what they wish to retrieve, begin your quest for a search tool with a retrieval algorithm that might address your users' information needs.

Query Builders

Besides search algorithms themselves, there are many other means of affecting the outcome of a search. *Query builders* are tools that can soup up a query's performance. They are often invisible to users, who may not understand their value or how to use them. Common examples include:

Spell-checkers
    These allow users to misspell terms and still retrieve the right results by automatically correcting search terms. For example, "accomodation" would be treated as "accommodation," ensuring retrieval of results that contain the correct term.

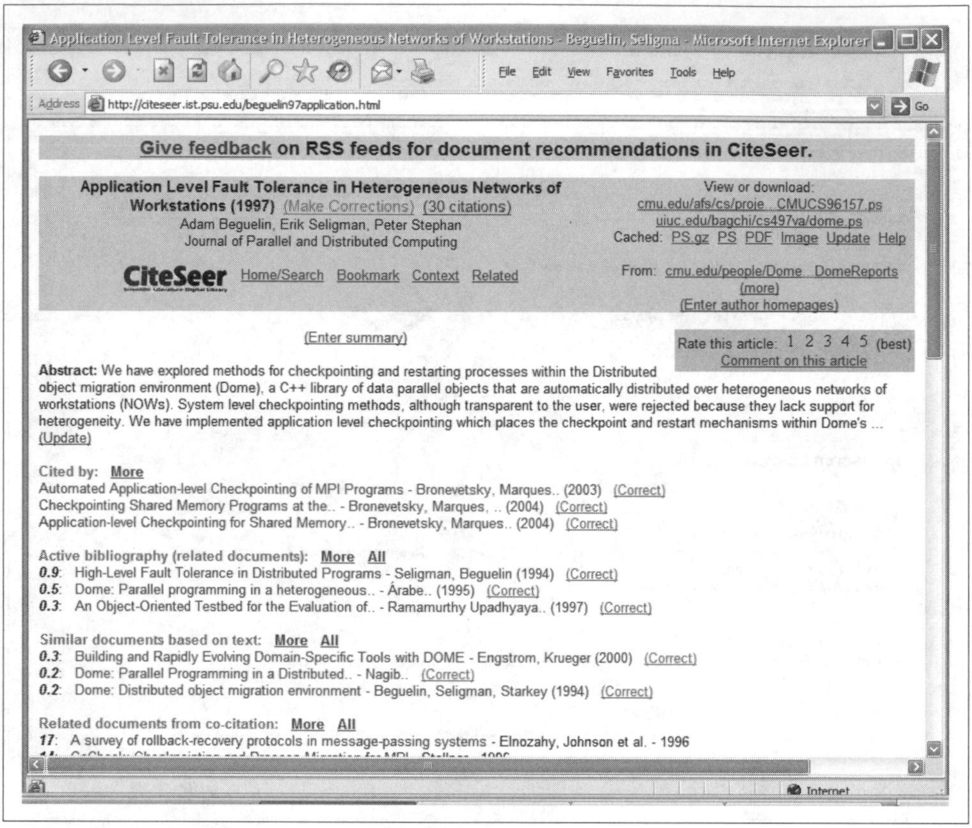

Figure 8-8. CiteSeer provides multiple ways to expand from a single search result

Phonetic tools

Phonetic tools (the best-known of which is "Soundex") are especially useful when searching for a name. They can expand a query on "Smith" to include results with the term "Smyth."

Stemming tools

Stemming tools allow users to enter a term (e.g., "lodge") and retrieve documents that contain variant terms with the same stem (e.g., "lodging", "lodger").

Natural language processing tools

These can examine the syntactic nature of a query—for example, is it a "how to" question or a "who is" question?—and use that knowledge to narrow retrieval.

Controlled vocabularies and thesauri

Covered in detail in Chapter 9, these tools expand the semantic nature of a query by automatically including synonyms within the query.

Spell-checkers correct for an almost universal problem among searchers and are well worth considering for your search system. (Look over your site's search logs, and you'll be amazed by the preponderance of typos and misspellings in search queries.)

The other query builders have their pros and cons, addressing different information needs in different situations. Once again, a sense of your users' information needs will help you select which approaches make the most sense for you; additionally, keep in mind that your search engine may or may not support these query builders.

Presenting Results

What happens after your search engine has assembled the results to display? There are many ways to present results, so once again you'll need to make some choices. And as usual, the mysterious art of understanding your site's content and how users want to use it should drive your selection process.

When you are configuring the way your search engine displays results, there are two main issues to consider: which content components to display for each retrieved document, and how to list or group those results.

Which Content Components to Display

A very simple guideline is to display less information to users who know what they're looking for, and more information to users who aren't sure what they want. A variant on that approach is to show users who are clear on what they're looking for only *representational* content components, such as a title or author, to help them quickly distinguish the result they're seeking. Users who aren't as certain of what they're looking for will benefit from *descriptive* content components such as a summary, part of an abstract, or keywords to get a sense of what their search results are about. You can also provide users some choice of what to display; again, consider your users' most common information needs before setting a default. Figures 8-9 and 8-10 show a site that provides both options to users.

When it's hard to distinguish retrieved documents because of a commonly displayed field (such as the title), show more information, such as a page number, to help the user differentiate between results.

Another take on the same concept is shown in Figure 8-11, which displays three versions of the same book. Some of the distinctions are meaningful; you'll want to know which library has a copy available. Some aren't so helpful; you might not care who the publisher is.

How much information to display per result is also a function of how large a typical result set is. Perhaps your site is fairly small, or most users' queries are so specific that they retrieve only a small number of results. If you think that users would like more information in such cases, then it may be worth displaying more content components per result. But keep in mind that regardless of how many ways you indicate that there are more results than fit on one screen, many (if not most) users will never venture past that first screen. So don't go overboard with providing lots of content per result, as the first few results may obscure the rest of the retrieval.

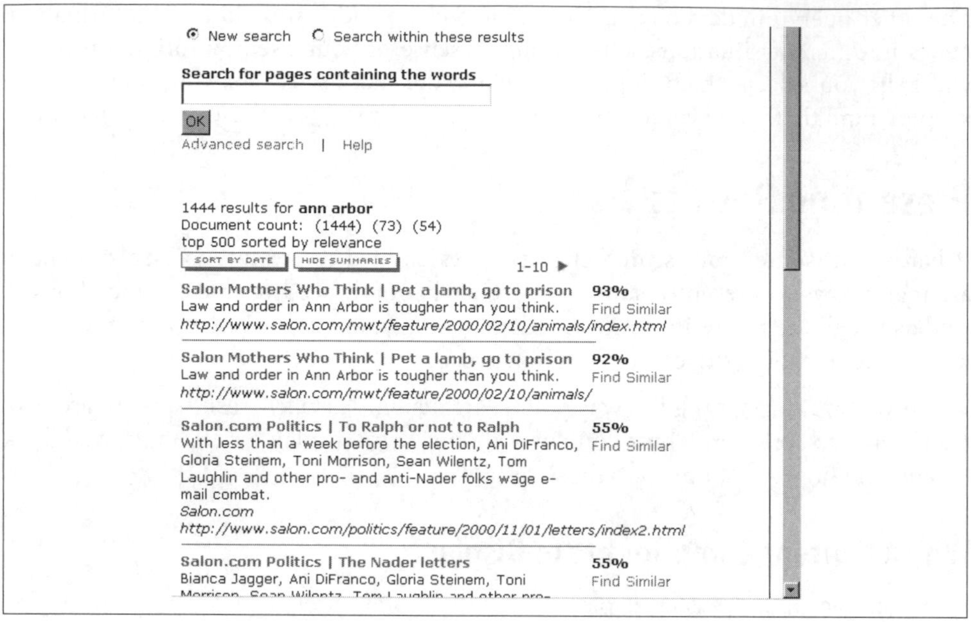

Figure 8-9. Salon uses search results with summaries to help users who want to learn about the documents they've retrieved…

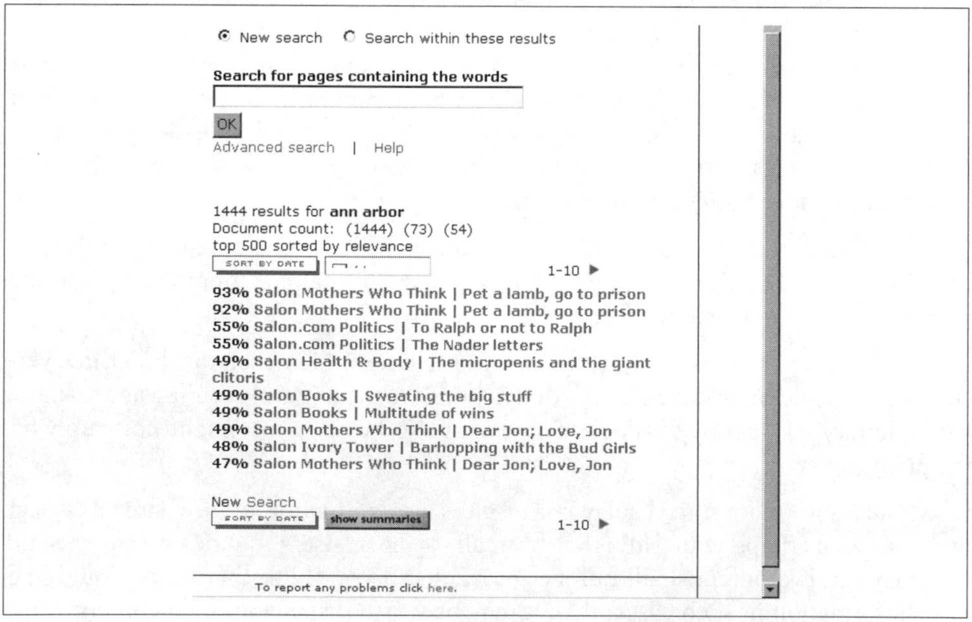

Figure 8-10. …and without summaries for users who have a better sense of what they need

Figure 8-11. Content components help distinguish three versions of the same book

Which content components you display for each result also depends on which components are available in each document (i.e., how your content is structured) and on how the content will be used. Users of phone directories, for example, want phone numbers first and foremost. So it makes sense to show them the information from the phone number field in the result itself, as opposed to forcing them to click through to another document to find this information (see Figure 8-12).

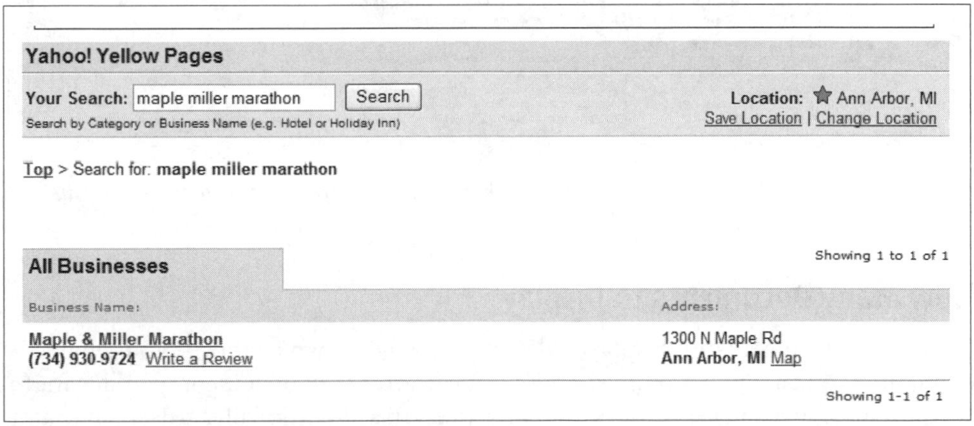

Yahoo! Yellow Pages

Your Search: [maple miller marathon]   [Search]   Location: ☆ Ann Arbor, MI
Search by Category or Business Name (e.g. Hotel or Holiday Inn)   Save Location | Change Location

Top > Search for: **maple miller marathon**

All Businesses   Showing 1 to 1 of 1

Business Name: Address:

Maple & Miller Marathon   1300 N Maple Rd
(734) 930-9724 Write a Review   **Ann Arbor, MI** Map

                                                      Showing 1-1 of 1

Figure 8-12. A yellow pages search doesn't force us to click through for a phone number

If you don't have much structure to draw from or if your engine is searching full text, showing the query terms within the "context" of the document's text is a useful variation on this theme (see Figure 8-13). In this example, E*Trade displays the query terms in bold—an excellent practice, as it helps the user quickly scan the results page for the relevant part of each result. E*Trade further augments this useful context by highlighting the surrounding sentence.

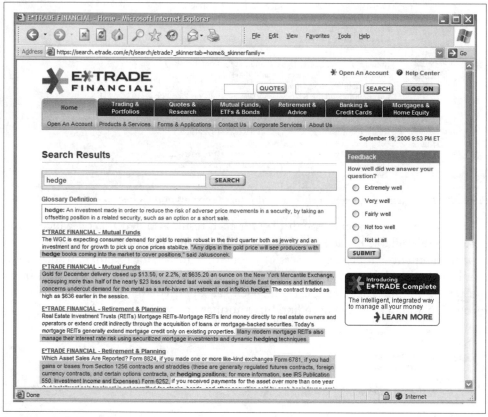

Figure 8-13. e*Trade bolds the search query, and highlights its surrounding sentence to show its context

How Many Documents to Display

How many documents are displayed depends mostly on two factors. If your engine is configured to display a lot of information for each retrieved document, you'll want to consider having a smaller retrieval set, and vice versa. Additionally, a user's monitor resolution, connectivity speed, and browser settings will affect the number of results that can be displayed effectively. It may be safest to err toward simplicity—by showing a small number of results—while providing a variety of settings that the user can select based on his own needs.

We do suggest that you let users know the total number of retrieved documents so they have a sense of how many documents remain as they sift through search results. Also consider providing a results navigation system to help them move through their results. In Figure 8-14, ICON Advisers provides such a navigation system, displaying the total number of results and enabling users to move through the result set 10 at a time.

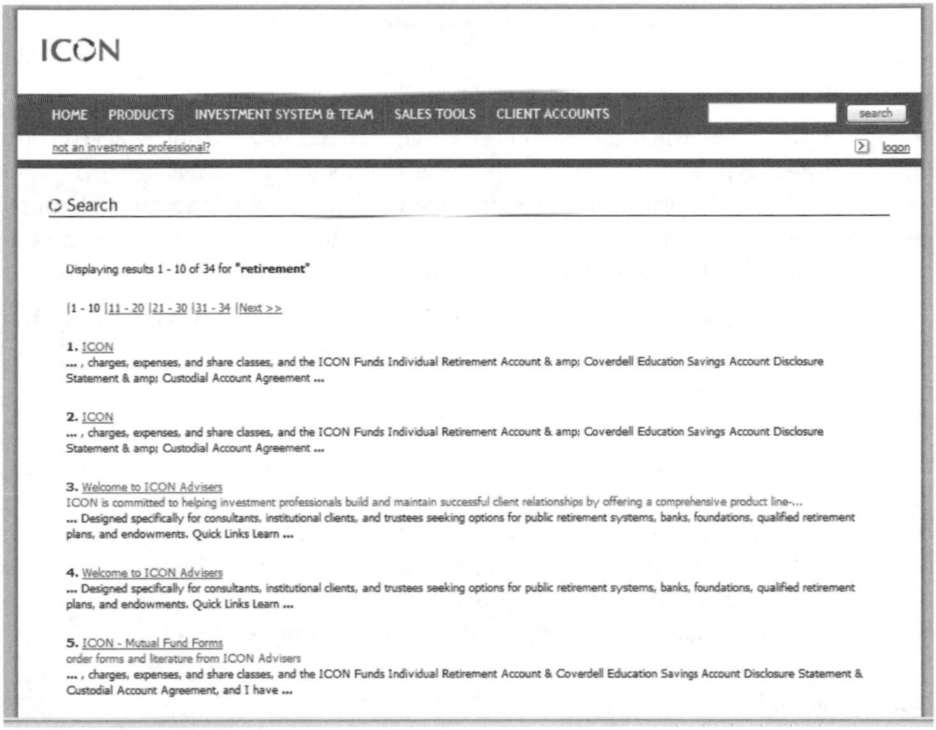

Figure 8-14. ICON Advisers allows you to jump ahead through screens of ten results at a time

In many cases, the moment a user is confronted by a large result set is the moment he decides the number of results is too large. This is a golden opportunity to provide the user with the option of revising and narrowing his search. ICON Advisers could achieve this quite simply by repeating the query "retirement" in the search box in the upper right.

Listing Results

Now that you have a group of search results and a sense of which content components you wish to display for each, in what order should these results be listed? Again, much of the answer depends upon what kind of information needs your users start with, what sort of results they are hoping to receive, and how they would like to use the results.

There are two common methods for listing retrieval results: *sorting* and *ranking*. Retrieval results can be sorted chronologically by date, or alphabetically by any number of content component types (e.g., by title, by author, or by department). They can also be ranked by a retrieval algorithm (e.g., by relevance or popularity).

Sorting is especially helpful to users who are looking to make a decision or take an action. For example, users who are comparing a list of products might want to sort by price or another feature to help them make their choice. Any content component can be used for sorting, but it's sensible to provide users with the option to sort on components that will actually help them accomplish tasks. Which ones are task-oriented and which aren't, of course, depends upon each unique situation.

Ranking is more useful when there is a need to understand information or learn something. Ranking is typically used to describe retrieved documents' *relevance*, from most to least. Users look to learn from those documents that are most relevant. Of course, as we shall see, relevance is relative, and you should choose relevance ranking approaches carefully. Users will generally assume that the top few results are best.

The following sections provide examples of both sorting and ranking, as well as some ideas on what might make the most sense for your users.

Sorting by alphabet

Just about any content component can be sorted alphabetically (see Figure 8-15). Alphabetical sorts are a good general-purpose sorting approach—especially when sorting names—and in any case, it's a good bet that most users are familiar with the order of the alphabet! It works best to omit initial articles such as "a" and "the" from the sort order (certain search engines provide this option); users are more likely to look for "The Naked Bungee Jumping Guide" under "N" rather than "T."

Sorting by chronology

If your content (or your user) is time-sensitive, chronological sorts are a useful approach. And you can often draw from a filesystem's built-in dating if you have no other sources of date information.

If your site provides access to press releases or other news-oriented information, sorting by reverse chronological order makes good sense (see Figures 8-16 and 8-17). Chronological order is less common and can be useful for presenting historical data.

Ranking by relevance

Relevance-ranking algorithms (there are many flavors) are typically determined by one or more of the following:

- How many of the query's terms occur in the retrieved document
- How frequently those terms occur in that document

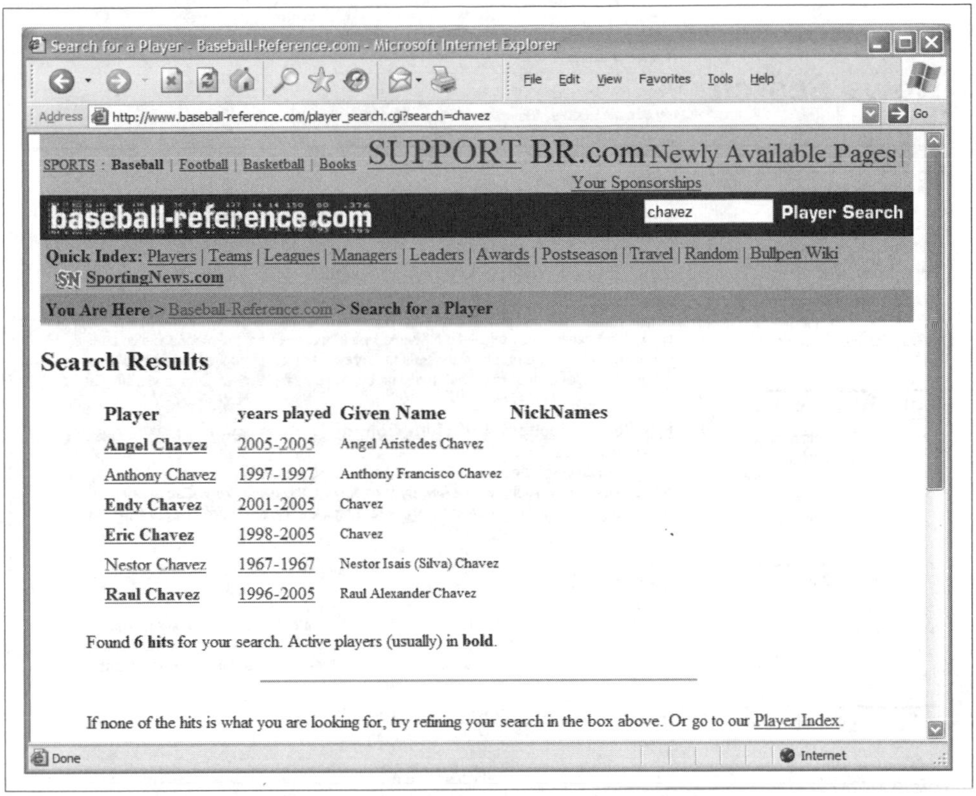

Figure 8-15. Baseball-Reference.com displays search results in alphabetical order

- How close together those terms occur (e.g., are they adjacent, in the same sentence, or in the same paragraph?)
- Where the terms occur (e.g., a document with the query term in its title may be more relevant than one with the query term in its body)
- The popularity of the document where the query terms appear (e.g., is it linked to frequently, and are the sources of its links themselves popular?)

Different relevance-ranking approaches make sense for different types of content, but with most search engines, the content you're searching is apples and oranges. So, for example, Document A might be ranked higher than Document B, but Document B is definitely more relevant. Why? Because while Document B is a bibliographic citation to a really relevant work, Document A is a long document that just happens to contain many instances of the terms in the search query. So the more heterogeneous your documents are, the more careful you'll need to be with relevance ranking.

Indexing by humans is another means of establishing relevance. Keyword and descriptor fields can be searched, leveraging the value judgments of human indexers. For example, manually selected recommendations—popularly known as "Best

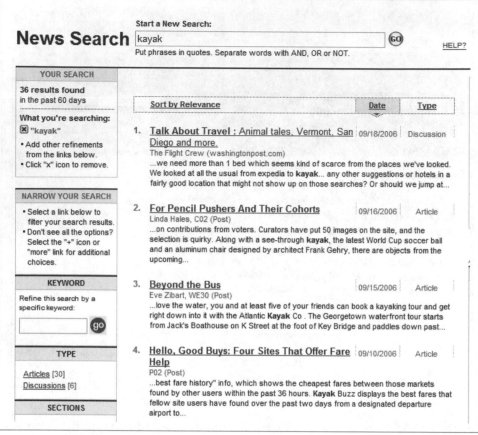

Figure 8-16. The Washington Post's default list ordering is by reverse-chronological order…

Bets"—can be returned as relevant results. In Figure 8-18, the first set of results was associated with the query "monty python" in advance.

Requiring an investment of human expertise and time, the Best Bets approach isn't trivial to implement and therefore isn't necessarily suitable to be developed for each and every user query. Instead, recommendations are typically used for the most common queries (as determined by search-log analysis) and combined with automatically generated search results.

There are other concerns with relevance ranking. It's tempting to display relevance scores alongside results; after all, those scores are what's behind the order of the results. In Figure 8-19, we searched for "storage" at Computer Associates' web site.

The first result does seem quite promising. But what exactly is the difference between a document with a relevance score of 50 percent and one with 49 percent? They are scored similarly, but the top result is CA's events calendar—which covers CA events. Interestingly, the events calendar doesn't even mention "storage." Other results are a

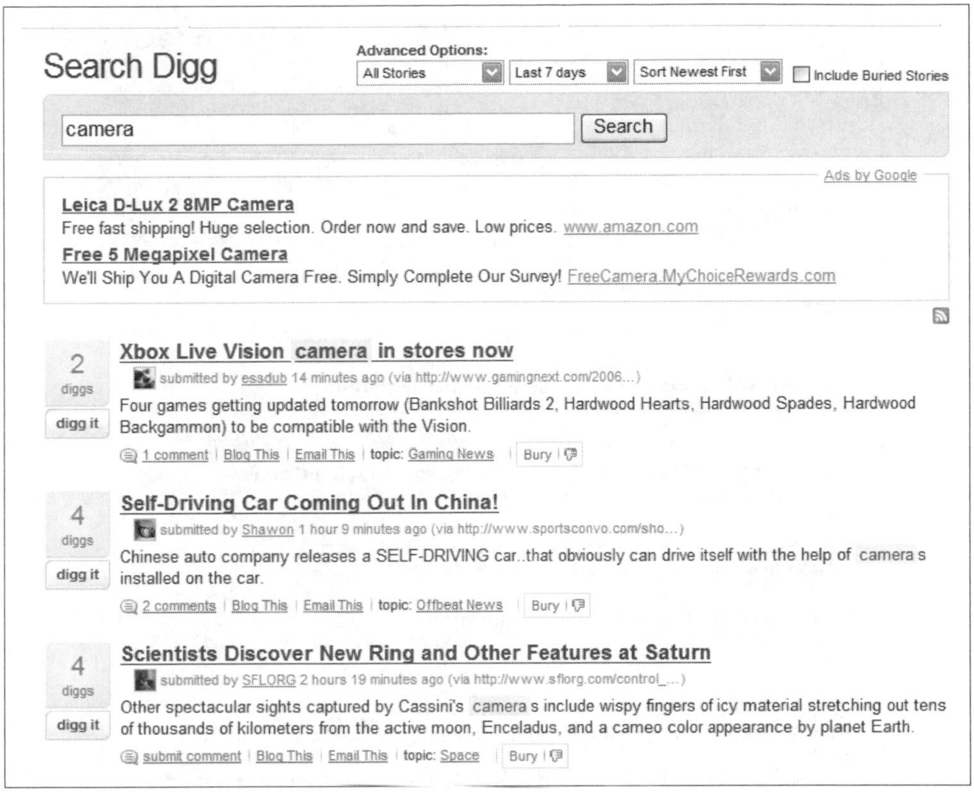

Figure 8-17. …as is Digg's

bit more relevant, but this is an excellent illustration of how relevancy algorithms do strange and complicated things behind the scenes. We don't really know why the results are ranked this way. Showing scores only aggravates that sense of ignorance, so these should be used with caution; leaving out scores altogether is often a better approach.

Ranking by popularity

Popularity is the source of Google's popularity.

Put another way, Google is successful in large part because it ranks results by which ones are the most popular. It does so by factoring in how many links there are to a retrieved document. Google also distinguishes the quality of these links: a link from a site that itself receives many links is worth more than a link from a little-known site (this algorithm is known as PageRank).

There are other ways to determine popularity, but keep in mind that small sites or collections of separate, nonlinked sites (often referred to as "silos") don't necessarily take advantage of popularity as well as large, multisite environments with many

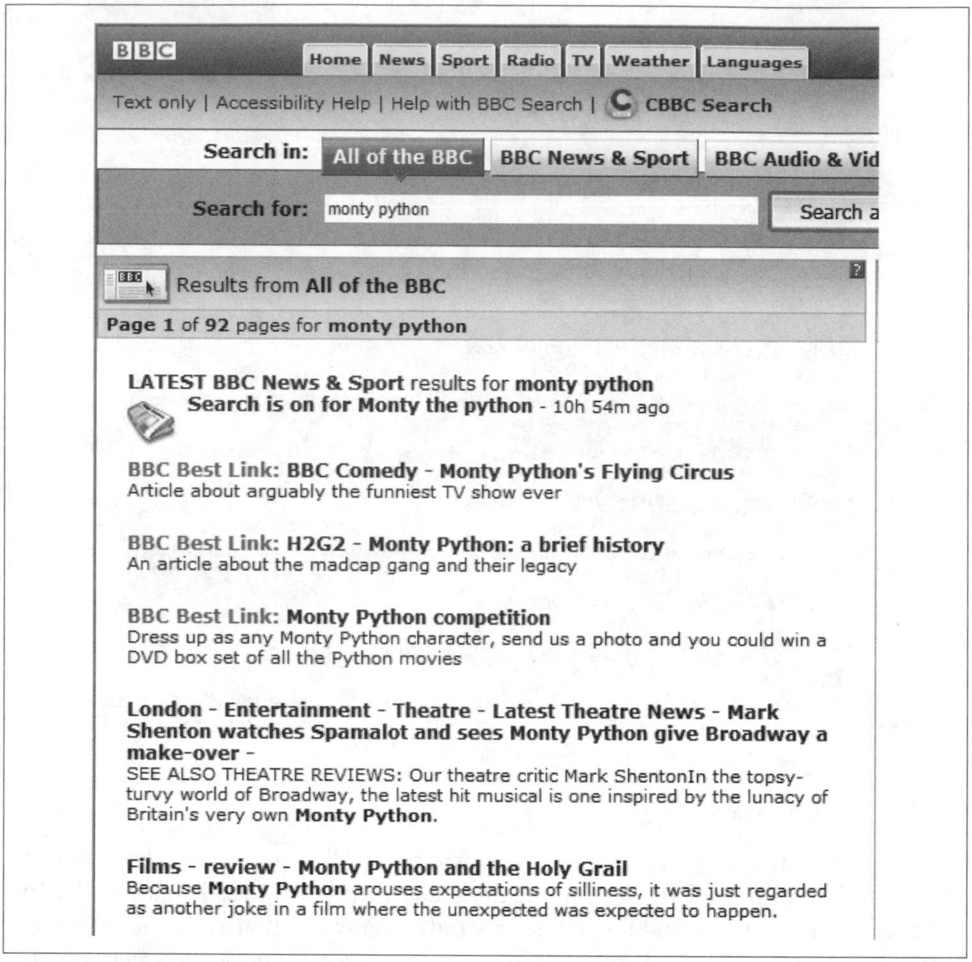

Figure 8-18. A search of the BBC site retrieves a set of manually tagged documents as well as automatic results; the recommendations are called "Best Links" rather than "Best Bets" to avoid gambling connotations

users. The latter have a wide scope of usage and a richer set of links. A smaller site isn't likely to have enough variation in the popularity of different documents to merit this approach, while in a "silo" environment, little cross-pollination results in few links between sites. It's also worth noting that, to calculate relevance, Google uses over 100 other criteria in addition to PageRank.

Ranking by users' or experts' ratings

In an increasing number of situations, users are willing to rate the value of information. User ratings can be used as the basis of retrieval result ordering. In the case of Digg (see Figure 8-20), these ratings—based on Digg users' votes on the pages

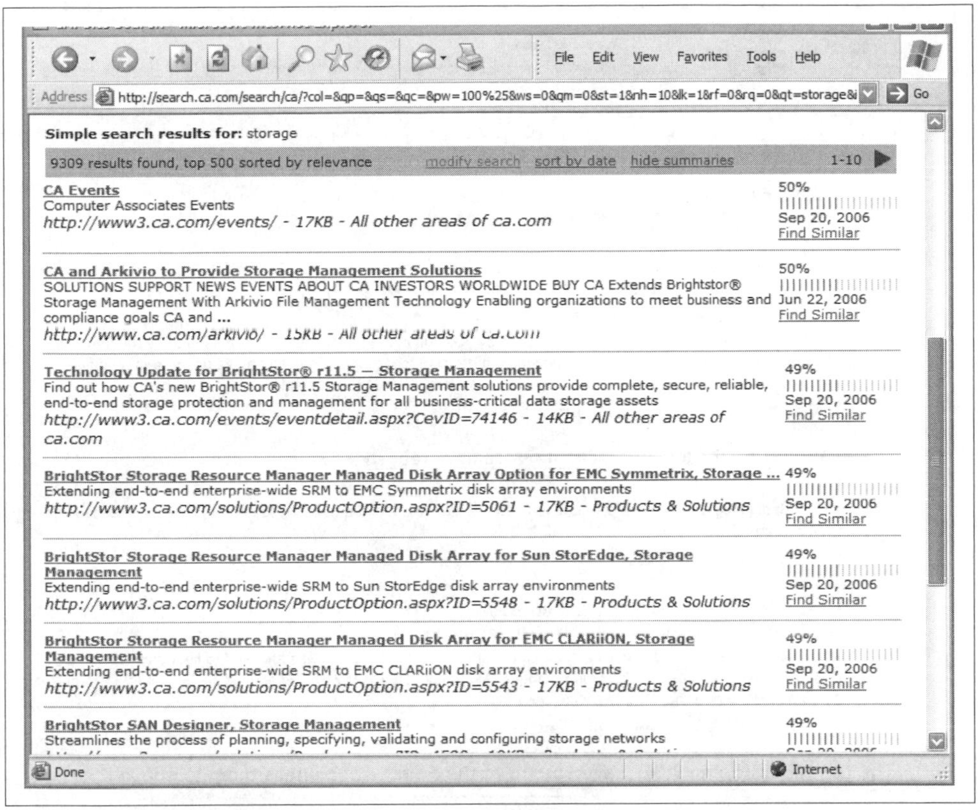

Figure 8-19. What do these relevance scores really mean?

submitted by other Digg users—are integral to helping users judge the value of an item, and form the foundation of an entire information economy. Of course, Digg has a lot of users who don't shrink from expressing their opinions, so there is a rich collection of judgments to draw on for ranking.

Most sites don't have a sufficient volume of motivated users to employ valuable user ratings. However, if you have the opportunity to use it, it can be helpful to display user ratings with a document, if not as part of a presentation algorithm.

Ranking by pay-for-placement

As banner-ad sales are no longer the most viable economic model, pay-for-placement (PFP) is becoming increasingly common to web-wide searching. Different sites bid for the right to be ranked high, or higher, on users' result lists. Yahoo! Search Marketing (Figure 8-21) is one of the most popular sites to take this approach.

If your site aggregates content from a number of different vendors, you might consider implementing PFP to present search results. Or if users are shopping, they might appreciate this approach—with the assumption that the most stable, successful sites

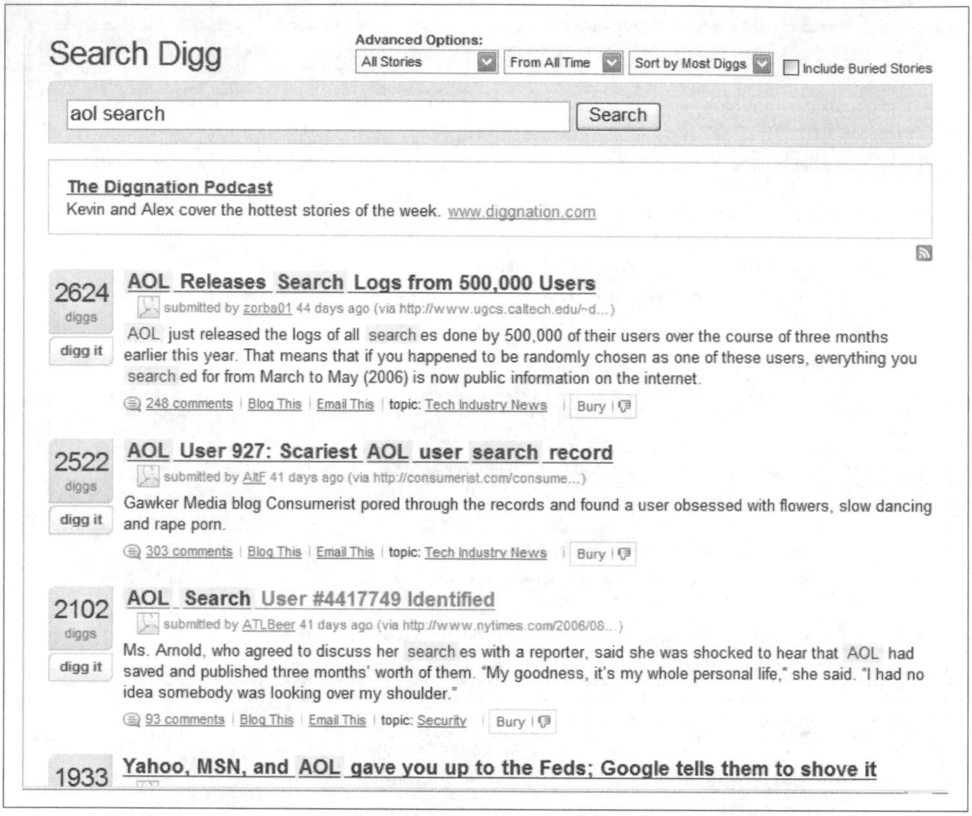

Figure 8-20. *User ratings fuel the ranking of these Digg results*

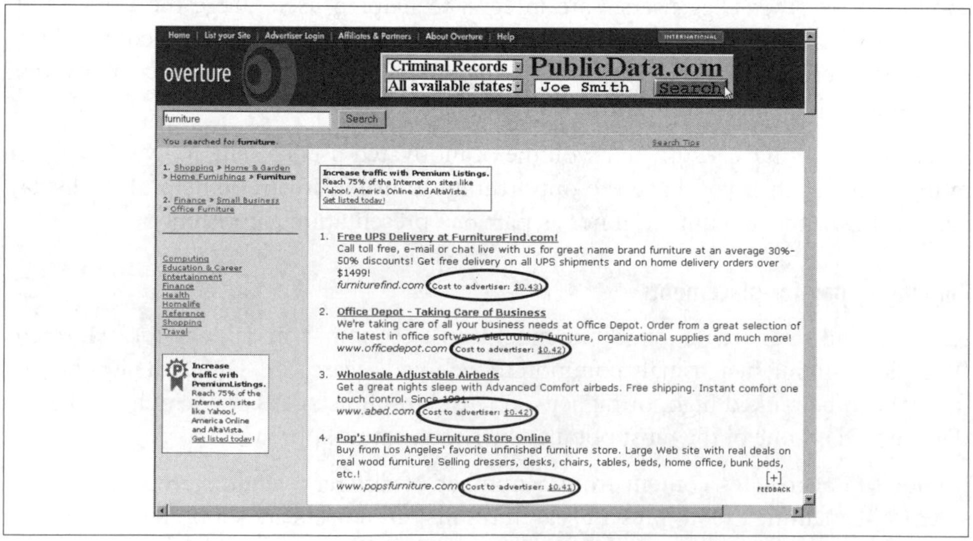

Figure 8-21. *Overture (now Yahoo! Search Marketing) used to auction the right to be ranked highly*

are the ones that can afford the highest placement. This is somewhat like selecting the plumber with the largest advertisement in the yellow pages to fix your toilet.

Grouping Results

Despite all the ways we can list results, no single approach is perfect. Hybrid approaches like Google's show a lot of promise, but you typically need to be in the business of creating search engines to have this level of involvement with a tool. In any case, our sites are typically getting larger, not smaller. Search result sets will accordingly get larger as well, and so will the probability that those ideal results will be buried far beyond the point where users give up looking.

However, one alternative approach to sorting and ranking holds promise: clustering retrieved results by some common aspect. An excellent study[*] by researchers at Microsoft and the University of California at Berkeley show improved performance when results are clustered by category as well as by a ranked list. How can we cluster results? The obvious ways are, unfortunately, the least useful: we can use existing metadata, like document type (e.g., *.doc*, *.pdf*) and file creation/modification date, to allow us to divide search results into clusters. Much more useful are clusters derived from manually applied metadata, like topic, audience, language and product family. Unfortunately, approaches based on manual effort can be prohibitively expensive.

Some automated tools are getting better at approximating the more useful topical types of clustering that often serve users best. In Figures 8-22 and 8-23, Clusty and WiseNut contextualize the query "RFID" with such topics as "Privacy," "Barcode," and "RFID implementation."

These clusters provide context for search results; by selecting the category that seems to fit your interest best, you're working with a significantly smaller retrieval set and (ideally) a set of documents that come from the same topical domain. This approach is much like generating search zones on the fly.

Exporting Results

You've provided users with a set of search results. What happens next? Certainly, they could continue to search, revising their query and their idea of what they're looking for along the way. Or, heavens, they might have found what they're looking for and are ready to move on. Contextual inquiry and task-analysis techniques will help you understand what users might want to do with their results. The following sections discuss a few common options.

---

[*] Dumais, S.T., Cutrell, E. and Chen, H. "Optimizing search by showing results in context." *Proceedings of CHI '01, Human Factors in Computing Systems* (April 2001).

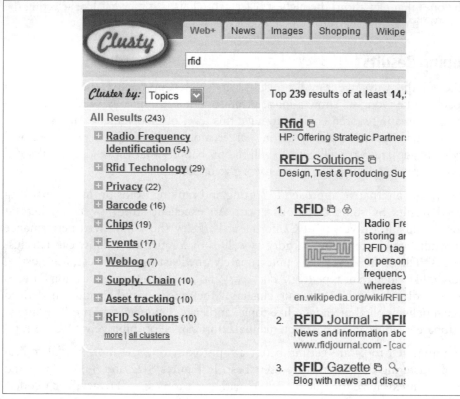

Figure 8-22. Clusty contextualizes search results for the query "RFID"…

Printing, emailing, or saving results

The user has finally reached his destination. He could bookmark the result, but he likely doesn't want to return to this document where it lives on the site. Instead, he wants to grab it and take it with him.

Obviously he can print it, but not all documents are designed to be printed—they may sport banner ads or be crowded with navigational options. If many of your users wish to print and your content isn't print-friendly, consider offering a "print this document" option that provides a clearer, more printable version of the document. Alternatively, users may want a digital version of the file. And as so many of us use our email programs as personal information managers, providing an "email this document" function can come in handy as well. Both functions are shown in Figure 8-24.

The *New York Times* also allows users to save articles for future retrieval. We wonder if many users take advantage of "Save," as most users rely on bookmarking options that aren't specific to a single site. The *Times* also provides a "reprints" option and enables users to toggle between multiple- and single-page views of the article. For the most part, these options are conceived with a good understanding of what users might want to do next, now that they've found an article of interest.

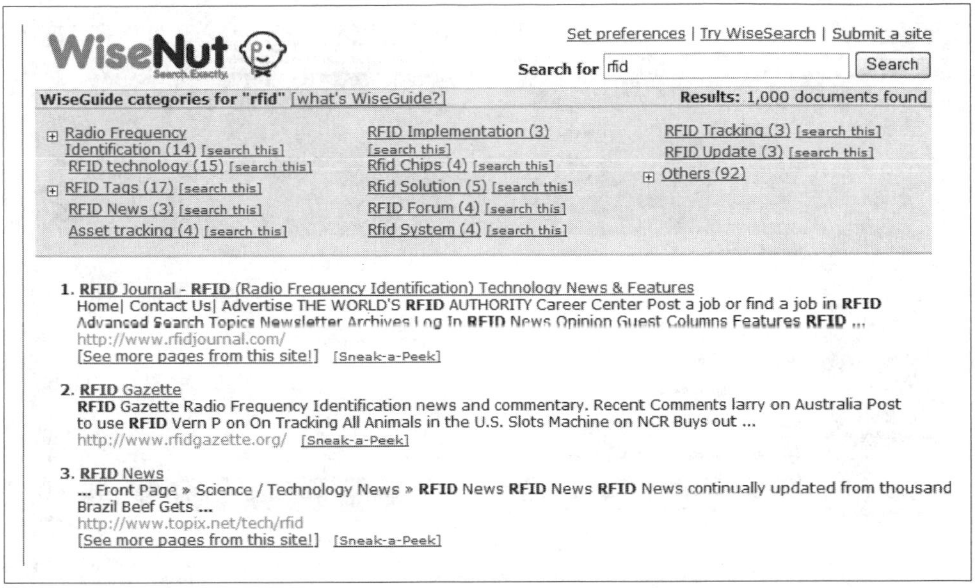

Figure 8-23. ...as does WiseNut; the positioning of related categories differs, as do the categories generated by both services

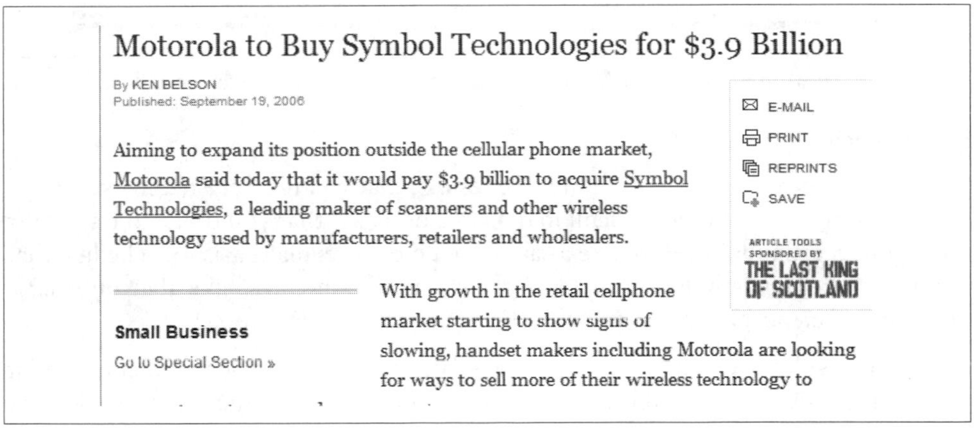

Figure 8-24. New York Times articles can be formatted for printing or emailed for later use

Select a subset of results

Sometimes you want to take more than one document along with you. You want to "shop" for documents just like you shop for books at Amazon. And if you're sorting through dozens or hundreds of results, you may need a way to mark the documents you like so you don't forget or lose track of them.

A shopping-cart feature can be quite useful in search-intensive environments such as a library catalog. In Figures 8-25 and 8-26, users can "save" a subset of their retrieval and then manipulate them in a "shopping basket" once they're done searching.

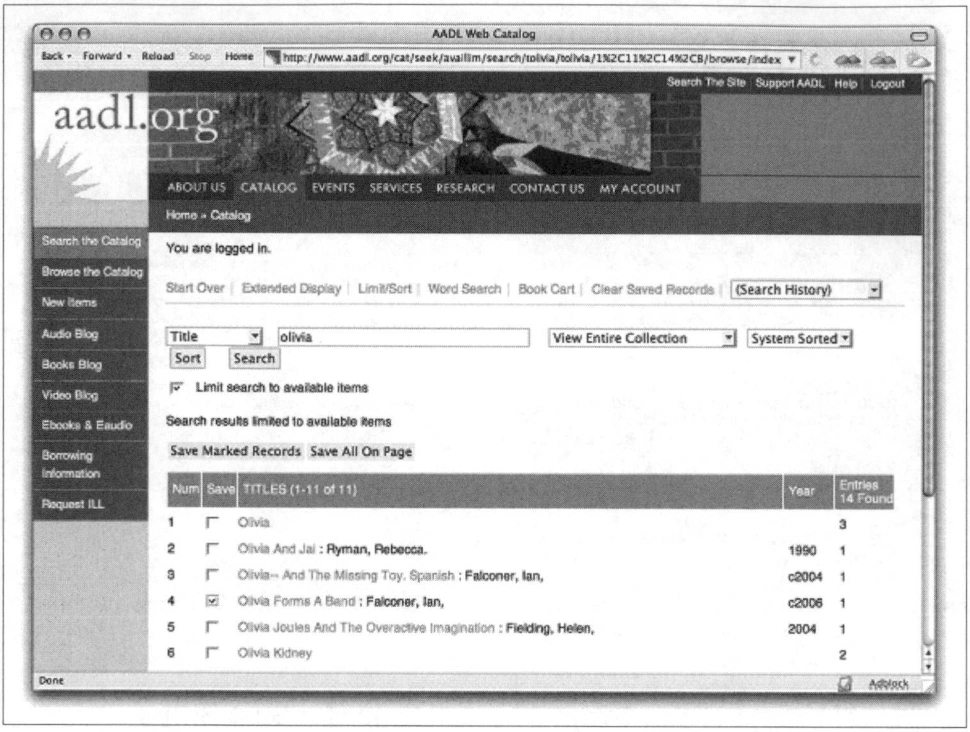

Figure 8-25. The Ann Arbor District Library catalog enables users to select a few records to "save"…

Save a search

In some cases it's the search itself, not the results, that you're interested in "keeping." Saved searches are especially useful in dynamic domains that you'd like to track over time; you can manually re-execute a saved search on a regular basis, or schedule that query to automatically be rerun regularly. Some search tools, like that of *Science Magazine*'s ScienceNOW service, allow both, as shown in Figure 8-27.

As search results become more "portable"—allowing users to access them without visiting the originating search system's site—they can be syndicated using RSS or Atom. For example, you can save and automatically re-execute a search in Google using the Google Alerts service, shown in Figure 8-28, and the results of your saved query can be monitored via an RSS or Atom feed (as well as by email).

Designing the Search Interface

All the factors we've discussed so far—what to search, what to retrieve, and how to present the results—come together in the search interface. And with so much variation among users and search-technology functions, there can be no single ideal search interface. Although the literature of information retrieval includes many studies of

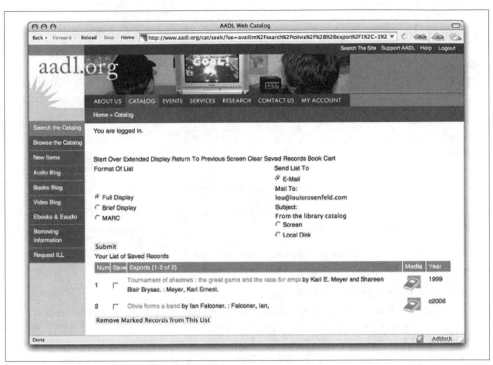

Figure 8-26. …and email the results or download them to a local disk

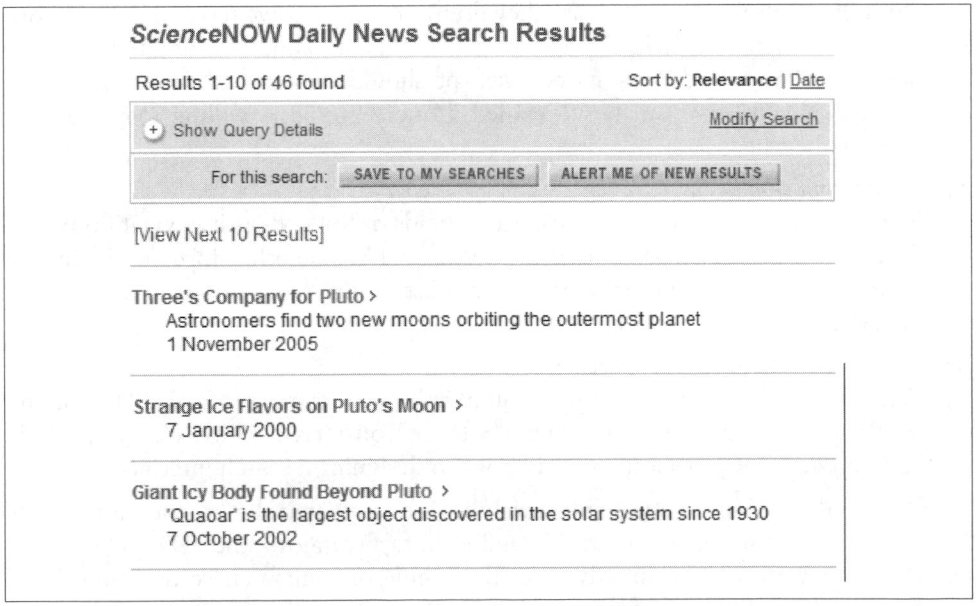

*Science*NOW Daily News Search Results

Results 1-10 of 46 found   Sort by: **Relevance** | Date

⊕ Show Query Details   Modify Search

For this search: SAVE TO MY SEARCHES   ALERT ME OF NEW RESULTS

[View Next 10 Results]

Three's Company for Pluto ›
Astronomers find two new moons orbiting the outermost planet
1 November 2005

Strange Ice Flavors on Pluto's Moon ›
7 January 2000

Giant Icy Body Found Beyond Pluto ›
'Quaoar' is the largest object discovered in the solar system since 1930
7 October 2002

Figure 8-27. Queries can be saved for future use and scheduled to be automatically re-executed on a regular basis

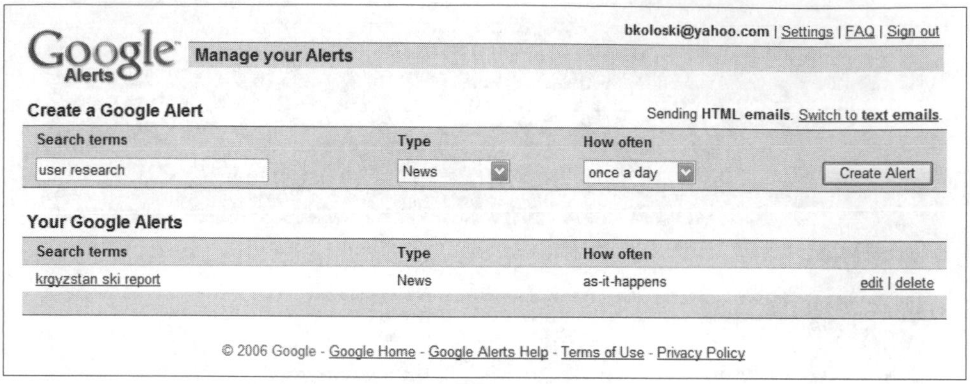

Figure 8-28. Monitoring queries using Google Alerts; results can be delivered via RSS or Atom feeds, as well as email

search interface design, many variables preclude the emergence of a "right way" to design search interfaces. Here are a few of the variables on the table:

Level of searching expertise and motivation
> Are users comfortable with specialized query languages (e.g., Boolean operators), or do they prefer natural language? Do they need a simple or a high-powered interface? Do they want to work hard to make their search a success, or are they happy with "good enough" results? How many iterations are they willing to try?

Type of information need
> Do users want just a taste, or are they doing comprehensive research? What content components can help them make good decisions about clicking through to a document? Should the results be brief, or should they provide extensive detail for each document? And how detailed a query are users willing to provide to express their needs?

Type of information being searched
> Is the information made up of structured fields or full text? Is it navigation pages, destination pages, or both? Is it written in HTML or other formats, including nontextual? Is the content dynamic or more static? Does it come tagged with metadata, full of fields, or is it full text?

Amount of information being searched
> Will users be overwhelmed by the number of documents retrieved? How many results is the "right number"? That's a lot to consider. Luckily, we can provide basic advice that you should consider when designing a search interface.

In the early days of the Web, many search engines emulated the functionality of the "traditional" search engines used for online library catalogs and CD ROM-based databases, or were ported directly from those environments. These traditional systems were often designed for researchers, librarians, and others who had some knowledge of and incentive for expressing their information needs in complex query languages. Therefore, many search systems at the time allowed the user to use Boolean operators, search fields, and so forth; in fact, users were often required to know and use these complex languages.

As the Web's user base exploded, overall searching experience and expertise bottomed out, and the new breed of user wasn't especially patient. Users more typically just entered a term or two without any operators, pressed the "search" button, and hoped for the best.

The reaction of search engine developers was to bury the old fancy tricks in "advanced search" interfaces, or to make them invisible to users by building advanced functionality directly into the search engine. For example, Google makes a set of assumptions about what kind of results users want (through a relevance algorithm) and how they'd like those results presented (using a popularity algorithm). Google makes some good assumptions for web-wide searching, and that's why it's successful. However, most search systems, web-wide or local, don't work as well.

For that reason, the pendulum may eventually swing back to supporting users who, out of frustration, have become more search-literate and are willing to spend more time learning a complex search interface and constructing a query. But for now, it's fair to assume that, unless your site's users are librarians, researchers, or specialized professionals (e.g., an attorney performing a patent search), they won't invest much time or effort into crafting well-considered queries. That means the burden of searching falls chiefly on the search engine, its interfaces, and how content is tagged and indexed; therefore, it's best to keep your search interface as simple as possible: present users with a simple search box and a "search" button.

The Box

Your site is likely to have the ubiquitous search box, as shown in Figure 8-29.

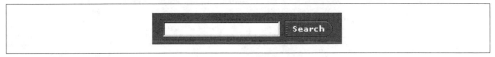

Figure 8-29. The ubiquitous search box (in this case, from ibm.com)

Simple and clear. Type in some keywords ("directions Somers") or a natural language expression ("What are the directions to the Somers offices?"), hit the "search" button, and the whole site will be searched and results are displayed.

Users make assumptions about how search interfaces work, and you may want to test for those as you design your own search system. Some common user assumptions include:

- "I can just type terms that describe what I'm looking for and the search engine will do the rest."
- "I don't have to type in those funny AND, OR, or NOT thingies."

- "I don't have to worry about synonyms for my term; if I'm looking for dogs, I just type 'dogs,' not 'canine' or 'canines.'"
- "Fielded searching? I don't have time to learn which fields I can search."
- "My query will search the *entire* site."

If your users have those assumptions and are not especially motivated to learn more about how your site's search works differently, then go with the flow. Give them the box. You certainly could provide a "help" page that explains how to create more advanced, precise queries, but users may rarely visit this page.

Instead, look for opportunities to *educate users when they're ready to learn*. The best time to do this is after the initial search has been executed and the user reaches a point of indecision or frustration. The initial hope that the first try would retrieve exactly what they were looking for has now faded. And when users are ready to revise their searches, they'll want to know how they can make those revisions. For example, if you search IBM's site for "servers" (see Figure 8-30), you'll likely get a few more results than you'd like.

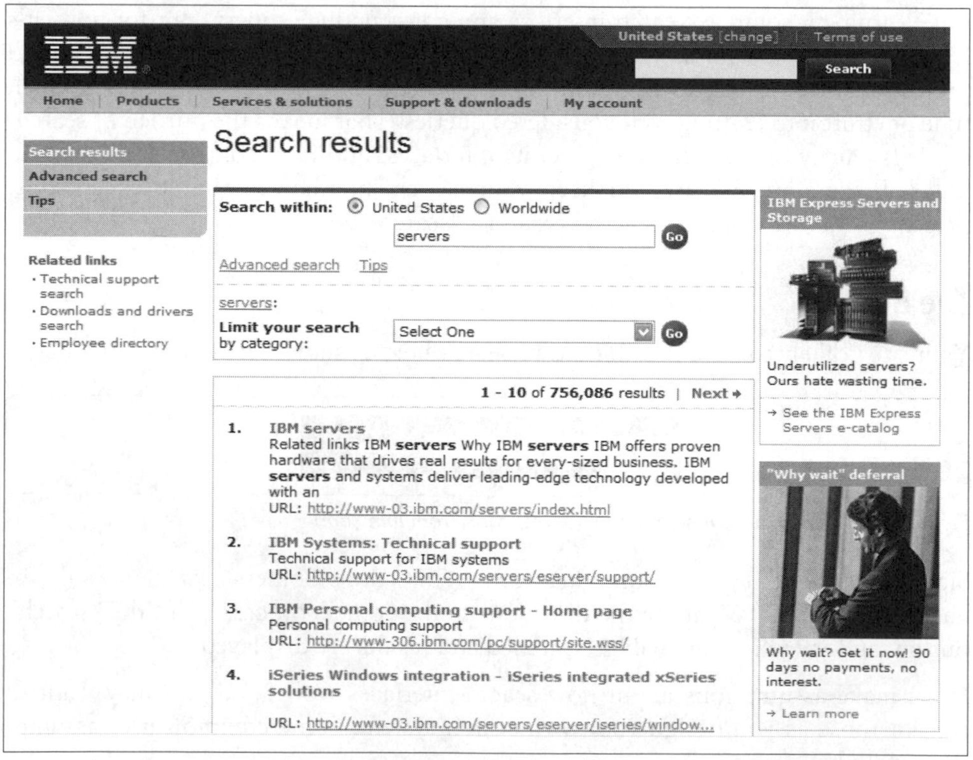

Figure 8-30. IBM's search results provide ample opportunities to revise your search…

At this point, IBM's search system goes beyond the box: it tells the user something to the effect of "Here are those 729,288 results that you asked for. Perhaps this is too many? If that's the case, consider revising your search using our souped-up 'advanced search' interface, which allows you to narrow your search, as shown in Figure 8-31. Or learn how to search our site better from our 'tips' page." Or, select from a list of categories (really search zones) to narrow your results further.

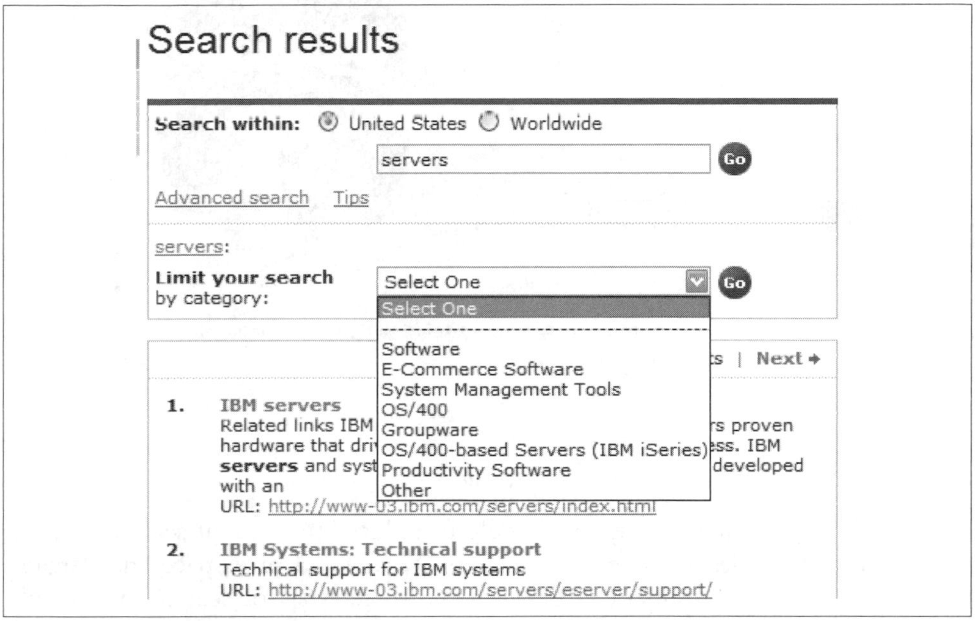

Figure 8-31. ...including the ability to narrow by category

In general, too many or too few (typically zero) search results are both good indicators for users to revise their searches; we'll cover more on this topic in the section "Supporting Revision" later in this chapter.

The box can cause confusion when it occurs alongside other boxes. Figure 8-32 shows a main page with many boxes, all of which come with the same "go" button, regardless of functionality. It's a good bet that users won't read the nice labels next to each box and will instead do all sorts of confounding things, like typing their search queries in the "password" box, not to mention URLs in the "search" box. (Search logs regularly turn up such "box bloopers.")

A better approach is to place the search box nearer to the site-wide navigation system at the top of the page and relabel its "go" button as "search." The other boxes could be made less prominent on the page or moved somewhere else altogether. Consistent placement of the search box alongside other site-wide navigation choices on every page in the site, along with the consistent use of a button labeled "search" that comes with that box, will go a long way toward ensuring that users at least know where to type their queries.

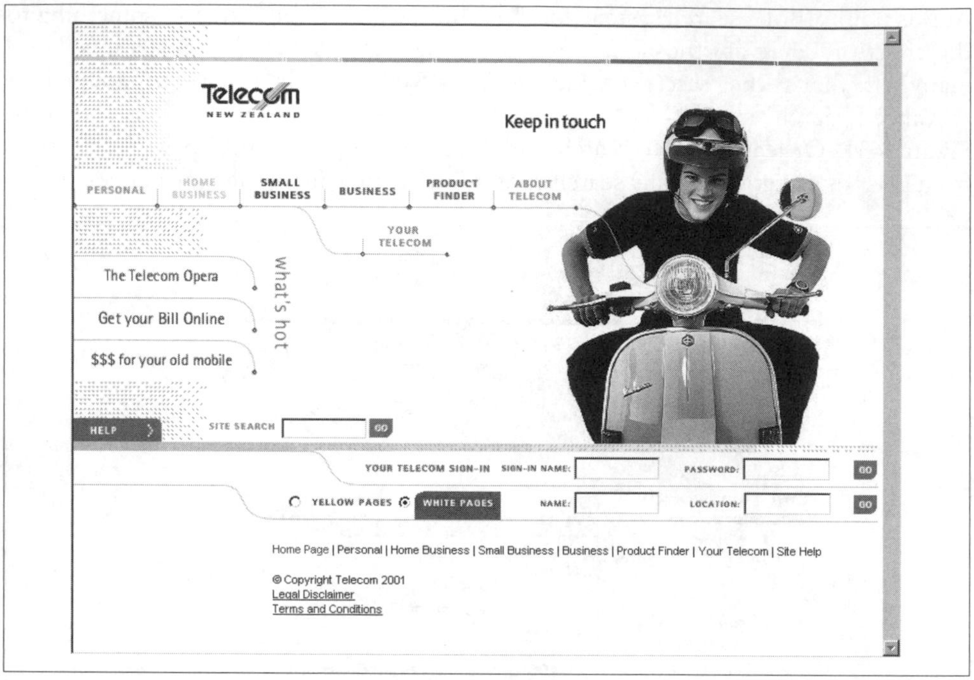

Figure 8-32. Where will users type in their search queries?

In Figure 8-33, the three search boxes could be reduced to one that searches a combined index of articles, comments, and users. This would save space and demand less of the user. The distinctions between the three types of search zones could always show up (and be made selectable) in a pull-down menu or advanced search interface.

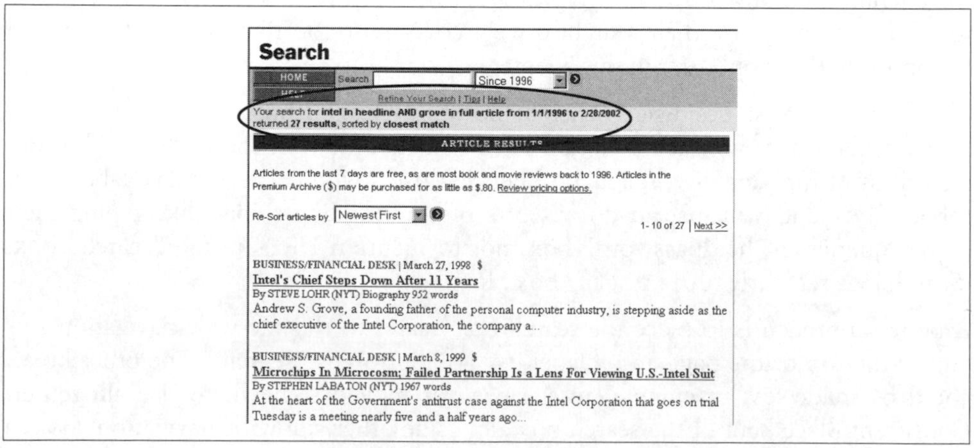

Figure 8-33. These three boxes could be combined into one

Clearly, there are many assumptions behind that innocuous little search box, some made on the part of the user, and some by the information architect who decides what functionality will be hidden behind that box. Determining what your users' assumptions are should drive the default settings that you set up when designing the simple search interface.

Advanced Search: Just Say No

Advanced search interfaces are where much of the search system's functionality is "unveiled" to users. In stark contrast to The Box, advanced search interfaces allow much more manipulation of the search system and are typically used by two types of users: advanced searchers (librarians, lawyers, doctoral students, medical researchers), and frustrated searchers who need to revise their initial search (often users who found that The Box didn't meet their needs).

Often, you find everything and the kitchen sink thoughtlessly stuffed into advanced search interfaces. Fielded searching, date ranges, search-zone selection, and specialized query languages all crop up here. In fact, these can often crowd the interface and make it difficult for users to know what to do. Gartner's advanced search interface, shown in Figure 8-34, for example, doesn't even fit on one page.

We won't cover these functions in this chapter because we've found that, contrary to our original assumptions, few users ever take advantage of them. Therefore, because few users will ever visit your advanced search page, we don't recommend investing much effort into its design. You're better off looking for ways to enable users to revise when they need to—in other words, in the appropriate context. More on that below.

As for advanced search, it can't be completely ignored, unfortunately. It is something of a convention, and many users will expect to see it. Perhaps a good rule of thumb is to unearth your search engine's various heavy-duty search functions on the advanced page for those few users who want to have a go at them, but design your search system with the goal of making it unnecessary for the vast majority of searchers to ever need to go to the advanced search page.

Supporting Revision

We've touched on what can happen after the user finds what she's looking for and the search is done. But all too often that's not the case. Here are some guidelines to help the user hone her search (and hopefully learn a little bit about your site's search system in the process).

Figure 8-34. Gartner's endless advanced search interface: who will use it?

Repeat search in results page

What was it I was looking for? Sometimes users are forgetful, especially after sifting through dozens of results. Displaying the initial search within the search box (as in Figure 8-35) can be quite useful: it restates the search that was just executed, and allows the user to modify it without re-entering it.

Explain where results come from

It's useful to make clear what content was searched, especially if your search system supports multiple search zones (see Figure 8-36). This reminder can be handy if the user decides to broaden or narrow her search; more or fewer search zones can be used in a revised search.

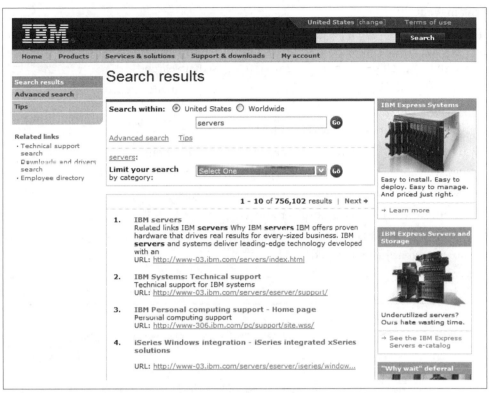

Figure 8-35. The original query is displayed on the results page and can be revised and re-executed

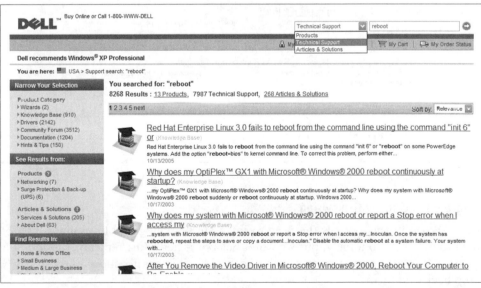

Figure 8-36. Dell's search system shows you where you searched (i.e., "Technical Support"), and makes it easy to reach results from other search zones

Explain what the user did

If the results of a search are not satisfactory, it can be useful to state what happened behind the scenes, providing the user with a better understanding of the situation and a jumping-off point should she wish to revise her search.

"What happened" can include the two guidelines just mentioned, as well as:

- Restate the query
- Describe what content was searched
- Describe any filters that might be in place (e.g., date ranges)
- Show implicit Boolean or other operators, such as a default AND
- Show other current settings, such as the sort order
- Mention the number of results retrieved

In Figure 8-37, the *New York Times* site provides an excellent example of explaining to the user what just happened.

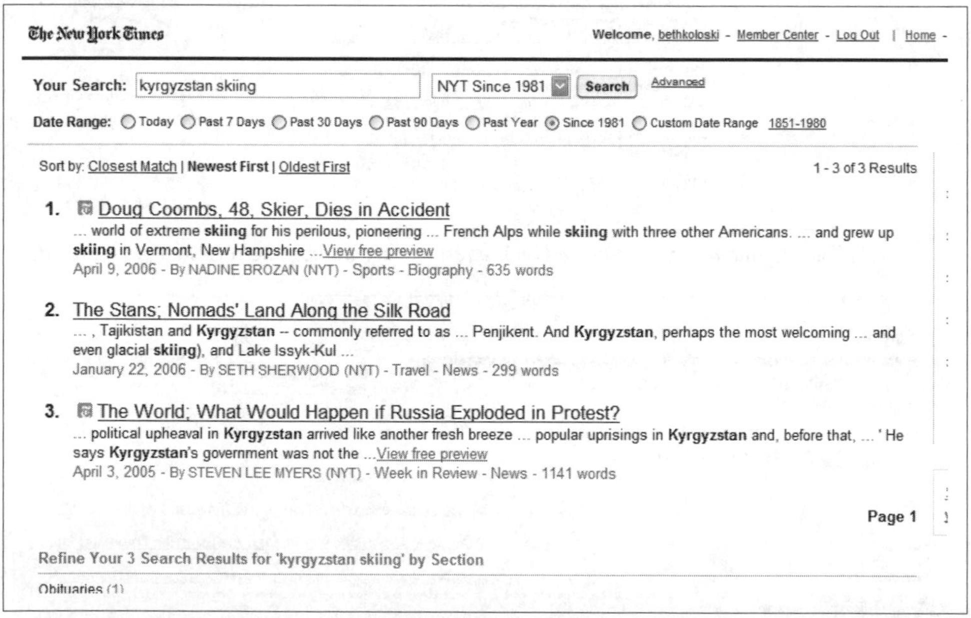

Figure 8-37. All aspects of the search are restated as part of these search results

Integrate searching with browsing

A key theme in this book is the need to integrate searching and browsing (think of them together as "finding"), but we won't belabor it here. Just remember to look for opportunities to connect your search and browse systems to allow users to easily jump back and forth.

In Figures 8-38 and 8-39, Amazon.com provides this functionality in both directions.

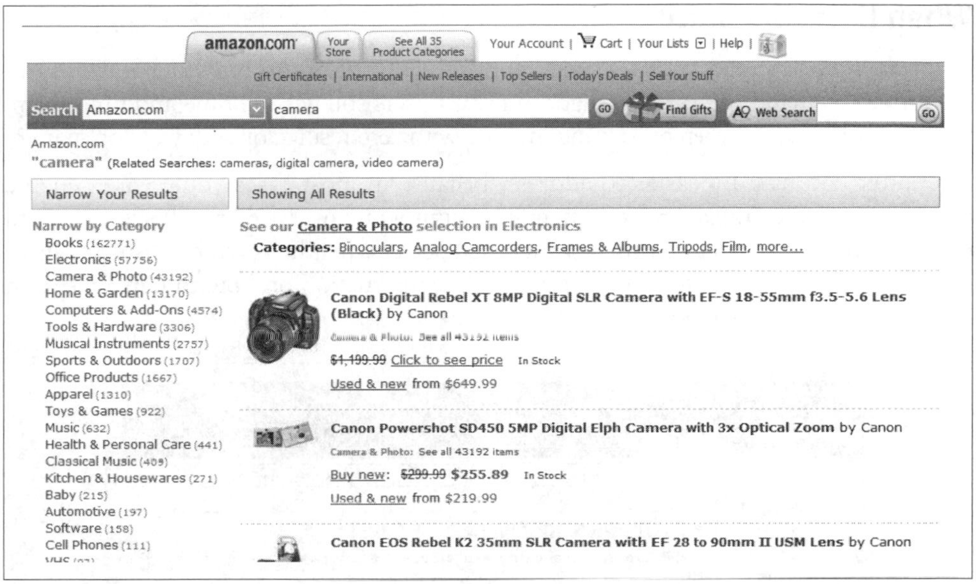

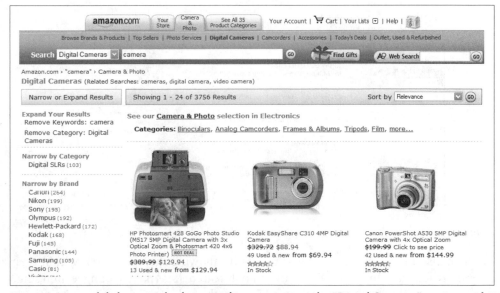

Figure 8-38. Searching leads to browsing: a search for "camera" retrieves categories as well as documents...

Figure 8-39. ...while browsing leads to searching: navigate to the "Digital Cameras" section, and you'll find the search box set to search that zone

When Users Get Stuck

You can strive to support iterative searching with fully integrated browsing and state-of-the-art retrieval and presentation algorithms, yet users still will fail time and time again. What should you do when presenting the user with zero results, or with way too many?

The latter case is a bit easier to address, because in most cases your search engine provides relevance ranked results. In effect, winnowing oversized result sets is a form of search revision, and often the user will self-select when he is ready to stop reviewing results. But it is still useful to provide some instruction on how to narrow search results, as shown in Figure 8-40.

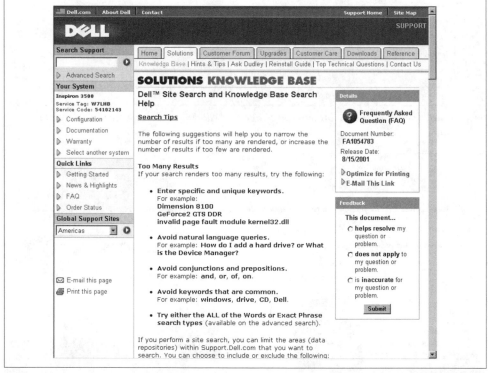

Figure 8-40. Dell's tech-support help page provides advice on how to deal with too many results

You can also help users narrow their results by allowing them to search within their current result set. In Figure 8-41, the initial search for "naked bungee jumping" retrieved over 9,000 documents; we can "search within these results" for "figure skating" to narrow our retrieval.

At the other end of the spectrum, zero hits is a bit more frustrating for users and challenging for information architects. We suggest you adopt a "no dead ends" policy to

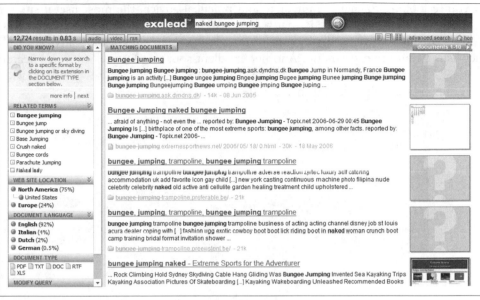

Figure 8-41. Exalead allows users to search within their result set

address this problem. "No dead ends" simply means that users always have another option, even if they've retrieved zero results. The options can consist of:

- A means of revising the search
- Search tips or other advice on how to improve the search
- A means of browsing (e.g., including the site's navigation system or sitemap)
- A human contact if searching and browsing won't work

It's worth noting that we've seen few (if any) search systems that meet all these criteria.

Where to Learn More

Although this is the longest chapter in this book, we've covered only the tip of the search system iceberg. If this piqued your interest, you may want to delve further into the field of information retrieval. Three of our favorite texts are:

- *Modern Information Retrieval* by Ricardo Baeza-Yates and Berthier Ribeiro-Neto (Addison-Wesley).
- *Concepts of Information Retrieval* by Miranda Lee Pao (Libraries Unlimited). This title is out of print, but you may be able to find used copies on Amazon.
- *On Search, the Series* by Tim Bray, an excellent collection of essays on search written by the father of XML (*http://www.tbray.org/ongoing/When/200x/2003/07/30/OnSearchTOC*).

If you're looking for more immediate and practical advice, the most useful site for learning about search tools is, naturally, Searchtools.com (*http://www.searchtools.com*), Avi Rappoport's compendium of installation and configuration advice, product listings, and industry news. Another excellent source is Danny Sullivan's Search Engine Watch (*http://www.searchenginewatch.com*), which focuses on web-wide searching but is quite relevant to site-wide searching nonetheless.

CHAPTER 9

Thesauri, Controlled Vocabularies, and Metadata

What we'll cover:
- Definitions of metadata and controlled vocabularies
- Overview of synonym rings, authority files, classification schemes, and thesauri
- Hierarchical, equivalence, and associative relationships
- Faceted classification and guided navigation

A web site is a collection of interconnected systems with complex dependencies. A single link on a page can simultaneously be part of the site's structure, organization, labeling, navigation, and searching systems. It's useful to study these systems independently, but it's also crucial to consider how they interact. Reductionism will not tell us the whole truth.

Metadata and controlled vocabularies present a fascinating lens through which we can view the network of relationships between systems. In many large metadata-driven web sites, controlled vocabularies have become the glue that holds the systems together. A thesaurus on the back end can enable a more seamless and satisfying user experience on the front end.

In addition, the practice of thesaurus design can help bridge the gap between past and present. The first thesauri were developed for libraries, museums, and government agencies long before the invention of the World Wide Web. As information architects we can draw upon these decades of experience, but we can't copy indiscriminately. The web sites and intranets we design present new challenges and demand creative solutions.

But we're getting ahead of ourselves. Let's begin by defining some basic terms and concepts. Then we can work back toward the big picture.

Metadata

When it comes to definitions, metadata is a slippery fish. Describing it as "data about data" isn't very helpful. The following excerpt from Dictionary.com takes us a little further:

> In data processing, meta-data is definitional data that provides information about or documentation of other data managed within an application or environment. For example, meta-data would document data about data elements or attributes (name, size, data type, etc.) and data about records or data structures (length, fields, columns, etc.) and data about data (where it is located, how it is associated, ownership, etc.). Meta-data may include descriptive information about the context, quality and condition, or characteristics of the data.

While these tautological explanations could lead us into the realms of epistemology and metaphysics, we won't go there. Instead, let's focus on the role that metadata plays in the practical realm of information architecture.

Metadata tags are used to describe documents, pages, images, software, video and audio files, and other content objects for the purposes of improved navigation and retrieval. The HTML keyword meta tag used by many web sites provides a simple example. Authors can freely enter words and phrases that describe the content. These keywords are not displayed in the interface but are available for use by search engines.

```
<meta name="keywords" content="information architecture, content management,
knowledge management, user experience">
```

Many companies today are using metadata in more sophisticated ways. Leveraging content management software and controlled vocabularies, they create dynamic metadata-driven web sites that support distributed authoring and powerful navigation. This metadata-driven model represents a profound change in how web sites are created and managed. Instead of asking, "Where do I place this document in the taxonomy?" we can now ask, "How do I describe this document?" The software and vocabulary systems take care of the rest.

Controlled Vocabularies

Vocabulary control comes in many shapes and sizes. At its most vague, a controlled vocabulary is any defined subset of natural language. At its simplest, a controlled vocabulary is a *list of equivalent terms* in the form of a synonym ring, or a *list of preferred terms* in the form of an authority file. Define hierarchical relationships between terms (e.g., broader, narrower) and you've got a classification scheme. Model associative relationships between concepts (e.g., see also, see related) and you're working on a thesaurus. Figure 9-1 illustrates the relationships between different types of controlled vocabularies.

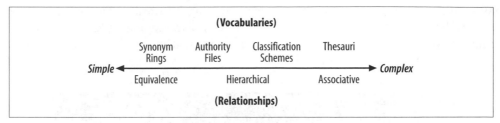

Figure 9-1. Types of controlled vocabularies

Since a full-blown thesaurus integrates all the relationships and capabilities of the simpler forms, let's explore each of these building blocks before taking a close look at the "Swiss Army Knife" of controlled vocabularies.

Synonym Rings

A *synonym ring* (see Figure 9-2) connects a set of words that are defined as equivalent for the purposes of retrieval. In practice, these words are often not true synonyms. For example, imagine you're redesigning a consumer portal that provides ratings information about household products from several companies.

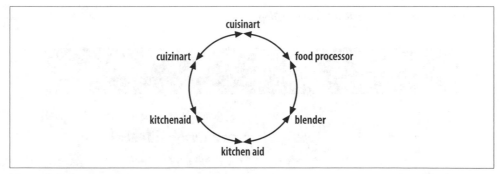

Figure 9-2. A synonym ring

When you examine the search logs and talk with users, you're likely to find that different people looking for the same thing are entering different terms. Someone who's buying a food processor may enter "blender" or one of several product names (or their common misspellings). Take a look at the content, and you're likely to find many of these same variations.

There may be no preferred terms, or at least no good reason to define them. Instead, you can use the out-of-the-box capabilities of a search engine to build synonym rings. This can be as simple as entering sets of equivalent words into a text file. When a user enters a word into the search engine, that word is checked against the text file. If the word is found, then the query is "exploded" to include all of the equivalent words. For example, in Boolean logic:

```
(kitchenaid) becomes (kitchenaid or "kitchen aid" or blender or
"food processor" or cuisinart or cuizinart)
```

What happens when you don't use synonym rings? Consider Figure 9-3, which shows the results of a search for "pocketpc." Pretty discouraging, huh? Looks like we might have to look elsewhere. But look what happens when we put a space between "pocket" and "pc" (Figure 9-4).

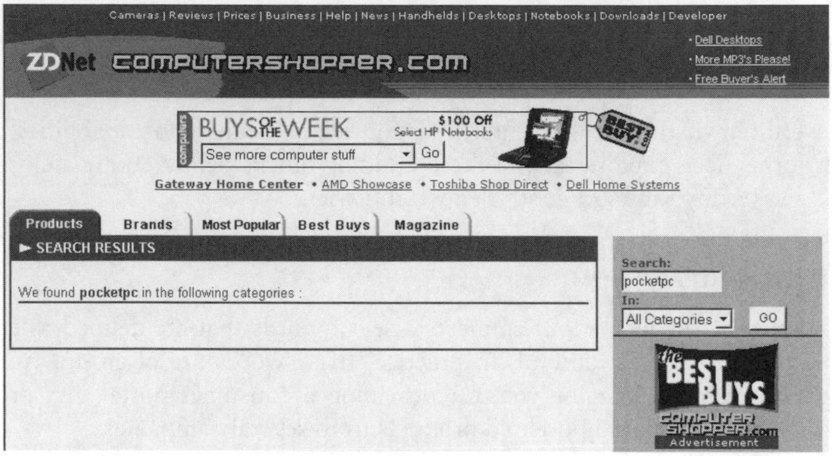

Figure 9-3. Results of a search at Computershopper

Figure 9-4. Another search on the same site

Suddenly, the site has oodles of information about the Pocket PC. A simple synonym ring linking "pocketpc" and "pocket pc" would solve what is a common and serious problem from both user and business perspectives.

However, synonym rings can also introduce new problems. If the query term expansion operates behind the scenes, users can be confused by results that don't actually include their keywords. In addition, the use of synonym rings may result in less relevant results. This brings us back to the subject of precision and recall.

As you may recall from Chapter 8, *precision* refers to the relevance of documents within a given result set. To request high precision, you might say, "Show me *only* the relevant documents." *Recall* refers to the proportion of relevant documents in the result set compared to all the relevant documents in the system. To request high recall, you might say, "Show me *all* the relevant documents." Figure 9-5 shows the mathematics behind precision and recall ratios.

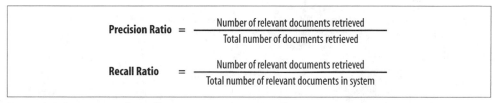

Figure 9-5. Precision and recall ratios

While both high precision and high recall may be ideal, it's generally understood in the information retrieval field that you usually increase one at the expense of the other. This has important implications for the use of controlled vocabularies.

As you might guess, synonym rings can dramatically improve recall. In one study conducted at Bellcore in the 1980s,[*] the use of synonym rings (they called it "unlimited aliasing") within a small test database increased recall from 20 to 80 percent. However, synonym rings can also reduce precision. Good interface design and an understanding of user goals can help strike the right balance. For example, you might use synonym rings by default but order the exact keyword matches at the top of the search results list. Or, you might ignore synonym rings for initial searches but provide the option to "expand your search to include related terms" if there were few or no results.

In summary, synonym rings are a simple, useful form of vocabulary control. There is really no excuse for the conspicuous absence of this basic capability on many of today's largest web sites.

Authority Files

Strictly defined, an *authority file* is a list of preferred terms or acceptable values. It does not include variants or synonyms. Authority files have traditionally been used largely by libraries and government agencies to define the proper names for a set of entities within a limited domain.

---

[*] *The Trouble with Computers: Usefulness, Usability, and Productivity*, by Thomas K. Landauer (MIT Press).

As shown in Figure 9-6, the Utah State Archives & Records Service has published a listing of the authoritative names of public institutions in the state of Utah. This is primarily useful from content authoring and indexing perspectives. Authors and indexers can use this authority file as the source for their terms, ensuring accuracy and consistency.

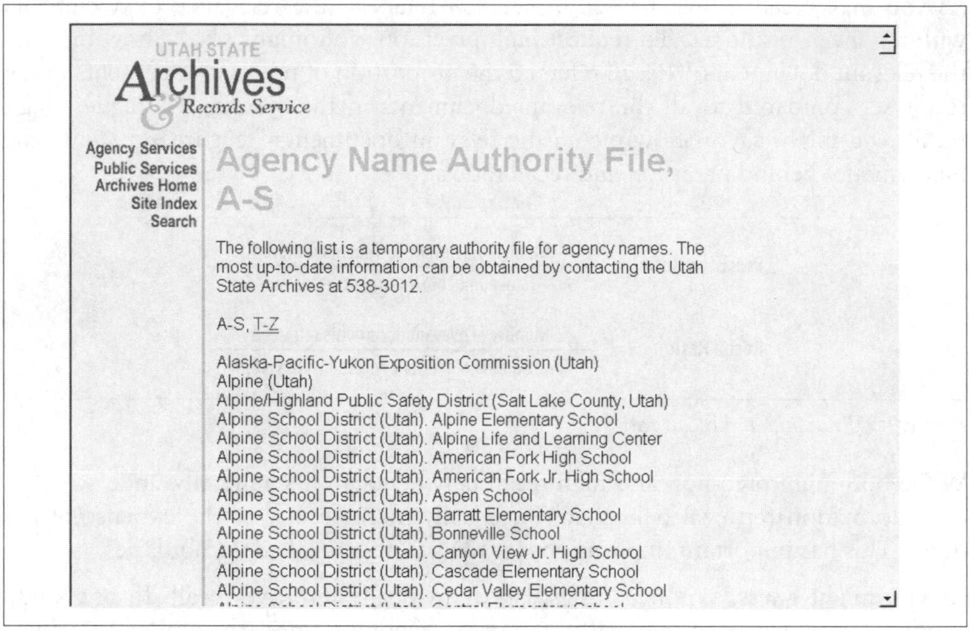

Figure 9-6. An authority file

In practice, authority files are commonly inclusive of both preferred and variant terms. In other words, authority files are synonym rings in which one term has been defined as the preferred term or acceptable value.

The two-letter codes that constitute the standard abbreviations for U.S. states as defined by the U.S. Postal Service provide an instructive example. Using the purist definition, the authority file includes only the acceptable codes:

```
AL, AK, AZ, AR, CA, CO, CT, DE, DC, FL, GA, HI, ID,
IL, IN, IA, KS, KY, LA, ME, MD, MA, MI, MN, MS, MO, MT, NE, NV, NH,
NJ, NM, NY, NC, ND, OH, OK, OR, PA, PR, RI, SC, SD, TN, TX, UT, VT,
VA, WA, WV, WI, WY.
```

However, to make this list useful in most scenarios, it's necessary to include, at a minimum, a mapping to the names of states:

```
AL Alabama
AK Alaska
AZ Arizona
AR Arkansas
CA California
CO Colorado
CT Connecticut
 . . .
```

To make this list even more useful in an online context, it may be helpful to include common variants beyond the official state name:

```
CT Connecticut, Conn, Conneticut, Constitution State
```

At this point, we run into some important questions about the use and value of authority files in the online environment. Since users can perform keyword searches that map many terms onto one concept, do we really need to define preferred terms, or can synonym rings handle things just fine by themselves? Why take that extra step to distinguish CT as the acceptable value?

First, there are a couple of backend reasons. An authority file can be a useful tool for content authors and indexers, enabling them to use the approved terms efficiently and consistently. Also, from a controlled vocabulary management perspective, the preferred term can serve as the unique identifier for each collection of equivalent terms, allowing for more efficient addition, deletion, and modification of variant terms.

There are also a number of ways that the selection of preferred terms can benefit the user. Consider Figure 9-7, where Drugstore.com is providing a mapping between the equivalent term "tilenol" and the authoritative brand name, "Tylenol." By showing users the preferred terms, you can educate them. In some cases, you'll be helping them to correct a misspelling. In others, you may be explaining industry terminology or building brand recognition.

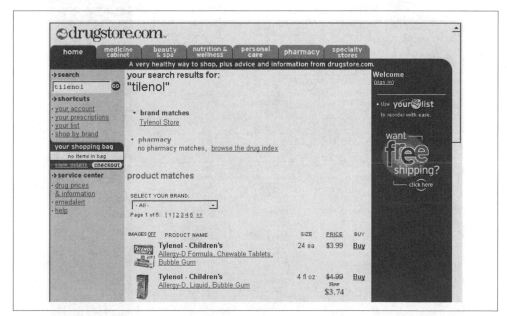

Figure 9-7. Mapping between equivalent terms

These "lessons" may be useful in very different contexts, perhaps during the next telephone conversation or in-store interaction a customer has with your organization. It's an opportunity to nudge everyone toward speaking the same language, without assuming or requiring such conformity within the search system. In effect, the search experience can be similar to an interaction with a sales professional, who understands the language of the customer and translates it back to the customer using the company or industry terminology.

Preferred terms are also important as the user switches from searching to browsing mode. When designing taxonomies, navigation bars, and indexes, it would be messy and overwhelming to present all of the synonyms, abbreviations, acronyms, and common misspellings for every term.

At Drugstore.com, only the brand names are included in the index (see Figure 9-8); equivalent terms like "tilenol" don't show up. This keeps the index relatively short and uncluttered, and in this example, reinforces the brand names. However, a trade-off is involved. In cases where the equivalent terms begin with different letters (e.g., aspirin and Bayer), there is value in creating pointers:

```
Aspirin see Bayer
```

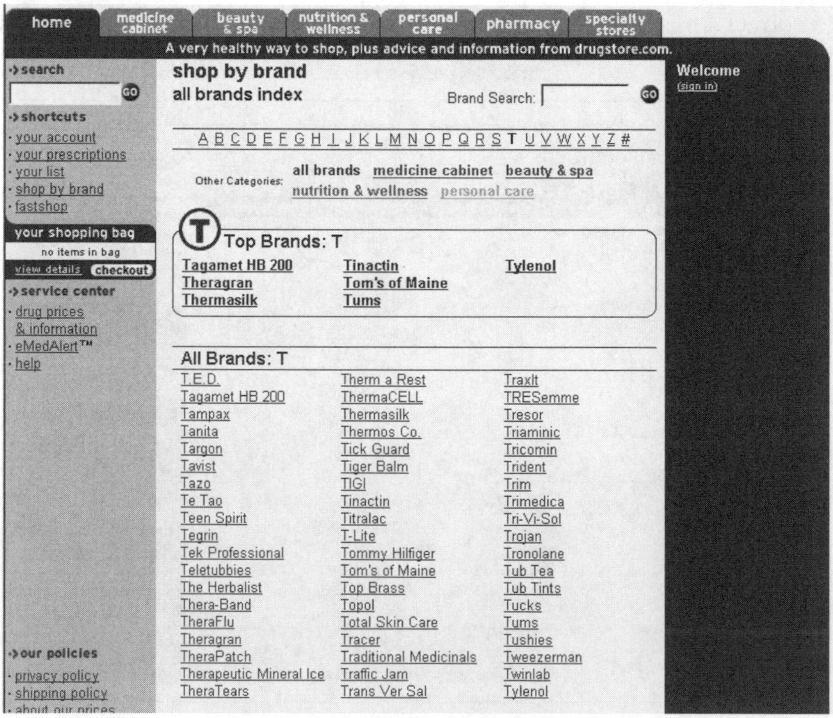

Figure 9-8. Brand index at Drugstore.com

Otherwise, when users look in the index under A for aspirin, they won't find Bayer. The use of pointers is called *term rotation*. Drugstore.com doesn't do it at all. To see a good example of term rotation used in an index to guide users from variant to preferred terms, we'll switch to the financial services industry.

In Figure 9-9, users looking for "before-tax contributions" are guided to the preferred term "pretax contributions." Such integration of the entry vocabulary can dramatically enhance the usefulness of the site index. However, it needs to be done selectively; otherwise, the index can become too long, harming overall usability. Once again, a careful balancing act is involved that requires research and good judgment.

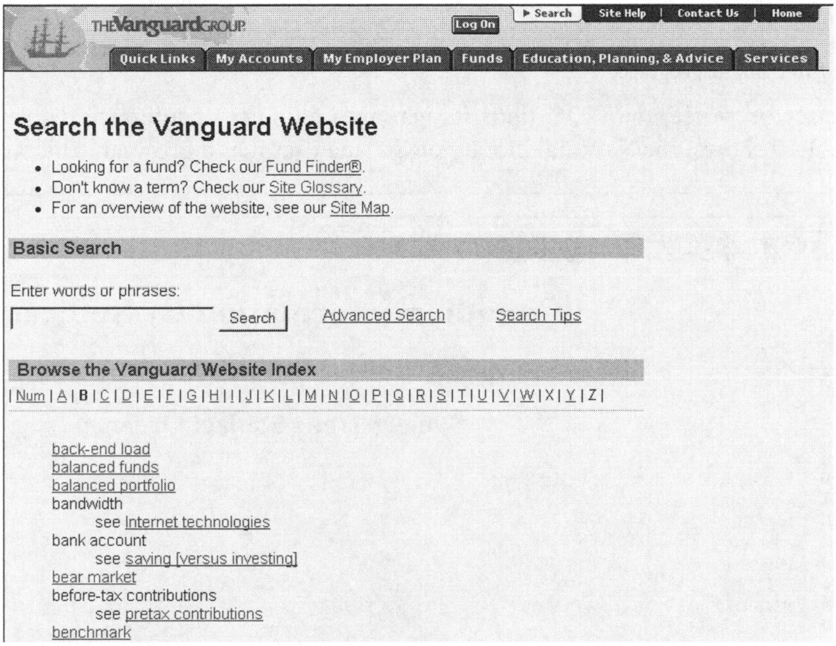

Figure 9-9. A site index with term rotation

Classification Schemes

We use *classification scheme* to mean a hierarchical arrangement of preferred terms. These days, many people prefer to use *taxonomy* instead. Either way, it's important to recognize that these hierarchies can take different shapes and serve multiple purposes, including:

- A frontend, browsable Yahoo-like hierarchy that's a visible, integral part of the user interface

- A backend tool used by information architects, authors, and indexers for organizing and tagging documents

Consider, for example, the Dewey Decimal Classification (DDC). First published in 1876, the DDC is now "the most widely used classification scheme in the world. Libraries in more than 135 countries use the DDC to organize and provide access to their collections."* In its purest form, the DDC is a hierarchical listing that begins with 10 top-level categories and drills down into great detail within each.

```
000 Computers, information, & general reference
100 Philosophy & psychology
200 Religion
300 Social sciences
400 Language
500 Science
600 Technology
700 Arts & recreation
800 Literature
900 History & geography
```

For better or worse, the DDC finds its way into all sorts of interface displays. As Figure 9-10 shows, the National Library of Canada uses it as a browsable hierarchy.

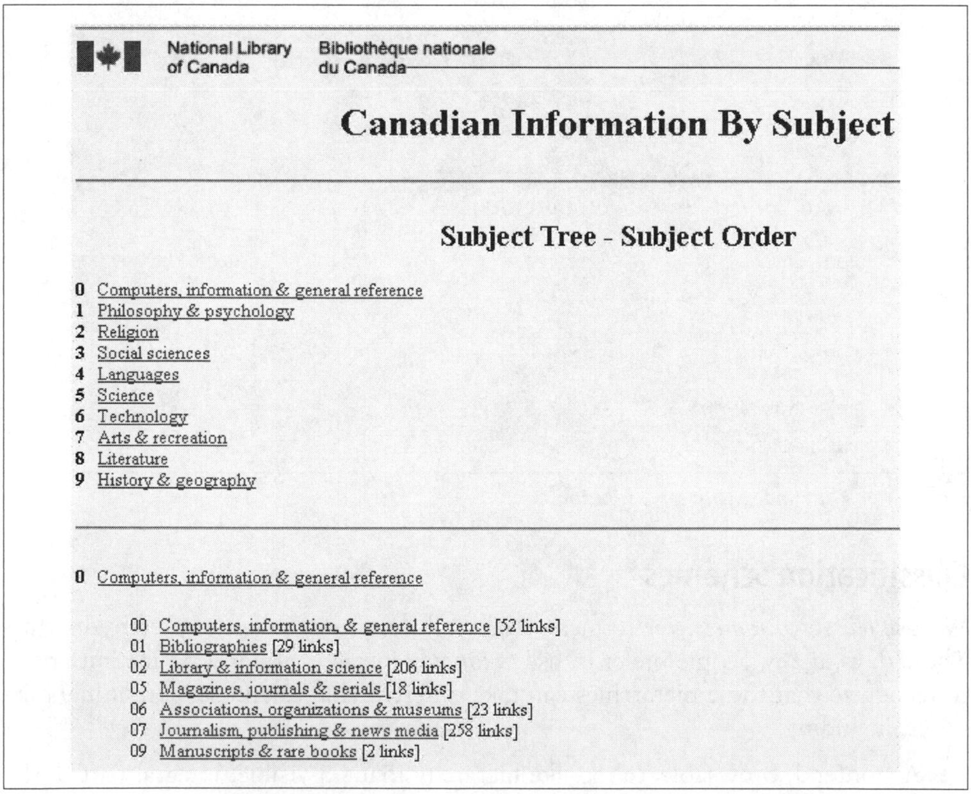

Figure 9-10. The Dewey Decimal Classification in action

---

* From OCLC's Introduction to the Dewey Decimal Classification at *http://www.oclc.org/dewey/about/about_ the_ddc.htm*.

Classification schemes can also be used in the context of searching. Yahoo! does this very effectively. You can see in Figure 9-11 that Yahoo!'s search results present "Category Matches," which reinforces users' familiarity with Yahoo!'s classification scheme.

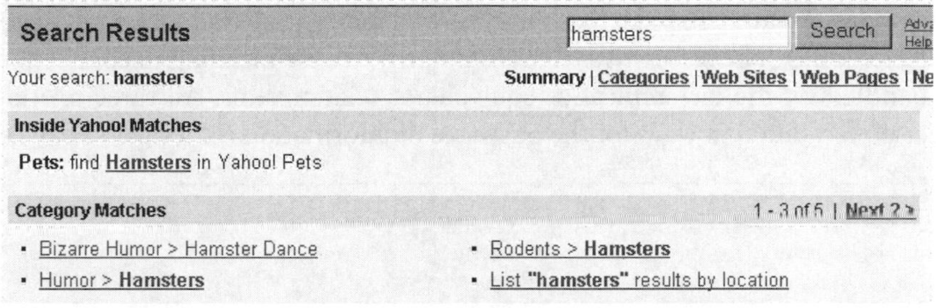

Figure 9-11. Category Matches at Yahoo!

The important point here is that classification schemes are not tied to a single view or instance. They can be used on both the back end and the front end in all sorts of ways. We'll explore types of classification schemes in more detail later in this chapter, but first let's take a look at the "Swiss Army Knife" of vocabulary control, the thesaurus.

Thesauri

Dictionary.com defines *thesaurus* as a "book of synonyms, often including related and contrasting words and antonyms." This usage hearkens back to our high school English classes, when we chose big words from the thesaurus to impress our teachers.

Our species of thesaurus, the one integrated within a web site or intranet to improve navigation and retrieval, shares a common heritage with the familiar reference text but has a different form and function. Like the reference book, our thesaurus is a semantic network of concepts, connecting words to their synonyms, homonyms, antonyms, broader and narrower terms, and related terms.

However, our thesaurus takes the form of an online database, tightly integrated with the user interface of a web site or intranet. And though the traditional thesaurus helps people go from one word to many words, our thesaurus does the opposite. Its most important goal is synonym management—the mapping of many synonyms or word variants onto one preferred term or concept—so the ambiguities of language don't prevent people from finding what they need.

So, for the purposes of this book, a thesaurus is:

> A controlled vocabulary in which equivalence, hierarchical, and associative relationships are identified for purposes of improved retrieval.[*]

---

[*] *Guidelines for the Construction, Format, and Management of Monolingual Thesauri.* ANSI/NISO Z39.19–1993 (R1998).

A thesaurus builds upon the constructs of the simpler controlled vocabularies, modeling these three fundamental types of semantic relationships.

As you can see from Figure 9-12, each preferred term becomes the center of its own semantic network. The *equivalence relationship* is focused on synonym management. The *hierarchical relationship* enables the classification of preferred terms into categories and subcategories. The *associative relationship* provides for meaningful connections that aren't handled by the hierarchical or equivalence relationships. All three relationships can be useful in different ways for the purposes of information retrieval and navigation.

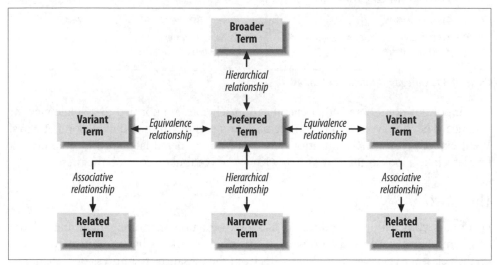

Figure 9-12. Semantic relationships in a thesaurus

Technical Lingo

If you're working with controlled vocabularies and thesauri, it's useful to know the core terminology used by experts in the field to communicate definitions and relationships. This specialized technical language can provide efficiency and specificity when communicating among experts. Just don't expect your users to recognize these terms. In the web environment, you can't require that users take a library science class before they use your information system.

Preferred Term (PT)
> Also known as the accepted term, acceptable value, subject heading, or descriptor. All relationships are defined with respect to the Preferred Term.

Variant Term (VT)
> Also known as entry terms or non-preferred terms, Variant Terms have been defined as equivalent to or loosely synonymous with the Preferred Term.

Broader Term (BT)

The Broader Term is the parent of the Preferred Term. It's one level higher in the hierarchy.

Narrower Term (NT)

A Narrower Term is a child of the Preferred Term. It's one level lower in the hierarchy.

Related Term (RT)

The Related Term is connected to the Preferred Term through the associative relationship. The relationship is often articulated through use of *See Also*. For example, Tylenol *See Also* Headache.

Use (U)

Traditional thesauri often employ the following syntax as a tool for indexers and users: Variant Term *Use* Preferred Term. For example, Tilenol *Use* Tylenol. Many people are more familiar with *See*, as in Tilenol *See* Tylenol.

Used For (UF)

This indicates the reciprocal relationship of Preferred Term *UF* Variant Term(s). It's used to show the full list of variants on the Preferred Term's record. For example, Tylenol *UF* Tilenol.

Scope Note (SN)

The Scope Note is essentially a specific type of definition of the Preferred Term, used to deliberately restrict the meaning of that term in order to rule out ambiguity as much as possible.

As we've seen, the preferred term is the center of its own semantic universe. Of course, a preferred term in one display is likely to be a broader, narrower, related, or even variant term in another display (see Figure 9-13).

Depending upon your experience with the classification of wines, you may already be questioning the selection of preferred terms and semantic relationships in this example. Should sparkling wine really be the preferred term? If so, why? Because it's a more popular term? Because it's the technically correct term? And aren't there better related terms than weddings and mimosas? Why were those chosen? The truth is that there aren't any "right" answers to these questions, and there's no "right" way to design a thesaurus. There will always be a strong element of professional judgment informed by research. We'll come back to these questions and provide some guidelines for constructing "good" answers, but first let's check out a real thesaurus on the Web.

A Thesaurus in Action

It's not so easy to find good examples of public web sites that leverage thesauri. Until recently, not many teams have had the knowledge or support to make this significant investment. We expect this to change in the coming years as thesauri become a key tool for dealing with the growing size and importance of web sites and intranets.

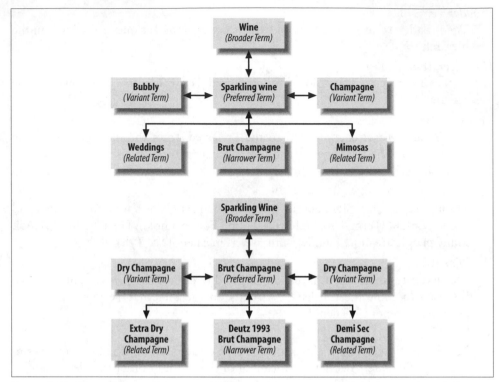

Figure 9-13. Semantic relationships in a wine thesaurus

Another barrier to finding good examples is that it's often not obvious when a site is using a thesaurus. When it's well integrated, a thesaurus can be invisible to the untrained eye. You have to know what you're looking for to notice one. Think back to the Tilenol/Tylenol example. How many users even realize when the site adjusts for their misspelling?

One good example that will serve throughout this chapter is PubMed, a service of the National Library of Medicine. PubMed provides access to over 16 million citations from MEDLINE and additional life science journals. MEDLINE has been the premier electronic information service for doctors, researchers, and other medical professionals for many years. It leverages a huge thesaurus that includes more than 19,000 preferred terms or "main subject headings" and provides powerful searching capabilities.

PubMed provides a simpler public interface with free access to citations, but without access to the full text of the journal articles. Let's first take a look at the interface, and then dive beneath the surface to see what's going on.

Let's say we're studying African sleeping sickness. We enter that phrase into the PubMed search engine and are rewarded with the first 20 results out of 2,778 total items found (Figure 9-14). So far, there's nothing apparently different about this search experience. For all we know, we might have just searched the full text of all 16 million journal articles. To understand what's going on, we need to look deeper.

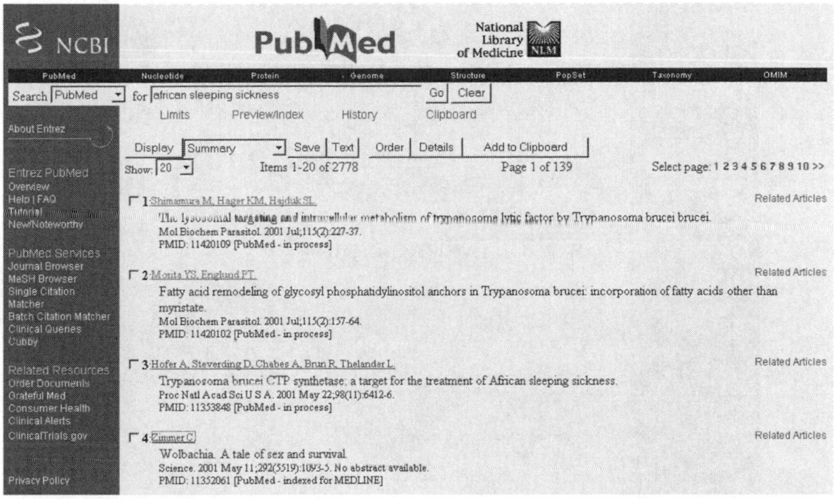

Figure 9-14. Search results on PubMed

In fact, we didn't search the full-text articles at all. Instead, we searched the meta-data records for these articles, which include a combination of abstracts and subject headings (Figure 9-15).

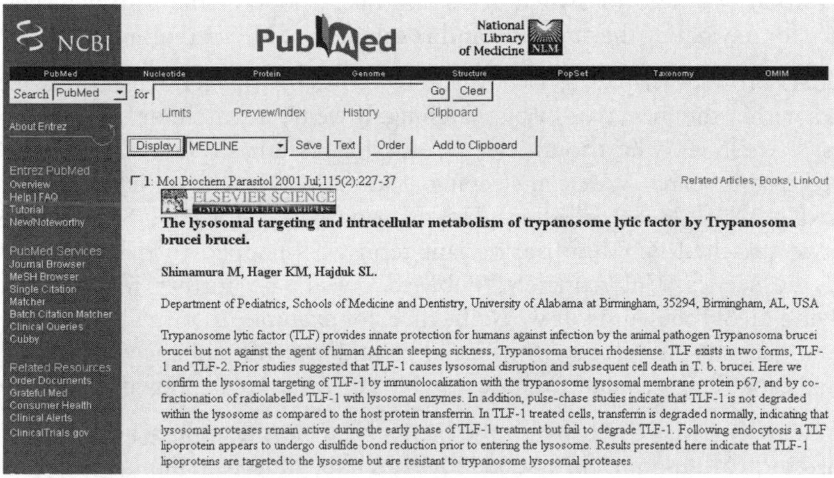

Figure 9-15. Sample record with abstract in PubMed

When we select another item from our search results, we find a record with subject headings ("MeSH Terms") but no abstract (Figure 9-16).

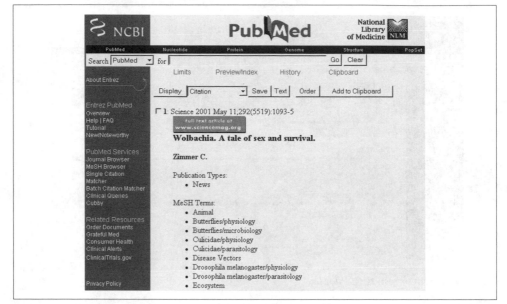

Figure 9-16. Sample record with index terms in PubMed

When we scroll down to look through the full list of terms, we see no entry for African sleeping sickness. What's going on? Why was this article retrieved? To answer that question, we need to switch gears and take a look at the MeSH Browser, an interface for navigating the structure and vocabulary of MeSH (Figure 9-17).

The MeSH Browser enables us to navigate by browsing the hierarchical classification schemes within the thesaurus or by searching. If we try a search on "African sleeping sickness," we'll see why the article "Wolbachia. A tale of sex and survival" was retrieved in our search. "African sleeping sickness" is actually an entry term for the preferred term or MeSH heading, "Trypanosomiasis, African." (See Figure 9-18.) When we searched PubMed, our variant term was mapped to the preferred term behind the scenes. Unfortunately, PubMed doesn't go further in leveraging the underlying MeSH thesaurus. It would be nice, for example, to turn all of those MeSH terms in our sample record into live links and provide enhanced searching and browsing capabilities, similar to those provided by Amazon, as shown in Figure 9-19.

In this example, Amazon leverages the hierarchical classification scheme and subject headings to provide powerful options for searching and browsing, allowing users to iteratively refine their queries. This surely could be a useful enhancement to PubMed.

One of the advantages to using a thesaurus is that you have tremendous power and flexibility to shape and refine the user interface over time. You can't take advantage

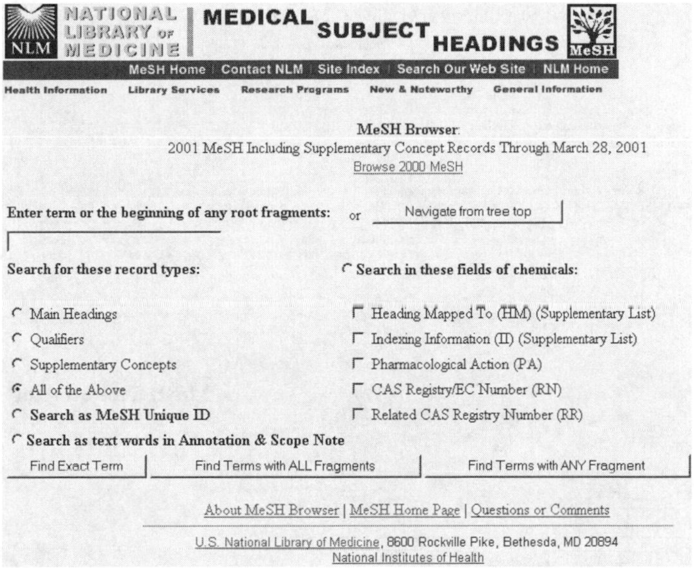

Figure 9-17. The MeSH Browser

of all the capabilities at once, but you can user-test different features, learning and adjusting as you go. PubMed may not have leveraged the full power of the MED-LINE thesaurus so far, but it's nice to have that rich network of semantic relationships to draw upon as design and development continues.

Types of Thesauri

Should you decide to build a thesaurus for your web site, you'll need to choose from among three types: a classic thesaurus, an indexing thesaurus, and a searching thesaurus (Figure 9-20). This decision should be based on how you intend to use the thesaurus, and it will have major implications for design.

Classic Thesaurus

A classic thesaurus is used at the point of indexing and at the point of searching. Indexers use the thesaurus to map variant terms to preferred terms when performing document-level indexing. Searchers use the thesaurus for retrieval, whether or not they're aware of the role it plays in their search experience. Query terms are matched against the rich vocabulary of the thesaurus, enabling synonym management, hierarchical browsing, and associative linking. This is the full-bodied, fully integrated thesaurus we've referred to for much of this chapter.

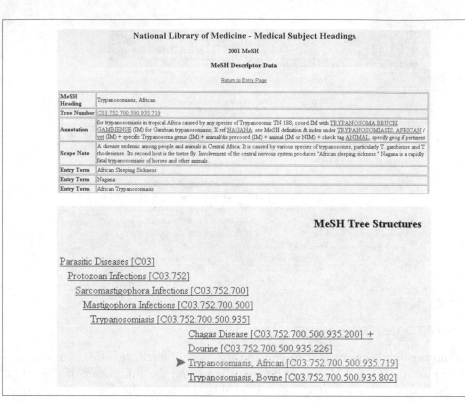

Figure 9-18. MeSH record for trypanosomiasis (top and bottom of page)

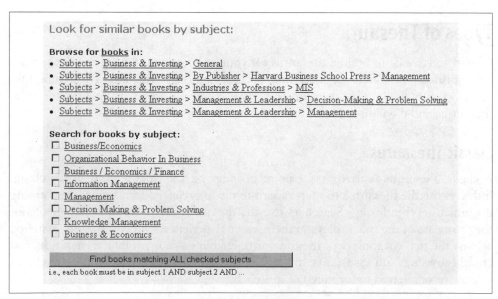

Figure 9-19. Amazon's use of structure and subject headings for enhanced navigation

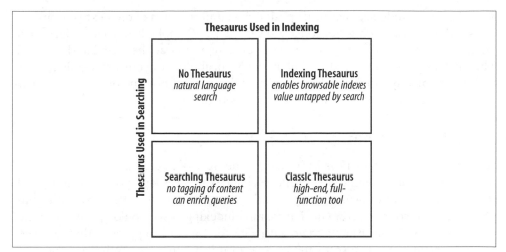

Figure 9-20. Types of thesauri

Indexing Thesaurus

However, building a classic thesaurus is not always necessary or possible. Consider a scenario in which you have the ability to develop a controlled vocabulary and index documents, but you're not able to build the synonym-management capability into the search experience. Perhaps another department owns the search engine and won't work with you, or perhaps the engine won't support this functionality without major customization.

Whatever the case, you're able to perform controlled vocabulary indexing, but you're not able to leverage that work at the point of searching and map users' variant terms to preferred terms. This is a serious weakness, but there are a few reasons why an indexing thesaurus may be better than nothing:

- It structures the indexing process, promoting consistency and efficiency. The indexers can work as an integrated unit, given a shared understanding of preferred terms and indexing guidelines.

- It allows you to build browsable indexes of preferred terms, enabling users to find all documents about a particular subject or product through a single point of access.

Such consistency of indexing can provide real value for information systems with captive audiences. When dealing with an intranet application that's used by the same people on a regular basis, you can expect these users to learn the preferred terms over time. In such an environment, indexing consistency begins to rival indexing quality in value.

And finally, an indexing thesaurus positions you nicely to take the next step up to a classic thesaurus. With a vocabulary developed and applied to your collection of documents, you can focus your energies on integration at the user interface level. This may begin with the addition of an entry vocabulary to your browsable indexes and will hopefully bring searching into the fold, so the full value of the thesaurus is used to power the searching and browsing experience.

Searching Thesaurus

Sometimes a classic thesaurus isn't practical because of issues on the content side of the equation that prevent document-level indexing. Perhaps you're dealing with third-party content or dynamic news that's changing every day. Perhaps you're simply faced with so much content that manual indexing costs would be astronomical. (In this case, you may be able to go with a classic thesaurus approach that leverages automated-categorization software, as described in Chapter 16.) Whatever the case, there are many web and intranet environments in which controlled vocabulary indexing of the full document collection just isn't going to happen. This doesn't mean that a thesaurus isn't still a viable option to improve the user experience.

A searching thesaurus leverages a controlled vocabulary at the point of searching but not at the point of indexing. For example, when a user enters a term into the search engine, a searching thesaurus can map that term onto the controlled vocabulary before executing the query against the full-text index. The thesaurus may simply perform equivalence term explosion, as we've seen in the case of synonym rings, or it may go beyond the equivalence relationship, exploding down the hierarchy to include all narrower terms (traditionally known as "posting down"). These methods will obviously enhance recall at the expense of precision.

You also have the option of giving more power and control to the users—asking them whether they'd like to use any combination of preferred, variant, broader, narrower, or associative terms in their query. When integrated carefully into the search interface and search result screens, this can effectively arm users with the ability to narrow, broaden, and adjust their searches as needed.

A searching thesaurus can also provide greater browsing flexibility. You can allow your users to browse part or all of your thesaurus, navigating the equivalence, hierarchical, and associative relationships. Terms (or the combination of preferred and variant terms) can be used as predefined or "canned" queries to be run against the full-text index. In other words, your thesaurus can become a true portal, providing a new way to navigate and gain access to a potentially enormous volume of content. A major advantage of the searching thesaurus is that its development and maintenance costs are essentially independent of the volume of content. On the other hand, it does put much greater demands on the quality of equivalence and mapping.

If you'd like to learn more about searching thesauri, try these articles:

- Anderson, James D. and Frederick A. Rowley. "Building End User Thesauri From Full Text." In *Advances in Classification Research*, Volume 2; Proceedings of the Second ASIS SIG/CR Classification Research Workshop, October 27, 1991, eds. Barbara H. Kwasnik and Raya Fidel, 1–13. Medford, NJ: Learned Information, 1992.

- Bates, Marcia J. "Design For a Subject Search Interface and Online Thesaurus For a Very Large Records Management Database." In *American Society for Information Science*. Annual Meeting. Proceedings, v. 27, 20–28. Medford, NJ: Learned Information, 1990.

Thesaurus Standards

As we explained earlier, people have been developing thesauri for many years. In their 1993 article "The evolution of guidelines for thesaurus construction," David A. Krooks and F.W. Lancaster suggested that "the majority of basic problems of thesaurus construction had already been identified and solved by 1967."

This rich history lets us draw from a number of national and international standards, covering the construction of monolingual (single-language) thesauri. For example:

- ISO 2788 (1974, 1985, 1986, International)
- BS 5723 (1987, British)
- AFNOR NFZ 47-100 (1981, French)
- DIN 1463 (1987–1993, German)
- ANSI/NISO Z39.19 (1994, 1998, 2005, United States)

In this book, we draw primarily from the original U.S. standard, ANSI/NISO Z39.19 (1998), which is very similar to the International standard, ISO 2788. The ANSI/NISO standard is entitled "Guidelines for the Construction, Format and Management of Monolingual Thesauri." The term "guidelines" in the title is very telling. Consider what software vendor Oracle has to say about its interpretation of this standard:

> The phrase . . . *thesaurus standard* is somewhat misleading. The computing industry considers a "standard" to be a specification of behavior or interface. These standards do not specify anything. If you are looking for a thesaurus function interface, or a standard thesaurus file format, you won't find it here. Instead, these are guidelines for thesaurus compilers—compiler being an actual human, not a program.
>
> What Oracle has done is taken the ideas in these guidelines and in ANSI Z39.19 . . . and used them as the basis for a specification of our own creation . . . So, Oracle supports ISO-2788 relationships or ISO-2788 compliant thesauri.

As you'll see when we explore a few examples, the ANSI/NISO standard provides simple guidelines that are very difficult to apply. The standard provides a valuable conceptual framework and in some cases offers specific rules you can follow, but it absolutely does not remove the need for critical thinking, creativity, and risk-taking in the process of thesaurus construction.

We strongly disagree with the suggestion by Krooks and Lancaster that the basic problems in this area have been solved, and we often disagree with guidelines in the ANSI/NISO standard. What's going on here? Are we just being difficult? No, what's really behind these tensions is the disruptive force of the Internet. We're in the midst of a transition from the thesaurus in its traditional form to a new paradigm embedded within the networked world.

Traditional thesauri emerged within the academic and library communities. They were used in print form and were designed primarily for expert users. When we took library science courses back in the 80s and 90s, a major component of online information retrieval involved learning to navigate the immense volumes of printed thesauri in the library to identify subject descriptors for online searching of the Dialog information service. People had to be trained to use these tools, and the underlying assumption was that specialists would use them on a regular basis, becoming efficient and effective over time. The whole system was built around the relatively high cost of processor time and network bandwidth.

Then the world changed. We're now dealing with totally online systems. We can't ask our customers to run to the library before using our web site. We're typically serving novice users with no formal training in online searching techniques. They're likely to be infrequent visitors, so they're not going to build up much familiarity with our site over time. And we're operating in the broader business environment, where the goals may be very different from those of academia and libraries.

Within this new paradigm, we're being challenged to figure out which of the old guidelines do and do not apply. It would be an awful waste to throw out valuable resources like the ANSI/NISO standard that are built upon decades of research and experience. There's a great deal that's still relevant. However, it would also be a mistake to follow the guidelines blindly, akin to using a 1950s map to navigate today's highways.

Advantages to staying close to the standard include:

- There's good thinking and intelligence baked into these guidelines.
- Most thesaurus management software is designed to be compliant with ANSI/NISO, so sticking with the standard can be useful from a technology-integration perspective.
- Compliance with the standard will provide a better chance of cross-database compatibility, so when your company merges with its competitor, you might have an easier time merging the two sets of vocabularies.

Our advice is to read the guidelines, follow them when they make sense, but be prepared to deviate from the standard when necessary. After all, it's these opportunities to break the rules that make our lives as information architects fun and exciting!

Semantic Relationships

What sets a thesaurus apart from the simpler controlled vocabularies is its rich array of semantic relationships. Let's explore each relationship more closely.

Equivalence

The *equivalence relationship* (Figure 9-21) is employed to connect preferred terms and their variants. While we may loosely refer to this as "synonym management," it's important to recognize that equivalence is a broader term than synonymy.

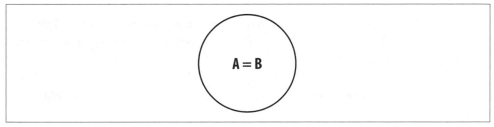

Figure 9-21. The equivalence relationship

Our goal is to group terms defined as "equivalent for the purposes of retrieval." This may include synonyms, near-synonyms, acronyms, abbreviations, lexical variants, and common misspellings; for example:

Preferred term
Palm m505

Variant terms (equivalents)
Palm, Palm Pilot, Palm 505, Palm505, Palm V, Handheld, Pocket PC, Handspring Visor

In the case of a product database, it may also include the names of retired products and of competitors' products. Depending on the desired specificity of your controlled vocabulary, you may also fold more general and more specific terms into the equivalence relationship to avoid extra levels of hierarchy. The goal is to create a rich entry vocabulary that serves as a funnel, connecting users with the products, services, and content that they're looking for and that you want them to find.

Hierarchical

The hierarchical relationship (Figure 9-22) divides up the information space into categories and subcategories, relating broader and narrower concepts through the familiar parent-child relationship.

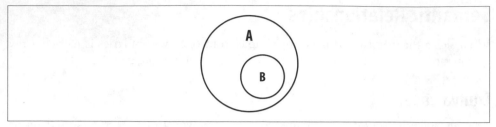

Figure 9-22. The hierarchical relationship

There are three subtypes of hierarchical relationship:

Generic
>   This is the traditional class-species relationship we draw from biological taxono-mies. Species B is a member of Class A and inherits the characteristics of its parent. For example, Bird *NT* Magpie.

Whole-part
>   In this hierarchical relationship, B is a part of A. For example, Foot *NT* Big Toe.

Instance
>   In this case, B is an instance or example of A. This relationship often includes proper names. For example, Seas *NT* Mediterranean Sea.

At first blush, the hierarchical relationship sounds pretty straightforward. However, anyone who's ever developed a hierarchy knows that it isn't as easy as it sounds. There are many different ways to hierarchically organize any given information space (e.g., by subject, by product category, or by geography). As we'll explain shortly, a *faceted* thesaurus supports the common need for multiple hierarchies. You also need to deal with the tricky issues of granularity, defining how many layers of hierarchy to develop.

Once again, we need to ground our work in the ultimate goal of enhancing the ability of our users to find what they need. The card-sorting methodologies (discussed in Chapter 10) can help you begin to shape your hierarchies based on user needs and behaviors.

Associative

The associative relationship (Figure 9-23) is often the trickiest, and by necessity is usually developed after you've made a good start on the other two relationship types. In thesaurus construction, associative relationships are often defined as strongly implied semantic connections that aren't captured within the equivalence or hierarchical relationships.

There is the notion that associative relationships should be "strongly implied." For example, hammer *RT* nail. In practice, however, defining these relationships is a highly subjective process.

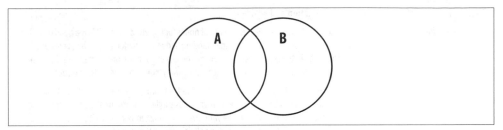

Figure 9-23. The associative relationship

The ANSI/NISO thesaurus discusses many associative relationship subtypes. For example:

Relationship subtype	Example
Field of Study and Object of Study	Cardiology RT Heart
Process and its Agent	Termite Control RT Pesticides
Concepts and their Properties	Poisons RT Toxicity
Action and Product of Action	Eating RT Indigestion
Concepts Linked by Causal Dependence	Celebration RT New Year's Eve

In the world of e-commerce, the associative relationship provides an excellent vehicle for connecting customers to related products and services. Associative relationships allow what marketing folks call "cross-selling," allowing an e-commerce site, for example, to say "Hey, nice pants! They'd go great with this shirt." When done well, these associative relationships can both enhance the user experience and further the goals of the business.

Preferred Terms

Terminology is critical. The following sections examine some aspects of terminology in detail.

Term Form

Defining the form of preferred terms is something that seems easy until you try it. All of a sudden, you find yourself plunged into heated arguments over grammatical minutiae. Should we use a noun or a verb? What's the "correct" spelling? Do we use the singular or plural form? Can an abbreviation be a preferred term? These debates can suck up large amounts of time and energy.

Fortunately, the ANSI/NISO thesaurus standard goes into great detail in this area. We recommend following these guidelines, while allowing for exceptions when there's a clear benefit. Some of the issues covered by the standard include:

Topic	Our interpretation and advice
Grammatical form	The standard strongly encourages the use of nouns for preferred terms. This is a good default guideline, since users are better at understanding and remembering nouns than verbs or adjectives. However, in the real world, you'll encounter lots of good reasons to use verbs (i.e., task-oriented words) and adjectives (e.g., price, size, variety, color) in your controlled vocabularies.
Spelling	The standard notes that you can select a "defined authority," such as a specific dictionary or glossary, or you can choose to use your own "house style." You might also consider the most common spelling forms employed by your users. The most important thing here is that you make a decision and stick to it. Consistency will improve the lives of your indexers and users.
Singular and plural form	The standard recommends using the plural form of "count nouns" (e.g., cars, roads, maps). Conceptual nouns (e.g., math, biology) should remain in singular form. Search technology has rendered this less important than in the past. Once again, consistency is the goal in this case.
Abbreviations and acronyms	The guidelines suggest to default to popular use. For the most part, your preferred terms will be the full words. But in cases such as RADAR, IRS, 401K, MI, TV, and PDA, it may be better to use the acronym or abbreviation. You can always rely on your variant terms to guide users from one form to the other (e.g., Internal Revenue Service See IRS).

Term Selection

Of course, selection of a preferred term involves more than the form of the term; you've got to pick the right term in the first place. The ANSI/NISO standard won't help too much here. Consider the following excerpts:

> Section 3.0. "Literary warrant (occurrence of terms in documents) is the guiding principle for selection of the preferred (term)."

> Section 5.2.2. "Preferred terms should be selected to serve the needs of the majority of users."

This tension between literary warrant and user warrant can be resolved only by reviewing your goals and considering how the thesaurus will be integrated with the web site. Do you want to use preferred terms to educate your users about the industry vocabulary? Will you be relying on preferred terms as your entry vocabulary (e.g., no variants in the index)? You'll need to answer these questions before deciding on the primary source of authority for term selection.

Term Definition

Within the thesaurus itself, we're striving for extreme specificity in our use of language. Remember, we're trying to *control* vocabulary. Beyond the selection of distinctive preferred terms, there are some tools for managing ambiguity.

Parenthetical term qualifiers provide a way to manage homographs. Depending on the context of your thesaurus, you may need to qualify the term "Cells" in some of the following ways:

Cells (biology)
Cells (electric)
Cells (prison)

Scope notes provide another way to increase specificity. While they can sometimes look very much like definitions, scope notes are a different beast. They are intended to deliberately restrict meaning to one concept, whereas definitions often suggest multiple meanings. Scope notes are very useful in helping indexers to select the right preferred term. They can sometimes be leveraged in searching or results display to assist users as well.

Term Specificity

The specificity of terms is another difficult issue that all thesaurus designers must face. For example, should "knowledge management software" be represented as one term, two terms, or three terms? Here's what the standards have to say:

ANSI/NISO Z39.19. "Each descriptor . . . should represent a single concept."

ISO 2788. "It is a general rule that . . . compound terms should be factored (split) into simple elements."

Once again, the standards don't make your life easy. ANSI/NISO leaves you arguing over what constitutes a "single concept." ISO leads you toward uniterms (e.g., knowledge, management, software), which would probably be the wrong way to go in this example.

You need to strike a balance based on your context. Of particular importance is the size of the site. As the volume of content grows, it becomes increasingly necessary to use compound terms to increase precision. Otherwise, users get hundreds or thousands of hits for every search (and every preferred term).

The scope of content is also important. For example, if we're working on a web site for *Knowledge Management* magazine, the single term "knowledge management software" or perhaps "software (knowledge management)" may be the way to go. However, if we're working on a broad IT site like CNET, it may be better to use "knowledge management" and "software" as independent preferred terms.

Polyhierarchy

In a strict hierarchy, each term appears in one and only one place. This was the original plan for the biological taxonomy. Each species was supposed to fit neatly into one branch of the tree of life.

```
kingdom:
  phylum:
    sub-phylum:
      class:
        order:
          family:
            species
```

However, things didn't go according to plan. In fact, biologists have been arguing for decades over the correct placement of various species. Some organisms have the audacity to exhibit characteristics of multiple categories.

If you're a purist, you can attempt to defend the ideal of strict hierarchy within your web site. Or, if you're pragmatic, you can allow for some level of polyhierarchy, permitting some terms to be cross-listed in multiple categories. This is shown in Figure 9-24.

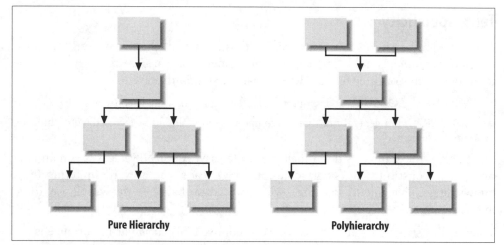

Figure 9-24. Hierarchy and polyhierarchy

When you're dealing with large information systems, polyhierarchy is unavoidable. As the number of documents grows, you need a greater level of precoordination (using compound terms) to increase precision, which forces polyhierarchy. For example, Medline cross-lists viral pneumonia under both virus diseases and respiratory tract diseases (Figure 9-25).

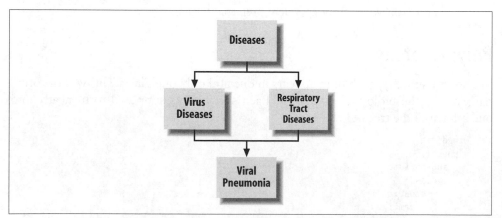

Figure 9-25. Polyhierarchy in Medline

Yahoo! is another large site that makes prolific use of polyhierarchy (Figure 9-26). The @ signs are used to note categories that are cross-listed under other branches within the hierarchy. In the classification and placement of physical objects, polyhierarchy causes a problem. Physical objects can typically be in only one place at one time. The Library of Congress classification scheme was developed so that each book in a library could be placed (and found) in one and only one location on the shelves. In digital information systems, the only real challenge introduced by polyhierarchy is representing the navigational context. Most systems allow for the notion of primary and secondary locations within the hierarchy. Yahoo!'s @ signs lead users from the secondary to the primary locations.

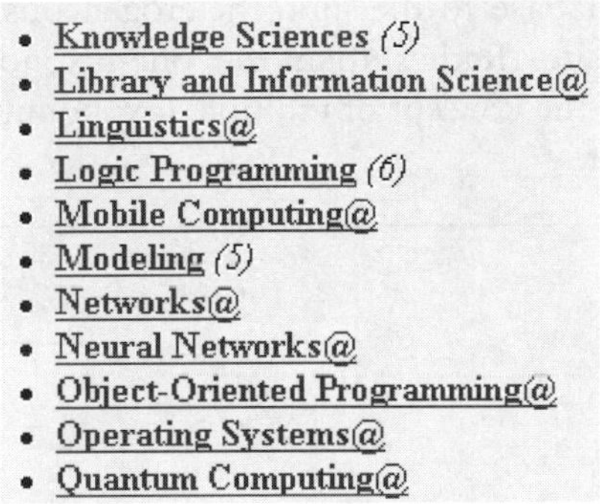

- Knowledge Sciences *(5)*
- Library and Information Science@
- Linguistics@
- Logic Programming *(6)*
- Mobile Computing@
- Modeling *(5)*
- Networks@
- Neural Networks@
- Object-Oriented Programming@
- Operating Systems@
- Quantum Computing@

Figure 9-26. Polyhierarchy within Yahoo!

Faceted Classification

In the 1930s, an Indian librarian by the name of S. R. Ranganathan created a new type of classification system. Recognizing the problems and limitations of these top-down single-taxonomy solutions, Ranganathan built his system upon the notion that documents and objects have multiple dimensions, or *facets*.

The old model asks the question, "Where do I put this?" It's more closely tied to our experience in the physical world, with the idea of one place for each item. In contrast, the faceted approach asks the question, "How can I describe this?"

Like many librarians, Ranganathan was an idealist. He argued that you must build multiple "pure" taxonomies, using one principle of division at a time. He suggested five universal facets to be used for organizing everything:

- Personality
- Matter
- Energy
- Space
- Time

In our experience, the faceted approach has great value, but we don't tend to use Ranganathan's universal facets. Instead, common facets in the business world include:

- Topic
- Product
- Document type
- Audience
- Geography
- Price

Still confused about facets? See Figure 9-27. All we're really doing is applying the structure of a fielded database to the more heterogeneous mix of documents and applications in a web site. Rather than the one-taxonomy-fits-all approach of Yahoo!, we're embracing the concept of multiple taxonomies that focus on different dimensions of the content.

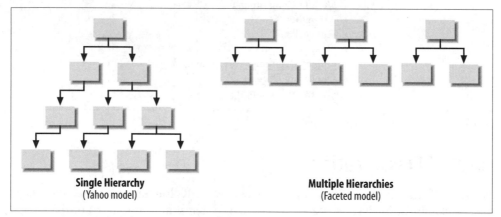

Figure 9-27. Single hierarchy versus multiple (faceted) hierarchies

Wine.com provides a simple example of faceted classification. Wine has several facets that we commonly mix and match in our selection process at restaurants and grocery stores:

Facet	Sample controlled vocabulary values
Type	Red (Merlot, Pinot Noir), White (Chablis, Chardonnay), Sparkling, Pink, Dessert
Region (origin)	Australian, Californian, French, Italian
Winery (manufacturer)	Blackstone, Clos du Bois, Cakebread
Year	1969, 1990, 1999, 2000
Price	$3.99, $20.99, < $199, Cheap, Moderate, Expensive

Note that some facets are flat lists (e.g., price) whereas some must be represented hierarchically (e.g., type). When we look for a moderately priced Californian Merlot, we're unconsciously defining and combining facets. Wine.com leverages a faceted classification to enable this experience online. The main shopping page in Figure 9-28 presents three ways to browse, providing multiple paths to the same information.

Figure 9-28. Faceted classification at Wine.com

The Power Search, shown in Figure 9-29, provides the ability to combine facets into the rich type of query we usually express in natural language.

Figure 9-29. Power Search at Wine.com

The results page (Figure 9-30) has our list of moderately priced Californian Merlot wines. Note that we're not only able to leverage facets in the search, but we can also use the facets to sort results. Wine.com has added ratings from several magazines (WE = *Wine Enthusiast*, WS = *Wine Spectator*) as yet another facet.

Figure 9-30. Flexible search and results display

The information architects and designers at Wine.com have made decisions throughout the site about how and when to leverage facets within the interface. For example, you can't browse by price or rating from the main page. Hopefully, these are informed decisions made by balancing an understanding of user needs (how people want to browse and search) and business needs (how eVineyard can maximize sales of high-margin items).

The nice thing about a faceted classification approach is that it provides great power and flexibility. With the underlying descriptive metadata and structure in place, information architects and interface designers can experiment with hundreds of ways to present navigation options. The interface can be tested and refined over time, while the faceted classification provides an enduring foundation.

In recent years, search solutions built atop faceted classifications have really come into their own, thanks in part to search vendor Endeca and its "Guided Navigation" model (Figures 9-31 and 9-32), which encourages users to refine or narrow their searches based on metadata fields and values.

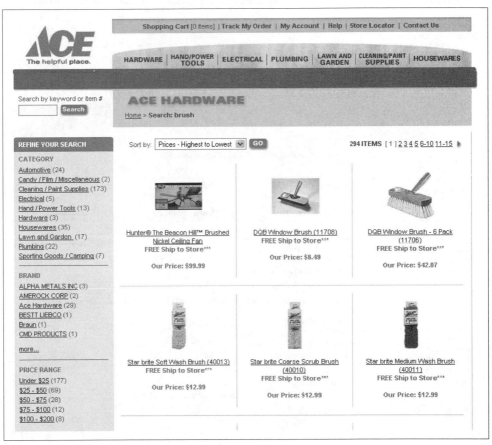

Figure 9-31. Guided navigation at Ace Hardware

Guided navigation was quickly embraced in the online retail arena, where there's a clear link between findability and profitability. More recently, this hybrid search/browse model has been widely adopted across industry, government, healthcare, publishing, and education. As Figure 9-32 shows, guided navigation is even being used to improve library catalogs. Ranganathan would be proud.

In addition to the increasing mainstream implementation of controlled vocabularies, we're also enjoying a growing wealth of resources to support these efforts. Here are just a few:

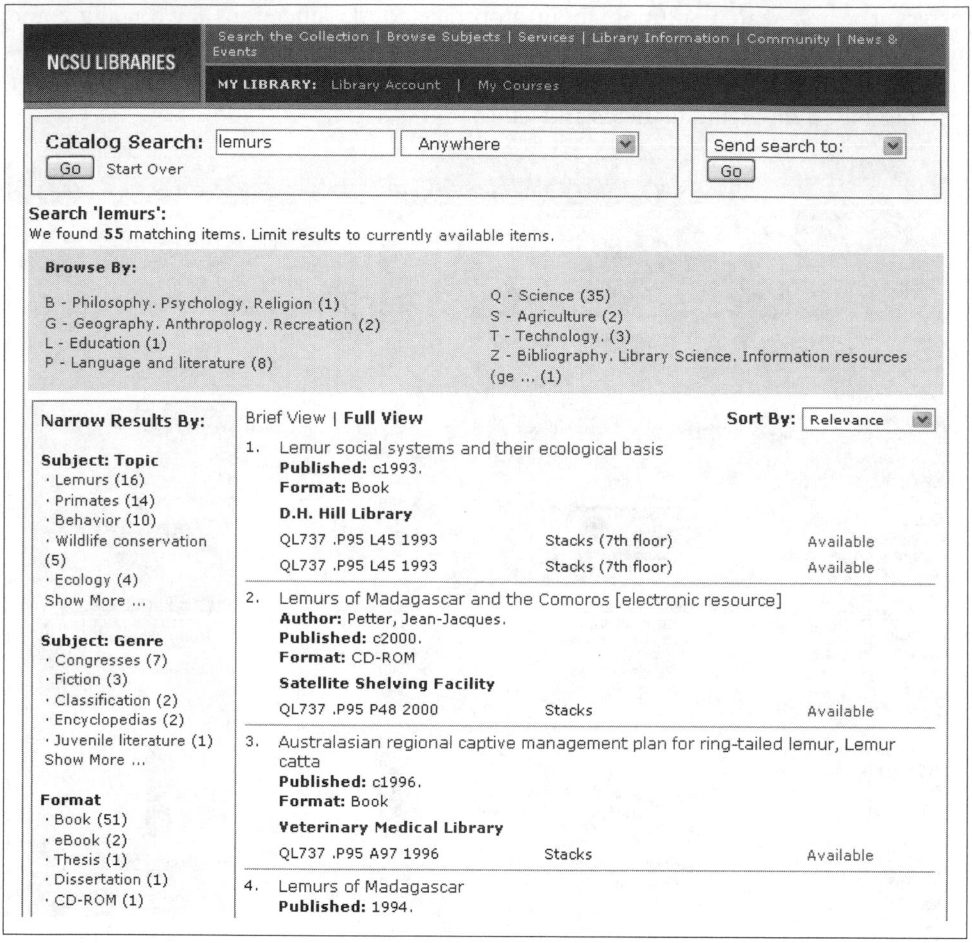

Figure 9-32. Guided navigation at NCSU

ANSI-NISO Z-39.19-2005

> *Guidelines for the Construction, Format, and Management of Monolingual Controlled Vocabularies.* Completely rewritten (and renamed) in 2005; *http://www.niso.org/standards/standard_detail.cfm?std_id=814*

Controlled Vocabularies: A Glosso-Thesaurus

> Written by Fred Leise, Karl Fast, and Mike Steckel; *http://www.boxesandarrows.com/view/controlled_vocabularies_a_glosso_thesaurus*

Dublin Core Metadata Initiative

> *http://dublincore.org*

Flamenco Search Interface Project

> *http://flamenco.berkeley.edu*

Glossary of Terms Relating to Thesauri
    http://www.willpowerinfo.co.uk/glossary.htm

Taxonomy Warehouse
    http://www.taxonomywarehouse.com/

ThesauriOnline
    http://www.asindexing.org/site/thesonet.shtml

Metadata, controlled vocabularies, and thesauri are increasingly becoming the building blocks of most major web sites and intranets. Single-taxonomy solutions are giving way to more flexible, faceted approaches. Put simply, if you're an information architect, we see facets in your future!*

---

* For more about Yahoo!, Wine.com, and faceted classification, see *http://www.semanticstudios.com/ publications/semantics/speed.html.*

PART III

Process and Methodology

CHAPTER 10

Research

> What we'll cover:
> - Integrating IA into the web development process
> - How and why to study users, context, and content
> - Research methods including stakeholder interviews, heuristic evaluations, user testing, and card sorting

So far, we've focused on concepts and components. Now we're going to shift gears and explore the process and methods for creating information architectures.

If it were just a matter of whipping up a few standard blueprints, our jobs would be easy. But as we've explained, information architecture doesn't happen in a vacuum. The design of complex web sites requires an interdisciplinary team that involves graphic designers, software developers, content managers, usability engineers, and other experts.

Effective collaboration requires agreement on a structured development process. Even for smaller projects, when teams are tiny and individuals fill multiple roles, tackling the right challenges at the right time is critical to success.

The following chapters provide an overview of the process and the challenges you'll encounter along the way. Our focus on the early stages of research, strategy, and design, rather than the later stages of implementation and administration, belies our consulting background. While the vast majority of our experiences have involved strategy and design for fast-paced information architecture projects, we are true believers in the importance of nailing the details in implementation and building sustainable information architecture programs. The dedicated in-house staff who protect and perfect information architectures over the long haul are the unsung heroes of the field.

Process Overview

In the early days of web design, many companies employed a one-step process called "Code HTML." Everyone wanted to jump right in and build the site. People had no patience for research or strategy. We remember one eager client asking us in the middle of a planning session, "So when are we going to start the real work?" Fortunately, after several years of painful lessons, there's a growing realization that designing web sites is hard work and requires a phased approach. Figure 10-1 illustrates the process of information architecture.

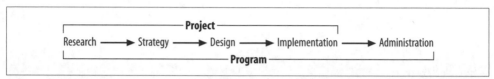

Figure 10-1. The process of information architecture development

The *research* phase begins with a review of existing background materials and meetings with the strategy team, aimed at gaining a high-level understanding of the goals and business context, the existing information architecture, the content, and the intended audiences. It then quickly moves into a series of studies, employing a variety of methods to explore the information ecology.

This research provides a contextual understanding that forms the foundation for development of an information architecture *strategy*. From a top-down perspective, this strategy defines the highest two or three levels of the site's organization and navigation structures. From a bottom-up perspective, it suggests candidate document types and a rough metadata schema. This strategy provides a high-level framework for the information architecture, establishing a direction and scope that will guide the project through implementation.

Design is where you shape a high-level strategy into an information architecture, creating detailed blueprints, wireframes, and metadata schema that will be used by graphic designers, programmers, content authors, and the production team. This phase is typically where information architects do the most work, yet quantity cannot drive out quality. Poor design execution can ruin the best strategy. For an information architect, the meat is in the middle and the devil is in the details.

Implementation is where your designs are put to the test as the site is built, tested, and launched. For the information architect, this phase involves organizing and tagging documents, testing and troubleshooting, and developing documentation and training programs to ensure that the information architecture can be maintained effectively over time.

And last but not least comes *administration*, the continuous evaluation and improvement of the site's information architecture. Administration includes the daily tasks of tagging new documents and weeding out old ones. It also requires monitoring site usage and user feedback, identifying opportunities to improve the site through major or minor redesigns. Effective administration can make a good site great.

Admittedly, this is a simplified view of the process. Clear lines rarely exist between phases, and few projects begin with a clean slate. Budgets, schedules, and politics will inevitably force you off the path and into the woods.

We don't aim to provide a paint-by-numbers design guide. The real world is far too messy. Instead, we present a framework and some tools and methods that may be useful when applied selectively within your environment.

Before we begin, we'll offer a word of encouragement. Much of this work looks tedious and boring when taken out of context. Not all of us can get jazzed up about poring over search logs and analyzing content. But when you do this work in the real world, it can be surprisingly engaging. And when that magic light bulb turns on, revealing a pattern that suggests a solution, you'll be glad you took the time to do it right.

A Research Framework

Good research means asking the right questions. And choosing the right questions requires a conceptual framework of the broader environment.

We have found our faithful three-circle diagram shown in Figure 10-2 to be invaluable in shaping a balanced approach to research. It helps us to decide where to shine the flashlight, and to understand what we see. Consequently, we have used this model to organize our exploration of the research process.

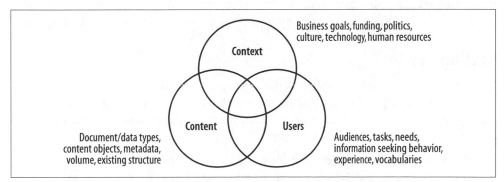

Figure 10-2. A balanced approach to research

We begin with an overview of tools and methods for research (see Figure 10-3). Obviously, it won't make sense or be possible to use every tool on every project. And, of course, you should absolutely seek out and try methods we haven't covered.

Our goal is to provide you with a map and a compass. The journey is left to you.

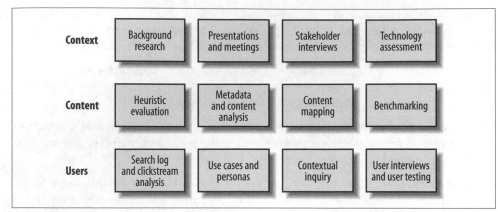

Figure 10-3. Tools and methods for research

Context

For practical purposes, an investigation of the business context can be a good place to start. It's critical to begin projects with a clear understanding of the goals and an appreciation of the political environment. Ignoring business realities is just as dangerous as ignoring users. A perfectly usable site that fails to support business goals won't last long. The term "user-centered design" is valuable insofar as it moves the pendulum away from executive-centered design, but don't let that pendulum swing too far.

Of course, context isn't just about politics. We also need to understand goals, budgets, schedules, technology infrastructure, human resources, and corporate culture. Legal issues can also be important, particularly in heavily regulated industries. All of these factors can and should influence the shape of the information architecture strategy.

Getting Buy-In

Research is not a one-way street. While conducting your investigation, it's important to recognize the value of building awareness and support for your project. After all, you're not a scientist studying rats. Your human subjects will have their own set of questions and concerns. For example:

- Who are you and why are you asking me these questions?
- What's information architecture and why should I care?
- What's your methodology and how does it relate to my work?

The way you answer these questions will influence the level of support you receive throughout the project. Since most large sites today depend upon interdepartmental collaboration and decentralized content ownership, it's impossible to succeed without broad buy-in. For this reason, you'll want to weave elements of presentation and persuasion throughout the research process.

Background Research

When a project begins, an information architect's head is filled with all sorts of good questions.

- What are the short- and long-term goals?
- What's the business plan? What are the politics?
- What's the schedule and budget?
- Who are the intended audiences?
- Why will people come to the site? Why will they come back?
- What types of tasks should users be able to perform?
- How will content be created and managed? And by whom?
- What's the technical infrastructure?
- What worked in the past? What didn't?

But just asking the right questions is not enough. You need to ask them of the right people in the right way at the right time. You must be very focused in how you use people's time and realistic about who can answer which questions.

Consequently, it's good to begin with a review of background materials. Sometimes the best way to learn about the future is to dig into the past. Get your hands on any documents that relate to the site's mission, vision, goals, intended audiences, and content. Also, try to find documents that provide a broader picture of the management structure and culture. Organization charts are really valuable if you're an outside consultant, particularly when working on intranets. They capture an important component of the users' mental model of the organization and will help you determine potential stakeholders and user groups for interviews and testing.

A revealing exercise is to compare the vision that preceded the current web site with the actual site itself. In some cases, we've seen elaborate PowerPoint presentations, hundreds of pages long, that paint a tremendously ambitious picture of what the web site should be. And then we've looked to the Web and found a small, poorly designed site with limited functionality. This gap between vision and reality is a red flag, suggesting misunderstanding between the managers who produce the slides and the team who must build the site. Great visions are useless without the time, money, and expertise to implement them. In these cases, you'll need to rein in expectations quickly.

Introductory Presentations

When you're kicking off an information architecture project, it's worth taking time for an introductory presentation. It's good to get authors, software developers, graphic designers, marketing folks, and managers all on the same page in understanding the following issues.

- What is information architecture and why is it important?
- How will the information architecture relate to the other components of the site and to the organization itself?
- What are the major milestones and deliverables?

These presentations and the discussions they provoke can identify potential landmines and foster productive relationships between teams. They are especially useful in building a common vocabulary that helps people communicate with one another more successfully.

Research Meetings

In the early 1990s, we held full-day marathon meetings with our clients' web teams to learn as much as possible about mission, vision, audience, content, and infrastructure, and to begin fleshing out a framework for the information architecture. In those days of small, centralized web design teams, one mammoth research meeting would often suffice. Today, the design and production of web sites is often more complicated, involving several teams drawn from different departments. This distributed reality may call for a series of targeted research meetings. Consider the following three meetings and their agendas.

Strategy team meeting

In many organizations today, there's a centralized strategy team or working group that's been tasked with management of the web or intranet effort. It's this strategy team that sets the high-level goals, defining the mission, vision, intended audience, content, and functionality. This is the group that deals with the big balancing act between centralization and autonomy.

Because of the need to establish trust and respect, face-to-face meetings with this team are essential. Only by having these meetings will you learn about the real goals of the project and the hidden landmines in your path. And only during face-to-face conversations will you reach a comfort level that allows both you and your colleagues to ask the difficult but necessary questions.

It's important to keep these meetings small and informal. Five to seven people is ideal. If the group gets too large, political correctness takes over and people won't talk. As far as the agenda goes, you'll want to hit on some of the following questions:

- What are the goals for this site?
- Who are the intended audiences?
- What is the planned content and functionality?
- Who will be involved in this effort?
- When do you need to show results?
- What obstacles do you anticipate?

However, the key in these meetings is to follow your nose. Be ready to dig deeper into the most interesting and important topics that come up. The worst thing you can do is rigidly stick to a formal agenda. Think of yourself as the facilitator, not the dictator. And don't be afraid to let the discussion wander a bit. You'll learn more, and everyone will have a more enjoyable meeting.

Content management meeting

The content owners and managers are the people you'll want to engage in detailed discussions about the nature of the content and the content management process. These people typically have lots of hands-on experience and a perspective more informed by bottom-up realities. If you can establish a rapport, you might also learn a lot about the culture and politics of the organization as well. Questions for these folks include:

- What are the formal and informal policies regarding content inclusion?
- Is there a content management system that handles authoring and publishing?
- Do those systems use controlled vocabularies and attributes to manage content?
- How is content entered into the system?
- What technology is being used?
- What content does each owner handle?
- What is the purpose of the content? What are the goals and vision behind this content area?
- Who is the audience?
- What is the format of the content? Is it dynamic or static?
- Who maintains the content?
- What future content or services are planned?
- Where does content originate? How is it weeded?
- What legal issues impact the content management process?

Information technology meeting

You should meet with the system administrators and software developers early on to learn about the existing and planned technical infrastructure that will support the web site or intranet. This provides a good opportunity to discuss the relationships between information architecture and technical infrastructure, as well as to build trust and respect. Remember, you depend on these folks to forge the connection between ideas and implementation. Questions include:

- Will we be able to leverage content management software (CMS)?
- How can we create a metadata registry to support distributed tagging?
- Does the CMS handle automated categorization of documents?

- What about automated browsable index generation?
- What about personalization?
- How flexible is the search engine?
- Will the search engine support integration of a thesaurus?
- Can we get regular access to search logs and usage statistics?

Unfortunately, the IT groups in many organizations are swamped with work and don't have the time to support information architecture and usability efforts. It's important to identify this problem early and develop a practical, realistic solution. Otherwise, your whole effort can stall when implementation time arrives.

Stakeholder Interviews

Interviews with opinion leaders or stakeholders are often one of the most valuable components of the business context research. These interviews with senior executives and managers from a variety of departments and business units allow for broader participation in the process and bring new perspectives, ideas, and resources to the table.

During these interviews, the information architect asks the opinion leaders open-ended questions about their assessment of the current information environment and their vision for the organization and its web site. It's worth taking the time to explain your project to these folks—their political support may be more important in the long haul than the answers they give during the interview. Sample questions for an intranet project include:

- What is your role in the organization? What does your team do?
- In an optimal world, how would your company use the intranet to build competitive advantage?
- In your opinion, what are the key challenges your company intranet faces?
- What enterprise-wide initiatives are occurring that the intranet strategy team should know about?
- Do you use the existing intranet? If not, why not? If so, what parts of the intranet do you use? How often?
- What incentives exist for departments and employees to share knowledge?
- What are the critical success factors for the intranet?
- How will these factors be measured? What's the ROI?
- What are the top three priorities for the intranet redesign?
- If you could tell the intranet strategy team one thing, what would it be?
- What question should we have asked that we didn't?

As with the strategy team meeting, these interviews should be informal discussions. Let the stakeholders tell you what's on their minds.

Technology Assessment

In our dream world, we would design our information architectures independent of technology, and then a team of system administrators and software developers would build the infrastructure and tools to support our vision.

In the real world, this doesn't happen very often. Usually, we must work with the tools and infrastructure already in place. This means that we need to assess the IT environment at the very beginning of a project so that our strategies and designs are grounded in reality.

This is why it's critical to talk with IT folks up front. You'll want to understand what's in place, what's in process, and who's available to help. Then you can perform a *gap analysis*, identifying the disconnects between business goals, user needs, and the practical limitations of the existing technology infrastructure.

You can then see if there are any commercially available tools that might help to close these gaps, and you can initiate a process to determine whether it's practical to integrate them within the context of the current project. (We'll discuss tools for information architects in more detail in Chapter 16.) Either way, it's much better to come to terms with these IT issues early on.

Content

We define content broadly as "the stuff in your web site." This may include documents, data, applications, e-services, images, audio and video files, personal web pages, archived email messages, and more. And we include future stuff as well as present stuff.

Users need to be able to *find* content before they can use it—findability precedes usability. And if you want to create findable objects, you must spend some time studying those objects. You'll need to identify what distinguishes one object from another, and how document structure and metadata influence findability. You'll want to balance this bottom-up research with a top-down look at the site's existing information architecture.

Heuristic Evaluation

Many projects involve redesigning existing web sites rather than creating new ones. In such cases, you're granted the opportunity to stand on the shoulders of those who came before you. Unfortunately, this opportunity is often missed because of people's propensity to focus on faults and their desire to start with a clean slate. We regularly hear our clients trashing their own web sites, explaining that the current site is a disaster and we shouldn't waste our time looking at it. This is a classic case of throwing out the baby with the bathwater. Whenever possible, try to learn from the existing site and identify what's worth keeping. One way to jump-start this process is to conduct a heuristic evaluation.

A *heuristic evaluation* is an expert critique that tests a web site against a formal or informal set of design guidelines. It's usually best to have someone outside the organization perform this critique, so this person is able to look with fresh eyes and be largely unburdened with political considerations. Ideally, the heuristic evaluation should occur before a review of background materials to avoid bias.

At its simplest, a heuristic evaluation involves one expert reviewing a web site and identifying major problems and opportunities for improvement. This expert brings to the table an unwritten set of assumptions about what does and doesn't work, drawing upon experiences with many projects in many organizations.

This practice is similar to the physician's model of diagnosis and prescription. If your child has a sore throat, the doctor will rarely consult a reference book or perform extensive medical tests. Based on the patient's complaints, the visible symptoms, and the doctor's knowledge of common ailments, the doctor will make an educated guess as to the problem and its solution. These guesses are not always right, but this single-expert model of heuristic evaluation often provides a good balance between cost and quality.

At the more rigorous and expensive end of the spectrum, a heuristic evaluation can be a multi-expert review that tests a web site against a written list* of principles and guidelines. This list may include such common-sense guidelines as:

- The site should provide multiple ways to access the same information.
- Indexes and sitemaps should be employed to supplement the taxonomy.
- The navigation system should provide users with a sense of context.
- The site should consistently use language appropriate for the audience.
- Searching and browsing should be integrated and reinforce each other.

Each expert reviews the site independently and makes notes on how it fares with respect to each of these criteria. The experts then compare notes, discuss differences, and work toward a consensus. This reduces the likelihood that personal opinion will play too strong a role, and creates the opportunity to draw experts from different disciplines. For example, you might include an information architect, a usability engineer, and an interaction designer. Each will see very different problems and opportunities. This approach obviously costs more, so depending on the scope of your project, you'll need to strike a balance in terms of number of experts and formality of the evaluation.

---

* For a good example of such a list, see Jakob Nielsen's *Ten Usability Heuristics* (*http://www.useit.com/papers/heuristic/heuristic_list.html*).

Content Analysis

Content analysis is a defining component of the bottom-up approach to information architecture, involving careful review of the documents and objects that actually exist. What's in the site may not match the visions articulated by the strategy team and the opinion leaders. You'll need to identify and address these gaps between top-down vision and bottom-up reality.

Content analysis can take the shape of an informal survey or a detailed audit. Early in the research phase, a high-level content survey is a useful tool for learning about the scope and nature of content. Later in the process, a page-by-page content audit or inventory can produce a roadmap for migration to a content management system (CMS), or at least facilitate an organized approach to page-level authoring and design.

Gathering content

To begin, you'll need to find, print, and analyze a *representative sample* of the site's content. We suggest avoiding an overly scientific approach to sample definition. There's no formula or software package that will guarantee success. Instead, you need to use some intuition and judgment, balancing the size of your sample against the time constraints of the project.

We recommend the Noah's Ark approach. Try to capture a couple of each type of animal. Our animals are things like white papers, annual reports, and online reimbursement forms, but the difficult part is determining what constitutes a unique species. The following dimensions should help distinguish one beast from another and build toward a diverse and useful content sample:

Format
> Aim for a broad mix of formats, such as textual documents, software applications, video and audio files, and archived email messages. Try to include offline resources such as books, people, facilities, and organizations that are represented by surrogate records within the site.

Document type
> Capturing a diverse set of document types should be a top priority. Examples include product catalog records, marketing brochures, press releases, news articles, annual reports, technical reports, white papers, forms, online calculators, presentations, spreadsheets, and the list goes on.

Source
> Your sample should reflect the diverse sources of content. In a corporate web site or intranet, this will mirror the organization chart. You'll want to make sure you've got samples from engineering, marketing, customer support, finance, human resources, sales, research, etc. This is not just useful—it's also politically astute. If your site includes third-party content such as electronic journals or ASP services, grab those, too.

Subject

This is a tricky one, since you may not have a topical taxonomy for your site. You might look for a publicly available classification scheme or thesaurus for your industry. It's a good exercise to represent a broad range of subjects or topics in your content sample, but don't force it.

Existing architecture

Used together with these other dimensions, the existing structure of the site can be a great guide to diverse content types. Simply by following each of the major category links on the main page or in the global navigation bar, you can often reach a wide sample of content. However, keep in mind that you don't want your analysis to be overly influenced by the old architecture.

Consider what other dimensions might be useful for building a representative content sample for your particular site. Possibilities include intended audience, document length, dynamism, language, and so on.

As you're balancing sample size against time and budget, consider the relative number of members of each species. For example, if the site contains hundreds of technical reports, you certainly want a couple of examples. But if you find a single white paper, it's probably not worth including in your sample. On the other hand, you do need to factor in the importance of certain content types. There may not be many annual reports on your web site, but they can be content-rich and very important to investors. As always, your judgment is required.

A final factor to consider is the law of diminishing returns. While you're conducting content analysis, you'll often reach a point where you feel you're just not learning anything new. This may be a good signal to go with the sample you've got, or at least take a break. Content analysis is only useful insofar as it teaches you about the stuff in the site and provides insights about how to get users to that stuff. Don't just go through the motions. It's unproductive and incredibly boring.

Analyzing content

What are you looking for during content analysis? What can you hope to learn? One of the side benefits of content analysis is familiarity with the subject matter. This is particularly important for consultants who need to quickly become fluent in the language of their client. But the central purpose of content analysis is to provide data that's critical to the development of a solid information architecture. It helps you reveal patterns and relationships within content and metadata that can be used to better structure, organize, and provide access to that content. That said, content analysis is quite unscientific. Our approach is to start with a short list of things to look for, and then allow the content to shape the process as you move forward.

For example, for each content object, you might begin by noting the following:

Structural metadata
>   Describe the information hierarchy of this object. Is there a title? Are there discrete sections or chunks of content? Might users want to independently access these chunks?

Descriptive metadata
>   Think of all the different ways you might describe this object. How about topic, audience, and format? There should be at least a dozen different ways to describe many of the objects you study. Now's the time to get them all on the table.

Administrative metadata
>   Describe how this object relates to business context. Who created it? Who owns it? When was it created? When should it be removed?

This short list will get you started. In some cases, the object will already have metadata. Grab that, too. However, it's important not to lock into a predefined set of metadata fields. You want to allow the content to speak to you, suggesting new fields you might not have considered. You'll find it helpful to keep asking yourself these questions:

- What is this object?
- How can I describe this object?
- What distinguishes this object from others?
- How can I make this object findable?

Moving beyond individual items, also look for patterns and relationships that emerge as you study many content objects. Are certain groupings of content becoming apparent? Are you seeing clear hierarchical relationships? Are you recognizing the potential for associative relationships, perhaps finding disparate items that are linked by a common business process?

Because of the need to recognize patterns within the context of the full sample, content analysis is by necessity an iterative process. It may be on the second or third pass over a particular document that the light bulb blinks on and you discover a truly innovative and useful solution.

With the exception of true bottom-up geeks (and we use the term respectfully), most of us don't find content analysis especially thrilling or addictive. However, experience has proven that this careful, painstaking work can suggest new insights and produce winning information architecture strategies. In particular, content analysis will help you in the design phase, when you begin fleshing out document types and metadata schema. But it also provides valuable input into the broader design of organization, labeling, navigation, and searching systems.

Content Mapping

Heuristic evaluation provides a top-down understanding of a site's organization and navigation structures, while content analysis provides a bottom-up understanding of its content objects. Now it's time to bridge these two perspectives by developing one or more content maps.

A *content map* is a visual representation of the existing information environment (see Figure 10-4). Content maps are typically high-level and conceptual in nature. They are a tool for understanding, rather than a concrete design deliverable.

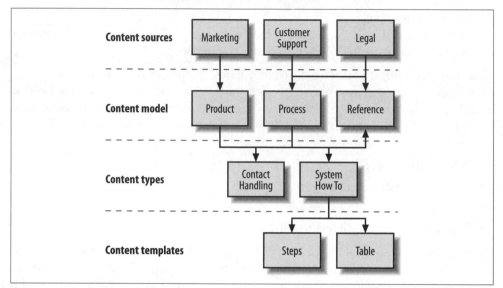

Figure 10-4. A small slice of a content map

Content maps vary widely. Some focus on content ownership and the publishing process. Some are used to visualize relationships between content categories. And others explore navigation pathways within content areas. The goal of creating a content map is to help you and your colleagues wrap your minds around the structure, organization, and location of existing content, and ultimately to spark ideas about how to provide improved access.

Benchmarking

We use the term *benchmark* informally to indicate a point of reference from which to make comparative measurements or judgments. In this context, benchmarking involves the systematic identification, evaluation, and comparison of information architecture features of web sites and intranets.

These comparisons can be quantitative or qualitative. We might evaluate the number of seconds it takes a user to perform a task using competing web sites, or take notes about the most interesting features of each site. Comparisons can be made between different web sites (competitive benchmarking) or between different versions of the same web site (before-and-after benchmarking). In both cases, we've found benchmarking to be a flexible and valuable tool.

Competitive benchmarking

Borrowing good ideas, whether they come from competitors, friends, enemies, or strangers, comes naturally to all of us. It's part of our competitive advantage as human beings. If we were all left to our own devices to invent the wheel, most of us would still be walking to work.

However, when we take these copycat shortcuts, we run the risk of borrowing bad ideas as well as good ones. This happens all the time in the web environment. Since the pioneering days of web site design, people have repeatedly mistaken large financial outlays and strong marketing campaigns as signs of good information architecture. Careful benchmarking can catch this misdirected copycatting before it gets out of control.

For example, when we worked with a major financial services firm, we ran up against the notion that Fidelity Investments' long-standing position as a leader within the industry automatically conferred the gold standard upon its web site. In several cases, we proposed significant improvements to our client's site but were blocked by the argument, "That's not how Fidelity does it."

To be sure, Fidelity is a major force in the financial services industry, with a broad array of services and world-class marketing. However, in 1998, the information architecture of its web site was a mess. This was not a model worth following. To our client's credit, they commissioned a formal benchmarking study, during which we evaluated and compared the features of several competing sites. During this study, Fidelity's failings became obvious, and we were able to move forward without that particular set of false assumptions.

The point here is that borrowing information architecture features from competitors is valuable, but it must be done carefully.

Before-and-after benchmarking

Benchmarking can also be applied to a single site over time to measure improvements. We can use it to answer such return-on-investment (ROI) questions as:

- How much did the intranet redesign reduce our employees' average time finding core documents?
- Has the web site redesign improved our customers' ability to find the products they need?
- Which aspects of our redesign have had a negative impact on user efficiency or effectiveness?

Before-and-after benchmarking forces you to take the high-level goals expressed in your statement of mission and vision, and tie them to specific, measurable criteria. This forced clarification and detail-orientation will drive you toward a better information architecture design on the present project, in addition to providing a point of reference for evaluating success.

Following are the advantages of before-and-after benchmarking, as well as those of competitive benchmarking:

Benefits of before-and-after benchmarking

- Identifies and prioritizes information architecture features in the existing site
- Encourages transition from broad generalizations (e.g., "Our site's navigation stinks") to specific, actionable definitions
- Creates a point of reference against which you can measure improvements

Benefits of competitive benchmarking

- Generates a laundry list of information architecture features, bringing lots of new ideas to table
- Encourages transition from broad generalizations (e.g., "Amazon is a good model") to specific, actionable definitions ("Amazon's personalization feature works well for frequent visitors")
- Challenges embedded assumptions (e.g., "We should be like Fidelity") and avoids copying the wrong features for the wrong reasons
- Establishes current position with respect to competitors and creates a point of reference against which to measure speed of improvement

Users

They're called users, respondents, visitors, actors, employees, customers, and more. They're counted as clicks, impressions, advertising revenues, and sales. Whatever you call them and however you count them, they are the ultimate designers of the Web. Build a web site that confuses customers, and they'll go elsewhere. Build an intranet that frustrates employees, and they won't use it.

This is the Internet's fast-forward brand of evolution. Remember the original Pathfinder web site from Time Warner? They spent millions of dollars on a flashy, graphical extravaganza. Users hated it. A complete redesign followed months after the original launch. This was an expensive and embarrassingly public lesson in the importance of user-sensitive design.

So, we've established that users are powerful. They're also complex and unpredictable. You can't blindly apply lessons learned by Amazon to the information architecture design of Pfizer.com. You've got to consider the unique nature of the site and of the user population.

There are many ways to study user populations.* Market-research firms run focus groups to study branding preferences. Political pollsters use telephone surveys to gauge the public's feelings about candidates and issues. Usability firms conduct interviews to determine which icons and color schemes are most effective. Anthropologists observe people acting and interacting within their native environments to learn about their culture, behavior, and beliefs.

No single approach can stand alone as the one right way to learn about users and their needs, priorities, mental models, and information-seeking behavior. This is a multidimensional puzzle—you've got to look at it from many different perspectives to get a good sense of the whole. It's much better to conduct five interviews and five usability tests than to run one test ten times. Each approach is subject to the law of diminishing returns.

As you consider integrating these user research methods into your design process, keep a couple of things in mind. First, observe the golden rule of discount usability engineering: any testing is better than no testing. Don't let budgets or schedules become an excuse. Second, remember that users can be your most powerful allies. It's easy for your colleagues and your boss to argue with you, but it's difficult for them to argue with their customers and with real user behavior. User research is an extremely effective political tool.

Usage Statistics

Most projects today involve redesigning an existing site. In these cases, it makes sense to begin by looking at data that shows how people have been using the site and where they've been running into problems.

Your site's usage statistics are a reasonable place to start. Most statistics software packages, such as Google Analytics shown in Figure 10-5, provide the following reports:

Page information
> The number of hits per day for each page in the site. This data will show which pages are most popular. By tracking page hits over time, you can observe trends and tie page popularity to events such as advertising campaigns or the redesign of site navigation.

Visitor information
> Statistics products claim they can tell you who is using your site and where the users are coming from. In reality, they'll tell you only the domains (e.g., aol.com, mitre.org) of those users' Internet service providers, which is often of limited value.

---

* If you'd like to dig deeper, we recommend reading *User and Task Analysis for Interface Design* by Joann Hackos and Janice Redish (Wiley). And then, of course, there are all sorts of wonderful articles and books by usability guru Jakob Nielsen (*http://useit.com*).

Your stats software may provide additional views into the usage data, indicating the times and dates when people are visiting, the referring sites your users are coming from, and the types of browsers being used, as shown in Figure 10-5.

Figure 10-5. Usage data presented by Google Analytics

The path that users trace as they move through a web site is known as the *clickstream*. If you want a higher level of sophistication in your usage statistics, you can buy software that handles clickstream analysis. You can trace where a user comes from (originating site), the path he takes through your site, and where he goes next (destination site). Along the way, you can learn how long he spends on each page of your site. This creates a tremendously rich data stream that can be fascinating to review, but difficult to act upon. What you really need to make clickstream data valuable is feedback from the user explaining why he came to the site, what he found, and why he left. Some companies use pop-up surveys to capture this information as users are leaving the web site.

Search-Log Analysis

A simpler and extremely valuable approach involves the tracking and analysis of queries entered into the search engine. By studying these queries, you can identify what users are looking for, and the words and phrases they are using. This is fantastic data when you're developing controlled vocabularies. It's also useful when prioritizing terms for a "Best Bets" strategy. (You'll learn more about Best Bets in the MSWeb case study in Chapter 20.)

At a basic level, search-log analysis will sensitize you to the way your users really search. Users generally enter one or two keywords, and you're lucky if they spell them right. Looking at search logs provides a valuable education for information architects who are fresh out of school and all steamed up about the power of Boolean operators and parenthetical nesting. You can achieve the same effect using a live search display* such as Metacrawler's metaspy, which shows the terms that real people are using to search right now (see Figure 10-6).

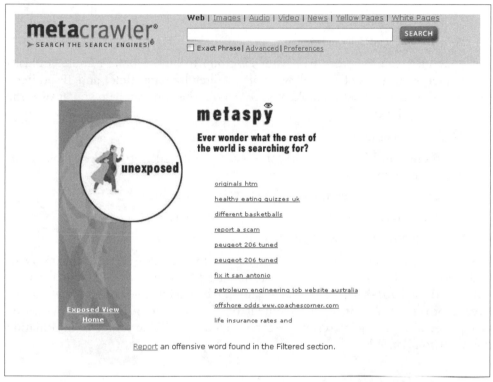

Figure 10-6. A public search voyeur service

But with your own site's search logs, you can learn much more. At a bare minimum, you should be able to get a monthly report that shows how many times users searched on particular terms during that month, as shown here:

```
54 e-victor
53 keywords:"e-victor"
41 travel
41 keywords:"travel"
37 keywords:"jupiter"
37 jupiter31 esp
```

---

* See *http://searchenginewatch.com/facts/searches.html* for more on live search displays.

```
30 keywords:"esp"
28 keywords:"evictor"
28 evictor
28 keywords:"people finder"
28 people finder
27 fleet
27 keywords:"fleet"
27 payroll
26 eer
26 keywords:"eer"
26 keywords:"payroll"
26 digital badge
25 keywords:"digital badge"
```

But hopefully, you can work with your IT group to buy or build a more sophisticated query-analysis tool that allows you to filter by date, time, and IP address. Figure 10-7 shows a good example of such a tool. This tool can help you answer the following questions:

- Which popular queries are retrieving zero results?
- Are these zero-hit users entering the wrong keywords, or are they looking for stuff that doesn't exist on your site?
- Which popular queries are retrieving hundreds of results?
- What are these hundred-hit users actually looking for?
- Which queries are becoming more popular? Less?

Based on the answers, you can take immediate and concrete steps to fix problems and improve information retrieval. You might add preferred and variant terms to your controlled vocabulary, change navigation labels on major pages throughout the site, improve search tips, or edit content on the site. Note that smart marketing groups are also getting interested in search logs as a valuable source of information about customer needs.

Customer-Support Data

In addition to reviewing web site statistics, it's worth looking to the customer- or technical-support departments to see if they've been capturing and analyzing the problems, questions, and feedback from the customers of your web site or intranet. Help-desk operators, call-center representatives, librarians, and administrative assistants can also be rich sources of information; in many large corporations, these are the people to whom customers or employees turn for answers. That means they are the people who know the questions.

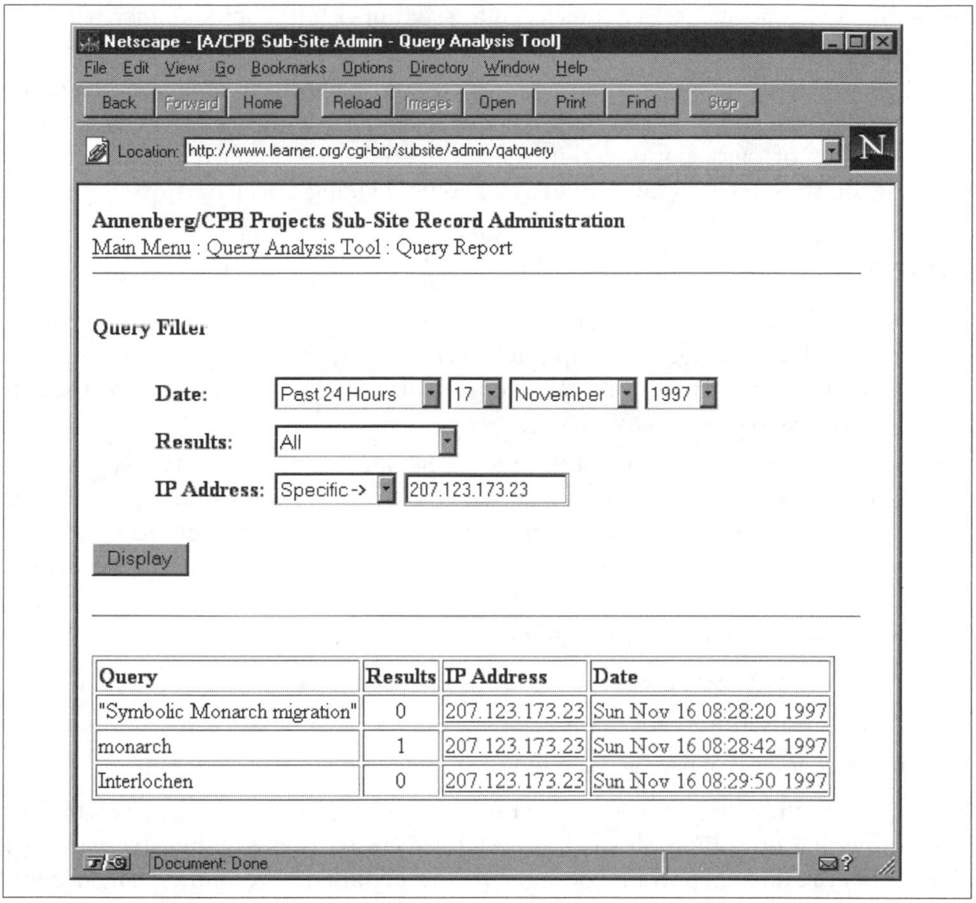

Figure 10-7. A query-analysis tool

Participant Definition and Recruiting

All of the remaining user research methods, including surveys, focus groups, interviews, and ethnographic studies, require the selection of representative samples of users to participate in the research studies. With the possible exception of surveys, it's rarely possible to study every user of a web site.

The definition and prioritization of intended and actual audiences for the site is obviously a critical factor. As we discussed earlier, there are myriad ways of slicing and dicing these audiences. Just as you define a primary hierarchy for your web site, you also need to define a primary hierarchy for participant selection. This hierarchy should strike a balance between the traditional ways that an organization views its customers (e.g., home users, business users, value-added resellers) and the distinctions an information architect is interested in (e.g., people familiar with the old site, people unfamiliar with the old site).

For large projects, the information architect should consider working with a traditional market-research firm that has experience defining audience categories, developing profiles of participants within those categories, recruiting participants, and handling logistics like facilities, incentives, and note taking.

Surveys

Surveys are a broad-and-shallow research tool that provide an opportunity to gather input from a large number of people relatively quickly and inexpensively. Surveys can be conducted via email, web, telephone, mail, or in person, and can be used to gather qualitative or quantitative data.

When designing a survey, you'll need to limit the number of questions if you want a reasonable response rate. You may also need to guarantee anonymity and offer an incentive. Since there's little opportunity for follow-up questions or dialogue, surveys don't allow you to gather rich data about users' information-seeking behaviors. Instead, they are best used for identifying:

- Which content and tasks users find most valuable
- What frustrates users most about the current site
- What ideas users have for improvement
- The current level of user satisfaction

In addition to the inherent value of real users' opinions, the survey results will provide you with a powerful political tool. If 90 percent of users say that the employee directory is the most important and most frustrating intranet resource, that's a compelling argument for improving it.

Contextual Inquiry

Field study is an important component of research programs in a variety of disciplines, from animal behavior to anthropology. Environmental context is tightly interwoven with behavior—you can only learn so much about the bald eagle or the bottle-nosed dolphin by studying them in a lab. The same applies to people and their use of information technology. In fact, a growing number of anthropologists are being tapped by the business world to apply their ethnographic research methods to product design.

These methods of contextual inquiry can be useful to the information architect.* For example, simply seeing the work spaces of users can be valuable in showing the spectrum of information resources they use on a daily basis (e.g., computer, phone, bulletin board, Post-it notes).

---

* To learn more about contextual inquiry, we recommend reading *Contextual Design* by Hugh Beyer and Karen Holtzblatt (Morgan Kaufmann).

If possible, it's also valuable to watch people interact with a site during the normal course of business. If you're redesigning a mission-critical call-center application that users interact with all day long, spend a few hours watching them. On the other hand, if you're redesigning a typical business web site, this observational approach won't be practical given the sporadic nature of site use. Most users will visit only once every several weeks or months. In these cases, you'll need to rely on user testing, though you still may be able to run the tests in the user's natural habitat.

In some cases, it can be valuable to simply watch people work. Observing users performing normal daily tasks—going to meetings, taking phone calls, and so on—can provide insight into how the intranet or web site might (or might not) help people be more productive. The difficult issue here (and, to some degree, with all the observation approaches) is that information architecture begins to bleed into knowledge management and business-process reengineering. In an ideal world, the roles and responsibilities of departments, teams, and individuals would all be designed in an integrated fashion. In the real world (and particularly in large organizations), most projects are limited by the scope, schedule, and budget of these different departments. The folks responsible for designing the information architecture rarely influence the way other departments do their work. For this reason, keep asking yourself throughout the research process whether you'll actually be able to act on the data. If you're going to get the job done, the answer better be yes.

Focus Groups

Focus groups are one of the most common and most abused tools for learning from users. When conducting focus groups, you gather groups of people who are actual or potential users of your site. In a typical focus-group session, you might ask a series of scripted questions about what users would like to see on the site, demonstrate a prototype or show the site itself, and then ask questions about the users' perception of the site and their recommendations for improvement.

Focus groups are great for generating ideas about possible content and function for the site. By getting several people from your target audiences together and facilitating a brainstorming session, you can quickly find yourself with a laundry list of suggestions. However, focus groups don't work as well for information architectures as they do for, say, consumer products. For example, people can tell you what they like, don't like, and wish for regarding their refrigerators, but most people don't have the understanding or language necessary to be articulate about information architectures.

Focus groups are also very poor vehicles for testing the usability of a site. A public demonstration does not come close to replicating the actual environment of a user who is navigating a web site. Consequently, the suggestions of people in focus groups often do not carry much weight. Sadly, focus groups are often used only to prove that a particular approach does or doesn't work, and they can easily be influenced in one direction or another through the skillful selection and phrasing of questions.

User Research Sessions

Face-to-face sessions involving one user at a time are a central part of the user research process. However, these sessions are also expensive and time-consuming. We've learned that you tend to get the most value out of these sessions by integrating two or more research methods. We typically combine an interview with either card sorting or user testing. This multimethod approach makes the most of your limited time with real users.

Interviews

We often begin and end user research sessions with a series of questions. Starting with a brief Q&A can put the participant at ease. This is a good time to ask about her overall priorities and needs with respect to the site. Questions at the end of the session can be used to follow up on issues that came up during the user testing. This is a good time to ask what frustrates her about the current site and what suggestions she has for improvement. This final Q&A brings closure to the session. Here are some questions we've used for intranet projects in the past.

Background

- What do you do in your current role?
- What is your background?
- How long have you been with the company?

Information use

- What information do you need to do your job?
- What information is hardest to find?
- What do you do when you can't find something?

Intranet use

- Do you use the intranet?
- What is your impression of the intranet? Is it easy or hard to use?
- How do you find information on the intranet?
- Do you use customization or personalization features?

Document publishing

- Do you create documents that are used by other people or departments?
- Tell us what you know about the life cycle of your documents. What happens after you create them?
- Do you use content management tools to publish documents to the intranet?

Suggestions

- If you could change three things about the intranet, what would they be?
- If you could add three features to the web site, what would they be?
- If you could tell the web strategy team three things, what would they be?

In determining what questions to ask, it's important to recognize that most users are not information architects. They don't have the understanding or vocabulary to engage in a technical dialogue about existing or potential information architectures. If you ask them if they like the current organization scheme or whether they think a thesaurus would improve the site's usability, you'll get blank stares or made-up answers.

Card Sorting

Want to get your hands on some of the most powerful information architecture research tools in the world? Grab a stack of index cards, some Post-it notes, and a pen. Card sorting may be low-tech, but it's great for understanding your users.

What's involved? Not a whole lot, as you can see in Figure 10-8. Label a bunch of index cards with headings from categories, subcategories, and content within your web site. About 20 to 25 cards is usually sufficient. Number the cards so that you can more easily analyze the data later. Ask a user to sort this stack of cards into piles that make sense to him, and to label those piles using the Post-it notes. Ask him to think out loud while he works. Take good notes, and record the labels and contents of his piles. That's it!

Figure 10-8. Sample index cards

Card-sorting studies can provide insight into users' mental models, illuminating the ways they often tacitly group, sort, and label tasks and content in their own heads. The simplicity of this method confers tremendous flexibility. In the earliest phases of research, you can employ exploratory, *open-ended* card-sorting methods like the one we just described. Later on, you can use *closed* card sorts in which users rely on your predefined labels to question or validate a prototype information architecture. You can also instruct users to sort the cards according to what's most important to them; they can even have a pile for "things I don't care about." The permutations are infinite. Consider the following dimensions of card sorting:

Open/closed

In totally open card sorts, users write their own card and category labels. Totally closed sorts allow only pre-labeled cards and categories. Open sorts are used for discovery. Closed sorts are used for validation. There's a lot of room in the middle. You'll need to set the balance according to your goals.

Phrasing

The labels on your cards might be a word, a phrase, a sentence, or a category with sample subcategories. You can even affix a picture. You might phrase the card labels as a question or an answer, or you may use topic- or task-oriented words.

Granularity

Cards can be high-level or detailed. Your labels might be main-page categories or the names of subsites, or you may focus on specific documents or even content elements within documents.

Heterogeneity

Early on, you may want to cover a lot of ground by mixing apples and oranges (e.g., name of subsite, document title, subject heading) to elicit rich qualitative data. This will really get users talking as they puzzle over the heterogeneous mix of cards. Later, you may want high consistency (e.g., subject headings only) to produce quantitative data (e.g., 80 percent of users grouped these three items together).

Cross-listing

Are you fleshing out the primary hierarchy of the site or exploring alternate navigation paths? If it's the latter, you might allow your users to make copies of cards, cross-listing them in multiple categories. You might also ask them to write descriptive terms (i.e., metadata) on the cards or category labels.

Randomness

You can strategically select card labels to prove a hypothesis, or you can randomly select labels from a pool of possible labels. As always, your power to influence outcomes can be used for good or evil.

Quantitative/qualitative

Card sorting can be used as an interview instrument or as a data collection tool. We've found it most useful for gathering qualitative data. If you go the quantitative route, be careful to observe basic principles of the scientific method and avoid prejudicing the outcome.

Due to the popularity of this research method, several companies have developed software to support remote card sorting (see Figure 10-9 for an example), so you don't even need to be in the same room as the users! Did we mention this method is flexible?

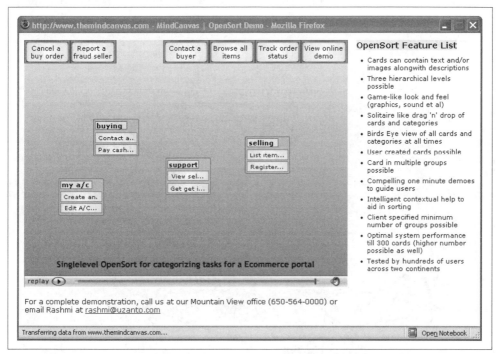

Figure 10-9. MindCanvas remote research software

Just as there are many ways to do card sorting, there are many ways to analyze the results. From a qualitative perspective, you should be learning and forming ideas during the tests, as users talk out loud about their reasoning, their questions, and their frustrations. By asking follow-up questions, you can dig into some specifics and gain a better understanding of opportunities for organizing and labeling content.

On the quantitative side, there are some obvious metrics to capture:

- The percentage of time that users place two cards together. A high level of association between items suggests a close affinity in users' mental models.

- The percentage of time a specific card is placed in the same category. This works well in closed sorts. For open sorts, you may need to normalize the category labels (e.g., Human Resources equals HR equals Admin/HR) to make this work.

These metrics can be represented visually in an affinity modeling diagram (see Figure 10-10) to show the clusters and the relationships between clusters. You may want to plug your data into statistical analysis software and have it generate the visuals automatically. However, these automatically generated visualizations are often fairly complex and hard to understand. They tend to be better for identifying patterns than for communicating results.

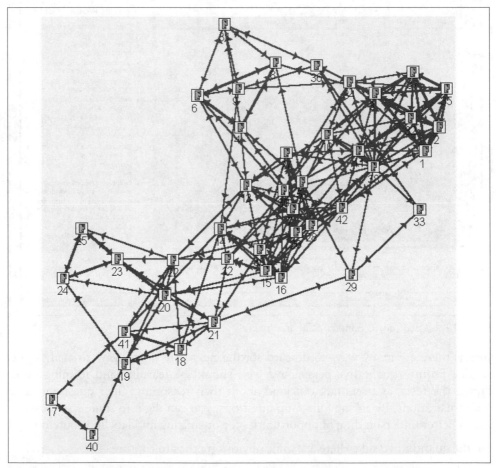

Figure 10-10. An automatically generated affinity model (prepared for Louis Rosenfeld and Michele de la Iglesia by Edward Vielmetti using InFlow 3.0 network analysis software from Valdis Krebs)

When you're ready to present research results to your clients, you may want to create a simpler affinity model by hand. These manually generated diagrams provide an opportunity to focus on a few highlights of the card-sorting results.

In Figure 10-11, 80 percent of users grouped the "How to set DHTML event proper-ties" card in the same pile as "Enterprise Edition: Deployment," suggesting they should be closely linked on the site. Note that "Load balancing web servers" is a boundary spanner and should probably be referenced in both categories on the site.

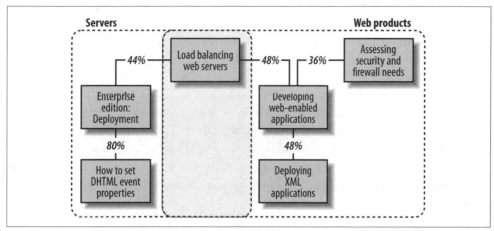

Figure 10-11. A hand-crafted affinity model

When used wisely, affinity models can inform the brainstorming process and are use-ful for presenting research results and defending strategic decisions. However, it's important to avoid masking qualitative research with quantitative analysis. If you conducted only five user tests, the numbers may not be statistically meaningful. So although card sorts produce very seductive data sets, we've found them most useful for the qualitatively derived insights they provide.

User Testing

User testing goes by many names, including usability engineering and information-needs analysis. Whatever you call it, user testing is fairly straightforward. As usability expert Steve Krug of Advanced Common Sense likes to say, "It's not rocket surgery."

In basic user testing, you ask a user to sit in front of a computer, open a web browser, and try to find information or complete a task using the site you're study-ing. Allowing roughly three minutes per task, ask the user to talk out loud while he's navigating. Take good notes, making sure to capture what he says and where he goes. You may want to count clicks and bring a stopwatch to time each session.

Once again, there are endless ways to structure this research. You may want to cap-ture the session on audio or video, or use specialized software to track users' click-streams. You might use the existing site, a high-fidelity web-based prototype, or even a low-fidelity paper prototype. You can ask the user to only browse or only search.

Whenever possible, include a range of audience types. It's particularly important to mix people who are familiar and unfamiliar with the web site; experts and novices typically demonstrate very different behavior. Another important element is choosing the right tasks. These need to be clearly defined by your research agenda. If you're in an exploratory phase, consider distributing your tasks along the following lines:

Easy to impossible
> It's often good to begin with an easy task to make the user feel confident and comfortable. Later, include some difficult or impossible tasks to see how the site performs under duress.

Known-item to exhaustive
> Ask users to find a specific answer or item (e.g., customer support phone number). Also, ask them to find everything they can on a particular topic.

Topic to task
> Ask some topical or subject-oriented questions (e.g., find something on micro-electronics). Also, give them some tasks to complete (e.g., purchase a cell phone).

Artificial to real
> Although most of your tasks will be artificial, try to build in some realistic scenarios. Rather than saying "find printer X," provide a problem statement. For example, "You're starting a home business and have decided to purchase a printer." Encourage the user to role-play. Perhaps she will visit other web sites, searching for third-party reviews of this printer. Maybe she'll decide to buy a fax machine and a copier as well.

As with content analysis, you'll also want to spread these tasks across multiple areas and levels of the web site.

User testing typically provides a rich data set for analysis. You'll learn a great deal just by watching and listening. Obvious metrics include "number of clicks" and "time to find." These can be useful in before-and-after comparisons, hopefully to show how much you improved the site in your latest redesign. You'll also want to track common mistakes that lead users down the wrong paths.

If you're a red-blooded information architect, you'll find these user tests highly energizing. There are few things more motivating to a user-sensitive professional than watching real people struggle and suffer with an existing site. You see the pain, you see what doesn't work, and you inevitably start creating all sorts of better solutions in your head. Don't ignore these great ideas. Don't convince yourself that creativity belongs only in the strategy phase. Strike while the iron's hot. Jot down the ideas during the research sessions, talk with your colleagues and clients between sessions, and expand on the ideas as soon as you get a spare minute. You'll find these notes and discussions hugely valuable as you move into the strategy phase.

In Defense of Research

The design or redesign of any complex web site should begin with research leading to the formation of an information architecture strategy. Through research, we aim to learn enough about the business goals, the users, and the information ecology to develop a solid strategy. By creating, presenting, and refining this strategy, we can work toward consensus on the direction and scope of the site's structure and organization.

This strategy will then serve as the roadmap for all subsequent design and implementation work. It will not only drive the information architecture process, but also guide the work of graphic designers, content authors, and programmers. While each of these teams will take different paths, the information architecture strategy ensures that everyone is headed toward a common destination.

Sometimes these are separate phases. Sometimes they are combined into a joint research and strategy phase. Either way, it's important to have the same team of people involved in performing the research and developing the strategy. In cases where these are done separately, the research team tends to lack direction and focus, seeking answers that are interesting but not necessarily actionable, while the strategy team lacks the richness of direct interaction with users, opinion leaders, and content. Only a small percentage of the hands-on learning can be conveyed through formal presentations and reports.

What happens if you don't make the time for research? There's no need to hazard a guess to this question—we've seen firsthand the very messy results of uncoordinated web development projects. On one occasion, we were brought into a large-scale e-commerce project in midstream. The client had chosen to skip the research and strategy phases because they wanted to "move fast." Graphic designers had created beautiful page templates; content authors had restructured and indexed large numbers of articles; the technical team had selected and purchased a content management system. None of these components worked together. There was no shared vision for how to connect users and content. In fact, nobody could even agree on the primary goals of the web site. The project entered what one participant eloquently called a "death spiral," as each team tried to convince the others that its vision was the right one. The client eventually pulled the plug, deciding it would be more efficient to start over rather than try to salvage the incompatible and fairly misguided efforts of each team.

Unfortunately, this scenario is not uncommon. In today's fast-paced world, everyone's looking for a shortcut. It can be very difficult to convince people, particularly senior managers with little hands-on web experience, of the importance of taking the time to do research and develop a solid strategy. If you're struggling with this problem, the next section might help.

Overcoming Research Resistance

In many corporate settings, mentioning the word *research* gets immediate resistance. Three common arguments include:

1. We don't have the time or money.

2. We already know what we want.

3. We've already done research.

There are good reasons behind these arguments. Everyone operates under time and budget constraints. Everyone has opinions (sometimes good ones) about what's working and how to fix what's not. And for all but the newest projects, some level of prior research that applies to the current situation has already been done. Fearing the perils of analysis paralysis, business managers tend to be very action-oriented. "Let's skip the research and get started with the real work" is a familiar sentiment.

However, for any major design or redesign project, the information architect must find a way to communicate the importance of conducting information architecture research. Without this careful investigation and experimentation aimed at the discovery of facts, you'll find yourself basing your strategy on the unstable foundation of biased opinion and faulty assumption. Let's review the common arguments for conducting information architecture research.

You're likely to save time and money by doing research

The propensity to skip research and dive into design is often the project manager's version of the paradox of the active user.* The immediate perception of progress feels good but often comes at the expense of overall efficiency and effectiveness. Since the information architecture forms the foundation of the entire web site, mistakes made here will have a tremendous ripple effect.

Our experience (summarized in Figure 10-12) constantly reinforces the idea that by spending the necessary time on research, you'll often shorten the design and implementation phases so much (by avoiding lots of arguments and redesign along the way) that you actually shorten the overall project.

However, the biggest savings will come from the fact that your site will actually work, and you won't have to completely redesign it six months later.

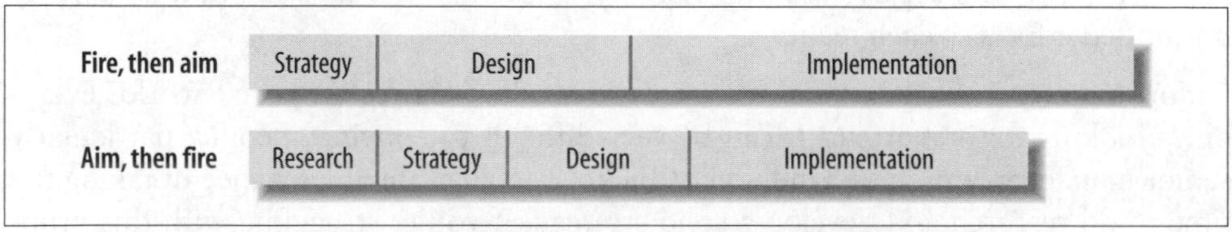

Fire, then aim	Strategy	Design	Implementation
Aim, then fire	Research	Strategy	Design	Implementation

Figure 10-12. The paradox of the active manager

---

* Users choose the illusion of speed over real efficiency. This explains why people repeatedly enter keywords into search engines despite bad results. Browsing feels slower.

Managers don't know what your users want

Most information architects have "gotten the religion" when it comes to recognizing the importance of user-centered design. Many business managers have not. They confuse what they want, what their bosses want, and what they think users want with *what users actually want*. The best way to convert these non-believers is to involve them in some user testing. There's no substitute for the humbling experience of watching regular people try to navigate your site.

We need to do information architecture research

Information architects need to ask unique questions in unique ways. Market-research studies and general-purpose usability tests may provide useful data, but they're not enough. Also, you want the same people involved in both testing and design. Throwing old research reports over the wall has limited value.

These battles to defend research are part of the broader war to defend the value of information architecture. To further fortify your defenses, see Chapters 17–19.

CHAPTER 11
Strategy

What we'll cover:

- The elements of an information architecture strategy
- Guidelines for moving from research to strategy
- Using metaphors, scenarios, and conceptual diagrams to bring your strategy to life
- Project plans, presentations, and the strategy report (including a detailed example from Weather.com)

Research can be addictive: the more you learn, the more questions you have. This is why doctoral students sometimes take more than a decade to complete their dissertations. Information architects rarely have that luxury. We typically need to move from research to design according to schedules measured in weeks or months rather than years.

The bridge between research and design is an information architecture strategy. It's critical that you start thinking about how you're going to build that bridge before research begins, and keep thinking about it throughout the research process. Similarly, as you're building the bridge, you need to continue your research efforts—continually testing and refining your assumptions.

In short, the line between research and strategy is blurred. It's not as simple as turning the page from Chapter 10 to Chapter 11. Though the process of moving from research to administration is linear at a high level, as shown in Figure 11-1 (also featured in the previous chapter), when you get down into the details this is a highly iterative, interactive process.

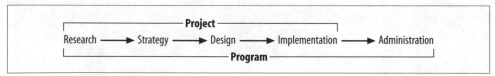

Figure 11-1. The process of information architecture development

The information architect must repeatedly switch back and forth, wearing both the researcher's hat and the strategist's hat against the backdrop of a budget and schedule. Oh, did we mention there's some stress involved? There's no question that this is hard work, but it can be fun and rewarding, too.

What Is an Information Architecture Strategy?

An information architecture strategy is a high-level conceptual framework for structuring and organizing a web site or intranet. It provides the firm sense of direction and scope necessary to proceed with confidence into the design and implementation phases. It also facilitates discussion and helps get people on the same page before moving into the more expensive design phase. Just as the operating plans of each department should be driven by a unifying business strategy, the design of a detailed information architecture should be driven by a holistic information architecture strategy.

To succeed, we need a solution that will work within the unique information ecology at hand. Based upon the results of our research into context, users, and content, we're striving to design a strategy that balances the needs and realities of each.

The information architecture strategy provides high-level recommendations regarding:

Information architecture administration
> It's critical to look ahead to the end game and create a realistic strategy for developing and maintaining the information architecture. This covers the inevitable centralization versus decentralization questions that are closely tied to politics, the departmental structure, and content ownership. Are you looking at a command-and-control model or a federated approach? Will your architecture deliver users to subsites or all the way through to content and applications? Can we trust content authors to apply metadata? Who will manage the controlled vocabularies?

Technology integration
> The strategy must address opportunities to leverage existing tools and identify needs for additional technologies to develop or manage the information architecture. Key technology categories include search engines, content management, auto-classification, collaborative filtering, and personalization.

Top-down or bottom-up emphasis
> Many factors influence where to focus your energies, including the current status of the site, the political environment, and the IA management model. For example, if there's already a solid top-down information architecture or a strong interaction design team that "owns" the primary hierarchy, bottom-up is probably the way to go.

Organization and labeling systems (top-down)
> This involves defining the major organization schemes for the site (e.g., users must be able to navigate by product, by task, and by customer category) and then identifying the dominant organization scheme to serve as the primary hierarchy.

Document type identification (bottom-up)
> This involves identifying a suite of document and object types (e.g., article, report, white paper, financial calculator, online course module) and requires close collaboration with the content authoring and management teams.

Metadata field definition
> This entails the definition of administrative, structural, and descriptive metadata fields. Some fields may be global (i.e., applied to every document), others may be local (i.e., applied only to documents within a particular subsite), and others may be associated only with a particular document type (e.g., for every news article, we need to identify the headline).

Navigation system design
> The strategy must explain how the integrated and supplemental navigation systems will leverage the top-down and bottom-up strategies. For example, search zones may allow users to leverage the top-down product hierarchy, while fielded searching may allow users to search for a particular white paper. This may also cover implications for customization and personalization capabilities.

While this may seem like a lot to cover, it's certainly not an exhaustive list. Each information ecology will place unique demands on the architect regarding what to include in the strategy and where to place emphasis. As always, you'll have to be creative and use good judgment.

The strategy is typically detailed in an information architecture strategy report, communicated in a high-level strategy presentation, and made actionable through a project plan for information architecture design. However, it's important to avoid placing too much focus on creating the perfect deliverables. Ultimately, an information architecture strategy must find understanding and acceptance within the minds of the designers, developers, authors, stakeholders, and anyone else involved in designing, building, and maintaining the site. Getting people to buy into your vision is critical to success.

Strategies Under Attack

While we're on the topic of buy-in, it's worth discussing some critical issues that crop up again and again when developing information architecture strategies. It's not unusual for a hostile stakeholder within a client's organization to ask the following questions during an interview:

- How can you develop an information architecture when we don't have a business strategy?
- How can you develop an information architecture before we have the content in place?

These questions can stop the inexperienced information architect in his tracks, especially when they're asked by a Chief Information Officer or a Vice President for Business Strategy within a Fortune 500 corporation. It's at times like that when you wish you'd read one of those books on how to deal with difficult people or how to disappear into thin air.

Fortunately, the lack of a written business plan or a complete content repository does not mean you need to fold up your blueprints and go home. In all our years of consulting for Fortune 500 clients, we've never seen a business plan that was complete or up to date, and we've never seen a content collection that wouldn't undergo significant change within a twelve-month period.

The reality is that you're dealing with a classic chicken-and-egg problem. There are no clean answers to the questions:

- What comes first, the business strategy or the information architecture?
- What comes first, the content or the information architecture?

Business strategies, content collections, and information architectures don't exist in a vacuum, and they don't hatch from the egg fully formed. They co-evolve in a highly interactive manner.

Developing an information architecture strategy is a wonderful way to expose gaps in business strategies and content collections. The process forces people to make difficult choices that they've thus far managed to avoid. Seemingly simple questions about organization and labeling issues can often set off a ripple effect that impacts business strategy or content policy. For example:

Innocent question posed by information architect:
"In trying to design the hierarchy for this Consumers Energy web site, I'm having a really hard time creating a structure that accommodates the content of Consumers Energy and its parent company, CMS Energy. Are you sure we shouldn't provide two different hierarchies and separate the content?"

Long-term implication of asking this question:
This simple question started a discussion that led to a business decision to build two separate web sites, providing a unique online identity and unique content collections for the two organizations:

> *http://www.consumersenergy.com/*
> *http://www.cmsenergy.com/*

This decision has held up for more than 10 years. Go ahead and check the URLs.

There's a similar bidirectional relationship between business strategy and content policy. For example, a colleague of ours was involved in the information architecture design of the Australian Yellow Pages. The business strategy was focused on increasing revenues by introducing banner advertising. It soon became obvious that the content policy was a key factor in executing this strategy, and the strategy ultimately led to real success.

Ideally, the information architect should work directly with the business strategy and content policy teams, exploring and defining the relationships between these three critical areas. Just as the business strategists and content managers should be open to the possibility that the development of an information architecture strategy may expose gaps or introduce new opportunities in their areas, the information architect needs to remember (and remind others) that the information architecture strategy is not set in stone either. As interaction designers and programmers become involved in later phases of the project, their work may expose gaps and introduce opportunities for improving the information architecture as well.

From Research to Strategy

A good information architect starts considering possible strategies for structuring and organizing the site before the research even begins. During the research phase, throughout the user interviews and content analysis and benchmarking studies, you should be constantly testing and refining the hypotheses already in your head against the steady stream of data you're compiling. If you're really committed (or ready to be committed, depending on how you look at it), you'll be wrestling with organization structures and labeling schemes in the shower. By the way, that's a great place for a whiteboard!

In any case, you should never wait until the strategy phase to start thinking and talking within your team about strategy. That's a given. The more difficult timing issue involves deciding when to begin articulating, communicating, and testing your ideas about possible strategies. When do you create your first conceptual blueprints and wireframes? When do you share them with clients? When do you test your assumptions in user interviews?

As usual, there's no easy answer. The research phase exists to challenge your (and everyone else's) preconceived notions regarding content, context, and users. You need a structured methodology in place to create the necessary space for learning. However, you'll reach a point in the research process when you begin to experience the law of diminishing returns. You're no longer learning anything new by asking the same questions in open-ended user interviews, and you're anxious to flesh out one or two hierarchies and start introducing your structures and labels to users, clients, and colleagues.

Whether or not the timing corresponds with the formal project plan, this is the point when you move from research to strategy. The emphasis shifts from open-ended learning to designing and testing. While you can continue to use research methodologies as you move through this phase, your focus should shift to articulating your ideas through visuals (conceptual blueprints and wireframes), sharing those visuals with clients and colleagues in strategy meetings, and testing your organization structures and labeling schemes with users.

Developing the Strategy

The transition from research to strategy involves a shift from a primary focus on process to a balance between process and product. Methodology is still important, but the work products and deliverables you create by applying that methodology move toward the center of attention.

Moving from a mode of absorption to one of creation is often a difficult transition for the information architect. No matter how much qualitative or quantitative research you've done, the development of an information architecture strategy is inherently a creative process, with all the associated messiness, frustration, pain, and fun.

Figure 11-2 presents an outline of the strategy development process and the resulting deliverables. Note the preponderance of arrows. This is a highly iterative and interactive process. Let's take a look at the four steps along the path: think, articulate, communicate, and test (TACT).

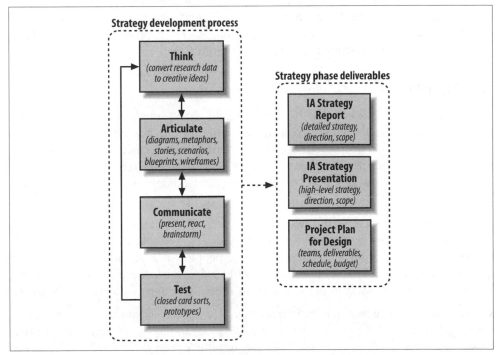

Figure 11-2. Developing the information architecture strategy with TACT

Think

The human mind is the ultimate black box. Nobody really understands the process by which input (e.g., research data) is converted into output (e.g., creative ideas). Our advice is to use whatever works best for you. Some people think best by themselves, while taking a long walk or doodling on a pad of paper. Others think best in a group setting. The key is to recognize that you need to create some time and space to digest all that you've learned during research and become ready to be productive.

Articulate

As your ideas begin to form, it's important to begin articulating them. It's best to start informally, scribbling diagrams and notes on paper or whiteboard. Stay away from visual design software at this point; otherwise, you'll waste energy on layout and formatting when you should be focused on developing your ideas.

Once again, some people work best alone whereas others need a sounding board. We've seen teams of two or three information architects work well together to flesh out ideas, collaborating around design of high-level visuals on a whiteboard. We've also seen environments where teams of eight or more people from a variety of backgrounds lock themselves in a room for day-long "collaborative design workshops." In our experience, these have been highly inefficient, unproductive exercises that lead to groupthink and exhaustion. Large group meetings may be good for brainstorming and sharing reactions, but not for designing complex systems.

Communicate

Eventually, you'll make the shift from creating ideas to communicating them. You'll need to identify the most effective ways to communicate these particular ideas to your target audience. Your architect's toolbox may include metaphors, stories, use case scenarios, conceptual diagrams, blueprints, wireframes, reports, and presentations. Let form follow function, selecting the right communication tools for your purpose.

It's often best to begin with informal communications with "safe" colleagues who will help you refine your ideas and build your confidence. You can then share your draft work products with "unsafe" colleagues, those people you can count on to ask hard questions and poke holes. This process should help you to develop your ideas and confidence so you're ready to present them to a broader group of clients or colleagues.

We've learned through much experience that it's good to communicate your ideas early and often. Many of us have a natural aversion to sharing partially formed ideas—our egos don't like the risk. One way to reduce your own sense of exposure is to suggest that this is a "strawman" work product, intended to provoke reactions and jump-start discussion. This explicit disclaimer will help everyone feel comfortable presenting and discussing alternate viewpoints and hopefully moving toward consensus. By proactively taking this collaborative approach, you'll end up with a better information architecture strategy and more buy-in from your clients and colleagues.

Test

Whether you're operating on a shoestring budget or have a multimillion-dollar project, there's no excuse for not testing your ideas before you lock into an information architecture strategy. Even running an informal usability test on your mom is better than nothing.

Many of the methodologies covered during the research phase can be applied with minor modification to the testing of possible strategies. For example, you might present your draft work products to a few opinion leaders and stakeholders to make sure you're on the right track in terms of business context. Similarly, you might test your model against documents and applications not included in the content analysis sample to make sure your strategy will accommodate the full breadth and depth of content. However, we've found the most valuable methods for testing at this stage of the game to be variations of card sorting and task performance analysis.

Closed card sorting provides a great way to observe user reactions to your high-level organization and labeling schemes. Create "category cards" for each of your high-level categories, using your recommended category labels. Then select a few items that belong in each of those categories. You may want to run this exercise a few times with items at differing levels of granularity (e.g., second-level category labels, destination documents and applications). Jumble up the cards and ask users to sort them into the appropriate categories. As users perform this exercise and think out loud, you'll get a sense of whether your categories and labels are working for them.

Task performance analysis is also a useful approach. Rather than testing users' abilities to navigate the existing web site as you did during research, you can now create paper or HTML prototypes for users to navigate. Designing these prototype tests can be tricky; you need to think carefully about what you want to test and how you can construct the test to yield trustworthy results.

At one end of the spectrum, you may want to isolate the high-level information architecture (e.g., categories, labels) from the interface components (e.g., graphic design, layout). You can get close to this ideal of testing the pure information architecture by presenting users with hierarchical menus and asking them to find some content or perform a task. For example, you could ask the user to find the current stock price of Cisco by navigating the following series of hierarchies:

> Arts & Humanities
> Business & Economy
> Computers & Internet

Of course, it's impossible to completely escape interface design implications. Simply deciding how to order these categories (e.g., alphabetical, by importance, or by popularity) will impact the results. More significantly, when presenting hierarchies, you need to make an interface decision regarding the presentation of sample second-level categories. Research shows that the presentation of second-level categories can substantially increase users' abilities to understand the contents of a major category. By adding second-level categories, you can increase the "scent" of information:[*]

Arts & Humanities
> Literature, Photography, etc.

Business & Economy
> B2B, Finance, Shopping, Jobs, etc.

Computers & Internet
> Internet, WWW, Software, Games, etc.

Advantages of these stripped-down information architecture prototype tests include:

- Very little work is necessary to build the prototypes.
- The tests ensure that users focus primarily on information architecture and navigation rather than interface.

Disadvantages include:

- The danger of thinking you've isolated information architecture from interface when you really haven't.
- You miss the opportunity to see how the interface might alter the users' experience of the information architecture.

At the other end of the spectrum is the fully designed, web-based prototype. In most situations, this testing occurs later in the process. Developing these prototypes requires a great deal of work, some of it involving interface designers and software developers. Additionally, the tests themselves introduce so many variables that you often lose the ability to learn about user reactions to the information architecture.

We often run a combination of tests, some aimed at isolating pure hierarchy and some that use simple wireframes. Wireframes are not fully designed prototypes, but they do allow us to see how users interact with the information architecture when it's embedded within the broader context of a web page, as illustrated in Figure 11-3.

Ideally, these tests will validate the information architecture strategy that you've developed. Realistically, they will help you to identity problems with your strategy and provide some insight into refining that strategy.

---

[*] The notion of *information scent* comes from an information-foraging theory developed at Xerox PARC.

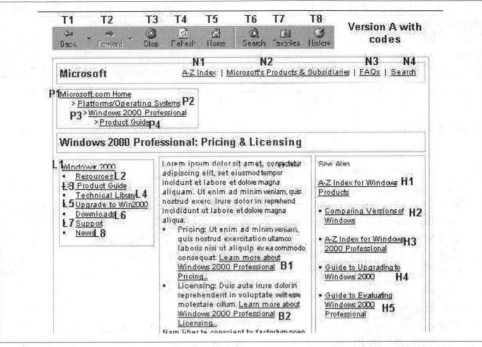

Figure 11-3. Sample wireframe with codes for tracking user choices during paper prototype testing

Remember that strategy development should be an iterative process. Within the parameters of budget and schedule, the more you can move from "think" to "articulate" to "communicate" to "test" and back again, the more confident you'll be that your information architecture strategy is on the right track.

Work Products and Deliverables

Throughout this chapter, we've referred to a variety of work products and deliverables (e.g., sample architectures, organizational schemas, and labeling systems) that may prove useful in communicating an information architecture strategy. Let's explore the advantages, disadvantages, and proper uses of a few.

Metaphor Exploration

Metaphor is a powerful tool for communicating complex ideas and generating enthusiasm. By suggesting creative relationships or mapping the familiar onto the new, metaphor can be used to explain, excite, and persuade.* In 1992, vice-presidential

---

* For more about the use of metaphor, read the book *Metaphors We Live By* by George Lakoff and Mark Johnson (University of Chicago Press).

candidate Al Gore popularized the term "information superhighway."[*] This term mapped the familiar metaphor of the physical highway infrastructure of the United States onto the new and unfamiliar concept of a national information infrastructure. Gore used this metaphor to excite the voters about his vision for the future. Although the term is oversimplified and has since been horribly overused, it did inspire people to learn about and discuss the importance and direction of the global Internet.

Many types of metaphors can be applied in the design of web sites. Let's look at three of the most important ones.

Organizational metaphors

These leverage familiarity with one system's organization to convey quick understanding of a new system's organization. For example, when you visit an automobile dealership, you must choose to enter new car sales, used car sales, repairs and services, or parts and supplies. People have a mental model of how dealerships are organized. If you're creating a web site for an automobile dealership, it may make sense to employ an organizational metaphor that draws from this model.

Functional metaphors

These make a connection between the tasks you can perform in a traditional environment and those you can perform in the new environment. For example, when you enter a traditional library, you can browse the shelves, search the catalog, or ask a librarian for help. Many library web sites present these tasks as options for users, thereby employing a functional metaphor.

Visual metaphors

These leverage familiar graphic elements such as images, icons, and colors to create a connection to the new elements. For example, an online directory of business addresses and phone numbers might use a yellow background and telephone icons to invoke a connection with the more familiar print-based yellow pages.

The process of metaphor exploration can really get the creative juices flowing. Working with your clients or colleagues, begin to brainstorm ideas for metaphors that might apply to your project. Think about how those metaphors might apply in organizational, functional, and visual ways. How would you organize a virtual bookstore, library, or museum? Is your site more like one of these things? What are the differences? What tasks should users be able to perform? What should the site look like? You and your colleagues should really cut loose and have fun with this exercise. You'll be surprised by the brilliant ideas you come up with.

---

[*] "The information superhighway metaphor goes back to at least 1988, when Robert Kahn proposed building a high-speed national computer network he often likened to the interstate highway system." *Internet Dreams*, Mark Stefik (MIT Press).

After this brainstorming session, you'll want to subject everyone's ideas to a more critical review. Start populating the rough metaphor-based architecture with random items from the expected content to see if they fit. Try one or two user scenarios to see if the metaphor holds up. While metaphor exploration is a useful process, you should not feel obligated to carry all or any of the ideas forward into the information architecture. The reality is that metaphors are great for getting ideas flowing during the conceptual design process, but can be problematic when carried forward to the site itself.

For example, the metaphor of a virtual community is one that has been taken too far in many cases. Some of these online communities have post offices, town halls, shopping centers, libraries, schools, and police stations. It becomes a real challenge for the user to figure out what types of activities take place in which "buildings." In such cases, the metaphor gets in the way of usability. As an architect, you should try to ensure that any use of metaphor is empowering, not limiting.

When first launched, the Internet Public Library (Figure 11-4) used visual and organizational metaphors to provide access to the reference area. Users could browse the shelves or ask a question. However, the traditional library metaphor did not support integration of such things as a multiuser object-oriented environment ("MOO"), and eventually the entire site was redesigned. Applied in such a strong way, metaphors can quickly become limiting factors in site architecture and design.

Also realize that people tend to fall in love with their own metaphors. Make sure everyone knows that this is just an exercise, and that it will rarely make sense to carry the metaphor into the information architecture design. For a lively discussion of the dangers of metaphor, see the section entitled "The Myth of Metaphor" in Alan Cooper's book, *About Face: The Essentials of User Interface Design* (Wiley).

Scenarios

While architecture blueprints are excellent tools for capturing an approach to information organization in a detailed and structured way, they do not tend to excite people. As an architect who wants to convince your colleagues of the wisdom of your approach, you need to help them "envision" the site as you see it in your mind's eye. Scenarios are great tools for helping people to understand how the user will navigate and experience the site you design,* and may also help you generate new ideas for the architecture and navigation system.

To provide a multidimensional experience that shows the true potential for the site, it is best to write a few scenarios that show how people with different needs and behaviors might navigate your site. Your user research is obviously an invaluable source of input for this process. Make sure you really take the time to wallow in the data before beginning to ask and answer these questions.

---

* For a more formal methodology, you may want to learn about use cases and use case scenarios (*http://www.usecases.org/*).

Figure 11-4. Metaphor use in the main page of the Internet Public Library

Who are the people using your site? Why and how will they want to use it? Will they be in a rush or will they want to explore? Try to select three or four major user "types" who will use the site in very different ways. Create a character who represents each type, giving him a name, a profession, and a reason for visiting your site. Then begin to flesh out a sample session in which that person uses your site, highlighting the best features of the site through your scenario. If you've designed for a new customization feature, show how someone would use it.

This is a great opportunity to be creative. You'll probably find these scenarios to be easy and fun to write. And hopefully, they'll help convince your colleagues to invest in your ideas.

Sample scenario

Let's now look at a brief sample scenario. Rosalind, a 10th grader in San Francisco, regularly visits the LiveFun web site because she enjoys the interactive learning experience. She uses the site in both "investigative mode" and "serendipity mode."

For example, when her anatomy class was studying skeletal structure, she used the investigative mode to search for resources about the skeleton. She found the "interactive human skeleton" that let her test her knowledge of the correct names and functions of each bone. She bookmarked this page so she could return for a refresher the night before final exams.

When she's done with homework, Rosalind sometimes "surfs" through the site in serendipity mode. Her interest in poisonous snakes leads her to articles about how certain types of venom affect the human nervous system. One of these articles leads her into an interactive game that teaches her about other chemicals (such as alcohol) that are able to cross the blood-brain barrier. This game piques her interest in chemistry, and she switches into investigative mode to learn more.

 This simple scenario shows why and how users may employ both searching and browsing within the web site. More complex scenarios can be used to flesh out the possible needs of users from multiple audiences.

Case Studies and Stories

It's not easy to take a complex, abstract subject like information architecture and make it accessible to a diverse audience. When you're communicating with other information architects, you can cut right to the chase, using a technical vocabulary that assumes familiarity and understanding. But when you're talking with a broader audience of clients and colleagues, you may need to be more creative in your communication approach in order to engage their interest and facilitate their understanding.

Case studies and stories (such as the ones featured in Chapters 20 and 21) can be a wonderful way to bring the concepts of information architecture to life. When trying to explain a recommended information architecture strategy, we find it very helpful to compare and contrast this case with past experiences, discussing what did and didn't work on past projects.

Conceptual Diagrams

Pictures are another way to bring abstract concepts to life. As an information architect, you often have to explain high-level concepts and systems that go beyond organization and labeling schemes.

For example, we often find ourselves needing to paint a picture of the broader information ecology within a business. When we work with an intranet team, it's not uncommon to find that they've succumbed over time to tunnel vision, seeing the intranet as the sole source of information for employees. You can tell them that this isn't true, but this really is a case where a picture is worth a thousand words.

The conceptual diagram in Figure 11-5 places the employee, rather than the intranet, at the center of the universe. The sizes of the "information clouds" roughly correspond to the importance of each resource as explained by employees during a series of user interviews. This diagram shows that people view personal networks and colleagues as the most important information resources, and see the current intranet as having relatively little value in their work lives. The diagram also presents a fragmented information environment, in which artificial boundaries of technology (media and format) or geography exist between pools of information. While it's possible to explain all of this verbally, we've found this type of visual to have a significant and lasting impact. It really gets the point across.

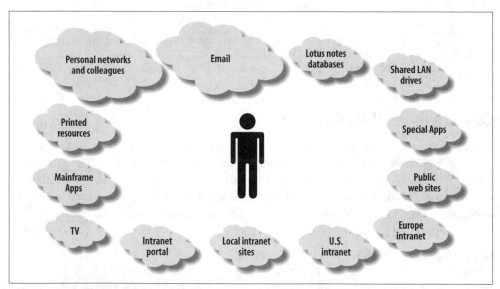

Figure 11-5. A conceptual diagram of how employees view the company's information ecology

Blueprints and Wireframes

The collaborative brainstorming process is exciting, chaotic, and fun. However, sooner or later, you must hole up away from the crowd and begin to transform this chaos into order. Blueprints (which show the relationships between pages and other content components) and wireframes (quick-and-dirty visuals that show the content and links of major pages on the web site) are the architect's tools of choice for performing this transformation. We discuss blueprints and wireframes in much greater detail in Chapter 12.

The Strategy Report

In our experience, this deliverable serves as the catalyst for the most detailed, comprehensive articulation of the information architecture strategy. The process of integrating the previous results, analysis, and ideas into a single written document forces tough decisions, intellectual honesty, and clear communication. Great ideas that don't fit within the broader framework must be discarded in the name of consistency and cohesiveness. Big, vague ideas must be broken down into components and explained so that all involved can understand their intention and implications.

For the information architecture team, the strategy report is often the largest, hardest, and most important deliverable. It forces the team members to come together around a unified vision for the information architecture, and requires them to find ways to explain or illustrate that vision so that clients and colleagues (i.e., people who are not information architects) will understand what the heck they're talking about.

One of the hardest things about writing the report is organizing it. Here you face yet another chicken-and-egg problem. An information architecture strategy is not linear, but a report forces a linear presentation. "How will they understand this section if they haven't read that later section?" is a common question. There's rarely a perfect solution, but the problem can be dealt with in a couple of ways. First of all, by including high-level visuals in the report, you can paint a nonlinear big picture and follow up with linear textual explanations. Second, remember that a strategy report cannot and should not stand completely alone. You should always have an opportunity to verbally explain your ideas and answer questions. Ideally, you'll have a face-to-face information architecture strategy presentation; at a minimum, you should have a conference call to discuss reactions and answer questions.

The only thing harder and more abstract than writing an information architecture strategy report is trying to write about how to write one. To bring this subject to life, let's examine a real strategy report that Argus created for the Weather Channel (*http://www.weather.com/*) in 1999.

A Sample Strategy Report

The Weather.com web site is a component of the broader Weather Channel family of services (including cable television, data and phone, radio and newspaper, and the Internet) that has provided timely weather information to the world since 1982. The Weather Channel web site is one of the most popular sites in the world, and features current conditions and forecasts for over 1,700 cities worldwide along with local and regional radars.

In 1999, the Weather Channel contracted Argus Associates to conduct research and recommend a strategy for improving the information architecture of Weather.com. Let's take a look at the table of contents of the final strategy report for this engagement (Figure 11-6).

Table of Contents

Executive Summary 1
Audiences & Mission/Vision for the Site 2
Lessons Learned from Benchmarking, User Interviews and Content Analysis 3
- Local Weather Organization and Content 3
- General Organization and Content 4
- Navigation 5
- Labeling 5
- Features 6

Architectural Strategies & Approaches 7
- Local Hub Architectural Strategy 8
  - Geographic Hub Architectural Strategy 10
  - Mockups of Content Areas 12
  - Customization & Personalization Strategy 21
  - Navigation Elements 25
- Distributed Content Architectural Strategy 26

Content Management 31

Figure 11-6. Table of contents for the Weather.com strategy report

This table of contents should provide a rough sense of the size and scope of the strategy report. While some of our reports (including blueprints and wireframes) have been more than 100 pages, we encourage our teams to strive for fewer than 50. If it gets much longer than that, you run the risk that nobody will have the time or inclination to read it. The major sections of this report are fairly typical. Let's take a look at each one in turn.

Executive summary

The executive summary (Figure 11-7) should provide a high-level outline of the goals and methodology, and present a 50,000-foot view of the major problems and major recommendations. The executive summary sets a tone for the entire document and should be written very carefully. It's helpful to think of this as the one page of the whole report that will be read by the big boss. You need to consider the political message you're sending, and generate enough interest to get people to continue reading.

The executive summary in Figure 11-7 does a nice job of accomplishing its objectives within one page. We were able to take such an upbeat tone because the Weather.com team was already well organized and had a fairly solid information architecture in place. This executive summary places an emphasis on recommendations for improving the information architecture to achieve greater competitive advantage.

Audiences, mission, and vision for the site

It's important to define the audiences and goals of the site to make sure that the report (and the reader) is grounded by the broader context. This is a good place to restate the mission statement for the web site.

Executive Summary

Weather.com contracted with Argus Associates, Inc. ("Argus") to develop recommendations for two top-level site architectural strategies, based on research on their audiences, competitors, content and an understanding of the company's strategic focus. Argus conducted user interviews, and performed benchmarking and content analysis to develop strategic recommendations for the site architecture.

The current Weather.com site garners huge numbers of hits and is the most recognized weather Web site on the Internet. The existing content on the site is attempting to please all audiences – those who want local weather, those who want to understand the weather, and those who only want weather information when it is convenient to get it. Although there is a great deal of valuable proprietary content, in addition to detailed weather data, it is essentially impossible to organize <u>all</u> of it in one site to fulfill the needs of <u>all</u> the audiences.

Consequently, our strategic recommendations are bi-fold:

- Develop a solid architecture that attracts and keeps users interested in accessing local weather and weather-related information, as well as providing a niche for users who want to understand more about the weather.

- Develop and promote Weather.com content for distribution to a wide variety of external sources including portals, software and hardware applications and specialized audiences. This will attract users who don't want to do much work to access the weather – convenience users – as well as users who are only interested in specific weather-related topics, e.g., gardening or stargazing.

The recommendations in this report address all 5 of the key focal areas noted as important for development of the Weather.com site:

- Making content more relevant to users – building a local hub architecture that allows users to access their local weather and related weather content from the same place.

- Improving personalization features – providing customization and personalization options that best suit weather users.

- Enhancing localization of the weather data – creating a local hub area that offers the most effective weather data, in an attracting layout.

- Developing customer loyalty – offering opportunities for users to customize weather data and content to suit their needs, distributing content to a wide variety of places outside the site and providing places for users interested in weather to talk to one another.

- Building and enhancing distribution opportunities – growing the user base by distributing Weather.com content via the Internet to a range of external sources.

By using the recommendations in this report to develop viable strategic solutions, Weather.com will be able to help all users find what they need more easily, attract a growing population of users and have these users return to the site. Weather.com is already in the lead of weather Web site development due to its branding and content – now it needs to use these recommendations to increase the narrowing gap between its site and competitor weather sites.

Figure 11-7. Executive summary for Weather.com

The following is the mission statement from the Weather.com strategy report:

Weather.com will be the best weather web site on the Internet. As the dominant brand leader of weather information on the Internet, Weather.com will provide relevant, up-to-the-minute information about the weather to any user. The primary focus of the site is to provide localized weather data and value-added proprietary and exclusive weather and weather-related content, supported by significantly related non-proprietary content. Weather.com will employ technology that effectively leverages personalization and customization of content, and that allows us to meet user demands during extraordinary weather conditions.

This is also a good place to define a vocabulary for discussing the roles of users and the audience segments. Figure 11-8 shows how this was accomplished for the Weather.com report.

Role	Abbreviation	Weather.com Audiences*
Care about weather only when it's convenient	Convenience	Commodity
Care about their city's forecast	My City	Planner: Scheduling, Activities
Care about other cities' forecast	Other Cities	Engaged: Caring, Tracking Planner: Scheduling, Activities
Care about weather anywhere and how it works	Understanding	Engaged: Understanding
* Taken from the Segmentation Study performed by Envision, 1996.		

Figure 11-8. Audiences and roles for Weather.com

Lessons learned

This section forms the bridge between your research and analysis and your recommendations. By showing that your recommendations are grounded in the results of competitive research (benchmarking), user interviews, and content analysis, you will build confidence and credibility.

In the Weather.com report, we organized this section into five subcategories. The following table shows a sample observation from each:

Observation	Conclusion	Implications for site architecture
Local Organization and Content		
Users said they wanted to see their city's weather first. (User Interviews)	Local, local, local.	Access to local weather should be through a prominent search box and browsing via a map or links.
General Organization and Content		
On weather sites, seasonal content is often scattered among several content areas. (Benchmarking)	Ephemeral content does not live in distinct areas that have a place within the site architecture.	Topically related content should live in a discrete, devoted area, even if it is seasonal. This will assist in providing effective content management of all content areas.
Navigation		
Users couldn't decipher where local and global navigation took them within portal sites that contained weather as well as other content. (User Interviews & Benchmarking)	Weather is only a portion of the content, and consequently what would be global navigation on a devoted weather site becomes local, which confuses users.	Weather- and non-weather-related content navigation shouldn't be co-located within the navigation frame.

Observation	Conclusion	Implications for site architecture
Labeling		
Many labels didn't accurately describe the content area underneath. (Benchmarking)	Labels need to describe exactly what is under them.	Use description or scope notes to help clarify a label. Avoid colloquialism and jargon.
Features		
No weather sites are providing effective personalization; in fact, some are doing a very poor job at it. (Benchmarking)	Personalizing using anonymous tracking and content affinity is most effective.	Use Amazon as a benchmark for this. Provide options such as "the top 10 weather stories" or "the top 5 purchases made by users from Michigan." Link these from the local weather pages.

Architectural strategies and approaches

Now we get to the meat of the report—the explanation of the recommended architectural strategies and approaches. This is a fairly extensive section, so we can't include it in its entirety, but we can present and briefly explain a few of the visuals used to illustrate the recommendations.

This report presents two strategies, *local hub* and *distributed content*, which are intended to be used in tandem. The local hub strategy centers on the fact that users are mainly focused on learning about their local weather. The conceptual blueprint in Figure 11-9 presents an information architecture built around this local hub strategy.

This blueprint is fairly difficult to understand without the accompanying text and context, some of which is shown in Figure 11-10. At a high level, it provides for geography-specific access (the local hub), and specifies major content areas and tasks that will ultimately be translated into navigation options on the local hub web page. These conceptual blueprints are followed by a series of wireframes that further illustrate the key points.

For each of the lettered call-outs in the wireframe, we included a textual explanation. The following table shows two examples.

Code	Elements	Description	Implications (from Lessons Learned)
A	City, state, or zip code search box.	Searching for local weather needs to be at the very top of the page. It should be prominent and obvious, or users will ignore it.	Access to local weather should be through a prominent search box and browsing via a map or links.
B	Find local weather (search, map, "breadcrumbs")	Users can click on the "Browse for local weather" link next to the search box, click on the map or the links to the right to access a region, or click on "World" to go up a geographic level. This allows users to navigate to weather at all levels. The map, if provided, cannot detract attention from the search box, which is the main method of access.	[Ditto.]

On the other hand, the distributed content architectural strategy is centered on the fact that there are a wide variety of portals other than Weather.com through which users access weather information. For example, Yahoo! serves as a general portal for many users. Weather information is one component of a wide range of information needs for Yahoo! users.

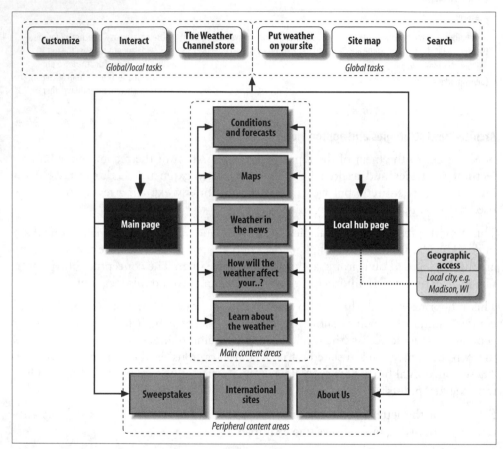

Figure 11-9. A conceptual blueprint for Weather.com

The Weather Channel has partnerships with some of these portals, providing customized access to Weather.com content. The distributed content architectural strategy shown in Figure 11-11 presents a model for how to structure the information architecture for these partnerships.

One of the major goals of this architectural strategy is to get users to return to the place that contains all the content: the Weather.com web site. When distributing content, it's not possible to offer users everything they need, so it's important to provide "teasers" to attract users to the site.

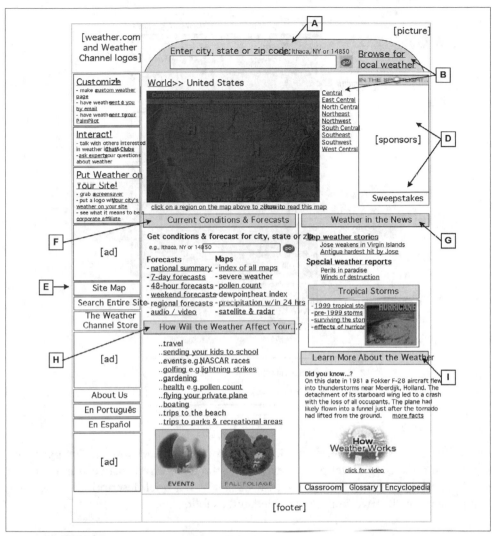

Figure 11-10. The accompanying wireframe for Weather.com

This architectural diagram places emphasis on the rate of return to the Weather.com site. It makes the point that it's more likely that users will come to Weather.com from topical web sites and general portals than from embedded software applications (e.g., a Java-based Miami heat index) or wireless hardware platforms (e.g., a Palm Pilot or cell phone).

Content management

The final section of this report provides a reality check by discussing how these information architecture recommendations will impact the content management infrastructure. Any discussion of content management is very context-sensitive,

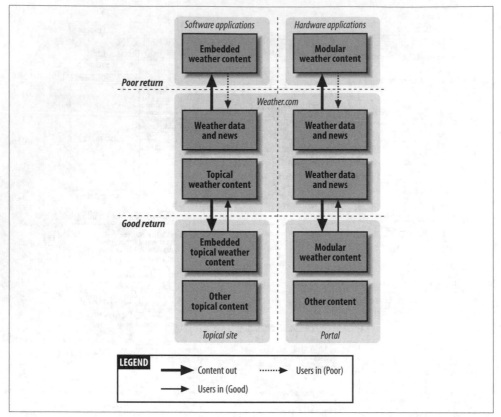

Figure 11-11. A distributed content architecture for Weather.com

depending upon the people, technology, and content in question. In this particular report, we took a high-level pass at explaining the relationship between information architecture and content management. It begins with a brief description of the three components of effective content management, as follows:

Rules

These are the processes whereby the content is managed. Usually these are workflows followed by staff to create, publish, and maintain content on the site. The workflow can be a part of, or external to, any content management software that is purchased or developed. Peripheral process documents include style guidelines and standards.

Roles

These are the staff that perform the content management processes. These people follow the processes and guidelines, as well as help create and maintain them. There may be highly specified roles for people who create metadata, review content, write content, act as a liaison with external content providers, or fix software when it breaks. There may be several people who have the same role, e.g., indexers.

Resources

These include the content itself in its various forms of creation, modification, or deletion, as well as the repository for holding static content and dynamic data. It also includes the management software that makes it easier for the Rules and Roles to be carried out.

We then go on to provide specific recommendations to Weather.com that might lead to more efficient content management. Here are just a few of the recommendations:

Templates

Much of the content that already exists on the site is dynamic data pulled from external sources (e.g., dew point, pollen count, flight arrival times). Data is very well suited for templates—it's simple to build common structured pages that are used over and over for the same type of data. Textual content isn't as easily placed in templates because it is more variable by nature, although it's necessary for some document types (e.g., a news story template). Both static and dynamic content need structured navigation templates, a consistent frame where users can easily see the types of navigation: global, local, and contextual.

Metadata

Descriptive metadata needs to be created to more easily populate the site architecture with relevant content. For instance, for each news story blurb on the "Weather in the News" main page, the following descriptive data should be noted:

Metadata element	Example
author	Terrell Johnson
publisher	Jody Fennell
title	Antigua hardest hit by Jose
date	Thu Oct 21 1999
expiration date	1031999 12:01:23
links	/news/102199/story.htm
document type	news story, glossary term
subject area	tropical storm
keywords	Jose, Antigua, damage, intensity
related to	breaking weather, news stories, severe weather maps
geographic access levels	local city, local regional, national
geographic areas	Antigua, North Carolina, South Carolina

Thesaurus

Building a thesaurus for your metadata helps users find information more easily. For instance, if a user is unsure whether to use the term "tropical storm" or "hurricane," accessing a thesaurus can identify the preferred term. It will be useful to create thesauri for weather terms and geographic areas, as well as one that allows for normalization of the "keyword" metadata field for indexing purposes. Generally, thesauri are built for behind-the-scenes use by staff who are creating the metadata for content chunks (e.g., looking up which term to assign to a chunk), but it is also useful at the searching and browsing stage on the site.

The Project Plan

We often find it useful to go beyond the content management discussion and actually create a project plan for information architecture design as part of the strategy phase deliverables.

This project plan can accomplish two major objectives. First, when developed in parallel with the strategy report, it forces the team to constantly ask questions such as:

- How will we accomplish that?
- How long will it take?
- Who will do it?
- What kinds of deliverables will be required?
- What are the dependencies?

This ensures that information architecture strategy is grounded in reality. The second objective of the project plan is to form the bridge between strategy and design. It can be integrated with plans from other teams (e.g., interaction design, content authoring, or application development) toward the development of a structured schedule for overall site design.

Given the common need to show some immediate progress, we usually provide short-term and long-term plans. In the short-term plan, we focus on low-hanging fruit, defining a process for design changes that can and should be made immediately to improve the information architecture. In the long-term plan, we present a methodology for fleshing out the information architecture, noting interdependencies with other teams where appropriate.

Presentations

You've done rigorous research and brilliant brainstorming. You've created a detailed, high-quality strategy report and a solid project plan. You've worked hard. You've successfully completed the strategy phase, right? Wrong!

We've learned through painful experience that information architecture deliverables can die a quiet death if they're left to fend for themselves. People are busy, have short attention spans, and generally don't enjoy reading 50-page information architecture strategy reports. Without some form of presentation and discussion, many of your best recommendations may never see the light of day.

It's often a good idea to make one or more presentations to the people who need to understand your recommendations. In some situations, this might take the form of a single presentation to the web site or intranet strategy team. In other situations, you make dozens of presentations to various departments to achieve organization-wide understanding and buy-in. You need to think about these presentations from a sales perspective. Success is defined by the extent to which you can communicate and sell your ideas in a clear and compelling manner.

First, make sure you've got the basics down. Select some highlights of your recommendations that will really get the attention of the particular group you're talking to. Then, organize your thoughts into a logical order to create a smooth presentation.

After you've figured all that out, you can consider ways to bring the presentation to life. Visuals such as charts, graphs, and conceptual diagrams can make a big difference, as can the use of metaphor. Remember, you're selling ideas. Metaphor can be a powerful tool for transforming garden-variety ideas into contagious, self-replicating memes.

Consider this example. We were designing an information architecture strategy for the primary web site of a Global 100 corporation. We had developed three possible strategies with the following working titles:

Umbrella Shell for Separate Hubs
> Develop a broad but shallow umbrella web site that directs users to independently maintained subsites or "hubs." Distributed control. Low cost, low usability.

Integrated Content Repository
> Create a unified, structured database for all content, providing powerful, flexible, consistent searching and browsing. Centralized control. High cost, high usability.

Active Inter-Hub Management
> Create standards for global metadata attributes, but allow for local subsite ("hub") attributes as well. Knit together with inter- and intra-hub guides. Federated model. Medium cost, medium usability.

The titles were very descriptive, but they didn't exactly roll off the tongue or stimulate interest. For our presentation, we came up with a musical metaphor that made this complex topic more fun and engaging:

Model	Working title	Description	Comments
Competing boom boxes	Umbrella Shell for Separate Hubs	Whoever has the loudest music wins	The "Status Quo." Works for neither company nor customers.
Symphony	Integrated Content Repository	Many instruments acting as one; a big investment	A "Bet the Farm" approach that carries many risks.
Jazz Band	Active Inter-Hub Management	A common key and beat; good teamwork; combination of tight rhythms and improvisation	Our favorite option. It provides rich functionality with less risk than the Symphony approach.

Not only can this use of metaphor make for a better immediate discussion, but people are more likely to talk about it with colleagues after the presentation itself, spreading your ideas like a virus.

Now, finally, you can congratulate the visionary within you, take a brief rest, and prepare for the detail-orientation of the design and documentation phase.

CHAPTER 12

Design and Documentation

What we'll cover:

- The role of diagrams in the design phase
- Why, when, and how to develop blueprints and wireframes, the two most common types of IA diagrams
- How to map and inventory your site's content
- Content models and controlled vocabularies for connecting and managing granular content within your site
- Ways to enhance your collaboration with other members of the design team
- Style guides for capturing your past decisions and guiding your future ones

When you cross the bridge from research and strategy into design, the landscape shifts quite dramatically. The emphasis moves from process to deliverables, as your clients and colleagues expect you to move from thinking and talking to actually producing a clear, well-defined information architecture.

This can be an uneasy transition. You must relinquish the white lab coat of the researcher, leave behind the ivory tower of the strategist, and forge into the exposed territory of creativity and design. As you commit your ideas to paper, it can be scary to realize there's no going back. You are now actively shaping what will become the user experience. Your fears and discomforts will be diminished if you've had the time and resources to do the research and develop a strategy; if you're pushed straight into design (as is too often the case), you'll be entering the uneasy realm of intuition and gut instinct.

It's difficult to write about design because the work in this phase is so strongly defined by context and influenced by tacit knowledge. You may be working closely with a graphic designer to create a small web site from the ground up. Or you may be building a controlled vocabulary and site index as part of an enterprise-level redesign that involves more than a hundred people. The design decisions you make and the deliverables you produce will be informed by the total sum of your experience.

In short, we're talking about the creative process. The information architect paints on a vast, complex, and ever-changing canvas. Often, the best way to teach art is through the time-tested practice of show-and-tell. So, in this chapter, we'll use work products and deliverables to tell the story about what the information architect does during the design phase.

Before we dive in, here's a caveat. Although this chapter focuses on deliverables, *process* is as important during design as it is during research and strategy. This means that the techniques covered previously should be applied to these later phases, albeit with more concrete and detailed artifacts—ranging from vocabularies to wireframes to working prototypes—being tested.

And another caveat: for reasons beyond your control, you'll occasionally—even frequently—find yourself in the uncomfortable situation of bypassing research and strategy altogether, skipping headlong into the abyss of design. Deliverables are especially critical in this context; they're anchors that, by forcing the team to pause, capture, and review its work, regulate and moderate an out-of-control project. You can also use deliverables to unmask design problems and force the project to backtrack to research and design tasks that should have been handled much earlier.

Guidelines for Diagramming an Information Architecture

Information architects are under extreme pressure to clearly represent the product of their work. Whether it's to help sell the value of information architecture to a potential client or to explain a design to a colleague, information architects rely upon visual representations to communicate what it is they actually do.

And yet information architectures, as we've mentioned many times, are abstract, conceptual things. Sites themselves are not finite; often you can't tell where one ends and the other begins. Subsites and the "invisible web" of databases further muddy the picture of what should and shouldn't be included in a specific architecture. Digital information itself can be organized and repurposed in an almost infinite number of ways, meaning that an architecture is typically multidimensional—and therefore exceedingly difficult to represent in a two-dimensional space such as a whiteboard or a sheet of paper.

So we're left with a nasty paradox. We are forced to demonstrate the value and essence of our work in a visual medium, though our work itself isn't especially visual.

There really is no ideal solution. The field of information architecture is too young for its practitioners to have figured out how best to visually represent information architectures, much less agree upon a standard set of diagrams that work for all audiences in all situations.* And it's unlikely that the messages we wish to communicate will ever lend themselves easily to 8.5 × 11 sheets of paper.

Still, there are a couple of good guidelines to follow as you document your architecture:

1. Provide multiple "views" of an information architecture. Digital information systems are too complex to show all at once; a diagram that tries to be all things to all people is destined to fail. Instead, consider using a variety of techniques to display different aspects of the architecture. Like the blind men and the elephant in John Godfrey Saxe's fable (see the section "Many Good Ways" in Chapter 18), no single view takes in the whole picture, but the combination of multiple diagrams might come close.

2. Develop those views for specific audiences and needs. You might find that a visually stunning diagram is compelling to client prospects, therefore justifying its expense. However, it probably requires too many resources to use in a production environment where diagrams may change multiple times per day. Whenever possible, determine what others need from your diagrams before creating them. For example, Keith Instone, an information architect at IBM, finds himself developing very different diagrams for communicating "upstream" with stakeholders and executives than for "downstream" communication with designers and developers.

Whenever possible, present information architecture diagrams in person, especially when the audience is unfamiliar with them. (If you can't be there in person, at least be there via telephone.) Again and again, we've witnessed (and suffered from) huge disconnects between what the diagram was intended to communicate and what it was understood to mean. This shouldn't be surprising, because there is no standard visual language to describe information architectures yet. So be there to translate, explain, and, if necessary, defend your work.

Better yet, work with whomever you're presenting your diagrams to—clients, managers, designers, programmers—to understand in advance what they will need from it. You may find that your assumptions of how they would use your diagrams were quite wrong. We've seen a large, respected firm fired from a huge project because it took too many weeks to produce bound, color-printed, sexy diagrams. The client preferred (and requested) simple, even hand-drawn, sketches because it needed them as soon as possible.

---

* It's worth noting that, while standards for deliverables haven't emerged, the diagrams themselves are maturing. The fall of 2006 saw the publication of *Communicating Design: Developing Web Site Documentation for Design and Planning* (New Riders), a book focused solely on deliverables, by Dan Brown, an information architect whose work is highly respected by many practitioners.

As we've seen in previous chapters, the most frequently used diagrams are blueprints and wireframes. These focus more on the structure of a site's content than its semantic content. Blueprints and wireframes are effective at depicting structure, movement, flow, and relationships between content, but not at conveying the semantic nature of content or labels. We'll discuss both types of diagrams in detail in the following sections, but first it would be helpful to understand the "language" that these diagrams use.

Communicating Visually

Diagrams are useful for communicating the two basic aspects of an information system's structural elements (semantic aspects, like controlled vocabularies, don't easily lend themselves to visual representation). Diagrams define:

Content components
> What constitutes a unit of content, and how those components should be grouped and sequenced

Connections between content components
> How components are linked to enable navigating between them

That's really pretty simple, and no matter how complex your diagrams may ultimately become, their main goal will always be to communicate what your site's content components are and how they're connected.

To help information architects and other designers create diagrams, a variety of visual vocabularies have emerged to provide a clear set of terms and syntax to visually communicate components and their links. The best-known and most influential visual vocabulary is Jesse James Garrett's,* which has been translated into eight languages. Jesse's vocabulary anticipates and accommodates many uses, but perhaps the greatest reason for its success is its simplicity; just about anyone can use it to create diagrams, even by hand.

Visual vocabularies are at the heart of the many templates used to develop blueprints and wireframes. Thanks to their developers' generosity, there are many free templates you can use to create your own deliverables; we've provided a table of useful examples below. Each requires one of the common charting programs, like Microsoft's Visio (for PC compatibles) or Omni Group's OmniGraffle (for Macintosh computers).

---

* *http://www.jjg.net/ia/visvocab*

Name	Creator	Application	URL
OmniGraffle Wireframe Palette	Michael Angeles	OmniGraffle	*http://urlgreyhot.com/personal/resources/ omnigraffle_wireframe_palette/*
Sitemap Stencil and Template	Garrett Dimon	Visio	*http://www.garrettdimon.com/resources/ templates-stencils-for-visio-omnigraffle*
Wireframe Stencil	Garrett Dimon	Visio	*http://www.garrettdimon.com/resources/ templates-stencils-for-visio-omnigraffle*
Wireframe Template	Garrett Dimon	Visio	*http://www.garrettdimon.com/resources/ templates-stencils-for-visio-omnigraffle*
Sitemap Stencil	Nick Finck	Visio	*http://www.nickfinck.com/stencils.html*
Wireframe Stencil	Nick Finck	Visio	*http://www.nickfinck.com/stencils.html*
Block Diagram Shapes Stencil	Matt Leacock, Bryce Glass, and Rich Fulcher	OmniGraffle	*http://www.paperplane.net/omnigraffle/*
Flow Map Shapes Stencil	Matt Leacock, Bryce Glass, and Rich Fulcher	OmniGraffle	*http://www.paperplane.net/omnigraffle/*
OmniGraffle GUI Design Palette	Robert Silverman	OmniGraffle	*http://www.applepi.com/graffle/*
Wireframe Stencil	Jason Sutter	OmniGraffle	*http://jason.similarselection.org/ omnigraffle/webwireframe.html*

What if you're a nonvisual person who cringes at the idea of learning Visio? Or the people you're communicating your ideas to aren't visually oriented? Does your work have to be visual?

Absolutely not. As ugly as it can be, you can render your blueprints as outlines in a word processor, or use a spreadsheet's cells in a similar fashion. You can write page descriptions that cover the same bases as your wireframes. Just about anything can be rendered in text, and ultimately, these deliverables are first and foremost communication tools. You need to play to your own communication strengths and, more importantly, take advantage of whatever style works best for your audience.

But remember, there's a reason they say "a picture is worth a thousand words." The lines between information archicture and the more visual aspects of design are blurry, and at some point, you'll have to connect your IA concepts, however textual, to the work that is the responsibility of graphic designers and interaction designers. Hence we spend most of our time in this chapter on visual means for communicating information architectures.

Blueprints

Blueprints show the relationships between pages and other content components, and can be used to portray organization, navigation, and labeling systems. They are often referred to as "site maps," and do in fact have much in common with the other definition of "site map," a type of supplementary navigation system that we describe in Chapter 7. Both the diagram and the navigation system display the "shape" of the information space in overview, functioning as a condensed map for site developers and users respectively.

High-Level Architecture Blueprints

High-level blueprints are often created by information architects as part of a top-down information architecture process (and, it's worth noting, they may also be produced during a project's strategy phase) Starting with the main page, the information architect might use the process of developing a blueprint to iteratively flesh out more and more of the architecture, adding subsidiary pages, increasing levels of detail, and working out the navigation from the top down. (Blueprints can also support bottom-up design, such as displaying a content model's content chunks and relationships; we discuss these uses later in the chapter.)

The very act of shaping ideas into the more formal structure of a blueprint forces you to become realistic and practical. If brainstorming takes you to the top of the mountain, blueprinting can bring you back down to the valley of reality. Ideas that seemed brilliant on the whiteboard may not pan out when you attempt to organize them in a practical manner. It's easy to throw around concepts such as "personalization" and "adaptive information architectures." It's not so easy to define on paper exactly how these concepts will be applied to a specific web site.

During the design phase, high-level blueprints are most useful for exploring primary organization schemes and approaches. High-level blueprints map out the organization and labeling of major areas, usually beginning with a bird's-eye view from the main page of the web site. This exploration may involve several iterations as you further define the information architecture.

High-level blueprints are great for stimulating discussions focused on the organization and management of content as well as on the desired access pathways for users. These blueprints can be drawn by hand, but we prefer to use diagramming software such as Visio or OmniGraffle. These tools not only help you to quickly layout your architecture blueprints, but can also help with site implementation and administration. They also lend your work a more professional look, which, sadly, will be more important at times than the quality your actual design.

Figure 12-1 shows a high-level blueprint that includes components within pages, groups of pages, and relationships between pages. The grouping of pages can inform page layout. For example, this blueprint dictates that the three guides should be presented together, whereas Search & Browse, Feedback, and News should be presented separately.

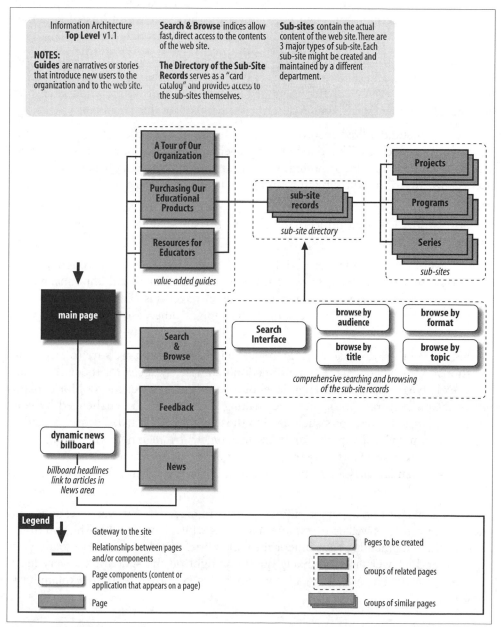

Figure 12-1. A high-level blueprint

Let's walk through the blueprint in Figure 12-1 as if we were presenting it to clients or colleagues. The building block of this architecture is the subsite. Within this company, the ownership and management of content is distributed among many individuals in different departments. There are already dozens of small and large web sites, each with its own graphic identity and information architecture. Rather than try to enforce one standard across this collection of sites, this blueprint suggests an "umbrella architecture" approach that allows for the existence of lots of heterogeneous subsites.

Moving up from the subsites, we see a directory of subsite records. This directory serves as a "card catalog" that provides easy access to the subsites. There is a record for each subsite; each record consists of fields such as *title*, *description*, *keywords*, *audience*, *format*, and *topic*, which describe the contents of that subsite.

By creating a standardized record for each subsite, we are actually creating a database of subsite records. This database approach enables both powerful known-item searching and exploratory browsing. As you can see from the Search & Browse page, users can search and browse by title, audience, format, and topic.

The blueprint also shows three guides. These guides take the form of simple narratives or "stories" that introduce new users to the site's sponsor and selected areas with the web site.

Finally, we see a dynamic news billboard (perhaps implemented through Java or JavaScript) that rotates the display of featured news headlines and announcements. In addition to bringing some action to the main page, this billboard provides yet another way to access important content that might otherwise be buried within a subsite.

At this point in the discussion of the high-level blueprint, you are sure to face some questions. As you can see, the blueprints don't completely speak for themselves, and that's exactly what you want. High-level blueprints are an excellent tool for explaining your architectural approaches and making sure that they're challenged by your client or manager. Questions such as "Do those guides really make sense, considering the company's new plans to target customers by region?" will surface, and present an excellent opportunity to gain buy-in from the client and to fire-proof your design from similar questions much later in the process, when it'll be more expensive to make changes.

Presenting blueprints in person allows you to immediately answer questions and address concerns, as well as to explore new ideas while they're still fresh. You might also consider augmenting your blueprints with a brief text document to explain your thinking and answer the most likely questions right on the spot. At the very least, consider providing a "Notes" area (as we do in this example) to briefly explain basic concepts.

Digging Deeper into Blueprints

As you create blueprints, it's important to avoid getting locked into a particular type of layout. Instead, let form follow function. Notice the difference between Figures 12-2 and 12-3.

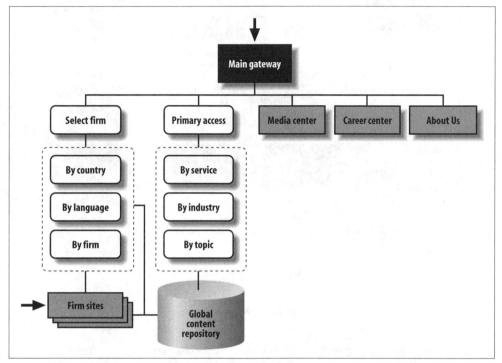

Figure 12-2. This blueprint illustrates the big picture for a consulting firm's public site...

Figure 12-2 provides a holistic view of the information architecture for a global consulting firm. It's part of an initiative to build support for the overall vision of unified access to member firms' content and services. In contrast, Figure 12-3 focuses on a single aspect of navigation for the Weather Channel web site, aiming to show how users will be able to move between local and national weather reports and news. Both blueprints are high level and conceptual in nature, yet each takes on a unique form to suit its purpose.

In Figure 12-4, we see a high-level blueprint for the online greeting card web site Egreetings.com. This blueprint focuses on the user's ability to filter cards based on format or tone at any level while navigating the primary taxonomy.

It's important for information architects (particularly those of us with library science backgrounds) to remind ourselves that web sites aren't just about content; we can also contribute to the design of online applications and e-services. This work requires task-oriented blueprints, which are similar to the process flow diagrams often created by interaction designers.

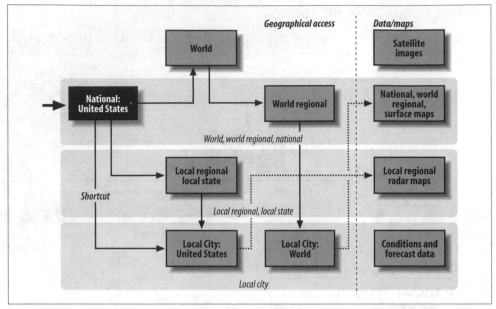

Figure 12-3. …while this one focuses on geographic hub navigation for the Weather Channel site…

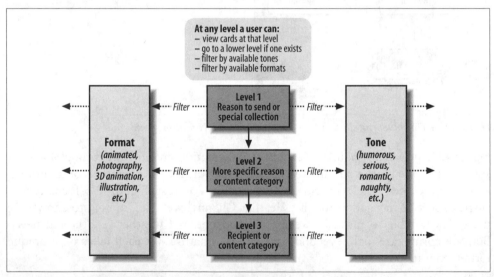

Figure 12-4. …and this one demonstrates how filtering might work at Egreetings.com

For example, Figure 12-5 presents a user-centered view of the card-sending process at Egreetings.com prior to a redesign project. It allows the project team to walk through each step along the web- and email-enabled process, looking for opportunities to improve the user experience.

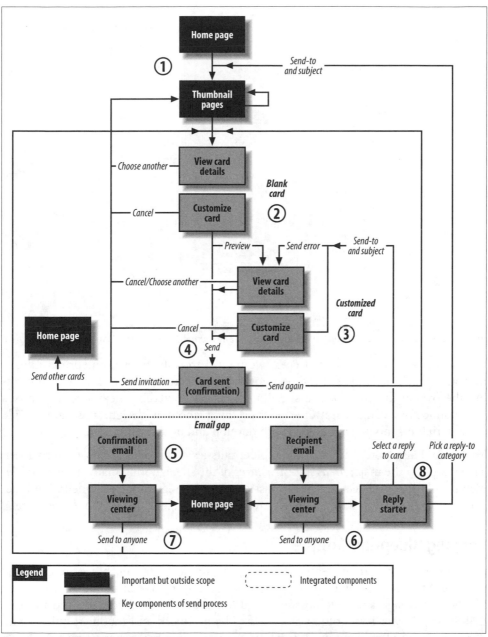

Figure 12-5. A task-oriented blueprint of the card-sending process

In Figure 12-6, information architect Austin Govella's blueprint demonstrates how casual browsers may become engaged in a political campaign over time by interacting with the site's content. This blueprint is as much about changes in the user's mind as it is descriptive of the site's content and navigation.

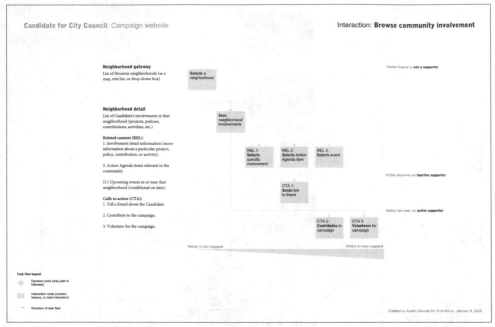

Figure 12-6. A blueprint depicting growing levels of engagement in a political candidate's campaign

You'll notice that as we dug deeper, we moved from high-level blueprints toward diagrams that isolated specific aspects of the architecture, rather than communicating the overall direction of the site. Blueprints are incredibly flexible; while boxes and connectors can't communicate everything about a design, they are simple enough that just about anyone can both develop and understand them.

You should also note that all of these blueprints leave out quite a bit of information. They focus on the major *areas* and *structures* of the site, ignoring many navigation elements and page-level details. These omissions are by design, not by accident. For blueprints, as with the web sites you design, remember the rule of thumb that *less is more*.

Keeping Blueprints Simple

As a project moves from strategy to design to implementation, blueprints become more utilitarian—enabling the information architect to communicate to others involved in design and development—and less geared toward strategy and product definition. "Lower-level" blueprints need to be produced and modified quickly and iteratively, and often draw input from an increasing number of perspectives, ranging from visual designers to editors to programmers. Those team members need to be able to understand the architecture, so it's important to develop a simple, condensed vocabulary of objects that can be explained in a brief legend. See Figure 12-7 for an example.

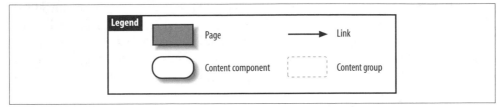

Figure 12-7. This blueprint legend describes an intentionally simple vocabulary

In this figure, the legend describes three levels of content granularity. The coarsest are content groups (made up of pages); these are followed by the pages themselves. Content components are the finest-grained content that makes sense to represent in a blueprint. The arrow describes a link between content objects; these can be one-way or bidirectional links.

This is a minimal set of objects; we've found that retaining a limited vocabulary helps the information architect avoid the temptation of overloading the diagram with too much information. After all, other diagrams can be used to convey other views of the architecture more effectively.

Detailed Blueprints

As you move deeper into the implementation stage, your focus naturally shifts from external to internal. Rather than communicating high-level architectural concepts to the client, your job is now to communicate detailed organization, labeling, and navigation decisions to your colleagues on the site development team. In the world of "physical" architecture, this shift can be likened to architecture versus construction. The architect may work closely with the client to make big-picture decisions about the layout of rooms and the location of windows; however, decisions regarding the size of nails or the routing of the plumbing typically do not involve the client. And in fact, such minutiae often need not involve the architect either.

Detailed architecture blueprints serve a very practical purpose. They map out the entire site so that the production team can implement your plans to the letter without requiring your involvement during production. The blueprints must present the complete information hierarchy from the main page to the destination pages. They must also detail the labeling and navigation systems to be implemented in each area of the site.

The blueprints will vary from project to project, depending upon the scope. On smaller projects, the primary audience for your blueprints may be one or two graphic designers responsible for integrating the architecture, design, and content. On larger projects, the primary audience may be a technical team responsible for integrating the architecture, design, and content through a database-driven process. Let's consider a few examples to see what blueprints communicate and how they might vary.

Figure 12-8 shows a blueprint from the SIGGRAPH 96 Conference that introduces several concepts (yes, we know it's an old example, but it remains useful and valid). By assigning a unique identification number (e.g., 2.2.5.1) to each component (e.g., pages and content chunks), the architect lays the groundwork for an organized production process, ideally involving a database system that populates the web site structure with content.

There is a distinction between a local and a remote page in Figure 12-8. A local page is a child of the main page on that blueprint, and inherits characteristics such as graphic identity and navigation elements from its parent. In this example, the Papers Committee page inherits its color scheme and navigation system from the Papers main page. On the other hand, a remote page belongs to another branch of the information hierarchy. The Session Room Layout page has a graphic identity and navigation system that are unique to the Maps area of the web site.

Another important concept is that of content components or *chunks*. To meet the needs of the production process, it is often necessary to separate the content (i.e., chunks) from the container (i.e., pages). Content chunks such as "Contact Us About Papers" and "Contact Us About This Web Site" are sections of content composed of one or more paragraphs that can stand alone as independent packages of information. (We'll discuss content chunking in more detail later in this chapter.) The rectangle that surrounds these content chunks indicates that they are closely related. By taking this approach, the architect provides the designer with flexibility in defining the layout. Depending upon the space each content chunk requires, the designer may choose to present all of these chunks on one page, or create a closely knit collection of pages.

You may also decide to communicate the navigation system using these detailed blueprints. In some cases, arrows can be used to show navigation, but these can be confusing and are easily missed by the production staff. A sidebar is often the best way of communicating both global and local navigation systems, as shown in Figure 12-8. The sidebar in the upper right of this blueprint explains how the global and local navigation systems apply to this area of the web site.

Organizing Your Blueprints

As the architecture is developed, it needs to accommodate more than just the site's top-level pages. The same simple notation can be used, but how can you squeeze all of these documents onto one sheet of paper? Many applications will allow you to print on multiple sheets, but you'll find yourself spending more time taping sheets together than designing. And if a diagram is too large to print on a single sheet, it's probably also too large to reasonably view and edit on a standard monitor.

In this case, we suggest *modularizing* the blueprint. The top-level blueprint links to subsidiary blueprints, and so on, and so on. These diagrams are tied together through a scheme of unique IDs. For example, in the top-level diagram in Figure 12-9, major

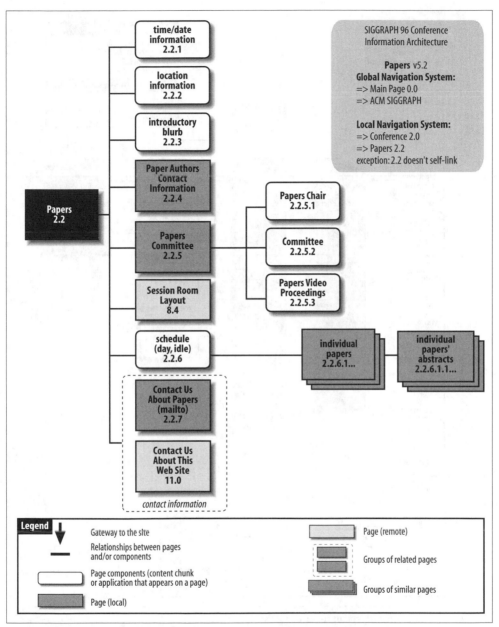

Figure 12-8. A blueprint of a major section of the SIGGRAPH conference web site

pages, such as the one representing "Committees and officers," are numbered 4.0. That page becomes the "lead page" on a new diagram (Figure 12-10), where it is also numbered 4.0. Its subsidiary pages and content components use codes starting with 4.0 in order to link them with their parent.

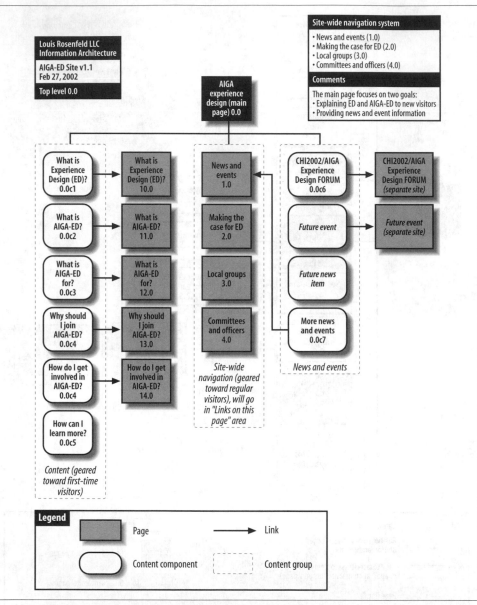

Figure 12-9. A detailed blueprint illustrating several concepts

Using a unique identification scheme to tie together multiple diagrams helps us to somewhat mitigate the tyranny of the 8.5×11 sheet of paper. (Although you may still find that your architecture requires dozens of individual sheets of paper.) This scheme can also be helpful for bridging a content inventory to the architectural process—content components can share the same IDs in both content inventory and

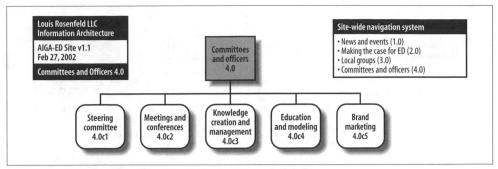

Figure 12-10. This subsidiary blueprint continues from the top-level blueprint

blueprint. This means that in the production phase, adding content to the site is not much different from painting by numbers.

If you'd like to learn more about blueprints, we suggest visiting the IAwiki site for some excellent discussion on the topic (*http://iawiki.net/SiteMaps*).

Wireframes

Blueprints can help an information architect determine where content should go and how it should be navigated within the context of a site, subsite, or collection of content. Wireframes serve a different role: they depict how an individual page or template should look from an architectural perspective. Wireframes stand at the intersection of the site's information architecture and its visual and information design.

For example, the wireframe forces the architect to consider such issues as where the navigation systems might be located on a page. And now that we see it on an early version of a page, does it seem that there are actually too many ways to navigate? Trying out ideas in the context of a wireframe might force you back to the blueprint's drawing board, but it's better to make such changes on paper rather than reengineering the entire site at some point in the future.

Wireframes describe the content and information architecture to be included on the relatively confined two-dimensional spaces known as pages; therefore, wireframes themselves must be constrained in size. These constraints force the information architect to make choices about what components of the architecture should be visible and accessible to users; after all, if the architectural components absorb too much screen real estate, no room will be left for actual content!

Developing wireframes also helps the information architect decide how to group content components, how to order them, and which groups of components have priority. In Figure 12-11, the information architect has determined that "Reasons to Send" is of a higher priority than the "Search Assistant." This priority is made clear by the content's prominent positioning and the use of a larger typeface for its heading.

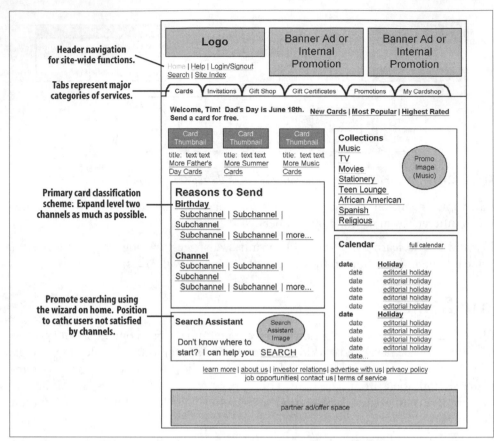

Figure 12-11. A wireframe of the main page of a greeting card site

Wireframes are typically created for the site's most important pages—such as main pages, major category pages, and the interfaces to search—and other important applications. They are also used to describe templates that are consistently applied to many pages, such as a site's content pages. And they can be used for any page that is sufficiently vexing or confusing to merit further visualization during the design process. The goal is not to create wireframes for every page in your site, but only for the ones that are complicated, unique, or set a pattern for other pages (i.e., templates).

Note that wireframes are not limited to describing pages. Figure 12-12 shows two stages of a user's interaction with a pop-up window.

Wireframes represent a degree of look and feel, and straddle the realms of visual design and interaction design. Wireframes (and page design in general) represent a frontier area where many web design-related disciplines come together and frequently clash. The fact that wireframes are produced by an information architect (i.e., a non-designer) and that they make statements about visual design (despite being quite ugly) often makes graphic designers and other visually oriented people very uncomfortable. For this reason, we suggest that wireframes come with a prominent

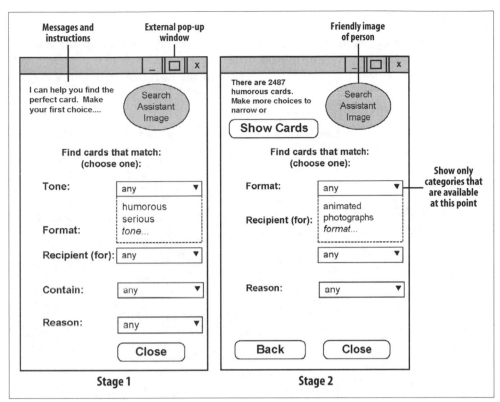

Figure 12-12. Wireframes can represent any type of content

disclaimer that they are not replacements for "real visual design." The fonts, colors (or lack thereof), use of whitespace, and other visual characteristics of your wireframes are there only to illustrate how the site's information architecture will impact and interact with a particular page. Make it clear that you expect to collaborate with a graphic designer to improve the aesthetic nature of the overall site, or with an interaction designer to improve the functionality of the page's widgets.

We also suggest making this point verbally, while also conveying how your wireframe will eliminate some work that visual designers and interaction designers might consider unpleasant or not within their expertise. For example, just as you'd prefer that a designer select colors or placement for a navigation bar, you've relieved the designer of the task of determining the labels that will populate that navigation bar.

Finally, because wireframes do involve visual design, their development presents a perfect opportunity for collaboration with visual designers, who will have much to add at this point. Avoid treating wireframes as something to be handed off to designers and developers, and instead use them as triggers for generating a healthy bout of interdisciplinary collaboration. Although collaboration slows down the project's schedule, the end product will be better for it (and besides, it may save you time during the project's development).

Types of Wireframes

Just like blueprints, wireframes come in many shapes and sizes, and the level of fidelity can be varied to suit your purposes. At the low end, you may sketch quick-and-dirty wireframes on paper or a whiteboard. At the high end, wireframes may be created in HTML or with a publishing tool like Adobe Illustrator. Most wireframes fall somewhere in the middle. Let's review a few samples.

Figure 12-13 is a relatively low-fidelity wireframe; there are no graphic elements and no real content. This enables the visual designer to focus attention on the global, local, and contextual navigation elements of the page.

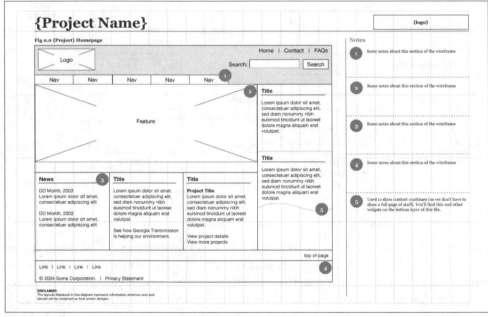

Figure 12-13. A low-fidelity wireframe developed by MessageFirst's Todd Warfel; note that all content is "greeked up" to ensure a focus on layout of content and visual elements

Figure 12-14, from a redesign project for Egreetings.com, is a medium-fidelity wireframe with a high degree of detail. This wireframe was intended to introduce several aspects of content, layout, and navigation into the discussion, and was one of many wireframes used to communicate the information architecture to managers, graphic designers, and programmers.

Finally, Figure 12-15 is a relatively high-fidelity wireframe that presents a close approximation of what the page will actually look like. This is about as far as most information architects can go without bringing a graphic designer into the picture.

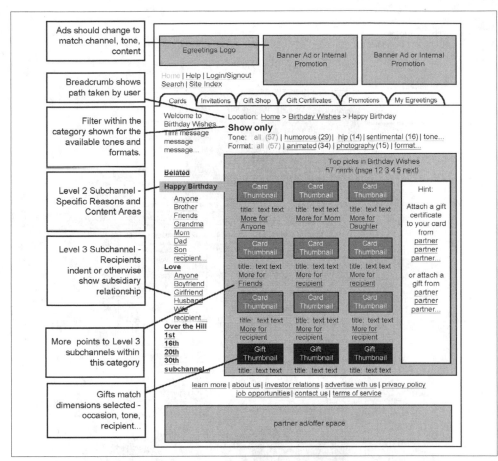

Figure 12-14. A medium-fidelity wireframe for Egreetings.com; more detail, more explanation, and more unique content

Such a high-fidelity wireframe has the following advantages:

- The content and color bring the page to life, helping to capture the attention of your clients or colleagues.
- By simulating actual page width and font size, the wireframe forces you to recognize the constraints of an HTML page.
- The fidelity is sufficient to support paper prototype-testing with users.

On the other hand, some disadvantages are:

- Higher fidelity requires greater effort. It takes a lot of time to design such a detailed wireframe. This can slow down the process and increase costs.
- As you integrate visual elements and content into a structured layout, the focus may shift prematurely from information architecture to interface and visual design.

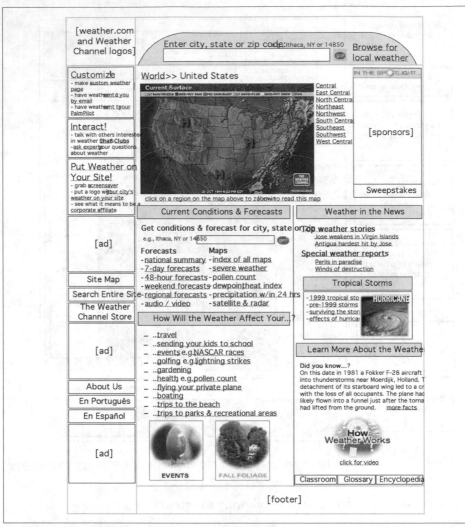

Figure 12-15. A high-fidelity wireframe for Weather.com

Provided that you recognize the strengths and weaknesses of these varying levels of fidelity, wireframes can be an extremely powerful tools for communication and collaboration during the information architecture design process.

Wireframe Guidelines

Chris Farnum, a former colleague at Argus Associates and a wireframe expert, suggests the following best practices to consider when creating wireframes:

- Consistency is key, especially when presenting multiple wireframes. It ensures that clients will be impressed by the professionalism of your wireframes. More importantly, colleagues take wireframes quite literally, so consistency makes their design and production work go more smoothly.

- Visio and other standard charting tools support background layers, allowing you to reuse navigation bars and page layouts for multiple pages throughout the site. Similarly, Visio's stencil feature allows you to maintain a standard library of drawing objects that can be used to describe page elements.

- Callouts are an effective way to provide notes about the functionality of page elements. Be sure to leave room for them at the sides and top of your wireframes.

- Like any other deliverable, wireframes should be usable and professionally developed. So tie your collection of wireframes together with page numbers, page titles, project titles, and last revision date.

- When more than one information architect is creating a project's wireframes, be sure to establish procedures for developing, sharing, and maintaining common templates and stencils (and consider establishing a wireframe "steward"). Schedule time in your project plan for synchronizing the team's wireframes to ensure consistent appearance, and for confirming that these discrete documents do indeed fit together functionally.

For an excellent discussion of information architecture deliverables and wireframes and additional information, see the IAwiki (*http://iawiki.net/WireFrames*).

Content Mapping and Inventory

During research and strategy, you are focused on the top-down approach of defining an information structure that will accommodate the mission, vision, audiences, and content of the site. As you move into design and production, you complete the bottom-up process of collecting and analyzing the content. Content mapping is where top-down information architecture meets bottom-up.

The process of detailed content mapping involves breaking down or combining existing content into content chunks that are useful for inclusion in your site. A content chunk isn't necessarily a sentence or a paragraph or a page. Rather, it is the most finely grained portion of content that merits or requires individual treatment.

The content, often drawn from a variety of sources and in a multitude of formats, must be mapped onto the information architecture so that it will be clear what goes where during the production process. Because of differences between formats, you cannot count on a one-to-one mapping of source page to destination page; one page from a print brochure does not necessarily map onto one page on the Web. For this reason, it is important to separate content from container at both the source and the destination. In addition, when combined with XML or a database-driven approach to content management, the separation of content and container facilitates the reuse of content chunks across multiple pages. For example, contact information for the customer-service department might be presented in context within a variety of pages throughout the web site. If the contact information changes, the modification need only be made to the database record for that content chunk, and it can then be propagated throughout the web site at the push of a button.

Even when you are creating new content for your site, content mapping is still necessary. It often makes sense to create content in a word processing application rather than an HTML editor, since tools like Microsoft Word tend to have more powerful editing, layout, and spell-checking capabilities. In such cases, you'll need to map the Word documents to HTML pages. The need for careful content mapping is even greater when new content is created by multiple authors throughout your organization; the mapping process then becomes an important managerial tool for tracking content from these disparate sources.

The subjective process of defining chunks should be determined by asking the following questions:

- Should this content be divided into smaller chunks that users might want to access separately?
- What is the smallest section of content that needs to be individually indexed?
- Will this content need to be repurposed across multiple documents or as part of multiple processes?

Once the content chunks have been defined, they can be mapped to their destinations, which can be web pages, PDAs, or some other medium. You will need a systematic means of documenting the source and destination of all content so that the production team can carry out your instructions. As discussed earlier, one approach involves the assignment of a unique identification code to each content chunk.

For example, the creation of the SIGGRAPH 96 Conference web site required the translation of print-based content to the online environment. In such cases, content mapping involves the specification of how chunks of content in the print materials map to pages on the web site. For SIGGRAPH 96, we had to map the contents of elaborately designed brochures, announcements, and programs onto web pages. Because it wouldn't have made sense to attempt a one-to-one mapping of printed pages to web pages, we instead went through a process of content chunking and mapping with the content editor. First, we broke each page of the brochure into logical chunks of content, inventoried the results, and then devised a simple scheme tied to page numbers for labeling each chunk (Figure 12-16).

As you saw in Figure 12-9, we had already created a detailed information architecture blueprint with its own content chunk identification scheme. We then had to create a content mapping table that explained how each content chunk from the print brochure should be presented in the web site (Figure 12-17).

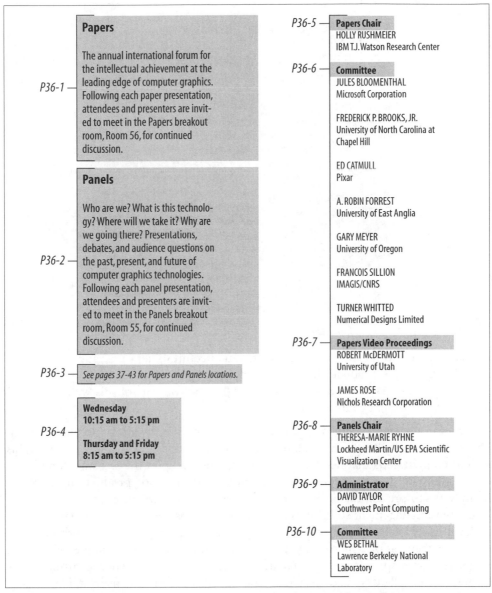

Papers

P36-1 — The annual international forum for the intellectual achievement at the leading edge of computer graphics. Following each paper presentation, attendees and presenters are invited to meet in the Papers breakout room, Room 56, for continued discussion.

Panels

P36-2 — Who are we? What is this technology? Where will we take it? Why are we going there? Presentations, debates, and audience questions on the past, present, and future of computer graphics technologies. Following each panel presentation, attendees and presenters are invited to meet in the Panels breakout room, Room 55, for continued discussion.

P36-3 — *See pages 37-43 for Papers and Panels locations.*

P36-4 —
Wednesday
10:15 am to 5:15 pm

Thursday and Friday
8:15 am to 5:15 pm

P36-5 — **Papers Chair**
HOLLY RUSHMEIER
IBM T.J. Watson Research Center

P36-6 — **Committee**
JULES BLOOMENTHAL
Microsoft Corporation

FREDERICK P. BROOKS, JR.
University of North Carolina at
Chapel Hill

ED CATMULL
Pixar

A. ROBIN FORREST
University of East Anglia

GARY MEYER
University of Oregon

FRANCOIS SILLION
IMAGIS/CNRS

TURNER WHITTED
Numerical Designs Limited

P36-7 — **Papers Video Proceedings**
ROBERT McDERMOTT
University of Utah

JAMES ROSE
Nichols Research Corporation

P36-8 — **Panels Chair**
THERESA-MARIE RYHNE
Lockheed Martin/US EPA Scientific
Visualization Center

P36-9 — **Administrator**
DAVID TAYLOR
Southwest Point Computing

P36-10 — **Committee**
WES BETHAL
Lawrence Berkeley National
Laboratory

Figure 12-16. Chunks from a print brochure are tagged with unique identifiers (e.g., "P36-1") so that they can be mapped out and inventoried

In this example, P36-1 is a unique ID code that refers to the first content chunk on page 36 of the original print brochure. This source content chunk maps onto the destination content chunk labeled 2.2.3, which belongs in the Papers (2.2) area of the web site.

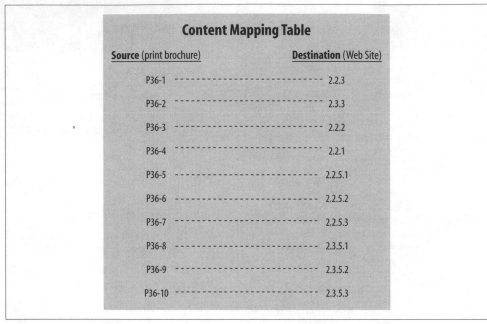

Figure 12-17. A content mapping table matches content chunks with their destinations

Armed with the original print documents, architecture blueprints, and the content mapping table, the production staff created and populated the SIGGRAPH 96 Conference web site. As you can see in Figure 12-18, the contents of this web page (2.2) include three content chunks from P36.

A byproduct of the content mapping process is a content inventory describing available content and where it can be found (e.g., the current site or the annual report), as well as content gaps that need to be filled. Depending upon the size and complexity of the web site and the process and technology in place for production, there are many ways to present this inventory. For larger sites, you might require a document or content management solution that leverages database technology to manage large collections of content. Many of these applications also provide a workflow that defines a team approach to page-level design and editing. For simpler sites, you might rely on a spreadsheet (see Figure 12-19). Sarah Rice of Seneb Consulting has created an excellent spreadsheet that you can download and use (at *http://www.seneb.com/example_content_inventory.xls*); in this example, she's applied it to the site of the Information Architecture Institute (formerly AIfIA).

Or, if you're feeling a bit more ambitious, you can create a web-based inventory that presents the titles and unique identification numbers of each page for the site, such as that shown in Figure 12-20. Selecting the hypertext numbers pops up another browser window that shows the appropriate web page.

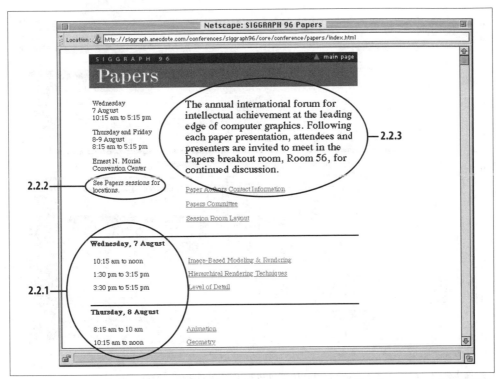

Figure 12-18. The web page produced by the content mapping process; P36-1 maps to 2.2.3, P36-3 maps to 2.2.2, and P36-4 maps to 2.2.1

You can create a content inventory* as soon as you have completed the content mapping process. At different points in time, it can serve as an inventory of pages that need to be created, an inventory of architectural page mockups that need to be designed, and an inventory of designed pages that need to be reviewed before integration into the web site.

Content Models

Content models are "micro" information architectures made up of small chunks of interconnected content. Content models support the critical missing piece in so many sites: contextual navigation that works deep within the site. Why a missing piece? Because it's easy—maybe too easy—for an organization to accumulate blobs of content, but extremely difficult to link those blobs together in a useful way.

---

* We suggest reading Jeff Veen's short and excellent take on content inventories, "Doing a Content Inventory (Or, A Mind-Numbingly Detailed Odyssey Through Your Web Site)" (*http://www.adaptivepath.com/ publications/essays/archives/000040.php*).

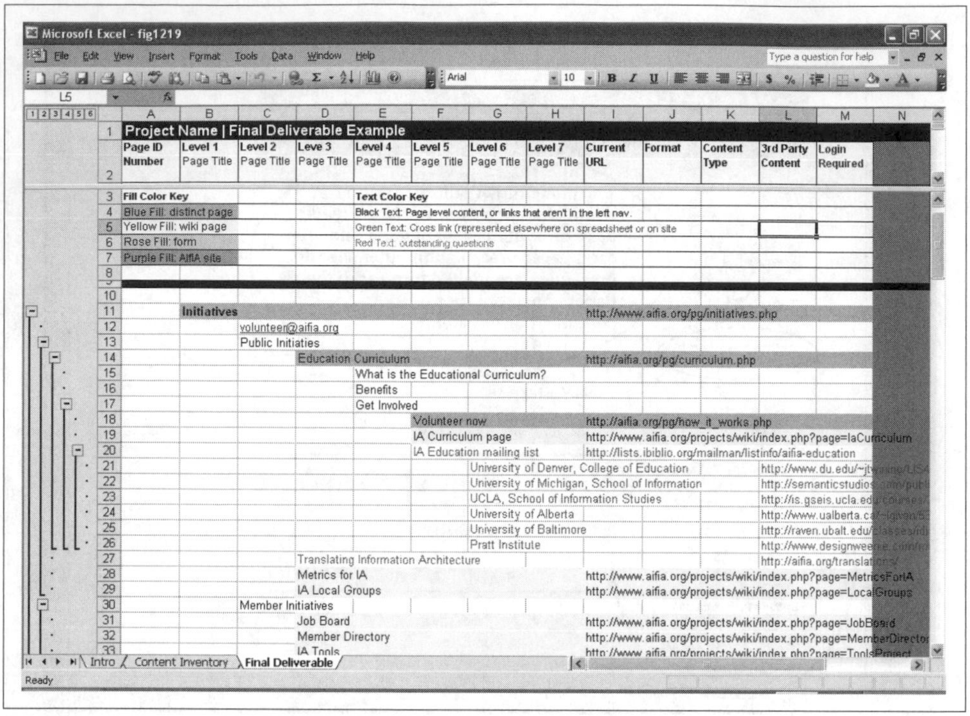

Figure 12-19. Section of a content inventory managed in Microsoft Excel

Why Do They Matter?

We encounter content models all the time on the Web and in more traditional media. A recipe is a great example. Its objects are a list of ingredients, directions, a title, and so on. If you "greek up" a recipe, it'll still be recognizable. But change the logic—by putting the steps before the ingredients or leaving out an important object—and the model collapses. Content models rely on consistent sets of objects and logical connections between them to work.

Supporting contextual navigation

Imagine that, by hook or by crook, you found your way deep into a clothing retailer's web site in your quest for a snazzy new blue oxford shirt. As a user, you've just clearly stated an incredibly specific information need. Such a need is far more precise than that of a user who has reached a site's main page. Wouldn't it be silly for the retailer not to apply this knowledge to your benefit (not to mention to its advantage)?

That's why most online retailers will, at this point, introduce you to some matching pants or other accessories. "You might also be interested in…." This is far more reasonable than the retailers hoping and expecting you to 1) guess that they sell these related items, and 2) actually find those items using the site's top-down organization

---

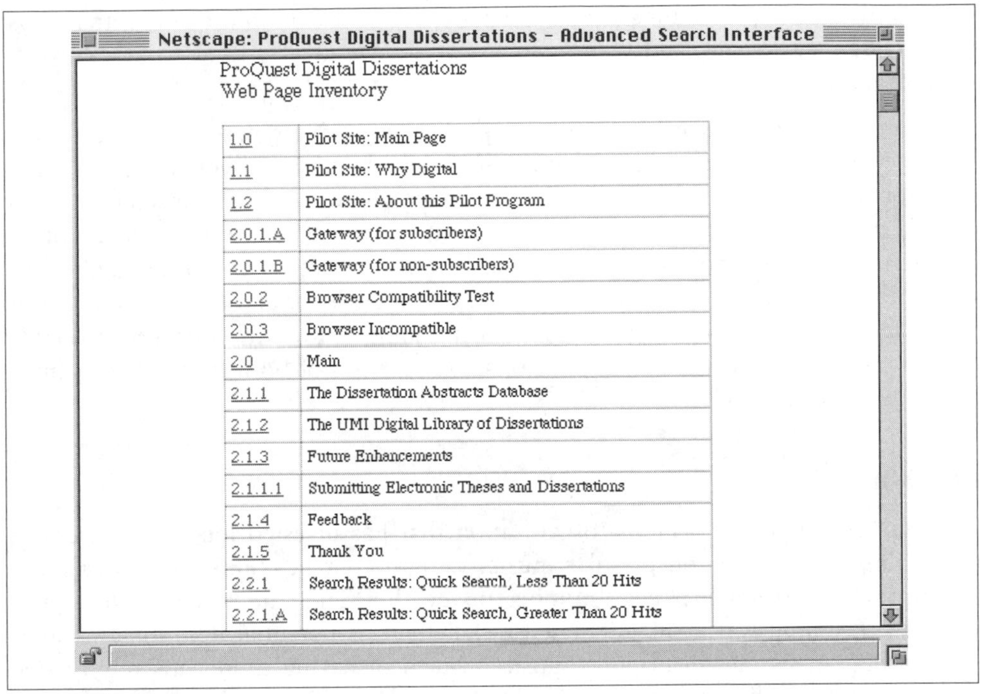
Netscape: ProQuest Digital Dissertations – Advanced Search Interface
ProQuest Digital Dissertations
Web Page Inventory
1.0 Pilot Site: Main Page
1.1 Pilot Site: Why Digital
1.2 Pilot Site: About this Pilot Program
2.0.1.A Gateway (for subscribers)
2.0.1.B Gateway (for non-subscribers)
2.0.2 Browser Compatibility Test
2.0.3 Browser Incompatible
2.0 Main
2.1.1 The Dissertation Abstracts Database
2.1.2 The UMI Digital Library of Dissertations
2.1.3 Future Enhancements
2.1.1.1 Submitting Electronic Theses and Dissertations
2.1.4 Feedback
2.1.5 Thank You
2.2.1 Search Results: Quick Search, Less Than 20 Hits
2.2.1.A Search Results: Quick Search, Greater Than 20 Hits

Figure 12-20. A web-based content inventory

and navigation systems. Horizontal hopping across the hierarchy is a form of contextual navigation, where your movement is based more on your needs as a user, rather than the site's structure. And content models exist primarily to support such navigation, whether for cross-selling retail products, connecting baseball fans to the story behind the boxscore, or introducing potential customers to a product's specs.

Coping with large amounts of content

Content models also help us deal with scale. When inventorying content, it's not uncommon to stumble upon large bodies of homogenous information buried in our content management systems and databases. For example, after a content inventory, a company that provides information on cellular phone products might find that it owns dozens of content chunks for each model's basic product information, thousands of reader reviews, and many more for information on related accessories. The phone product pages look, work, and behave the same. So do the review pages and the accessory pages.

If each type of content chunk works the same, why not take advantage of this predictability by linking them? Allow those users to move naturally from a specific cell phone's page to its product reviews and accessories. Better yet, do this in an automated fashion so the links can be generated instantly, rather than having an army of HTML coders deciding what should be linked to what. Automating the creation of links between content chunks means your users benefit from more and better ways to navigate contextually, and your organization derives greater value from its investment in the content.

So content models can be especially helpful when we've got a lot of high-value homogeneous content chunks that aren't well linked and some technology on hand to automate those links. You can certainly create content models for smaller numbers of content chunks—for example, information associated with the dozen or so people that serve on your company's board—but it's pretty easy to manually connect these objects. You could also create content models for all of your content, but the process is a bit involved, so we recommend doing so for only your most valuable content (with value defined as a judicious combination of both user and organizational needs, of course).

An Example

Let's say you work for a media organization that has invested lots of resources in assembling information on popular music. Certain content chunks—such as artist descriptions and album pages—number in the thousands, and they all look and work in the same way. You might sense that there is potential here for a content model that serves fans of popular music. Instead of having those fans rely on the site's hierarchy to find content relevant to a particular artist or album, why not create a content model?

Based on content inventory and analysis, there are a few music-related content objects that may emerge as good candidates for a content model, shown in Figure 12-21.

Figure 12-21. Content objects that might be the basis of a content model for album information

How should these objects be linked? We can certainly decide that an album page ought to link to its corresponding review, artist bios and descriptions should link to each other, and so on. But it won't always be so easy to come up with the most obvious links; even if it is fairly obvious, you may need to produce some user research to validate your work.

In such cases, consider a variation of the card sort exercise. Print out a sample of each content object and cut out the navigation options (to prevent biasing users with the current information architecture). Then ask subjects to look at each content object and consider where they'd want to go next. Then have them cluster the objects and draw lines between them that indicate navigation (they can do this with string, or they can tape the content object samples to a whiteboard and use dry-erase markers to draw their lines). Arrows indicate whether users wish to navigate in both directions or prefer a one-way link.

To perform a simple gap analysis, ask subjects which missing content objects would be nice to include in the mix. By doing so, you'll get a sense of what should be added to your content model. If you're fortunate, the missing objects might already exist somewhere else in your site. Otherwise, you'll at least have some guidance in deciding which content to create or license.

At the end of the process—whether based on user research or your own hunch—you'll have an idea of how your content model ought to work. The result might look like Figure 12-22.

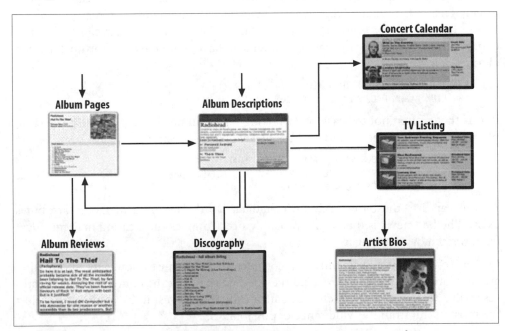

Figure 12-22. An ideal content model, showing navigation and missing content objects

So you've identified new content objects, like a discography, that you might need to create. And you've linked to other content, like TV listings for televised concerts and events in a concert calendar, that is a logical extension of the content model (and possibly, a connection to candidates for future content models). You've also identified logical "tops" or common points of entry to this content. And ultimately, you have a sense of how users might want to navigate an area deep in the guts of your site.

Unfortunately, you're not quite done. How do these links between content objects get made?

If you're Amazon, you've got reams of usage data to draw from. Amazon employs customer-behavior data to make connections between related products in its content model; familiar examples are the products listed under "Customers who bought this item also bought" and "What do customers ultimately buy after viewing this item?" But not every organization has the traffic volume from which to cull this kind of useful data.

So the rest of us typically rely on metadata as the basis of the logic that connects our content chunks. Shared metadata does the work of linking a pair of content chunks. For example, if we want to link an album page and an album review, the logic might look like this:

```
IF ALBUM PAGE'S ALBUM NAME = ALBUM REVIEW'S ALBUM NAME
THEN LINK ALBUM PAGE AND ALBUM REVIEW
```

Now, this rule might suffice for albums with unique titles, like "Sergeant Pepper's Lonely Hearts Club Band." But what if the title is the ubiquitous "Greatest Hits"? If you're lucky, the object has a unique identifier, like an ISBN, that can be used as connecting metadata (many classical albums do have unique IDs; unfortunately, pop albums don't):

```
IF ALBUM PAGE'S UNIQUE ID = ALBUM REVIEW'S UNIQUE ID
THEN LINK ALBUM PAGE AND ALBUM REVIEW
```

But as that's often not the case, your linking logic will need to get a little more complicated, and additional metadata attributes will be necessary:

```
IF ALBUM PAGE'S ALBUM NAME = ALBUM REVIEW'S ALBUM NAME
AND ALBUM PAGE'S ARTIST NAME = ALBUM REVIEW'S ARTIST NAME
THEN LINK ALBUM PAGE AND ALBUM REVIEW
```

As you can see, these rules rely on metadata. Do the required metadata attributes exist? The bad news is that you'll probably need to invest in creating new metadata from scratch or acquiring it.

Of course, metadata availability is a consideration with just about any information architecture project of any size. And the good news is that the content modeling process will help you decide which metadata attributes to invest in by helping you select the most useful from the wide range of possibilities.

Consider our arrows in Figure 12-22. Which metadata will be necessary to drive the logic behind each link? Make a simple table listing each content object, which other objects it should link to, and the metadata attributes required to make those connections. It might look something like this:

Content objects...	...link to other content objects...	...by leveraging common metadata attributes
album page	album review, discography, artist	Album Name, Artist Name, Label, Release Date
album review	album page	Album Name, Artist Name, Review Author, Source, Pub Date
discography	album review, artist description	Artist Name, Album Name, Release Date
artist description	artist bio, discography, concert calendar, TV listing	Artist Name, Desc Author, Desc Date
artist bio	artist description	Artist Name, Individual Artist Name
concert calendar	artist description	Artist Name, Tour, Venue, Date, Time
TV listing	artist description	Artist Name, Channel, Date, Time

Notice a pattern here? Certain metadata attributes show up more frequently than others. These are the attributes that are most necessary for the content model to succeed. If you're operating with limited resources (and who isn't?), now you'll have an excellent way to prioritize your investment in metadata attributes.

A Valuable Process

As you can see, content models are as much an exercise as a deliverable. While the primary output is a useful IA deliverable that informs the design of contextual navigation deep within a site, the process also generates two invaluable, if secondary, benefits.

First, content modeling forces us to determine which content is most important content to model. As you can see, it's work—not necessarily terribly difficult, but not trivial. Most likely you can't create content models for all of your content. So you'll have to ask yourself: which content fulfills the requirements of homogeneous, high volume, and, most of all, high value? You might find a set of priorities falls out of this exercise; for example, perhaps this year you'll develop a product-area content model, next year a support-area content model, and later you'll link those two models together for even greater benefit.

Second, content modeling also forces you to choose which of the many metadata attributes are the ones that will make your content model operational. The combination of focusing on and narrowing down to critical content and critical metadata means a huge simplification and clarification of a large and complex problem space. And that's what the *Pareto Principle*, the information architect's best friend (and commonly referred to as the 80–20 rule), would recommend.

Controlled Vocabularies

There are two primary types of work products associated with the development of controlled vocabularies. First, you'll need metadata matrixes that facilitate discussion about the prioritization of vocabularies (see Table 12-1 for an example). Second, you'll need an application that enables you to manage the vocabulary terms and relationships.

Table 12-1. A metadata matrix for 3Com

Vocabulary	Description	Examples	Maintenance
Subject	Terms that describe networking	Home networking; servers	Difficult
Product type	Types of products that 3Com sells	Hubs; modems	Moderate
Product name	Names of products that 3Com sells	PC Digital WebCam	Difficult
Product brand	Brands of products that 3Com sells	HomeConnect; SuperStack	Easy
Technology	Types of technologies associated with products	ISDN; Broadband; Frame relay	Moderate
Protocols	Types of standards and protocols associated with products	TCP/IP; Ethernet	Moderate
Hardware	Types of devices that products are used in	PDA; Wireless phone; Internet appliances; PC	Moderate
Geographic location: region	Name of geographic region	Europe; APR	Easy
Geographic location: country	Name of country	Germany; Czech Republic	Easy
Language	Name of language	German; Czech	Easy
Technology applications	Names of applications for technologies	Call center; e-business	Moderate
Industries	Types of industries that 3Com works with	Healthcare; government	Easy
Audiences	Kinds of audiences the 3Com site attracts	Consumers; First-time visitors; media	Easy
Customer group: workplace	Type of workplace that customers work in	Home; office	Moderate
Customer group: business	Size or scale of business that customers work in	Small business; large enterprise; service provider	Moderate
Roles	Type of role that people have in their business	IT manager; consultant	Moderate
Document type	Purpose of content object	Form; instructions; guide	Easy

As you can see from Table 12-1, there's no shortage of possible vocabularies. The information architect's job is to help define which vocabularies should be developed, considering priorities and time and budget constraints. A metadata matrix can help you to walk clients and colleagues through the difficult decision-making process, weighing the value of each vocabulary to the user experience against the costs of development and administration.

As you shift gears from selecting vocabularies to building them, you'll need to choose a database solution to manage the terms and term relationships. If you're creating a sophisticated thesaurus with equivalence, hierarchical, and associative relationships, you should seriously consider investing in thesaurus management software (see Chapter 16 for further discussion). However, if you're creating a simple vocabulary with only preferred and variant terms, you should be able to manage with just a word processor, spreadsheet program, or basic database package.

When we created a controlled vocabulary to be used by thousands of representatives at AT&T's inbound call centers, we managed the accepted and variant terms in Microsoft Word (see Table 12-2).

Table 12-2. Excerpt from a controlled vocabulary database created for AT&T

Unique ID	Accepted term	Product code	Variant terms
PS0135	Access Dialing	PCA358	10-288; 10-322; dial around
PS0006	Air Miles	PCS932	AirMiles
PS0151	XYZ Direct	DCW004	USADirect; XYZ USA Direct; XYZDirect card

For this project, we were dealing with 7 distinct vocabularies and around 600 accepted terms.

- Products & Services (151 accepted terms)
- Partners & Competitors (122 accepted terms)
- Plans & Promotions (173 accepted terms)
- Geographic Codes (51 accepted terms)
- Adjustment Codes (36 accepted terms)
- Corporate Terminology (70 accepted terms)
- Time Codes (12 accepted terms)

Even given the relatively small size and simplicity of these vocabularies, we found Microsoft Word was barely sufficient for the task. We created one very long document with tables for each vocabulary. This document was "owned" by a single controlled vocabulary manager and shared via our local area network. Our team of indexing specialists was able to search against accepted and variant terms in the "database" using MS Word's Find capability. And we were able to output tab-delimited files to assist the programmers who were building the site at AT&T.

Design Collaboration

Once you've developed blueprints, wireframes, content models, and vocabularies, you'll find yourself collaborating more with other people involved in developing the site—visual designers, developers, content authors, or managers. You'll move from capturing and communicating your own design concepts to integrating them with the visions of other members of your team. Naturally, this is as challenging as design gets—everyone wants his own ideas to play a role in the final product, and because the group's members often come from interdisciplinary backgrounds, there are often competing vocabularies and breakdowns in communication. But if each person goes in with an open mind and good tools for collaborating, this difficult phase is also the most gratifying one, ending with a shared vision that's far better than anyone was likely to arrive at individually. Design sketches and web prototypes are just two tools for merging differing ideas.

Design Sketches

In the research phase, the design team developed a sense of the desired graphic identity or look and feel. The technical team assessed the information technology infrastructure of the organization and the platform limitations of the intended audiences, and they understood what was possible with respect to features such as dynamic content management and interactivity. And, of course, the architect designed the high-level information structure for the site. Design sketches are a great way to pool the collective knowledge of these three teams in a first attempt at interface design for the top-level pages of the site. This is a wonderful opportunity for interdisciplinary user interface design.

Using the wireframes as a guide, the designer now begins sketching pages of the site on sheets of paper. As the designer sketches each page, questions arise that must be discussed. Here is a sample sketching-session dialog:

> *Developer*: "I like what you're doing with the layout of the main page, but I'd like to do something more interesting with the navigation system."

> *Designer*: "Can we implement the navigation system using pull-down menus? Does that make sense architecturally?"

> *Information Architect*: "That might work, but it would be difficult to show context in the hierarchy. How about a tear-away table-of-contents feature? We've had pretty good reactions to that type of approach from users in the past."

> *Developer*: "We can certainly go with that approach from a purely technical perspective. How would a tear-away table of contents look? Can you sketch it for us? I'd like to do a quick-and-dirty prototype."

As you can see, the design of these sketches requires the involvement of members from each team. It is much cheaper and easier for the group to work with the designer on these rough sketches than to begin with actual HTML pages and finished graphics. These sketches allow rapid iteration and intense collaboration. The final product of a sketching session might look something like Figure 12-23.

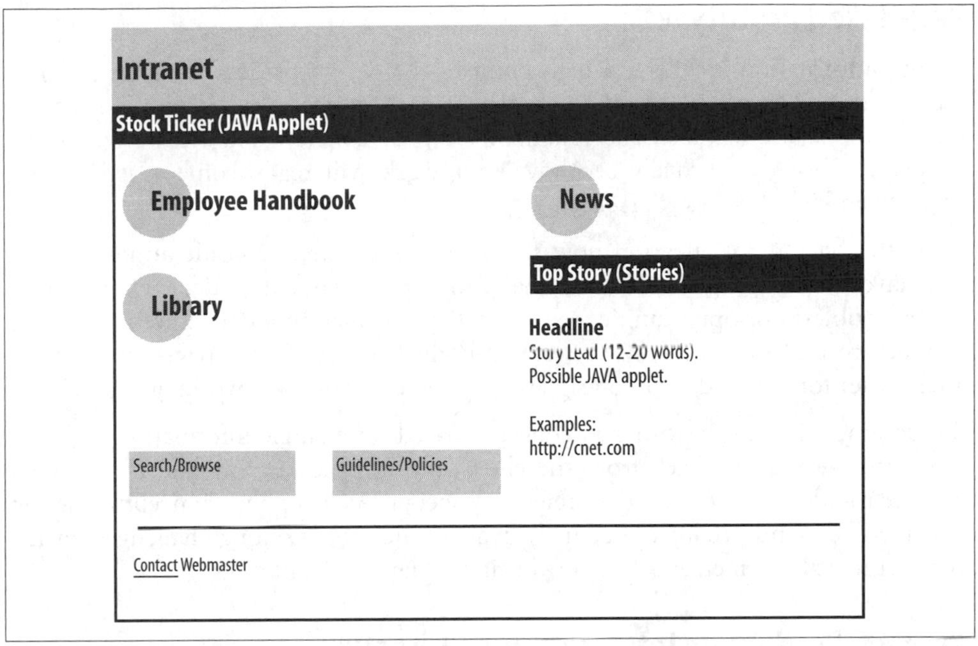

Intranet

Stock Ticker (JAVA Applet)

Employee Handbook

News

Library

Top Story (Stories)

Headline
Story Lead (12-20 words).
Possible JAVA applet.

Examples:
http://cnet.com

Search/Browse

Guidelines/Policies

Contact Webmaster

Figure 12-23. A basic design sketch

In this example, Employee Handbook, Library, and News are grouped together as the major areas of the web site. Search/Browse and Guidelines/Policies make up the page navigation bar. The News area defines space for a dynamic Java-based news panel. This sketch may not look much different from a wireframe. In fact, the team may have begun with an information architect's wireframe, then iterated on the design until arriving at this sketch, which in turn may be the basis for a revised and final wireframe.

Starting with a sketch—whether a formal wireframe or something more "back-of-the-napkin"—is critical to the success of interdisciplinary meetings. The sketch provides a common focus for each participant, minimizing the attention paid to the individual personalities around the table. It also makes it more likely that participants will be using the same terminology to discuss the design; shared terms for design concepts often emerge directly from the sketch itself.

Finally, note that design sketches aren't necessarily "owned" by the information architect. For example, sketches that describe functional requirements may be under the purview of the designer or developer. Be wary of getting caught up in ownership issues; contributing to the design, regardless of who is driving Visio, OmniGraffle, or Illustrator, is far more important to the project's outcome.

Web-Based Prototypes

For the information architect, a high point of the design process is the creation of web-based prototypes. More than sketches or scenarios, these digital renditions show how the site will look and function. They are concrete and often aesthetically compelling; you can actually see how your work will really come together, and maybe even kick the tires yourself.

While the balance of attention now shifts toward aesthetic considerations such as page layout and graphic identity, the prototypes frequently identify previously unseen problems or opportunities related to the information architecture. Once your architecture and navigation system are embodied in actual web pages, it becomes much easier for you and your colleagues to see whether they are working.

The designer may begin with two concepts based on a single information architecture. After getting feedback from the client, the designer and architect may work together to adapt and extend the preferred concept. At this point, conceptual design officially ends, and production actually begins. The most exciting challenges for the architect have been met, and you now begin the days of detail.

Point-of-Production Information Architecture

Ideally, the production process would proceed smoothly in a paint-by-numbers manner, and the architect could sit back and relax. In reality, you must be actively involved to make sure the architecture is implemented according to plan and to address any problems that arise. After all, no architect can anticipate everything.

Many decisions must be made during production. Are these content chunks small enough that we can group them together on one page, or should they remain on separate pages? Should we add local navigation to this section of the site? Can we shorten the label of this page? Be aware that at this stage, the answers to these questions may impact the burden on the production team as well as the usability of the web site. You need to balance the requests of your client against the sanity of the production team, the budget and timeline, and your vision for the information architecture of the web site.

You shouldn't need to make major decisions about the architecture during production because hopefully these have already been made. Discovering a major flaw in the architecture at this point is an information architect's nightmare. Fortunately, if you've followed the process of research, strategy, and design, this is unlikely. You have worked hard to define the mission, vision, audiences, and content for the web site. You have documented the decisions made along the way. You have resolved the top-down and bottom-up approaches through content mapping and detailed blueprints. Through careful planning, you've created a solid information architecture that should stand the test of time.

Still, it's worth reminding yourself that an information architecture can never be perfect. Factors of content, users, and context are constantly changing, and the architecture will, too. It's more important to invest your energy in educating your colleagues that information architecture design is an ongoing process, rather than fighting with them to get it "right."

Putting It All Together: Information Architecture Style Guides

A web site is always growing and changing. As an information architect, you must help guide its development—even after the site launches—or risk architectural drift. It's frustrating to see your carefully and flexibly designed organization, navigation, labeling, and indexing systems get mangled as site maintainers add content without heeding the architectural implications. While it may be impossible to completely prevent the effects of entropy, an information architecture style guide can steer content maintainers in the right direction.

An *architecture style guide*[*] is a document that explains how the site is organized, why it is organized that way, who it's for, and how the architecture should be extended as the site grows. The guide should begin with documentation of the mission and vision for the site, as it's important to understand the original goals. Continue with information about the intended audiences. Who was the site designed for? What are their goals? What assumptions were made about their information needs? Then, follow up with a description of the content development policy. What types of content will and won't be included and why? How often will it be updated? When will it be removed? And who will be responsible for it?

The "Why" Stuff

Documenting the lessons learned and the decisions made during the research, strategy, and design phases is critical. These underlying philosophies not only drive the design and maintenance of the information architecture, they also guide your site through the zigs and zags of major changes that your organization will surely encounter in the future.

For example, your organization may merge with another or spin off a unit. It may offer new products, or try to reach new markets and go global in the process. Major changes like these often coincide with major organizational changes such as new senior managers, many of whom wish to leave their mark in all areas, including the

---

[*] For an excellent example of a general style guide that includes information architecture and other areas, see the "Best Practices for PBS Member Stations" design guidelines, developed with assistance from Adaptive Path: *http://www.pbs.org/remotecontrol/bestpractices*.

site's design. But do new requirements and major changes to the organization require major changes to the site's information architecture? Ideally, not; a clearly documented rationale serves to explain an information architecture and demonstrate its flexibility, thereby mitigating against the extremes that plague so many redesigns.

Perhaps the biggest "why" you'll encounter is the one that comes so often from senior vice presidents, marketing managers, and product managers, which, in effect, boils down to: "why can't my favorite feature/my department's content be made more prominent/become your highest priority?" An information architecture style guide provides you with concrete documentation to help you prioritize the many such requests you'll likely encounter. It'll even provide you with cover when you absolutely have to say no.

The "How" Stuff

Your style guide should include some basic nuts-and-bolts components to help various people maintain the site. Consider including such sections as:

Standards
> There are usually at least a few rules that must be followed while maintaining and changing the site. For example, newly-created documents must be indexed with terms from the appropriate controlled vocabulary before they are published to the site. Or there may be specific procedures that must be followed to ensure that new content is immediately spidered and indexed by the site's search system. Here's the place to note the rules…

Guidelines
> …and distinguish the rules from the guidelines, which suggest—but don't mandate—how the information architecture should be maintained. These may be drawn from information architecture best practices,* and often require interpretation for each situation in which you'll find yourself; examples include advice on how to avoid overly long lists of links and page-titling recommendations.

Maintenance procedures
> Regular tasks that are required for the site's survival should be fully documented, such as when and how to add new terms to a controlled vocabulary.

---

* For a few examples of IA heuristics, visit the following links: Lou Rosenfeld's "IA heuristics" at *http://www.louisrosenfeld.com/home/bloug_archive/000286.html,* Lou Rosenfeld's "IA heuristics for search systems" at *http://louisrosenfeld.com/home/bloug_archive/000290.html,* and James Robertson/StepTwo's "Intranet Review Toolkit" at *http://www.intranetreviewtoolkit.org.*

Pattern library

> Consider creating a pattern library* that documents and provides access to reusable aspects of your site's design—such as a navigation widget that helps users scroll through pages of results—to cut down on reinventing the wheel.

Your style guide should also present both the blueprints, wireframes, controlled vocabulary information, and other documentation that came from the design process and will be reused throughout the site's lifetime. Since you won't always be there to explain these deliverables, it may be necessary to provide written explanations to accompany the blueprints. You also need to create guidelines for adding content to ensure the continued integrity of the organization, labeling, navigation, and indexing systems. This can be a challenge. When should a new level in the hierarchy be added? Under what conditions can new indexing terms be introduced? How should local navigation systems be extended as the web site grows? By thinking ahead and documenting decisions, you can provide much-needed guidance—a user's manual, really—to the site maintainers.

Keep in mind the different audiences that might use the style guide. For example, in a large organization, content authors working from far-flung parts of the globe may not need to know the site's overall strategy so much as the maximum number of characters they should use for a document title. Interaction designers may need to understand the rules that guide construction of the ALT tags that a navigation system's mouse-overs rely upon. Consider an information architecture style guide as a sort of "how and why" document that should be designed for use, just like any other information system. And remember that your organization may already have a style guide for its branding, its content, and other aspects of its online presence; when possible, integrate information architecture guidelines into existing style guides.

---

* To learn how Yahoo! developed its excellent library, read "Implementing a Pattern Library in the Real World: A Yahoo! Case Study," by Erin Malone, Matt Leacock, and Chanel Wheeler (*Boxes & Arrows*, April 29, 2005): *http://www.boxesandarrows.com/view/implementing_a_pattern_library_in_the_real_world_a_yahoo_case_study*.

Information Architecture in Practice

CHAPTER 13

Education

What we'll cover:

- The current state of IA education
- The value of relevant educational credentials to IA employment
- Universities that offer IA degrees and coursework

We get lots of email from people who want to become information architects. A technical writer in Australia states her desire to make an ambitious career change toward information architecture and asks, "What are my chances, and what advice do you have for me to increase my skill set?" A library and information science student in Florida explains that he's committed to becoming an information architect but notes that clear directions are hard to find.

We also talk with many practicing information architects who are searching for ways to improve their expertise. Some want a broad introduction that covers all the bases, while others need advanced skills in a specific area of practice. A few are willing and able to pursue a graduate degree, but most are searching for educational formats that better fit their busy schedules.

And last but not least, we regularly meet with people who have no interest in becoming information architects but want to learn more about information architecture. They may be decision makers or managers with broad responsibilities for web and intranet development; their core expertise may be in marketing, software development, interaction design, or a dozen other areas. Information architecture plays a small but important role in their activities.

In short, all of these people are searching for ways to learn about information architecture, and many are having a hard time finding what they need.

Transition in Education

It's not surprising to see all this confusion. In such a new discipline, all the paths are "less traveled." Schools are not sure what to teach, and students don't know what they need to learn.

In the established professions of medicine, law, and business, a vast array of educational programs has been tested by the evolutionary pressures of the market. Only those programs that add value have survived. The independent forces of supply and demand have moved toward equilibrium.

In our field, both the employment and education markets are still somewhat immature. The hiring of professional information architects by consulting firms and large corporations is a relatively new phenomenon. It's still unclear how much information architecture design will be done in the coming years and who will do it. The recent economic turbulence in the IT industry has further muddied the waters—and our field is not alone in this chaos. A powerful assortment of forces is driving change in the broader realms of government, economics, communication, entertainment, and education. As individuals, it's not easy to make sense of the fast-paced world around us, particularly when it comes to our careers. In such a dynamic and competitive environment, we must take responsibility for our own education, and we must all be lifelong learners.

A World of Choice

A wonderful aspect of life in the 21st century is our freedom as consumers to choose what we want. In education, awareness of the rich array of opportunities is a key to success. Never before have there been so many different ways to learn. This is especially true in fields like information architecture that have become early adopters of Internet technologies for communication and collaboration. Resources and methods for learning include:

Experience
> There's no substitute for the time-tested method of learning by doing. Most of today's information architects learned their craft on the job. Volunteering at a nonprofit organization or building a personal web site can jump-start beginners.

Apprenticeship
> The fastest and most reliable way to move from novice to expert is to work closely with someone who's already an expert. Try to find a mentor who's willing to share his tacit knowledge.

Formal education
> As the field matures, we expect that growing numbers of information architects will seek and find formal education. Ultimately, employers will prefer candidates with a blend of education and experience. We tackle this important topic in the next section.

Conferences and seminars

Whether you're searching for a quick introduction or an in-depth study, you'll find all sorts of courses, workshops, and seminars offered by universities, conferences, and consulting firms. If you have to choose just one, we recommend the annual ASIS&T Summit (*http://iasummit.org/*).

Literature

The volume of books and articles relevant to information architecture is staggering. If you look carefully, you can also find research reports, survey results, and sample deliverables.

Communities

Professional associations and online communities offer great ways to learn about best practices and network with people in the field. Online discussion lists are often a good place to begin.

News and opinion

News feeds and blogs that cover information architecture and experience design can also be invaluable for keeping up with the latest people and ideas.

While it's impossible to be comprehensive, we have provided selective pointers to education resources in the Appendix. This guide to essential information architecture resources should get you started on your quest to learn more.

But Do I Need a Degree?

You don't need a specialized degree to become an information architect, but it helps. As our field matures and becomes more competitive, the emphasis on formal educational credentials grows more pronounced.

At present, only a few schools offer a degree in information architecture, but a much wider collection of universities offers relevant degrees that include coursework in information architecture.

For instance, many information architects have chosen graduate programs in Library and Information Science (LIS) or Human–Computer Interaction (HCI), in which they can knit together a custom curriculum relevant to their future. Some LIS programs have stretched beyond the traditional library, exploring information organization in the online environment, and some HCI programs have escaped the boundaries of the software interface to explore rich content environments and information-seeking behavior.

In fact, you can build a solid foundation for an information architecture career in a variety of programs. It's important to consider the mix of core courses, the interests of faculty, and the availability of cognate classes. For example, as a student in an LIS program, can you take classes in the university's business and engineering programs?

As you wind your way through a program, you might consider using our three circles (users, content, and context) to help shape a major and a minor. For example, in an HCI program, you could major in users (understanding how users interact with interfaces) but minor in content (taking some LIS courses in information organization and retrieval). It's important to have a core area of expertise but also to be well rounded.

The State of the Field

We recently surveyed information architecture educators and practitioners to get a clear snapshot of this fast-changing environment.* As Table 13-1 shows, we found that roughly half of practitioners have formal education in a relevant field.

Table 13-1. Formal education

Do you have any *formal* (e.g., college, university) education in Information Architecture, Human–Computer Interaction, Usability, Library Science or a related field?	
Yes	48.6%
No	48.6%
Not Sure	2.8%

Among those with a formal education, roughly 70 percent hold a Master's degree, and as Table 13-2 shows, library science clearly stands out.

Table 13-2. Major field of study

What was your major field of study? (if you responded "Yes" above)	
Library Science	40.3%
Human–Computer Interaction	12.3%
Information Management	8.4%
Information Architecture	4.5%
Human Factors	3.9%
Information Science	3.9%
Usability	3.2%
Interaction Design	2.6%
Technical Communication	2.6%
Cognitive Psychology	1.3%
Computer Engineering	1.3%
Design	1.3%
Information Systems	1.3%
Multimedia Design	1.3%

* For complete survey results, see *http://iainstitute.org/pg/polar_bear_book_third_edition.php*.

Table 13-2. Major field of study (continued)

What was your major field of study? (if you responded "Yes" above)	
Software Development	1.3%
Communications Design	0.6%
Computer-Based Instructional Design	0.6%
Computer Science	0.6%
Ergonomics	0.6%
Industrial Design	0.6%
Interactive Multimedia	0.6%
Learning Design and Technology	0.6%
Library Science and Human Factors	0.6%
User-Centered Design	0.6%
Visual Communication	0.6%

And, among those practitioners with hiring responsibilities, roughly 50 percent responded that when making a hiring decision, they consider formal education in a related field to be either valuable or extremely valuable.

Fortunately, the volume and diversity of programs that offer information architecture coursework is increasing to meet demand. Schools that offer information architecture degrees include:

- University of Baltimore, Master of Science in Interaction Design and Information Architecture
- Illinois Institute of Technology, Master of Science in Information Architecture
- Kent State University, Master of Science in Information Architecture and Knowledge Management

And, schools that offer substantive information architecture coursework include:

- University of California—Berkeley, School of Information
- Carnegie Mellon, School of Design
- University of Michigan, School of Information
- University of Texas, School of Information
- University of Washington, Information School

In summary, the field of information architecture is in transition. After more than a decade, the field is no longer in its infancy, but there's still plenty of room to grow. Whatever your goals and educational credentials, there are two things you can count on as you look ahead. First, change will be rapid and relentless. Second, time and attention will be limited. So you can never learn everything, but your education is an ongoing process. Choose carefully and learn to love learning.

CHAPTER 14
Ethics

What we'll cover:
- The politics of categories and classification
- Issues of intellectual and physical access to information
- The ethical responsibilities of information architects

You've almost finished the book. You understand the concepts. You're familiar with the methods. But before you move onward and upward, consider the following questions:

- Are you aware that the practice of information architecture is riddled with powerful moral dilemmas?

- Do you realize that decisions about labeling and granularity can save or destroy lives?

- Will you be designing ethical information architectures?*

If you've never considered these questions, don't worry. It's not your fault. Blame your parents. Did they ever take the time when you were a small child to clarify that the story of Hansel and Gretel is really a metaphor for the horrors of ineffective breadcrumb navigation? Did they ever explain that Spiderman symbolizes the virtuous hypertextual power of the Web? Without information architect superheroes and archvillains to serve as role models, how you could be expected to recognize your own potential for good or evil?

---

* This chapter is based on a *Strange Connections* article written by Peter Morville (*http://argus-acia.com/ strange_connections/strange008.html*).

Ethical Considerations

The truth is that ethics is one of the many hidden dimensions of information architecture. As Geoffrey Bowker and Susan Star state in their book *Sorting Things Out* (MIT Press):

> Good, usable systems disappear almost by definition. The easier they are to use, the harder they are to see.

> Large information systems such as the Internet or global databases carry with them a politics of voice and value that is often invisible, embedded in layers of infrastructure.

Through the course of the book, Bowker and Star uncover the serious ethical dimensions of organizing and labeling information.

Now, don't worry. We're not about to stand on a soapbox and tell you how to save the world. Instead, we present a framework that illuminates six ethical dimensions faced by information architects, so you can make your own decisions. Once again, we humbly seek to make the invisible visible.

Intellectual Access

Much information architecture work is focused on helping people find information or complete tasks efficiently and effectively. We hope to reduce senseless friction, thus avoiding wasted time, money, and frustration.

But we also go beyond connecting users with the information they're explicitly seeking, by leveraging thesauri and recommendation engines to educate them about additional products, services, or knowledge that they didn't know existed. This work is no more ethically neutral than designing the first atomic bomb.

Recently, Amazon changed its search engine after an abortion-rights organization complained that results were skewed toward anti-abortion books.[*] Apparently, when users searched on "abortion," Amazon's autosuggest presented them with the question "Did you mean adoption?" Amazon explained this was an algorithmic rather than editorial suggestion, but its choice to disable that suggestion was clearly an editorial decision with ethical (as well as political and financial) implications.

A great information architecture can help a medical researcher discover the missing puzzle piece that results in the cure for a disease. A great information architecture can also connect an angry teenager with instructions on how to build a pipe bomb.

Whether you're working for a business, a nonprofit organization, a university, a government, a political candidate, the military, or a nuclear power station, the ethics of the information architecture depends on the unique situation. So before you take on a new job or project, you'd do well to consider the broader ethical context.

---

[*] "Amazon Says Technology, Not Ideology, Skewed Results," by Laurie J. Flynn. *New York Times*. March 20, 2006.

Labeling

There are few things as quietly powerful as labels. We are completely surrounded by them, and for the most part their influence is invisible. They are seen only by the people they hurt.

Bowker and Star provide a couple of good examples. They discuss the politics and pain involved in the transition over several years from the label "gay-related immune disorder" (GRID) through a chain of other labels to the now-accepted "acquired immune deficiency syndrome" (AIDS). In another example, they explain that "many patients feel that one of the greatest burdens of having chronic fatigue syndrome is the name of the illness." The word "fatigue" indicates everyday tiredness, making it less likely that friends, family, employers, and coworkers will take the condition seriously.

When we develop labeling systems and controlled vocabularies, we struggle to balance literary warrant (use of authors' terminology) with user warrant (anticipated terms to be employed by users). We strive for clarity, predictability, and conciseness. Perhaps we should also consider the potential impact our labels can have on people and perceptions.

Categories and Classification

The presence or absence of categories and the definition of what is and is not included in each category, can also have powerful consequences. Bowker and Star explain that although child abuse surely existed before the 20th century, you couldn't tell from the literature; that "category" did not exist. The very creation of the category made it more socially and legally visible.

They also discuss the problems that occur when things don't fit into an existing category ("monsters") and when they fit multiple categories ("cyborgs"). They include a quote from Harriet Ritvo about the proliferation of monsters in the 18th and 19th centuries, which notes that "monsters were united not so much by physical deformity or eccentricity as by their common inability to fit or be fitted into the category of the ordinary."

As we design classification schemes, are we responsible for our own Frankensteins? The taxonomies we build subtly influence people's understanding and can inject undesirable bias into sensitive topics. Let's make sure we classify with care.

Granularity

Bowker and Star examined the work of a group of nursing scientists to develop a Nursing Intervention Classification (NIC). They hoped that the classification would help make the work of nurses more visible and legitimate.

During the project, granularity took center stage in a balancing act between the politics of certainty and the politics of ambiguity:

> The essence of this politics is walking a tightrope between increased visibility and increased surveillance; between overspecifying what a nurse should do and taking away discretion from the individual practitioner.

It's interesting to consider the ethics of granularity in the context of web sites and intranets. What unintended consequences might result from our chunking of content? Who might suffer if we alter the balance between certainty and ambiguity? Sometimes, the devil is in the level of detail.

Physical Access

From ramps and elevators to large-print and audio books, architects, librarians, and designers are familiar with issues of physical access to traditional libraries. Unfortunately, the difficulty is carrying this experience into the digital environment.

Despite the ready availability of the W3C Web Content Accessibility Guidelines[*] and Section 508 Standards,[†] even today many software applications and web sites are designed with little sensitivity to the physical capabilities and limitations of various audiences. The ACM Code of Ethics states:

> In a fair society, all individuals would have equal opportunity to participate in, or benefit from, the use of computer resources regardless of race, sex, religion, age, disability, national origin or other such similar factors.

Ben Schneiderman, a leader in the field of human–computer interaction, extended this code of ethics into the notion of universal usability:

> Universal Usability will be met when affordable, useful, and usable technology accommodates the vast majority of the global population: this entails addressing challenges of technology variety, user diversity, and gaps in user knowledge in ways only beginning to be acknowledged by educational, corporate, and government agencies.[‡]

Surely, information architects have a role to play in creating useful, usable systems that work for diverse audiences. Have you been designing for universal usability?

Persistence

As we've mentioned before, information architecture is not about surface glamour; it's about mission-critical infrastructure. And infrastructure has widespread and long-term impact. The ripples of our designs spread outward, affecting the work of

---

[*] Web Accessibility Initiative, *http://www.w3.org/WAI*.

[†] Section 508 of the Rehabilitation Act, Electronic and Information Technology, *http://www.access-board.gov/508.htm*.

[‡] Ben Schneiderman, *Communications of the ACM*, 2000. See *http://universalusability.org*.

interface designers, programmers, authors, and eventually, users. And from experience, we know that the quick-and-dirty placeholder site can become an enduring monument to the axiom, "Do it right or don't do it at all." As we design the legacy information architectures of tomorrow, we should consider our responsibility to the big here and the long now (we'll discuss this topic in more detail in the section "Fast and Slow Layers" in Chapter 15). Remember the Y2K bug? Enough said.

Shaping the Future

As humans, we collectively avoid a huge percentage of ethical dilemmas by defining them out of existence. We decide that they are beyond our control and are someone else's responsibility.

As an information architect, you can define any or all of these ethical dimensions as "not my problem." Maybe the responsibility really belongs with the client, the business manager, the authors, the usability engineers, or the users themselves. Or, maybe we'll all just wait for a superhero to save the day.

Speaking of which, a handful of user-experience superheroes have written books that tackle these thorny issues head on. For example, B.J. Fogg's *Persuasive Technology: Using Computers to Change What We Think and Do* (Morgan Kaufmann) includes a chapter about the ethics of persuasive technology. Jeffrey Zeldman's *Designing with Web Standards* (Peachpit Press) details the ethics and economics of designing for accessibility. And, Adam Greenfield's *Everyware: The Dawning Age of Ubiquitous Computing* (Peachpit Press) presents ethical guidelines for user experience design in ubiquitous computing environments. We encourage you to read these books and put their ideas into action so you can help shape a better future.

Building an Information Architecture Team

What we'll cover:
- Striking a balance between innies and outies
- The implications of pace layering to IA team formation
- Staffing IA projects and programs (short-term and long-term considerations)
- The case for professional information architects

Since even the title of this chapter may incite quiet fury among our colleagues, we'd like to begin with a few qualifications. First, our focus on staffing an information architecture team in no way suggests a desire to build walls between roles and disciplines. To the contrary, we are firm believers in the value of closely knit, multidisciplinary teams. Second, we fully recognize that our description of an information architecture dream team is provocative and ambitious. The complete vision will be realized only in the largest of projects and organizations.

Our intent is to push the envelope, and to explore scenarios for the small but influential community of professional information architects. How will the world's most massive sites be designed and managed? Who will do the work? Will it be outsourced or done internally? Will staff be centralized or distributed?

These questions loom large in the minds of many. Should I become an in-house information architect, or is it better to stay in a consulting firm? Innie or outie? Which is safest? Where can we expect the most growth?

Intranet and web managers are asking the same questions. How do I get this information architecture designed? Do I need a permanent staff, or can I get by with a consultant? Either way, who do I hire? What mix of skills is required?

These are hard questions. They drive debates about the role and discipline of information architecture. They force us to imagine the future of our web sites, intranets, and companies. They demand that we make distinctions between the transient and the enduring. They make us feel confused and insecure. In other words, these are exactly the right questions to be asking.

These questions are especially difficult because we're compelled to fix the airplane while we're flying it. Even worse, we haven't yet reached cruising altitude. As we struggle to climb above the clouds and gain greater visibility, it's important to recognize that we're in the midst of a powerful transition.

In the 1990s, companies viewed their web sites and intranets as short-term projects. They expected to engage a design or IT consultancy for a few months and be done with it. Fortunately, this naïve attitude is gradually giving way to more enlightened perspectives. Many managers see the growing mission-critical nature of their web sites and intranets. They recognize the long-term value of strategy and architecture, and they're aware that information architecture challenges multiply as their sites become larger and more complex.

Consequently, many leading companies have created positions for in-house information architects. This is a positive step for the field as a whole, but it's unnerving to consultants and consultancies. Does this mean all information architecture design will soon be done in-house? No, of course not. But it does mean that we must figure out which approaches work best in which situations and at what times, and that leads us to the critical issue of the web design life cycle.

Destructive Acts of Creation

What bothers us most about web and intranet redesign projects is the widespread practice of throwing out the baby with the bathwater.* The site development process moves from strategy to design to implementation. Then, after a period of maintenance often measured in months, not years, someone decides a redesign is required. Perhaps there's a new CEO who wants a "fresh look," or the IT department purchases a content management system. Maybe the User Experience team just gets bored with maintenance.

Whatever the justification, someone commits to a take-no-prisoners redesign that obliterates all elements of the prior site. In the worst cases, an entirely new team is assigned to "do the job right this time," assuring no organizational learning whatsoever.

We're optimistic that we can break out of the infinite loop of destructive creation (Figure 15-1), but first we must better understand and disentangle the currently interwoven layers of information architecture, content, and interface.

---

* Sections of this chapter are drawn from "The Speed of Information Architecture," an article by Peter Morville (*http://semanticstudios.com/publications/semantics/000003.php*).

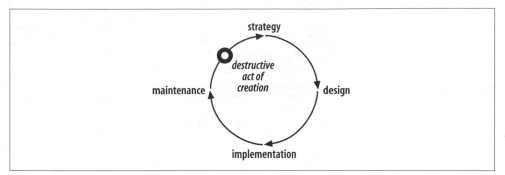

Figure 15-1. The infinite loop of destructive creation

Fast and Slow Layers

In his book *The Clock of the Long Now*, Stewart Brand introduces the notion that society is a construct of several layers, each with a unique and suitable rate of change (Figure 15-2). The slow layers provide stability; the fast layers drive innovation. The independence of speed between layers is a natural and healthy result of societal evolution. Imagine the alternative. How about commerce moving at the pace of federal bureaucracy? Remember the Soviet Union?

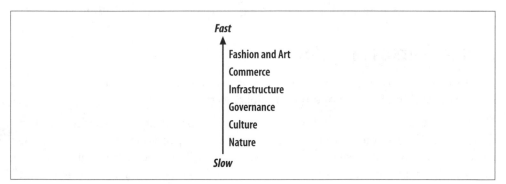

Figure 15-2. Societal layers

This recognition of independently dynamic layers holds great promise within the narrower domain of information architecture. By isolating enduring IA from adaptive IA, we can invest sensibly in long-term infrastructure while creating flexibility where it's needed. Figure 15-3 is an early attempt to identify these layers.

The lowest and slowest layers are facets and their hierarchies. These constitute the foundation of the enterprise IA infrastructure.

Next, the embedded navigation system composed of browsable taxonomies, indexes, and the search system defines at a fundamental level how users are able to search and browse. These two bottom layers should be stable. They become intertwined with

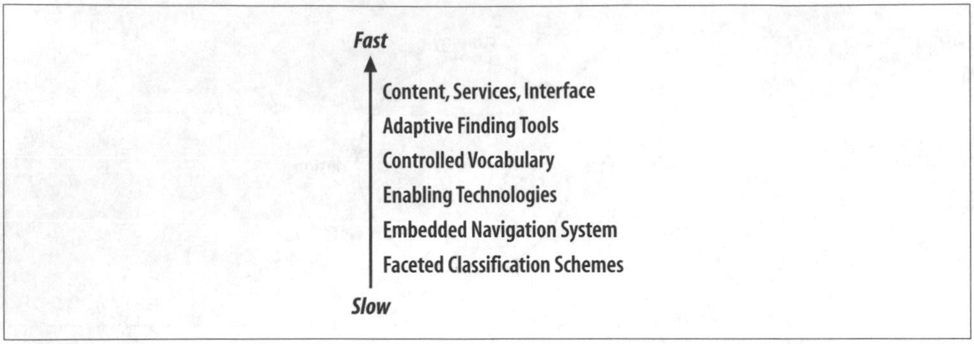

Figure 15-3. *Information architecture layers*

content, technology, and process, and become the core to users' mental models. Change at the bottom is painful and expensive. You also don't want to frequently switch enabling technologies such as content management systems, search engines, and portal software, as they too become enmeshed with content and process.

Moving to the faster layers, controlled vocabulary terms will evolve with product and service offerings and with the broader language of business and technology. Adaptive finding tools such as project-specific guides, indexes, and collaborative filtering devices will benefit from continuous adaptation. And, finally, the site's content and services may change on a regular basis, along with tweaks to the user interface.

Project Versus Program

All of this points toward the importance of evaluating information architecture staffing needs from both project and program perspectives.

First, companies must staff a short but intensive information architecture *project* to design an enduring foundation. Depending on the scale of your site, the project may require anywhere from 6 weeks to 18 months, and will involve research and the eventual development of an information architecture strategy. You need "big-picture" information architects who can design an overall strategic framework that integrates organization and navigation systems with the software, processes, and staffing responsibilities needed to bring it to life and keep it living. You also need "detail-oriented" information architects who can do the critical work of developing the controlled vocabularies for each facet. And, of course, the work of these individuals needs to be coordinated. In other words, you must staff this project with a well-organized team of professional information architects who bring real expertise and experience to the table. The quality of the work they do on this project will be something your organization lives with for a long time.

Second, you need to build an information architecture *program* that is focused on administration and continuous improvement. This will mostly require detail-oriented information architects who will be responsible for manual indexing and controlled vocabulary management. You may also want a "cartographer" who converts patterns in content, structure, and usage into useful maps and other navigation tools. And, if you're staffing at the enterprise level, you may want to hang on to your strategic information architects. (To learn more about information architecture for the enterprise, see Chapter 19.) They can provide the long-term vision and continuity to keep your site on track, and can also serve as consultants to the businesses and functions on subsite projects, promoting consistency throughout the organization.

Buy or Rent

The question remains: how does a company strike a balance between consultants and in-house staff? Let's begin with the outies. There are all sorts of reasons why companies hire consultants in general, and most of these can be applied to information architecture specifically.

Projects

Companies often hire consultants to complete a project with a limited duration. This relates to the project/program distinction we just made. You don't want to hire a full-time, permanent employee for a six-month project. For this reason, companies should consider using consultants heavily (but not solely) to make that initial investment in an information architecture foundation or a major redesign.

Money and politics

Because of the short-term nature of the investment, it's often easier to get a budget for consultants than for in-house staff. In addition, there's a tendency for managers within an organization to respect "objective expert advice" coming from outside the company much more than the "biased opinions" of people within the company. Given the new and insecure position of information architecture practices within many companies, "high-powered consultants" are often needed to establish internal credibility and launch the operation successfully.

Perspective

Although they're never completely unbiased, consultants really can bring a fresh, outsider's perspective. This is particularly important when you're trying to get outside the organizational mindset and understand the needs and behavior of your users. Consultants can also draw upon the "best practices" they've seen at other companies, helping you learn from the successes and failures of others.

On the other hand, there are some very good reasons why companies hire employees, and these too apply to information architects.

Programs

For ongoing programs, it's typically more cost effective to hire full-time, permanent employees. You'll probably want to hire a staff to manage those fast-moving layers of information architecture (e.g., controlled vocabularies, secondary navigation structures). As web sites and intranets are increasingly recognized as mission-critical, the question will shift from "Do I hire an information architect?" to "How many do I hire, and what types of information architects do I need?"

Business context

Over time, in-house information architects gain a rich understanding of the business context, which is a real advantage over consultants. Their deep knowledge of the strategy, customers, and culture of the organization can provide insight into needs and opportunities that are invisible to an outsider.

Relationships

In-house information architects have the opportunity to build the long-term strategic relationships with employees, customers, and partners that are often needed to effect real change in a large organization.

In large organizations, it's often best to begin with a mix of consultants and staff. You'll need the added firepower of consultants to work through the initial information architecture project. By carefully selecting a mix of consultants, you can use this as an opportunity to learn about your staffing requirements and the types of available skill sets. This will be helpful as you begin to transition from project to program and from consultants to staff. Of course, it's a good idea to maintain a consulting budget so that you have the ability to handle ad hoc projects and expose your in-house staff to fresh perspectives from time to time.

In a smaller organization with only a handful of web-focused employees, you're less likely to be able to justify a full-time information architect. In such cases, our advice is to engage a professional consultant to develop a framework, and then make someone inside your organization responsible for the minimal amount of ongoing maintenance.

Do We Really Need to Hire Professionals?

We are continually amazed by the scale of business blunders caused by the false assumption that anybody can do this work. In our consulting experience with dozens of Fortune 500 companies, we have seen several situations where literally millions (if not tens of millions) of dollars have been wasted by web and intranet development teams that lack even a single professional information architect.

Inside large companies, the policy of promote-from-within sometimes results in newly anointed "information architects" who may know the business context but lack understanding of users and content. Consulting firms can produce even worse results. Not so long ago, it was fairly common practice for consultants to respond to a client's request for an information architect by rebranding one of their graphic designers. A quick change on a business card and *voilà*, you've got your information architect!

In all walks of life, we hire professionals when we want some assurance that the work will be done quickly and effectively. We constantly make judgments about when and when not to pay the added price. I cut my finger on a piece of glass, decide stitches probably aren't necessary, and go the self-help route with Band-Aids and antibiotic cream. But if the bleeding is bad, I'm off to the emergency room for stitches. We make the same judgments when deciding to hire lawyers, accountants, and plumbers.

In some of these cases, our definition of a professional includes education and certification requirements as well as experience. We want a lawyer who has been to law school, passed the bar exam, and spent some time in practice. In other cases—for example, when we need a plumber—we may be satisfied with experience and a good reference.

So, we're not saying you need a professional information architect in all situations. If you're developing a small web site or maintaining a large one, an intelligent, detail-oriented person with a professional attitude may be all you need. And we're not demanding that a "professional information architect" must have a relevant graduate degree.

But, for Pete's sake (and for Lou's sake, too), if you're investing several million dollars in the development of a corporate web site or enterprise portal, don't you think it might be a good idea to have someone involved who actually has information architecture design experience? Someone who understands and cares about structuring and organizing information?

This stuff is really difficult! Even with relevant graduate degrees, a decade each of consulting experience, and the opportunity to work with some of the best and brightest in the field, we (the authors) are still learning how to design information architectures more effectively. Information architecture is not something you can pick up by reading a couple of books and taking a class.

We apologize for the soapbox rant, and we know we're preaching to the choir. The good news is the overall trend over the past decade has been toward hiring professional information architects. The best companies we've worked with in recent years have blended in-house information architects with specialized information architecture consultants to design powerful, flexible sites that last. The success of these early adopters will eventually result in broader recognition of the value of investing in professional information architects. Until then, let's all keep our soapboxes handy.

The Dream Team

The projects and programs of today are lucky to have one information architect involved. In the coming years, as sites become increasingly mission-critical and the industry matures, we will see teams of specialists blended to meet the unique challenges of each context.

Given a web site or intranet of sufficient value and complexity, Table 15-1 shows some of the information architecture specialists we'd want as part of our dream team.

Table 15-1. Information architecture dream team

Position title	Description
Strategy Architect	Responsible for overseeing design of the overall information architecture and working with other teams to ensure good integration. Familiarity with the business context and an ability to establish relationships with senior management are critical.
Thesaurus Designer	Develops classification schemes, controlled vocabularies, and thesauri. Requires education, experience, and a passion for detail.
Controlled Vocabulary Manager	Manages evolution of controlled vocabularies, including addition, modification, and deletion of preferred and variant terms. May coordinate a team of indexing specialists.
Indexing Specialist	Tags content and services with controlled vocabulary metadata. Requires attention to detail and commitment to quality and consistency.
Interaction Designer	Works in the gray area between information architecture and graphic design. Creates navigation schemes and page layouts with a focus on user interaction.
IA Software Analyst	The critical link between the IA and IT teams, focusing on ways to leverage software to create, manage, and drive the user experience. Requires familiarity with content management systems, search engines, auto-classification, collaborative filtering, and thesaurus management software.
IA Usability Engineer	Focuses on the intersection of usability and information architecture. Conducts studies that isolate IA elements (e.g., category labels). Background in HCI or ethnography.
Cartographer	Converts patterns in content, structure, and usage into maps, guides, indexes, and other useful navigation tools.
Search Analyst	Leads the design, improvement, and ongoing analysis of the search system. Works closely with the design, technical, content management, and information architecture teams.

This is only a partial inventory of the specialized roles information architects will be filling in the coming years. Other roles we expect to see include:

- Enterprise Information Architect
- Social Navigation Architect
- Content Management Architect
- Knowledge Management Architect
- Web Services Architect

Some may consider these ideas foolish, a fantasy constructed by information architects for information architects. But the complexity, sophistication, and importance (real and perceived) of information architecture work will continue to grow, and before too long we'll start to see most large organizations putting together these rich teams of specialists.

In fact, we've already witnessed the beginnings of these niche roles in some of the most progressive organizations. We've worked with controlled vocabulary managers and indexing specialists at AT&T. We've seen strategy architects and interaction designers at Vanguard. And we've collaborated with thesaurus designers and search analysts at Hewlett-Packard.

Let's close this chapter with the immortal words of William Gibson: "The future is already here. It's just unevenly distributed."

CHAPTER 16

Tools and Software

What we'll cover:
- The tools most useful to information architects, and how to select the right software
- Diagramming products such as Visio and OmniGraffle
- Prototyping tools such as Dreamweaver and iRise
- Portals and content management systems
- Search engines and tools for analytics, automated categorization, and user research

Information professionals have a love/hate relationship with information technology.* We love IT because it made our jobs necessary by enabling the creation and connection of tremendous volumes of content, applications, and processes. We hate IT because it constantly threatens to replace the need for us. If you've seen the 1957 film *Desk Set* in which the librarians fear the "electronic brain" threatening to steal their jobs, you understand the enduring nature of this struggle.

Love it or hate it, we are all participants in a co-evolutionary journey with technology that is defined by rapid change. As information architects, we have a real opportunity (if not an ethical obligation) to positively influence outcomes by injecting our understanding and healthy skepticism into the information technology acquisition and integration process.

A Time of Change

We are living in the stone age when it comes to software for information architects. The products are crude, as is our understanding of what we really need. When people get together to discuss experiences with enterprise-wide applications to support

---

* This chapter is based on a *Strange Connections* article written by Peter Morville (*http://argus-acia.com/ strange_connections/strange011.html*).

web sites and intranets, pain and suffering are dominant themes. Many organizations become so distracted and discouraged by their first web application that they fail to explore the products in related categories.

This will change. In the coming years, all large web sites and intranets will leverage software applications from a wide variety of categories. We will not choose between automated classification software and a collaborative filtering engine—we will need both, and more. And information architects will play an integral role—working closely with business managers, content managers, and software engineers to select, acquire, integrate, and leverage this sophisticated suite of applications. None of these people can successfully do this work alone.

Categories in Chaos

It's ironic that one of the toughest challenges in understanding software for information architects involves trying to define meaningful categories for the darned stuff. There are huge overlaps between products, exaggerated by overzealous marketing efforts that claim the software can create taxonomies, manage content, fix dinner, and tie your shoes. And, of course, the vendors and their products are multiplying, merging, and mutating at a terrific pace. Given this fluid, ambiguous context, this chapter is an early attempt to define a few of the product categories relevant to information architects.[*] They include:

- Automated Categorization (16.2%)[†]
- Search Engines (56.4%)
- Thesaurus Management Tools (19.7%)
- Portal or Enterprise Knowledge Platform (37.6%)
- Content Management Systems (65.8%)
- Web Analytics / Tracking (62.4%)
- Diagramming Software (79.5%)
- Prototyping Tools (70.9%)
- User Research and Testing (not included in survey)

Within each category, we list the most popular tools (according to our survey results), and in some cases we list additional tools worth mentioning. Our lists of product examples are by no means comprehensive. We hope only to provide a framework and a starting point.

---

[*] To draw upon the insights of the wider community, we conducted an online survey. The complete results are available at *http://iainstitute.org/pg/polar_bear_book_third_edition.php*.

[†] Survey participants were asked about the categories of software with which they had direct experience.

Automated Categorization

Software that uses human-defined rules or pattern-matching algorithms to automatically assign controlled vocabulary metadata to documents. This is equivalent to assigning documents to categories within a taxonomy.

Synonyms

Automated classification, automated indexing, automated tagging, clustering

Examples

- Interwoven's Metatagger, *http://www.interwoven.com/products/content_intelligence/index.html*
- Entrieva's SemioTagger, *http://www.entrieva.com/entrieva/semiotagger.htm*
- Vivisimo's Clustering Engine, *http://vivisimo.com/html/vce*
- Autonomy IDOL Server, *http://www.autonomy.com/content/Products/IDOL/index.en.html*

Comments

We see great potential to integrate human expertise in designing taxonomies with software that populates those taxonomies quickly, consistently, and inexpensively. However, note that this software:

- Works best on full-text document collections
- Can't index images, applications, or other multimedia
- Does not adjust for user needs or business goals
- Does not understand meaning

And, we believe that attempts to automatically generate the taxonomy itself, as Vivisimo and Autonomy attempt to do, will generally fail to produce categories and labels of sufficient quality for most applications.

Resources

- "Extracting Value from Automated Classification Tools" by Kat Hagedorn, *http://argus-acia.com/white_papers/classification.html*
- "Tools for Creating Categories and Browsable Directories" from Search Tools, *http://www.searchtools.com/info/classifiers-tools.html*
- "Little Blue Folders" by Peter Morville, *http://argus-acia.com/strange_connections/strange003.html*

Search Engines

Software that provides full-text indexing and searching capabilities.

Examples

- Endeca Information Access Platform, *http://endeca.com*
- Google Enterprise Solutions, *http://www.google.com/enterprise*

- Fast, *http://www.fastsearch.com*
- Autonomy, *http://autonomy.com*

Comments

As content volume grows, search will become the heart of most web sites and intranets. Yet few vendors admit they're selling a search engine; they all have "solutions." Meanwhile, the true challenge involves getting the IT people, who currently own the search engines within most corporations, to share their toys with people who understand how and why to connect users and content. The current difficulties in this category are not due to technology. It's a people problem! However, there are some interesting developments in the technology area. Multi-algorithmic solutions like Google and guided-navigation solutions like Endeca are gaining popularity, forcing the other vendors to play catch-up.

Resources

- "Search Tools for Web Sites and Intranets" by Avi Rappoport, *http://searchtools.com*
- "Search Engine Software for Your Web Site" by Danny Sullivan, *http://www.searchenginewatch.com/resources/software.html*
- Enterprise Search Report, *http://www.cmswatch.com/Search/Report*
- "In Defense of Search" by Peter Morville, *http://www.semanticstudios.com/publications/semantics/search.html*

Thesaurus Management Tools

Tools that provide support for the development and management of controlled vocabularies and thesauri.

Examples

- MultiTes, *http://www.multites.com*
- Factiva Synaptica, *http://www.factiva.com/products/taxonomy/synaptica.asp*
- Lexico, *http://www.pmei.com/lexico.html*
- WebChoir, *http://www.webchoir.com*
- Term Tree, *http://www.termtree.com.au*
- DataHarmony, *http://www.dataharmony.com*

Comments

The bleeding edge! Most early adopters have had to rely on custom development and integration. The hard part is supporting controlled vocabulary management in today's decentralized publishing environments.

Resources

- "Thesaurus Management Software" from the American Society of Indexers, *http://www.asindexing.org/site/thessoft.shtml*
- "Software for Building and Editing Thesauri" from Willpower Information, *http://www.willpower.demon.co.uk/thessoft.htm*

Portal or Enterprise Knowledge Platform

Tools that provide "completely integrated enterprise portal solutions."

Examples

- Microsoft SharePoint Portal Server, *http://www.microsoft.com/sharepoint/portalserver.asp*
- Bea's AquaLogic, *http://bea.com*
- Oracle Portal, *http://www.oracle.com/technology/products/ias/portal/index.html*
- IBM's WebSphere Portal, *http://www.ibm.com/websphere/portal*

Comments

The vision of seamless, intuitive access to all enterprise and third-party content independent of geography, ownership, and format is compelling and completely unrealized. These tools claim to do everything. Make sure you know what they do well.

Resources

- "Portal Software" by Janus Boye, *http://www.cmswatch.com/Feature/120*
- "Pandora's Portal" by Peter Morville, *http://www.semanticstudios.com/publications/semantics/portal.html*

Content Management Systems

Software that manages workflow from content authoring to editing to publishing.

Examples (Enterprise)

- Interwoven, *http://www.interwoven.com*
- Vignette, *http://www.vignette.com*
- Microsoft Content Management Server, *http://www.microsoft.com/cmserver*
- Stellent, *http://www.stellent.com*

Examples (Personal and Workgroup)

- WordPress, *http://wordpress.org*
- Movable Type, *http://www.sixapart.com/movabletype*
- Drupal, *http://drupal.org*
- Plone, *http://plone.org*
- SocialText, *http://www.socialtext.com*

Comments

At the enterprise level, Forrester Research calls these product offerings "immature." The problems stem from the fact that content management is very complex and very context-sensitive. Inevitably, you'll need to buy and then customize extensively. This is a headache that few large organizations will be able to avoid. At the personal and workgroup level, the products are relatively quick and easy to set up. They've powered the blogging revolution and are now having a positive impact in corporate environments.

Resources

- CMSWatch, *http://www.cmswatch.com*
- CM Professionals, *http://www.cms-list.org*

Analytics

Software that analyzes the usage and statistical performance of web sites, providing valuable metrics about user behavior and characteristics.

Examples

- WebTrends, *http://www.webtrends.com*
- Google Analytics, *http://www.google.com/analytics*
- Omniture, *http://www.omniture.com/products/web_analytics*
- CoreMetrics, *http://www.coremetrics.com*
- Mint, *http://www.haveamint.com*

Comments

This is a fast-growing category that's generated tremendous interest in recent years due to the advertising and marketing value derived from tracking and understanding user behavior.

Resources

- Wikipedia on Web Analytics, *http://en.wikipedia.org/wiki/Web_analytics*
- "Search Analytics for Your Site" by Louis Rosenfeld and Richard Wiggins, *http://www.rosenfeldmedia.com/books/searchanalytics*

Diagramming Software

Visual communication software that information architects use to create diagrams, charts, wireframes, and blueprints.

Examples

- Microsoft Visio, *http://www.microsoft.com/office/visio*
- OmniGraffle, *http://www.omnigroup.com/applications/omnigraffle*
- Illustrator, *http://www.adobe.com/products/illustrator*
- PowerPoint, *http://microsoft.com/powerpoint*
- Intuitect, *http://www.intuitect.com*

Comments

These are the visual communication tools that information architects use to create work products and deliverables, particularly blueprints and wireframes.

Resources

- "Diagramming Tools" on IAwiki, *http://www.iawiki.net/DiagrammingTools*
- "Where the Wireframes Are" by Dan Brown, *http://www.boxesandarrows.com/view/ where_the_wireframes_are_special_deliverable_3*

Prototyping Tools

Web development software that enables you to create interactive wireframes and clickable prototypes.

Examples

- Dreamweaver, *http://www.adobe.com/products/dreamweaver*
- Visio, *http://www.microsoft.com/office/visio*
- Flash, *http://www.adobe.com/products/flash/flashpro*
- Serena Composer, *http://www.serena.com/Products/composer*
- iRise, *http://www.irise.com*
- Axure, *http://www.axure.com*

Comments

As Rich Internet Applications (RIA) further blur the lines between web sites and software applications, prototyping tools provide a powerful way to show navigation, interaction, and other functionality during the design process.

Resources

- "HTML Wireframes and Prototypes" by Julie Stanford, *http://www.boxesandarrows. com/view/html_wireframes_and_prototypes_all_gain_and_no_pain*
- "A Designer's Guide to Prototyping Ajax" by Kevin Hale, *http://particletree.com/features/ a-designers-guide-to-prototyping-ajax.*

User Research

Software that supports user research, including online card sorting and remote usability testing.

Examples

- MindCanvas, *http://www.themindcanvas.com*
- Morae, *http://www.techsmith.com/morae.asp*
- Macromedia Captivate, *http://www.adobe.com/products/captivate*
- Ethnio, *http://www.ethnio.com*
- xSort, *http://www.ipragma.com/xsort*

Comments

These products can reduce the time and cost associated with user research, and may provide you with new ideas about how best to study user behavior and preferences. However, when it comes to developing empathy for the user, remember that there's no substitute for being in the same room. It's often best to combine in-person and remote testing methods, so you don't miss out on the human element.

Resources

- "Remote Online Usability Testing" by Dabney Gough and Holly Phillips, *http://www.boxesandarrows.com/view/remote_online_usability_testing_why_how_and_when_to_use_it*
- Remote Usability Testing Wiki, *http://remoteusability.com*

Questions to Ask

Whatever the category, when you're involved in selecting complex, expensive software, there are a number of important questions to ask.

You'll need to determine whether it's best to build it yourself, buy a product, or contract with an ASP (application service provider). You'll want to know about the total cost of ownership, from purchase to integration to customization to maintenance to upgrade. You'll want to know about the long-term outlook for the vendor; in other words, will she be there to answer the phone in six months?

Most importantly, you need to find an *engineer* in the vendor's firm who will answer these questions. One of the many truisms from the world of Dilbert is that engineers are like Vulcans; they cannot tell a lie. They will happily contradict their company's marketing hype—usually without even the slightest provocation—and tell you:

- What their product does well
- What their product does poorly
- What they wish their product could do

So, even though engineers are the ones who are actually working hard to automate us out of a job, we should still like them because they're helpful and honest. And they will only need us more in the coming years—to make productive use of the fascinating new tools they are building.

PART V

Information Architecture in the Organization

CHAPTER 17

Making the Case for Information Architecture

What we'll cover:
- The unavoidability of selling
- The ROI case for information architecture
- The fallacy of ROI thinking when it comes to information architecture
- Other ways to make the case for information architecture
- The value of information architecture: a checklist

Wherever information architecture is happening or could be happening, someone is trying to decide whether or not the pursuit is worth the investment of resources. And that person often needs a lot of convincing. You, as an information architect, must be prepared to make a case for what you do.

You Must Sell

Perhaps you've never found yourself trying to sell information architecture to a client; that's what the sales folks do, or if you're an in-house information architect, your boss worries about this. Your job is to just show up and generate those blueprints and wireframes. If this describes your attitude, skip this section. (But don't be surprised if you suddenly find yourself unemployed.)

When it comes to others' perceptions of information architecture, be prepared to change negative thinking into positive. Most people still haven't heard the term "information architecture," many don't think it's real or worth their attention, and many simply don't understand the value of anything so "fuzzy," especially when compared to concrete things like, say, the intensively marketed software tools that promise to solve their problems.

Some people do recognize the value of information architecture but don't know how to convince their colleagues. And others implicitly recognize its value in theory, but simply don't yet have the practical experience to tell the people in charge just how valuable it is compared with the many other ways they can spend their money.

You need to be ready for all of these situations—not just getting the point across initially, but being able to "sell" what you do on the ground. Because the worst can and often does happen after the sale. In fact, in a May 2002 survey of the information architecture community,* we found that the most challenging aspect of promoting information architecture was not getting the opportunity to promote it until it was too late in the design and development process. We've sold many large information architecture consulting engagements only to find that as soon as we sent our consultants off, some unanticipated and terrible event happened that jeopardized the entire project. For example, one person who hired us for a Fortune 50 company retired the day before we showed up for work. Worse, despite his assurances to us, he never had the political power within the organization to pave the way for our work. And even worse, he hadn't prepared his successor in any way; the successor didn't have a clear vision of the value of information architecture and obviously couldn't advocate for it to his colleagues. So our own consultants had to sell their expertise on his behalf. This made it difficult for them to actually get any work done, but they were ready to sell themselves, and it made a big difference. If our people couldn't have made a case for information architecture, the whole project would have been torpedoed.

So all information architects need to be salespeople at one time or another, both before a project is set up and while the project is underway.

The Two Kinds of People in the World

Now that we've covered the need to sell it, just what is involved in making the case for information architecture? That depends on the person to whom you're making the case. To grossly overgeneralize, we've found that business people typically fall into two groups: "by the numbers" folks, and "gut reactionaries."

The "by the numbers" people require data to help them make their decisions. They need to see figures: "If we invest X dollars into this information architecture thing, we'll make or save 2X dollars." They rationally consider return on investment (ROI) as the basis for their business decisions. Makes sense, right? Well, as we'll see, it doesn't. But you still need to understand this mindset because you'll encounter it again and again.

"Gut reactionaries" do what *feels* right. They trust their instincts and often have plenty of good experience to draw on. They consider the intangibles when they make decisions. And they're often suspicious of numbers and how well they depict the "real world." The success of the case you make to gut reactionaries often depends on luck as much as anything else; the intangibles are as dubious as they are fuzzy. So, just in case, you'd better dust off that suit before sitting down with a gut reactionary.

---

* *http://www.surveymonkey.com/DisplaySummary.asp?SID=106148&U=10614882722.*

Ultimately, when you're making the case for information architecture, you don't know which of these narrow and extremely unfair stereotypes will describe your client. So be prepared to discuss both the numbers and the intangibles.

Running the Numbers

OK, so here's the big question: what is information architecture actually worth?

The best source of numbers is white papers created by such analyst firms as Forrester Research and The Gartner Group. These numbers often don't focus on the ROI for information architecture per se, but they do address similar or overlapping areas of practice (e.g., user experience) or a hot technology (e.g., portals) that may involve a specific architectural approach.

For intranets, most utilize an opportunity cost approach to assessing ROI, drawing on a technique that was popularized in the web design community by Jakob Nielsen.[*] Table 17-1 shows the basic calculation.

Table 17-1. ROI case for investing in the Sun intranet's information architecture

Factor	Cost
Time lost due to a design-related problem (determined through user testing)	10 seconds/occurrence
Time lost over course of a year per employee (10 seconds/occurrence $\times$ 3 occurrences/day $\times$ 200 days/year)	6000 seconds (1.67 hours)/year
Cost per employee (e.g., $50/hour/employee, including benefits)	$83.33/employee
Number of employees that experience this problem	5,000
Total cost due to this design-related problem	$416,667/year

For example, if the design problem at hand is a confusing labeling system, and you feel confident that investing $150,000 will make it go away, then you can claim an ROI of 178 percent ($416,667–$150,000 / $150,000). Not bad, especially if you consider that this particular design problem may be just one of many that can be addressed.

Here are some more examples of this opportunity cost approach:

- Bay Networks invested $3 million into organizing 23,000 documents for its 7,000 users. Among other benefits, Bay estimated that each member of the sales staff would save a minimum of two minutes a day searching for documents, or roughly $10 million a year.[†] That's a 233% return on investment.

---

[*] "Intranet Portals: The Corporate Information Infrastructure" (*http://www.useit.com/alertbox/990404.html*).

[†] Fabris, P. "You Think Tomaytoes, I Think Tomahtoes" (*http://www.cio.com/archive/webbusiness/040199_nort.html*).

- In its November 2001 report "Intranets and Corporate Portals: User Study,"[*] Agency.com surveyed 543 employees from different companies regarding their use of portals. Respondents reported that portal use saves on average 2.8 hours per week, or 7 percent of their time. Assuming $55,000/year per employee (fully loaded), a well-designed portal would save employers $3,908 per employee. A 5,000-person company would therefore save about $20,000,000/year.

- Applying this approach to intranet portals, Nielsen states that "The cost of poor navigation and lack of design standards is . . . at least ten million dollars per year in lost employee productivity for a company with 10,000 employees."

The last two examples don't provide investment costs, so we can't determine the actual ROI. Regardless, the number jockeys will be extremely impressed.

These examples focus on ROI for intranets, which is measured primarily in cost savings. What about external sites, such as e-commerce sites, that are geared toward increasing revenue? The most powerful numbers come from examining sales lost due to sites that confuse and frustrate customers. For example, Creative Good tested the BestBuy.com e-commerce site and found that over 78 percent of customers' purchase attempts failed.[†] Creative Good then designed a prototype of the BestBuy.com site with improvements made to, among other things, some aspects of the information architecture. Among customers who used the prototype, 88 percent could complete a purchase, exactly quadruple that of the live site's rate.

It's not clear what the improvements would cost, but Creative Good estimated that they would require less than one month to develop and implement. Let's be conservative and assume that this effort cost $1,000,000 (a reasonably high number). If BestBuy.com's current sales are $100,000,000, and the improvements only doubled (not quadrupled) sales to $200,000,000, the ROI would still be quite healthy: ($100,000,000–$1,000,000) / $1,000,000 = 9,900%!

There are many other similar and exciting numbers for e-commerce sites.[‡] For example, IBM spent millions over a 10-week/100+ employee effort to improve ibm.com's information architecture, resulting in a 400 percent increase in sales.[§] And Tower Records was able to double the rate of purchases made by visitors to its site by improving its search system.[**]

---

[*] See *http://research.agency.com/*.

[†] "Holiday 2000 E-Commerce: Avoiding $14 Billion in 'Silent Losses'" (*http://www.creativegood.com/holiday2000*).

[‡] Another good article: Najjar, L. J. "E-commerce user interface design for the Web." (*http://mime1.gtri.gatech.edu/mime/papers/e-commerce%20user%20interface%20design%20for%20the%20Web.html*).

[§] Tedeschi, B. "Good Web site design can lead to healthy sales." (*http://www.nytimes.com/library/tech/99/08/cyber/commerce/30commerce.html*).

[**] Guernsey, L. "Revving up the search engines to keep the e-aisles clear." *New York Times*, February 28, 2001.

Many of the metrics used to judge a site's success can be positively impacted by an improved information architecture. And for each of those architectural improvements, there is likely an exciting number that matches it. If LL Bean is trying to sell more ties, better contextual navigation from the shirts area to connect to matching ties might raise revenue. If the Sierra Club is trying to increase awareness of environmental issues, perhaps a more prominent link to its mailing lists and feeds would raise subscription levels. If American Express is drowning in costs associated with printing, maintaining, and distributing product literature to financial advisors across the country, a well-architected extranet might save them big bucks. And if Dell is trying to reduce technical-support call volumes, perhaps reconfiguring its site's search system will result in higher usage levels and allow for a reduction in technical support staff.

Ultimately, certain aspects of information architecture, like any other UCD-influenced improvement, *should* have a direct and quantifiable impact on just about any site's performance. Because the cost of information architecture work can be measured, ROI calculations *should* be attainable. And you *should* therefore be able to have fruitful and productive conversations with the "by the numbers" people.

Debunking the ROI Case

By now, you should be getting nervous because we italicized "should" three times in the last paragraph. Unfortunately, it's almost always impossible to calculate true ROI for an information architecture. We can discuss it as theory, but information architects must be careful not to fall into the trap of false claims of attaining proven ROI numbers.

There are three major reasons why ROI measurements of information are, at best, unreliable:

The benefits of a complete information architecture cannot be quantified
> It's generally possible to measure the value (and ROI) of some of an architecture's individual components. For example, we may be able to determine how well users navigate a broad and shallow hierarchy versus a narrow and deep one. Or we might measure how users respond to one way of presenting search results versus another.
>
> However, an information architecture is made up of many such components. And it's generally wrong to measure an individual architecture component, as there's a good chance that its performance will be impacted by that of another component. As mentioned earlier, users often integrate tools for both searching and browsing in a single effort to find information. Although the natural tendency is to separate these tools for testing purposes, it makes more sense to measure searching and browsing performance together—after all, that's how the site is used. But measuring both concurrently is exceedingly difficult; it soon becomes apparent that you can't isolate the impact on performance that each component makes.

Measuring the performance of a component of an information architecture is useful as long as such measurements are not confused with the measure of the overall architecture.*

The benefits of many information architecture components can't ever be quantified

Though an information architecture is greater than the sum of its parts, the performance of many of its parts can't ever be quantified.

For example, many efforts to measure search performance focus on how long and how many clicks it takes users to find the answer. This is reasonable if users are performing only known-item searches, where there is a "right" answer to their question and a consistent and measurable endpoint to their search sessions. But as discussed earlier in this book, the majority of many sites' users are not performing known-item searches. Instead, they're looking to perform comprehensive research, learn a few tidbits about a topic, pick up some news, or be entertained. These types of searches usually don't have an endpoint. If there is no endpoint, it's not possible to confirm (and therefore quantify) success.

Another consideration is that many users *don't* find what they need from a site. There are potentially huge numbers associated with this cost, but how would it ever be measured? In these situations, you might ask subjects if they were satisfied with their results. And their answers might suggest that they were indeed pleased. But when it comes to finding information, ignorance is often bliss: users don't know what they don't know. They may miss out on the best, most relevant content, but they simply have no idea that it exists.

Most claims for quantified information architecture benefits can't be validated

Most quantifications of information architecture, like those discussed above, can't be proven. When we read about how many minutes per day an employee would save, or how many more sales a redesigned shopping cart would convert, we are essentially reading predictions. We ultimately have no way of proving that those minutes are used productively and not for playing *Tetris*, or that customers bought more or less due to the redesign. It's unfortunate, but efforts at validation are rarely made because they're too expensive and time-consuming. And many, many factors might influence a before-and-after outcome besides the redesign. Would an e-commerce site's numbers go up because the information architecture was better, because more redundant connections were added to the site's servers, or because the overall number of web users had grown? There are an incredible number of uncontrollable and, at times, unknown variables to consider that make it difficult, if not impossible, to validate such measurements.

---

* A good source of evaluation techniques for information architecture components is the November 2000 ACIA white paper "Evaluating Information Architecture" by Steve Toub (*http://argus-acia.com*).

Information architecture is a human issue. For that reason, it doesn't lend itself to the type of quantification that one might expect of other areas, such as determining what type of router to purchase to accommodate more network traffic. Unfortunately, it is often confused with such technical areas by those who have insufficient knowledge of information architecture.

Numbers associated with information architecture should be seen for what they are: predictions based on soft numbers that haven't been or can't be validated. That doesn't mean they're not useful. ROI cases are simply one of many tools that, if they sound reasonably valid, make people feel comfortable with an unknown. And after all, we do have to survive, and sometimes the only way to convince a "by the numbers" person is to show them numbers.

But if you do provide ROI numbers to a manager or potential client, be honest that you're not really proving anything; you're simply predicting value that probably can never be measured but is real nonetheless. It's our responsibility, not to mention in our own interest, to educate our market. After all, our work will always be easier and more effective if we're selling to and working with smart people. If we continue to hammer away at the honest truth about ROI numbers, perhaps information architecture will eventually be broadly accepted as a valuable (but not quantifiable) field such as public education or psychotherapy.

Or, for that matter, management, marketing, human resources, and IT.

Talking to the Reactionaries

The "gut reactionaries" aren't necessarily interested in numbers and often go with what feels right or is in line with their experience. This approach is excellent if the reactionary has direct experience with information architecture or related issues. Then you can simply draw on that frame of reference as you discuss future plans.

But what if the reactionary has no relevant experience to draw from? In such cases, we've found that telling firsthand "stories" is often the best way to engage and educate this type of person. Stories put him in the shoes of a peer who faces a comparable situation, feel that peer's pain, and help him see how information architecture helped in that situation. Case studies also end on a useful note of redemption, but don't sufficiently personalize the story by connecting the person you're telling it to with his peer within the story.

An effective story should provide the listener with both a role and a situation to identify with. The role and the scenario should set up a painful, problematic situation so that the listener feels that pain and can see how investing in information architecture can help make it go away.

Following is an example of a true story that we've found useful in communicating both a problem scenario and a set of information architecture-based solutions. It goes like this:

A client who came to us was a mid-level manager of a huge technical-support operation for a Fortune 50 company. This person was responsible for the documentation used by thousands of operators manning the phones and answering customers' questions 24/7. The answers to these questions had originally been published in huge three-ring-bound manuals that were expensive to produce, unwieldy to use, could not be searched, and were exceedingly difficult to update and maintain.

When the Web grew in popularity, the company decided to convert all of this printed documentation into HTML pages and house it on an intranet. And that's exactly what it did: thousands of pages were converted, with no thought given to how the content would be browsed and searched in the context of a web site, how the content templates should be designed, or how maintenance would be handled. It was as if the printed manuals were dropped into an HTML meat grinder. The output was so bad that it caused some major problems.

The biggest problem was that the operators couldn't find the information quickly, or at all. Speed was certainly an important factor; faster meant that staff could help more customers per hour. More importantly, it also meant that customers spent less time on hold getting angrier and angrier. But the site was so poorly designed that operators often had to look in ten or twenty different places to find all the information on one product because the content wasn't labeled consistently. Of course, the staff usually gave up and ended up providing incomplete answers.

Sometimes staff would spend so much time searching for a single piece of information that when they finally did find it, they'd breathe a sigh of relief, print the information, and tack it to their cubicle walls so they'd never have to undergo that ordeal again. Of course, if that information was time-sensitive, like a product rate sheet, the support operator would be providing inaccurate, out-of-date answers from then on. Even worse, there were documented instances of operators making up answers. This wasn't surprising at all: at $10 per hour, they simply didn't have the motivation or loyalty to their employer or customers to go through the hell of sifting through the intranet.

As you might imagine, all of these factors—time on hold, and incomplete or wrong answers—had a devastatingly negative impact on customers, whose brand loyalty was damaged in a real, if unquantifiable, way.

And the impact on the support staff was also quite expensive. Training costs, already high, were going higher. It now cost $10,000 to train each one, a staggering figure considering that these employees earned only $10 per hour. Worse, turnover was 25 percent annually, meaning that even with expensive training, staff were finding work at the local fast-food restaurant comparable in pay and better in job satisfaction. Anything would be better than using that horrible intranet!

So the client had some huge headaches when they came to us. They'd already tried one consulting firm, which utterly failed. That firm's consultants took a database design perspective, treating all this messy text like a data set. When that approach went down in flames, the client tried to fix their problems in-house, using their own staff. But it soon became clear that their people didn't have the breadth of skills or experience with information architecture to take on a problem so huge.

Then they hired us to help them design a new information architecture. We helped them tackle the problem in a number of ways:

- We worked with them to reduce the amount of content that the users had to sift through and the company had to manage by identifying what was and wasn't "ROT": redundant, outdated, and trivial content. We designed policies and procedures that reduced ROT at the point content was initially created, and that helped identify and weed out ROT throughout the lifetime of the site.

- We devised ways to organize their content and standardize their labeling. Now their staff could browse through content, find what they were looking for where they expected to find it, and feel confident that everything they were looking for was located right there, all in one place.

- We developed a small set of templates that were consistent with one another, and we taught their content authors how to use these templates. The result was content that was predictable: all the pages worked the same way, making it easy for operators to scan quickly for answers.

- Finally, we taught their tech-support operators how to use and maintain controlled vocabularies to index their content. Three years later, they were still using our system, and it was still working. We did our work, trained our replacements, and got out.

There you have it: a painful situation and a happy ending. As you read it, we hope you identified with the actors and their problem (including its humorous aspects), and were glad to see it resolved. Telling stories is fun, doesn't require messy calculations, and can be incredibly effective: stories enable your prospect, client, or colleague to take on the perspective of the story's hero. In effect, the person you're telling the story to inserts himself within the story, and in doing so lets his own imagination take over. Storytelling is really a participatory experience, and that participation will help educate "gut reactionaries" and others who are new to information architecture.

What's your favorite information architecture story? You might document a past problem and how your information architecture design improved the situation. Or you might borrow from your own experience as a user frustrated by a site similar to your client's. If you don't have any good stories handy, just use ours.

Other Case-Making Techniques

Storytelling is just one way to make the case for information architecture. There are other approaches, and which one you select depends on many different factors, including whether or not you're involved in a marketing effort, a sales call, or an interaction with colleagues during a project. (Most of these techniques are discussed at greater length elsewhere in this book.)

User sensitivity "boot camp" sessions

The premise here is simple: get decision makers who aren't too web-savvy in front of a web browser. Ask them to try to accomplish three or four basic and common tasks using their own web site (or, if none is available, a competitor's). Just as you would in a standard task-analysis exercise, have them "think" aloud, and jot down the problems they encounter on a white board. Then review those problems, identifying which are caused by a poor information architecture versus other aspects of design. You'll be surprised at how many of the problems are indeed information architecture problems, and the decision makers will be enlightened by, as information architect Steve Toub says, "eating their own dog food."

Expert site evaluations

Information architecture evaluations of a site can be done quickly and easily. You can probably identify 5 or 10 major information architecture problems within the first 10 minutes of exploring a site. Whether you deliver this evaluation in writing or in the context of a sales call, it can make a huge impression. Not only will you appear knowledgeable about your potential client's site, but you'll probably be exposing problems that they didn't know they had, or that they were aware of but didn't know how to articulate. Evaluations by outsiders, especially experts, are taken very seriously within organizations, because outside opinions often mean much more to internal decision makers than the opinions of their staff. If you're an in-house information architect and have room in your budget, bring in an outside expert when you need to hammer home the value of information architecture to colleagues.

Strategy sessions

These one- to two-day sessions are geared toward bringing together decision makers and opinion leaders, providing them with a brief introduction to information architecture, and then facilitating a discussion on the company's strategy and how issues of information overload, organization, and accessibility can have a strong impact on that strategy. As with site evaluations, strategy sessions are often effective because they educate clients about a problem set that was an unknown, or because they provide language to articulate problems that were already known. Strategy sessions have an added benefit: because they're done in groups, participants often discover that they are not alone in their "information pain."

Competitive analyses

A site's information architecture issues can be riveting when the site is placed alongside its competitors. "Keeping up with the Joneses" is one of the most powerful forms of psychological manipulation, and you should use it here. Always look for opportunities to compare architectural components and features to help prospects and clients see how they stack up. You'll find ample opportunities to slip in information architecture education in the process. Or if you're working in-house, use competitive analyses to expose the differences between business units' subsites within your organization.

Comparative analyses

Not everyone has a competitor, but you can still compare your site to comparable sites. Also consider comparing specific features, such as search interfaces or shopping carts, with the "best in class" from other sites that may not be from the same industry.

Ride the application salesman's wake

Huge amounts of money are being invested by vendors of information architecture-related software applications (e.g., search engines, content management tools, and portals). Whether you partner with such vendors or simply pick names from their client lists, it's often valuable to follow them into a client project. These vendors have already spent heavily on client education, so you can leverage their nickel, but because they focus on the "solution" provided by their own technology, that education is generally incomplete. Clients will inevitably need information architects to configure and add value to the technology, and therefore will be more open to your case-making.

Be aggressive and be early

OK, this isn't so much a technique, but we can't overstate the importance of promoting information architecture as early in the process as you possibly can. For example, if you work at an agency or consulting firm, you should do your best to make sure information architecture is included in the marketing and branding that comprise your firm's public face, not to mention its list of services. Your active participation in the sales process can ensure that information architecture is part of your company's proposals and, more importantly, its project plans. And whether or not you work in-house or for a consulting firm, aggressively educate the other members of your design team; they need to know your value as much as anyone else. After all, it's the intangible stuff, like information architecture, that gets pushed to the side when time and budgets get tight.

Whatever technique you use, consider these three pieces of advice:

Pain is your best friend

More than ROI numbers—more than anything else—work hard to identify the source of a prospect or client's pain. While this may sound obvious, there's more to it than meets the eye. Although many people have heard terms like "information overload," few have actually thought about information as important and strategic stuff. They may not have realized that accessible information is a valuable commodity, and that it takes special efforts and expertise to make it easier to access and manage. And many decision makers don't deal directly with information systems like corporate intranets; employees do it for them. Your best tools here are stories that broaden perspectives, competitive analyses that produce anxiety, and experiences, such as "boot camps," that force people to confront the pain their sites cause.

Articulation is half the battle

Even when people realize what is causing them pain, they often don't have the words to express it. Information problems are new to them, and unless they can articulate what ails them, no amount of consulting will help. That's why information architecture is so important: it provides a set of concepts, terms, and definitions that provide the language to express information pain. If you can educate prospects and clients in the language of information architecture, you can communicate and begin collaborating on addressing their pain. Strategy sessions that begin with a one- or two-hour-long primer on information architecture are a great way to educate clients. Inserting some tutorial material into your initial reports or including a copy of your favorite information architecture book (!) are also useful ways to "spread the word."

Get off your high horse

Let's face it: the term "information architecture" sounds pretty high-falutin'. The jargony nature of the term was the second-biggest challenge in promoting information architecture, according to our May 2002 survey. Be ready for this reaction with a good-natured acknowledgment of this problem (poking fun at oneself and one's profession always seems to go over well). Then defuse the jargon with alternative, "real-language" descriptions of what information architecture really is and what problems it addresses. This is the precise moment that the elevator pitches described in Chapter 1 come in handy, so make sure you stock them along with the case studies and stories in your bag of evangelization tricks.

The Information Architecture Value Checklist

Whatever technique you use to make the case for information architecture, and whether you're making a quantitative or qualitative case, there is a checklist of points that might be relevant to your case or story. Some of these points pertain more to intranets, while others are more relevant to external sites. We suggest that you first consider your situation (the type of site you're working on, whether you're a consultant or in-house information architect, etc.) and where you are in the process of case-making (pre-sales, sales, or while the project is underway). Then, as you prepare to make your case, review this checklist to make sure you're not missing an important point:

- Reduces the cost of finding information
- Reduces the cost of finding wrong information
- Reduces the cost of not finding information at all
- Provides a competitive advantage
- Increases product awareness
- Increases sales

- Makes using a site a more enjoyable experience
- Improves brand loyalty
- Reduces reliance upon documentation
- Reduces maintenance costs
- Reduces training costs
- Reduces staff turnover
- Reduces organizational upheaval
- Reduces organizational politicking
- Improves knowledge sharing
- Reduces duplication of effort
- Solidifies business strategy

A Final Note

Whichever points and approaches you use to make your case for information architecture, keep in mind how difficult this challenge is. After all, you're promoting something that's abstract, intangible, and new, and each situation demands a unique solution. This is generally a lot harder than selling a mass-produced tool that everyone uses in the same way, like a spreadsheet application, or something that can be grasped visually, like a graphic design firm's portfolio.

On the other hand, the information stored in most web sites and intranets is growing at a ridiculous rate. And the content already on those sites may be good today, but will be spoiled tomorrow if there's no good plan for maintenance. Problems associated with the information explosion are only going to get worse. In the long run, your efforts to market and promote information architecture should get easier as more and more people experience information pain. Hold firm: time is on your side.

CHAPTER 18
Business Strategy

In strategy, surprise becomes more feasible the closer
it occurs to the tactical realm.
—Carl von Clausewitz
  On War, 1832

What we'll cover:
- Competing definitions of business strategy
- Strategic fit: a case study at Vanguard
- The relationship between IA and business strategy
- How IA can contribute to competitive advantage

What is business strategy doing in a book about information architecture? Do they have anything in common? After all, we didn't have any business strategy courses in our library and information science programs, and it's safe to say there are very few information architecture courses in the MBA curriculum.

In truth, these two fields have existed independently and in relative ignorance of each other heretofore. This historical isolation is about to change. As the Internet permeates our society, managers and executives are slowly recognizing the mission-critical nature of their web sites and intranets, and this awareness is inevitably followed by a realization that information architecture is a key ingredient for success. Once they've seen the light, there's no going back. Managers will no longer leave information architects to play alone in the sandbox. They'll jump in and start playing, too, whether we like it or not. The good news is they'll bring some toys of their own to share, and if we look at this as an opportunity rather than a threat, we'll learn a lot about the relationship between strategy and architecture along the way.

In practice, information architecture and business strategy should have a symbiotic relationship. It's obvious that the structure of a web site should align with the goals and strategy of the business. So, business strategy (often called "business rules") drives information architecture. What's less obvious is that the communication should go both ways. The process of information architecture design exposes gaps and inconsistencies in business strategy. Smart organizations make use of the feedback loop shown in Figure 18-1.

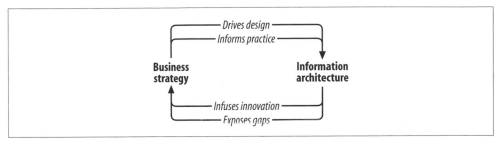

Figure 18-1. The feedback loop of business strategy and information architecture

On a more theoretical level, we believe the emerging discipline of information architecture has much to learn from the established field of business strategy. This is not an accidental match-up; the two fields have much in common. Both suffer from a high degree of ambiguity and fuzziness. They're intangible and don't lend themselves to concrete, quantitative return on investment analysis. Also, both fields must embrace and influence the whole organization to be successful. Information architects and business strategists can't afford to work in ivory towers or be limited by narrow departmental perspectives.

And finally, information architecture, along with the umbrella disciplines of experience design and knowledge management, creates new opportunities and challenges for business strategy innovation. As the Internet continues to blow gales of creative destruction* through our industries, firms that see technology as their salvation will die. Success will belong to those who understand how to combine technology, strategy, and structure in keeping with their unique position in the marketplace. Information architecture will play a role in this vital and relentless search for competitive advantage.

The Origins of Strategy

Dictionary.com defines strategy as "the science and art of using all the forces of a nation to execute approved plans as effectively as possible during peace or war." As this definition suggests, strategy has a military history. In fact, its etymology leads us back to ancient Greece, where we find the term "strat-egos" ("the army's leader").† Early works such as Sun Tzu's *Art of War* and Carl von Clausewitz's *On War* are still often quoted in the business world.

---

* The concept of "creative destruction" was first formulated by economist Joseph Schumpeter (1883-1950).

† "The Historical Genesis of Modern Business and Military Strategy: 1850–1950," by Keith Hoskin, Richard Macve, and John Stone, *http://les.man.ac.uk/ipa97/papers/hoskin73.html*.

This explains why the language of business strategy is filled with military terminology—positioning the marketplace as a battlefield, competitors as enemies, and strategy as a plan that must be well executed to assure victory. It also helps to explain why the field of business strategy has been largely dominated by men who project power and confidence and who convincingly build a case that their plan or model or philosophy is the "one best way." This is a world where indecisiveness is taken as a sign of weakness.

And yet, notice the use of the term "art" in both the dictionary definition and the title of Sun Tzu's famous text. This is an acknowledgment that business strategy is not pure science. It involves a certain degree of creativity and risk taking, much like our nascent field of information architecture.

Defining Business Strategy

Over the past few decades, Michael Porter, a Harvard Business School professor and successful entrepreneur, has played an influential role in leading and shaping the field of business strategy and our understanding of competitive advantage.

In his brilliant book *On Competition* (Harvard Business School Press), Porter defines strategy by contrasting it with operational effectiveness:

> Operational effectiveness means performing similar activities better than rivals perform them. Operational effectiveness includes but is not limited to efficiency.

He notes that operational effectiveness is necessary but not sufficient for business success. He then answers the question, what is strategy?

> Strategy is the creation of a unique and valuable position, involving a different set of activities.

He goes on to explain that "the essence of strategy is in the activities—choosing to perform activities differently or to perform different activities than rivals." It is this strategic fit among activities that provides a sustainable competitive advantage, which is ultimately reflected in long-term profitability.

Alignment

So how do we align our information architecture activities with business strategy? Well, we need to begin by finding out what strategies our business is pursuing. This can be nearly impossible in large organizations.

As consultants to Fortune 500 firms, we've rarely had much access to the senior executives who (we assume) could articulate their company's business strategy. And the people we've worked with often haven't had a clear idea about the overall strategic direction of their organization and how their web site or intranet fits into that bigger picture. They've often been left in the dark.

While we wait for the senior executives and corporate strategists to become more involved in their sites, there are things we can do. Stakeholder interviews provide an opportunity to talk with senior managers. While they may not be able to rattle off a concise explanation of their company's strategy, these managers can be helpful if you ask the right questions. For example:

- What is your company really good at?
- What is your company really bad at?
- What makes your company different from your competitors?
- How are you able to beat competitors?
- How can your web site or intranet contribute to competitive advantage?

It's important to keep digging. You need to get beyond the stated goals of the web site or intranet and try to understand the broader goals and strategy of the organization. And if you don't dig now, you may pay later, as we learned the hard way. A few years ago, we had an uncomfortable consulting experience with a dysfunctional business unit of a Fortune 100 firm.

We had completed an evaluation of the company's existing web site and were in the process of presenting our recommendations to a group of senior managers. Halfway through the presentation, the vice president of the business unit began to attack our whole project as a misguided effort. The thrust of her assault can be summed up in the following question: "How can you design our web site when we don't have a business strategy?"

Unfortunately, we didn't have the understanding or vocabulary at the time to clearly answer this question. Our ignorance doomed us to a half hour of suffering, as the VP cheerfully pulled out our fingernails. It turned out that her hidden agenda was to get us to write a blunt executive summary (which she could then pass to her boss), stating that if this business unit didn't have more time and resources, their web efforts would fail.

She was asking the right question for the wrong reasons. We were more than happy to satisfy her request for a brutally honest executive summary (connecting the dots between our IA and their BS), and we managed to escape the relationship with only a few bruises.

The more permanent outcome of this engagement was a personal conviction that information architects need a good understanding of business strategy and its relationship to information architecture.

Strategic Fit

Let's draw an example from Porter's *On Competition* to learn how to connect the dots between business strategy and information architecture. Porter uses "activity-system maps" as a tool for examining and strengthening strategic fit. Figure 18-2 shows an activity-system map for Vanguard, a leader in the mutual fund industry.

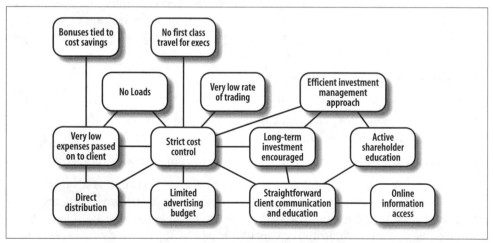

Figure 18-2. An activity-system map for Vanguard

As Porter explains, Vanguard is widely respected for providing services to the conservative, long-term investor, and the company's brand is very different from that of competitors such as Fidelity and T. Rowe Price.

Vanguard strives for a strategic fit between all its activities, from limiting the costs of advertising and business travel to fostering shareholder education and online information access. Low costs and informed investors go hand in hand.

This strategy is no accident. As founder John C. Bogle explains, early in its history, Vanguard established "a *mutual* structure without precedent in the industry—a structure in which the funds would be operated solely in the best interests of their shareholders."* Noting that "strategy follows structure," he suggests that it was logical to pursue "a high level of economy and efficiency; operating at bare-bones levels of cost, and negotiating contracts with external advisers and distributors at arms-length. For the less we spend, the higher the returns—dollar for dollar—for our shareholder/owners."

What's exciting is that this strategy is evident in the design of Vanguard's web site, the main page of which is shown in Figure 18-3. First of all, notice the clean page with minimal branding. There are no fat logos or banner ads; usability is obviously a high priority. Second, notice the lack of technical vocabulary for which the financial industry is renowned. Vanguard makes an explicit point of using "plain talk."

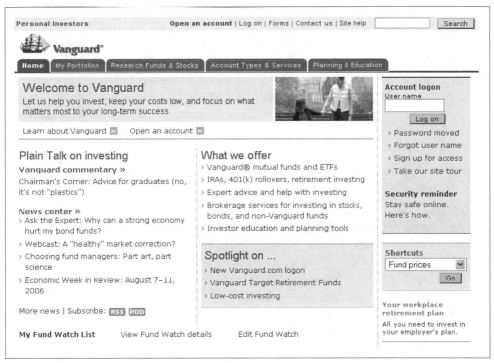

Figure 18-3. Main page of the Vanguard web site

And as you explore, you see an emphasis on education, planning, and advice woven throughout the site. Tools like a site glossary, a site map, and a site tour help customers to navigate and educate themselves at the same time.

---

* John C. Bogle, "The Vanguard Story," *http://www.vanguard.com/bogle_site/october192000.html.*

Vanguard's web site is distinctive, and that's how it should be. It's different by design and reflects the company's unique strategy. For web sites, structure follows strategy, and the best companies exhibit individuality in both areas. That's why Dell.com is different from Compaq and IBM, and Landsend.com is different from L.L. Bean and J. Crew.

Rather than copy their competitors and engage in zero-sum price wars, these companies work to understand, leverage, and strengthen their unique positions within their industries. And their web sites are increasingly acknowledged as important strategic assets that can be used to achieve competitive advantage.

Exposing Gaps in Business Strategy

Information architectures should solve problems and answer questions. Consequently, information architects must find problems and ask questions. In our quest to understand how context, users, and content all fit together, we often expose serious inconsistencies and gaps within business strategy, particularly in how it relates to the web environment.

In many cases, the problems are fixable. A company known for excellent customer service has neglected to integrate customer support into its web site. Or a widely respected online bookstore risks violating its customers' trust by secretly featuring search results for publishers who pay a fee. In a healthy organization, the architect can raise these issues and get them resolved.

In other cases, the problems are symptoms of an organization in real trouble. Consider the following examples, with names omitted to protect the guilty.

- A Global 500 company has recently been through a large merger. The U.S. division has a formal, centrally managed, top-down corporate intranet. The European division has several decentralized, informal, bottom-up departmental intranets. Stakeholders on opposite sides of the Atlantic have very different goals and ideas for their intranets. The plan? Design a single integrated intranet to foster the sense of a single, unified company. The reality? Two disparate cultures clashing on a global scale. The tail of information architecture can't wag this dog.

- A Fortune 100 company decides to enter the e-commerce gold rush by throwing $40 million into development of a consumer health portal. After discovering dozens of domestic competitors, they decide to target several European countries, all at once. One tiny problem. They know almost nothing about the health-related information needs or information-seeking behaviors of the people in those countries. And they never get to find out. Eventually the plug is pulled on this out-of-control e-business.

When we find ourselves in situations that feel crazy, it's human nature to pretend things will work out. We assume the executives really do know what they're doing and that the master plan will become clear soon. But painful experience suggests otherwise. If it looks crazy, it probably is crazy. Trust your gut. Remember, the executives who develop strategy are human, too. It is not uncommon to find situations where the people involved are aware of major gaps and flaws in the plan, but they're too afraid or unmotivated to point them out. As the information architect, you may be well positioned to be the one who cries out, "the emperor has no clothes," and then proceeds to work with the managers, strategists, and stakeholders to put together a more sensible plan.

One Best Way

Figure 18-4 illustrates SWOT, the best-known model for strategy formulation. SWOT stands for the analysis of internal Strengths and Weaknesses of the organization informed by the Opportunities and Threats posed by the external environment.

	Strengths	Weaknesses
Internal capabilities		
External environment	Opportunities	Threats

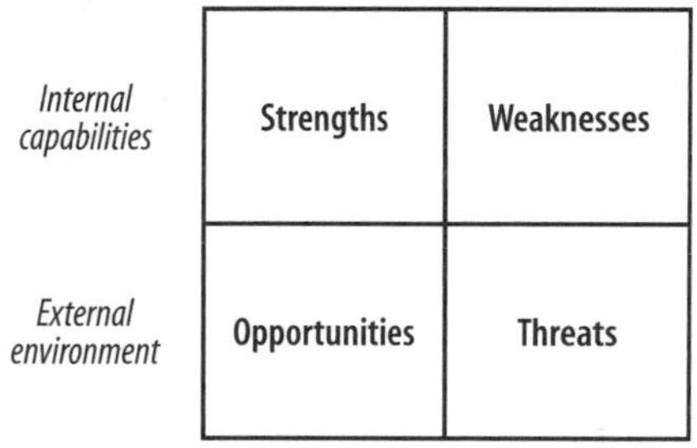

Figure 18-4. The SWOT model of strategy formulation

SWOT has been a favorite model of business schools, textbooks, management consulting firms, and senior executives. SWOT analysis can be performed in a classroom or an executive's office with a small group of people in a short amount of time. These "strategists" or "thinkers" can objectively assess internal capabilities and the external environment, and then deliberately and consciously craft a strategic plan to be implemented by the "doers" of the organization. This model is highly adaptive and can be applied to virtually any type of organization at any time. In many contexts, SWOT has been presented as the "one best way" to formulate a business strategy.

You may have guessed that we don't agree. And if you're wondering what all of this has to do with information architecture, stick with us. We're getting there.

Many Good Ways

In their fascinating book *Strategy Safari* (Free Press), Henry Mintzberg, Bruce Ahlstrand, and Joseph Lampel approach the subject of business strategy in a manner we as information architects would do well to emulate. The book begins with the fable of "The Blind Men and the Elephant," (Figure 18-5), which they note is often referred to but seldom known. We decided to follow their lead.

THE BLIND MEN AND THE ELEPHANT
By John Godfrey Saxe (1816-1887)

It was six men of Indostan
To learning much inclined,
Who went to see the Elephant
(Though all of them were blind)
That each by observation
Might satisfy his mind.

The first approached the Elephant,
And happening to fall
Against his broad and sturdy side,
At once began to brawl:
"God bless me but the Elephant
Is very like a wall."

The Second, feeling of the tusk,
Cried, "Ho! What have we here
So very round and smooth and sharp?
To me 'tis mighty clear
This wonder of an Elephant
Is very like a spear!"

The Third approached the animal,
And happening to take
The squirming trunk within his hands,
Thus boldly up and spake:
"I see," quoth he, "The Elephant
Is very like a snake!"

The Fourth reached out an eager hand,
And felt around the knee,
"What most this wondrous beast is like
Is mighty plain," quoth he;
"Tis clear enough the Elephant
Is very like a tree!"

The Fifth, who chanced to touch the ear,
Said: "E'en the blindest man
Can tell what this resembles most;
Deny the fact who can,
This marvel of an Elephant
Is very like a fan!"

The Sixth no sooner had begun
About the beast to grope,
Than seizing on the swinging tale
That fell within his scope,
"I see," quoth he, "the Elephant
Is very like a rope!"

And so these men of Indostan
Disputed loud and long,
Each of his own opinion
Exceeding stiff and strong,
Though each was partly in the right,
And all were in the wrong!

Moral
So oft in theologic wars,
The disputants, I ween,
Rail on in utter ignorance
Of what each other mean,
And prate about an Elephant
Not one of them has seen!

Figure 18-5. The Blind Men and the Elephant

The authors of *Strategy Safari* proclaim, "We are the blind people and strategy formation is our elephant. Since no one has had the vision to see the entire beast, everyone has grabbed hold of some part or other and 'railed on in utter ignorance' about the rest." Swap "strategy formation" with "information architecture," and you've just described many of the heated debates at our conferences and on our discussion lists.

Strategy Safari extends the philosophy of "many good ways" by describing 10 schools of thought within the business strategy field:

The school	Strategy formation as
The Design School	A process of conception
The Planning School	A formal process
The Positioning School	An analytical process
The Entrepreneurial School	A visionary process
The Cognitive School	A mental process
The Learning School	An emergent process
The Power School	A process of negotiation
The Cultural School	A collective process
The Environmental School	A reactive process
The Configuration School	A process of transformation

The authors describe an evolution over the past 50 years from the top-down, highly centralized design and planning schools toward the bottom-up, entrepreneurial learning and cultural schools. In today's information economy, there's greater recognition that thinking can't be isolated to the CEO and an elite team of corporate strategists. Knowledge workers must play a role in strategy formation. The doers must also be thinkers, and the plan must be informed by the practice. This evolution is driven by advances in information technology, increased maturity in business management theory, a better-educated workforce, and changing social dynamics.

The authors note that during this 50-year evolution, the business community has desperately embraced each new school as the "one best way," only to abandon it when something better came along. They explain that just like the blind men, each school is partly right and partly wrong. None deserves a full embrace, but none should be completely thrown aside either.

Understanding Our Elephant

The information architecture community has much to learn from this expansive, honest, multifaceted approach to strategy. We are a young field, and we often resemble the illustration that accompanies "The Blind Men and the Elephant" (Figure 18-6). We have yet to develop our schools of thought. And our elephant is a complex, dynamic, and elusive beast. Building toward a collective understanding of information architecture is exasperatingly difficult.

As we continue to formulate our ideas and methods, we should be wary of those who expound a "one best way." We should embrace many definitions, many methods, and many facets. We should also be on the lookout for early indicators of trends that suggest new directions and new schools of thought for information architecture. It would be naïve to think our practice has matured in less than a decade.

Figure 18-6. The Blind Men and the Elephant (image from http://www.jainworld.com/literature/ story25i1.gif)

This is not to say that we haven't made great progress already. The practice of information architecture has come a long way since the early 1990s. We began with highly centralized, top-down approaches, attempting to leverage careful planning into stable solutions. We did some good work but learned the hard way that change is a constant and surprises should be expected. More recently, we've been exploring bottom-up approaches that tap the distributed intelligence within our organizations to nurture emergent, adaptive solutions. The following table compares classic or "top-down" IA to modern or "bottom-up" IA:

Classic IA	Modern IA
Prescriptive	Descriptive
Top-Down	Bottom-Up
Planned	Emergent
Stable	Adaptive
Centralized	Distributed

As we struggle with these ideas, an interesting question arises: do we create information architectures or reveal them?

In *Information Ecology*, Thomas Davenport and Laurence Prusak have this to say on the topic:

> From an ecological perspective, identifying what information is available today and where it can be found is a much better use of architectural design than attempting to model the future. Information mapping is a guide to the present information environment. It may describe not only the location of information, but also who is responsible for it, what it is used for, who is entitled to it, and how accessible it is.

This provocative statement is partly true, but it's also partly false. Information mapping is a useful approach that more of us should embrace, but it doesn't negate the value of other approaches. Remember, we are all blind men, and information architecture is our elephant.

Competitive Advantage

The fact that we can't see the whole picture doesn't mean we shouldn't forge ahead. The disciplines of business strategy and information architecture are dauntingly abstract and complex. But we can't fall victim to analysis paralysis. In the world of business, both disciplines are useless if they don't contribute to the development of sustainable competitive advantage.

On this vital subject, business strategy can teach us one more lesson. In short, the invisible nature of our work can contribute to our competitive advantage. Geoffrey Moore reveals this hidden opportunity with respect to business strategy. In *Living on the Fault Line*, Moore presents a competitive-advantage hierarchy to show the multilayered foundation upon which strategy is built (Figure 18-7).

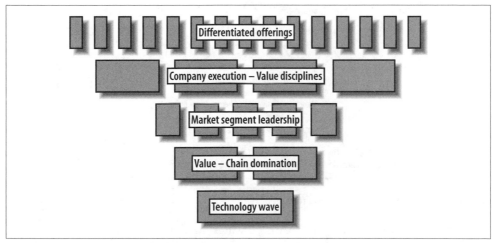

Figure 18-7. A competitive-advantage hierarchy

Moore explains that while most people focus on the top layer of differentiated offerings (e.g., branding and positioning), businesses can achieve lasting competitive advantage only by building from the bottom up.

> At the base lies the technology itself, the core of cores. On top of it form value chains to translate its potential into actuality. Atop this evolution lie specific markets . . . Within all markets, companies compete against each other based on their ability to execute their strategy . . . The ultimate expression of this competition, the surface stratum that is visible for all to see, is an array of differentiated offerings that compete directly for customers and consumers on the basis of price, availability, product features, and services . . . In technology-enabled markets, corporations, like tall buildings, must sink their foundations down through all the strata to secure solid footing in competitive advantage.

While the media pundits and water-cooler jockeys rant and rave about branding and positioning, the strategic decisions with long-term implications are happening beneath the surface, invisible to the outside world and to many corporate "insiders." The invisible nature of this strategy work confers greater gains to leaders and thwarts copycat competitors.

The End of the Beginning

As information architects, we can also use invisibility to our advantage. There is no question that our discipline suffers from the iceberg problem, as illustrated in Figure 18-8. Most of our clients and colleagues focus on the interface, without appreciating the underlying structure and semantics.

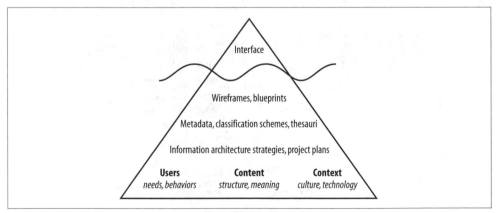

Figure 18-8. The information architecture iceberg

Savvy designers know to look beneath the water line, understanding the importance of blueprints and wireframes to site development. But few people, even within the web design community, realize the critical role the lower layers play in building a successful user experience. This ignorance of deep information architecture results in short, superficial, and often doomed projects.

Those who recognize the need to build structures from the bottom up have an immediate advantage over those who skim along the surface. And because this structural design is hidden from the outside world, these early adopters get a big head start. Once competitors see what the Episcopalians call "the outward and visible signs of inward and spiritual grace," it's often too late. By the time Borders Books & Music realized the power of Amazon's user experience, they were already years behind.

But invisibility doesn't automatically confer sustainable advantage. In today's fast and fluid economy, easily duplicated best practices spread like wildfire. This is why companies can no longer look to technology for their salvation. By lowering the barrier to entry and fostering open standards, the Internet has created a more level playing field.

Michael Porter says it best in a *Harvard Business Review* article:[*]

> As all companies come to embrace Internet technology, the Internet itself will be neutralized as a source of advantage. Basic Internet applications will become table stakes—companies will not be able to survive without them, but they will not gain any advantage from them.

Today's cutting-edge technology is tomorrow's commodity. If it *can* be copied, it *will* be copied. Porter goes on to explain:

> To gain these advantages, companies need to stop their rush to adopt generic "out of the box" packaged applications and instead tailor their deployment of Internet technology to their particular strategies. Although it remains more difficult to customize packaged applications, the very difficulty of the task contributes to the sustainability of the resulting competitive advantage.

That last line resonates strongly in the context of information architecture. In effect, we can transform the invisibility and difficulty of our work from a liability into an asset. The possibilities for aligning information architecture and business strategy to produce sustainable competitive advantage are exhilarating.

We have much to learn, and we've only just begun. When we look back many years from now, we will chuckle at the foolishness of our earliest efforts on the Web. We will wonder how we ever thought that information architecture and business strategy could exist independently. We haven't yet figured out all the answers, but at least we're starting to ask the right questions.

As Winston Churchill once said, "This is not the end. It is not even the beginning of the end. But it is, perhaps, the end of the beginning."

---

[*] Porter, Michael. "Strategy and the Internet," *Harvard Business Review*, March 2001.

CHAPTER 19

Information Architecture for the Enterprise

What we'll cover:

- What enterprise information architecture is, and why you should care about it
- What the goal of EIA is (it's not centralization)
- Practical EIA design techniques for top-down and bottom-up navigation, search, and emergent or "guerrilla" approaches
- How in-house EIA competency can and often does grow, both strategically and operationally
- What EIA work needs to get done, and what kinds of people should do it
- How to pay for and position an in-house EIA group
- What EIA services should be provided
- How to grow an EIA group over time

Information Architecture, Meet the Enterprise

What's enterprise information architecture (EIA)? Quite simply, the practice of information in the enterprise setting.

Sorry, that definition was accurate but not too helpful. Let's back up and make sure we understand what an enterprise is. Most would say that it's a large, physically distributed organization—usually a corporation or a government agency, but we'd also count substantial academic institutions and nonprofits. Enterprises suffer from problems big and complicated enough to merit serious, expensive solutions. (Hence, software marketers have found that prepending the term "enterprise-class" to their products' names is a reasonably reliable path to a condo in Aspen.)

But "large" and "physically distributed" aren't what really defines an enterprise. In fact, the most telling attribute is a place where "one hand doesn't know what the other one's doing." Or, one hand ignores or doesn't care what the other's doing. Or that first hand absolutely despises the second hand, and will do anything to undermine it.

Interestingly, these attributes can be found in just about any organization, regardless of size or physical distribution. So while you might not work at ExxonMobil, Thomson, or the UN, it's likely that you're dealing with enterprise-class IA challenges.

Enterprises have been characterized by a constant tug-of-war between forces of centralization and autonomy. A new management regime comes in, finds wasteful duplication of effort and expense, and discovers a lack of coordination and collaboration among business units. The new managers try to reign things in by centralizing as much as they possibly can. Typically this process fails to have its intended impact and even creates some unintended negative consequences, such as choking off local innovation. Then a new regime enters the picture, sees a new set of problems, and in its hurry to leave its mark, swings the pendulum hard the other way: "let a thousand flowers bloom." Staff in far-flung units are empowered to take things into their own hands but may do so in a wasteful, duplicative, uncoordinated manner. And we're back where we started.

This constant tug-of-war impacts an organization's web presence, whether public or internal. In fact, the Web, by dint of its democratizing ways, actually aggravates the naturally innate tension between local and central. The end result is, typically, a web environment consisting of hundreds or even thousands of separate mini-web sites that don't work together in any coherent way, or failed efforts to enforce compliance with common design standards and platforms. Designing a successful information architecture against this insane backdrop is perhaps the biggest challenge we face today. And if it's hard for us as designers, consider the even more horrible experience users face.

Finding Your Way Through an Enterprise Information Architecture

Let's say that you work for a global consulting firm. You just returned from a client trip with a wad of receipts in your wallet or purse. Now you want to get repaid. It's a common task, so it should be feasible to complete using your company's intranet. But where do you begin?

Unfortunately, like many intranets, the company's information architecture mirrors its organization chart and is structured like Figure 19-1. Do you know how your company is organized? (Grab a sheet of paper right now and try jotting it down. Not so easy, is it?) Imagine how confused you'd be if you were a new employee. And considering the "constant revolution" of ongoing reorgs that churn so many enterprises, even long-timers might not have a clue.

So you begin to poke around the intranet. The legal department might or might not have some information on how much your client's contract allows you to be compensated for. But HR has various policies and procedures that you'll need to take into account as well. They point to tools, forms, and other materials that might or might not help you get reimbursed.

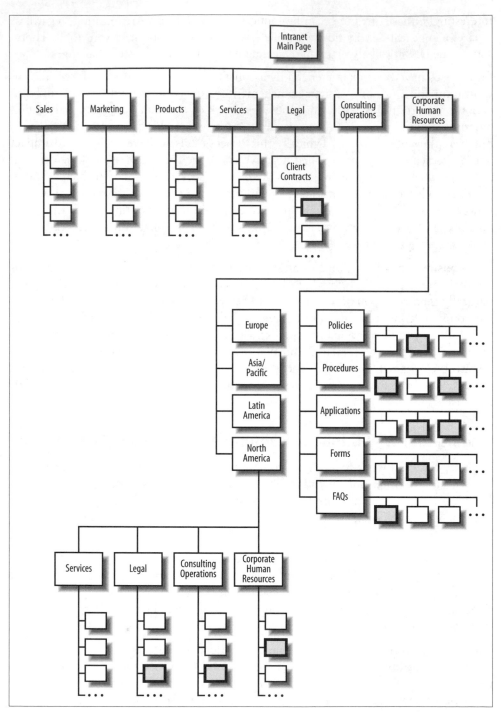

Figure 19-1. An intranet that looks like an org chart; common tasks can't be supported because relevant information is buried in departmental "silos"

Of course, if you work for the North American division, there might (or might not) be a similar array of contractual information, policies, tools, and so forth that only pertain to doing business in North American countries.

You'll probably become tired of guessing and hunting. So what happens?

Maybe you give up, making your employer happy because they've just saved the expenses you'll eat. But in the long run, they won't be well served by the according decline in employee loyalty.

Or, more typically, you'll go ask someone who you think can help. Now you've thrown the intranet—which hasn't been exactly cheap for your company to build and maintain—out the window, and you'll go bother an expensive human "expert," who's got other work to do and isn't by any means guaranteed to give you the correct information.

Either way, it's a bad outcome, and it's why we're devoting a chapter to enterprise IA. It may not be the most interesting or exciting of topics—most of us in the field would probably prefer to spend our time poking around at the intersection of Web 2.0, design patterns, and semantic webs (with a little Ajax thrown in for good measure). But more and more of us find ourselves thrust into the role of balancers—not of budgets, but of centralized and autonomous content, and the motivations, urges, people, and egos behind those conflicting forces. And we have precious little to go on to help us address information architecture challenges in this setting. Our goal in this chapter is to provide you with at least a little practical advice on improving an enterprise's information architecture.

What's the Goal of EIA?

We haven't yet encountered an enterprise site that didn't suffer from problems associated with decentralization. Put another way, it's the rare site that is too centralized. Now that the Web's novelty has started to wear off, and web sites are recognized as a foundational component of doing business in the 21st century, many early sources of resistance to centralization are wearing down. Business units are beginning to understand the benefits of shared resources and coherent user experience, for their sites' users as much as for their own bottom lines.

Getting Everyone on the Same Page

But it's still not clear to everyone why some measure of centralization is worth pursuing. So the following list of benefits of centralization might come in handy:

Increased revenues
> Especially in e-commerce situations, customers don't want to be exposed to the enterprise's org chart as they try to navigate the site. They want to make a purchase and go on with their lives. A centralized information architecture will help users focus on *their* needs, not your organization's politics and structure.

Reduced costs

Centralization helps the enterprise save money in so many ways. One is that you can avoid purchasing multiple and redundant licenses for such technologies as search engines, and can instead collectively negotiate for a single enterprise-wide license. Another is that pooling resources may allow the enterprise to afford the development of customized tools (or customization of shrink-wrapped tools) and specialized staff. Yet another is that duplication of effort, such as having two research teams working on the same project, can be eliminated. And, of course, reducing the time needed to find information can really add up when that time is paid for by the enterprise.

Clearer communication

Whether they're employees who access the intranet or investors wondering about new acquisitions, all users can expect a consistent and accurate message on behalf of the enterprise if centralization is in place.

Shared expertise

Centralization implies that there is some means for cooperating and reaching decisions as a group. Besides indicating an organization with a healthy attitude toward communicating and sharing knowledge in a general sense, it also means that the organization is collectively learning about information architecture and other areas that will help "glue" together content from its disparate silos. Which, of course, can only be a good thing.

Reduced likelihood of corporate reorganization

Perhaps it's a stretch, but if poor communication and coordination are major causes of corporate reorganizations, then having a strong centralized information architecture will reduce the need for reorgs. Reorgs are often the most painful and expensive event that organizations face, so anything that reduces their likelihood should be considered valuable.

Centralization is inevitable anyway

Most enterprises have already begun the process of centralizing their information architectures, consciously or not. Why not acknowledge this reality, tap it, and if possible, shape, hasten, and direct it with a conscious, intelligent strategy?

Centralization Above All?

Considering all those good outcomes, it's tempting to consider centralization as the ultimate goal of enterprise IA (which, admittedly, we did in this book's second edition). It does sound like a nice way to deal with the problematic intranet described in the example above. Just design an information architecture that knits together all units' content silos in a rational, usable way, and then implement across the organization.

This kind of thinking is common in many enterprises. And anyone who's been through such an exercise knows just how difficult it is to force business units to comply with common standards. It's not completely impossible—for example, IBM.com's pages now all use standard templates, which is quite an impressive achievement considering the size of the site and diversity of its numerous owners—but many aspects of a centralized IA are more difficult to understand and, therefore, to comply with. For example, while common page templates are a tangible aspect of the user experience, the more abstract concepts, like shared metadata, are not quickly grasped—much less adopted—by many enterprise decision-makers.

So What Is the Goal?

The goal of enterprise IA is *not* to centralize everything you see. In fact, the goal of EIA is no different than any other flavor of IA: *identify the few most efficient means of connecting users with the information they need most.* That often might involve adopting some centralizing measures, but it could also mean a highly decentralized approach, such as enabling employees to use a social bookmarking tool to tag intranet content (as the aforementioned IBM is doing). The point, as always, is to apply whatever approach makes the most sense given your organization, its users, content, and context.

Naturally, this is a more thoughtful approach than simply seeking to centralize the information architecture; put another way, it's more work. But don't dismay: patterns are emerging to describe common enterprise IA challenges and solutions. In the remainder of this chapter, we'll describe how an EIA typically evolves in terms of design, strategy, and operations, and how you can have a positive impact in each case.

Designing an Enterprise Information Architecture

As with any other flavor of information architecture, there's no "right way" to design an enterprise information architecture. However, over time certain IA design approaches, when pursued in the appropriate sequence, have emerged as making the most sense in the enterprise setting.* In this section, we've broken the wide range of possible IA design components into four categories, and for each we provide a few nuggets of practical advice on what to do and what not to do. We could fill up an entire book on enterprise IA design, but we hope you'll find this tip of the iceberg to be useful.

Top-Down Navigation and EIA

Thanks to improved search engines and the advent of RSS syndication, users are finding more ways to bypass top-down navigation. But top-down navigation isn't going away any time soon, and top-down elements provide ample opportunities for you to improve EIA.

---

* Lou Rosenfeld's *Enterprise Information Architecture Roadmap* represents an effort to capture what makes sense to do and when; you can download the latest version (in PDF) from *http://louisrosenfeld.com/publications/index.html#enterpriseia.*

Bypass the main page

You read it right. Many large IA projects get completely derailed by this one page among the millions that comprise your site. Granted, there are an increasing number of other ways to reach your site's content, such as via a web-wide search engine, an RSS feed, and your advertisements. Still, you know that the main page is the single most important page on your site; the problem is that everyone else in your organization knows that, too. The result: design meetings where senior vice presidents joust over dozens of main-page pixels.

Of course, you could try to shepherd such a meeting to a productive end—a place where the main-page design is conceived with the needs of the enterprise as a whole and the users it serves, rather than the setting where interdepartmental strife plays out. But that might take years, and you've got other fish to fry. So we advise you to be prepared to step away from your normal urge to care about the main page. Consider it an unfortunate chunk of real estate that could be so nice if only the warring gangs would cease and desist. You'll have a chance to rehabilitate it later; for now, move on...

Repurpose your sitemap

...to other pieces of real estate that might be quite useful if only anyone bothered to pay attention to them. For example, your sitemap (aka table of contents, as discussed in Chapter 7) may already be linked to throughout your site. That makes it a property with considerable value. And yet, it's often something of an orphan; it may not be clear whose responsibility it is, and few people bother to use it. Can you blame them? Most sitemaps simply mirror the site's main organization system, and in many enterprise sites, that's the org chart. Not very useful.

Normally, your attention would be focused on improving the organization system, weaning your enterprise from an org-chart-driven self-view. But that's quite difficult to pull off in an enterprise setting, and requires considerable agreement and coordination.

If you want to get things done in the enterprise, it's often better to ask forgiveness than to beg permission. So you should consider sneaky, Machiavellian means for improving your organization's information architecture. One trick is to redesign the sitemap so that it stops mirroring what is, and instead suggests what could be. In other words, use the sitemap as a sandbox to try out a new, more user-centered organization system. Chances are, few will complain, and you may be able to monitor traffic to this page to see how well your changes have gone over. This might help you build a case for eventually revising the site's organization system; or, when your enterprise is ready to seriously consider improving site-wide navigation, you can point to a readily available model for how to do it. This whole messy undertaking may leave you feeling a little impure, but what the heck: life is short, and besides, no lives will be lost or damaged by your noodling around with your enterprise's sitemap.

Slim down your site index

Another prime piece of real estate is the site index (also covered in Chapter 7). Like the sitemap, an index ties together content from silos all over your enterprise, thereby making it a great EIA tool. But indices are expensive to develop and maintain. And, in fact, site indices are often superseded by search systems; both support known-item searching, but search is more automated and comprehensive.[*]

Does this mean you should throw out your site's index? Generally, no. Many search systems aren't well designed, so users might still need to rely upon an index as a backup. What can you do to make that backup effective while cutting back on its maintenance costs?

Consider a specialized site index. Instead of trying to index everything in your site, focus on one critical type of information. For example, the Centers for Disease Control's index, shown in Figure 19-2, doesn't include directions to its campus or biographies of its directors. Instead, it provides an A–Z list of health topics and issues—the primary kind of content that users come to the site for.

A specialized index is far simpler to maintain than a soups-to-nuts version, and because it's focused on the important content type, it can provide value to a wide array of your enterprise site's users.

As an alternative, you might consider another variety of less-than-comprehensive site index. Michigan State University builds its site index, shown in Figure 19-3, automatically, using the same common keywords derived from search-log analysis that have been assigned Best Bet results. Essentially, if the query is good (common) enough to merit a Best Bet, it's good enough to be included in the site index. Note that each entry links directly to its Best Bet result:

Develop guides

Guides, also covered in Chapter 7, are different from other forms of supplementary navigation. While they can link to content from any silo, guides don't offer comprehensive coverage of your site's content like sitemaps and traditional site indices do. Guides, like the one in Figure 19-4, are selective—they're something of an enterprise FAQ—and for that reason they're ideal "glue" for your enterprise site.

We recommend developing a handful of guides that address users' top information needs and tasks. What do users really want and need from your site? Here's your opportunity to serve those needs in an especially simple and low-tech way; guides are

---

[*] Our former company, Argus Associates, was once hired by a Fortune 500 company to develop a custom A–Z index for its public site. We'd recommended investing in search improvements, but the search engine was off-limits at the time, so we began work on the index. Many months and $250,000 later, a comprehensive index was built and launched, and a team of indexers trained to maintain it. And two years later, it was thrown away, as the IT department acceded to improvements to the search system. So it goes in the enterprise environment.

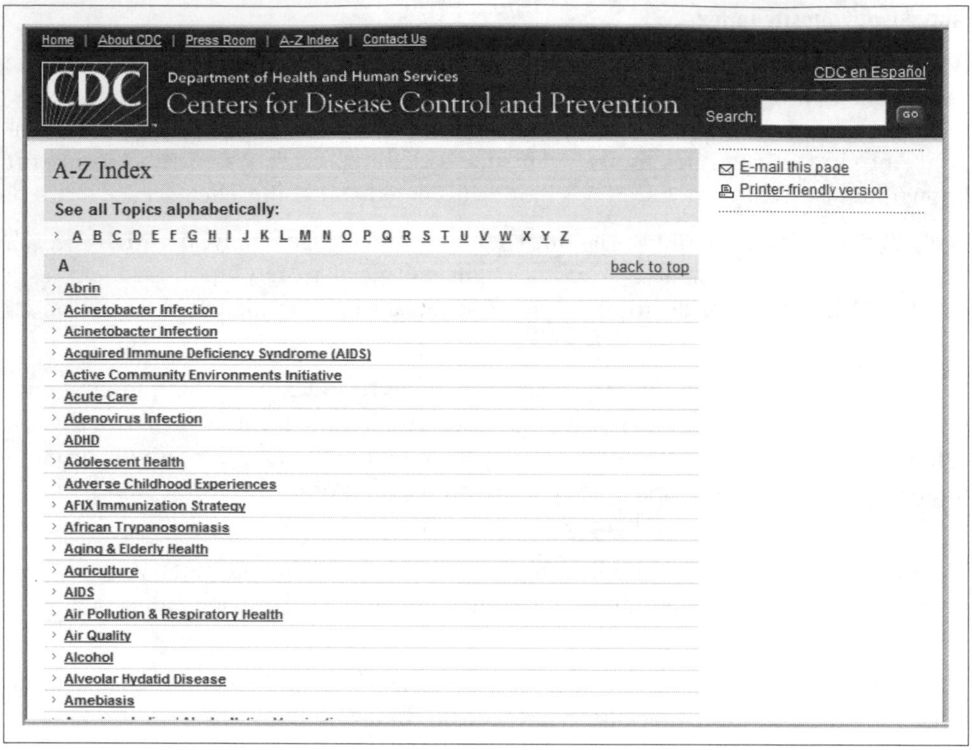

Figure 19-2. The Centers for Disease Control's specialized index on health topics

simply single pages of HTML code, and therefore don't require specialized technical expertise or applications to implement. And you can use a variety of methods to determine common needs, such as search-log analysis (discussed in Chapters 6 and 10), persona development, and even talking to your organization's switchboard operators.

We're especially enthusiastic about guides in the enterprise context because they scale well. You can develop as many guides as your resources allow. The largest bottleneck typically comes from identifying subject matter experts. But in many cases, the expert—in the example above, the poor person besieged by requests for help processing travel expenses—will often be glad to encapsulate his knowledge so he doesn't have to answer the same question over and over.

Guides are also a good reminder of how you should think about allocating your EIA resources. Let's face it: you could spend decades trying to develop the ideal information architecture to serve all of your content to all of your users. No one has that luxury—or patience—as far as we know. Prioritization is the only viable alternative, and guides are an ideal tool to aid in efforts to prioritize your EIA development. Build a few guides to address common tasks and information needs, and you'll see how a little effort can go a very long way.

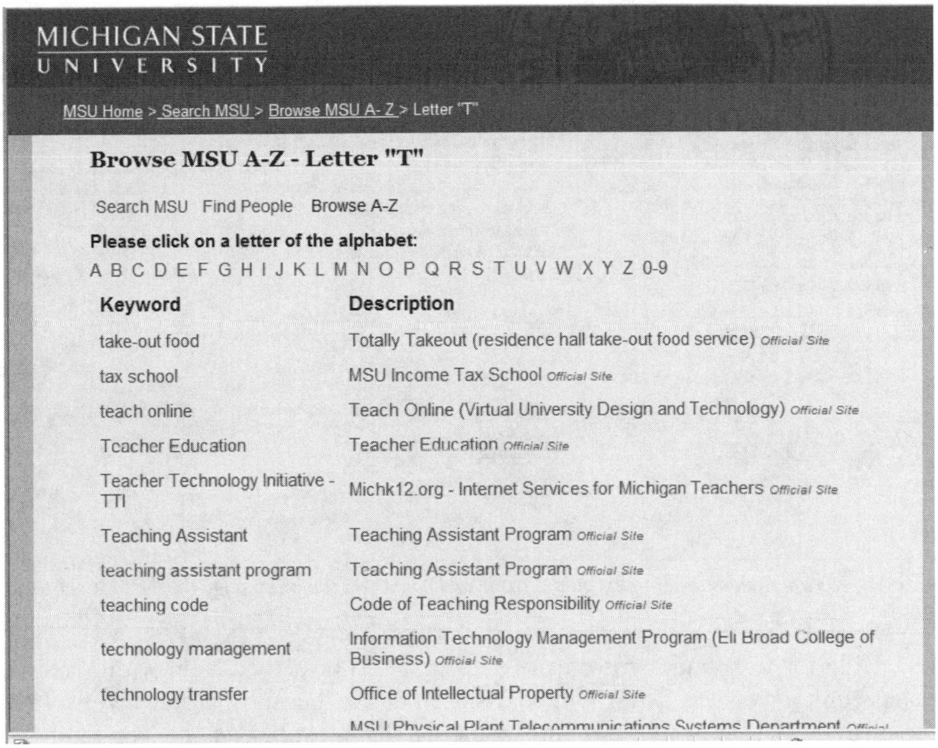

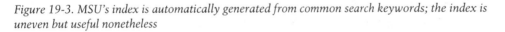

Figure 19-3. MSU's index is automatically generated from common search keywords; the index is uneven but useful nonetheless

Bottom-Up Navigation and EIA

While top-down navigation offers a few quick win opportunities, bottom-up navigation is much trickier. It's difficult to integrate the upper layers of several separate information architectures, but because there are so many more "moving parts," it can be far more difficult to integrate the more granular content from the collection of sites that make up an enterprise intranet or public web environment.

Build single-silo content models

To build momentum toward ambitious content-integration projects, you've got to start with baby steps. First among them is building a handful of content models (which we've introduced in Chapter 12).

Think back to the common information needs and tasks that we discussed earlier. Each might require navigating deep into the guts of your site; strong contextual navigation requires strong content models. Of course, some of the most critical tasks and information needs will require content models that cross departmental silos; set

Figure 19-4. Vanguard introduces its guides front and center on the main page (in the "I want to…" section)

those aside for now and focus on the ones that can be served from within a single business unit's web site. These will be easier to tackle, because 1) they involve fewer people, and 2) they won't run into some of the metadata challenges that we'll describe shortly.

Your goals are to get other people in your enterprise familiar with the idea and execution of content models, which is already a lot to ask of them. So focus on simple tasks and needs that can be addressed by content within a single silo. What useful content model could you build within Human Resources? Marketing? Within your staff directory? Or for each of your products? Your site's users will benefit from even limited contextual-navigation improvements, and your organization will benefit in the long run from both the experience with content modeling that it gathers, and, ultimately, the ability to connect those content models across silos.

Limit dependence on metadata

As much as we'd like to build interconnected semantic webs throughout the guts of our enterprise's content, metadata keeps getting in our way. Figure 19-5 shows a simple illustration, using the BBC content model. Here we want to connect our model with relevant content—let's say events from a concert calendar and TV listings—from other silos within the BBC.

This should work—*if* we've got the same metadata to use to make the connection. Unfortunately, this isn't always the case. For example, let's assume that the artist's

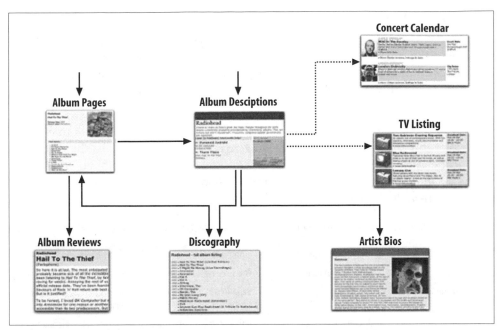

Figure 19-5. We'd like to connect (along the dotted lines) our content model to other models from other business units; do we have the right metadata to make this happen?

name is the metadata that connects "artist descriptions" and "TV listings." If the people who maintain the TV listings use a different version of an artist's name—say, an abbreviated or all-caps version, and you list artist names differently, it can be tricky to automate the creation of a link between those two chunks of content.

Usually, software can be taught to understand and deal with simple differences like these. But as metadata becomes more descriptive, even the best artificial intelligence falls flat. For example, if one unit at the BBC classifies Johnny Cash's music as "country," while another unit deems it "Americana," genre metadata wouldn't be very useful or usable for automating connections between content models. Achieving agreement—such as on a standard usage of controlled vocabulary terms—is quite difficult, often for political reasons. And expensive efforts to retrospectively reclassify content might serve as yet another roadblock to relying on shared metadata across the enterprise.

It's not all gloom and doom, though. Whenever you create a content model, you're forced to select the most useful metadata attributes to build from a wide variety of possibilities. The same is true when you connect content models across silo boundaries—this exercise reveals the few types of metadata that you should focus your efforts on across the enterprise. So efforts to build enterprise-wide content models will have a useful byproduct: in the process, you'll identify the few most important varieties of metadata to invest in.

"Telescoped" metadata development

In the above example from the BBC, you can see that some metadata types are easier to standardize than others. Because EIA is an expensive, long-term undertaking, you've got to prioritize whenever possible, taking on the easy wins first while building momentum toward tougher challenges. In the case of metadata, some varieties are indeed easier than others, though nothing's ever easy.

Use content model exercises to help you choose which types of metadata to develop or acquire. But also keep in mind that, in general, the less ambiguous the metadata, the cheaper and easier you'll find it to develop or acquire, and maintain. Table 19-1 orders some common (but by no means comprehensive) types of metadata attributes, from least to most difficult.

Table 19-1. Relative difficulty among metadata attributes; start with the simple ones

Level of difficulty	Metadata attribute	Comments
Easy	Business unit names	These are typically already available and standardized
Easy to Moderate	Chronology	Variations in formats (e.g., 12/31/07 versus 31/12/07) usually can be addressed by reasonably intelligent software
Moderate to Difficult	Place names	Although many standards exist (e.g., state abbreviations and postal codes), many enterprises (and their business units) use custom terms for regions (such as sales territories)
Moderate to Difficult	Product names	Product granularity can vary greatly; marketing may think in terms of product families; sales in terms of items with SKU numbers, and support in terms of product parts that can be sold individually
Difficult	Audiences	Audiences, such as customers or types of employees, vary widely from unit to unit
Difficult	Topics	The most ambiguous type of metadata; difficult for individuals, much less business units, to come to agreement on topical metadata

Similarly, as we know from examining thesauri in Chapter 9, metadata can support a complexity of semantic relationships, ranging from synonyms to broader/narrower terms to related terms (see Table 19-2). Consider beginning your enterprise metadata journey by relying on simpler vocabularies that provide only synonyms, rather than full-blown (and more expensive) thesauri.

Table 19-2. Relative difficulty of developing semantic relationships within metadata; again, start with the simple ones

Level of difficulty	Type of relationship	Examples
Hard	Synonymous	Synonym rings and authority lists
Harder	Hierarchical	Classification schemes
Hardest	Associative	Thesauri

Simpler vocabularies mean simpler information architectures. You might be able to assemble the metadata you'll need for the top few layers of a site-wide navigation system before politics and your own lack of expertise with local content get in the way of going deeper. And your architecture almost certainly won't be able to take advantage of "see alsos" and other related terms in any substantial way until your organization achieves some measure of "EIA maturity."

It's amazing that, after years of kicking around in the backwaters of corporate consciousness, "metadata" has suddenly emerged as a buzzword. Yet many senior decision-makers now see it as a panacea in much the same way they held out hopes for portals, personalization, and search in the past. We should all realize that there's no such thing as a silver bullet, especially when it comes to information architecture; each interesting approach, new or not, comes with many hidden costs. Understanding the varying degrees of difficulty involved with metadata implementation will help you—and your enterprise—scale up its investment in metadata-driven solutions in a reasonable and ultimately successful manner.

Search Systems and EIA

As pessimistic as we are about instituting descriptive metadata across the enterprise, we see great potential for enterprise search systems. They're the closest thing to a killer application for enterprise information architectures. Search systems can provide access to most or all of your enterprise content, regardless of silo. The query logs they create generate valuable data that can help you diagnose and fix your information architecture's biggest problems. And because, typically, the same retrieval algorithm is applied to all of your enterprise's content, search is as apolitical as things can get in the enterprise environment. Put another way, you might have a product manager scream at you about your design of your site's navigation, organization, and labeling systems, but we'd be surprised that she'd come after you for reasons related to search.

That said, we don't advise purchasing the latest and best enterprise search engine, installing it, and simply walking away. Small modifications can go a long way toward improving the interface. We've already covered many search system improvements in Chapter 8, but we'll reiterate a few here, recast for enterprise consumption.

Simple consistent interface

If it's important anywhere, it's especially important in the enterprise: a simple search interface—"The Box"—should behave consistently and be consistently located on each page, like the one shown in Figure 19-6, regardless of who owns that page. Thankfully, this is becoming a convention, partly due to the advent of content management systems and their use of standard templates, which can be customized to include a simple search interface.

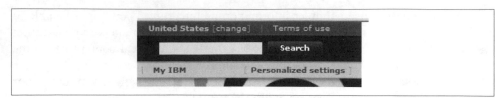

Figure 19-6. If IBM can pull off a simple search interface on each of its pages, so can you!

Perhaps your enterprise isn't able or willing to provide a standard interface. Don't let that stop you; simple search is a good cause around which you can build a campaign for some measure of enterprise centralization. Not only is it everywhere (you don't have to look far to see how it's emerged as a convention), but you can find good supporting data; for example, you can always cite a guru like Jakob Nielsen, who makes the point* that roughly 50 percent of all users begin their sessions on any given site by searching. Very few people can muster a strong case against ubiquitous simple search interfaces, and once you succeed with this particular battle, you'll have momentum to take on bigger challenges that require some measure of coordination across the enterprise.

Analyze those logs

If search systems are the killer app for enterprise sites, then search-log analysis is the killer enterprise diagnostic tool. You don't need to spend months analyzing your query data to reveal some critical problems with your search system and content. Common examples: users' preponderance to misspell and mistype queries (fix it by implementing a spell-checker to your search system), frequent entry of acronyms and jargon (address with a glossary), searches for product codes (make sure your product pages include those codes!), and so on.

Prioritize your queries

Additionally, search-log analysis is a means for revealing which are the most commonly searched queries on your site. You can use this data to prioritize your efforts at developing Best Bet search results (covered in Chapter 8) and in a similar vein, guides, which could be considered Best Bets for main pages.

The numbers are really in your favor here: let's say you create Best Bet results for the 200 most common queries. These 200 queries account for 25 percent of your all queries executed on your site. If, as Jakob Nielsen suggests, 50 percent of your site's users start by searching, multiply that 50 percent by 25 percent; the result is an improvement in the user experience for 12.5 percent of all users. These numbers, like all IA-related numbers, can be easily challenged, but the message behind the numbers—improved performance—still rings loud and true.

---

* Jakob Nielsen, "Search and You May Find." AlertBox, July 15, 1997. *http://www.useit.com/alertbox/9707b.html*.

While you're at it, look over those top queries, identify which have zero results, and plug those content gaps. Might that bring you another three to five percent improvement in the user experience? Not bad. Add in some percentage for users who'd previously been defeated by spelling errors and typos, and the numbers start to add up.

Reverse-engineering content and metadata

No matter what you do to improve your enterprise search system, poor content and metadata can conspire to derail your efforts. Garbage in, garbage out. And in a distributed environment, it's hard to even find authors, much less to convince them to do a better job preparing their content for consumption via the web site or intranet.

When you do have the opportunity to bend an author's ear, you'll need a good tool to help convince him to do a better job authoring content, applying metadata tags to it, and titling documents. Whether this comes up in the context of an enterprise style guide or a face-to-face meeting, come prepared with an example of poor search results—which include some of his own documents—to demonstrate just how much his work impacts users down the line.

For example, a search for "financing" on the DaimlerChrysler site returns poorly formatted, poorly titled results, as shown in Figure 19-7.

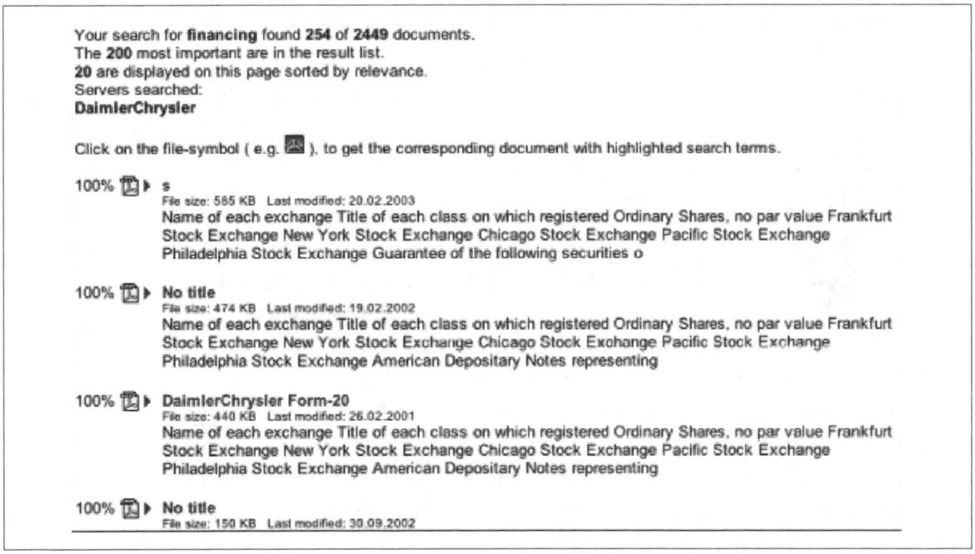

Figure 19-7. Wouldn't you be a bit embarrassed if you were the author of one of these documents? (Or, for that matter, responsible for the search system?)

You now have the opportunity to show authors of these documents the importance of well-considered document titles. Conversely, you could show content authors how their documents don't show up as highly as they should in search results, and explain to them how they might improve their rankings by following the enterprise's guidelines on writing titles and good copy, and assigning metadata.

Poor search results are an effective way to communicate to authors just what happens when they fail to see their content, and their work, as part of something much larger—namely, an enterprise web site or intranet that serves thousands of users. "Reverse-engineering" search results uncovers opportunities for authors to do better, makes the case for doing so quite clear, and provides you with a way to accomplish "organizational change" in a small but important way: author by author.

"Guerrilla" EIA

The three tracks described so far all have to do with overlaying existing content from different silos with user-oriented ways to navigate and search. Increasingly, these approaches are being complemented with newer, often emergent methods of connecting users and content in the enterprise setting. One "guerrilla" approach is predicated on enabling the creation of content that is, by definition, cross-departmental (mostly through the use of blogs and wikis). Another is the growing use of folksonomic tagging to provide access to content. Both guerrilla approaches make sense primarily on intranets.

Klogs for internal experts

Remember the person who knew so much about filing expense reports at our fictional consulting firm? She's an SME (Subject Matter Expert) whose expertise spans multiple business units' content. It serves the goal of EIA to enable her knowledge to be captured and shared more broadly within the enterprise. To that end, many companies are providing simple blog tools to their SMEs—sometimes describing them as "klogs," or knowledge blogs[*]—to help them share what they know.

Implementing klogs internally is technically fairly simple; however, identifying SMEs—especially ones with valuable cross-departmental knowledge—may be a bit difficult. Even more challenging, your enterprise's culture may not support its employees sharing their knowledge. It's an unfortunate fact that many organizations encourage its opposite: knowledge hoarding. Additionally, many SMEs aren't willing to share what they know simply to protect their job security. So klogs aren't a slam dunk, especially in settings where there is little incentive to share information. But their technical barrier to entry is low, and they at least merit consideration. Many individuals already do share their knowledge, especially if it raises their personal visibility as an expert within the enterprise (and if it helps them to avoid answering the same questions over and over again).

---

[*] It should be noted that many public-facing web sites increasingly feature blogs from their employees as a way to positively influence customers. This is especially the case in technical areas where it is beneficial to showcase in-house technical expertise.

Wikis for groups

Just as klogs enable individuals to capture and share their cross-departmental knowledge, wikis and other shared-authoring tools have similar potential for groups. Every enterprise has projects that require collaboration from multiple business units; these are typically tackled by temporarily constituted committees and working groups.

Wikis can make it relatively easy for these committees to capture their work—which, by definition, has cross-departmental value. In many cases, the content these groups develop will eventually receive official blessing and be published in a more traditional format, perhaps as a Word document or a PDF. But even in its relatively fluid and unfinished state, such content can have significant value to enterprise users. Additionally, wiki-based content is more likely to be accessible via search systems than Word or PDF files.

Accessing internal expertise through the staff directory

In so many cases, we search intranets for *people* rather than content. As cross-departmental information systems, staff directories are already excellent demonstrations of the value of EIA. We can extend their value by linking directory entries to corresponding klog and wiki content. The result: users can find out more about coworkers than their email addresses; they can learn about colleagues' expertise, what projects they've served on, and who they served with. Users can also search a topic and ultimately find a person.

Traditional directories can also be expanded to include more relationships between coworkers, such as reporting relationships. For example, it can be useful to know what to expect from the new boss by grilling a few of his past supervisees. Look to social-network services like LinkedIn (shown in Figure 19-8) and Ryze for models of how staff directories can be expanded and enhanced.

Aggregating staff expertise…and everything else

If your enterprise does begin investing in blogs and other means for capturing cross-departmental content, the good news is that most of these new publishing tools generate RSS or Atom feeds for recently posted content (blogs especially, of course). The better news is that there are many tools, both web-based* and standalone, that allow users to aggregate the feeds they've subscribed to. Imagine in-house researchers relying on aggregators to easily monitor the findings of their colleagues from research centers throughout the enterprise as soon as they're published.

---

* If you're not familiar with aggregators, we recommend kicking the tires of the excellent and free web-based service Bloglines (*http://www.bloglines.com*).

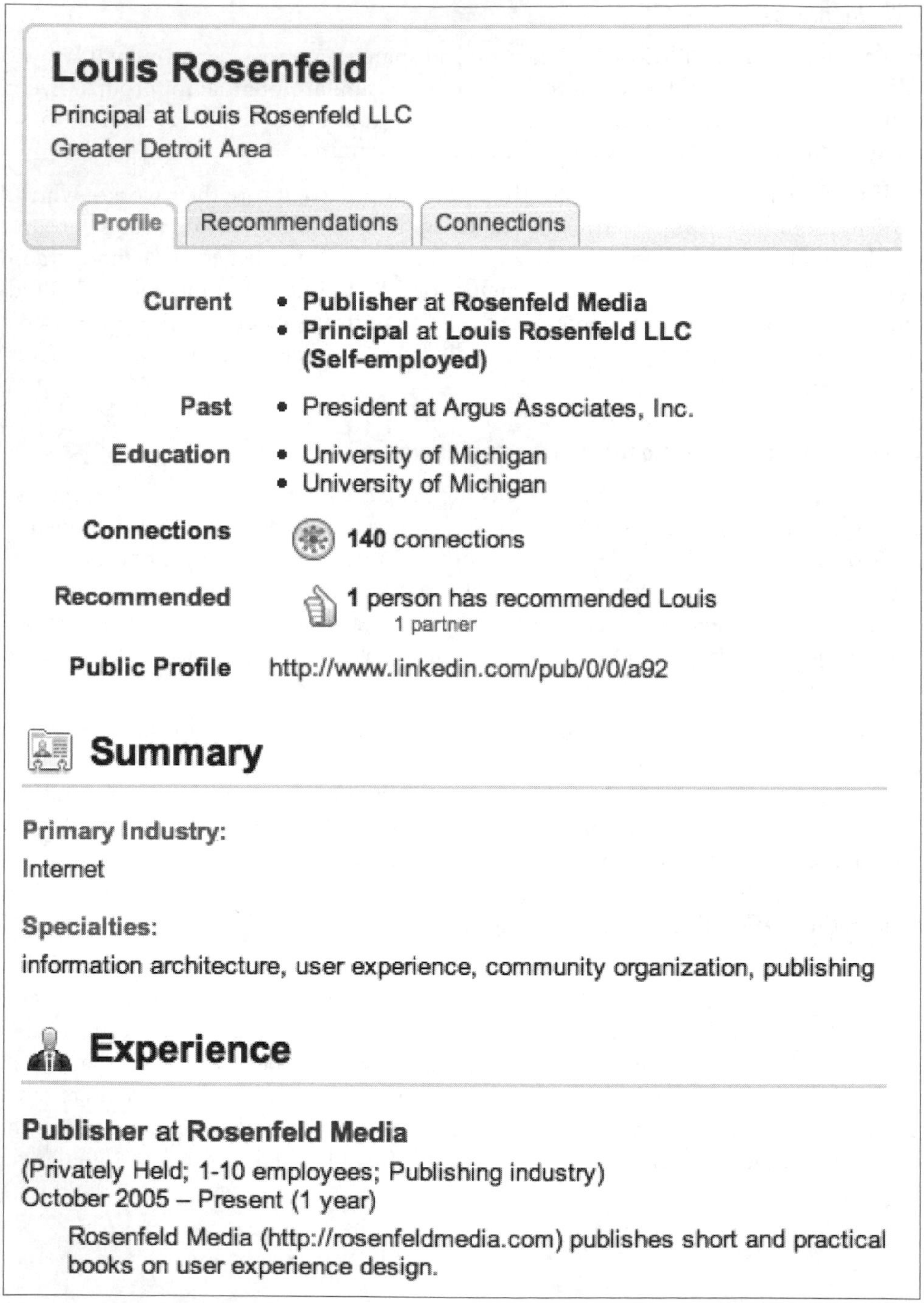

Louis Rosenfeld

Principal at Louis Rosenfeld LLC
Greater Detroit Area

| Profile | Recommendations | Connections |

Current
- **Publisher** at **Rosenfeld Media**
- **Principal** at **Louis Rosenfeld LLC (Self-employed)**

Past
- President at Argus Associates, Inc.

Education
- University of Michigan
- University of Michigan

Connections
- **140** connections

Recommended
- **1** person has recommended Louis
  1 partner

Public Profile   http://www.linkedin.com/pub/0/0/a92

 Summary

Primary Industry:

Internet

Specialties:

information architecture, user experience, community organization, publishing

Experience

Publisher at **Rosenfeld Media**

(Privately Held; 1-10 employees; Publishing industry)
October 2005 – Present (1 year)

Rosenfeld Media (http://rosenfeldmedia.com) publishes short and practical books on user experience design.

Figure 19-8. An entry from LinkedIn; is this your staff directory's future?

The even better news is that, as feeds become common for just about any type of web site, your enterprise's users could subscribe to feeds from a variety of departmental subsites. The aggregator becomes the means for accessing an enterprise's new content—regardless of originating silo—in one window. Imagine aggregating news releases from their many sources within your enterprise so you can keep up with what your own employer is actually doing—or enabling a public site's users to do the same.

Social bookmarking in the enterprise

Social bookmarking applications like del.icio.us have succeeded at helping users tag and return to visited content from across the Web. And by seeing what others have tagged with the same tags, del.icio.us subscribers also benefit from the wisdom of the hive, learning about other relevant documents (and who shares a similar interest).

Could the same approach work in the enterprise? Although it's too soon to say, large enterprises like IBM are hoping to find out.[*] Enterprise environments are obviously smaller than the Web as a whole, but they certainly exhibit web-like characteristics, such as overwhelming growth, frustrating organization, and swirling change. Bookmarking tools could help enterprise users benefit from one another's tagging efforts, and as an additional benefit, find like-minded colleagues. Collectively, tags also provide excellent fodder for helping improve traditional controlled vocabularies and bring them up-to-date.

EIA Strategy and Operations

We've described EIA design work that focuses on small steps and quick wins that don't necessarily require a huge outlay of resources, time, or staff. Because so many of these improvements can be made "under the radar," they often can take hold without requiring management sign-off up and down the chain of command.

Of course, there are far more ambitious designs that you can tackle within each of the four areas we covered above. But whether the focus is on short- or long-term goals, someone has to be responsible for design, implementation, maintenance, and governance of an enterprise information architecture. And management will ultimately have to be involved in setting policies, finding funding, and settling the political disputes that will inevitably arise.

Unfortunately, most enterprises have not dedicated staff to this work, or if they have, those staff are buried inside other business units that distract them from their primary goals. And management, despite its talking the talk of "information is our most strategic commodity" doesn't yet walk the walk. How does ownership of an enterprise information architecture evolve?

---

[*] David Millen, Jonathan Feinberg, and Bernard Kerr, "Social Bookmarking in the Enterprise" in *ACM Queue*, vol. 3, no. 9. Nov. 2005 (*http://acmqueue.com/modules.php?name=Content&pa=showpage&pid=344&page=1*).

A Common Evolutionary Path

The following table charts a common path for both *operational* and *strategic* aspects of EIA. Strategic work focuses on the growth, positioning, funding, and governance of EIA resources and staff, while the operational side addresses who actually does the work of developing and maintaining an EIA. This table shows how both tracks can evolve side by side over time, often in concert, in a "typical" enterprise environment.

Operational EIA	Strategic EIA
Individuals recognize that EIA issues exist	**Managers stuck in redesign mode**
A handful of people "in the trenches" responsible for some aspect of their business units' respective information architectures independently become aware that there are IA challenges that affect the entire enterprise. They may see the need for their own work (e.g., managing a search engine, developing product metadata or a style guide) to be coordinated or shared with others, but have little or no contact with like-minded peers within the enterprise. Nor do they have incentive to coordinate efforts.	Management is mostly unaware of and disinterested in EIA issues, although it may occasionally grapple with other relevant enterprise issues, such as branding. Typically, the enterprise web site is in the hands of the marketing function, and the enterprise intranet is managed by IT. Efforts to improve either site tend to be of the one-shot comprehensive "redesign" variety; accordingly, momentum quickly dissipates, and little institutional knowledge is retained.
	At this point, there is little value in attempting to engage decision-makers in the process of developing a coordinated EIA. However, some managers may begin to emerge as possible future champions of EIA projects.
Community of interest emerges	**Friendly managers lend tacit support**
As IA becomes more accepted throughout the enterprise, more people assume the job title "information architect"; it becomes easier to find similarly titled peers. Other triggers for bringing IA peers together include external events, such as attending local professional meetings and IA conferences, or the installation of an enterprise-class application (e.g., CMS, portal, or enterprise search engine), which requires significant configuration by internal staff.	A few "enlightened" managers emerge; their recognition of EIA issues often comes directly from analyzing the failures of past redesigns. These enlightened managers aren't yet in a position to provide resources or to allocate a portion of staff time to EIA efforts, but are supportive (or at least don't disapprove) of their staff who wish to participate in the informal activities of the community of interest.
An informal community of shared interest within the enterprise emerges, typically through the efforts of one or a few instigators, and is usually managed via an email discussion list and regular brown-bag lunches. At this point, few efforts are made to coordinate IA activities; it's more typical to compare notes on "how we did it" (e.g., how best bets are being implemented locally), as well as sharing external best practices gleaned at conferences.	

Time

Operational EIA	Strategic EIA

Community of practice achieves formal recognition

The community of interest becomes one of practice, with IAs from different units quietly coordinating efforts with enterprise implications. Examples include developing user-centered requirements for inclusion in functional specifications when new enterprise applications are being selected, and sharing budgets to cover software licenses or consulting from IA specialists (e.g., taxonomists). A semi-formal leadership structure emerges within the community of practice, mostly to manage communications within the group (rather than activities or resources). Local business units' respective IA activities still trump EIA work for all involved.

Advisory Committee emerges

Formalization of an in-house EIA community comes in the form of an official "blessing" on the part of managers. These managers are often drawn from a combination of friendly managers and "squeaky wheels" (vocal managers responsible for major content areas, product groups, or user constituencies), and they take on a semi-official role as an Advisory Committee. Meetings are irregular and often draw attendance from a different subset of managers each time.

Official Advisory Committee responsibilities are minimal. At this point, its chief role is to serve as a means for communicating about EIA and related issues between departments and, occasionally, to advocate to senior managers on behalf of the community of practice when it identifies specific needs or requires help dealing with policy issues and internal politics.

Distributed teams assigned to specific EIA projects

Growth in demand for better EIA coordination leads to formal allocation of IA staff to specific enterprise projects, especially around the implementation and configuration of enterprise-class applications, as well as metadata and interface design guidelines. IAs from business units continue to work primarily on local projects, but their enterprise allocation continues to increase—even if only for temporary projects—and they begin to take on formal responsibility for EIA-related projects.

EIA teams that are initially constituted for specific projects increasingly become permanently established. External IA specialists are more commonly brought in to assist in EIA efforts.

Advisory Committee matures; Strategic Board backs it up

The Advisory Committee becomes a formal decision-making group, advising EIA teams, formulating EIA policy and strategy, and paving the way for projects when EIA teams need more senior-level assistance. The Committee meets more regularly, and its membership becomes increasingly representative of important constituencies and internal units (extending especially beyond IT and Marketing).

The Advisory Committee recognizes that its growing scope of responsibility requires additional authority and funding; it advocates for the creation of a very senior Strategic Board (akin to a company's Board of Directors) to put at least the appearance of teeth into proposed policies through visible support (even if this support takes the form of rubber-stamping new policies). The Board, which meets every few months, also helps identify sources of funding for major EIA-related projects.

Business unit dedicated to EIA in place

A permanent EIA unit, usually drawn from internal staff, are now in place, with its own management structure. Team size varies, often based on scope (some units are more broadly focused on enterprise user experience or knowledge management). As team size reaches double digits, specialists in such areas as metadata development, user testing, search systems, and metrics are brought on as full-time staff. Though their primary responsibility is the enterprise architecture, both generalists and specialists also provide IA consulting to local business units on an as-needed basis. The EIA team also takes on a leadership role in training local IA staff and with EIA "intellectual property," such as the enterprise-wide style guide and metadata standards.

Strategic players formalize and expand their roles

Seeing the strategic nature of enterprise information, the Strategic Board takes on a greater role, paving the way for the creation of a new cost center, a business unit dedicated to EIA and related areas.

Other groups that have a role in EIA strategy begin to form, such as a user-advocacy board (useful for maintaining an enterprise-wide pool of users for testing and evaluation purposes).

The Advisory Committee also takes on a more formal, active role as the primary decision-making group, serving as executive managers of the EIA business unit.

Time

This isn't how it always happens, but it's a relatively close approximation of the mean. (Another common path toward in-house EIA competence involves the migration of an e-commerce team or web development group to a group that addresses EIA as well.) More importantly, this evolution will provide you ideas and, if nothing else, a straw man that you can react to as you chart your own course.

The EIA Group's Ideal Qualities and Makeup

As with an actual information architecture, you should consider assembling an in-house EIA group from both the top down and bottom up. Think of the top-down approach as the strategy end of things, where senior people figure out the big picture of where the EIA unit should be headed and how it will get there. The bottom-up side is comprised of the operational tasks involved in actually doing the work at hand. As much as possible, separate these two areas; their respective missions, tasks, and members will be quite different.

The strategists

The strategists—members of the Advisory Committee and Strategic Board—focus on the role of the EIA unit within the broader enterprise. Their mission is to ensure that the enterprise benefits from a quality information architecture through the efforts of the EIA group. Their goals are to:

- Understand the strategic role of information architecture within the enterprise
- Promote information architecture services as a permanent part of the enterprise's infrastructure
- Align the EIA operations team and its services with the enterprise's goals
- Ensure the financial and political viability
- Inform EIA operations of changes in strategic direction that may impact the enterprise's information architecture plans
- Help develop EIA operating policies
- Support the EIA team's management
- Assess the EIA team's performance

In effect, strategists are responsible for the success of EIA operations. That means navigating politics, getting buy-in from management across the enterprise, and acquiring funding and other resources. It also requires the development of metrics to help judge the success of the enterprise information architecture broadly, and EIA operations specifically.

People who would be effective and available in the director's role exhibit these qualities:

- Have been in the enterprise long enough to have wide visibility, an extensive network, and the ability to draw on years of institutional memories and experiences
- Are entrepreneurial; can read and even write a business plan
- Have a track record of involvement with successful enterprise initiatives
- Have experience with centralized efforts, successful or not (failures are as informative as successes)
- Can navigate political situations
- Can "sell" a new, abstract concept; have experience finding internal funding
- Resemble or can at least understand your clients in terms of outlook, position within the org chart, personality, and golf handicap
- Have experience with consulting operations, either as a provider or a purchaser
- Have experience negotiating licensing agreements with vendors

Operations People

The EIA operations team takes on the tactical work of information architecture: researching and analyzing factors related to content, users, and business context; designing information architectures that address those factors; and implementing that design. Besides delivering the EIA Unit's services, the operations unit follows (and upholds) policies and procedures for content management and architectural maintenance.

How should this team be staffed? There are many roles that would be nice to have on your team, including:

- Strategy Architect
- Thesaurus Designer
- Interaction Architect
- Technology Integration Specialist
- Information Architecture Usability Specialist
- Search Analyst
- Controlled Vocabulary Manager
- Indexing Specialist
- Content Modeling Architect
- Ethnographer
- Project Manager

Of course, staffing each of these areas is a fantasy for most of us, but this ideal gives you something to shoot for. More importantly, it helps you line up outside consulting expertise. Don't have a usability specialist on staff? Your entrepreneurial business model might allow you to pass a consultant's costs to your clients.

When you do get around to hiring staff for your interdisciplinary operations team, look for these qualities:

- Entrepreneurial mindset
- Ability to consult (i.e., do work *and* justify IA *and* navigate difficult political environments)
- Willingness to acknowledge ignorance and seek help
- Ability to communicate with people from other fields
- Experience within the organization
- Experience of prior enterprise-wide centralization efforts
- Sensitivity to users' needs
- Knowledge about information architecture and related fields (of course)

Finally, consider what gaps your EIA unit is filling within the enterprise. You may find that you want to broaden your scope, branching toward conventional IT services such as hosting, or toward visual design, editorial, or other areas under the broader umbrella of experience design. Select your staff and consultants accordingly to fit the needs of the enterprise.

Doing the Work and Paying the Bills

The evolutionary path described earlier ends with the seemingly optimistic outcome of a separate EIA business unit, independent of the baggage of IT, Marketing, Corporate Communication, or other parent groups. Why are we fans of the go-it-alone approach?

Efforts to knit together an enterprise's information architecture naturally require extensive cross-departmental communication and involvement. And business units typically don't trust other business units to do the right thing. An effort to centralize an enterprise-wide architecture will be tough enough *without* including the baggage of that effort's foster parent, Department X. And if Department X's mission in life is operating the corporate WAN or maintaining the corporate brand, its managers won't typically understand—much less fully support—EIA efforts; they're not likely to fit any existing department's core mission and goals. So why force it?

Additionally, because efforts to centralize are long-term and ongoing, and information architecture and content management have become a permanent part of the scene, a support infrastructure for these efforts is a necessity. Enterprises simply can't afford to "re-do" their information architectures every year or two; the direct costs are high, and no organizational learning is retained. For these reasons, EIA is ideally owned and operated by an independent infrastructural unit with its own budget and managers.

Interestingly, when the second edition of this book (published in 2002) suggested standalone EIA groups, the idea wasn't popular; it seemed too optimistic given both the lack of acceptance of IA in many enterprises and the economic conditions of the time. Yet today this model is becoming widespread, because many organizations find it impossible to make progress with EIA unless it's the responsibility of an (at least somewhat) autonomous and baggage-free business unit. There really are few viable alternatives.

Build a New Business Unit

The idea of a standalone business unit begs the question: how will it be funded? New cost centers do get established from time to time—at some point, IT, HR, and other groups found the funding they needed to address the needs of the entire enterprise. But, admittedly, such events are infrequently witnessed in the enterprise landscape. So where will the money come from?

Nothing is impossible, and there are a variety of potential sources of income that merit consideration. Here are five possibilities:

Seed capital

> In some cases, organizations see enough value in a new project to at least grant it an initial investment. Seed money is a fixed financial injection, usually to be used over a predetermined block of time and intended to support the new business unit until it can stand on its own feet. It should be carefully budgeted to cover the initial years of a project, gently winding down as revenues projected from other sources begin to grow.

Operating expenses

> Central funding can also come in the form of operating expenses that all business units (including new ones and especially cost centers) can count on to pay for the basics, like desks, roofs, and possibly administrative staff. These funds aren't typically available to cover much else beyond a business unit's basic "cost of living."

Flat tax

> Some cost centers derive income from client business units to cover the cost of basic services and shared services that address the needs of the entire enterprise. A good example in the EIA context is the ongoing maintenance and tuning of a search system that provides access to the enterprise's entire body of content, regardless of its originating business units.

Income for special enterprise-wide projects

> Occasional big-ticket items, like a new content management platform and content migration, are also costs likely to be borne by all business units. These are usually assessed as one-time fees, requiring agreement from all other business units; alternatively, the bill is footed by the enterprise's central administration, which sees such projects as being important to the success of the enterprise as a whole.

Income for services rendered

The standard "chargeback" model; services are paid for by client business units just as they'd pay external vendors. In an ideal world, the EIA unit ensures its independence by sustaining itself on the fees of a loyal in-house clientele; unfortunately, this model often runs counter to certain organizational cultures, especially those in the nonprofit and academic sectors.

Figure 19-9 shows how these sources of income might vary over the first few years in the life of an EIA business unit.

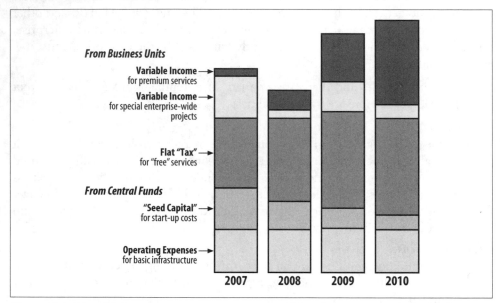

Figure 19-9. Diversified revenue stream to support a standalone business unit responsible for EIA

Which (if any) of these revenue sources makes sense for you depends on how business gets done internally within your organization. For example, some organizations live and die by the chargeback model, while it wouldn't even receive 10 seconds of consideration in other settings. Clearly, the best approach is to try to "diversify your revenue stream" and not place too many eggs in one basket. And, hopefully, your Advisory Committee and Strategic Board (or equivalent thereof) will take the lead in determining the appropriate revenue model; ideally, they have prior experience doing so within your enterprise.

Build an Entrepreneurial Business Unit

We especially advocate reliance on one of the above-mentioned revenue streams: billing internal "clients" for services rendered. Obviously, a standalone cost center will be better off if it becomes responsible for its own income. Seeing the enterprise environment as a local economy, and seeking to function as a service provider in that environment, acknowledges a critical truth of the enterprise: nothing succeeds without trust and incentive.

We've already discussed how business units don't tend to trust other business units, and how the new and baggage-free EIA unit might fly under the radar. It may not achieve trust, but at least it might avoid mistrust. A more important way to achieve trust is to behave in a way that's familiar to your "clients." In other words, if they're operating within the corporate economy—functioning with budgets, costs, and revenues—then you should, too. If they see you operating by the same rules, they'll understand and trust you more than if you appear to be some vice president's ephemeral pet project. By acting as an entrepreneurial *service provider* to the enterprise, you will craft a menu of services catered to your clients' true needs (more on these services shortly).

In terms of trust, people can't trust what they don't understand. So, like any entrepreneurial organization, a standalone EIA team needs to take seriously the role of marketing its efforts. We've found that one of the best ways to market an abstract concept like information architecture is through education. A program of introductory information architecture seminars, repeated regularly throughout the year, can help potential clients understand that their problems aren't unique, that there is a nomenclature they can use to express these problems, that a field (information architecture) exists to guide them, that others within the enterprise suffer similar pain, and, ultimately, that the EIA group is there to provide real assistance with such problems.

Where does incentive fit in? Simply put, a self-funded business unit has greater incentive to do good work, especially because it often faces competition from external service providers. Self-support means that the EIA group will become better at listening to clients and discerning their pain, developing appropriate services, and communicating the benefits of its own services versus those of competitors.

Incentive is a two-way street. Should the EIA unit not justify its budget to clients, those clients will not have a good sense of what value information architects bring. They often don't know what these services cost, never having purchased them before. Divorcing level and quality of service from some monetary equivalent muddies the waters, leading to relationships between the EIA team and its clients that are more likely to be fraught with misunderstandings and miscommunication. In effect, other business units don't have incentive to be good clients.

Provide Modular Services to Clients

What types of services should you sell to clients? Naturally, they will be limited by the EIA team's expertise. Basic market-research techniques will help you understand what exactly your clients need, whether it's help configuring that search engine or designing better navigation systems. The important thing is to delineate services that are concrete and modular. By doing so, you are in effect making information architecture itself more concrete and less of an intimidating unknown. Therefore, it's more likely to be an attractive and justifiable purchase for your clients.

Table 19-3 shows just some of the services the EIA unit might provide to clients around the enterprise.

Table 19-3. Possible services of the EIA unit

Content acquisition	Content archiving
Content authoring	Content management tool acquisition
Quality control and editing	Content management tool maintenance
Link checking	Search engine acquisition
HTML validation	Search engine maintenance
Designing templates	Autoclassification tool acquisition
Applying templates	Autoclassification tool maintenance
Overall information architecture design	Training of business unit staff in IA/CM
Overall information architecture maintenance	Publicity of new and changed content
Indexing (manual)	Standards development
Indexing (automated)	User testing and feedback evaluation
Controlled vocabulary/thesaurus creation	Search-log evaluation
Controlled vocabulary/thesaurus maintenance	Interaction with visual-design staff
Content development policy creation	Interaction with IT staff
Content development policy maintenance	Interaction with vendors
Content weeding and ROT removal	

This list of services is focused on information architecture and, to a lesser degree, content management. It could be expanded to include other aspects of the user experience, such as visual design, interaction design, application development, media production, copyrighting, hosting, and publicity.

Developing a list of potential services is also a useful exercise to help you determine just what your team can and can't do. Don't have anyone on staff who can develop a thesaurus? Now you know that you'll need to find that expertise, whether in-house or from external vendors. This exercise helps you begin the process of resolving your team's strengths and weaknesses, and points out expertise gaps that could be filled with external talent. In effect, you'll now have the answers to your questions regarding when to bring in outside expertise, as well as what kind of staff to hire in-house once there's sufficient demand. (This is a much better method for incorporating external expertise than is typical; outside contractors and consultants are often brought in at the wrong time and for the wrong reasons.)

Consider creating two versions of each service: a free "loss leader," and a premium version that clients pay for. Because IA is still so new to so many within your enterprise, you should provide them a chance to dip their toes in and try your offerings.

Ideally, they'll like what they see, find it indispensable, and eventually "upgrade" to the premium version. Table 19-4 shows an example of one such item on the menu.

Table 19-4. Free versus premium versions of a service

Service: Content Acquisition				
Basic-level service description	Basic service pricing	Premium-level service description	Premium service pricing	Client requirements
Interview client and no more than 5 users to determine content needs. Identify free and proprietary sources of content.	First 25 hours free; then $125/hr.	Same as basic level, plus: interview 15 users total, and develop plan for integrating new and existing content, including plan for metadata integration.	$5,000 for 60 hours; then $125/hr.	Client agrees to identify, contact, and arrange meetings with content stewards and sample users for interviews regarding content needs.

Aside from free versus fee, consider other ways of making your fee structure attractive. For example, clients may appreciate the opportunity to pay for certain service charges as *fixed*, such as a retainer fee for weekly spidering of content, versus *flexible*, such as an hourly charge for occasional search engine configuration.

Finally, you might also consider incentive programs; for example, you might reward a business unit with a discount for frequently updating its content or religiously following certain manual-tagging guidelines. There are whole information economies, like evolt.org (described in Chapter 21), that manage to inspire broad community participation and exchange of information without a single penny ever changing hands. Blogs and wikis are increasingly being explored as knowledge management tools within enterprise contexts. It's worth reviewing such innovative approaches when considering how your own business model will function.

Before determining service fees, consider the models already in place within your enterprise. Are there organizations that already provide centralized services? The IT department is one logical place to look; others include the library or research center, the division that manages the enterprise's office space, human resources, and so on. Your goal is to find out how they provide their services. How do they study market demand, how do they publicize their services, and how are they funded? What works and what doesn't?

Timing Is Everything: A Phased Rollout

EIA efforts are often tripped up by efforts to work with everyone and to do so all at once. Obviously, this is a recipe for disaster, but what's the alternative? It's pretty simple, really: choose your battles wisely, and take your time. Here's our advice.

Identifying Potential Clients

You don't want to work with all clients. Some are simply too stuck in "cowboy" mode, playing the rugged individualist to your information architecture communalist. Some are too busy to work with you. Some are too cautious when it comes to new things. Some would like to work with you but don't have the resources, or perhaps they don't have particularly valuable content. Some, frankly, just don't get this information architecture stuff, regardless of your best educational efforts. And don't forget: some will actually have a much more sophisticated understanding of information architecture than you do.

In such a mixed environment—with both ends of the evolutionary spectrum coexisting on the same floor of the corporation—you must accept the reality that you'll be working with only the few clients with whom success is immediately likely, and waiting for the others to catch up over time.

Some clients shouldn't be using your information architecture at all; they may be better suited to managing the information that lives within their department. You need to figure out how to pull out that information and integrate it with other information. For example, HR data is probably never going to be something you have control over, but it is exposed through various interfaces (web, database, etc.). You can work with HR to extract the information you need and integrate it with your architecture, but you'll have to build a bridge to HR to keep this functioning. Your task is to integrate all these scenarios into an overall strategy, and accommodate the different needs and requirements in your information architecture.

So who are the "right" clients? Once again, use the three-circle Venn diagram of information architecture to guide you. The right clients exhibit the following characteristics:

Content

What's the "killer" content within the organization? It might be the stuff that's used the most broadly and therefore has the highest visibility within the enterprise. A great example, at least for enterprise intranets, is the staff directory; not only does it have high value, but everyone uses it. For public sites, the product catalog is a good candidate. Both are often examples of excellent information architecture design. So whoever owns it is potentially an excellent client. Also, who has content that already comes with reasonably good metadata, or that is well structured? This stuff has already undergone at least some information architecture design, and therefore is ripe for inclusion in your architecture.

Users

The clients you want to work with are trying to please the most important and influential audiences within the enterprise. These users may already be complaining about some information architecture-related issue and pushing for change. Aside from throwing their weight around the enterprise, these users might also have the deepest pockets, which is always a good thing. A great example of a key audience is the Research and Development group—they're influential within the enterprise, and they live and die by quality access to quality content. The clients who cater to them are probably already knowledgeable about information architecture (even if they call it something else) and are less likely to require "missionary" sales efforts on your part.

Context

Where's the money (and the good technology and the knowledgeable staff)? Ultimately, you want a paying client; you can't be doing charity work for too long. Which clients do you think will present the fewest headaches to work with? How far along is each on the autonomy/centralization evolutionary path? Who will be in the best position to provide testimonial support as you approach other potential clients throughout the enterprise? If your prized client is infamous and unpopular throughout the enterprise, its support may actually be counterproductive.

In your quest to find the best clients to work with, consider these issues as part of your market research and selection process. Also keep in mind that your initial round of projects is a marketing tool, providing models of your work and work style to longer-term potential clients.

After your first pass at assessing who's out there, you might go a level deeper in your analysis. Using the list we devised earlier, create a checklist for your "sales" staff to use as they delve deeper into each business unit's needs. This will help to determine how "information architecture-ready" each business unit is, and to assess the market for your EIA unit's services. The following checklist addresses the services listed in Table 19-1.

Service	What are they doing now?	Do they have in-house expertise in this area?	Do they have tools or applications available in this area?	Other considerations
Content acquisition				
Content authoring				
Quality control and editing				
Link checking				
HTML validation				
Designing templates				
Applying templates				
Overall information architecture design				
Overall information architecture maintenance				
Indexing (manual)				
Indexing (automated)				

Service	What are they doing now?	Do they have in-house expertise in this area?	Do they have tools or applications available in this area?	Other considerations
Controlled vocabulary/thesaurus creation				
Controlled vocabulary/thesaurus maintenance				
Content development policy creation				
Content development policy maintenance				
Content weeding and ROT removal				
Content archiving				
Content management tool acquisition				
Content management tool maintenance				
Search engine acquisition				
Search engine maintenance				
…and so on				

Interestingly, this exercise is also beneficial in determining what each unit has to offer to centralization efforts. For example, you might learn that a far-flung, little-known unit has acquired an expensive license for a new search engine. Perhaps it can bring this tool to the table? Sharing license fees helps the unit, and the enterprise as a whole may benefit by using the technology at a lower cost.

Phasing in Centralization

Of course, the best potential client in Q3 of 2007 could be very different from the best in Q2 of 2009. If the previous section is about helping you identify the "low-hanging fruit" that is ready to be plucked right now, then this one is about being ready to catch the next batch as it ripens.

There is a natural evolution toward greater centralization among the enterprise's business units. The modularization of information architecture services is the perfect way to tap this evolution because you can hook clients for basic "must-have" services right away, and sign them up for additional services over time. The idea is that today's basic-service clients will evolve into clients of higher-end services as their needs become more sophisticated and their aversion to centralization wanes.

Strive for a plan that's built upon a "timed release" of your services throughout the enterprise. For example, your market research may allow you to come up with projections like those shown in the following table. This worksheet tracks the evolution of demand for more and more sophisticated services over time, allowing the EIA Unit to make a case for additional headcount.

BUSINESS UNITS (16 total): service usage (past and projected)								
	Historical Performance →			Projected Performance →				
	2007 Q3	2006 Q4	2008 Q1	2008 Q2	2008 Q3	2008 Q4	2008 Q1	2008 Q2
Designing templates								
No service	11	11	10	10	9	9	8	7
Basic service	4	4	5	4	4	4	5	5
Premium service	1	1	1	2	3	3	3	4
Indexing (manual)								
No service	14	6	1	1	0	0	0	0
Basic service	2	8	11	11	10	10	8	8
Premium service	0	2	4	4	6	6	8	8
Controlled vocabulary maintenance								
No service	8	3	3	3	3	1	0	0
Basic service	4	7	6	5	4	5	6	4
Premium service	4	6	7	8	9	10	10	12

A glimpse at future demand will help you allocate the EIA unit's resources more effectively, enabling you to develop a phased plan to approach each tier of potential clients over time and ensuring that the EIA unit's services are ready to meet the demand. The predictive power of this approach will give you a better idea of when to bring in outside specialists and other types of help. Perhaps most importantly, realistic projections of demand will be quite useful as you approach senior management for additional investment.

Finally, phasing in modular services allows various business units to have differing levels of centralization. In other words, cavemen can coexist with the highly evolved folks down the hall. What might result is something like the following "snapshot" of the enterprise, where the three business units are at very different points on the spectrum of autonomy/centralization. A flexible framework supports the unique needs of each. The following table once again deals with the items in Table 19-1.

	Business Unit		
Service	Human Resources	Corporate Communications	Procurement and Supply
Content acquisition	-	Premium	-
Content authoring	-	-	Basic
Quality control and editing	-	Basic	-

	Business Unit		
Link checking	Basic	Basic	-
HTML validation	Basic	Premium	-
Designing templates	-	Premium	Basic
Applying templates	-	Basic	-
Overall information architecture design	Basic	-	-
Overall information architecture maintenance	Basic	-	-
Indexing (manual)	-	Basic	Basic
Indexing (automated)	Basic	Basic	-
Controlled vocabulary/thesaurus creation	Basic	-	-
Controlled vocabulary/thesaurus maintenance	Basic	-	-
Content development policy creation	Basic	Basic	-
Content development policy maintenance	Basic	Basic	-
Content weeding and ROT removal	-	-	-
Content archiving	Basic	-	Basic
Content management tool acquisition	Basic	Basic	-
Content management tool maintenance	Basic	Basic	-
Search engine acquisition	-	Premium	Basic
Search engine maintenance	-	Basic	Basic
Autoclassification tool acquisition	-	-	-
…and so on			

A Framework for Moving Forward

In this chapter, we've mapped out a loose and ambitious framework that, even if you don't agree with our specific recommendations, will provide you with ideas to mull over and react to as you develop your own approach. By breaking up overwhelming problems into digestible pieces, we hope that this framework will ensure that information architecture becomes a permanent fixture within enterprises that need it. By taking a phased approach, we believe this framework can stand the test of time. And by staying true to an entrepreneurial approach, this framework might defuse the urge to "force" autonomous business units to comply with centralizing efforts.

Ideally, this framework will be flexible enough to roll with the inevitable punches of corporate mergers, spin-offs, and reorganizations. We hope that it helps you and your organization avoid the waste and frustration of developing elegant information architectures on paper that can never be implemented in the unruly distributed information environments that have proliferated within the modern enterprise.

PART VI

Case Studies

CHAPTER 20

MSWeb: An Enterprise Intranet

What we'll cover:

- The story of how a large enterprise information architecture was improved
- How three types of "taxonomies"—an indexing vocabulary, schema, and category labels—were successfully utilized to describe high-value content
- The technical architecture that was developed to maintain these taxonomies
- How a modular approach and an emphasis on service helped the MSWeb team succeed in revamping the MSWeb intranet

What is the Holy Grail for information architects? It's the secret that will help them develop and maintain a user-centered information architecture for a large, distributed enterprise—the kind made up of all sorts of autonomous, bickering business units that have their own goals, their own sites, their own infrastructures, their own users, and their own ideas of how to go about things (see Chapter 19 for more on enterprise information architecture).

It's nearly impossible to develop a successful information architecture against a backdrop of explosive content growth, content ROT, and the political twists and turns common in any organization. And, we're sorry to say, no one can claim to own the Grail. But we've had the privilege of getting up close to a large number of corporate intranets. And one of the best approaches we've seen so far is the one taken by Microsoft's intranet portal (MSWeb) team.

Before you protest, we admit that yes, we understand that you probably don't have the same resources at your disposal as Microsoft's team did. But we think everyone can learn from Microsoft's efforts; what it's doing today is what most intranets will be doing in three to five years, for two reasons. First, MSWeb's approach is flexible enough to be customized for many large organizations. And second, knowing Microsoft, it's a reasonable bet that the good ideas described here will soon enough find their way into Microsoft's product offerings and into your IT department. So perhaps you'll own a piece of this approach in the not-too-distant future. Let's preview it here so you'll be ready.

Challenges for the User

Like Microsoft itself, MSWeb is insanely huge and distributed. Let's use some numbers to paint a picture of the situation. MSWeb contains:

- 3,100,000+ pages
- Content created by and for over 50,000 employees who work in 74 countries
- 8,000+ separate intranet sites

With apologies to Herbert Hoover, Microsoft has put a web server in practically every employee's pot. Employees, in turn, have responded by embracing the technology (as you'd expect from one of the world's largest technology companies), and by churning out an impossibly huge volume of content.

But if you're a typical Microsoft employee, these numbers also represent a bit of a problem. Microsoft estimates that a typical employee spends 2.31 hours per day engaging with information, and 50 percent of that time is used *looking for that information*. Although you already know how ambivalent we are about using such calculations to estimate actual costs to the organization, we think these numbers show that at least some valuable employee time is being wasted flailing about in this huge environment in search of information.

Here are just a few examples of how this chaotic environment hurts Microsoft employees.

Where to begin?
> This is your typical case of "silo hell." With as many as 8,000 possibilities available, employees have a hard time determining where they should begin looking for the information they need. While some starting points are obvious—check the human resources site for information on your medical insurance or 401K plan—other areas, such as technical information, are scattered throughout Microsoft's intranet environment.

Inconsistent navigation systems
> Navigation systems are quite inconsistent because they employ many different labeling schemes. Therefore, users are confused each time they encounter a new one. Not only does this inhibit navigation, it also muddles the user's sense of place.

Same concept, different labels
> Because different labels are used for the same concepts, users miss out on important information when they don't search or browse for all the possible labels for those concepts. For example, users may search for "Windows 2000" without realizing that they also need to hunt for "Microsoft Windows 2000," "Windows 2000," "Win 2000," "Win2000," "Win2k," "Win 2k," and "w2k."

Different concepts, same label

Conversely, a term doesn't always mean what you think it does. For example, ASP can mean "active server pages," "application service providers," or "actual selling price." And the term "Merlin" has been used as the code name for three very different products.

Ignorance is not bliss

Often, users are happy when they get *any* relevant information. But in a knowledge-intensive environment like Microsoft's, users are much more demanding—their jobs depend on finding the best information possible. In this case, employees often get frustrated because they don't know when to stop searching. Is the content simply not there? Or is a server down somewhere? Or maybe they didn't enter a good search query?

It's not hard to see how a typical employee's 1.155 hours per day might get burned up. In short, Microsoft employees face an expansive and confusing information environment that's about as intimidating as the Web itself.

Challenges for the Information Architect

The flip side of this problem is how these numbers affect the people who are responsible for making Microsoft's content or aggregating that content into portals. Let's make another comparison to the broader Web. Building and maintaining the Yahoo! portal was a huge undertaking, spanning years and a gigantic collection of content—the Web as a whole. MSWeb is a portal, too, and though 8,000 sites is a much more manageable number than what Yahoo! faced, consider the varying motives and concerns of those who own and maintain those independent sites. And Microsoft can't charge or compel site owners within the company to register. Instead, the MSWeb team has to create incentives for participation in its model. But the owners of the intranet's various sites are too distracted by other concerns (such as serving their own constituencies) to consider how their site fits into the bigger picture of Microsoft's intranet.

When a site is brought into the MSWeb fold, it comes with its own information architecture. Its organization, labeling systems, and other tricky information architecture components must be integrated into the broader MSWeb architecture or be replaced altogether. For example, as many as 50 different variants of product vocabularies had been created in the Microsoft intranet environment. Fixing such problems is a messy and complicated challenge for any information architect.

And it gets even worse: all of those Microsoft intranet sites are backed up by a technical architecture of some sort. Some are designed, built, and maintained by in-house technical staff and are quite advanced and elaborate. At the other extreme are sites maintained by hand or by a simple tool like MS FrontPage. The technology architectures that support the Microsoft intranet environment vary widely in complexity, and the MSWeb team must determine ways to normalize and simplify the environment to make content management easier and more efficient. Additionally, many of these technology architectures are not designed to support a portal or any other sort of enterprise-wide information architecture, so that's another crucial factor the MSWeb team must account for.

Does your head hurt yet?

We Like Taxonomies, Whatever They Are

Well, many heads were throbbing at Microsoft. And an odd and often misunderstood term—"taxonomies"—began to be heard in corridors at Redmond. Although they share a common x, "taxonomies" and "sexy" are two words that aren't often seen together in public. So when "taxonomies" become a part of everyday conversation, it's a sure sign that an organization is ready for a deeper look into information architecture.

So Microsoft's MSWeb team heard the word and knew that the time had come for a more ambitious approach to improving MSWeb. The team—fewer than 10 people, but populated by an impressive mix of information scientists, designers, technologists, and politically savvy managers—began to consider what users meant when they called for better (or any) taxonomies. Instead of the traditional biology-inspired definition, Microsoft's employees thought of taxonomies as constructs that would help them search, browse, and manage intranet content more effectively.

In response, the MSWeb team developed a more generalized operating definition of taxonomies that would be more in line with how other employees were using the term. This flexibility—the willingness to speak the language of clients, rather than rigidly clinging to a "correct" but ultimately unpopular meaning—was key. It set the tone for successful communications between the MSWeb team and its clients throughout the organization.

Three Flavors of Taxonomies

The team defined taxonomies as any set of terms that shared some organizing principle. For example, *descriptive vocabularies* were seen as controlled vocabularies that described a specific domain (e.g., geography, or products and technologies) and included variant terms for the same concept. *Metadata schema* were collections of labeled attributes for a document, not unlike a catalog record. *Category labels* were sets of terms to be used for the options of navigation systems. These three areas comprised the foundation of the MSWeb approach. Better searching, browsing, and managing of information would be achieved by designing taxonomies that could be shared throughout the enterprise.

Descriptive vocabularies for indexing

Developing terms to manually index important pieces of content seemed a smart proposition for the MSWeb team. It would complement automated indexing by the search engine, which was currently the primary means of making the site's content available. But creating and applying descriptive vocabularies is an expensive proposition, especially within an information environment as large as Microsoft's. And there are so many different ways to index content, so half the battle was in selecting which vocabularies would deliver the most value to the organization as a whole.

The MSWeb team considered a number of issues when deciding which vocabularies to develop. Not surprisingly, characteristics of the content drove many of the decisions.

Search-log analysis

Queries from MSWeb's search-query logs are stored in an SQL database and can therefore be searched and more easily analyzed. Search-log analysis helped the MSWeb team gauge user content needs in users' own words and determine appropriate vocabulary terms. Studying the search log's most common queries also helped the team get a good overview of which content areas were generally most valuable to users.

Availability

The team looked for decent controlled vocabularies that had already been developed in-house or that were available commercially. Vivian Bliss, MSWeb Knowledge Management Analyst, puts it simply: "Don't reinvent the wheel!" If there's a useful vocabulary out there, it's much cheaper to license and adapt it than to create a new one. Unfortunately, most of the required vocabularies were very specific to Microsoft's content and had to be custom-built in-house.

Other decisions were driven by business context. The MSWeb team considered such issues as:

Politics

The team was careful to talk with content stakeholders about what they felt was needed to make their content more accessible. In some cases, stakeholders were interested both in information architecture concepts and in committing to working with the MSWeb team. Others were interested in neither. Through such discussions, it became apparent which stakeholders were ready to participate and which weren't.

Applicability

Some vocabularies were too specific to have broad value for users across the company. The MSWeb team instead focused on vocabularies with broader appeal and value.

After taking all of these considerations into account, Microsoft narrowed its vocabulary development to the following vocabularies:

- Geography
- Languages
- Proper names
- Organization and business unit names
- Subjects
- Product, standards, and technology names

Developing some of these vocabularies was trickier than you might think. Geography, for example, had to be split into two separate vocabularies: general place names, and locations of Microsoft installations. On the other hand, the subject vocabulary development was simpler than it might have been: its development was constrained primarily to addressing equivalence relationships. The MSWeb team hasn't added extensive hierarchical and associative relationships; that would require a huge effort and take resources away from developing other vocabularies that could provide broad benefits right away. (In the future, the team does plan to selectively address these other relationships as time and resources permit.)

Metadata schema

Developed hand-in-hand with controlled vocabularies, metadata schema describe which metadata to use to describe or catalog a content resource. While Microsoft's descriptive vocabularies were driven by content and context, metadata schema were informed more by issues of users and content.

The MSWeb team developed a single schema that has value for both MSWeb and other intranet sites. Borrowing from the Dublin Core Metadata Element Set (see *http://dublincore.org*), MSWeb's schema was intended to be sufficiently "stripped down" so that content owners would use it to describe resources, resulting in more records and therefore a more useful collection of content. The schema's simplicity was balanced with the goal of providing enough descriptive information to augment searching and browsing by users.

The team also had to ensure that records produced using the schema would include fields useful for resource description, display, and integration with other parts of the information architecture (namely by integrating with search results and browsing schemes). The process used to develop this metadata schema was, in the words of one team member, "down and dirty." Although more polished methodologies exist, sufficient resources were not available at the time for this initial schema development project. For this reason, it was important to structure the schema to include both a required "core" set of fields and the flexibility to support future extensions of the schema by other business units. To date, seven other major portals are using the metadata schema, and many have extended and customized it for their own context.

The schema's core fields are:

URL Title
   The name of the resource

URL Description
   A brief description of the resource; suitable for display in a search result

URL
   The address of the resource

ToolTip
   Text displayed for a mouseover

Comment
   Administrative information that helps manage a record (not seen by the end user)

Contact Alias
   The name of the person responsible for this resource

Review Date
   The date that the resource should be reviewed next (default setting is six months from when the record was created or last updated)

Status
   The record's status; e.g., "active" (the default), "deleted," "inactive," and "suggestion"; used for content management purposes

The schema has been commonly extended with these optional fields:

Strongly Recommended
   Flags resources that are especially appropriate

Products
   Terms from the product, standards, and technology names vocabulary that describe the subject matter of the resource

Category Label
   Terms from the vocabulary of category labels; used to ensure that the resource is listed under the appropriate label in the site's navigation system

Keywords
   Terms from descriptive vocabularies used to describe the resource

MSWeb began to use the metadata schema to create resource records in 1999; since then, over 1,000 records have been created. These fuel the immensely useful "Best Bets" search results and hold huge potential for improving areas such as content management. We'll describe the role of both metadata schema and "Best Bets" at Microsoft in greater detail later in this chapter.

Category labels

The third type of taxonomy—labels for the categories in site-wide navigation systems—was geared toward providing users of Microsoft intranet sites with navigational context. Category labels help users know where they are and where they can go. The MSWeb team employed a user-centered process for designing navigation systems, relying upon useful standbys as card sorting and contextual inquiry. In Figure 20-1, the category labels are shown on the lefthand side of the screen. Descriptions of nodes, displayed on the righthand side, help catalogers choose the appropriate category label.

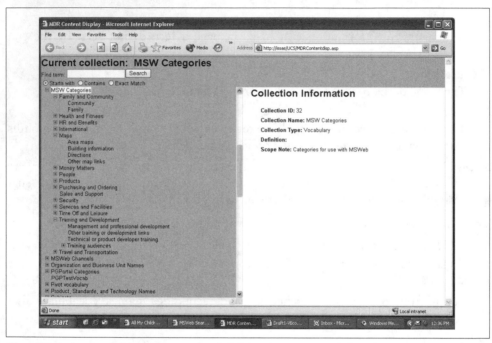

Figure 20-1. A subset of MSWeb's category labels, with some expanded to show subcategories

The initial set of category labels was developed solely for the MSWeb portal's navigation system. But because the portal is so widely used and because the revised navigation represented a major upgrade for many users, the owners of other intranet sites began to approach the MSWeb team for assistance in developing their own navigation systems.

The MSWeb team responded by making its user-centered design process and expertise into a *service* that other site owners could utilize. As collaboration with other sites increases, a "standard" intranet navigation system will eventually be created, likely a combination of predetermined intranet-wide options (e.g., another "core") and a locally determined selection of choices ("extensions") that would be informed by a shared set of guidelines. For now, the transitional stage of raising awareness and providing support to other site owners is considered a great leap forward and a prerequisite to further navigation standardization.

How It Comes Together

The impact of all three taxonomies is clear from the MSWeb search results shown in Figure 20-2. Category labels provide contextual navigation at the end of each "Best Bet" result (the first two displayed) and populate the "categories" site-wide navigation system on the lefthand side. Below that, the "terms" area displays two variants of the search term that come directly from the descriptive vocabularies. The "Best Bet" search results themselves are drawn from resource records based on a metadata schema.

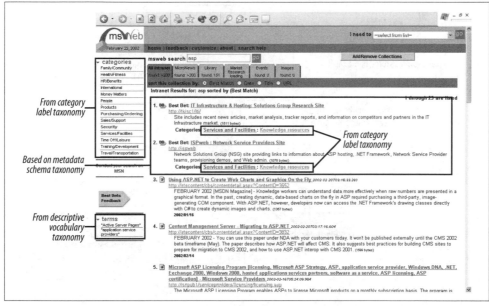

Figure 20-2. All three taxonomies are used to create these search results

MSWeb's "three taxonomies" approach is steeped in traditional library science, which isn't surprising considering the backgrounds of many of those on the MSWeb team. But it's important to note how willing the team was to abandon the traditional library science concepts that didn't make sense in the intranet environment. For example, the team did not try to create "traditional" thesauri for its metadata schema and category label taxonomies. Other standards familiar to the LIS community, such as Dublin Core, weren't initially adopted for MSWeb's metadata schema because they were not appropriate at the time (although the Dublin Core schema may be partially or completely adopted by MSWeb at some point).

The Technical Architecture: Tools for Taxonomies

The MSWeb information architecture is certainly informed by library science ideas. But it's important to remember that the team (not to mention the company) has its share of technical smarts, too. Out of that combined expertise was born a suite of advanced tools for managing MSWeb's various taxonomies. And, as mentioned earlier, we wouldn't be shocked to see these tools on the shelves in the near future.

Figure 20-3 shows a simplified view of the MSWeb technical architecture. The tools are the Metadata Registry (MDR), which is used for storing, managing, and sharing taxonomies used on the Microsoft intranet; VocabMan, which provides access to the MDR; and the URL Cataloging Service (UCS), which is used for creating records based on the metadata schema, category labels, and descriptive vocabularies.

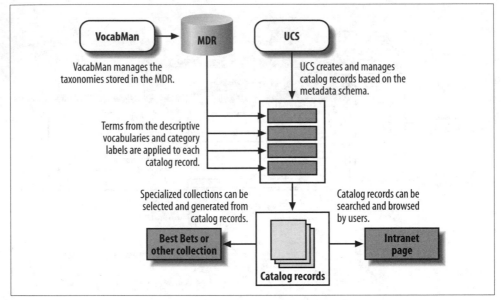

Figure 20-3. A simplified view of the MSWeb technical architecture

VocabMan and the MDR feed terms from descriptive and category label vocabularies into records generated from the metadata schema stored in UCS.

The ultimate goal is the creation of a valuable catalog record that improves searching and browsing for users, and makes content management easier.

Creating and managing the taxonomies: VocabMan and the Metadata Registry

VocabMan and the Metadata Registry (MDR) are separate tools that are used together for taxonomy management. The MDR is simply a SQL-based relational database that uses an associative data model to store MSWeb's taxonomies. VocabMan is a Visual

Basic client that provides taxonomy specialists with access to the MDR, allows the creation and editing of taxonomies, and supports the creation of relationships between them.

Pictures are definitely worth thousands of words, so we'll let screenshots tell the story of how VocabMan works. The following sequence shows how a taxonomist might find a specific term to see if it is listed in an existing vocabulary, or simply to understand its context in a particular vocabulary.

VocabMan's initial screen (Figure 20-4) displays available taxonomies for MSWeb and for subsites in the lefthand column. These can be either browsed in "tree" format or searched. The fields in the righthand column support the creation of a new "collection" or taxonomy of vocabulary terms.

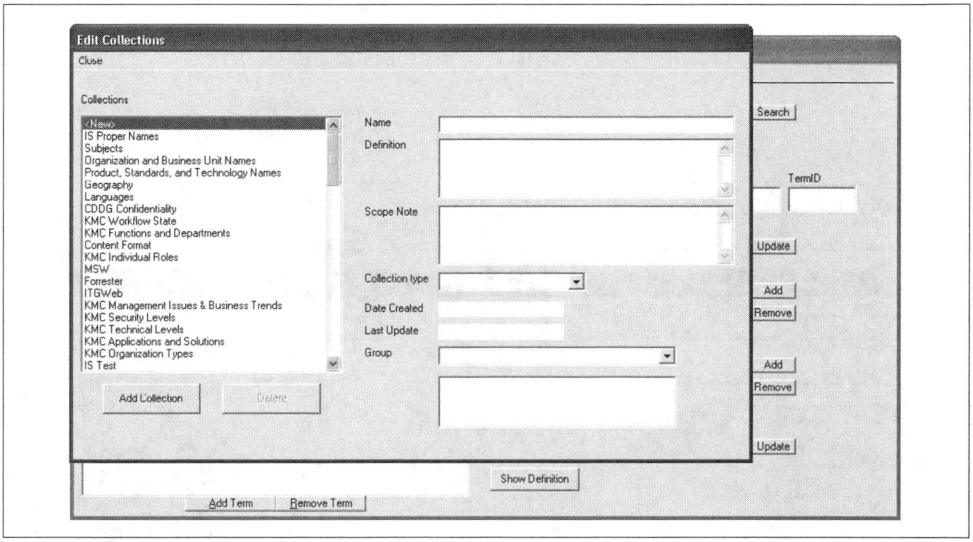

Figure 20-4. Creating and editing taxonomies in VocabMan

Once an existing taxonomy is selected (in Figure 20-5, the descriptive vocabulary "Geography"), it can be searched or modified from this screen. Note that "Relation to Parent," "Related Terms," "Entry Terms," and "Scope Note" are attributes of a specific term drawn directly from traditional thesaurus design.

To find a specific term, we can browse the tree on the lefthand side or search on the righthand side (Figure 20-6). Here, "entry terms" are equivalent to variant terms.

In Figure 20-7, a search on "Chicago" shows that it is an authorized term in several taxonomies—a test vocabulary, the products vocabulary, and twice in the geographic vocabulary (once as a place in Illinois, and once as a subdistrict in Microsoft's Midwest Sales District).

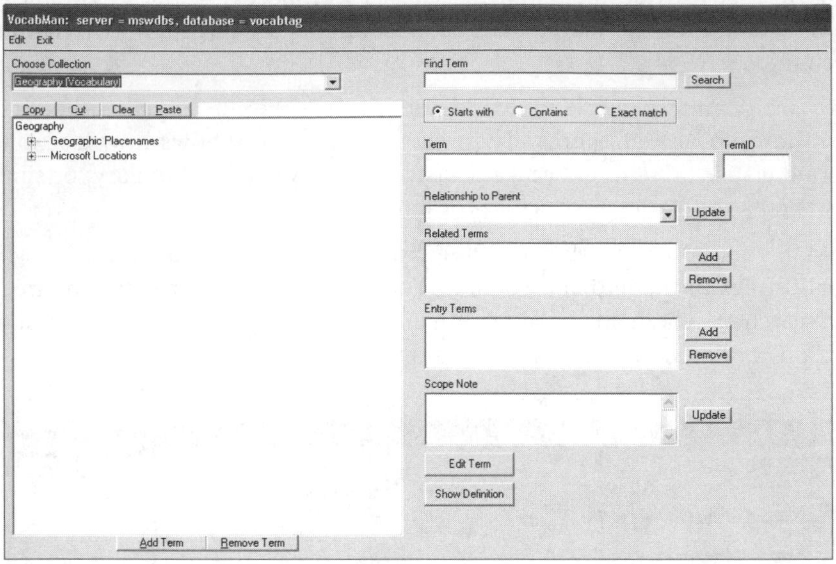

Figure 20-5. Selecting a taxonomy in VocabMan

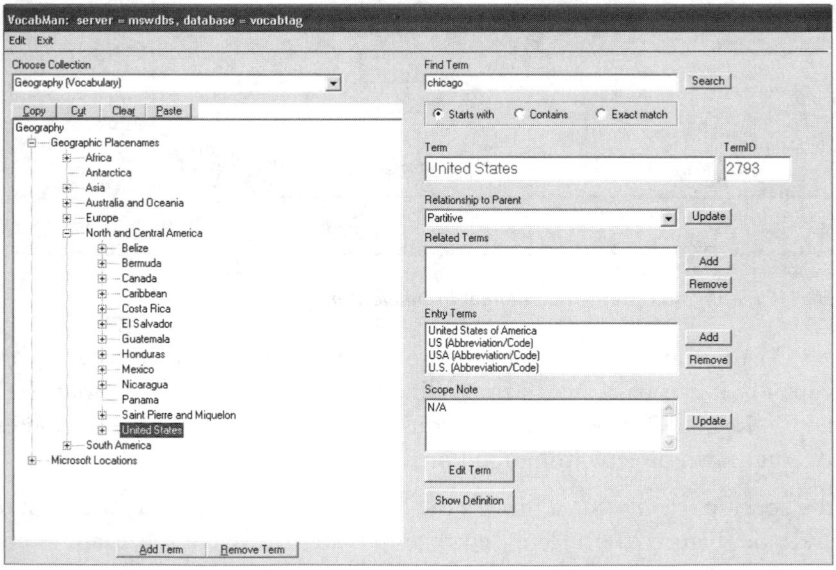

Figure 20-6. Finding a term in VocabMan

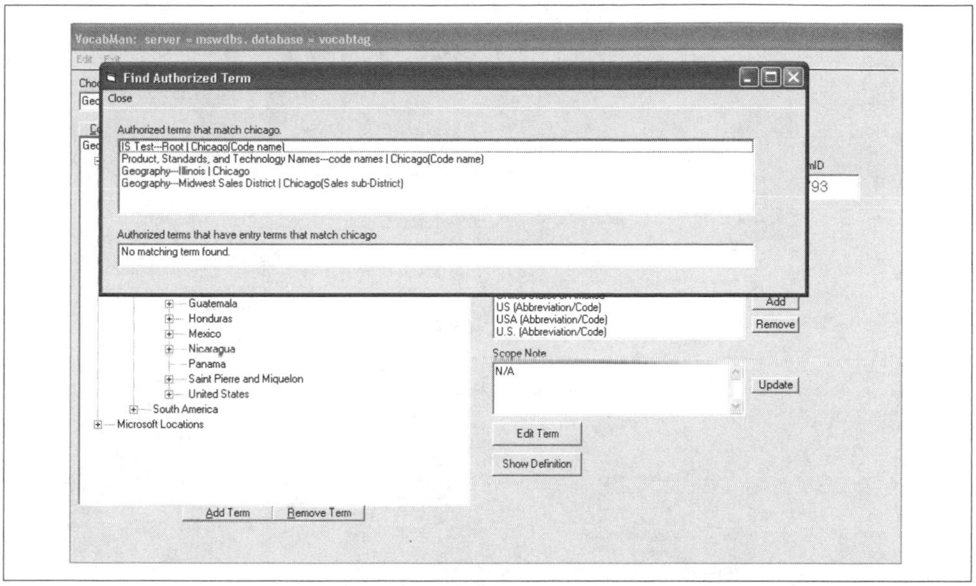

Figure 20-7. Searching for a term in VocabMan retrieves source taxonomies

After selecting "Chicago" as a place in Illinois, the term is displayed in the broader context of the geographic descriptive vocabulary (Figure 20-8). The lefthand side shows us that Chicago is a city in Illinois, a Great Lakes state, and a part of the United States. On the righthand side, we see that it is a major city in relation to its parent term ("Illinois") and is related to the Chicago Sales subdistrict (no entry terms or scope notes are available for this term). Note that the same interface allows the editing of this term's entry.

VocabMan can also be used to create thesaural relationships (i.e., hierarchical, equivalence, and associative) between terms within specific taxonomies and between terms in different taxonomies. The screenshot shown in Figure 20-9 has a specific schema (for "Best Bets") displayed on the lefthand side. Highlighting "Keywords" displays the vocabularies associated with this particular schema tag in the "Related Vocabularies" field on the righthand side. "IS Proper Names," "Subjects," and "Organization and Business Unit Names" are the descriptive vocabularies that supply the terms for the "Keywords" tag. ("Pivot vocabulary" is an administrative vocabulary that is not used for indexing.)

Creating and managing the records: the URL Cataloging Service

Drawing from taxonomies stored in the MDR, the URL Cataloging Service (UCS) is a "workbench" for creating, managing, and tagging records; it enables the creation of shared catalog records for useful resources in the Microsoft intranet (such as "Best

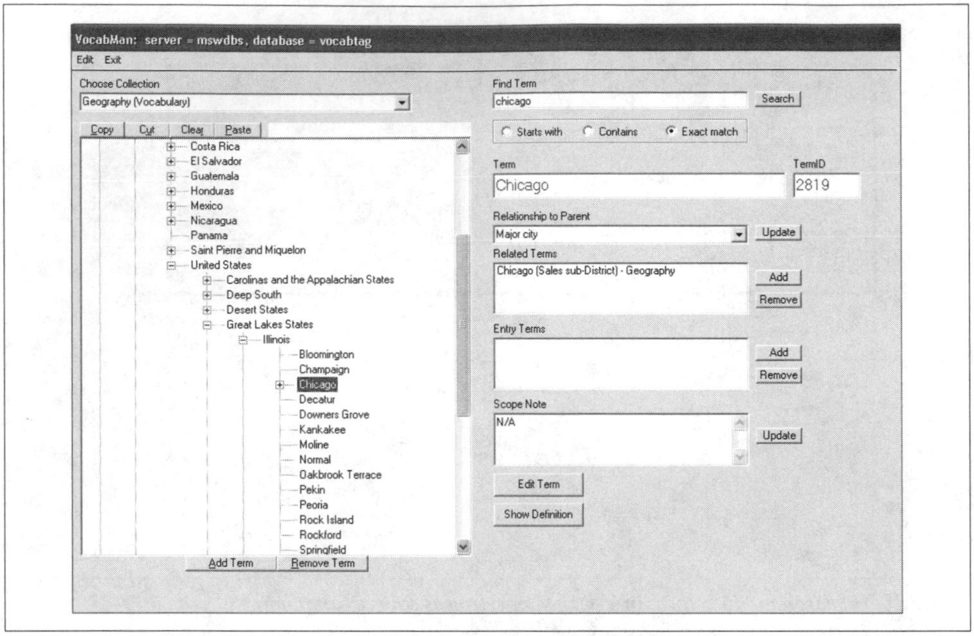

Figure 20-8. VocabMan provides context for a taxonomy term

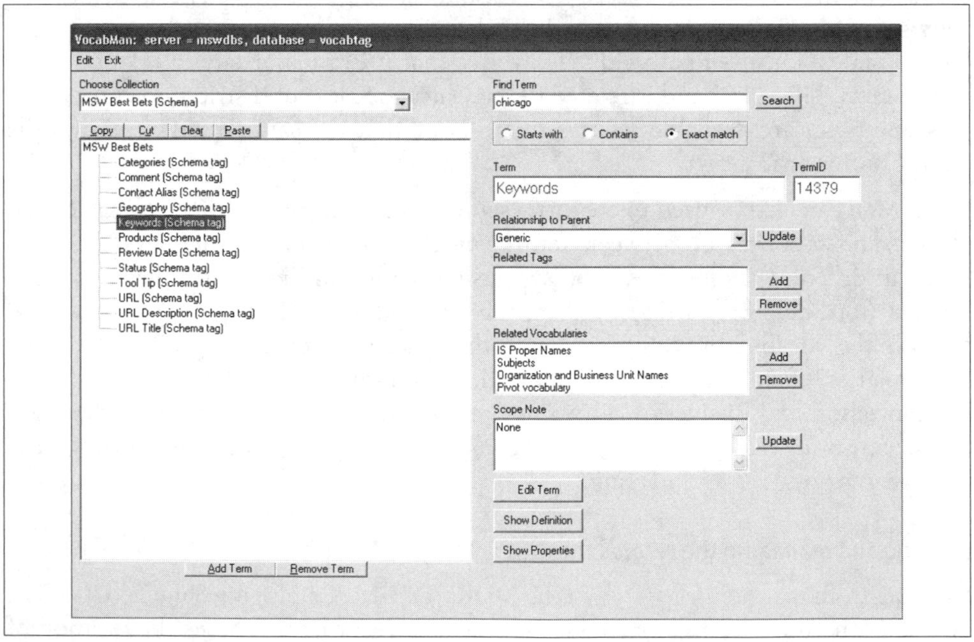

Figure 20-9. Viewing a metadata schema's tags and associated vocabularies in VocabMan

Bets"). It's based on a relational database and uses SQL Server. Like VocabMan and the MDR, UCS was initially designed for use by the MSWeb team, but its value was soon recognized by other groups, and UCS eventually became another service offered by MSWeb to other players in the Microsoft intranet environment.

Using UCS, catalogers create quality resource records that directly improve the user's experience because they can be indexed for searching and browsing. These records are created quite simply: when invoked, UCS displays the metadata schema's attributes as fields within a form. Record creators fill out the form, selecting from category labels to classify the record and from the various descriptive vocabularies available to index the record. Catalogers have access to all the vocabularies stored in the MDR; however, they don't have modification privileges for all records, as do the taxonomists who access the MDR via VocabMan.

The initial screen of UCS (shown in Figure 20-10) describes an array of services, ranging from cataloging resources to link checking. It is accessed from the SAS console, which also provides read access to the MDR. SAS (Search As Service) is the bundle of information architecture and content management services that the MSWeb team offers to other Microsoft business units, and the console is the control panel that MSWeb puts in its clients' hands. (We'll describe SAS in greater detail later in this chapter.)

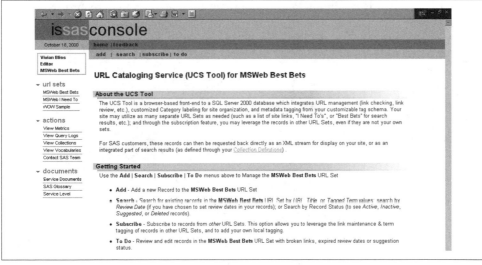

Figure 20-10. The initial screen of UCS, accessed from the SAS console

In this case, the user can edit or add resource records to any of the three URL sets or collections listed in the lefthand column of Figure 20-10. Catalogers are limited to modifying only those collections that they own and are responsible for; however, the MSWeb team has permissions to modify any collection. This despotism is used benevolently; for example, if a cataloger wishes to create a collection of 60 resources, the MSWeb team might find that 28 of these resources are already cataloged. As the cataloger can "subscribe to" (but not modify) these 28 resource records or incorporate them into his collection, a significant amount of duplicated effort can be eliminated. Figure 20-11 shows a new record being added to the "Best Bets" Collection.

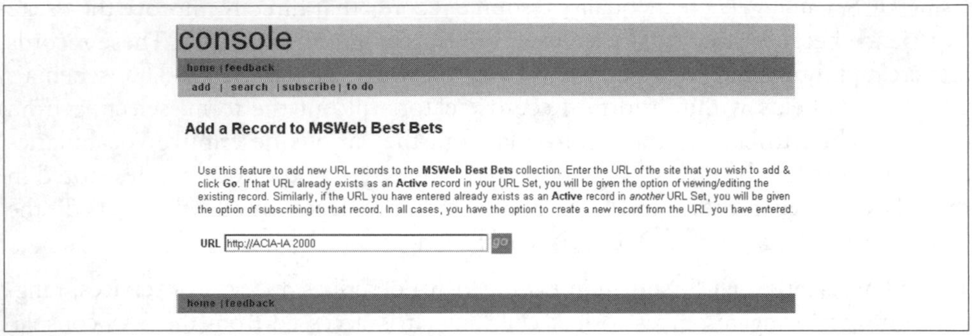

Figure 20-11. Using UCS to add a new resource record

UCS automatically checks the URL of the record to be added to see if one has been created already for that resource. In this case, no record exists, so we'll create a new one, as shown in Figure 20-12. The fields in this form are essentially an interactive version of the metadata schema, and filling them out creates a new record. Note that this process is fairly simple and straightforward, sacrificing a degree of richness and data validation for the ease of creating new records.

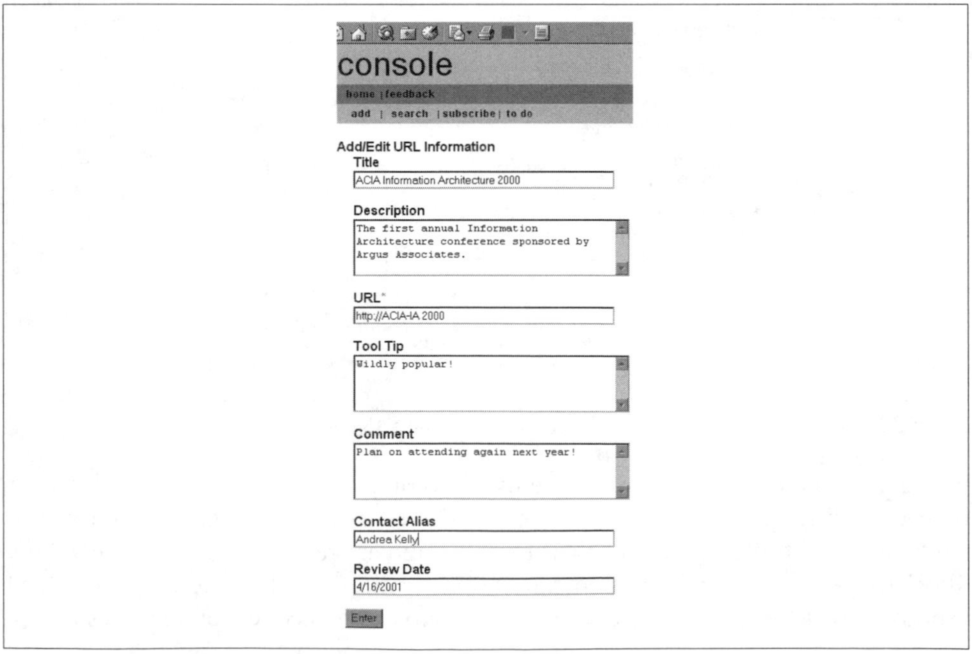

Figure 20-12. Filling out the fields of the new resource record

The righthand side of the new form displays the ways it should be indexed, which are encoded in the metadata schema (Figure 20-13).

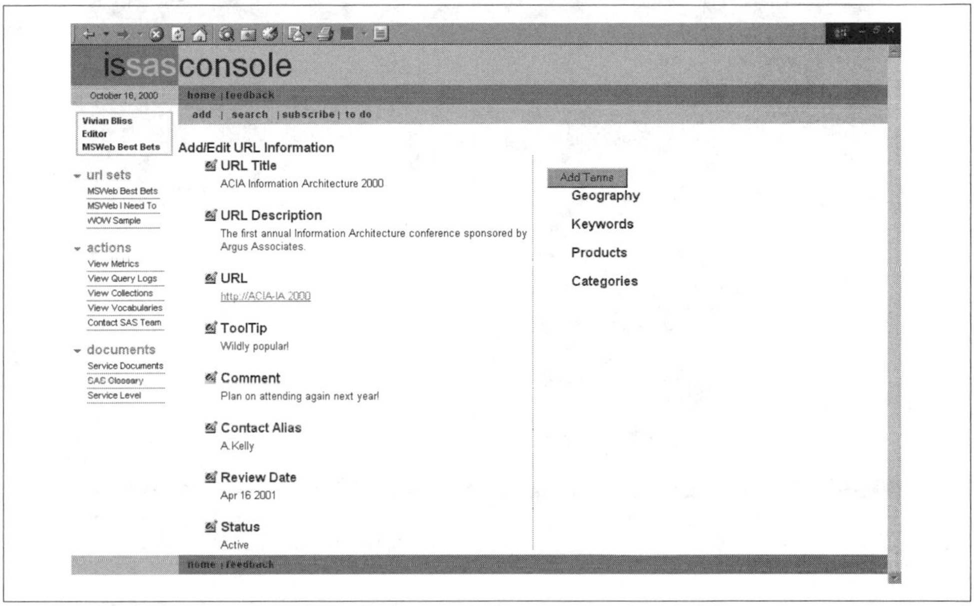

Figure 20-13. The new record is ready for indexing

These taxonomies draw from the category labels and descriptive vocabularies managed in the MDR. Clicking "Add Terms" brings up a pop-up window for selecting vocabulary terms to be added to the record. These are displayed as hierarchies for easier browsing, as shown in Figure 20-14. Or, if the cataloger prefers, he can search the descriptive vocabularies for terms that match his interest, as shown in Figure 20-15. Search results display a full path—"breadcrumb" style—to provide fuller context for the matching terms.

Selecting a term (or "node," as shown in Figure 20-15) displays its relationships to other terms. These thesaural relationships are all stored in the MDR and managed by taxonomy specialists with access to VocabMan.

On the other hand, if the record for a resource already exists, the cataloger can simply modify the record if it's part of a collection he controls. If it's part of another collection, he can't modify the original record, but he can "subscribe" to that record and add custom tags to it that are locally used (record subscription is described later in this chapter). In all cases, the cataloger can elect to create a duplicate entry.

For example, the cataloger might know from search-log analysis that his site's users are often looking for product information. The product history information at *http://msw/products* would be an excellent "Best Bet" for his site's users. He enters the URL and learns that two records already exist for this resource (see Figure 20-16). One

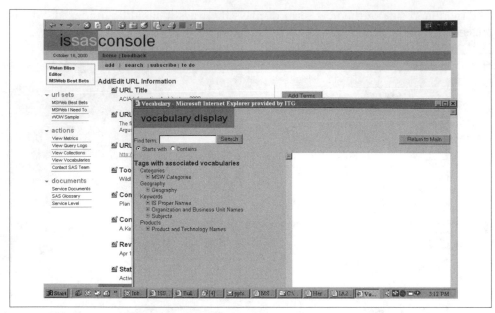

Figure 20-14. The cataloger can browse for a term from a taxonomy associated with this schema…

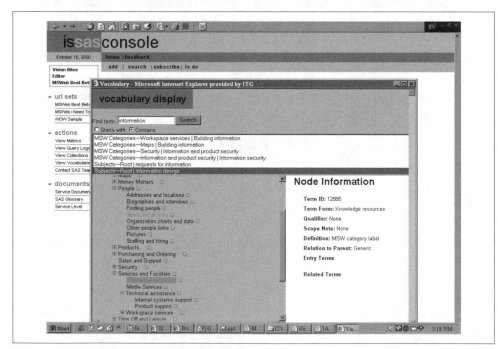

Figure 20-15. …or the cataloger can search for a taxonomy instead (note the helpful information displayed for this node)

record is from the MSWeb "Best Bets" collection, and the other is from Microsoft's Museum "I Need To" collection (another high-value record collection used in MSWeb, similar to "Best Bets"). Note that only the URL is the same; the two records have different titles, descriptions, and other metadata associated with them, and different contexts often require different tags. In this case, the cataloger chooses the Museum record for this resource.

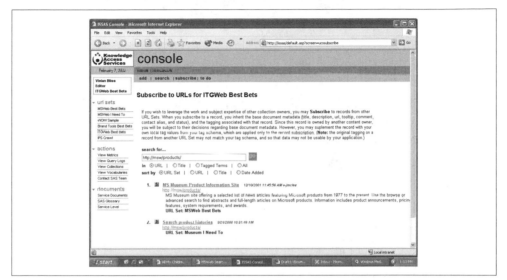

Figure 20-16. Two records have already been created for this resource

Because this record was created as part of a separate collection, its core tags can't be modified. However, subscribed records can be extended for local use. In this case, the cataloger can apply the metadata schema extensions that are used by his own collections (Figure 20-17). These fields—"Keywords" and "Products"—are displayed in the upper-right corner. The cataloger can populate these fields with terms from the descriptive vocabularies that his organization has decided will have the most value for its users and content owners.

UCS also provides other useful tools for helping manage resource records, including link checking, broken-link reports (Figure 20-18), and a calendar of tasks for periodically revisiting and checking the quality of a resource record. But perhaps the most important aspect of UCS is how well it balances a core of requirements with a flexible set of extensions. By bringing together taxonomies and other resources in a straightforward interface, UCS makes it easy to create more records. Similarly, because UCS supports the sharing of those records, intellectual effort is not duplicated. Sharing is made even more effective by the metadata schema's extensibility— resource records can be better customized for local use, resulting in more incentive to "borrow" rather than re-create. In other words, UCS supports the investment of

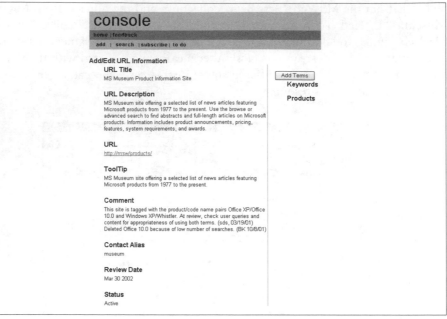

Figure 20-17. The selected record, created by another cataloger, can be extended with fields from the metadata schema utilized by this editor's collection

human capital in the creation and customization of content rather than the duplication of effort—something all too common in most enterprise environments.

This philosophy of flexibility and sharing extends throughout the MSWeb approach and suite of tools. For example, Microsoft's library doesn't use UCS at all, opting instead for its own homegrown tool for creating resource records. However, its tool can access the MDR and its taxonomies in much the same way that UCS does. In this case, flexibility through modularity accommodates other business units' needs (i.e., for a specialized record-creation tool) without forcing them to reject all aspects of MSWeb's approach (i.e., the taxonomies stored in the MDR).

The use of open standards further illustrates this flexible, modular approach. XML is employed in exporting taxonomy terms to tools like UCS and the library's similar tool; other units' approaches could easily utilize XML exporting in the same way. Similarly, XML is employed by UCS as the basis for exporting resource record data to be used as search results by numerous Microsoft intranet sites.

Beyond Taxonomies: Selling Services

The MSWeb team started out with a vision of the very broad but tricky area of taxonomies, and went to work figuring out how they could be built for use on the MSWeb portal. The team tested and developed tools and vocabularies that improve content management as well as searching and browsing of the MSWeb site.

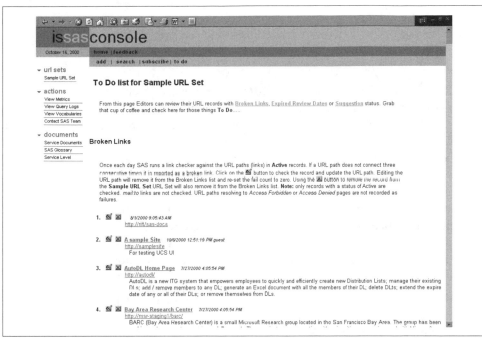

Figure 20-18. UCS's reporting features help catalogers maintain the quality of resource records

This project has begun to have an impact far beyond the MSWeb site. Other major Microsoft intranet sites—those for human resources, finance, the library, and the information technology group—have begun to use some or all of the tools and taxonomies that were developed by the MSWeb team. And more than two dozen major subportals have implemented aspects of MSWeb's search system. How has the MSWeb team succeeded at spreading its gospel through a huge organization like Microsoft when similar efforts at smaller companies often fail?

There are many reasons for MSWeb's success. Let's examine them.

Location, location, location

Because MSWeb is the company's major intranet portal, just about everyone in the company uses it—94 percent of all Microsoft employees. The site is large and complex, providing the team with ample challenges and a test bed for trying out new solutions. Additionally, MSWeb's enterprise-wide prominence has made for an excellent marketing opportunity for the team's efforts and for information architecture in general.

Indeed, as a candidate site for an information architecture redesign, MSWeb is the ultimate low-hanging fruit: highly visible, frequently used by many in the company, rich in valuable content, important to management, and, finally, managed by an enlightened team that was aware of information architecture. You couldn't ask for a better showcase for the value of good information architecture.

Helping where it hurts

Every information architecture project ultimately has two audiences: users and site managers/owners. It's important to make both audiences happy, and the best way to do so is to fix what hurts.

The MSWeb team intentionally selected a major area—search—that would greatly benefit both users and managers, and designed its taxonomies to specifically improve search performance. Users' experiences with searching were greatly improved through the integration of Best Bets into search results (more on Best Bets below). And the MSWeb team began to help site managers address search, sometimes by simply providing informal consulting, but also in more concrete ways such as providing a centrally managed crawling and indexing service. By encouraging units to develop resource records, the MSWeb team spawned a collection of content surrogates that references some of the most valuable content in the Microsoft intranet environment. And once these records were created, they made for great starting points for site crawling—robots simply followed the links embedded in the UCS's records.

Just as the prominence of MSWeb gained exposure for the team's efforts, the success of Best Bets validated the MSWeb approach. Both paved the way for improved collaboration between the MSWeb team and many other business units that were players in the Microsoft intranet environment.

Modular services

From the very start, the MSWeb team has looked for opportunities to develop its taxonomies and tools in a modular and therefore reusable fashion, and package them as services for the rest of the company. In fact, it's even branded its offerings as "Search and Taxonomies as a *Service*" (originally "Search as a Service," and still referred to as SAS). The SAS console, displayed in Figure 20-19, provides an excellent visualization of what SAS offers to its users.

The MSWeb team recognized that other business units would have a wide variety of needs as well as existing tools on hand to address their own information architecture and content management challenges. It knew that no one could compel those business units to adopt 100 percent of the MSWeb approach. So the team designed SAS to be extremely modular; Microsoft business units could take advantage of some services while passing on others.

For example, SAS offers access to MSWeb's taxonomies through the MDR. Other units can manage and store their own taxonomies through the MDR as well, as long as they are willing to share their work. And to ensure quality in their taxonomies, those other business units can take advantage of taxonomy-related consulting services provided by SAS.

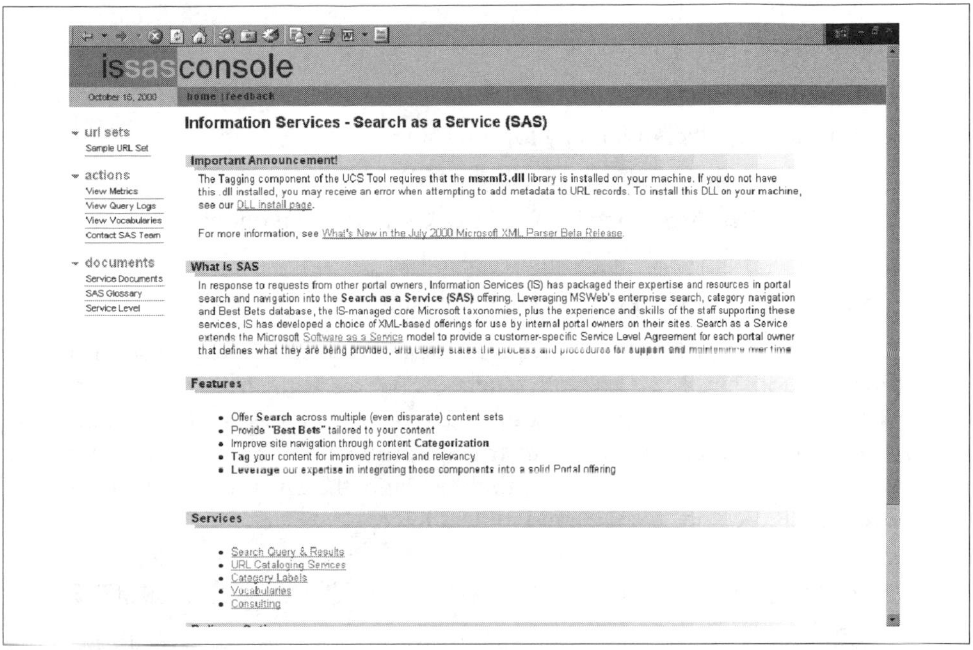

Figure 20-19. The SAS console

Different business units can access taxonomies from the MDR through the SAS console. Or, because the taxonomies are exportable in XML, units can develop their own interfaces, as did Microsoft's library. This flexibility means that existing tools, homegrown or not, don't need to be thrown out in favor of MSWeb's version. Similarly, XML is used to export search results; this enables another unit's site to leverage the records stored in UCS (assuming that its engine can accommodate XML). Even the MSWeb search interface is exportable since it's written using XSL.

As discussed earlier, metadata schema are extensible, in effect allowing different business units to create customized versions of any schema. Records created using those schema are reusable through a highly flexible subscription process. And last but not least, optional crawling and indexing services are also made available by SAS to its client business units.

All of this flexibility leads to a huge number of possible SAS service configurations. A Microsoft business unit could handle most of its information architecture and content management needs using everything SAS has to offer, or it could operate its own publishing system that only imports taxonomies from the MDR. Or it might choose to go it completely alone. The decision is up to that business unit and is impacted by the factors of users, content, and context that guide all information architecture work.

In the case of HRWeb, Microsoft's human resources portal, the team decided to use most SAS services. SAS was used to:

- Identify content for crawling and indexing for use in searching
- Create a category label taxonomy for browsing
- Create Best Bets specifically for use in the HRWeb portal
- Classify those Best Bets using HRWeb's category label taxonomy
- Provide access to the SAS high-quality search engine
- Export Best Bets search results to HRWeb's site

Perhaps most importantly, HRWeb drew on the MSWeb team's expertise through a consulting relationship. MSWeb staff taught HRWeb's team how to develop category labels through user-centered design (UCD) techniques such as contextual inquiry. The HRWeb team was also instructed in the art and science of cataloging resource records using descriptive vocabularies and the shared metadata schema. The resulting HRWeb site is shown in Figure 20-20.

Figure 20-20. Microsoft's HR group is a full-fledged SAS "client," using all of SAS's services

Currently, most units have small web development-related teams and limited resources, and are just beginning to delve into the sticky topics of taxonomies, searching, and browsing. As they learn about SAS, they are generally quite glad to take advantage of the tools and expertise already developed by the MSWeb team. But as each unit's expertise and budget for information architecture grows, it will likely want to take on more and more control. The flexibility of its service modules will ensure that SAS can be configured to keep up with those changes.

Different kinds of flexibility

Aside from a focus on taxonomies, the major components of MSWeb's approach—the tools and a flexible, modular, and somewhat entrepreneurial service model—draw little from library science. And as noted earlier, the taxonomies themselves, not to mention MSWeb's operating definition of the word "taxonomy," do not adhere to an orthodox library science approach.

This is a different flexibility than the kind that drives the SAS approach. The MSWeb team has been driven by a philosophy built on a flexibility of *mind*. Although many team members have library science backgrounds, they have left their disciplinary baggage at the door in order to achieve buy-in and support from colleagues from different backgrounds and with different perspectives.

For example, few (if any) graphic designers get excited by the thought of developing taxonomies. But anyone will listen to an open-minded colleague describing a good approach to solving a big problem. Because the MSWeb team was willing to be flexible in its terminology and outlook, it could communicate its taxonomy-based solutions more effectively to colleagues and clients who might be turned off by "library talk." One senior designer on the MSWeb team described his realization of the value of the taxonomy approach and its basis in UCD techniques as the moment he "drank the Kool-Aid." From that point on, he bought into the approach 100 percent.

The team was also successful because it was flexibly designed—not just LIS people, but technologists, technical communicators, designers, and strategists. In addition to lending the team more credibility with outsiders, the team's interdisciplinary nature meant that many ideas were explained, translated, and fought over before they were ever exposed to outsiders. Interdisciplinary perspectives lead, as always, to a better and more marketable set of services.

Company savings

The MSWeb team members understand the need for baby steps in any significant information architecture project. They've spent years developing taxonomies and supporting tools to use on MSWeb. And they've taken a gradual approach to rolling them out as SAS services to other business units.

But it's also important to note that within three months of launching SAS, nine subportals had already implemented SAS-based search on their sites. Two of those had created site-specific category label taxonomies to support browsing, and another was in the process of doing so. All leveraged the MSWeb Best Bets results as part of their own search systems.

Quick adoption of SAS represents success for the MSWeb team, but it has much greater significance to Microsoft as a whole. Besides the benefits to users, which we'll describe in the next section, an incredible amount of labor has been saved. It's estimated that SAS has resulted in a cost savings of 45 person years in avoided work (based on calculating the development efforts—estimated at 5 person years—and multiplying by 9—the number of business units that didn't have to reinvent the SAS wheel). These savings were achieved with no increase in the MSWeb team's staffing levels, and what was developed for MSWeb has been completely reusable by other business units.

Benefits to Users

As Microsoft's intranet environment matured in the mid-90s, it began to suffer from the same afflictions as most enterprise intranets: too many clicks required to get to desired information, difficult site-wide navigation, and the best documents buried deep within search results. And, as mentioned earlier, users and their champions began to ask for taxonomies to make these problems go away.

The MSWeb team's response is a work in progress. What we've described represents only a brief moment in the lifespan of a large company and its information systems. The team is taking an evolutionary approach, avoiding unrealistic goals of fixing all problems for everyone in a few years. In this way, there are no false expectations. But even in a short time span, many concrete benefits have been realized, and taxonomies are at the forefront of these improvements. With category label taxonomy, for example, the labels are more representative and consistent, improving navigation within MSWeb and between Microsoft intranet sites.

Searching is also greatly improved. By encouraging resource record creation with UCS, MSWeb is able to identify valuable content in the intranet environment and therefore can do a better job of crawling remote intranet content. Better crawling leads to more comprehensive indexing. Users are now querying indexes that represent a much larger body of content and a higher-quality collection of content. More importantly, users' queries are more powerful than before—they are able to take advantage of MSWeb's descriptive vocabularies to reduce the ambiguity of individual search terms. Consider a search on "asp," a very ambiguous term. During a search, the descriptive vocabularies stored in the MDR are automatically invoked to expand the search by including the different meanings ("Active Server Pages" and "application service providers"). These terms are also displayed as executable searches on the search results page to narrow or refine the search.

The MSWeb team has also helped pioneer a positive and increasingly common trend: "Best Bets." These are search results that are the product of manual efforts (they are also discussed in Chapter 8). Often displayed before other, automatically generated results, Best Bets link a user to documents that a cataloger has determined to be highly relevant to the user's initial search query. Best Bets are designed to address the "sweet spot" in searching, which consists of the few unique search queries that constitute the majority of all searches executed. Why not add value to the small number of frequently executed searches by adding Best Bets to their results?

Figure 20-21 shows the results for the search query "asp" from the MSWeb intranet, and you'll note that the first five are all Best Bets. The components of the search results—resource title, URL, description, and categories—are drawn from the meta-data schema, since the query searched an index of the controlled vocabulary terms assigned to these Best Bet records when they were indexed with UCS.

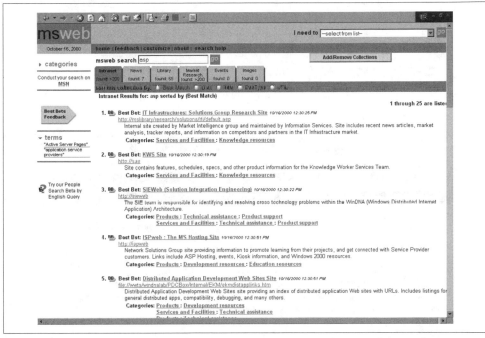

Figure 20-21. Best Bets search results are drawn directly from resource records created using UCS

The MSWeb team uses a function provided as part of the SAS console to determine which searches merit Best Bet coverage. By invoking the console's "View Query Logs" command (Figure 20-22) and specifying a date range and collection, it's possible to determine how many documents each query retrieved. If the "Where Query Returned" option is set to "0 Best Bets," we can learn which of those high retrieving queries do not have Best Bets associated with them, and create new Best Bets accordingly.

Another SAS Console function is "View Metrics." Its "Ranked Hit Clickthrough" option provides a graphic representation of the rank of documents in a particular query's search results that are being clicked through (Figure 20-23). Typically, the Best Bets, ranked at the top, have a far higher clickthrough than other documents.

So, does this hybrid approach—the combination of manually and automatically gen-erated results—actually help users? It may be too early to tell, but the initial data is promising. Users are performing 18 percent fewer searches since Best Bets were implemented; this might suggest that the results of their initial searches are more successful, reducing the need to submit follow-up searches. And, as shown in

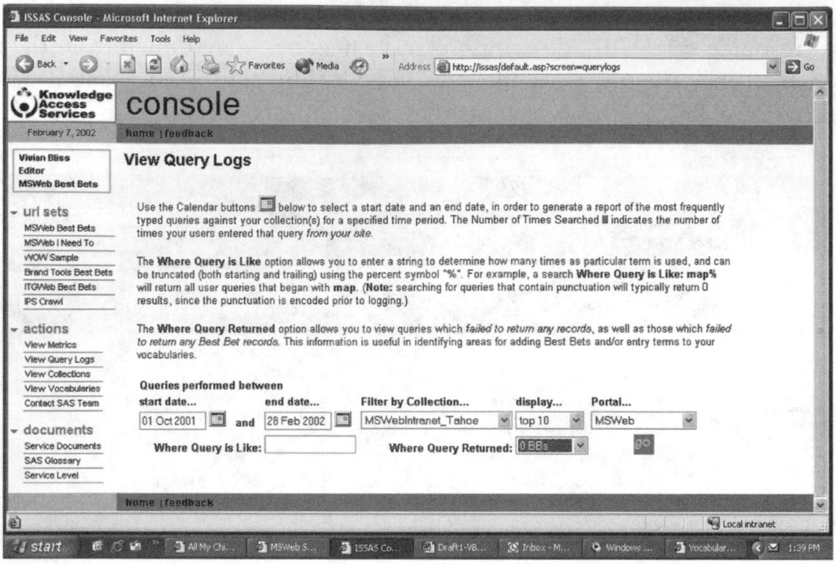

Figure 20-22. The "View Query Logs" function is useful in determining popular queries

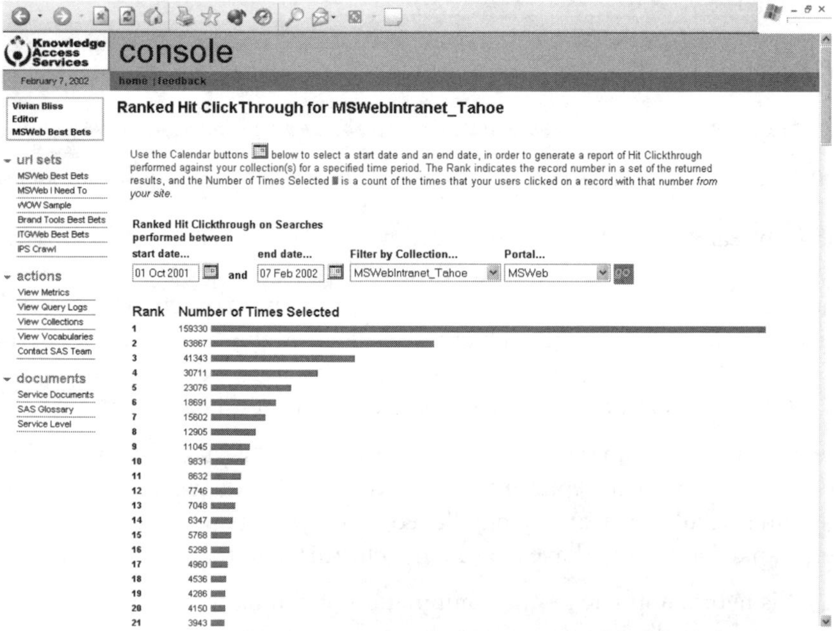

Figure 20-23. Best Bets are typically the most clicked-through documents

Figure 20-24, users are clicking through the top results' links close to twice as much as they had before Best Bets were implemented. This may suggest that users are finding Best Bets results to be more relevant than automatically generated results.

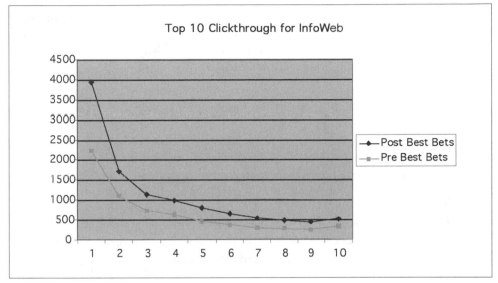

Figure 20-24. Best Bets seem to have increased search-result clickthrough

Overall, the MSWeb team has attempted to measure the cumulative impact that better browsing, searching, and content have had on users. By performing a task-analysis exercise both before and after a major redesign, the team was rewarded with some hopeful results in terms of success rate, time on task, and number of clicks. The following table displays the results of the task analysis. The version 3.0 results were recorded in February 1999, prior to the implementation of the taxonomy-driven approach, and the version 4.01 results were recorded in July 1999, after the implementation of the taxonomy-driven approach.

Measure	v.3.0 Average	v. 4.01 Average	Change
Task success rate	68.30%	79%	+10.7%
Time on task	3 minutes 26 seconds	3 minutes 10 seconds	−16 seconds
Number of clicks	13	5	−8 clicks

Certainly, other factors may have had an impact on these numbers. But even if we discount them, there is still ample anecdotal evidence to demonstrate the value of the MSWeb team's efforts.

What's Next

The initial success of MSWeb's approach is exciting, but it's just the first step over the course of many years and phases to come. To some degree, the team expects continued growth in what's currently in place: more resource records, more robust taxonomies, and more sites coming on board and utilizing an increasing array of SAS services and MSWeb consulting. But the MSWeb team also hopes to try out some interesting new plans in the not-too-distant future.

One exciting possibility is an increased role for other business units in the creation of an even more mature infrastructure to support enterprise-wide information architecture and content management. MSWeb isn't looking to own this endeavor but to move into a leadership role, with other units playing the role of partners. In this scenario, Microsoft will save money because its business units will engage in increased sharing of taxonomies and related tools and efforts. Additionally, a greater degree of awareness among content managers might result in more willingness to go along with future centralizing initiatives, such as requiring the registration of resources in order for them to be indexed for searching. This trade-off might make for a little more work on the part of content owners, but it will result in improved searching for users, as well as much more efficient content management practices, by establishing who's responsible for what content, when it should be updated, and so on.

Even more exciting is the possibility of creating something of a Microsoft "semantic web" along the lines of what Tim Berners-Lee, creator of the Web, and others have proposed.* Much like the content models covered in Chapter 12, a semantic web allows connections to be made automatically between related content objects. Some of the tools described in this chapter could be extended to support such automatic associations; for example, the taxonomies developed by different Microsoft business units could be "cross-walked," meaning that relationships between similar terms or "nodes" in the taxonomies could be established. These relationships could go a long way toward improving search across Microsoft's intranets because content with different tags and similar content would be retrieved together. VocabMan and the SAS console already have built-in support for related tags, which will enable future cross-walking of taxonomies.

The concept of a semantic web offers much more potential. Alex Wade, Manager of Knowledge Access Services, sees a future where semantic objects—not physical documents—are the atoms that make up the MSWeb universe. He states: "We don't draw many lines between objects today, and when we do, these are rarely delineated; now we're moving to semantically derived relationships." He'd like to see a semantic MSWeb provide access to people, places, and things that are connected by

---

* Tim Berners-Lee, James Hendler, and Ora Lassila, "The Semantic Web," *Scientific American*, May 2001 (*http://www.sciam.com/2001/0501issue/0501berners-lee.html*).

"strong rules" or relationships; once an initial set of rules is seeded, new rules can be inferred. This web of relationships could have a hugely beneficial impact in an intranet environment like Microsoft's, where it's often as important to find the right person as it is to find the right information. This transition requires a paradigm shift for information architects: as Alex suggests, we'll need to "stop tagging documents and start drawing relationships between objects. Eventually they'll have different types of hierarchical, associative, and equivalent relationships."

MSWeb's Achievement

Nothing that the MSWeb team did—whether considering the initial problem, coming up with an approach, and developing the tools and expertise to make it happen—can be described as revolutionary. Rather, these were rational steps taken to address complicated problems. So why discuss its work here?

Well, if you have ever worked in a large organization—or even many smaller ones— you know that what's rational isn't often what happens. The rational, the obvious, and the good often never make it off the drawing board, thanks to corporate strategies that change with the wind, extreme fluctuations in budgets, and, worst of all, the dreaded reorganization. And Microsoft isn't immune to such problems; one MSWeb team member went through seven different managers and had three title changes in just five months.

The MSWeb team has developed some neat taxonomies and tools. But we're recognizing the team for its most impressive achievement: successfully implementing a rational plan in a large, corporate environment. The team members understood that only a holistic approach—one that accommodated content, users, and context— could make a difference. They also knew that enterprise-wide solutions require sufficient time—years, not months—to take hold.

If you're taking on a similar challenge, we suggest you follow Vivian Bliss's advice:

> . . . Improving information systems affects people, process and technologies. To not recognize that will spell doom. In other words, technology alone is not the answer. Just as merely tweaking the UI is not the answer, nor is building a taxonomy that is not flexible or able to be leveraged in publishing and finding. Another key is to have a multi-disciplinary team. Just one discipline does not have the answer.

CHAPTER 21

evolt.org: An Online Community

What we'll cover:
- How an online community developed (and developed around) an innovative information architecture with almost no budget
- How incentives can serve to drive an economy of participation among content creators and consumers

The building of online communities has been going on since the Web began. Some have succeeded, but most have failed spectacularly. Yet again and again, the allure of thousands of paying customers happily discussing the benefits of a company's latest widget makes even the most hardboiled and pragmatic businesspeople throw caution to the wind. Fanning the flames of the online community fire were all sorts of new and intensely marketed community-enabling technologies, such as chat applications, that promised that "if you build it—with our technology, of course—they will come."

Clearly, online communities require more than cool tools to succeed. Technologies enable people with shared interests to converse and exchange ideas, but it's up to those people to contribute interesting and relevant information, stay on topic, be patient with one another, and police themselves when things get out of hand. Every community is unique in who it allows to join, how it welcomes and initiates new members, what types of events and milestones it promotes, and what types of behaviors it honors. So it's not grandiose to claim that each successful online community truly has its own culture.

Cultures and communities don't just happen; they require careful nurturing. On the other hand, they wither when overmanaged. A well-designed information architecture can help balance these two extremes, flexibly encouraging freedom of expression and action while organizing and structuring content for better findability. And where other architectures have to fit within a context, an online community architecture *creates* that context—it is often the only place where its members meet. In effect, online-community information architecture is the ultimate exercise in designing for context. This case study describes evolt.org, a real live online community that is grappling with, and succeeding at, providing and nurturing the context for its members.

evolt.org in a Nutshell

What is evolt.org? That's simple—it's explained at the bottom of each page in the site:

> evolt.org is a world community for web developers, promoting the mutual free exchange of ideas, skills and experiences.

> What "evolt" means: "evolt" combines the best elements of evolution, revolution, with a bit of voltage thrown in for good measure. "evolt" embodies our goals and enthusiasm!

The evolt.org site provides an interesting case study in online-community information architecture—its membership has grown quickly in its short life, and yet the site has hung together despite its distributed membership, rapid growth, competition, reliance on volunteers, noncommercial approach, and other factors that can potentially cause trouble. We learned some interesting lessons from evolt.org and its members, who have taken a novel and completely nontraditional approach to information architecture.

Architecting an Online Community

Online communities aren't built upon compulsory participation; to succeed, they must attract members who are already busy doing other things. And sometimes online communities compete with other communities that are doing much the same thing.

evolt.org, for example, is focused on web development. As you might guess, there are *many* other communities that share the same focus. So the evolt.org folks must be doing something right—in five years' time, they've built four active mailing lists, the largest of which ("thelist") has over 3,000 members. And the evolt.org web site has over 24,000 registered users. These growing numbers are impressive, even more so when you consider evolt.org's budget, which is minute. Volunteers contribute their time and passion, and they've cobbled together a few servers to make this work.

Obviously, passion and today's incredibly cheap and powerful information technologies are a potent combination. But they aren't enough to guarantee success; an environment must be created to tie them together. Someone has to play God, setting up the rules and infrastructure that create an environment that becomes self-sustaining, and where people join in and participate. And that's where information architecture comes in. Information architecture provides much of the structure that ties together the people, passion, content, and technology in one cohesive place.

So how exactly does information architecture figure into evolt.org?

The Participation Economy

The major challenge faced by every online community is how to get people to participate. Participation requires a balance of give (creating content) and take (consuming content). It's difficult to ensure reciprocity between givers and takers; it's often human nature to lurk and learn, while creating good information takes time and hard work. If everyone consumes and no one produces, online communities fail. Those responsible for online communities therefore have a harder job than Ben Bernanke (the head of the U.S. Federal Reserve Board). Beyond tweaking economic performance, they have an even larger job: to create the economy from scratch. And since they can't force people to participate, a healthy online-community economy must therefore err in the direction of free-market principles—enabling, not overmanaging—the creation of content in a way that keeps up with its consumption.

Information architecture comes into play here in two ways. First, it provides a critical set of rules and guidelines that make up part of the economy's infrastructure, much in the same way that the international banking system structures transactions in the global economy. So information architecture is a key part of "setting up" an economy.

Second, information architecture can be used to tweak levels of "transactions" in the participation economy, much like the Federal Reserve Board's adjustments to interest rates can invigorate or cool down economic activity. Information architecture greases the participation economy by supporting different levels of content creation that fit with human nature, and by "monetizing" that participation so that members better understand what their content creation—and consumption—is worth.

Supporting Different Levels of Participation

Some sites put up a huge wall that must be scaled in order for users to participate. For example, they may require all sorts of personal information from participants before they're "allowed in." This speakeasy model may work in unique situations, but it generally fails in today's competitive environment of plentiful community venues and sources of content. A better approach is to accommodate the different levels of participation sought by many sorts of people, ranging from the quiet lurkers to the hyperactive gadflies.

evolt.org supports different levels of access to its content and other resources. Anyone, member or not, can be involved in evolt.org, but higher levels of participation are accorded to members, and even higher levels to administrators. These social strata are detailed in Table 21-1.

Table 21-1. evolt.org's "classes" and their allowed levels of participation

Class	Participation level
Anyone	Allowed abilities: • Search and browse the entire site and mailing list archives. • Read articles. • Download browsers from the browser archive. • Submit items to the directory of web development resources.
evolt.org members	Can do all of the above plus: • Subscribe and post to any of the discussion lists. • Rate and comment on articles. • Contribute articles for publication in evolt.org. • Create an entry in the member directory. • Search the member directory. • Apply for a members.evolt.org ("m.e.o.") account, which provides disk space and tools for experimentation. • Make suggestions about how to improve the lists or the site. • Have input on decisions affecting evolt.org through participating in "theforum" discussion list. • In certain cases, implement changes to the site and its back end.
evolt.org administrators	Can do all of the above plus: • Edit and approve/deny submitted articles. • Answer messages submitted by users. • Write FAQ articles.

Although this scheme is by no means revolutionary, it does set in place a system of "classes" and a logical migration path that taps people's desire to be "upwardly mobile." Nonmembers get an initial taste of the site that may encourage them to increase their level of participation over time.

More classes could be developed, but that would make for too complex and weighty a caste system. evolt.org has judiciously chosen to keep things simple so that users understand which class they belong to and where they can go from there. And the rite of passage from "anyone" to a decision-making member is quick and relatively painless (no tattooing, branding, or other forms of hazing are required).

Capital in the Economy

Perhaps even more interesting is the way that participation is "monetized." The evolt.org economy runs on many types of "money" that take on two major forms: payments made by producers, and payments received by consumers. More specifically, evolt.org's "payments" are transacted through such commonplace actions as posting to a discussion list, writing an article, or creating a personal directory entry, as we describe next.

Discussion list postings

When someone posts a question, answer, comment, or idea to an evolt.org discussion list, she isn't necessarily conscious of conducting a transaction in evolt.org's participation economy. In fact, such postings are essentially the backbone of the economy, as most people come to evolt.org for the discussions. And, because evolt. org supports four major discussion lists—each addressing different aspects of web development and the management of evolt.org itself—the needs of many types of users are addressed. "thelist" is where evolt.org's raison d'être—web development—is discussed. "theforum" and "thesite" are oriented more toward building and improving evolt.org itself. And "thechat" is the place to take inevitable off-topic conversations. (See Figure 21-1.)

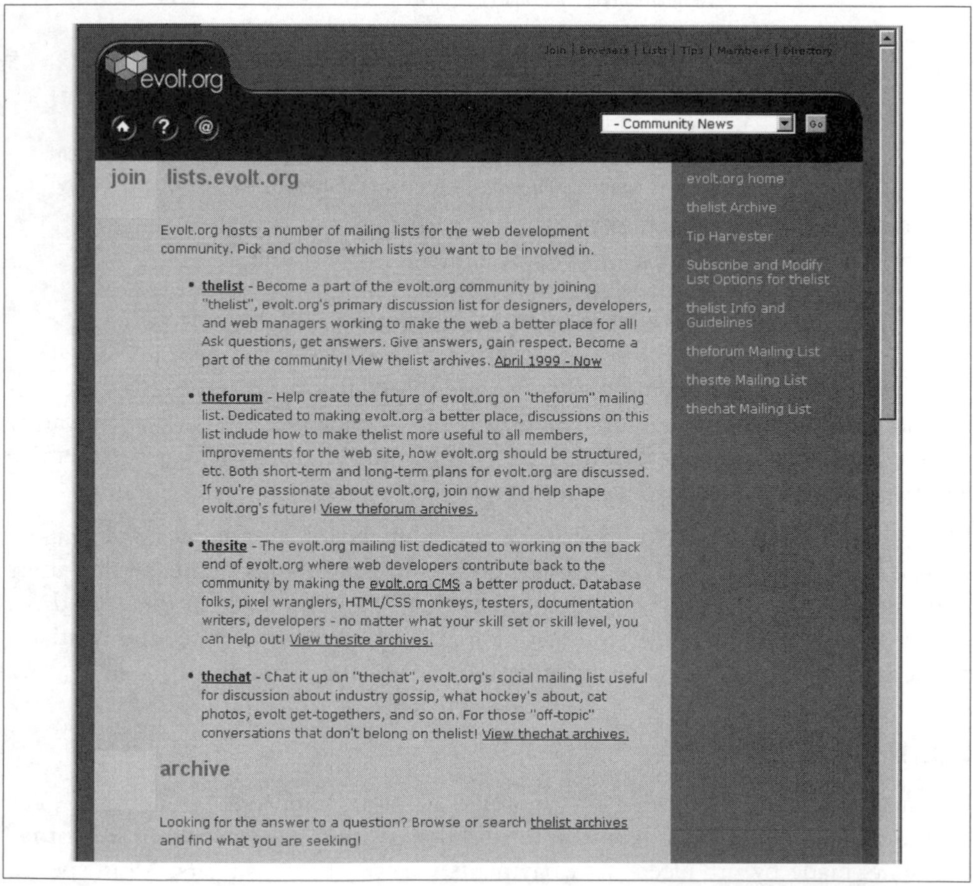

Figure 21-1. evolt.org's mailing lists

Tips

But while evolt.org encourages contributions to its discussion lists, it also must balance quantity with quality. Low signal–noise ratio is probably the leading cause of list collapse, so evolt.org uses a variety of methods and guidelines to maintain quality in its discussion-list postings (see Figure 21-2). While it can't force posters to stay on topic, it does ask them to prefix their subject lines with the warning "[OT]" (for Off-Topic) when necessary. That way, a reader can quickly scan a subject line and spot an off-topic posting without having to read the full posting.

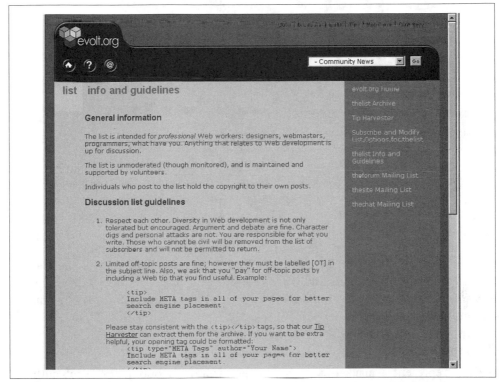

Figure 21-2. Guidelines for participating in evolt.org's discussion lists

More ingeniously, evolt.org employs a policy that makes those responsible for off-topic postings "compensate" the community. Negligent authors are asked to include "tips," consisting of useful web development-related wisdom, in their off-topic postings. They typically comply; in fact, many authors compose tips just for the sake of it.

Authors must mark up their tips in a way that enables evolt.org's automated "Tip Harvester" to index them for future use by the community. This is done with a simple open tag (<tip>) and close tag (</tip>). Tip authors are also encouraged to make use of additional markup options, such as <tip type="..."> and <tip author="...">.

This markup supports impressive searching capabilities for a site that's not tightly controlled (Figure 21-3).

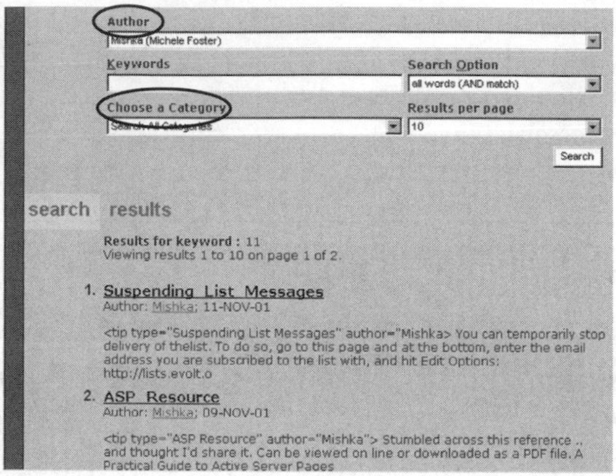

Figure 21-3. These two simple metadata schemes make tips more easily searched

Economies based on compulsion don't survive for long. And evolt.org really doesn't have the infrastructure, much less the desire, to police communications and punish violators. That's why tips are so important—after all, it's a given that we can't *always* stay on topic, and it's difficult to participate in a community without revealing any of your personal thoughts and feelings. Tips allow members to make up for their off-topic postings by contributing capital elsewhere in the community. In effect, tips are an examples of transactions in evolt.org's economy; they enable members to "pay" for their participation. And what's considered a plague in many other community discussion lists is transmogrified into a win–win situation in evolt.org's online community.

"Published" articles

Articles represent a major investment in the evolt.org economy, both for authors, who are expected to put significant effort into writing them and receive recognition in return, and for evolt.org itself, which is often measured by the quality of such articles. Additionally, evolt.org accords articles prime real estate on the site's main page, as shown in Figure 21-4.

And evolt.org makes the investment equally risky for authors by prominently featuring readers' comments and ratings. This enables other readers to quickly determine how their peers are reacting to a particular article. These comments and ratings help evolt.org assure a degree of quality in its articles. Table 21-2 further explores the capital being exchanged in this content "transaction."

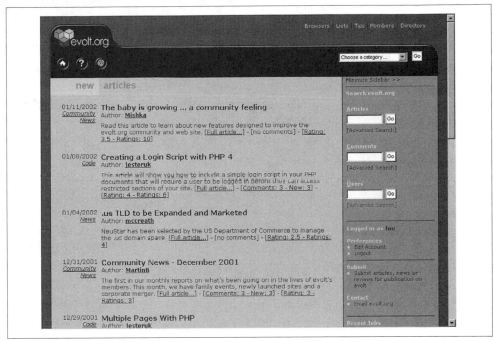

Figure 21-4. Recent articles occupy roughly 75 percent of evolt.org's main page

Table 21-2. Content transaction

Transactor	"Pays"	"Receives"
Authors	Articles	Comments
		Ratings
		Recognition
Readers	Comments	Articles
	Ratings	Guidance from other readers' comments and ratings
		Participatory role in the community; sense of ownership
evolt.org	Valuable screen space	Assurance that reader comments and ratings will prevent the contribution of low-quality articles

As authors create content over time, they can accrue more capital. This is reflected on article pages, where "cubes" and other cumulative information are displayed, as well as on authors' biographical sketches in the evolt.org member directory.

Cubes are simply graphical representations of how prolific an author's output is. The cube in Figure 21-5 shows that Mishka has authored one to five articles. The sidebar on the right shows us that she has in fact written exactly five articles, which have been rated 54 times at an average score of 3.86 (on a 1–5 scale). And there's a cute photo to boot.

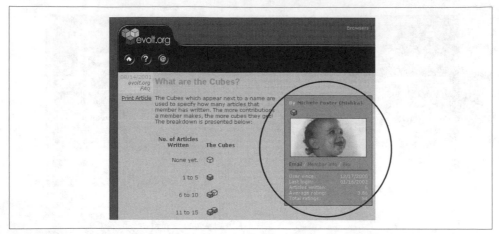

Figure 21-5. Cubes give a sense of who authors are, how prolific their output is, and how good it is

This information is useful to readers, who can quickly judge the quality of the author's output; the photo and links to email address and other author information serve to personalize her. By making authors more familiar to readers, evolt.org's information architecture may help increase the sense of community that reading an article brings. It's also helpful to authors, whose initiative to contribute articles (not to mention their self-esteem!) may be driven by knowing that evolt.org colleagues are reading their articles, posting comments, and reacting strongly enough to rate the articles. (Writing with an audience in mind is a wonderful author motivator.)

Biography listings

Should readers wish to learn more about an author, or if members want to know more about one another in general, evolt.org provides more detailed biographical information in its member directory. Directory pages include member-entered information (e.g., email address and brief bio), and automatically display their contributed tips and articles with reader comments and ratings (Figure 21-6). Although evolt.org hasn't chosen to do so, it might also be useful to link to a member's recent discussion-list postings.

New ventures

One of the great benefits of this era of cheap and powerful information technology is that, well, information technology is cheap and powerful! Cheap and powerful enough that a free community site like evolt.org can make it available as a sort of "venture capital" to its more entrepreneurial members.

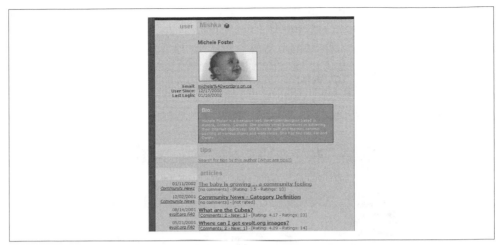

Figure 21-6. Member directory records serve as the "main page" for evolt.org members

This is the goal of members.evolt.org (m.e.o.): it serves as a development environment or "sandbox" for evolt.org members. It provides members with access to such web development essentials as ColdFusion, MySQL, Perl, PHP, Python, server-side includes, JSP and ASP capabilities, FTP, POP3 email, and, of course, disk space (currently 15 Mb per person). Instead of serving as an ASP or hosting service for operational sites, m.e.o. allows members to hone their web development expertise by working on experimental projects. Figure 21-7 shows a list of the projects that were being developed in the m.e.o. skunk works (which is unfortunately now defunct).

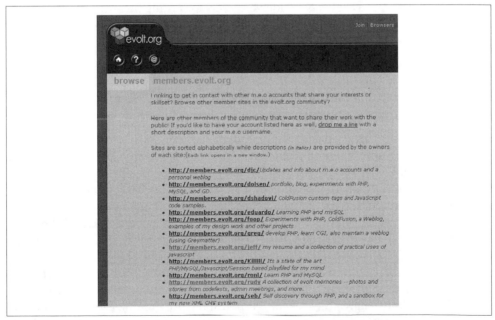

Figure 21-7. The members.evolt.org area is home to an eclectic set of projects

What does evolt.org get out of making all these goodies freely available? Besides goodwill, m.e.o. also inspires members to be entrepreneurial—to develop new concepts that might serve the greater good of the evolt.org membership. One evolt.org administrator describes m.e.o. as akin to a "government grant for scientific research," and that investment has started to pay dividends. One member's coding experiment has evolved into a live directory that allows members to contribute to a growing collection of web development resources (see Figure 21-8).

Figure 21-8. The Directory, one of m.e.o.'s successful progeny

The evolt.org community also spawned the creation of a well-regarded archive of browsers, shown in Figure 21-9. The Browser Archive is handy for web developers who want to download copies of various browsers for testing their designs.

Decision-making

Decisions regarding evolt.org's direction are another type of transaction in the evolt.org economy. Initially, the site placed decision-making in the hands of administrators, many of whom were founders of the community. In their Godlike role, admins created the rules, roles, economy, and infrastructure that allow evolt.org to function on its own.

As the community matured and the maintenance workload increased, decision-making became more democratized and was placed directly into the hands of evolt.org members. Two discussion lists were created specifically for decision-making: "theforum" (for the community's general direction and policy) and "thesite" (for decisions and work on the site's "back end"). This democratization and expansion of decision-making was possible and sensible once the size of the community and its members' sense of ownership and responsibility had reached a critical mass. In effect, evolt.org's creators set up the community's infrastructure and waited for members to "move in" and achieve the ability to self-police their community. When they moved in and began to feel comfortable and invested in the place, they could be expected to take on responsibility for guiding evolt.org's future.

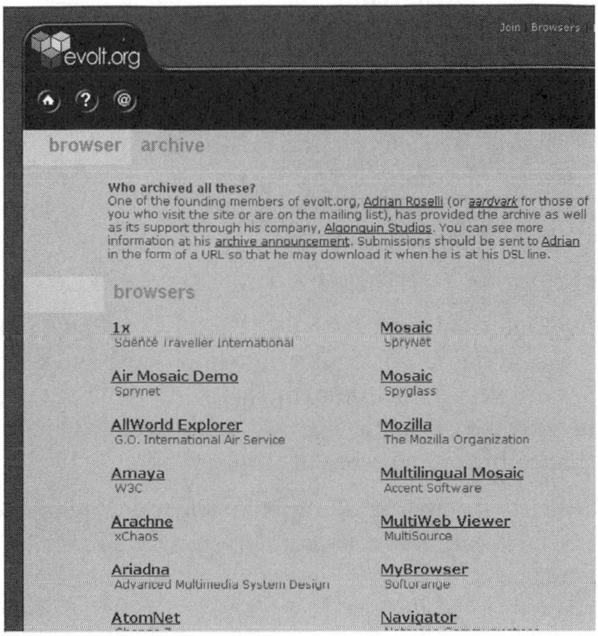

Figure 21-9. The Browser Archive

In this context, decisions are made informally: the community's size renders decision-making by consensus infeasible, and formal majority voting cumbersome. Despite this informality, the system works; members are neither shut out of decision-making nor overburdened by it.

And despite shedding much of their decision-making power, admins still play an important role—they approve or deny article submissions, and they have the ability to edit those submissions. They also answer user questions, help write the site's FAQs, settle ties, and occasionally represent evolt.org in public settings. This broader set of roles is the most demanding of any in evolt.org; however, it's also considered an honor since not everyone gets to be an admin. To be admitted to the "club," one must be invited by its current members. The honor typically falls to long-time members who have made active and visible contributions to the community.

How Information Architecture Fits In

In this discussion of evolt.org, we haven't covered much in terms of the basic nuts and bolts of information architecture; we haven't shown a single blueprint or wireframe, or discussed how users might search and browse the site.

In fact, evolt.org's information architecture is extremely simple, and perhaps not all that interesting if examined in a vacuum. However, it *is* extremely interesting to see how the site's information architecture enables the community to create and share content—this, after all, is the ultimate challenge in online-community sites. The architecture's minimalism is what makes it superlative.

The information architecture simply doesn't get in the way of people who wish to create content, but it does actively support getting that content in all sorts of volumes, sizes, and degrees of structure. It displays content captured elsewhere—ratings, comments, biographical information, and so on—in new settings, such as member directory entries, and in new forms, such as cubes. It provides an open canvas for experimentation that leads to innovation.

Therefore, evolt.org's information architecture has a lot to do with many of the characteristics of a successful online community. It shows how and why one might participate, provides valuable original content, helps promote a sense of ownership among its members, makes sure that contributors are recognized, and taps and repays members' philanthropy and sense of altruism.

Of course, this isn't to say that evolt.org's information architecture couldn't be improved. Like any information architecture organically developed by a geographically disparate community, evolt.org's silos could be better integrated from the bottom up. And certain areas of the site haven't yet found an "economic model" to ensure their survival.

Cracking the Nut of Integration

evolt.org's information architecture features some major silos:

- Discussion lists and their respective archives
- Tips and their archive
- Articles
- The member directory
- The web development resource directory
- The browser archive
- The developmental area (m.e.o.)

These are reasonably well integrated. For example, articles and tips link to their author's entries in the member directory; additionally, articles embed biographical content directly in the page. Tips are ingenious in that they are created specifically to be used again and again, either by being read on the fly or accessed from the tips archive.

On the other hand, there are additional opportunities for further bottom-up integration. For example, the discussion-list postings don't link to their authors' entries in the member directory, and vice versa. The discussion postings are an incredibly rich resource, but it's a bit of a hassle to find out who's responsible for them; you'd need to go to the evolt.org site, log in, and search the member directory to find out the source of that brilliant posting. Threads aren't treated as objects that can be searched or browsed. The discussion archives themselves aren't easily searchable, and it could be useful to search them all together, instead of one by one.

Integration is also tricky from the top down. While the site's primary organization scheme (Join, Browsers, Lists, Tips, Members, and Directory) works well for now, it probably won't scale well as new content areas spring from the m.e.o. skunk works.

Fit Enough to Survive?

Integration aside, the other major architectural challenge that online communities face is ensuring that each of their components has a sufficiently robust "economic model." The best example of this concern can be found in evolt.org's resource directory (Figure 21-10). Created and maintained by one person, the Directory accepts suggestions for resources to include from anyone who wishes to submit them. The obvious concern is that if not enough resources are submitted, the Directory will have limited utility. If too many are submitted, the maintainer will drown in a sea of cataloging and classification.

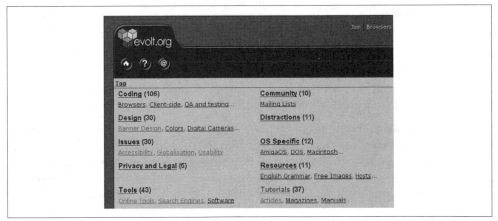

Figure 21-10. A useful directory, but will it last?

How should this problem be addressed? Typically, evolt.org would look to broaden participation by incenting other members to help manage the Directory. However, developing controlled vocabularies, identifying resources, and consistently indexing and classifying content are not easy tasks for lay people (especially volunteers) in distributed environments. Controlled vocabularies in particular require a high degree of central control, something that may not be practically (or *philosophically*) in accord with how evolt.org works.

The Yahoo! directory faced similar challenges in 1996, but Yahoo! had ample venture capital to fund its efforts. Despite that, the Yahoo! directory's quality began to erode over time, and in fact, most people now use Yahoo! for services *other* than its directory. The Open Directory Project, staffed completely by volunteers, has also encountered similar scaling problems. It will be difficult for evolt.org to solve this one; online communities don't typically spawn or operate by approaches that rely on significant central control. Perhaps this would be a great place to apply user tagging—folksonomies, à la del.icio.us and Flickr. Certainly, metadata control would be sacrificed, but a more sustainable model—one in line with evolt.org's philosophy—would take its place.

The "Un-Information Architecture"

Despite these concerns, evolt.org and its information architecture are impressive and successful. We should celebrate its very existence and also congratulate its founders on developing a flexible model that is likely to survive through the next generation of administrators.

Yet the process by which evolt.org took shape is anathema to "traditional" information architecture; there was minimal planning, formal process, or methodology. The whole approach has a "throw it against the wall and see what sticks" flavor to it.

And you know what? That's OK.

When a site operates on the goodwill of volunteers who create its infrastructure and populate it with content, it's hard to get them to follow a plan. Nothing about evolt.org—including its information architecture—can be forced. Accommodation, flexibility, and the willingness to experiment (and to live with those experiments!) are what drive the information architecture, not the other way around.

So, like the site itself, the architecture is a work in progress. Someone comes up with a good idea and floats it, others encourage him to try it, and suddenly there's a new section of the site. Integration with the rest of the site comes afterward, if at all. This constant morphing is the case with more than just the actual site architecture; it applies to the people involved—the volunteers and decision-makers—and the policies as well.

Transitional architectures can succeed only if the community is true to its goal of broad participation. In an environment where ideal methods such as contextual inquiry and content analysis are too expensive to be practical, volunteers must be counted on to take an active role in coming up with ideas that contribute to a better information architecture in their own way. Members ultimately design the information architecture for one another. Like the participatory economy, participatory information architecture will ultimately be the reason why sites like evolt.org survive and prosper.

Essential Resources

When the first edition of this book was published, we couldn't have included this appendix; there were few (if any) books, sites, and communities dedicated to information architecture. Now there are far too many to include them all.

And by the time this book finds its way into your hands, some of these resources will have been superseded by better competitors, some will have gone the way of all flesh, and some will have morphed into entirely different resources. URLs will change, too, but enough excuses. This is a reasonable snapshot of what we feel are today's most essential information architecture resources.

Another caveat: we said that these are what *we* feel are essential. This is a subjective selection, by no means comprehensive in coverage. For each topic, we've listed the few items that we think are the best or most appropriate. That means we've had to leave out some great stuff, and to those responsible for those resources, please accept our apologies in advance. When we could, we took into account others' views of what's essential, but what you'll find here is the information architecture resources *we* would take to that proverbial desert island. Your mileage will, of course, vary.

Communities

Typically, people are the best source of information, especially on a fairly new topic. And the best places to find people who know about a topic are the communities that are organized around that topic.

Since this book was last published, new opportunities have been created for IAs to meet and discuss information architecture as a community. The first organization dedicated solely to information architecture—the Information Architecture Institute (*http://iainstitute.org*, originally the Asilomar Institute for Information Architecture)— was started and now has more than 1,000 members. In a few short years, this organization has gathered members from over sixty countries. Additionally, grassroots efforts such as local information architecture "cocktail hours" have been a popular way of meeting fellow information architects. Meetings typically involve a guest speaker or discussion facilitator and a cocktail or two. Track local meetings from the IAwiki (*http://www.iawiki.net/cgi-bin/wiki.pl?search=CategoryEvent*), or consider starting a local group yourself.

Speaking of volunteerism and community building, it's important to note that no field can transform itself into a community without the "sweat equity" of its practitioners. Information architecture is still a young field. While more resources exist now, there is still much room for growth. In other words, if you feel that the information architecture community should provide its members with more—whether that means conferences, a job board, a library, or more local events—then you should make it happen. Happily, the Information Architecture Institute may be able to provide much of the resources and infrastructure you'll need to make it happen.

Discussion Lists

The information architecture community meets most frequently on discussion lists, specifically the IAI members list and SIGIA–L. These two lists are probably the most important resources for information architects. They will help you learn who your peers are, what they're working on, and what challenges they face. In this section we also list information on some highly relevant professional associations and SIGs that you might consider joining.

IA Institute Members

http://lists.iainstitute.org/listinfo.cgi/iai-members-iainstitute.org/

The IAI sponsors a moderated members-only discussion list. Considering its signal–noise ratio and civil tone, it alone makes it worthwhile to join the Institute. This list has anywhere from 100 to 300-plus postings per month.

SIGIA–L

http://www.info-arch.org/lists/sigia-l/

Sponsored by ASIS&T, SIGIA–L attracts roughly 2,000 subscribers with a large international contingent, and gets approximately 10–20 messages per day. List postings are not moderated, so the level of civility tends to swing back and forth substantially.

AIGA–Experience Design

http://groups.yahoo.com/group/AIGAExperienceDesign/

The American Institute of Graphic Arts (AIGA), the professional association for design, includes an Experience Design community that sponsors this lively mailing list of approximately 1,900 members. Traffic varies widely; a month with 141 postings has been followed by a month with 1 posting. Established in 1998, the AIGA–ED list is a great place to learn from and mix it up with a highly interdisciplinary crowd interested in the broad area of experience design.

CHI–WEB

http://www.sigchi.org/web/

If you want to take the pulse of the usability engineering community, sign up for CHI–WEB. Sponsored by the ACM SIG on Computer–Human Interaction, CHI–WEB is a highly moderated (and therefore high-quality) list with about 100–200 postings per month.

IxDA

http://www.ixda.org/en/join_us/ixd_discussion_list/index.shtml

IxDA, the Interaction Design Association, is a nonprofit organization started in 2003. It sponsors an active discussion list, with about 15 posts a day.

Professional Associations

While we don't suggest you go out and join each of these associations, they're all certainly worth knowing about. Most produce high-quality conferences, journals, and other valuable resources. And although these particular associations are not the only ones relevant to the field, each has expressed a desire or taken active steps to provide information architects and other experience designers better and more coordinated professional support.

ACM SIGCHI

http://www.acm.org/sigchi/

One of the Association for Computing Machinery's 35 SIGs, the Special Interest Group on Computer–Human Interaction sponsors the CHI–WEB discussion list, the bimonthly *Interactions* and *SIGCHI Bulletin* magazines, and the SIGCHI annual conferences each spring, and it is the force behind many other useful HCI resources and events. SIGCHI has about 5,000 members.

ASIS&T

http://www.asis.org

The American Society for Information Science and Technology, ASIS&T, sponsors SIGIA (Special Interest Group for Information Architects), as well as its corresponding SIGIA–L discussion list and the annual Information Architecture Summits. ASIS&T has approximately 3,000 members, many of them information scientists from academia and business.

CM Pros

http://www.cmprofessionals.org

The Content Management Professionals Association (CM Pros) was started in 2004 to allow content management professionals to share content management information, practices, and strategies.

IA Institute

http://iainstitute.org

The Information Architecture Institute (formerly the Asilomar Institute for Information Architecture, "AIfIA") was founded in 2002. To date, the Institute has over 1,000 members in more than 60 countries. The Information Architecture Institute has already made excellent progress on developing an Information Architecture Library, a job board, a calendar of events, a mentoring program, and more.

IxDA

http://www.ixda.org

The Interaction Design Association (IxDA) is a nonprofit organization started in 2003. It is committed to serving the needs of the international interaction design community.

STC

http://www.stc.org

The Society for Technical Communication has about 25,000 members worldwide. Two of its most popular SIGs—Information Design with 3,200 members, and Usability with 2,500 members—are most relevant to information architects. STC publishes *Intercom* 10 times annually. The spring annual event draws a large audience, and STC's 150 local chapters are also quite active.

UPA

http://www.upassoc.org

Established in 1991, the Usability Professionals' Association focuses on the needs of usability practitioners; UPA now has approximately 2,500 members. Its annual conference takes place in the summer. UPA publishes *User Experience* magazine three to four times a year.

UXnet

http://uxnet.org

The User Experience Network (UXnet) was started in 2002 to help further the field of user experience by facilitating collaboration and cooperation among relevant organizations and individuals. Although it's not a membership-based organization, UXnet now includes 95 local ambassadors in 29 countries.

Directories

When something is "comprehensive," that typically means it covers everything on a particular domain. However, in the case of directories on the Web, comprehensive is a relative term; there are no absolutes. No single site covers every resource related to information architecture. And if one tried, no business model could support its ongoing maintenance.

So, while there are a few directories of information architecture resources, none will provide you with *everything*. Instead, it's a good idea to regularly visit multiple directories to find information about the field.

The IAwiki

In the fall of 2001, Eric Scheid established the IAwiki as a "collaborative discussion space for the topic of Information Architecture." Think of the IAwiki as a wonderful shared collection of hyperlinked, annotated bookmarks that anyone can add to, modify, or delete, regardless of who that person is. (You can learn more about wikis from the original wiki—*http://c2.com/cgi/wiki?FrontPage*.) Of course, this is good and bad. The IAwiki is self-propagating, packed with useful resources, and updated daily. But it's difficult to design and maintain a shared information architecture, so it's not always a snap to find what you're looking for in the IAwiki. The IAwiki's "Recent Changes" page, which lists what's new on the site, is the best place to start.

The Information Architecture Library

The Information Architecture Library on the IA Institute's web site (*http://iainstitute. org/library/*) contains a growing list of resources for IAs. The library is organized by subject, resource type, author, and languages, and it is actively seeking to expand its non-English resources.

InfoDesign

Peter Bogaards deserves acclaim for his regular, consistent, and expert filtering of an incredibly huge amount of material (*http://www.informationdesign.org/*). This site covers information design, usability, visual design, and information visualization as well as information architecture. Also available via email.

IxDA's Resource Library

IxDA has begun developing a categorized resource library on all aspects of interaction design (*http://resources.ixda.org/*).

Additional Resources

Two additional resources that are no longer updated but still contain lots of great information, especially for those who are newer to the field, are Usable Web (*http://www.usableweb.com/*) and the Argus Center for Information Architecture IA Guide (*http://argus-acia.com/ia_guide/*).

Books and Journals

Online Journals and Magazines

There are a growing number of online journals, and even a few print magazines, that cover information architecture and user experience. A few of the ones we enjoy are:

A List Apart (http://alistapart.com)
> An online magazine covering web design development as well as information architecture and user experience topics.

BASIS&T, the Bulletin of the American Society for Information Science and Technology (http://www.asis.org/bulletin.html)
> ASIS&T's bimonthly bulletin; it includes a regular column on information architecture.

Boxes and Arrows (http://www.boxesandarrows.com)
> The field's "peer-written journal dedicated to discussing, improving and promoting the work of this community, through the sharing of exemplary technique, innovation and informed opinion."

Digital Web (http://www.digital-web.com)
> An online magazine covering a broad range of web development, design and information architecture topics.

GUUUI (http://www.guuui.com)
> Billed as "The Interaction Designer's Coffee Break," this journal offers well-written articles on a range of interaction design topics.

Interactions (http://www.acm.org/interactions)
> A publication of ACM, the Association for Computing Machinery. It has covered human–computer interaction topics since 1994. The magazine is a print publication, but its contents are also available online to subscribers.

OK/Cancel (http://www.ok-cancel.com)
> *OK/Cancel* publishes less frequently, but it deserves a visit for introducing us to the World's First HCI Rap, "We Got It," and for its frequently updated usability and user interface-related comics.

User Experience (http://www.upassoc.org/upa_publications/user_experience)
This print publication is published by the Usability Professionals' Association and covers usability and user experience topics in depth.

UXmatters (http://uxmatters.com)
An online magazine started in late 2005 that covers user experience and the design of user interfaces for digital products.

Books

There are also precious few books dedicated to information architecture. But thousands of titles are relevant to the field, and perhaps hundreds merit reading. We can't hope to narrow that list down to four or five, so we'll instead rely on a survey conducted to determine which books IA educators use to teach their classes.[*]

Responses to the question "What books or other teaching materials do you use in your courses?"

About Face: The Essentials of User Interface Design by Alan Cooper (Wiley)

Ambient Findability by Peter Morville (O'Reilly)

Designing Web Usability: The Practice of Simplicity by Jakob Nielsen (Peachpit Press)

Designing with Web Standards by Jeffrey Zeldman (New Riders)

Don't Make Me Think: A Common Sense Approach to Web Usability by Steve Krug (New Riders)

GUI Bloopers: Don'ts and Do's for Software Developers and Web Designers by Jeff Johnson (Morgan Kaufmann)

Handbook of Usability Testing: How to Plan, Design, and Conduct Effective Tests by Jeffrey Rubin (Wiley)

How to Build a Digital Library by Ian H. Witten and David Bainbridge (Morgan Kaufmann)

Human Computer Interaction in the New Millennium by John M. Carroll (Addison-Wesley)

Human–Computer Interaction: Concepts And Design by J. Preece et al. (Addison-Wesley)

Information Anxiety 2 by Richard Saul Wurman, David Sume, and Loring Leifer (Que)

---

[*] *http://iainstitute.org/documents/research/results/polar_bear_survey_4.html*

Information Architecture for the World Wide Web by Louis Rosenfeld and Peter Morville (O'Reilly)

Information Architecture: Blueprints for the Web by Christina Wodtke (New Riders)

Metadata Solutions: Using Metamodels, Repositories, XML, and Enterprise Portals to Generate Information on Demand by Adrienne Tannenbaum (Addison-Wesley)

Modern Information Retrieval by Ricardo Baeza-Yates and Berthier Ribeiro-Neto (Addison-Wesley)

Observing the User Experience: A Practitioner's Guide to User Research by Mike Kuniavsky (Morgan Kaufmann)

Organizing Knowledge: An Introduction to Managing Access to Information by J. E. Rowley and John Farrow (Gower)

Paper Prototyping: The Fast and Easy Way to Design and Refine User Interfaces by Carolyn Snyder (Morgan Kaufmann)

Persuasive Technology: Using Computers to Change What We Think and Do by B.J. Fogg (Morgan Kaufmann)

Rapid Contextual Design: A How-to Guide to Key Techniques for User-Centered Design by Karen Holtzblatt, Jessamyn Burns Wendell, and Shelley Wood (Morgan Kaufmann)

Task-Centered User Interface Design by Clayton Lewis and John Rieman (Lewis and Rieman)

The Design of Everyday Things by Donald A. Norman (Basic Books)

The Humane Interface: New Directions for Designing Interactive Systems by Jef Raskin (Addison-Wesley)

The Inmates Are Running the Asylum: Why High Tech Products Drive Us Crazy and How to Restore the Sanity by Alan Cooper (Sams)

The Organization of Information by Arlene G. Taylor (Libraries Unlimited)

The Practical Guide to Information Design by Ronnie Lipton (Wiley)

The Usability Engineering Lifecycle: A Practitioner's Handbook for User Interface Design by Deborah J. Mayhew (Morgan Kaufmann)

Usability for the Web: Designing Web Sites that Work by Tom Brinck, Darren Gergle, and Scott D. Wood (Morgan Kaufmann)

Usability Inspection Methods by Jakob Nielsen and Robert L. Mack (Wiley)

Visual Revelations: Graphical Tales of Fate and Deception From Napoleon Bonaparte To Ross Perot by Howard Wainer (LEA, Inc.)

Additional Resources

In addition to subscribing to discussion lists, other good places to find out what books IAs read are the IAWiki Canon (*http://www.iawiki.net/IACanon*), *Boxes and Arrows* Staff Recommendations (*http://www.boxesandarrows.com/view/our_favorite_books_recommendations_from_the_staff_of_boxes_and_arrows*), and the IA Institute's list of information architecture books (*http://iainstitute.org/pg/books.php*).

Formal Education

As discussed in Chapter 13, academia is still struggling with where to fit and how to teach information architecture, not to mention the many other emergent fields under the collective umbrella of user experience design. While many more courses are offered today than when this book was last published, programs focusing specifically on information architecture are still few and far between. If you are interested in formal education in IA, it's still a good plan to consider graduate-level programs in established fields related to information architecture (such as library science, cognitive psychology, and human–computer interaction) and augment your studies with cognate courses from other fields.

IA Institute Education

http://iainstitute.org/pg/schools_teaching_ia.php

In 2003, the IA Institute published a very detailed and well-organized list of institutions worldwide that offer courses and full degree programs dedicated to information architecture.

Educators Survey

http://iainstitute.org/documents/research/results/polar_bear_survey_4.html

In 2006, an extensive but less-detailed list of educational institutions offering courses or programs related to IA was compiled as part of one of the surveys conducted to inform this book. This list includes all programs mentioned by any survey respondent. This is also available on the IA Institute web site. (See question 5.)

IxDA Education Resources

http://resources.ixda.org/archive/category/education

IxDA has begun a list of education resources for interaction designers.

Human Factors International

http://www.humanfactors.com/downloads/degrees.asp

Human Factors International has published a list of graduate human–computer interaction programs.

IAwiki Degree in IA Page

http://www.iawiki.net/DegreeInIA

The most up-to-date collection of resources on the topic; includes listings of programs and discussion of syllabi.

U.S. News and World Report

http://www.usnews.com/usnews/edu/grad/rankings/lib/libindex_brief.php

U.S. News and World Report publishes the "Complete Guide to Library and Information Studies Programs."

HCI Bibliography

http://www.hcibib.org/education/#PROGRAMS

This HCI Education Survey Report lists 76 HCI programs.

University of Texas on Information Architecture

http://www.gslis.utexas.edu/~l38613dw/readings/InfoArchitecture.html

R.E. Wyllis's excellent article on IA education. It "discusses ideas associated with the phrase 'information architecture' and relates them to aspects of the library- and information-science (LIS) professions." Published in 2000.

Conferences and Events

Quite a few conferences have been held since we last published this book. While a few of the bigger ones are listed below, you can find out about many more conferences and events by keeping up with discussion lists and the event calendars listed below.

Information Architecture Summit (ASIS&T)

The longest-running and most specific conference dedicated to information architecture—the ASIS&T-sponsored Information Architecture Summit—has been held in

North America each spring since 2000. The Summit is organized by volunteers and typically attracts 300–400 attendees. ASIS&T also organizes the European IA Summit. Visit the ASIS&T web site (*http://www.asis.org*) for information on the next Summit.

DUX

DUX (Conference on Designing for User eXperience) began in 2003 as a collaboration of ACM SIGCHI, ACM SIGGRAPH, and AIGA, with the intent of holding a conference every second year. Information for the most recent conference is available at *http://www.dux2005.org*.

Additional Conferences

The IAI is organizing or sponsoring IA conferences and meetings around the world, including IA Retreats, the IDEA Conference, and more. Keep up by viewing the IAI's events calendar (*http://iainstitute.org/calendar*). Many more conferences and events can be found through the events calendars listed below.

- *Boxes and Arrows* (interaction, experience, and other design): *http://events. boxesandarrows.com/events*
- Brint (knowledge management): *http://www.brint.com/calendar/cal/calendar.cgi*
- IAwiki Conferences page (information architecture): *http://www.IAwiki.net/ IAconferences*
- InfoDesign: (information design and many related areas): *http://www. informationdesign.org/events/index.php*
- Interaction Design Calendar: *http://www.interaction-design.org/calendar*
- SearchTools (information retrieval): *http://www.searchtools.com/info/conferences. html*

Examples, Deliverables, and Tools

There are no definitive ways to create architectural documentation, no standards for diagrams, and no consensus tools to help you do your work as an information architect. It's not clear if there ever will be. Thankfully, there are more and more useful resources to provide you with options and ideas, primarily from the IAwiki.

IA Institute Tools

http://iainstitute.org/tools

The IA Institute has organized quite a few sample documents within its Tools section.

IAwiki Deliverables and Artifacts

http://www.iawiki.net/DeliverablesAndArtifacts

From site maps and wireframes to examples and advice, this page provides an extremely impressive collection of links on the products of information architecture design.

IAwiki Diagramming Tools

http://www.iawiki.net/DiagrammingTools

The IAwiki doesn't have quite as much information on actual tools, but this page is a good start and is the best source on the topic so far.

IxDA Resource Library

http://resources.ixda.org

The IxDA Resource Library contains a growing repository of content about Patterns, Work Products, Software and Tools, Research, and more.

jjg.net's Visual Vocabulary

http://www.jjg.net/ia/visvocab

Originally released in October of 2000, Jesse James Garrett has regularly updated this collection of tools, templates, and thoughts. His goal is "to describe, at a high level, the structure and/or flow of the user experience of a web site." He's done so in a highly systematic way, and both information architects and interaction designers will find it quite useful.

Index

We'd like to hear your suggestions for improving our indexes. Send email to *index@oreilly.com*.

N

narrow-and-deep hierarchies, 70
narrower terms, 205
narrowing search results, 190
National Library of Canada, 202
National Library of Medicine, 206
natural language processing tools, 162
navigation, 43, 46
    bottom-up, in EIA, 401
    site-wide, 50
    top-down, in EIA, 398
navigation bars, 122, 129
navigation features of web browsers, 117
navigation pages, 153
Navigation Stress Test, 48, 120
navigation systems, 115–144
    advanced navigation approaches, 139
    blueprints and, 304
    context, 118
    embedded, 122
    flexibility, 120
    integration, need for, 129
    labels within, 92
    problematic, 146
    strategy recommendations on design
        of, 266
    supplemental navigation systems, 131
    types of, 116
navigation tools, human's use of, 115
need for information architecture, the, 17
neologisms, 85
Netscape Navigator, 117
New York Times web site, 124, 155, 188
NIC (Nursing Intervention
        Classification), 342
Nielsen, Jakob, 125, 367, 406
Noah's Ark approach to content
        gathering, 241
nonverbal communication, 83
Northern Light, 175
Northwest Airlines, 92
Nursing Intervention Classification
        (NIC), 342

O

observation, as user research technique, 253
OK/Cancel, 480
OmniGraffle, 294, 359
On Competition (Porter), 381, 382
On War (Clausewitz), 379
one best way (SWOT analysis), 385

online communities, 460–474
open audience-specific organization
        schemes, 66
open card sorts, 106
Open Directory Project, 474
open standards, of MSWeb tools, 448
Open URL (browser command), 118
open-ended card sorting, 256
operational effectiveness, 381
operations teams, of EIA Units, 415
opinion leader (stakeholder) interviews, 238,
        381
opportunity cost approach to assessing
        ROI, 367
Oracle, 213
organization charts, 235
organization systems, 53–81
    ambiguity, 55
    components, 58
    creating cohesive, 80
    heterogeneity, 56
    internal politics and, 58
    organization schemes, 59
    organization structures, 58, 69, 73, 76
    personal, 57
    perspectives, differences in, 57
    strategy recommendations on, 266
organizational jargon, 86
organizational learning, 346
organizational metaphors, 274
organizing blueprints, 304
organizing information, 54, 81
outies (consultants), innies versus, 349
outside opinions, 374

P

page hits, 247
page paradigms, 130
pages, 302–307
pain, value of, 375
Pao, Miranda Lee, 191
paper prototypes, 271
paradox of the active user, 262
parent-child (hierarchical) relationships, 215
parenthetical term qualifiers, 218
participant definition and recruiting, for user
        research, 251
participation, in online communities, 462
participatory information architecture, 474
Pathfinder, 246
pattern-matching algorithms, 159
patterns, in labeling systems, 102

pay-for-placement (PFP) ranking, 173
pearl-growing model, 37
Peppers, Don, 139
permutation of index terms, 135
persistence, 344
personalization, 65, 139
perspective, consultants', 349
perspectives, differing, of organization system
    creators, 57
PFP (pay-for-placement) rankings, 173
phased rollouts, 421
phone books, 59, 165
phonetic tools, 162
phrasing, of cards for sorting, 256
physical access, 343
physical objects, polyhierarchy and, 221
pictures, 97, 277
pitch, ambiguity of term, 55, 98
places, organization schemes for, 60
planning school of business strategy, 387
PMEST (Ranganathan's facets), 222
point-of-production architecture, 328
politics, 58, 349
polyhierarchy, 70, 219
popularity ranking, for search results, 171
portal solutions, 358
portals, 212, 284
Porter, Michael, 380, 382, 391
positioning school of business strategy, 387
Powell's Books, 147
power school of business strategy, 387
Power Search (Wine.com), 223
precision, 159, 197
precoordination, 220
preferred terms, 199, 204, 217
presentation, consistency of, 99
presentations, 235, 279, 288, 293
printing, of search results, 176
problem statements, 260
processes, labeling steps in, 92
product management and information
    architecture, 20
product vocabularies, 431
professionals, hiring, 350
profitability, long-term, 381
programs, hiring information architects
    for, 348, 350
project plans (strategy phase work
    product), 288
projects, 348, 349
prospective view, of web browsers, 118

prototypes, 271, 272, 328
    software for, 360
Prusak, Laurence, 389
PubMed, 206

Q

qualifications for practicing information
    architecture, 18–23
qualifiers, parenthetical term, 218
qualitative card sorting, 256
quantifying benefits of information
    architecture, 370
quantitative card sorting, 256
query builders, 161
questions
    for content owners, 237
    about software, 361
    for stakeholders, 238, 381
    strategic, effects of, 267
    for strategy teams, 236
    for system administrators, 237
    user research, 254

R

randomness, card sorts and, 256
Ranganathan, S. R., 221
Rappoport, Avi, 192, 357
reality, 235
recall, 159, 197
recent content, 155
recruiting, for user research, 251
REI web site, 126
related documents, 160
related terms, 205
relational databases, 74
relationships, 215, 350, 458
relevance ranking of search results, 168
remote pages, 304
reports, strategy, 279
representation, 82
representational content components, 163
representative samples, for content
    analysis, 241
research, 231–263
    business context research, 234
    conceptual framework for, 233
    content research, 239
    defense of, 261
    importance, 261
    meetings for, 236

T

tables of contents, 132
> for strategy reports, 279

tablets, scrolls, books, and libraries, 6

TACT (think, articulate, communicate, and test), 269

task-oriented organization schemes, 64

tasks
> analysis of, 271, 457
> for user testing, 260

taxonomies, 69
> cross-walking of, 458
> depth versus breadth of, 70
> designing, 70
> for MSWeb, 432
> multiple, 222
> stability of, 347

Taxonomy Warehouse, 227

teams, information architecture, 345

technical architectures, 431, 438

technical writing and information architecture, 20

technology, 265, 391

technology assessments, 239

telling stories, 373

templates, 287, 308

term definition, 218

term forms, 217

term rotation, 135

term selection, 218

term specificity, 219

terminology, for controlled vocabularies, 204

testing, 89, 271

textual navigation bars, 129

The Clock of the Long Now, 347

The One to One Future (Peppers and Rogers), 139

thechat, 464

theforum, 464, 470

thelist, 464

thesauri, 52, 203
> classic, 209
> definition, 203
> descriptions of, in strategy report, 288
> designers of, 352
> examples, 206
> indexing (thesaurus type), 211
> Internet as disruptive force, 214
> as label sources, 102
> management tools for, 357
> preferred terms, 217
> as query builders, 162
> searching (thesaurus type), 212
> semantic relationships, 215
> standards, 213
> terminology, 204
> types of, 209

ThesauriOnline, 103, 227

thesite, 464, 470

thinking, in strategy development, 270

three circles diagram, 233

Time Warner, Pathfinder web site, 246

time, organizational schemes for, 60

tips, in evolt.org postings, 465

TITLE tag (HTML), 96

titles, organization schemes for, 61

tomatoes, classification of, 56

tool salesmen, following, 375

tools and software, 354–361

too-simple information model, the, 31

top-down business strategy development, 387

top-down information architecture, 44, 266
> bottom-up information architecture versus, 388
> high-level blueprints and, 296
> strategy recommendations on, 265

top-down organization structures, 69

topic to task distribution, 260

topical organization schemes, 63

Toub, Steve, 374

tours, as guides, 136

Tower Records, 368

trench warriors, 22

tutorials, 136

two-step model, corporate portals and intranets, 37

Tzu, Sun, 379

U

U.S. News and World Report, 484

U.S. states, Postal Service two-letter abbreviations for, 198

UCS (URL Cataloging Service), 438

U-Haul, 83

Umbrella Shell for Separate Hubs strategy, 289

unified vision, importance, 261

universal usability, 343

University of Texas on Information Architecture, 484

unlimited aliasing, 197

About the Authors

Considered one of the founders of the field, **Lou Rosenfeld** works as an independent information architecture consultant, helping such clients as Accenture, Caterpillar, the CDC, Ford, Microsoft, and the NCAA develop information architecture strategies and in-house expertise. Lou cofounded industry leader Argus Associates in 1990 and was its president from 1993–2001. He played a leading role in creating ASIS&T's successful series of annual information architecture summits and cofounded the field's professional association, the Information Architecture Institute, as well as UXnet, the User Experience Network.

Lou's recent work includes founding Rosenfeld Media, a publishing house focused on user experience books. He also teaches his popular seminars on enterprise information architecture in six cities yearly.

Lou has an advanced degree in information and library studies from the University of Michigan, where he has also taught graduate courses. Lou lives in Ann Arbor, Michigan with his wife, Mary Jean Babic, their daughter, Iris, and Schwa the cat. He blogs at *www.louisrosenfeld.com*

Peter Morville (*morville@semanticstudios.com*) is president and founder of Semantic Studios, a leading information architecture and strategy consultancy. Since 1994, he has played a major role in shaping the modern practice of information architecture design. As chief executive officer of Argus Associates (1994–2001), Peter helped build one of the world's most respected information architecture firms, serving clients such as AT&T, Barron's, Ernst & Young, HP, IBM, L. L. Bean, Microsoft, Procter & Gamble, Vanguard, and the Weather Channel. An internationally distinguished speaker, Peter provides keynotes and seminars on such topics as user experience, knowledge management, and findability. His work has been featured in many publications including *Business Week*, *Fortune*, MSNBC, and the *Wall Street Journal*.

Peter holds an advanced degree in library and information science from the University of Michigan, where he now teaches a popular graduate course.

Colophon

Our look is the result of reader comments, our own experimentation, and feedback from distribution channels. Distinctive covers complement our distinctive approach to technical topics, breathing personality and life into potentially dry subjects.

The animal featured on the cover of *Information Architecture for the World Wide Web*, Third Edition, is a polar bear (*Ursus maritimus*). Polar bears live primarily on the icy shores of Greenland and northern North America and Asia. They are very strong swimmers and rarely venture far from the water. The largest land carnivore, male polar bears weigh from 770 to 1,400 pounds. Female polar bears are much smaller, weighing 330 to 550 pounds. The preferred meal of polar bears is ringed seals and bearded seals. When seals are unavailable, the bears will eat fish, reindeer, birds, berries, and trash.

Polar bears are, of course, well adapted to living in the Arctic Circle. Their black skin is covered in thick, water-repellent, white fur. Adult polar bears are protected from the cold by a layer of blubber that is more than four inches thick. They are so well insulated, in fact, that overheating can be a problem. For this reason they move slowly on land, taking frequent breaks. Their large feet spread out their substantial weight, allowing them to walk on thin ice surfaces that animals weighing far less would break through. Because food is available year-round, most polar bears don't hibernate. Pregnant females are the exception, and the tiny one to one and a half pound cubs are born during the hibernation period.

Polar bears have no natural enemies. Their greatest threat comes from hunting, but in the past 15 years, most governments have placed strict limits on hunting polar bears. Their population has more than doubled in that time and is now estimated to be between 21,000 and 28,000. They are not considered to be endangered. They are extremely aggressive and dangerous animals. While many bears actively avoid human contact, polar bears tend to view humans as prey. In encounters between humans and polar bears, the bear almost always wins.

The cover image is from a 19th-century engraving from the Dover Pictorial Archive. The cover font is Adobe ITC Garamond. The text font is Linotype Birka; the heading font is Adobe Myriad Condensed; and the code font is LucasFont's TheSans Mono Condensed.

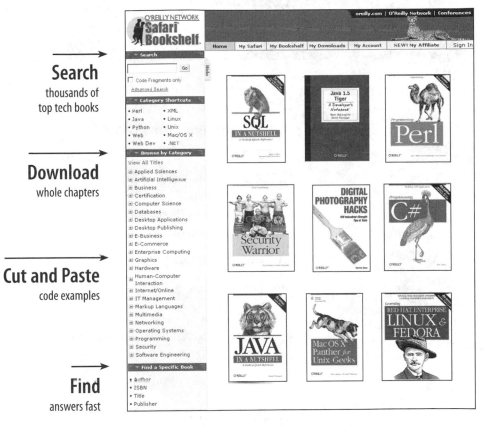